Helen and Larry Eisenberg

THE OMNIBUS OF FUN

Drawings by Ed Goddard

ASSOCIATION PRESS / NEW YORK

THE OMNIBUS OF FUN

Copyright © 1956 by
National Board of Young Men's Christian Associations

Association Press, 291 Broadway, New York 7, N. Y.

Library of Congress catalog card number: 56-10663

 55

Printed in the United States of America
American Book–Stratford Press, Inc., New York

DEDICATION

In appreciation for their warm encouragement and their open-hearted and openhanded sharing of ideas, of material, and of themselves with us through the years, we dedicate this book to some long-time colleagues:

Lynn and Katherine Rohrbough
Ruth and James Norris
Dr. George Steinman
Mary Ann and Michael Herman
Wilma Mintier
James McGiffin
Vytautas Beliajus
Elizabeth Burchenal
Howard Tanner
Harry D. Edgren
Jane Farwell Hindricks
R. Harold Hipps
M. Leo Rippy

Bruce "Uncle Tom" Tom
A. D. Zanzig
Dr. Lloyd Shaw
F. L. "Mac" McReynolds
Rev. Henry Lewis
Richard Chase
H. G. Williamson
The late E. O. Harbin
Warren Willis
Bert Lyle
Mary Elizabeth McDonald
Wally Chappell

Foreword

Why do publishers and authors launch into as big a book as this one (or its companion volume, *The Program Encyclopedia*)?

Both parties recognize that if an extensive job is done in one volume to show some of the needs and "whys" of recreation programs, some of the "hows," and "with what," it takes many pages. Much hard work, too, is required to "boil down" the information, yet to treat it fully enough so that the meanings are clear.

The Omnibus of Fun is the result of several years spent in collecting material. Most of it has been used by the authors in groups all over the United States. As we were outlining the book, together with our publishers, we agreed that it would be for three kinds of leaders:

1. The casual leader who has responsibility only once in a while.
2. The intermittent leader who leads more often but not regularly.
3. The "recreation leader," full time and volunteer, who needs a wide variety of activities and helps at his finger tips. (The thought was that this person might also use *The Omnibus of Fun* as a loan volume for volunteers.)

We also agreed that we would attempt to include material for workers with children (Clubs, Brownies); for leaders of Hi-Y and Hi-Tri, Y-Teen, Girl Scout, Campfire Girl groups; for workers with church schools, vacation church schools, and church youth groups; for camp leaders; for workers with youth in school clubs, playgrounds, community centers; for rural youth groups, college clubs, and other organizations. We kept in mind also the workers with adults: community centers, men's and women's clubs, church groups, luncheon clubs, informal community groups, older adults.

As a special emphasis, we planned help for workers with the handicapped: deaf and hard-of-hearing, blind, bed-ridden persons, mental patients, older folk. There was also to be family fun.

Most important of all was the task of setting up the great volume of material for easy use and quick reference. The more pages to a book, the harder this becomes. We acknowledge deep indebtedness for invaluable assistance from Director James Rietmulder and his associate, Roland Burdick, of Association Press, and from Miss Lucile Lippitt, who helped to rewrite and rearrange the manuscript.

OUR PERSONAL HALL OF FAME

We are eternally indebted to pioneers and veterans who have paved (and are paving) the way for broader understanding in the full use of leisure time for personality growth. Most of these tireless workers we have known personally—many are personal friends. All have rendered a large contribution to their segment of the broad field of use of leisure time. We'd appreciate having your nominations!

Philosophy. L. P. Jacks, Jay Nash, Ott Romney, Dr. William C. Menninger, Howard Braucher, Joseph Lee, Harry Overstreet, S. R. Slavson, Harry Edgren, Neva Boyd, Evelyn Millis Duvall.

Church Recreation. Lynn Rohrbough, Ed Schlingman, Maurice Bone, Howard Irish, Wally Chappell, Chet Bowers, Owen Geer, Bob Tully, Art Henke, DeWitt Ellinwood, Bob Fakkema, Wilma Mintier, Paul Weaver, Sibley Burnett, Mrs. Agnes Pylant, M. Leo Rippy, Don Snider, Jack and Edith Fellows, Don Clayton, Joe Bell, Gene Hibbard, Fred Smith, Bob Nolte, Neal Griffith, T. B. Maston, Eulalie Ginn, Lawton and Sally Harris, Alan T. Jones, Raymond Veh, Bob Clemmons, Virginia Stafford, Gene Durham.

Extension. F. L. McReynolds, Stewart Case, Jane Farwell Hindricks, Bruce Tom, Verne Varney, E. C. "Duke" Regnier, Ruth McIntyre, Bill Carpenter, Max V. Exner, Pauline Reynolds, Bernard V. Beadle, George Boehnke.

Music. A. D. Zanzig, Peter Dykema, Janet Tobitt, the late Russell Ames Cook, Lynn Rohrbough, Max and Bea Krone, Mary Lib McDonald, the late Leonard Deutch.

Folk and Square Dancing. Mary Ann and Michael Herman, Vytautas Beliajus, Dr. Lloyd Shaw, Elizabeth Burchenal, Paul and Gretel Dunsing, the late Lawrence Loy, Grace Ryan, Benjamin Lovett, Ed Durlacher, Sally and Lawton Harris, Lynn Rohrbough, Jane Farwell Hindricks.

Nature and Outdoor Fun. "Cap'n Bill" Vinal, Reynold E. Carlson, L. B. Sharp, Bernard Mason, Elmer D. Mitchell, Kit Hammett, Herb Sweet, Wes Klusmann, "Daddy" Drew, Bert Lyle, Argyle Knight.

Crafts and Equipment. Howard Tanner, Ruth Faison Shaw, Lester Griswold, the Paul Bunnings, Frank Staples, Walter Cowart, Wally Dodd, Art Bell, Edna and John Clapper.

Informal Dramatics. Ruth and Jim Norris, Jack Knapp, Charles F. Wells, Grace Walker, Amy Loomis, Margaret Palmer Fisk, Harold Ehrensperger, Fred Eastman.

Stories. Richard Chase, Ben Botkin, "Col. Stoopnagle."

General Recreation. Buford and Betty Bush, Bert Kessel, Ethel Bowers, Ben Solomon, the late Joseph Lee, Willard Sutherland, Charlie Reed, Virginia Musselman, Tom Rivers, Dorothy Donaldson, Rose Schwartz, Bob Gamble, Ruth Ehlers, Mildred Scanlon, Ann Livingston, Frank Staples, Joseph Prendergast, and, of course, the National Recreation Association.

All these people have been at work in the recreation vineyard for ten years—some of them thirty to forty years! Space prevents mentioning many more, especially those who have labored closer to the local scene.

OUR CONTRIBUTORS

We extend special thanks to those who have written sections or chapters for us: Valerie V. Hunt, Bert Lyle, Mary Elizabeth McDonald, Amy Goodhue Loomis, Dr. George Steinman, Walter Cowart, Reynold E. Carlson, Edna and John Clapper, and to Ed Goddard who created the sprightly drawings. Dr. Steinman made available files that he had accumulated for years.

Here are our contributors to this volume as we have listed them, along with their states (which, by the way, reveal how widespread is our recreation leadership). If we have inadvertently left out a name, please let us know and we'll correct the omission in a future edition.

Bannermann, Glenn, N. C.
Barden, Mrs. Isabelle, N. H.
Battle, Gerry, Tenn.
Beadle, Bernard V., Minn.
Beatty, Bill, Pa.
Beliajus, Vytautas, Calif.
Bell, Jennie Lee, Ill.
Bierly, Ethel, Ind.
Blair, Viola, Ark.
Bogardus, LaDonna, Tenn.
Boon, Fannie, Va.
Bowers, Richard, Va.
Brightbill, Charles H., Ill.
Brothers, Sue, Ark.
Brown, Mrs. Elmore, Va.
Budrow, Ted, N. Y.
Burnett, Sibley, Tenn.
Carlson, Bernice, Tenn.
Case, Stewart, Colo.
Cassell, Fern, Okla.
Chappell, Wally and Stell, Tenn.
Clapper, Edna and John, Ill.
*Clark, Dr. Homer, Pa.
Colby, Dick, R. I.
Coffey, Ellen, Tenn.
Cowan, Mark, Ind.
Daly, Mrs. Joan, Ind.
Davenport, Gene, Ala.
Davis, Leland, Texas
DeHainaut, Mrs. R. K., La.
Dence, Carlton, N. Y.
Desjardins, Lucille, Tenn.

Dicks, Dorothy, N. C.
Dixon, Ruth Wohr, Mass.
Eccles, Richard, Mich.
Edgren, H. D., Ind.
Ellinwood, DeWitt, Ill.
Ellis, Howard, Tenn.
Elson, Irving, N. Y.
Fakkema, Bob, La.
Fellows, Edith and Jack, Ind.
Flynn, Jim, Texas
Garrison, Webb, Tenn.
Gordon, Sol, N. Y.
Grano, Rose, Pa.
Griffith, Neal, Pa.
Haas, Peter, N. Y.
Haines, Vergie R., Ill.
Hammond, Pixie, Colo.
Hampton, Jack, Texas
Harper, George, Mont.
Herman, Mary Ann and Michael, N. Y.
Hibbard, Eugene, Ohio
Hinman, Adele, Pa.
Hipps, R. Harold, N. C.
Holbrook, Leona, Utah
Holbrook, Robert, Nebr.
Horn, Sue, N. C.
Huffines, Virginia and David, N. C.
Hurston, Zora Neale, Fla.
Jesperson, Christence, Nebr.
Jones, Wyatt, N. Y.
Irish, Howard, Mich.

* Deceased.

Jennings, Bill, Ohio
Jones, Alan, Ind.
Johns, Mrs. Ralph, Ind.
Johnson, Hilda, N. C.
Justi, June and Wib, D. C.
Kessel, Bert, Mass.
Keyser, Paul, Wash.
Kleinkauf, Myrtle and Jack, Minn.
Koster, Norma, Ind.
Kuether, Ralph, Wis.
Leonard, Carolyn
Linegar, D. Ned, Texas
Lindsay, Allen, Miss.
Matthewses, The Cecil, Texas
Matthews, George and Elmore, Texas
McIntyre, Jim, Fla.
McReynolds, F. L., Ind.
Miller, Levi, Md.
Mintier, Wilma M., Pa.
O'Farrell, Una and Sean, Calif.
Page, Ralph, N. H.
Parish, Helen, Tenn.
Phifer, Lyndon, Tenn.
Pylant, Mrs. Agnes, Tenn.
Reeves, Nina, Ala.

Reynolds, Pauline F., N. D.
Ross, Charles
Ruesink, David
Schoonover, Barbara, Miss.
Severance, Roy, N. Y.
Shill, Rose, N. Y.
Short, Timothy, Texas
Smith, Kathryn and Howard, Mich.
Smith, Quay, Miss.
Stevens, Mrs. Ardis, Vt.
Stewart, Martha, Ga.
Stinnett, Betty
Stout, Marge and Ozzie, Calif.
Stuntz, Hugh C., Tenn.
Sunley, Mamie, Ind.
Tennant, Wirth, Mich.
Upton, Edward, Miss.
Veh, Raymond E., Pa.
Wakefield, Forrest W., Iowa
Walkup, Frank, Alaska
Will, Herman, Jr., Ill.
Willis, Warren W., Fla.
Wilson, John E., Texas
Winkler, Don, Tenn.
Winterberg, Lois, Ill.
Wright, Mrs. Nan, Texas
Yoh, Robert, Ala.

Contents

PART III: PLANNING FOR FUN

PART IV: MATERIALS FOR FUN

for Teaching and for Recreation . . . Scrapcraft (*by John and Edna Clapper*) . . . Craft Projects and Sources of Project Materials . . . Some Handcraft Supply Companies

PART ONE

Your Role

as a

Fun

Leader

_____1

New Ways to Fun and Fellowship

What wise men—ancient and modern—have said about recreation:

- The whole end and object of education is the right use of leisure.—ARISTOTLE, 384 B.C.
- Whatever enriches life has spiritual value.—E. O. HARBIN
- The hours that make us happy make us wise.—JOHN MASEFIELD
- You can discover more about a person in an hour of play than in a year of conversation.—PLATO

TIMES HAVE CHANGED. And how they have changed! In 1792 this was the attitude of a pioneer civilization in the United States, as interpreted in *Discipline,* the official guide of the Methodist Episcopal church: "We forbid play in the strongest terms. Those who play when they are young will play when they are old!"

Play was a luxury, to come only after material wants were met. And since they were never met, there was no time for play, even for the children. Work was virtue. Play was thought of as trivial.

Some leaders began to doubt this in the latter part of the nineteenth century. Playgrounds in cities began to spring up. A new consciousness of the need for play for children grew. Adults still lacked time to play. Men still worked 12 hours a day or more, for $1 a day.

Since 1900 the times have changed radically. The machine has liberated Americans from long hours of work. Instead of being scarce and precious, leisure time has become plentiful, even a problem. Delinquency is resulting from misdirected energy which, in former days, had to be devoted to work in order to survive.

More than ever, people are seeing the need for play—realizing that it is not only all right but necessary for folk of all ages. We are learning from the psychologist that recreation meets deep-seated psychological demands, far beyond superficial enjoyment. People must have release from the routine and tension of modern living. They must find expression for their interests and capabilities. Fun time becomes self-discovery time.

WHAT IS RECREATION?

Many people have attempted definitions of recreation. One of the best is attributed to a little boy, "What you do when you don't have to." Here are some others:

"Recreation—to create anew, to restore to a good condition the body or mind, to refresh."

"Recreation is the joyful exercise of body, mind, and social spirit, of performing and creating skill."

"Recreation is any pleasant voluntary activity apart from occupation."

Whatever the definition, these are words which pertain to recreation:

release	relaxation	bridge activity
renewal	recuperation	exhilaration
revitalization	fun	drive leading to
restoration to normal	change from the usual	love, beauty, and
sharing	spontaneity	fullness of life
refreshment	joyfulness	

Leisure is the *time* away from work or other necessary activity. Play is the *spirit* of true recreation.

THE TOTAL PERSON

The new approach acknowledges man to be a whole person, in keeping with the findings of the "ologies"—psychology, sociology, physiology. Leaders now recognize that the personality operates simultaneously through mind, muscles, emotions, spirit. Where the earlier approaches to organized recreation emphasized heavily the physical and competitive, the newer one looks on an individual as having need for social, creative, spiritual, and adventurous outlets, as well as physical.

Encouraging is the new recognition of the whole person by the churches. In former days the churches felt that they need minister only to the "spiritual" aspect of man's nature. (A wag replied to that argument, "I have yet to see a disembodied spirit!") Churches are coming to accept their responsibility for developing wholesome programs for the use of leisure time. Now they recognize that it is in the choices of leisure time that people "go right" or "go wrong." They are saying that people need to play together (fellowship of man with man) as well as to pray together (fellowship of man with God). "Religion embraces all things that improve a person's stature mentally, physically, spiritually, and socially, enabling him to grow toward a 'whole' person," says a statement of a conference of church recreation leaders.

Leaders are placing increasing importance on satisfaction through creative activities: doing things, making things, experiencing things. More than ever, drama, hobbies, crafts are getting attention in the forms of festivals, hobby nights, hobby shows, talent nights.

The best groups are doing more perspective planning. They are looking ahead months (some, years) to make sure that they bring to the members new and varied experiences and adventures, indoors and outdoors: parties, hikes, hobbies, crafts, music, festivals, athletic events, service projects. They are attempting to make the program "add up" so that members will grow in their abilities and expressions. Those who take the long look see recreation as making a vastly more significant contribution to lives than simply occupying time pleasantly for a few hours occasionally.

THE IMPORTANCE OF GROUPS

Richard Cabot has indicated man's needs as work, play, love, and worship, with a balance among them. Others have phrased man's needs in such terms as new experience and adventure, group regard, security, recognition, expression of creative abilities, expression of altruism, and the like. Nearly all these satisfactions will be gained (or missed) in *groups*. The most basic need of all is for a person to feel that he is of personal worth—that he is wanted, needed, missed when absent. Absolutely essential to the mental health of individuals is to be loved, understood, appreciated—to have a place in the group.

The fellowship of play can build that foundation of acceptance and understanding.[1] This is the reason that no matter what the purpose of a group, its social life is of great importance to its members.

The good group now attempts to find opportunity for adequate expression for all its members. Each is encouraged to do what he can do best. The new approach to group life calls for democracy in planning. Interest indicators, group discussions, surveys can help to show the planners what the group really wants. Democratic leadership consults frequently with the people planned for, especially at significant points, and before plans are crystallized. (An excellent guide to leadership is Lawrence Frank's *How to Be a Modern Leader*.[2])

Co-operative and creative activities are finding new importance in the programs of groups. There is a great increase in the use of intercultural materials such as folk songs, folk crafts, folk games and dances. New friendships across cultural and racial lines spring up. Recreation offers an effective bridge from person to person, group to group.

Competition is not being ruled out here. Through competitive games people can express and release aggressive tendencies enjoyably. (A successful technique of the psychologist is to have a patient name a golf ball for an enemy and sock it to the next county!) In competitive activity some people will find their only opportunity to express adventure and daring. If a boy cannot steal a base in a ball game he may steal something else to satisfy his need for adventure and daring. However, cumulative competition often does more harm than good in group life. The weak players, who need play for recreation, are eliminated. Pressure to win makes a "game" into work, takes the joy from it. Often only a few can play. Mass participation is more desirable.

DOING FOR OTHERS

Groups with lofty motives are finding a deepening of their togetherness by doing for others. This is one of the newer realizations in the building of group fellowship. Recreation has been called more a matter of emotions than motions. Therefore, the joyful, voluntary work of the work camp, service project, caravan, becomes pleasure because of the motive.

Work camps attract all ages, particularly high school and college youth. They help build playgrounds, reconstruct needed buildings, clear camp sites and the like. Caravans carry on play and education programs in communities and in churches. Projects like The Lord's Acre (see Index) are popular.

Many groups are getting enjoyment through sponsoring social affairs for the handicapped or the aged. In helping to relieve the loneliness of others, group members find their own lives refreshed. (See Table of Contents for location of fuller discussions of these projects.)

SOME CONCERNS

Most thoughtful persons are vitally concerned about many of the aspects of the use of leisure time. With 50 million new people having crowded into American cities during the past fifty years, urban residents are finding life becoming more depersonalized. Go where you want to go, do what you want to do—who cares? Who knows you? Along with this urbanizing of life has come "quick and easy" recreation, especially of the spectator type, a disease which Jay Nash called "spectatoritis" and another person, "sit-itis." The easy pleasures of watching, reading cheap literature, aimless riding around are not totally satisfying. They kill time, they pile up to make life dull. Many people take to drink as a futile "way out" from life's dullness.

Unused facilities are a matter of concern—the unlighted school or church, or other community service building—in the face of community need. Many schools and churches are concerned about this and are doing something about it. The film, "Leisure for the Lord," [3] attempts to deal realistically with this very problem from the standpoint of the church.

The need for training is a concern. Every year colleges and universities are adding courses for professional training, not only in physical education but also in the leadership skills and understandings of social recreation. Short-term, informal training opportunities are growing with extended service from city recreation departments, schools, churches, extension service, and such groups as the National Recreation Association.[4] Autonomous recreation leadership laboratories [5] are growing in strength and effectiveness. Most church groups now sponsor such laboratories. Schoolteachers are increasingly interested in the skills of recreation for use in the classroom and in other groups to which they belong.

GETTING VALUES STRAIGHT

So many problems face our group life that we sometimes forget that progress is being made. Martha M. Eliot, Chief of the U. S. Children's Bureau, reminded us recently that "last year some 18,-000,000 girls and boys between the ages of 10 and 17 were *not* (italics ours) picked up by the police for any crime whatsoever."

It could be that the many who have not been "picked up by the police for any crime whatsoever" and, more positively speaking, the many who have found joy in releasing others, have got their values straight. The two bits of verse which follow express, in different styles and from different approaches, certain values of recreation—the wisdom of preventing wrongdoing by constructive use of leisure, and the pleasure of "helping others to . . . make of their lives a thing of beauty."

FENCE OR AMBULANCE

'Twas a dangerous cliff, as they freely confessed,
Though to walk near its crest was so pleasant;
But over its dangerous edge there had slipped
A duke, and full many a peasant;
So the people said something would have to be done,
But their project failed all to tally,
Some said: "Put a fence around the edge of the cliff."
Some: "An ambulance down in the valley."

But the cry for the ambulance carried the day,
And it spread through the neighboring city,
A fence may be useful or not, it is true,
But each heart became brimful of pity,
For those who slipped over the dangerous cliff,
And the dwellers in highway and alley,
Gave pounds or gave pence, nor for a fence,
But an ambulance down in the valley.

"For the cliff is all right if you're careful," they said.
And if folks ever slip and are dropping,
It isn't the slipping that hurts them so much
As the shock down below when they're stopping!
So day after day as these mishaps occurred,
Quick forth would these rescuers sally
To pick up the victims who fell off the cliff
With the ambulance down in the valley.

Then the old sage remarked: "It's a marvel to me
That people give far more attention
To repairing results than to stopping the cause
When they'd much better aim to prevention.
Let us stop at its source all the mischief," he said.
"Come, neighbor and friends, let us rally;
If the cliff we would fence we might almost dispense
With the ambulance down in the valley."

"Oh, he's fanatic," the others rejoined,
Dispense with the ambulance? Never!
He'd dispense with all charity too, if he could:
No! No! We'll support them forever!
Aren't we picking folks up just as fast as they fall?
Why should he prevail on us all?
Why should people of sense stop to put up a fence
While their ambulance works in the valley?

Better guide well the young than reclaim them when old.
For the voice of true wisdom is calling;
To rescue the fallen is good, but 'tis best
To prevent other people from falling.
Better close up the source of temptation and crime
Than deliver from dungeon or galley;
Better put up a fence round the top of the cliff
Than an ambulance down in the valley.[6]

FINDING RENEWAL

Then said one who was fear-filled
    and frightened because he had no skills
        of music
           or art
              or crafts;
    who was not free of self enough to share the thoughts
        that enveloped his mind;
    and whose song was not of joy—

"What can I do to be a part of the fellowship of life?"

And he answered, saying:

"We, being many, are each members of one body
    but all members have not the same office;

Having then gifts *differing,*
    find what is renewal for your own mind and heart.

And you who are leaders—
      and you are *all* leaders—
Be careful lest you lose yourself in a game, a song, a craft—
      and keep in mind only what is
            re-creative for you.

If you are indeed wise,
      you will not bid others enter the house of your joy
            but rather help each to the threshold of his own joy.

And even as there are many paths to the Kingdom of God above,
      so there are many paths to abundant, creative living
            here on earth,

Be it ever your good pleasure to find new ways of helping others
      to release their imprisoned splendor;

      And make of their lives a thing of beauty." [7]

2

What the Leader Does

IT MAY BE TRUE that to many recreation leaders the art of leadership has come "naturally," but it is a safe guess that by far the majority of them are made, not "born." In other words, to be a good recreation leader takes not only a strong yen to be one and a keen love of good fun, but also conscious, plugging effort, and some self-examination.

THE LEADER HIMSELF

Ask yourself which of these qualifications needed for a good leader you can claim or can develop:

He loves fun and radiates the spirit of fun to the group.
He likes people and deals with them kindly and considerately.
He is democratic and gives the group a chance to share in making decisions.

Leader examines himself

11

He is group-minded. He feels that individuals are important but that to get them to participate happily in the group is his goal as a recreation leader.

He is prepared. He has checked over his material, tried out ideas, and rounded up more than he thinks will be needed.

He is creative. He can work under all kinds of conditions, can improvise, and encourages others to do so.

He is humble, though confident. Sometimes he is not so confident— he is apprehensive or "just plain scared."

He has faith in God the Father and faith in people. The best leader, however he phrases his goal, is attempting to bring more abundant life to those with whom he works.

Every leader finds that certain ways of attaining his goal, certain devices or techniques, bring better results than others. The "how to do's" are the skills, the tools of the recreation leader's trade.

GENERAL AIDS TO LEADERS

Within the later sections of this book many "how to do's" are given. Some practical techniques, however, that are of general interest are included at this point:

Getting the Attention of the Group. Using a whistle is out of date for most social recreation. In its place leaders use a chord of music, or speak in a low tone so that people must become quiet, or sometimes stand calmly until the group has quieted down. Sometimes a raised hand is the "get quiet" signal. On a public address system a musical whistle of two or three notes indicates time to get quiet. The best device is to get the group to applaud, then to raise their right hands as you raise yours. Try it!

Standing in the Right Place. Take your place where the group can see you easily. This may mean standing on a stool or a raised platform. Sometimes it means standing in the center of a circle, but turning so that people can lip-read what you are saying.

When coaching a large standing group, ask all to stoop while the demonstration goes on in the center of the room. A group of several hundred can thus see the steps of the process easily and will try them more readily.

Making Corrections. Accept any responsibility for your own mistakes. Be pleasant; use humor if it comes naturally. Look at any situation from the viewpoint of the people involved. As leader, you are the representative of the entire group. Don't hesitate to show how something should be done, or even to correct errors if need be, but always do it tactfully, kindly, and firmly.

Handling Dissenters. These folk want attention. They are often tense, so help them to relax if possible. They want people to notice them. Sometimes letting them do a demonstration or run an errand will help. Give them something useful to do. Ask their opinion if you can do so sensibly. Give them alternate choices. Be pleasant with them—joke with them if you can.

However, don't hesitate to discipline them if it is necessary. With willingness to accept defeat if need be, put the possibilities to a vote of the entire group, and put it firmly to the dissenters if they lose. Try to do it in a face-saving way for them.

Sometimes choosing activities divided into small groups will "do the trick." They may be jealous of your position, but now they have their own group to lead.

Being Adaptable. The best leader is always ready to come up (if he or she can) with the *right thing,* at the *right time,* done in the *right way.* This may mean shifting gears quickly. Here are some sample situations you may meet:

1. There is too small a space, unexpectedly so. (Do group starters, or divide into groups.)
2. There is an unexpected excess of males or females. (Use trio musical games and those which can take extras, also games and activities requiring no partners.)
3. Equipment promised has not been provided. (Do the best you can. Shift games or activities.)
4. Another leader who was to help doesn't show up. (Anticipate this, if you can, and have in mind what you will do.)
5. It rains, for an outdoor situation. (Plan in advance for this. Consider whether to cancel the affair or find an indoor spot. Shift to indoor fun.)
6. No accompanist shows up for the music. (Try singing without the piano, or shift to humor, group starters, skits, and stunts.)
7. An unusually small group shows up, or an unusually large one.

(Try to fit your activities to the mood of the group. If it's unusually small, relax and make the program a gentle, genial
experience with small group games, mystery games, humor,
group starters, music, and such. If it's very large, you may
want to divide it into several smaller units for several activities.)

8. Seats are unexpectedly screwed to the floor. (You had thought
the people could move around. Here group starters, humor,
mystery games, skits, and stunts are valuable. Some equipment games may be placed around the sides of the room for
fun. Do things in two's.)

9. You find unanticipated noises, competition. (Try to go with
the situation, not against it. Complaining bitterly may relieve
feelings, but it doesn't stir courageous joy! Move location, request the noise to be stopped if feasible, wait until the noise is
over, or shift to another activity. Laugh if the situation is
funny.)

10. Two groups are scheduled for the same room. (Usually one
must leave!)

11. The lights go out. (Like the rain situation, think ahead for
this as a possibility. A couple of candles in the leader's kit
would be a good idea.)

12. The building is locked, and you don't have a key. (Grind your
teeth. . . . See if anyone knows where a key can be had. . . .
Send somebody for it. . . . Sing, do knock-knocks, play mystery games, until the person gets back unless it's too cold.)

Using Helpers. Multiple leadership is often planned for a social
affair so that one at a time, different people lead. Sometimes,
however, an individual is in complete charge of an entire period
of fun. It is good to have from one to several helpers in the
group who will assist with anything that needs to be done,
whether it is to open windows as the leader motions to him or
her, or to help in a demonstration, or to run an errand. When
a recreation leader from outside is visiting a group, the group's
regular leader either ought to occupy this "helper" role or get
someone to do it.

Helpers can often encourage folk to join in the fun by a little
enticement. (Always be careful not to force people into activity

especially adults. There may be some good reason for the person's staying out.)

Giving Advance Warning. Don't create a bump! Groups will cooperate better if they know what's coming, therefore experienced leaders try to move smoothly from one thing to the next.

"In five minutes we're going to put away the equipment games." That warning gives time to adjust minds. In musical games, to call out, "Once more through" or "Last time," keeps the end from coming too abruptly.

In group singing, move the mood of the singing gradually toward a climax (which may be very loud or very soft). Consider carefully moving from one formation to another. Transitions are important here, too.

Developing "Groupness." Groups of different sizes feel quite different, both to leader and to participants. A little group of three is very chummy. To double it, does not change its nature too

Examining the group

much. However, fifteen seems much larger, and a little more impersonal. There is a next breaking point at about fifty, and the group takes on additional formality. Many "party games" are not good if played in groups larger than this. A group of a hundred is more formal, and not radically different from a thousand or more, except that over a period of time the hundred can get to know each other, but the thousand people probably never will.

To bring that spirit of "groupness" into large groups, it is advantageous to divide into smaller ones, by birth month, date of birth, counting off, or some such system. Then simultaneously, in these small groups, a few people begin to get acquainted with each other.

The advantage of a small group is that members can get to know each other quite well. "Groupness" comes from doing things together. There is a sense of common fellowship and a common goal. Some naïve individuals think that group spirit can be verbalized into being, simply by saying, "We have a fi-i-ine group here." On the contrary, "groupness" is built slowly by group-minded leadership.

Here is an illustration of how a conference might open, moving toward "groupness":

1. Everybody has a name tag. Everyone is to speak to every person he sees wearing a name tag.
2. At the first meeting in the auditorium the leader begins with some group starters and motion songs, getting the people to do "Rolling O'er the Billows" with arms over each others' shoulders. (If it is a religious group, they may end the song period with a spiritual or a hymn.)
3. Later in a recreation period they do easy group mixers, both with and without music. Time is given for each person to visit a bit with each new person he faces. "Group Interview" is used in small groups, so that a few persons really get acquainted. Later there are refreshments and a closing sing.
4. During the program, the leadership is introduced in an informal way, perhaps with a skit. Without belittling what they are to do, they do not set themselves on a pedestal. The "ordinary conferee" gets the impression that "we are all in this together."
5. At the end the leader announces, "Everybody shake hands with fifteen people before you leave," and counts for them, for the first one or two.

At the end of such a combination of effort, a group spirit is already beginning to emerge. It often takes two to three days to break through, sometimes longer, depending on the group.

Showing Honor. Developing groupness comes also through showing appreciation, honor, and respect for those in the group and for people serving the group. Whether it's just "We want a cook's parade" (to the tune, "Farmer in the Dell") or whether it's recognition of fifty years of service by a much loved officer, the very showing of honor and appreciation draws the group together mightily.

Recognizing the Value of Formations. The very way a group is formed has much to do with how it feels about itself! Nothing surpasses having a group sit close together for group singing, or for doing stunts, or even for just watching entertainment put on for their benefit. It is often worth while to move to a smaller room so that people feel almost crowded. When many people are jammed in close together on the steps, sitting on a pier, in the back of a bus, or up close around the fire on a cold night, a quick sense of fellowship develops.

The circle is another good form, especially if not too large. A circle of over fifty persons begins to lose the sense of intimacy and merely shows that a big crowd is present. The usual table setup, where people are eating and talking, can become very sociable, simply because they form themselves unconsciously into little groups. (Conversation starters will help prime this pump.)

Lines are good to develop a sense of mild competition, especially in relays. The grand-march sort of line gives people security in that the men (or boys) join *their* line and the girls (or women) join *theirs*.

Dealing with Ideas of Right and Wrong. Some leisure-time pursuits are regarded as generally wrong, but there are many borderline situations, in which people have convictions that certain kinds of activities are wrong. The wise leader will deal with these instances as they arise.

In the first place, every good leader is guided by his own insights and conscience, doing nothing that is not right in his own sight. Then he listens sympathetically to viewpoints different from his own. There are so many interesting things to do in group recreation that no one activity need be the only one. Often to shift to something acceptable to all is the solution. Then too, people are often "down on what they're not up on." When they see what is being done, they may change their minds. This often happens, particularly among fair-minded church folk in relation to their youth.

Handling the All-Male Situation. Actually there is not too much difference in what you do there from what is done in a mixed group. It may be chiefly in the way you present it!

For instance, in all-male groups, half may have been given ribbons or some other identification to be "ladies," and partner affairs have been conducted. An ingenious woman leader in a camp in Germany asked the fellows to go to their bunks for a pillow, and had them do several dances with a pillow as a partner. It was all in good fun.

Most mental games are fun; most group starters would be fine. Skits and stunts can become hilarious when men take the parts of women. Men's groups like to sing, they like to eat, and they like to talk about themselves. They enjoy humorous material. (Most of 'em can top yours!) All-male camping trips are very usual. Equipment games go well with this group, too.

Active games, low-organized, sportlike games, and regular sports would be acceptable to an all-male group. Select some games in which all can play. Have plenty of good food, and close on a good-fellowship note, perhaps with singing. (Men like to hear men's voices, as well as women do.)

Handling All-Girl or Woman Groups. Much the same devices work as for the all-male groups. A girl can put on a painter's cap and become a man for a while without being too much bothered.

Group singing, humor, skits and stunts, most group starters, equipment games would all have some interest. Cook-outs and other outdoor affairs are enjoyed by girls and women.

THE LEADER'S KIT

A leadership kit, for which a carton or old suitcase is used as container, is a necessary and practical tool for any leader of recreation, whether he is an old hand or a nervous beginner. It consists merely of gathering an assortment of simple equipment and utilizing these odds and ends for many purposes. For example, pieces of 4-foot rope can be used for making a loop for a hoop relay, a three-legged race, the handcuff puzzler, a bulldog pull. Many recreation leaders make cards on which directions for games are kept separately.

A list of simple articles and equipment, along with several games that can be played with each, is given below. (See other sections for directions to these games.)

Kit for General Use

ALPHABET CARDS. Alphabet Race, Split Affinities, Alphabet Soup, Scrambled Alphabet, Post Card Relay (hold cards between lip and nose)

BALLOONS. Balloon Pop Relay, Balloon Battle Royal, Balloon Basketball, Balloon Swat, Balloon Shave (lather balloon, then shave it)

BEANS. Guess How Many (in jar), Bean Pass Relay, Stock Market, Barnyard I Spy

BEAN BAGS. Bean Bag Toss, Pass It, Bean Bag Relay, Football Party, Steal the Bacon, Pass Fast

BOTTLES. Use as bases, or to mark off playing area for Bean Drop (kneel on chair and drop beans into bottle on floor), Ping-pong Flip.

CANDLES (*see* MATCHES). (Candles are handy when lights go out!)

CHALK. Writing Relay, Drawing Relay, Blind Artist (blindfolded person tries to draw object on board). Use chalk to draw playing areas and diagrams for other games on floor.

HANDKERCHIEFS (BANDANA). Handkerchief Laugh (group must laugh when leader drops handkerchief and remain quiet while he holds it): games in which blindfold is needed: Blind Artist, Hot Potato, Blind Feeding the Blind (two blindfolded players feed ice cream to each other)

JAR TOP RINGS. Quoits, Bottle Toss (throw over neck of bottle), Chair Leg Toss, Twirl Relay (twirl pencil around while hopping on one foot), Indoor Washers (three circles drawn on floor—5, 10, and 15 points)

LIFESAVERS. Lifesaver Relay (pass from person to person on soda straw held in teeth), Lifesaver Push (push across yardstick or floor with soda straw held in teeth), Find the Lifesaver (on a string, passed from person to person behind their backs), Hand Clap Relay

MATCHES (AND PENNY MATCH BOXES). Match Box Relay (nose to nose); Firebuild Race, Lighted Candle Relay, Candle Light-and-Blow Relay (matches with heads off can be used in place of toothpicks for some games)

NEWSPAPERS. Steppingstone Relay, Making Doilies (best design wins prize), Swat Tag, Balloon Swat. Use for costume designing. Delete names of products of familiar ads and let group guess.

PAPER BAGS. Blow and Burst Relay (blowing up and sitting on sacks), Elephant Race (tie large bags on feet and run to goal), Paper Bag Handshake (mixer—tie bags on everybody's hand and introduce to others), Hammer Throw (inflate and tie with long string). Paper bags may also be used as blindfold.

PAPER AND PENCILS. "Draw It" version of "Act It Out," Blind Artists, Hidden Words, Split Proverbs (mixer), Tit-Tat-Toe, Battleship, Dot, Pencil Jump (hold toes with fingers and try to jump over pencil). Use pencils in relays as objects to pass or carry.

PING-PONG BALLS. Ping-pong Rounders, Toss for Accuracy, Ping-pong Relay (couples hold ball between their foreheads); Ping-pong Football (two teams try to blow ball across opposite line—use floor or table), Monacle Relay (place ball on eye and pass it from eye to eye down line); Ping-pong Bounce (try to bounce ball into hat or wastebasket), Ping-pong Fan Relay, Dodgeball Game, Flip the Ball (like Flip the Cork).

PINS. Use in decorations, pinning paper or other material on players' clothing, costuming.

ROPE. Loop Relay, Three-Legged Race, Handcuff Puzzler, Bulldog Pull, Rope-Skipping Relay, Tug of War.

SCISSORS. Use in decorations, cutting doilies, Scissors Race (contestants race to cut strip of paper ten feet long and one inch wide).

SONGBOOKS. Have two copies at least, one for accompanist. Try to use familiar songs.

STRING. Chew the String Race, Marshmallow Race (first one to marshmallow on middle of string wins), Wrap-Around Relay, Pass the Ring. Quoits may also be made from string.

TAPE MEASURE. Handy for use in the Indoor Track Meet (hammer throw, shot, javelin, broadest grin). Measure tiniest waist, longest nose, biggest feet.

BOTTLE CAPS. For counters in games, for tossing games

CHECKERS. For sliding, in table shuffleboard

ALPHABET SPAGHETTI. For spelling word games, glued on for name tags

SOAP. For carving

CLAY. For modeling

SHEET. For use in shadow plays

SOCKS. For puppets

PIPE CLEANERS. As creative art medium

TOOTHPICKS. As counters in games, substituting for matches

CRAYONS. For adult drawing and coloring as well as for children

COMBS. For comb band

SUITCASE. To contain your kit supplies

BUBBLE GUM. Just for fun—see who can blow biggest.

CLOTHESPINS. Drop them in games, dress them.

CORKS. For cork-tossing games, water games, flipping cork from top of coke bottle

MAGAZINES. For number of creative games (see Magazine Games)

CAMERA. For taking pictures, camera hike, making movie, publicity pictures

POSTAL CARDS. For card shower to group member absent by illness

CLOTHES HANGERS. For wire to make Christmas wreaths, to hang with bell for tossing game

NAME TAGS. To use as name tags, as belt blocks (if with four holes), or as place cards

DRIED BEANS, PEAS. As counters for games, like Even or Odd

PAPER PLATES. For eating, decorating, discus throwing

RUBBER HEELS. For tossing games

LARGE METAL WASHERS. For washer tossing, or for tossing board indoors

MIMEOGRAPHED FORMS. For Quiz, Scrambles, other games that appeal

Additional Items for Outdoor Kit

BAGS (BURLAP). Sack Race, Blind Boxing, Swat Tag. Use also as bases for ball and tag games.

BALLS (PLAYGROUND, TENNIS, VOLLEYBALL, SOFTBALL). Old Plug, Dodge Ball, Safety Zone Ball, Bottle Baseball, Stop Ball (see Active Games section)

BAT (SOFTBALL BAT). Sock-a-Ball, Flies and Grounders, Work Up, Hit the Bat

BROOMSTICKS. Dizzy Izzy Relay, Broomstick Hurdle Relay, Broom Hockey, Pull Up Contest, Stick Acrobatics, Siamese Centipede Race

LIME (SMALL BAG). Use in laying out playing areas.

WASHERS. Washer Pitching (3 holes in line two inches apart; 15 feet away, a like number of holes; first hole counts 5, second 10, third 15; 60 is the game; each contestant pitches 3 washers, alternating throws)

Kit Items for Use with Younger Children

PAPER BAGS. For puppets, painting faces on them, masks, funny faces, for sack of surprises or as storytelling sack (full of objects to be shown)

NEWSPAPERS. To stuff paper-sack puppets, to use in dry-paper modeling, as protective aprons when working with paints

KLEENEX TISSUES. Dresses for clothespin or pipe-cleaner puppets

PAPER PLATES. For decorating, with jingling objects on edge for tambourine; to contain clay, to hold crayons

FINGER-PAINTING MATERIALS. From stationery store, for doing finger painting (old shirts for children to wear while painting)

TEMPERA PAINTS. In preference to water colors

TEXTILE PAINTS. For older children, to make gifts of cloth for parents

CRAYONS. Get in large boxes, larger crayons for younger children.

CHALK (WHITE AND COLORED). For blackboard and construction paper

PAINT BRUSHES. For painting

GLUE, PASTE, RUBBER CEMENT. For pasting (rubber cement most satisfactory)

SCISSORS. Blunt-edged ones for little children

MAGNETS. With paperclips, nails, iron filings, for informal fun

MAGAZINES. For cutting out paper dolls, making quick scrapbook

DOILIES. For making hats, bonnets, decorations, skirts for doll dresses, valentines, place cards

PAPER CUPS. As foundations for clothespin dolls, puppet hats

CONSTRUCTION PAPER, NEWSPRINT (BLANK). Bought respectively from stationery store, newspaper office (ends of rolls)

BOXES FOR BUILDING. Blocks also, of course

ODDS AND ENDS. For making place cards (including cards, of course)

RHYTHM INSTRUMENT SUPPLY BOX. With lard cans covered with inner tubes, bells, nails long enough to strike with, boxes or cans with something in them that rattles, pieces of broomstick sawed off to be struck together, old pot lids for cymbals

THE USE OF A RECREATION INTEREST INDICATOR

An excellent device both to reveal program desires of a group and to discover skills already developed is a brief interest finder in questionnaire form. The leader might have mimeographed copies run off of either chart which follows,[1] to be filled out by members of each new group.

RECREATION INTEREST INDICATOR

Name (Mr. Mrs. Miss) _____Nickname_____

Address_____Phone_____

Occupation _____Business Phone_____

Age Group: (Please circle) 9-11 12-14 15-17 18-23 24-34 35-65 65 over

I would participate in planned programs (circle): Mon. Tue. Wed. Thu. Fri. Sat. Sun.

I have most leisure time (circle) Morning Afternoon Evening

My hobbies _____

Special skills, training, experience in any field relating to Recreation and Social Life _____

STORYTELLING

Storytelling is one of the oldest, most natural forms of recreation or entertainment. It was part of a recreation pattern forced upon people because there were few other diversions. Now it is more of an acquired art.

Stories are nearly always welcome, especially if well told. "Have you time for a story?" usually brings an enthusiastic "Yes."

One becomes a good storyteller by observation and practice.

Activity	Interested	Would Do	Could Lead
Arts			
Art Exhibits			
Drawing			
Painting			
Poster making			
Sculpturing			
Sketching			
Crafts			
Ceramics			
Copper			
Flower arranging			
Jewelry			
Leather			
Metal			
Needlework			
Photography			
Plastics			
Textile painting			
Tin			
Weaving			
Wood			
Model Building			
Drama			
Acting			
Choral Speaking			
Costumes			
Directing plays			
Informal Drama			
Interpretive dance			
Making scenery			
Public speaking			
Puppets			
Radio and TV Programs			

Activity	Interested	Would Do	Could Lead
Reading plays			
Stage lighting			
Theatrical make-up			
Writing plays			
Literature			
Book club			
Creative writing			
Debating			
Discussions and forums			
Library work			
Storytelling			
Music			
Chorus or choir			
Creative song writing			
Music appreciation—			
Listening group			
Playing in orchestra			
Play piano			
Play other instruments			
Singing for fun			
Quartette (barber shop)			
Trio			
Outdoor Recreation			
Bird study			
Campfires			
Camping			
Conducted tours			
Cook-outs			
Gardening			
Hiking			
Nature study			
Picnics			
Playground			

Activity	Interested	Would Do	Could Lead
Star study			
Social Recreation			
Banquets			
Conversation			
Equipment games			
Folk games and dances			
Parties			
Party games			
Social dancing			
Square dancing			
Table games			
Sports			
Badminton			
Baseball			
Basketball			
Boating			
Bowling			
Croquet			
Field events			
Fishing			
Football (tag)			
Golf			
Handball			
Horseshoes			
Hunting			
Ping-pong			
Roller skating			
Shuffleboard			
Softball			
Swimming			
Track			
Tennis			
Volleyball			

There is no short cut to this art. Here are some pointers that may help you in your own quest to become a storyteller:

1. Select an appropriate story for the age group and for the occasion, not too long.
2. Check it to see if it has a good ending, and if it is plausible in its development.
3. If dialect is involved, try to do justice to the dialect, but admit that you are an amateur if you are. The best storyteller will use only that material which laughs *with* the dialect, never *at* it. (*Making fun of any person or any region or any nationality is not a worthy act in storytelling—or at any time.*)
4. Try to make the characters seem real, with personalities that are consistent. Practice telling your story to a small experimental group and let them give you some suggestions for improvement.
5. Many stories allow for interruptions, or should do so. Children especially respond. "What do you think he did next?" If their answer is good, you may want to incorporate it into the story. Small children like themselves to be the hero-heroine of a story.
6. The pattern of a good story will include an interest catcher at the beginning. It will move through the development of a conflict or struggle or obstacle to minor crises. Things often go against the hero-heroine in the early or middle part of the story. There is usually a big struggle, with the hero or heroine winning at least a partial victory over his enemy or antagonist, over a bad situation, or over himself, and then an ending. Sometimes there will be a surprise as in the "tall tale" kind of story.
7. Practice telling a story different ways, letting your imagination carry you. Place yourself as much as possible in the situation of the people involved. (However, be careful to distinguish between the imaginative "tall tale" kind of story and the *lie,* which deliberately misleads people to think that you actually participated in something in which you did not. "Tall tale" has an element of the tongue-in-cheek.)
8. Have a few short stories, of the punch-line variety, ready to tell. There are more situations in which this can be done than those in which long stories may be told. (See Humor section.)
9. Read stories from collections such as those mentioned in the Bibliography. Public libraries usually have a good collection of

books with stories to be told to all ages. Read-aloud stories (such as those included in this book) may be memorized and told.

RELIGION AND THE RECREATION LEADER

Since the aim of recreation is to re-create, there is an important role for religious expression in connection with recreation.

The best leadership in the field is found in people who have a religious philosophy of life, whatever their faith. They believe in the fatherhood of God, the brotherhood of man, and the worth of every individual person. Such leadership will demonstrate its source of power in the way it handles group situations and persons in groups. The best leaders pray for their members, for insights, and for the renewal of ability. The best planning is preceded by prayer, whether the group does it in the planning meeting or not.

A religious philosophy (this is not necessarily sectarian) will make itself known through group operation in these ways:

1. An over-all spiritual quality in the relationship of the members with each other and with others. (If religion is not lived in relationships, it is hard to believe that it is there at all.)
2. Concern for others—the needy, the lonely, the helpless. One of the best exercises in thinking and planning would be to say, "Who in our community is lonely and might be cheered by something we could do, or *get him to do?*"
3. Service projects, both in the community and on a wider basis, perhaps world-wide, enjoyed by the group as recreational activity, yet having significant consequences.
4. Worship and meditation services, often informal, sometimes brief, but always sincere. Many groups close every party or social with a fellowship circle or a quiet song period and prayer, sometimes with a thought for the week. A simple sentence or two in prayer or meditation expressing a thought that is really related to the occasion, is far more desirable and more impressive than an extraneous poem or prayer dragged in.
5. Some groups like to have special places for quiet meditation. In some camps a chapel is open for meditation. The council circle or council fire is often used as a rallying center for meditation and closing service in camps. Even hikes and cook-outs may

offer a natural occasion for silent worship. (The Indian always regarded his council fire as sacred. He did his cooking on another fire.) The "green temple" idea also has been used out of doors—a special wooded place with log seats, set aside for quiet and meditation. (A recreational work project might construct such a place for meditation.)

6. Music and drama can reflect the religious philosophy of a group. Recreationally it may mean singing and enjoying hymns, carols, spirituals in informal "sing," or reading plays and discussing them. (See Bibliography.) A well-chosen play may impel the group to action in bettering relationships or in sponsoring service projects, even though the play was undertaken from a recreational standpoint.

7. Religious appreciation and concern will be reflected in the material used in programs, especially at the closing. Passages of Scripture, such as Psalm 8, Psalm 23, Psalm 19, reflect the glory of God and nature; the 13th chapter of I Corinthians or the 12th chapter of Romans outline duties in relationships, Psalm 90 a trust in God. Many groups love Malotte's "The Lord's Prayer" to be sung by all as a closing. (A good project would be to have a committee look up suitable scripture references for closings, for outdoor services and the like, keeping a card file on their findings.) The search for meaningful passages would help members to become better acquainted with the Bible.

8. Some groups call the endings of their programs "Signatures." Should the name at the end be the leader's or another's? The ending should be in the spirit of togetherness, a "we" experience. In religious groups it would recognize the fellowship of man and the fellowship with God. To be effective it does not have to be long, but it needs to be single-minded and sincere.

WHERE CAN THE LEADER GET HELP?

From books and materials (as listed in the Bibliography) the recreation leader can get help, but in many communities he can find it in person if he looks around. Here are some suggestions:

1. City or county recreation department
2. County agent's office
3. Staffs serving churches, 4-H, Scouts, Grange, YMCA, YWCA, community centers

4. Handicraft shops
5. Highschool and college departments of arts and crafts, dramatics, physical education, social group work
6. Radio announcers (who are MC's)
7. Hobby clubs and individual hobbyists
8. Callers' Associations for squares
9. Forestry Service, Parks Department
10. Camp leaders, camp operator. (Many agencies operate camps.)
11. Drama clubs, Little Theater
12. National headquarters of churches and group work agencies and national suppliers of records, craft materials, books (see Bibliography)

PART TWO

Selecting the

Right Activities

for

Each Group

3

Children

THE CHILDREN FROM preschool age to twelve years are considered in this chapter. Even in this short age span different approaches are needed in planning recreation.

> Come listen now to the good old days
> When children, strange to tell,
> Were seen, not heard, led a simple life—
> In short, were brought up well.
> —Based on an observation made by ARISTOPHANES, 448–380 B.C.

From time immemorial the older generation has looked at the younger one with wonder, amazement, disapproval. The elders have

Children

been shaking their heads. Yet children keep coming into the world, and keep growing up into elders—who in turn shake their heads.

The problems of the modern child have to do with the fact that the family is, in a sense, displaced in the city, where more and more people are living. This often denies a child the opportunity for play in nature's settings. Many times children are not situated where they can run and make noise freely. Spectator activities, particularly television, present real problems for the normal growth and development of the child.

But some good things have come, too. The family is becoming more of a companionship group than one ruled by a dictator. We know much more about the needs of childhood and its struggles for expression.

UNDERSTANDING CHILDREN BY AGE GROUPS

Children 2 to 5. These children are homebound, dependent largely on parents, other children in the family, playmates, perhaps grandparents for their companionship. Some in later years may go to nursery school.

This is the age which is learning to talk, to use creative and muscular skills. Their world is that of play. They learn to pull wheeled toys, stack blocks, play with other children. They can learn to play alone with sandbox, paper and crayon, clothespins, pans, play records. The older they are, the more they want outdoor play with swings, slides, jungle gyms, climbing trees, doing "stunts." A "Yard Party" is right down their alley. They imitate Western heroes, like stories, like to sing. They are quite able, in their world of make-believe, to pretend that things are quite different—the tricycle representing a horse or chariot, the doll being a beautiful princess. "Let's Pretend" activities they enjoy.

Children of this age are quickly influenced by others. They learn initiative, self-reliance, co-operation through playing with other children. It is well to know what kind of children these playmates are, however, for the little tots learn from each other to cheat, to do wrong things, as well as to play fair.

Younger children like to "make up things," and often compose simple little songs. They will not always perform when requested, of course.

As with all other children, leaders need to remember that they differ. Each child has a different response pattern. The best leaders are those who can "empathize" (feel into the situation) with a child. The most important single thing to remember is that young children need to feel warmth and to be loved. Corrections can be made if the child feels basically that the person correcting is fond of him.

Children 6 to 8. This is the age of starting to school, developing independence, breaking home ties. The attention span of 6-to-8'ers is not very long. Because of the many changes coming in their lives, 6-year-olds may not like too much variety in play and recreation. They are fond of old stories retold, reread. However, they are learning new songs, games, and skills, and can perform them. Seven-year-olds like dramatic play with dolls, paints, clay, guns, planes, and cars; outdoor play in the water; big blocks and sandboxes, for imaginative construction; running games. Tall tales are a part of being seven, just as "taking things" may be a part of being six. These children especially need love and understanding.

The 8-year-olds are beginning to read, thus broadening their recreational interests. They enjoy reading almost anything for pleasure. They like to have a special friend. They like signs of being "grown up" in allowances, small responsibilities. They like to play store, play with money. They have hobbies. They still need love and understanding from the leadership. They will accept a leader as being a special friend (not a mama substitute). Because of the need for much exercise they horseplay and scramble a lot. The girls begin to enjoy dressing up like mama. This is the beginning of the comic book age. Guidance in what to read here may help greatly. They like lots of activity, running games.

Children 9-11. These children like some of the same things that they did earlier, such as singing; but they often shift from creative activities (painting, making things of clay and other art media) to intellectual pursuits. The 9-year-olds are undergoing a change in that they are entering the "gang age" where the group becomes important. They are inclined toward hero worship. They need love and understanding, and certainly not comparisons.

In the "gang age" the children may "gang up" on their elders. They are not difficult to work and play with if a leader is understanding and sympathetic with their needs and points of view. They need guidance, not dictatorship. They must have opportunity and room for noise, and they must express emotions.

Organized games they will enjoy, including competition. They need to learn to win and lose. However, *cumulative* competition is not wholesome, and this age is generally not ready for "league play." There are many "low-organized games" (see Index) in this book highly suitable for their needs for exercise and group competition.

PARTY PLANNING FOR YOUNGER CHILDREN

Children enjoy parties as much as their elders do in celebration of birthdays, holidays—or just for fun, like a yard party. They like to help plan a party themselves. The amount of help given depends on the age of the children, but they feel as if it is "their party" if they can help. This is true whether the party is done by a group or by and for an individual child, and whether the adult planner is a teacher or other leader, or whether it is a mother or perhaps father.

The occasion may be any of the holidays or it might be a birthday or (in a group) birthdays. Here are some planning pointers to help:

WHAT SHALL THE PARTY BE? The child or children can help to decide that—also when it shall be.

WHO WILL BE INVITED? Friends of the same age are most congenial. With very young children the number should be small, about the same number of guests as the child's age. Above 5 you can double it. (Numbers are exciting to young children.)

SHALL WE INVITE MOTHERS TOO? If you do, have something else for them to do. Two adults in most parties is enough.

WHAT ARE THE MOST IMPORTANT THINGS? The favors or gifts, the food, the games, probably in that order, for younger children. Therefore the table should be decorated nicely. Food does not need to be elaborate, but there should be plenty. Some like to serve things the children can eat with their fingers entirely, with drinks in paper cups.

DECORATIONS. Children like colorful decorations. From them they can get the party spirit whether the games are too good or not. Let them help plan and prepare decorations (even if the effect is not perfect).

FOOD. Simple refreshments are preferred by children. If the party is in midmorning or midafternoon, don't serve too much too close to mealtime, unless what you serve is intended to be a meal.

GAMES, ACTIVITIES. For children 2-5, such things as rolling balls to each other, playing records, coloring pictures (selected in keeping with the party theme), cutting out dolls, making valentines, Santa Clauses, kites, jack-o-lanterns are good. They may enjoy "Pin the tail on the donkey" (adapted, such as pin Santa's pack on his back), or identifying pictures of animals. They enjoy playing with familiar toys. Also they can sing songs learned at home, nursery school, Sunday School. Building blocks, finger painting are fun. Only one or two games of any kind are needed for them.

Children 5 and above can do more things. They still enjoy singing, but you can add dramatic play (house, dolls, cowboys, storytelling). They still enjoy play in the sand and of course water play, if possible.

Eight-and-nine-year-olds may enjoy games involving dressing up, putting on a stunt. They can enjoy most of the equipment games, and many of the active games in this book. Most children like contests. Alternate active and quiet games where needed. (See the other Party Planning helps.)

FAVORS, GIFTS, PLACE CARDS. The child or children could help to select gifts for the guests (perhaps to make them), or favors, place cards. Nut cups, pipe cleaners, doilies, paper cups and plates may be used in constructing and decorating. Some party planners prefer not to have very many contests with prizes, but rather to give gifts to every child so that no one is left out. For some parties children will exchange gifts.

INVITATIONS. Make them appropriate, such as: large candle made of cardboard or construction paper for birthday party (or cake, big numeral with year of child, or party hat). For seasonal parties log cabin for Lincoln's Birthday, pig for St. Patrick's Day, Uncle Sam's Hat for July 4, egg for Easter, cut-out turkey or jack-o-lantern for Thanksgiving or Hallowe'en, Santa's pack for Christmas.

MAKE A CHECK-OFF LIST of things to do to be sure all are done, and in order.

CLOSE THE PARTY PROMPTLY. After refreshments it is nice to have the children do one more activity, perhaps sing. If the children know the tune, you might have them end with (to "Good Night, Ladies") "Good-bye, Everybody." (The fact that the words don't exactly fit will not bother children.)

STAY WITH THEM DURING THE PARTY. If mothers come, let them play by themselves in another room. For younger children 5 or under, constant help is needed. For the others it needs to be regulated. The proper role for the adult is that of assisting the children in having a good time, giving them as much freedom as is wise, but not hesitating to stop a game, settle an argument (pleasantly), and otherwise keep group spirit moving. As a companion, the adult will play with the children either actually or in spirit.

EQUIPMENT GAMES FOR YOUNGER CHILDREN

Younger children can enjoy many of the rolling, sliding games, using balls, bean bags, marbles.

Blocks (2 x 4's, sawed proper length, sanded smooth, painted) are good, also boxes of various sizes.

Tin cans (no rough edges) of various sizes can be used for building.

Peg boards can be bought or made, using golf tees.

Little children of preschool age will enjoy soft animals and equipment for housekeeping: tables, chairs, beds, bureaus, carriages, stoves, refrigerators. (The orange crate is a standard basic piece here.)

Blackboard and chalk, story books, picture books are sure-fire aids.

Younger children like to help make toys such as those of box lumber.

NOTE: Shelves, child-height, help to keep equipment in place. (Youth and adult equipment will probably be kept in closets or basement.)

4

Teens

THE DISCUSSION OF recreation in this chapter covers first the early teens of seventh or eighth grade or junior high school, moves on to the senior high school boy or girl, and includes the young college student. It looks at the needs of youth with understanding, at his relationship to the adult leader, at the kinds of fun he can have on dates, at the types of recreation that can be offered at school, church, and teen center, at the kinds of works projects that appeal to youth, and at numerous other youth concerns.

Young People

WHAT ARE TEENS LIKE?

Youth is a time of growing and changing. Almost daily there is some new phase of life to deal with that was not present yesterday! Youth is a time of constant change in body and nature. Youth needs steadiness and security, yet it is a time for throwing off apron strings and for finding independence.

36

Young people are generally daring where parents and adults are cautious. They have not yet been hurt—do not yet know what they can't do. So they are willing to try.

Therefore teen-agers are willing to challenge "taboos" (those "do-nots"). They want to find out for themselves whether they are right or not. This can be wholesome, if not carried to extreme, and adults should recognize this God-given quality.

Youth has an exploring spirit, ready to go places, move out, see what's beyond the horizon. This should be understood and encouraged, and especially taken into account in planning for fun times.

Youth is frank, but often clams up when adults are around. This is because young folk traditionally do not trust adults. An adult leader therefore may have to win his way with them, by trying not to be one of them but to be an adult friend to them, one who recognizes and respects them and has faith in them.

Youth is naturally religious, although the spirit of exploration and rebellion is there too. With characteristic frankness, youth wants to know why, and intends to find out. Herein lies the key to many rich and interesting discussions and exchanges of opinions with other young people and their elders. The development of church summer camps and programs is an attempt to help them here. If the purpose is to indoctrinate them, however, they may rebel. Unfettered youth is after truth in a recreational search— with broad and deep consquences.

NEEDS OF YOUTH

Youth's needs grow out of its essential nature. One of the greatest needs is for self-expression. Youth is skill hungry, and the creative urge, fanned by the desire of independence, makes youth want to excel. This is for the sake of the expression itself, and for the admiration that always goes toward those who excel. Yet youth may be shy, halting, timid. This may cause a tremendous sense of conflict in its being and, of course, in its conduct.

Youth needs the security of knowing that it can do some things well—a sense of power, status, and accomplishment. A young boy or girl very likely will reassure himself or herself with such thoughts as these:

"I am somebody. I am desirable, attractive. I am the equal (or superior) of my fellows. I can do a lot of things. I know a lot of things—including the social graces. I can get along with people. I can take it. I'm smart enough to get, learn, do, or be *that*. I am capable of handling my own affairs, money, and time. I am capable of supporting myself, going away to college, running my own life." (Many of these declarations may be partial truths. To a trusted friend, youth may readily admit error.)

A young person needs security in group relationships. Since he himself is in such a process of change, he needs much that is stable, and the assurance that even if he fails, his group and his leader will hold him in high regard.

He needs discipline, external and internal. He needs some rules to go by (although he may deny it). It is good when youth can be a part of the rule-making process. Young people who have lived in homes where discipline is lacking present a problem to other groups, for they still must learn the rules of restraint (both self-imposed and imposed from without).

Youth needs opportunity for wholesome expressions of fellowship with the opposite sex. (Here special allowance must be made for stages of maturity. Junior high girls mature more rapidly in this interest than boys. While girls are beginning to be interested in boys, the boys themselves may be devoting most of their interest to roughhousing, vigorous games, athletics. In the senior high years and later, the mutual interest develops.) Until later senior high years, teen-agers do not usually date the same person. This means that much responsibility for boy-girl fellowship falls upon groups, actually a wholesome development. It assures a good time to those who cannot date or who are too timid to do so. Part of this developing interest includes a hunger for information. Discussions, "bull sessions," reading may help a young person to develop wholesome attitudes here.

The teen-ager needs the give-and-take of group experience. In the group he needs to learn to win or lose. To use a figure of speech, in the best group experience he (a) gets the spotlight on occasion (b) operates the spotlight, helping point it toward someone else (c) serves by cleaning the lens or changing the bulb. Here he is manifesting group status, regard for others, service to the group.

Youth needs, under guidance, many opportunities to carry out

responsibility and to perform leadership for his own group. The
guidance is greater for junior high boys and girls, much less for
older youth. A democratic group gives youth the opportunity of
helping to plan, and to succeed or fail.

The teen-ager needs to try his abilities and his hands in the fields
of arts and crafts, music, drama. Here he can develop confidence
in himself by discovering and expressing his abilities in creating
something useful, beautiful, satisfying.

Youth needs a variety of new experience in all fields, especially
in relationships. Youth needs informal opportunities to talk with
other youth, with adult leaders, and to talk and share with other
folk, quite different from themselves, especially from other parts of
the world.

WHAT YOUTH NEEDS FROM ADULT LEADERS

AFFECTION, SYMPATHY, UNDERSTANDING. Even if a leader has not
had training or experience, he or she may be highly successful
with youth by giving them these essentials to their spirit and
growth.

DEMOCRATIC SPIRIT AND PLAN OF OPERATION. A democratic
leader plans *with* youth, not *for* them, and is willing for young
folk to make mistakes and learn from them. He will counsel
and guide, not tell them what to do. (The other extreme is the
perfectionist-dictator, who sees to it that the group is run by
his standards.)

BELIEF IN YOUTH. This kind of adult will not think youth are *all*
wrong, even if they are *often* wrong nor that youth are "automatically delinquent just because they are youth."

HELP IN DEVELOPING RESPONSIBILITY. A good adult will help
each young person find his own pace of taking responsibility and
developing into good leadership or followership. He will en-
force reasonable discipline.

ADVENTURESOME SPIRIT. A youth-minded adult will help young
people choose wholesome adventure for group life, not always
following the old beaten path.

PATIENCE, "THE LONG VIEW." Teen-agers need perspective from
their adult leaders, who have lived longer and should have developed this quality to a greater degree.

A DEPENDABLE PERSON FOR HERO WORSHIP. This quality of hero

worship is strongest in the junior-high age, but continues, gradually diminishing. The leader need not be a perfect person, but he should know how to handle this quality in youth, not taking advantage of it for personal reasons.

LEADERSHIP WITH FAITH. Youth is unsure of its faith, since it is in the process of forming its own set of beliefs. The good youth leader has a faith in God and in man, just as he does in individual young persons. He does his best to live up to it. Prayer is a needed tool in working with any groups of people, particularly youth.

FUN WITH "JUNIOR HIGHS"

When you're just beyond grade school, changing every day, growing like wildfire, hungry, sometimes moody, you are an "intermediate" in more ways than one.

You can't sit still very long or concentrate very long. You want action much of the time (or you may want to be alone). If you are a girl you may be physically bigger than many of the boys. If you're a boy, you may be either too small or too large, even gangly.

If you're a girl, you may be concentrating on grace and charm. If a boy, you may be concentrating on how to be more athletic and strong.

This intermediate age is a mixed-up, noisy one—but warm, usually loyal, highly appreciative of adults who are at all sympathetic.

The boys may be skittish about girls, not too anxious to play with them—certainly not to hold their hands! (This evens out at the age of 14 in some cases.) Every leader of junior high school youth needs to keep these facts in mind.

Junior high is the time for great activity, yet these youngsters tire easily and need to rest. They can get overtired and then become antisocial. Any leader who has in mind to "wear 'em down" should remind himself of this.

These intermediates need much help, individually and in the group. The adult helpers need to be especially patient and understanding. A person who does not know youth and believe in youth has difficulty here.

Much help is needed in planning and in carrying out the plans, in most groups. There are many jobs which can be handled adequately by "junior highs" with proper adult help—decorations, invitations, selection of games and activities, refreshments, clean-up, telephoning, and the like. Adults usually need to keep tab on how things are going, remembering that these young people will learn to do by doing, and that they need to learn to become adequate for their responsibilities in high school and beyond.

Parties and banquets are always fun for these folk, likewise stunt and talent nights. Though they are quite capable of working out skits and stunts, they enjoy taking a good one already prepared and "going to town" with it, especially if it contains good material.

Likewise, hobbies offer much for "junior highs." Often they are the ones who sponsor a hobby show in a community center, church, or other organization, and their hobbies are many and varied.

Skill and equipment games interest this age, but the interest may be for a shorter span. Do not let them misuse the equipment. One leader has a rule for equipment: if he sees anyone misusing a piece of equipment and this misuse goes unchallenged by the other youth present, he puts it away, knowing that they are tired of it.

"Junior highs" can sing well, and they like good music. They like to sing "crazy" songs, and should be permitted to do so, even encouraged. But their potential for good music should be emphasized, too, and they should go home from group or camp with some nice folk songs, spirituals, hymns committed to memory.

In folk games, this age may be skittish. They may enjoy them and play without any difficulty, but to hold a girl's hand is a very "personal" thing to the boys. Sometimes it is better to select those games which emphasize partners the least, if at all. And if the group shows an aversion for this kind of rhythmic activity, simply shift quickly to another activity, bearing in mind that in a few months they may be quite ready for "this boy-girl stuff."

Hiking, camping (including day camping), outdoor activities are especially good for "junior highs" because they represent a strong mutual interest of girls and boys. Picnics and most outdoor activities are enjoyed by them, as well as vigorous outdoor games like tether ball, tennis, water games, and the like. (Don't forget some rest and quiet time, not labeled that, but in the schedule anyway.)

FUN WITH "SENIOR HIGHS"

Youth who are in high school are not all delinquents, do not all love the juke box and ball field, and do not all take to hot-rodding!

They are developing young persons, usually with plenty of energy, ready for almost anything that is fun, except that they are often shy, inexperienced, and in desperate need of help and guidance. Like any other group at any age, they need friends who are very fond of them and who believe in them. "High schoolers" need adults to whom they can go in confidence. A person who is otherwise inadequate may, with a warm interest and a sympathetic ear, help high school youth greatly.

More ably than intermediates ("junior highs") they can take their own leadership responsibilities, although they are somewhat erratic in carrying out the obligations. They need to be encouraged. This is a part of growing up. (Some adults have not grown up in this way!)

High school youth may be at a loss as to how to express themselves and to present ideas. Wise leadership will help them find the words, perhaps in vocabulary-building games.

Here are youth who want wholesome, satisfying relationships with the opposite sex but who are confused, especially with the artificial pictures of "how you get along" coming from movies, radio, television. Simple questions like "What is a date?" "What should you do on one?" "What do boys expect of girls, girls expect of boys?" "What is fair for their parents to expect?" These questions involve their whole recreational outlook. You can always get a discussion on boy-girl relationships. (Here it is well to have at hand some good books on the subject, like *Facts of Life and Love for Teen-Agers* (see Bibliography). Dating is more common. Some youth "go steady," but it is best not to encourage this. Boys and girls doing things in a congenial group is better. Each boy has the chance to come to know a number of girls, and vice versa. They can have a pleasant time together without commitments. Marriages taking place in this age are often based on immature judgments.

Time is a big problem for high school youth. School and social activities take many hours of the day. There are numerous groups and agencies bidding for their services. (Each group, if interested in the youth as persons, should try to add to their activity what they need for balance instead of simply demanding time from them.) Some communities need to get agencies together and talk this over, to keep from running youth ragged.

Commercial amusements capitalize on high school boys and girls because they have some spending money, are ready for fun, and are easily swayed. Many commercial records with love themes are beamed at them. Wise groups will select some of the wholesome commercial opportunities, like a decent swimming pool or bowling alley, a good skating rink, certain worth-while movies, plays, concerts, and arrange to have the boys and girls go to them "in a group," perhaps dropping back by the regular meeting place to whip up refreshments, or going to the sweet shop for ice cream and fun. (Use some of the "Humor" section here, for fun.)

These young people like active fun, generally, and the hike-swimming party-active game-dancing-running sort of thing appeals. (Remember that all youth are not alike. Individual differences should be taken into account in the planning.) They also need rest. Remember the rest hour at camps. Though the boys and girls both need "big muscle" activity, these muscles need a chance to be quiet.

The boys still like to do some things together (with no girls present), and in groups should have some opportunities to do so. Perhaps a stag affair could be planned at the same time as a hen or chick affair, with friendly, youth-minded adults in both groups.

Some leaders assume that high school youth know more than they actually do, because they have the appearance of being grown up. In some ways they are grown up, but too much should not be expected, nor should adult leaders get too discouraged at lack of responsibility, "silly action," and the rest. Adults should be participant-helpers. (An adult on the sidelines, maintaining that his place is "in the background" is not doing the best job of helping youth.) In the present philosophy of youth work, youth and their adults work and play *together*.

High school youth like to demonstrate skills learned at school, skills involving the use of the mind (quiz), the body (swimming, athletic games, showing how high you can jump), and such personal skills as craft ability, creative arts, skits and stunts. Such things as a beauty show or a male beauty show would usually be enjoyed.

Mother-daughter and father-son affairs are enjoyed, but the youth usually don't want parents around during ordinary groupings or meetings. It is natural for them to want to keep love relationships somewhat secret, especially from parents. (This is a part of the apron-string breaking that some parents find hard to understand. It is an impersonal dislike of parents that most youth have at this time.)

Some groups help this situation by having parent-youth discussion groups where problems of relationships are discussed. Usually parents are surprised when their children in such a group take them down a peg. Likewise, youth are moved to know of parents' concern for them. One minister-parent in such a group was telling about their fine, democratic relationship at home, only to have his daughter rise and say quietly, "No, it isn't a very democratic one, Dad." (This became the basis for talking over their problems. A closer mutual understanding developed.) Such a discussion (or series of them) might be far better than a mother-daughter or father-son affair which skims the surface of relationships.

Hobbies are important to high school youth. The opportunity to display them at a hobby show, or a "roving hobby show" in which the group goes from home to home, seeing hobbies on display in the home setting, helps the teen-ager to feel a sense of importance about something dear to him. (This is true of all ages about hobbies.) Drama and role playing are also enjoyed as well as lighter skits and stunts, and are important.

COLLEGE-AGE FUN

Students of college age are different from those in high school. They are more sophisticated in that they have developed broader background and interests. They are more interested in complicated fun. (The same game, played in a college group, will take on a different flavor from one in a high school group.)

This group is more likely to be word conscious, with a bigger vocabulary and word interest. They like to play with words.

Because they are a little older and more removed from childhood, collegians will often get a big kick from "kid games" which high school and junior high would not dare to appear to enjoy.

College age is old enough not to be bothered by the appearance of being kiddish. Yet there is also the pressure to be more sophisticated.

"Bull sessions" form an important part of the recreation of this group, though they probably do not think of this as recreation. The informal exchange of ideas is increasingly important. By this time youth's philosophy of life, self, religion, attitudes about life work, life mate, standards of living, are beginning to crystallize, and most of them want to talk about it. (This fact should be remembered in program planning.)

The "Coffee-and-Discussion" or "Coke Hour" therefore may be fun, but dead-serious, too. Many college student groups sponsor such affairs, and find these informal meetings with chosen leaders very rewarding.

The out-of-school group in this age must do more to arrange its group recreation than college students need to, for much of the fun on the college campus is automatically there. Students get their recreation going to events on the campus. Student centers frequently encourage this, having their groups gather at the center for refreshments after the campus affair is over.

The group itself is fun, in college, whether the group is a fraternity or a sorority, a student club or a religious student center. A well-equipped lounge is important, with reading material, easy-to-play table games, sometimes equipment and equipment games (see Equipment and Skill Games in Index) available for informal play. A well-stocked kitchen, with students free to go in to cook a hamburger or its equivalent and pay the "kitty" adds to the "home away from home" attractiveness.

Many student centers have "hi-fi" enthusiasts who will install a good record player with records. This is best if done in a room where serious listening, if desired, can be done. Hi-fi isn't worth too much in a passageway room.

Students like to work on committees, prepare meals, run a co-op. This, too, is recreation, since it is joyful, voluntary use of leisure time.

Most college student groups find that singing is important. Get a good songbook and become familiar with it. Use the piano for a rallying center, even if only a few are present. Learn some songs of lasting quality as well as frothy music, popular music. (The "popular" actually doesn't last. College should be the center of some experiences that are lasting.)

Dramatics, from heavy drama to play reading to informal skits and stunts to dramatic games, are "right down the alley" of the college student group. Many groups find time to present plays; but play reading, "walking rehearsals," problem-introducing original skits, role playing are important too—and they furnish fun on a cultural level.

Deputation teams and other service projects appeal to college students. The team goes out to small communities, to clubs, churches, children's groups to provide leadership and leadership training in recreation (and other fields, too). Usually a team consists of three or four students. Often an adult interested in the program will go along too.

Service projects (see Index) give students a kind of expression not found elsewhere—the expression of the desire to do something helpful for others. If the project is big enough, it can become the unifier for a group. One group, sensitive to the world need of food, started a Meager Meal project in a church basement. From the first this group was interfaith and interracial. No effort was made to grind axes—a low-cost meal (less than the normal amount) was served, students paid a regular meal price, and the money was sent to a world student relief organization. Although started in a church, soon fraternities, sororities, and other social groups volunteered to take it on for one week at a time, prepare the food, and serve it. (The rule was that the materials must not cost over 3 cents per person. That was a real challenge to the buyers.) Volunteer leadership services in children's homes or community centers are often done in the name of a campus religious group.

Retreats, week-end work camps, are very popular with student groups. These programs combine fun with instruction and work in a happy experience of real significance to the students involved.

This is the age for increased couple activity. Wise planners, however, will keep in mind those who are not in couples and those who may never be! This is a special function for the religious student group—to help fill that gap for those who have not yet mastered the art of dating, love, mating or whatever they want to call it. Interesting things to do at the student center fill the void. Position, group regard, group affection are very important to the collegian whose life is quite different from that at home. (During the first ten days in college, there are more appendectomies than during any one year, medical reports say. The cause might be attributed to homesickness.)

WHAT YOUTH CAN DO FOR ITSELF

The learn-by-doing concept in education holds just as true in recreation, and self-reliance can be one of the by-products developed through fun.

1. Youth can do much of the planning. It is best to have an experienced adult present to guide in such matters as wisdom of choice of activities, interpreting the folk ways of adults, reminding that chaperones are still needed. A youth-minded adult can help.
2. They can lead individual games and singing. This is usually not too much responsibility.
3. Some young persons can direct an entire social time or party.
4. They can plan, or help to plan, and buy and put up the decorations.
5. They can plan, prepare, and serve refreshments.
6. They can get together the equipment needed and often operate it, such as projectors, record players, tape recorders, equipment games, properties for a circus, blackboard.
7. They can help with publicity—posters, mimeographing, announcements, radio spots, telephoning.
8. Some exceptional youth can take charge and move right ahead with the entire responsibility without adult help. The older they are, the more likely youth are to be able to do this, of course.

THINGS YOUTH LIKES TO DO

Big muscle activities

Hiking	Water sports	Folk and square
Boating	Treasure hunts	dancing
Swimming	Softball	Exploring
Tennis	Football	Cycling—hosteling
Volleyball	Active games	Paddle tennis
Skating	Tether ball	Badminton
Toboganing	Dancing	

Less strenuous activities

Fishing	Bowling	Auto driving, riding
Skill games	Croquet	Picnics
Camping	Horseshoes	
Ping-pong	Campfires	

Music—art—drama—writing

Group singing	Puppetry	Painting, sketching
Choral groups	Acting in plays	Choral speaking,
Orchestra	Backstage work	verse choirs
Trips to hear	makeup	Play reading
chorus, orchestras,	setting	Creative writing
opera, see plays	lighting	(poetry, stories)

Other fun

Trips to sight-see	Reading	Parties, socials
Mystery trips for	Watching television,	Conversation
adventure	athletic contests,	Discussion
Stunt nights—hobby	movies	Entertaining
nights	Dressing up, down	Dancing

DATING FUN

Dating is said to be a uniquely American custom. Whether it is or not, most American youth practice it to enjoy companionship, to gain prestige, to get acquainted with a person of the opposite sex, to pursue mutual interests, and because they genuinely like each other.

There is an easy temptation for young people to drop into the habit of "necking" when they get together, especially since it is easy to drive to places of seclusion with a car. Studies have shown that many boys do it because they think the girls expect it, and that the girls do it because they think the boys expect it.

Dating is an important part of our American recreation pattern. There are many interesting things one can do on a date. Here are some of them:

1. Sit with a coke or milkshake and talk. Be natural. That in itself can be fun.

2. Go roller skating, bowling, dancing, to the movies, plays, concerts.

3. Watch TV.

4. Play records.

5. Play ping-pong, Canasta at home.

6. Double-date, shop, and cook (and clean up).

7. Paint together, draw together. (Aha!)

8. Make things together of a craft nature, Christmas cards, woodwork.

9. Play table games, skill games.

10. Go on hikes, picnics together. (Good double-date idea.)

11. The two of you cook for the gang, invite them in for a meal or for a dessert party.

12. Play archery, badminton, tennis, goofy golf, clock golf, washer tossing.

13. Do gardening together (usually for couples "going steady").

14. Read together (one reads aloud, the other rests).

15. Penny-walk as a couple. (Flip a coin at each intersection. If it's heads, you go to the right; tails, you go to the left.)

16. Have fun by window shopping.

17. Go on a breakfast hike. (Get up early, go out to cook breakfast.)

18. Hunt out small, unknown eating places.

19. Go to museums, galleries, circus, zoo.

20. Work as a couple in a settlement house on volunteer basis.

21. Wash the car, paint a barn or fence together.

22. Attend school, church affairs together.

23. Study together.

24. Fry hamburgers, fix "black cows," pop corn, cook fudge, toast marshmallows.

25. Wash the car of a person who has furnished a lot of transportation personally or for a group.

26. Write letters to mutual friends.

27. Take pictures. Later, develop and print them.

28. Go on a cook-out together.

29. Attend spectator sports.

30. Listen to radio, TV. See who can answer the quiz-questions first.[1]

WORK PROJECTS POPULAR WITH YOUTH

Mimeographing, putting out paper

Painting

Repairing

Putting on special breakfast or
other meal

Mending books, hymnals

Making things for an orphanage

Fellowship teams (go to groups
to conduct recreation, serve)

Trick or Treat for UNICEF

Collecting and selling, like paper,
coat hangers, scrap metal

Entertaining in children's home,
or for shut-ins

Planting flowers in school or
church yard, or for shut-ins

Keeping an animal, sharing it
(like a caged bird, cow)

Making and selling things:
candles, tin craft

Collecting parties:
books, shoes, clothes, food

Helping harvest perishable crops

Slave Day (boys and girls hire
out their labors for money)

Chinese Auction to raise money

Lord's Acre project

Reading to older folk

Performances or tape recorded
programs for shut-ins

Promoting worth-while causes

Meager Meal, Starvation Banquet
(for benefit of needy, hungry)

One of the most important expressions of all in groups is that of tender concern for the need of others. Altruism (doing for others) and empathy (feeling into the need and situation of others) are qualities which most youth want to express to some degree.

Any project (see Projects in Index) should be agreed upon heartily by all. Such a list as the one above may stimulate a group to further thought and action, along a somewhat different line. That is fine. Any group which does only for itself reaps the reward for such shallowness in the kind of program and fellowship that it has. Most of the projects listed above require some action, and youth likes action.

Groups build a sense of togetherness by doing things together. Service projects bring wonderful results in that group feeling, for in most of them youth can sing, play, "cut up," and have a good time, with something to show for their efforts in the end.

FUN AT SCHOOL

Much of the material in this book would be useful for school groups. The skits and stunts, for instance, would be appropriate for a fun program in the school auditorium, for club and class activities, at parties, and at banquets.

Helps for party and banquet planning are "right down the alley."

The musical mixers are appropriate for school affairs, dances, after-game parties, to get people to participate. The humorous material and gags can be used all the way from little groups in the soda shop to "just standing around," to club and class functions, private parties, at camp, and in conventions. Songs (stunts, too) would be useful at meetings of all kinds, at parties, and on trips.

Service projects would give classes and clubs some ideas to go on. The helps for a circus, carnival, football party, could be used not only to provide fun but to raise money.

Group starters will be priceless at meetings and parties. One or two may be used even when the meeting is of fairly serious nature. They serve to "get the students warmed up."

FUN AT THE CHURCH

Youth fun at the church is like that of other situations, but there are some aspects deserving special attention.

Church groups should do a specially good job of planning for service projects. They should have parents' nights, mother-daughter and father-son banquets, and should co-operate in family affairs. This means publicizing and attending.

Church groups should do a good job of "long-term planning," looking three to twelve months ahead. (Some groups do this in a fall or spring retreat.) Big dates are blocked into a calendar, some responsibility fixed. Later the details are filled in, and smaller social affairs planned.

Discussions on right and wrong in recreation, friendships, dating and courtship, getting along at home with parents and brothers and sisters, are appropriate, important, and recreational.

Fun at church should include some emphasis on international friendship, with festivals, banquets, visits from international guests and speakers, world parties in the planning.

Church parties will place more emphasis on a "religious ending," such as a fellowship circle with spirituals, hymns, prayer; singing around the piano or fire; readings from the Bible or religious literature, and prayer. These closings should not be laborious, but they should reflect the togetherness of the group with each other and with God. Otherwise, an element of religious expression is left out.

The church may serve as headquarters for groups of youth who go to plays, movies, concerts, athletic contests, or out on a membership drive, such as a Bike Roundup. The youth come back, with their leaders, to the church for refreshments and conversation. Talking over a movie may be more important and impressive than "studying the lesson."

Church youth groups will find much use for "Short Parties" of 20 to 45 minutes duration, especially in connection with the Youth Fellowship meeting, or after church. These should be planned with care, even though they are short.

Building equipment games should occupy interest in most churches. They may be stored when not in use. Adults who have sewing or carpentry skill (women can help make bean bags, men can supervise the construction of a game cabinet, for example) will be glad to help youth equip a social room. It should be for the use of others in addition to youth, incidentally, especially young adults, older adults. Perhaps a joint committee among them could be formed to get materials and build the equipment.

Whatever committee of youth for recreation is organized, at least one adult should work in connection with it. This adult can then interpret to other adults what they are planning and doing, often keeping down misunderstanding.

Most churches have a manual of recreational activities and suggestions. Get in touch with your denominational or faith headquarters.

OPERATING A TEEN CENTER

Responding to the knowledge that young people need "a place of their own," many groups are sponsoring teen centers. This is a good idea if it is carefully worked out. If not, it can be a very bad idea indeed, becoming the center of unwholesome or aimless activity instead of good things, as originally intended.

One statement may be made with certainty. A juke box and a milk bar are not enough to sustain interest of youth for any extended period of time. Youth-minded adult leadership is absolutely essential. This is the kind of person (or persons) who will say,

"Let's work this out together" and mean it. Then he (or she) will stay on the job with the youth until things are accomplished.

Before going into a teen center project, it should be determined accurately whether it is really needed (do the youth have time and interest for it?) or is it somebody's hobby idea? Youth should be in on the planning, and should actually have power to influence decisions. Adults who "do *for*" instead of "do *with*" youth find the youth quickly tiring of this new project, which is actually an adult's hobby-brainchild.

The Good Teen Center. The good teen center has most of the following elements or characteristics:

1. Is strategically placed, where youth have access to it.
2. Is operated by youth and youth-minded adults together. Neither can do it alone for any lengthy period of time.
3. Has a regular place with assurance that such place will be available for a considerable period of time.
4. Is assured of enough continuing adult help for planning and chaperonage—experienced, trained adults if possible, but always those who understand youth and who are sympathetic with youth.
5. Has a program, agreed upon by youth and their adult leaders. Just keeping the youngsters off the streets is not enough to sustain their interest very long. Service projects, like adult service clubs, are fine if the youth can be interested in them.
6. Has a financial plan for meeting bills for the months ahead. The money may come jointly from youth and adults, or from community, school, or church funds; but there should be assurance that the budget will be balanced. (This may involve paying for some adult leadership or furnishing leadership from a staff.)
7. Has a membership plan for youth. Most of those who do not have one, fail. Usually a membership card is used, with a small fee for joining (25 cents to $1) and the rules printed on the card, to be signed by the young person joining. A few will not live up to the rules and must be disciplined or ejected.
8. A set of rules, made by the youth themselves. One group of youth made up these:

a. No drinking
b. No smoking inside the building
c. Admittance by membership or visitor's card, sponsored by a member
d. No card playing or gambling of any kind
e. Reasonable co-operation with the youth and adult leaders
f. No profanity

Persons violating the rules were to be warned and possibly ejected from the club.

9. Has a schedule of activities, fair for all age groups involved. Some centers operate for "junior highs," "senior highs," and out-of-school youth, each having special times when they may come and not come. Sometimes other ages than teen-agers are involved in the use of facilities, from children to older adults. Each group must then come only at the scheduled time.

10. Maintains the air of "something interesting to do if you drop in." Table games, equipment and skill games, and music are nearly always available. If organized activity is used for some of the time, freedom is usually given to do "just what you want to" for the rest.

5

Adults

ADULTS LIKE AND NEED FUN, just as youth and children do, but for somewhat different reasons. Adults need to seek more consciously for exercise and emotional release that comes from recreation. Most adults need it for a change of scene, change of pace. (Young adults may need to be free from their children for a while, yet older adults may get together for a similar reason—to be away from a noisy, bothersome, restricting household.)

Adults need fellowship with each other. They need to rediscover old joys of play. They may need to relearn, for instance, the joy of painting pictures as well as floors!

Adults

Unlike youth, it's not *independence* that bothers adults—it's their *dependents!* Particularly is this true of the young mother. Therefore, an excellent group service to her may be to have a nursery twice a week during shopping hours so that her child can be cared for while she does some buying and breathes freely, for a bit.

Adults like much the same recreation as youth, but again for somewhat different reasons. Where youth want to use folk games and outdoor activities as methods of getting acquainted with persons of the opposite sex, most adults have solved that problem. The folk dance group gives them a chance to have fun with the husband (or wife) of someone else—without disturbing after-effects.

The situation of the single young adults among married couples needs to be considered in planning. If some of these unwed folk are coming to an affair, it is best not to plan games and activities that call for couples all the way. Do some activities in threes, and in other number combinations. Among adult groups, a husband is often out of town on business during the week. Affairs planned then should include freely the wife, who may be very lonely at the time. The wise adult group will seek to make a warm place for every person who needs it, whether married or not.

Adults are old enough to be free from kiddish taboos. They may enjoy a kid party immensely, as a matter of fact. Any planning committee should be careful to take into account the wants and desires of its group. Some adult groups mimeograph an interest finder which they themselves have compiled, and plan their program ahead from the answers.

Though adults need a change from their work, they may enjoy work projects immensely, either because of the change from regular work, or because of the opportunity to show others what they know from their daily work. (See Projects in Index for ideas.)

Skits and stunts, drama informal and more formal are all interesting to adults. Given an organizing idea, adults can work up interesting stunts, and prepared stunts are "right down their alley." Among most adult groups are good storytellers. At least they can read some of the humorous story material in this book, for breathers, for home situations around the fireplace or in the living room. Though adults may not have time to present full-fledged dramas, play reading is becoming quite popular, and some groups do have time for productions.

Hobbies are worthy of attention for adult groups. A hobby show not only will give the hobbyist a chance to show his wares, but also may stimulate others to undertake interesting hobbies, and to get acquainted with others who have similar hobbies. Investigate the possibility of the "roving hobby show," based on the "progressive party" idea. On a certain afternoon or evening, several homes hold "open house" during a specified period of time, to display hobbies. Anyone can drop by to see these hobbies and perhaps to have refreshments.

Adult groups may sponsor also neighborhood parties or cooperative endeavors, such as encouraging two or three men to get together and mow each other's lawn.

If responsibilities permit it, the "Slave Day" idea may appeal as a way of raising money. In advance of the day the services of several members of the group are offered for a price (the money to go to the group treasury). Then on the appointed day, such as a Saturday, these folk move out to their "jobs" to wash windows, help clean house, paint, and do the various jobs they agreed to do.

Adults need from their groups affection, response, new experience, recognition, opportunities to express altruism, just as the younger folk do. Therefore, opportunities need to be given to each adult to achieve and shine—likewise to take note of achievements outside the group. Birthdays, anniversaries, and other celebrations should be noted and honored. (Pay no attention to adult protests —they like it!) And of course, observe Mother's Day and Father's Day, as well as Family Week.

Physical problems of adults should be noted and watched, especially by the leader or leaders. Heart troubles, other physical difficulties, even women who are "expecting," may need to be considered in any group. (Some special suggestions for older adults are given later in this chapter.)

FUN WITH YOUNG ADULTS—MARRIED AND SINGLE

There are two kinds of young adults—the married and the single. Their problems are quite different.

The married ones are occupied with problems and thoughts of establishing a home, having and rearing children, their own relationships, getting ahead in the world. They need play apart from their children, but much of their play time, of necessity, will have to be *with* their children. Therefore, they may be involved more in "family affairs" than in "young adult affairs" in connections with their organizations. They are likely to be interested in school affairs, civic affairs, social clubs. The time for any one of them is limited, especially if they must spend much time at home. Baby sitters may become one of the large problems, especially from a cost standpoint.

The single young adult, on the other hand, probably has no home of his own or her own. This person may live in a boarding house or a Y, may live at home, may have an apartment. Often he or she lives alone. The consciousness that the rest of his age group is busy establishing home and relationships may create a problem. Most single adults really want marriage and its companionship, which is a perfectly reasonable desire.

It is quite possible to put the two groups together, but when the emphasis is solely on married life the single young adult feels left out, especially if a group is thoughtless enough to call itself "the couples' club."

All young adults need and like:

Group singing	Active, athletic games (for
Hobbies, crafts (when useful)	exercise)
Social games, folk dancing	Table games, equipment games
	Banquets

Single young adults, because they may have more leisure time, may do more hosteling (cycling), swimming, dancing, projects, individual sports. They may devote more time to hobbies, and would be more available for trips, picnics, and the like. Often they find great satisfaction in group service projects and in individual service, like assisting in a community center, children's home.

Unmarried young adults need co-ed parties in homes, at the beach, in the mountains. They need to have meetings beyond the "local level" in any organization in the hope of finding a mate. City-wide or community-wide gatherings may give them the time and opportunity to make the contact with pleasant persons of the opposite sex that they have lacked.

Single young adults enjoy a non-institutional drop-in place. This may be the home of a married young couple. It might be a homey room arranged at a community center or church or other organization, so decorated and arranged that it does actually seem homelike and not institutional.

Married young adults need to have outings such as picnics, hikes, trips without their children. It is hard to leave the children, but all are refreshed from having been apart. On such affairs as these, if the activities are impersonal and the conversation is not about home and family all the time, single young adults may get considerable delight from a joint experience.

Some churches have done a good job with single young adults, having a special "fireside" time or "friendly fellowship" for them. More churches should attempt to bring this group together in fellowship. They can do for themselves if they have the chance and the encouragement.

In planning for young adults, remember those in unusual circumstances. Some of the women are "expecting." Many times the husband is away when socials are held, and "the girls" must come alone, if at all. They may need to come because they are lonely. Some young adults are caring for aged parents. It would be a nice gesture for someone to "swap off" with the person so burdened, so that he or she could enjoy a bit of freedom.

FUN WITH MIDDLE ADULTS

Middle adults like to take it easier, and do not enjoy vigorous activity quite so much as they used to. Anything of a social nature, however, is enjoyed by middle adults quite as much as by young adults, and their lists of interests would be similar, with a little de-emphasis on active games, skating, swimming, and the like. Middle adults are a little slower at new tricks.

The children of middle adults are in the upper grades of grade school or in high school, so the parents are facing the problems of this age bracket. Part of the fun for middle adults is talking about their children, comparing notes. Often they belong to parents' groups.

Middle adults like mental games, table games, in general. They enjoy banquets, can do a good job at dramatics. They enjoy talking. A good kind of activity is one around a card table, such as simple crafts or puzzles, which gives these folks plenty of time to talk.

Some middle adults need to relearn to play. They grew up in a generation which thought that work was a virtue, and play senseless. The "happy medium" for some of them might be work projects of the group instead of out-and-out play. For example, a group of middle-aged women may enjoy a hooked rug class more than a bridge club; the men, a course in cabinet making.

Middle adults are beginning to reminisce. They are looking forward but also backward. Occasionally they like to remember how things used to be. (For suggestions see the Older Adults section which follows.)

The single person and the widowed person in a group of middle adults may be happily occupied, but they are just as likely to be lonely. Special thoughtfulness in planning needs to take them into consideration. Often they need transportation. Single adults need jobs to do, hobbies, the encouragement to do for others.

These activities are of interest to middle adults, married or single:

Going to the movies	Week-end trips
Athletic contests	Having and using a cabin
Bowling	Enjoying music, concerts, the
Swimming	opera
Dancing	Vacations, family trips
Skating	Golf
Hiking	Producing plays, opera,
Boating	operetta, musical shows

Adults like to show off:

Home	Babies
Car	Photography hobby
Yard	Scrapbooks

For this reason you can get homes for meetings rather easily! Adults also enjoy hobbies. They will help build a house, work in the yard or garden, basement; they enjoy sewing and sawing, ripping and reaping.

Raising flowers and vegetables, keeping the yard as a children's playground, having bull sessions, gadgeteering (for car, workshop). (Adults have toys. A car may be a man's toy; kitchen gadgets or the telephone, the woman's.)

Many adults also enjoy doing good works, helping people in need. Many persons do these things in the spirit of hobbies.

FUN WITH OLDER ADULTS

There are as many older adults in the U. S. A. as the entire population of the Dominion of Canada. During the first half of the century, the general population doubled, the number of older adults quadrupled. More groups, particularly in public and church recreation, are attempting to meet the need of this rising group in the population.

Needs. Older adults have the same needs as any other age group, but they have some intensified needs that should be borne in mind in planning for fun. Often older adults are lonely because of the loss of a spouse. Children have married, moved away, and the parent does not feel needed.

This leads to a sense of futility and fatalism, "I might as well die." Many older adults are unwilling to accept the fact of age and its limitations. Some have worked all their lives and never played. Now work is taken away, with no hobbies to replace work. Physically their processes are slowing, and poor hearing, eyesight, co-ordination may set in.

Love, affection, belonging, being wanted and needed, are therefore very important to older adults, who must feed on these instead of the status they once enjoyed.

Because men do not live so long as women, there may not be many men in any older adult group. Activities should be planned to include men, and they should be on committees.

How to Start. Any person who is conscious of the need for fun and fellowship for older adults may take the lead to get started. People to be invited are older adults themselves, community center directors, ministers, case workers, recreation workers, directors of religious education and persons likely to help follow through.

Facilities. It is best to have a cheerful room as near the ground level as possible, easily accessible, one permitting a wide range of games, activities, refreshments. If at all possible, have a room that can be called "their room," for a place of their own is a need for older adults. It would be good to have toilets close by, if possible.

Choosing a Name. Older adults themselves are ingenious with names. Here are some, as reported by Dr. George Steinman and Virginia Stafford:

Fun After 60   OAYF (Old As You Feel)
XYZ (Extra Years of Zest)   Senior Citizens
Live Long and Like It   Borrowed Time
Old Timers   Golden Age

How to Operate. Get a person who is interested (and perhaps trained) to work with the older adult group. A young adult is often available, using funds for initial operation furnished by a young adult group. The group should decide, as soon as it is ready, on such details as place, time, and frequency of meeting; officers and their functions, committees. Every person who is willing should be given some responsibility.

Some Things to Keep in Mind. Encourage the group to plan ahead. Consult them at all points. Arrange meetings at times convenient to them. Move at an easygoing tempo. (Time is not of the essence with older adults.) Simplicity as the key to older adult activities is best.

Help elderly people to feel welcome whether in a group activity or on the sidelines. Some groups like to have several things going (at least two) so that there is some choice. The folks will get satisfaction from the fact that they are all in the same place together, enjoying it.

It is good, in a large group, to have several persons, younger than this age group, as cheerful helpers. Recruiting is usually done from younger women, though it would be good to have men around, too.

Be careful where stairs or steps are involved.

Activities for Fun. In choosing activities, keep in mind the physical problems that older adults may face. There should be good light and large type or notes for material to be read or sung from notes by the group. Because fingers are not so supple, or are sometimes shaky, crafts involving fine work may not fit. The sense of balance is less secure in older adults, so musical games, mixers, and the like, should not require them to stand on one foot, kicking the other up or out. A slow-fast regulator on a record player (if one is used) would permit slowing down a record. (This should be done in many cases.)

Some activities enjoyed by older adults would be these:

1. Singing (A piano is helpful, using songs mother sang, favorite hymns, carols.)
2. Listening to music (performances or records)
3. Skits and stunts (presented by them or for them)
4. Conversation, informal talk (about things of yesteryear, particularly)
5. Handwork, crafts: carving, painting, crocheting, knitting, sewing, quilting, painting pictures, working with wood or metal
6. Group games, guessing games, pencil and paper games
7. Celebrations, anniversaries, complete with presents
8. Horseshoes, croquet, shuffleboard, golf, and the like
9. "Do as you please," with several things to do such as table games of the checker, chess variety, on card tables

Other suggestions by an older adult, John E. Wilson, who is working with older adults, are as follows:

1. Hold quizzes on things with which the people are familiar. Don't forget to choose up for a spelling bee, using an old speller.
2. Quote or sing lines from the oldest song you know.
3. Name a novel read over forty years ago and its author. What authors were popular then?
4. Tell a story as old as your father. Who can tell the oldest yarn?
5. Offer a prize for the oldest book or magazine brought in.
6. Identify articles in common use fifty to seventy-five years ago such as shoe button, bustle, whalebone stay, bed warmer, shaving mug, kid curler, curling iron, button hook, cuff holders, tintype, ferris waist.
7. Name ten Bible women. Name ten Bible men in the Old Testament and ten in the New Testament.
8. Hold an "Exhibit from Yesterday." Old letters, personal or business. Old bills (an 1860 plumbing bill recently brought interest). Old love letters when the persons involved are not present. Old stamps, old ads of high-wheel bicycles, high-wheel buggies, old typewriters, corsets, shoes.
9. Play table games like Anagrams, Scrabble, crossword puzzles, and the like.
10. Charades, recite "pieces."

Older adults like the thrill and success of winning. However, they tire of a contest that lasts too long.

Some may like to sing while others are playing games and doing activities. A special group might practice and present their music later. Many older adults can play musical instruments. Some successful orchestras have been organized among the group.

Service Activities. Dr. George Steinman has suggested a number of service activities that might be performed by anyone, but especially by older adults:

1. Serve as historian, perhaps of church.
2. Help beautify grounds.
3. Serve on art committee.
4. Act as librarian, keeper of music.
5. Provide flowers for meetings.
6. Keep literature table.
7. Sponsor special meetings, such as prayer meetings.
8. Sew costumes for dramatic group.
9. Keep picture files.
10. Teach others his own art or skill, such as woodworking, quilting, tatting.
11. Meet to quilt, send quilts to orphanage.
12. Raise funds for scholarship.
13. Correspond with service men who are gone from community.
14. Make favors for banquets.
15. Collect and sell paper, coathangers.
16. Sponsor home visit to shut-in, with covered dish supper, perhaps having pastor serve communion as part of activity.
17. Serve as consultants in areas in which their experience qualifies them.
18. Help organize other older adult groups.

(See also Service Projects in Index.)

THE CHINA TEA SET

A china tea set—just to own
A china tea set was her dream—
Dear fragile cups, quaint little bowl,
A cunning pitcher for the cream.

So graciously she'd pour the tea,
Her friends would chatter bright and gay:
"Such perfect tea! Such lovely cups!
I'm glad I happened in today!"

But he to whom her life was joined
Thought money would be better spent
For land, for implements and stock—
And to his will her will was bent.

His toil and gain were all for her—
And when the two were old and gray
That she might have no wish denied
He brought the tea things home one day.

Dear fragile cups, quaint little bowl!
She thanked him with her patient smile.
She placed them in a shining row
Admired them there a little while
Then packed them all away. You see
No friends were left to drink the tea.

MRS. B. Y. WILLIAMS
Ladies Home Journal, March, 1927

Senile Older Adults. In the younger years of older adulthood, many people have a great deal of vigor and interest in life. As older adults get older, many become very feeble. These elderly folk enjoy having things done for them—presents, entertainment, being read aloud to (although their attention may be of short span). Some are almost incapable of any kind of participation. This should be kept in mind as activities are planned which include these "older" older folk.

_____ 6

Families

It has often seemed that with all the talking and writing these latter days about the family as a sociological this and a psychological that, or a cosmological something else, one is likely to lose sight of the first and foremost fact of all.

The family, considered simply and not "approached" from this angle or that, is just a household composed of individuals who in the natural order of things have come "out of the everywhere into the here" with a certain set of relationships already established for them.

All things being usual and normal, we live with our families for all our growing years. Our first social experiences are in our own homes, and they are of far-reaching importance, helping or hindering us all our lives long. Members of families who get into a good stride with each other, who give and take fairly, and who manage to enjoy each other and to have fun in their homes, have a great advantage over those who merely live under one roof! [1]

FAMILY FUN is more than "games for the children." It is the kind of activity that brings the entire family together, on the under-standing level and participation level of all. The home, called a bulwark of democracy, is being pulled apart in these confusing times. Family worship and family fun are two of the keys to keeping it together.

In families old enough to have one, a family council is valuable. Here the members of the family get together as equals, with each one in rotation acting as chairman, and under certain rules that they establish themselves. Planning for family fun takes place in the family council.

PLANNING FOR FAMILY FUN

If a family is sincere about attempting to organize its fun, it will take an inventory of its places and equipment, asking such questions as these:

What could we do in our yard?
How could we equip a playroom?
What about the living room, dining room, kitchen?

From the family itself many ideas may develop. Here are some idea starters.

Kitchen. In the kitchen you can prepare meals, refreshments. The children can help to cook. You can have a Co-operative Dinner, inviting another family and having each person draw slips for the chore he is to do for the meal. In the refrigerator you can freeze ice cream, make frozen suckers.

Some of the members can make fudge, popcorn balls, surprise drinks. You can take turn about, cooking meals (with father and some of the children working together). You can bake birthday cakes, prepare mother her breakfast in bed for Mother's Day. (Any day could be Mother's Day!)

Dining Room. You can decorate the table, fix up fancy place cards. Spend some time in making an attractive centerpiece. Have joke or conundrum night (use some material from this book). You can sing table graces (and compose some new ones), play mental games of all sorts (especially mystery games), have surprises, birthday celebrations, play any kinds of table games.

Living Room (and Bedroom). Family singing, reading, games, scrapbook making, storytelling, forming a rhythm band, pursuing some hobbies or crafts such as making Christmas cards and ornaments, keeping up family records, showing slides and movies, entertaining guests.

Playroom. All the things suggested for a living room would be suitable for a playroom and, in addition, most of the equipment games in this book. This would be a good room also for hobbies and crafts, although some of them may be kept in individual rooms. Sometimes a family will rig up a darkroom for developing pictures.

Yard. Both the young and the older have a right to a share in the yard. A family garden tended by all, a barbecue pit or outdoor grill, picnic table, equipment games (such as horseshoes, washer tossing, tether ball, badminton court, tennis court, volleyball court, basketball goal, unigoal—a basketball goal on a 10-foot pole, specially constructed—croquet set. Here family parties could be held, with other families invited. Dessert parties (they eat at home, get dessert here) or a Yard Party would be fun.

Family Nights. Increasingly, groups such as clubs and churches are sponsoring family nights. These are usually served meals or "pot-luck dinners." Sometimes they are picnics. (An "indoor picnic" would be appropriate.)

There are many ideas suitable for family nights in *The Family Fun Book*. If a group does not otherwise have family nights, it might want to participate in National Family Week, coming the week previous to, and including the Sunday of, Mother's Day.

A SAMPLE FAMILY AFFAIR

Ten families, along with some "unattached" folk, gathered in a large back yard for a picnic and fellowship. There was a field next to the yard, and a ball game materialized among some of the boys and the more active fathers. The other adults stood around and talked, and the girls gathered to gripe because they couldn't play ball.

Actually there was not much time. Girls joined their mothers to prepare the picnic, and soon all were eating after having a singing grace. The parents and older children filled plates for the younger ones.

The "group fellowship" then began indoors, where this collection of families—children ages 2-12, their parents beginning in the 30's and going up—got together. The children sat on the floor near the leader, and the adults sat in chairs or wherever they could.

What to do? The leader had some ideas, but actually worked most of them from the group. One child suggested I Spy, which of course was impractical, but Imaginary I Spy (see Index) was played instead. After playing two or three times the group began to waver. It was necessary to get them back together again.

"How many of you have been on a Lion Hunt?" asked the leader. Few had, so they did "The Lion Hunt" (*The Handbook of Skits and Stunts*) in animated manner. It ended with a vigorous cheer, as it usually does.

Here an adult suggested playing The Organ Grinder Man. (Send someone from the room and choose something he is to do. When he returns, sing softly when he is far away from the object or task; loudly when he is close.) Several children wanted to be "It," so we eliminated by having them guess a number between 1 and 25, the successful guesser leaving the room.

"What songs do you like to sing?" the group was asked. They named several. Starting with popular songs that the children knew from radio and television (led by children) we asked what songs they liked at Sunday School, closing with one of these, "Fairest Lord Jesus," because of its general appeal to the age span. We learned, sang, and hummed a spiritual in closing.

FAMILY FUN IN THE CAR
by Reynold E. Carlson *

Barnyard Madness. Riders on the left side of the car form one team; those on the right, another. One point is given to each team for each cow, horse, chicken, sheep, dog, or cat which it finds on its side of the road. Each white horse counts two points. Each pig deducts one point (provided that the opposing team sees and reports it). If a large group of animals (like a herd of cows) is passed so quickly that the animals cannot be individually counted, the team is granted 25 points. Passing a graveyard reduces to zero the score of the team on whose side it lies, provided that the opponents report it. The game continues until a certain town, chosen at the start of the game, is reached.

How Many Miles? A good game for the "wide open spaces."

One player points out a distant object—a tree, barn, hill—toward which the car is traveling and quickly gives an estimate as to its distance. The remaining players quickly give their estimates, and the mileage on the speedometer is checked. If the car is traveling fast, distances of less than about two miles should not be chosen. The winner of course is the one whose guess is the nearest correct.

I'm Thinking of Something. One player says, "I'm thinking of

* "Family Fun in the Car" was written by Reynold E. Carlson especially for *The Omnibus of Fun*.

something" (a natural object, preferably one which has been seen from the car). The others ask him questions which can be answered with "Yes" or "No" (as in Twenty Questions). The person who guesses the object correctly gets the next turn at "thinking of something."

"HOW WE KEPT MOTHER'S DAY"

As Related by a Member of the Family
by Stephen Leacock †

Of all the different ideas that have been started, I think that the very best is the notion of celebrating once a year "Mother's Day." . . .

It is especially in a big family like ours that such an idea takes hold. So we decided to have a special celebration of Mother's Day. We thought it a fine idea. It made us all realize how much Mother had done for us for years, and all the efforts and sacrifice that she had made for our sake.

So we decided that we'd make it a great day, a holiday for all the family, and do everything we could to make Mother happy. Father decided to take a holiday from his office, so as to help in celebrating the day, and my sister Anne and I stayed home from college classes, and Mary and my brother Will stayed home from high school.

It was our plan to make it a day just like Christmas or any big holiday, and so we decided to decorate the house with flowers and with mottoes over the mantelpieces, and all that kind of thing. We got Mother to make mottoes and arrange the decorations, because she always does it at Christmas.

The two girls thought it would be a nice thing to dress in our very best for such a big occasion, and so they both got new hats. Mother trimmed both the hats, and they looked fine, and Father had bought silk ties for himself and us boys as a souvenir of the day to remember Mother by. We were going to get Mother a new hat too, but it turned out that she seemed to really like her old one better than a new one, and both the girls said that it was awfully becoming to her.

Well, after breakfast we had it arranged as a surprise for Mother that we would take her for a beautiful drive away into the country. Mother is hardly ever able to have a treat like that, because we can only afford to keep one maid, and so Mother is busy in the house nearly all the time. And of course the country is so lovely now that it would be just grand for her to have a lovely morning, driving for miles and miles.

† From *Laugh with Leacock* (New York: Dodd, Mead & Company, Inc., © 1923, 1930). Used by permission.

But on the very morning of the day we changed the plan a little bit. It occurred to Father that it would be better to take her fishing. Father said that we might just as well drive up into the hills where the streams are. As Father said, if you just go out driving without any object, you have a sense of aimlessness, but if you are going to fish, there is a definite purpose in front of you.

So we all felt that it would be nicer for Mother to have a definite purpose. Father had just got a new rod the day before, which made the idea of fishing all the more appropriate, and he said that Mother could use it if she wanted to; in fact, he said it was practically for her, only Mother said she would much rather watch him fish and not try to fish herself.

So we got everything arranged for the trip, and we got Mother to cut up some sandwiches and make up a sort of lunch in case we got hungry, though of course we were to come back home again to a big dinner in the middle of the day, just like Christmas or New Year's Day. Mother packed it all up in a basket for us ready to go in the car.

Well, we got the car packed and it turned out that there hardly seemed as much room in it as we had supposed, because we hadn't reckoned on Father's fishing basket and the rods and the lunch, and it was plain enough that we couldn't all get in.

Father said not to mind him, he said that he could just as well stay home. He said that we were not to let the fact of his not having had a real holiday for three years stand in our way; he wanted us to go right ahead and be happy and have a big day, and not to mind him.

But of course, we all felt that it would never do to let Father stay home, especially as we knew he would make trouble if he did. Anne and Mary would gladly have stayed and got dinner, only it seemed such a pity to, on a lovely day like this, having their new hats. But they both said that Mother had only to say the word, and they'd gladly stay home and work. Will and I would have dropped out, but unfortunately we wouldn't have been any use in getting the dinner.

So in the end it was decided that Mother would stay home and just have a lovely restful day around the house, and get the dinner. It turned out anyway that Mother doesn't care for fishing, and also it was just a little bit cold and fresh out of doors, though it was lovely and sunny, and Father was rather afraid that Mother might take cold if she came.

He said he would never forgive himself if he dragged Mother round the country and let her take a severe cold at a time when she might be having a beautiful rest. He said it was our duty to try and let Mother get all the rest and quiet that she could, after all that she had done for all of us, and he said that that was principally why he had fallen in with this idea of a fishing trip, so as to give Mother a little quiet.

So we all drove away with three cheers for Mother, and Mother stood and watched us as long as she could see us, and Father waved his hand back to her every few minutes till he hit his hand on the back edge of the car, and then said that he didn't think that Mother could see us any longer.

Well, we had the loveliest day up among the hills that you could possibly imagine, and Father caught such big specimens that he felt sure that Mother couldn't have landed them anyway, if she had been fishing for them, and Will and I fished too, though we didn't get so many as Father, and the two girls met quite a lot of people that they knew as we drove along, and there were some young men friends of theirs that they met along the stream and talked to, and so we all had a splendid time.

It was quite late when we got back, nearly seven o'clock in the evening, but Mother had guessed that we would be late, so she had kept back the dinner so as to have it just nicely ready and hot for us. Only first she had to get towels and soap for Father and clean things for him to put on, because he always gets so messed up with fishing, and that kept Mother busy for a little while, that and helping the girls get ready.

But at last everything was ready, and we sat down to the grandest kind of dinner—roast turkey and all sorts of things like on Christmas Day. Mother had to get up and down a good bit during the meal fetching things back and forward, but at the end Father noticed it and said she simply mustn't do it, that he wanted her to spare herself, and he got the walnuts from the sideboard, himself!

The dinner lasted a long while, and was great fun, and when it was over all of us wanted to help clear the things up and wash the dishes, only Mother said that she would really much rather do it, and so we let her, because we wanted just for once to humor her.

It was quite late when it was all over, and when we all kissed Mother before going to bed, she said it had been the most wonderful day in her life, and I think there were tears in her eyes. So we all felt awfully repaid for all that we had done.

_____7

Handicapped

By *Valerie V. Hunt, R.P.T., Ed.D.* *

EVERY VOLUNTEER LEADER today finds some handicapped persons in average recreational groups. Actually there are more handicapped now than in the past. People are concerned about them and their well-being. And because they are more accepted they feel freer to participate in social recreation with "normal" people.

When we learn that there are handicapped persons in average groups we frequently react with pity, or an increased desire to take care of them, or at least we feel that they are different and unique. Handicapped people do have some differences which may limit them from doing everything which others do or from doing things in the same way, but they are not sick people. They are not greatly different from the average—they are more like the "normal" than they are unlike them.

In the past we have labeled a physical difference a handicap and have called the person a handicapped person. This gave us a skewed idea about him. It led us to believe that the amount of handicap was in direct proportion to the physical limitation; that a person with an extreme physical limitation was inevitably a very handicapped person, and one with a slight limitation was only mildly handicapped. But we have learned that the degree of physical limitation does not always determine the person's ability. What his difference means to him in living with and adjusting to

* Author of *Recreation for the Handicapped*. Dr. Hunt is executive officer, Division of Physical Therapy, University of California at Los Angeles. Under the title "Fun with the Handicapped" this chapter was written especially for *The Omnibus of Fun*.

others and in meeting everyday living demands is more important. Except with very severe multiple physical problems, the person's emotional adjustment to his disability is more significant in determining his handicap than his actual physical limitations.[1]

In a sense, each one of us is handicapped. If we cannot swim, dance, or play golf, bridge, or a musical instrument we are handicapped when we are with those who can. Our ability is limited either for lack of experience or lack of interest, but nonetheless we are limited more than we need to be.[2] Since the physically handicapped have a legitimate reason it is even easier for them to be restricted more than is necessary.

Because the handicapped person at all ages is more normal than abnormal he has the same interests and drives and needs as all of us. Oftentimes his needs are exaggerated because they are unsatisfied. He wants to play, to have fun, to be with others, and to be like others. Frequently he hesitates because he lacks courage to start things that he has never done or that he does poorly or differently.[3] Leaders must supply security to the handicapped which gives him courage to do and to succeed. When we are sure that he can participate someway we find out that he can and he will succeed. Our satisfactions are great when we see how much recreational activities mean to him and when we realize that without our help he might not have played.

Sometimes leaders are afraid to have a handicapped person in their groups because they know nothing about his physical problems. They fear that he will injure himself or worsen his condition. Volunteers should take average precautions with all recreational activities, but physically limited people are generally quite cautious. With the exception of children, most handicapped people know what they can and cannot do. Parents and family physicians can tell you about an individual child's limitations. Remember that the best recreation leaders of disabled people are those who view the physically disabled the same as the "normal."

PHYSICAL LIMITATIONS

Blind and Partially Seeing. Seeing people believe that the loss of sight is the greatest handicap. Blindfold yourself for a day and you will learn what the blind person knows, that blindness is not an insurmountable handicap. You will find out that your senses of hearing and smell and touch become more acute. You will learn that what you have called sight is more than seeing with your eyes. Sight is an impression, an understanding of the world about you, and visual sight is only a part of this understanding. As we grow from a child to an adult the visual part of perception becomes dominant because we rely upon it. If you became blind you could develop that sixth sense, the combination of other senses, to give you similar pictures and impressions that the seeing person enjoys.

Many blind people have some visual perception of light and dark, of shadow and color. Some fear approaching objects and noises which they cannot anticipate. Their tension is high and their movements are frequently limited. Blindisms of rhythmic rocking, nodding, rubbing eyes or hands are indications of this tension. Those with little or no sight tend to move slowly, to shuffle their feet, and to hold their head and body slightly bent.[4]

The Deaf and the Hard of Hearing. Deafness from birth is the most difficult single handicap to overcome. The deaf child does not understand the world in which he lives. "The deaf infant is a little animal who must learn to be human while his greatest tool, hearing, is restricted, and his most important skill, verbal communication, is made difficult for him." [5] The term "deaf and dumb" commonly used to describe the deaf is a misnomer. Since the totally deaf cannot hear they do not speak. But deafness does not mean that they will not be able to speak; it means rather that they have to be taught to speak since they do not casually learn like hearing children.[6] This is a long and arduous task, but once they have learned to speak and to read lips they also can understand the world they live in and their handicap diminishes.

The emotional turmoil and frustration of the deaf child may be expressed in behavior problems. If he has learned to speak before deafness occurs he is much less handicapped. However, adults who become suddenly deafened experience profound depression, as though they were in a vacuum. They feel insecure when they cannot hear the noises of the world around them.[7] Most deaf persons are otherwise healthy.

The Orthopedically Incapacitated. The orthopedically handicapped people who are commonly called crippled have difficulty moving their bodies—they creep or move with slowness. When bones, muscles, or joints are abnormal, regardless of the cause, the person has an orthopedic or movement disability.[8] There are more orthopedically handicapped in normal groups since these constitute the largest number of disabled people.

Each orthopedically handicapped person is indeed different from all others in degrees of disability and parts of the body that are affected. Frequently volunteer leaders believe that each orthopedic problem is entirely different from any other because of the many causes, such as osteomyelitis, poliomyelitis, tuberculosis, Perthes disease, traumatic injury, amputation, paraplegia, and congenital birth malformations. Actually this is not true. Regardless of the cause the end result is the same, that the person has difficulty moving parts of his body. The leader should not be concerned with why he moves poorly but rather how he moves. A postpolio with paralysis can have the same movement difficulties as a paralytic from an automobile accident. A person with a congenital defect of the hip joint can have the same difficulties running as an amputee.

The gravest adjustment problems of the orthopedically handicapped are related to the appearance of the limbs which are involved.[9] Emotional adjustment is far more difficult when the body is distorted in appearance, as compared with average people, than when it looks normal although it moves poorly.

Through the use of braces, crutches, walkers, and supports most orthopedically disabled compensate for movement handicaps and perform average tasks. Each person learns ingenious methods to do the things he needs and wants to do.

The Neurologically Incapacitated. Neurological handicaps are the most complex of all. Cerebral palsy, the most common, is likewise a problem of moving, but the movements are exaggerated, excessive, and uncontrolled rather than decreased as in the orthopedic disability. The source of the difficulty lies in destruction of nerve cells in the brain which control the muscles.[10] Although cerebral palsied people may have multiple handicaps from sensory, emotional, intellectual, and movement limitations the diagnosis is determined by the distorted movement.

We observe that some cerebral palsied persons move normally in most parts of their body yet are palsied in some parts. Or we see that most movements are excessive or in-co-ordinated. These differences in movement give some indication of the amount of brain cell damage. We observe also that some cerebral palsied persons have thin tense bodies with flexed positions and sudden jerky movements; that some have rhythmic, unpurposeful, squirming movements; that some have rigid coglike movements. These different types of movements signify approximately where in the brain the nerve destruction has occurred and the name given to the type. Spastic paralysis is a prevalent type, but not all cerebral palsied people are spastic.

Because they have excessive movements and because they try to control their movements they fatigue more easily than average people. If they drool, grimace, or display grotesque movements people may believe that they are mentally deranged or dumb. Their biggest adjustment problems are related to the reactions of normal people to them.

For practical purposes of recreation the volunteer should be concerned more with what they can do and how they can do it than about their type of cerebral palsy or what caused the nerve destruction. They ". . . have numerous limitations, but medically they are not sick." [11] There is no cure for cerebral palsy, but it rarely grows worse.

The Epileptic. We cannot distinguish an epileptic by appearance since he looks like any average person. The person himself knows if he has seizures, and he is often secretive about his condition. Leaders may first become aware of an epileptic during his seizure. The first witnessing of a *grand mal* seizure is somewhat upsetting to the average adult because of the unnatural paroxysmal movements, the unconsciousness, and the blue pallor of the victim. Children who first see a seizure are less deeply affected particularly if the adults around them are undisturbed.[12]

The exact cause of epileptic seizures is unknown. We do know that the normal rhythm of the operation of the brain is upset, causing sudden jerking, thrashing movements with loss of consciousness, falling and frequently frothing at the mouth. Seizures are self-terminating in a few seconds. The person slowly gains consciousness and is generally exhausted and disoriented for a few hours. He needs quiet rest. Afterward he knows that he has had a seizure, but since amnesia accompanies major seizures he remembers nothing specific about the seizure. He may hurt himself from falling or striking objects during his violent movements but he does not purposefully inflict injury to himself or to others.

Most epilepsy begins before adulthood and remains somewhat constant. With modern methods of treatment many epileptics have no seizures or only rare seizures. Generally the person is aware of an impending seizure before it occurs and he can get to a place where he is unlikely to injure himself and where he is less conspicuous. Awareness, called an aura, may occur a few seconds, or hours, or even days before a seizure and is noticed by vague sensations of twitchings, sounds, tastes, or flashes of light.

Although the true cause is unknown, boredom, anxiety, and physical discomfort appear to precipitate seizures. Comfort and happiness appear to lessen them. Except during seizures most epileptics are healthy and appear normal.

The commonly referred to "epileptic personality" does not exist. Most emotional abnormalities result from inability to adjust to the social problems connected with epilepsy rather than from the disordered brain wave pattern.[13]

The Cardiac. "Because heart disabilities are the most common cause of death in the Western World, they are the most feared of all disabilities." [14] Heart conditions range from extreme, in which the person is bedridden and unable to care for himself, to mild with no major limitations of activity. In ordinary recreational groups there may be mildly to moderately cardiac disabled people. And since rheumatic fever, prevalent in childhood, is the most common cause of heart damage, the cardiac handicapped belong to all age groups. Cardiac adults are well versed in their problems and limitations. Children need cautious supervision. Parents and physicians should be consulted about the amount of activity permitted each child. The volunteer should know what the cardiac can do but more importantly how he can do it. Recreational activities are either mild or strenuous by how they are done. If the child's skin turns blue and he breathes heavily through the mouth, it will be wise to engage him in less strenuous activities or, better, in really quiet games for a period.

LEADING THE HANDICAPPED

You as a volunteer leader can learn more about the handicapped by working with them than anyone can tell you. Be aware of the activities which are successful and why these are. Don't be over-solicitous; they have fun trying new things and working out successful ways to do them. The more you forget their limitations and remember what they can do the more successful you will be. The following general suggestions should make your first experiences easier.

The Blind. The biggest difficulty of the blind is moving around unfamiliar places. They must get acquainted with new rooms and playgrounds themselves. You can help them by talking to them, by identifying yourself and by seeing that there are not a lot of unnecessary things which they may bump into. They will follow your voice and alter their direction accordingly. Don't be afraid to use the word "see." To them "see" means understanding and they do understand. Give them a chance to learn by feeling things. Give directions slowly and progress slowly. The seriously blinded are unable to move rapidly to sound, as in ball games, or to handle too fine objects.[15] They will surprise you by the things they do and the skill they gain. They may need manual help on uneven ground. But don't underestimate their potential ability, and don't assist them with the things they can do alone.

The Deaf and the Hard of Hearing. The problems of communication are paramount when working with the deaf. Most deaf people read lips, yet not all deaf are equally skilled and not all hearing people are equally easy to understand by lip reading. To lip-read there must be good light on the person speaking; the deaf should be directly in front of the person speaking. Normal gestures help but should not supplant speech. If they do not understand what you have said, say it another way.[16] Use simple sentences, not phrases, and speak distinctly without exaggerated lip movements. In general, those leaders who are most easily understood by hearing people are better understood by the hard of hearing. Establish a hand signal which means that you want their attention.

Although some deafened persons lose their balance more easily than the hearing they can do all normal activities.

The Orthopedically Incapacitated. The orthopedically handicapped may hesitate to enter wholeheartedly into recreation with average people, even though they can participate in some way. They move more slowly but they can accomplish if they take a longer time. Those who are unstable of body should support themselves by sitting or leaning against a wall, a post, or crutches in order to move their arms and legs. Gadgets like recessed tables, three-wheeled bicycles and light-weight equipment are helpful. They will help you figure out how they can do an activity or how you can change the rules. Arrange some way for them to participate even though it looks different from the way others play; decrease the space required for the game, slow up the game. Adapt the rules, give them a less active position, or let another player assist them.[17]

The Neurologically Incapacitated. Cerebral palsied persons have expansive movements and strong movements. They have difficulty if equipment is too small or fragile or space so confined that they strain to control their movements. They need a slower pace, sturdy equipment, and the modification of many game rules similar to the orthopedically handicapped. Those who are very tense should be protected from falling on hard surfaces since they hurt themselves when they land.

The two best ways for the cerebral palsied to move are (1) to sit or stand relaxed and quiet until time to move—then to relax between movements; or (2) to establish a rhythm by gently swinging the part of the body they intend to move until it is relaxed—then to perform the movement.[18] If they have difficulty dancing, for example, the leader should suggest that they try both methods to see which works better. The leader does not need to know the type of cerebral palsy. One method is always more satisfactory with an individual.

The cerebral palsied do things best in the mid-day before they become fatigued. Loud noises, bright colors, competition, or too much movement of others around them increases their tension. Remember that they have fun doing what others do, and active games do not hurt them.

The Epileptic. There are no special suggestions for working with epileptic persons except cautions against injury from falling. The use of slides, swings, sharp tools, or bicycling, swimming, and horseback riding are questionable for those without auras, and those with poorly controlled seizures.[19] Strenuous physical exercise if it is fun generally wards against seizures.

If a person has a seizure, remove sharp objects or large objects that he may strike, loosen tight clothing, and calm the anxiety of others. Following the seizure keep him warm and let him rest. Do not resist his movements or try to give him stimulants. If you are in doubt do nothing.[20]

The Cardiac. Fatigue must be minimized for all cardiac handicapped people. They must use moderation in exercise. Moderation means what they do and how they do it. Guard against long standing or holding an uncomfortable position; eliminate fast movements, handling heavy objects, walking up steep elevations, strong competition, exposure to extreme heat or cold, prolonged activity, and excessive emotional experiences.[21] See that they stop activity before they are tired. Mouth breathing and blue skin coloring are warning signs that the heart is under strain.

SUGGESTED ACTIVITIES

Sports. The blind like team activities with modified rules. Use bigger balls rolled on the ground instead of batted or thrown; call a seeing runner out if a blind person touches a hit ball; use a medicine ball in volleyball, or give them a specific position such as goalie. Individual sports like archery with a buzzer under the target, shuffleboard, horseback riding, tandem bicycle riding, and golf are popular activities when with seeing people.[22]

If necessary modify the sports rules for orthopedically handicapped. You can change the rules in these ways: declare them safe in baseball if they hit the ball or have someone else run for them; allow them several hits in volleyball or let them hit with any part of their body; give them a score if they hit the basketball backboard; let them throw and catch and kick a ball even if they cannot run. One-armed persons can team with one-legged persons; individual sports like badminton, quoits, ping-pong, and deck sports are easily adapted for each individual.

Team-type sports are difficult for serious neurologically handicapped, but milder cases participate like the orthopedically handicapped. Table games with sports elements can be substituted. Box hockey, dart baseball, table football, table bowling, and table shuffleboard are examples.

Many cardiacs can play restricted positions in sports activities like pigtail, goalie, referee, or active positions with limitation on time and running. Call ball, nine-court basketball, captain ball, passing, throwing, basketball goal shooting are fun and less strenuous. Cardiacs enjoy table sports, and most deck sports are within their capacities.

Arts and Crafts. The blind particularly like crafts in which they can feel and assemble material like ceramics, woodcrafts, paper crafts, and sculpture. Blind children enjoy creating pictures by gluing shapes and textures of wood, cloth, wire, and plastics on cardboard, or constructing cardboard houses, or making wood block designs. Avoid crafts where the material is too small or the patterns too complicated. Painting and drawing are not satisfying for the severely blinded.

The orthopedically and neurologically handicapped also enjoy crafts and art work in which they can manipulate materials such as clay, ceramics, spatter painting, finger painting, wood block design, and designs from objects. The material may have to be partially cut or made for their assembly. Let them do as much as they can do; they have fun trying.

Even those with arm and hand disabilities can draw and paint by holding the brush or pencil in their teeth, their other hand, or the crook of the elbow.[23]

Dramatics. The deaf are generally highly skilled in pantomime. They are real "ham actors" in copying people's movements and actions, and they enjoy all types of dramatics. Speaking parts are more difficult but not impossible for them.

The blind display feelings and movement by changing their voice, but generally they leave out body movement and facial mimetics. They love to watch action movies and plays with a seeing person who describes what is taking place.[24]

Orthopedically and neurologically disabled enjoy all forms of dramatics. They can use gestures in place of words or words in place of moving about a stage. Dramatic guessing games, Charades, and singing dramatic games like Ring Around the Rosy, Farmer in the Dell, Did You Ever See a Lassie, are excellent expressive activities for children.

Music. Active and passive music experiences have a profound place in the recreation of all handicapped people. The blind are extremely sensitive to music and are frequently skilled in playing instruments and in singing. The deaf enjoy the rhythm of music and imagine a melody even if they cannot hear it. They like to put their hands on a piano, a phonograph, a radio or instrument to feel the sound. They may be off pitch but they do have fun singing.

The orthopedically and neurologically disabled possess the same appreciation of music as average persons. The orthopedic can play many instruments, and singing presents no problem. The neurologic dislike harsh, loud music or that with a long, strong, continuous beat. Those who cannot play standard instruments enjoy rhythm instruments like bells, drums, and rattles, which they easily manipulate. They like to sing although their sounds seem distorted to the average person.

Games. Blind persons enjoy contest table games with seeing persons who explain where their "men" are situated or the number on cards and dominoes. Braille equipment is available for chess, dominoes, cards, checkers, and most popular games from American Foundation for the Blind, 15 West 16th Street, Boston, Massachusetts.

Even orthopedically and neurologically handicapped who are unable to move their hands participate if another player moves their "men." Special large checkers and large recessed playing boards help them from upsetting "player" positions. Sliding boards where "men" cannot be moved out of a grooved line assist some to play without help.

Dance. All handicapped people can dance. If they are too severely crippled to stand another person can push their wheel chair through dance patterns while they move their feet, hands, or head. Remember that dance entails the use of any part or parts of the body to rhythm.

The blind accomplish all types of dance from social to complicated square dances. It is easier if each blind person dances with a seeing partner or next to a seeing person in line, circle, and square dances. They rarely bump into others in social dance, but they get mixed up in folk dances which have turning and change of position unless they have a seeing partner.

Deaf persons feel the rhythmic beat through the floor, or by following a hearing person, and stay in time with the music. In square dances there should be hearing leaders of their square whom they follow.

Camping and Swimming. All handicapped persons should experience fun with nature. The blind enjoy nature through feeling trees and rocks, through the smell of flowers and the sounds of birds. Seeing people describe to them color and distant objects. They hike smooth trails unassisted, or rocky terrains with help.

Orthopedically and neurologically handicapped can camp. Their hike may involve a slow pace or a short distance, or even an automobile ride down a woodsy lane. An overnight trip may be within sight of habitation, but most can roast a marshmallow, help build a fire, and make a bed. Their fun is as great for them as a strenuous hike for the "normal."

Cardiacs camp at low altitudes in mild weather of neither too hot nor too cold temperature. They walk at a slow pace on level ground and rest often to observe nature about them.

Swimming and bathing are universally fun. The blind have difficulty swimming in a straight line. They need protection from getting into deep water, if they cannot swim, and from divers who might hit them.

Generally the orthopedically and neurologically handicapped are uncomfortable in water cool enough for normal people. The cerebral palsied enjoy water with the temperature in the nineties. All can learn to swim if they overcome their fear of water. Some need the support of inner tubes or floats because they move slowly and tend to sink.

Cardiac persons require warm water and should stay in for only short periods of time. Form swimming, bathing, and mild play should be encouraged rather than speed or distance swimming.

For detailed discussion of those handicapped and for suggested activities for the aged, the psychotic, the mentally defective, the diabetic, and the convalescent refer to the book *Recreation for the Handicapped.*

PART THREE

Planning

for

Fun

8

How to Organize Your Plans

WHETHER RECREATION takes the form of a simple gathering, like a picnic, or a formal party, some advance planning will help people to enjoy it far more. Details that a committee responsible for the affair need to think about, devices for "getting folks started," things that can be done in crowded places, at big meetings, at camp, fun that develops intercultural and international appreciation, the importance of publicity, qualifications that a master of ceremonies needs to have, interesting and unusual refreshments for parties and picnics—all these and more are discussed in this chapter.

A TESTING OUTLINE

Here is the newspaper testing outline that can be used in making the decision whether to have a recreational event, whether you are a recreation leader or a committee:

WHY? Some groups plunge ahead to have social affairs without determining why. "Do we really need and want it?" Be honest— or you may have a flop!

WHO? HOW MANY? Who should, could come? What age range? Ratio of males to females.

WHAT? The why determines the what. In other words, what are our real goals? Sociability? To get acquainted? (If the group are already well-known to each other, there is no point in playing "get acquainted" games.) If they are not, many get-acquainted games, mixers, "name callers" may be needed.

WHEN? The time is important, particularly when considered in relation to other events taking place in the community. Is there stiff competition with something else?

WHERE? Often that is settled by the headquarters of the group that is doing the planning, but sometimes other facilities are needed, such as social halls, skating rinks, or even an outdoor spot which needs to be booked, such as a park area.

In addition, the planning committee should consider things like these:

1. What are the likes and the dislikes of the group?
2. What have they had before? (Too much of a good thing is a bad thing!)
3. Do we have a general plan for recreation for the whole year? How does this event fit the plan? What should it accomplish?
4. What kind of leadership do we need to carry this through properly?

THE PLANNING COMMITTEE

There should be enough people of varied backgrounds on the planning committee to make sure that the affair is a success. Some insist on ten or twelve, although many groups would have to operate with fewer people. Whether it is an elaborate or a simple undertaking is a factor, of course.

Sometimes a committee has been directed to plan a certain kind of party, like a Valentine Party. Often, however, the committee has the freedom to choose its own theme and work it out. Preparation for any particular planning session might consist of duplicating on paper or writing on the board a number of possible themes and, in addition, getting members of the group to think up some ideas themselves. (The party themes suggested in this book should stimulate thought, even though none of them be adopted.)

Often a committee will use an interest finder, similar to the one in this book (see Index), to determine what activities interest people the most. There is no substitute, of course, for talking with people to see how they react to the social life of the group.

Every skillfully planned party will include most of these elements:

1. Fellowship and "at-easeness," release from tension.
2. Chance to "mix and mingle," especially in small groups.

3. Opportunity for self-expression, especially in creative activity of some sort.
4. Opportunity to win or lose.
5. Rhythmic activities, if appropriate, to demonstrate skill in forming pattern.
6. Creation of something beautiful, especially in music and art.

In other words, most parties will include:

1. Mixers, get acquainted, group starter activities.
2. Music (performed by or for the group, or both).
3. Drama, skits (even improvised "quickies").
4. Active (moving around) games and quieter (seated) ones.
5. Rhythmic activities.
6. Refreshments (something new is nice).
7. Final opportunity for togetherness before leaving. A closing fellowship period.

This means that all aspects of the person attending will be taken into account:

HANDS (representing shaking hands for fellowship, or using them in some creative activity, such as paper-sack puppets); HEAD (for mental games, creative activities); FEET (for active games, rhythmic activities); "TUMMY" (refreshments); VOICE (for music); HEART, SOUL (representing emotion, religious expression).

A little rhyming formula has been devised:

MEET. Committee meets, plans, delegates responsibility in advance.

HEAT. Temperature is checked, condition of room. If too hot, effort made to cool it; if too cool, to get it comfortable.

GREET. One or more persons are ready to greet first-comers, show them something interesting to do. (Name tags are involved here.)

SEAT—FEET. Throughout the party or social affair there is a happy blending of activities on the feet and on the seat, so that folks won't be too tired of either way of doing it.

TREAT. Something special, a big surprise sprung unexpectedly, adds fun and flavor.

FEET—SEAT. Some more alternation, keeping it as active as the situation warrants.

EAT. Make it fun but not the most important part of the affair.

HEAT. Here this represents the fire in the fireplace, campfire, or other *rallying center* around which people gather after refreshments for stories, songs, closing fellowship, and worship expression.

NEAT. It is a rule of good sociability that a group leaves the place as neat or neater than it was found. Here all may be asked to help with the clean-up, especially picking up paper, clearing tables, dismantling decorations.

Multiple Leadership. It is easier for one person to be the leader of an entire social affair. However, there are many occasions in which it is very desirable to use many people to lead.

They need to have their signals straight, their order of doing things straight. Someone should be designated as the over-all leader, chairman, director. That person should have freedom to adjust the program and cut out items if absolutely necessary.

There follows a time schedule worked out for a large party, directed by several committees. This might become a sample to your group for a good plan, flexible enough and yet clear enough. Note that they planned activities for "couples" but also for a situation in case the relationship was 2-1 (usually girls to boys, or women to men).

RALLYING CENTERS

Experienced recreation leaders have learned that certain spots are "naturals" as rallying centers for a group which is slowly ingathering. (Often they won't ingather until some rallying starts around a rallying center!) Here are some of the centers, and what you might do at (or in) them:

1. Piano or accompaniment instrument	Sing.
2. On the porch, on the steps	Sing, do stunts, challenges, tell jokes, read humorous material, play small group games.
3. On the pier	Same as 2.
4. Around a basket of fruit	Stand and talk, sing, tell jokes, do tricks, physical feats.

SADIE HAWKINS SHINDIG *

Sample Party Time Schedule and Plan for Large Group

Time	Activity 2 to 1 Balance	Leader	Equipment	Preparation, Formation Notes
7:00 to 7:30	Even Numbers Equipment games Name tags Affinities Word Hunt Skunk Hollow Football	Early Comers Committee	Pins, green and red paper guns, pencils, sheets of wrapping paper with inscription, prize	(Games leaders get equipment ready)
7:30 to 7:55	Games Turnip Race Skunk Hollow Special	Games Committee	Large turnips, teaspoons, string, paper napkins. Blindfolds for all girls	Leave partners in a single file, either by 2's or 3's, ready for Grand March leader
7:55 to 8:10	Grand March by 2's or Grand March by 3's	Grand March Leader, musician, and trained leaders	Music Cowbell or whistle	
8:10 to 8:45	Musical Games	Musical Games Leader, musician, and trained leaders	Music Cowbell or whistle	Lunch Committee gets ready to serve. Leader quiets group to listen to Lunch Committee announcement
8:45 to 9:15	Refreshments, polkas	Lunch Committee "Records Jockey" or musician	Refreshments Music for polkas	
9:15	Talent Festival, or more musical games or squares	Musical Games Committee	Records Player	Leave group in large circle or have squares move close together for closing songs
9:50	Closing songs Songbooks distributed	Song leader Party chairman	Music for musician Songbooks	Clean-up Committee ready

5. In the lounge	Get in one corner where several people are together, do as in No. 2.
6. Cool spot (under tree) Warm spot (around stove)	Spin yarns, read aloud, sing, tell jokes, use humorous material.
7. Around game tables	Play simple games, do quickie crafts. Try puzzles, puzzler games, match games.
8. Equipment games	Play or watch.
9. Fireplace	Sit and talk; warm selves; swap yarns; sing; do crafts; tell jokes; do physical feats of mild variety.
10. Sweet shop	Carry on conversation; do puzzles, tricks; use humorous material; play small group games.
11. In the bus for a trip	Sing, converse, compose songs; play trip games; have jokes, humorous material, guessing games.
12. Walled or enclosed backyard	Play equipment games, all kinds of outdoor games, many indoor games. Sit and talk, joke, sing, eat.
13. A "Green Temple"	Sit and rest, meditate, in this outdoor spot.
14. Refreshment table	Stand and talk, joke, have informal fun.
15. Set-up tables	Do simple crafts, paper-sack puppetry; make up stunts; make name tags.

FUN FOR CROWDED PLACES

(From platform, for banquets, rallies, conventions)

When people cannot budge, or at least cannot move around freely, you need to shift gears a bit, but there are plenty of fun possibilities. The situation can be handled in three ways:

1. Put on things for them to enjoy, such as skits, monologues, films, and the like.
2. Do things in which all can participate as a group, such as singing, certain group stunts.
3. Break the larger group down to two's or small groups to be doing some fun activity simultaneously.

Under No. 1 above, the leader may become a performer and do a number of "one person stunts," may read aloud some material such as "boners," may do an individual performance, such as "Lot's Wife." Or persons staging pre-prepared skits and stunts, quartets, and other performers may do their stuff. Many group starters fit here.

Under No. 2, the group have more fun if they can join in themselves. Singing is perfect for this. Often exercisers or stretchers are what is needed. Such activities as having all shout their names at the same time, standing on tiptoes, or doing "Football" (see Index) or responding to the story of the "King with a Terrible Temper" (in *Handy Stunts*—see Bibliography) or Stagnet, or Clappertown (in *The Fun Encyclopedia*) are fun. Most of these are noisy.

Under No. 3 get each person to face a neighbor and play Fingers Up or Fox, Gun, Hunter, involving two players facing each other (there are many more in the Group Starter section). Also it is possible to get four persons to play together and to do such things as Group Interview, or small group games like Imaginary I Spy (if there is time). It is important to keep the spirit moving.

The Group Starter section has many kinds of material for this purpose. See also music and humor.

FUN AT BIG MEETINGS
(Conference—camp—retreats—rallies—conventions)

One of the most important things to do at the opening of a big gathering is to have several persons as *greeters* who know how to welcome people, help them find their rooms or cabins, get to the registration line, find the facilities they need, help them get a name tag, find some other people to talk with, or simple games to play. (Equipment games are good for this purpose.)

Some groups use the leaders for this "greeter" function. It is impressive to have your bag carried to your room by a person who later is to be a teacher or featured speaker.

Hello! Often a group will start with a tradition from the very first of asking all who meet each other anywhere, to say "Hello" or "Hi" or "Hey," or whatever is said in that section. No one passes another person of the camp or conference without speaking.

Likewise, a rule which keeps name tags on people puts a penalty of the price of a "coke" for anyone caught without name tag. (Some excellent wooden ones may be had from The Handcrafters, Waupun, Wisconsin, at low cost.)

Words on Trees, Buildings. Many camps and conferences have tastefully made signs with friendly and thoughtful words on them, in the halls, over doors, on trees, some of them permanently made, the wording appropriate for the group age. "Welcome to . . . ," "We're glad you came to . . ." Outdoors on trees, the signs may take quotations from Psalms, like: "I will lift up mine eyes to the hills" (if appropriate) or "He leads me beside still waters" by a quiet stream or lake. Don't make the signs promotional—make them warm and personal and thoughtful, so that the new individual begins to feel a sense of fellowship with the purposes and causes of the camp or group.

At the Table. During the first two or three meals, the table gives an excellent opportunity for getting acquainted. Unless absolutely necessary to keep them together, have the leaders spread out at different tables, getting acquainted with the people, and the people with them.

Use conversation starters like these: "What is the funniest joke you have heard recently?" or "What was the funniest thing that ever happened to you?" or "How are they doing it in your section?" (This assignment can be made by announcement or by a card on each table.)

Let the tables discuss alternative choices involved in the program or schedule, and report through a representative or a note to the steering or planning committee. This quickly brings people together in a small group or natural setting, and helps them to become acquainted.

Group Interview (see Index) may be done at the table, if there is time.

Getting Acquainted. Right away, people are interested in four kinds of "get acquainted": (1) with each other, (2) with the program or schedule, (3) with the leaders, (4) with the facilities.

In this book are many get-acquainted games, mixers and the like, for "each other." It is well to have the leaders mix with the group in these get-acquainted times. (Leaders might have a different kind of name tag to distinguish them quickly from group members.)

Acquainting the group with the program and schedule can be done by talks, skits, and other presentation. Introducing the leaders with a skit is excellent. ("The Legend of Instant Postum," with each leader assuming a role, was used very effectively in one camp. Found in *Skit Hits*—see Bibliography.)

The game Camouflage is a fine way of introducing the people to the facilities, if they are not too widespread. Also, if at a certain time, interesting things are going on in different rooms and buildings, and the campers or delegates are free to roam from one to the other, they may come up with a good knowledge of facilities. Sometimes this is done on a group basis.

One camp found a "Round the World Party" (see Index) excellent for orientation. Here pretrained "pilots" carried the people around the camp to see different shows. This could be modified to a simple presentation of facilities.

Sample Planning for Opening of Camp or Conference. Committee meets, decides who will greet people as they arrive. They plan it so that someone will be at the regular points of arrival at all times. They help newcomers find their rooms, carry baggage.

A specially creative name tag situation is worked out in which they are to "wood-burn" (with wood-burning tools) their names on wooden name tags. Several people are there to assist. (They also institute the rule, "Each One Teach One," and urge those who have learned, to show others how to do wood-burning.)

Refreshments—like lemonade, iced or hot tea, coffee—are available, with enough people to serve them, either free or for a small charge. (Here people may stand, talk, get acquainted. They ask some of the featured leaders to help serve refreshments.)

Simple skill and equipment games are in a good-sized room close by, and several people are in charge. Frequently they will invite newcomers to come in and will teach them how to play the games, especially of the rolling-tossing-sliding variety.

At the first meal, a get-acquainted plan is used at the table. At the end of the meal, some fellowship singing is in charge of a good leader.

During the opening social fellowship period, musical mixers

and get-acquainted games are to be used, followed by Group Interview. Then the leaders present a stunt, followed by a presentation of the program and schedule.

Next is Camouflage, with people scattering all about, coming back at a bell signal, telling what they saw and where, as the leader reads out the names of the items and asks where they were.

This is followed by more musical mixers, refreshments, and a closing ceremony which includes singing and a brief talk about the purposes of the meeting.

Taking Advantage of the Setting and Personnel. A good recreation leader (or committee) will do everything possible to take advantage of the setting.

In a camp with a nice waterfront, it is good to schedule swimming and water games. With excellent hiking trails available, have hikes or trips to points of interest. If material and time permit, offer nature crafts or bird walks.

In a conference in town, the opportunities might lean more toward visiting an unusual park or museum, seeing special shows, including telecasts, visiting Chinatown, taking in a special concert, or athletic contest. Skating rinks or bowling alleys might provide some fellowship and recreation for delegates.

In any kind of gathering, there are interesting people with interesting skills and stories. This is particularly true of those who have come from other countries. See to it that they have opportunities for informal chats, for displaying souvenirs, showing slides and films. If these people have skills which others would like to learn, and if there is time, schedule meetings for them.

Animated Bulletin Board. If someone good at drawing is available, let him draw some animated pictures showing the possibilities in the "free choosing" time for fun. This is particularly good if you are "selling" a new idea with which conferees or campers are not too well acquainted. Informal posters spotted around can help to stir interest in recreational possibilities.

Sample Big Group Program. This example is from a meeting of 150 youths in a church basement after a meeting upstairs. (Much of this could be done in a one-room church.) The group is seated at the start, in movable chairs.

1. Clapping Stunt. (See Index.)
2. Handkerchief drop. While leader drops handkerchief and before it hits floor, everyone is to applaud loudly until it touches the floor.
3. Let's Get Acquainted. Have everyone stand and shout his name as loud as he can. Then call, "Louder, I couldn't hear." Then again, "Louder." "Now sit down."
4. Sing song or two, such as "In a Cabin in a Wood" (see Index).
5. Play march music, have chairs put back to wall, get boys into center of room, then ask girls to make circle around them, boys facing girls. As music plays, each circle moves to its own left. When music stops, each person does one "funny handshake" (see Index) with one or two persons in opposite circle facing him or her. Repeat five or six times.
6. Do simple musical game for couples, such as Circle Virginia Reel or other musical mixer.
7. March them past refreshment service.
8. Back in fellowship circle for two songs: "Vive l'Amour" (or other lively song that they know) then "Kum Ba Yah" (or other spiritual or hymn). Close with prayer and benediction.

Parties for Five or Six Hundred. Annually the great influx of freshmen into colleges calls for a Freshman Week, with all its social affairs. Here is the way six hundred were handled on a Saturday.

The Student Christian Association co-operated and furnished fifty leaders, who worked in pairs. They met at noon on Saturday for a briefing session, in which they learned in detail what was to go on and what were the objectives. There was a question period, and then they played the games to be used later, just to get familiar with them.

Scheduled for outdoors, the group had to go into the gym because of weather. The freshmen walked by several serving stations in lines, where they were handed their hot dogs and picnic material, also a number. There were guides at each door to show them where the leaders with cardboard numbers on 5-foot poles were located.

As the freshmen gathered in these little groups, the SCA leaders took charge and saw that the freshmen came to know each other, and that they completed a name tag. All ate together who were assigned the same number. The SCA students also told the freshmen about the program of SCA and welcomed them to become members.

When the meal was finished, all were invited, in groups, to go to the gym floor, where they regrouped around their numeral and played two games while seated in circles: Pass It On and Spin the Bottle (see Index). They were then asked to come, by groups, close to the stage and sit on the floor to do group singing. Several motion songs were done, then a group starter, and some "boners" read.

Following this was a brief devotional service, a break, and a mixer dance (using selected musical mixers to allow students to come to know each other). The Bunny Hop was used to draw students in after the break because it did not require partners. A dance with orchestra finished the evening.

In another group serving five hundred students, instead of having SCA people alone, couples who lived in town were present, one couple for each of the 25 groups into which the 500 were divided. Each group met on the green outdoors at a pole bearing the name of one couple, so that they were in the "Norris" family, or the "Park" family. There the couple greeted the students, and games were played, directed by a college student, who had been pretrained.

(Later, then, each group of twenty visited in the home of the local couple whom they had met, for a social time. This meant that, even though these freshmen had been in town only a few days, they at least knew one *town* family!)

The program was concluded by some all-group singing, presentations, and a brief worship service.

FUN AT CAMP

Whether camping is done by children, youth, or adults, it is community living in the out-of-doors. There are three important factors involved: the people, living in groups, the camp itself, its outdoor location. Some enthusiasts are likely to forget one or two factors and overemphasize their favorite.

In camp, people should do some different things from those they do back home. They should do things differently, too. However, the camp that forgets completely to educate people for their way of life back home is not taking advantage of its full opportunity.

Generally, the objectives of camp would include helping people to enjoy and to come to love the out-of-doors; to find happy expression of their total selves (physical, social, mental, creative, aesthetic, spiritual) in the camp community; to gain new knowledge and new skills and therefore to grow in a wholesome, constructive way.

The recreational aspects of camp can provide for each camper a framework of expression. Through camp fun life the camper can come to enjoy the natural setting, the pure air, the free schedule, the specialized (and perhaps spiritualized) fellowship. He can learn to "rough it," sleeping in tents or outdoors, eating plain food, taking strenuous activities, going on trips, being teased. Camp gives a wonderful opportunity for learning the skills of problem solving, whether these be problems in group relationships, improvising repairs to equipment, or making up new games.

Camp is a setting for forming new friendships. The wise camp staff will have present some people who are of different cultural, perhaps racial, background from the campers. The skillful recreation director or committee will see to it that there are fellowship times in which the campers can come to know these folk. Many church camps deliberately send a "national" from another country to help enrich the fellowship.

Recreation at camp often takes on several groupings: (1) the entire camp, (2) cabins or groups of cabins or buildings, (3) "tribes" or other groupings, which may or may not follow cabin lines. Each of these will develop its own fun, much of it of an informal nature, "pulling gags," and the like.

Cabins enjoy such fun as singing, working out skits together, writing new songs or graces for the table, sharing jokes and tricks, carrying on letter writing projects and storytelling, learning new instruments and playing them, mastering other skills together.

The organization of tribes or other groupings may be a little more formal because there are more people. They will enjoy the same things that cabins do, if the pressure of numbers does not prevent.

For the entire camp, such fun ideas as these are good:

1. Singing after meals (especially made-up songs). In one camp the leader, who has eaten first, visits the tables and helps them start songs.

2. Dramatics, skits, especially improvised, also role playing. Effort should be made to keep such times from dropping into the old ruts of stale threadbare stunts.

3. Rainy day fun. (There might be cabin competition for the best ideas for rainy day fun.)

4. Using "nationals," that is, people from other countries. Often they can play, sing, tell of life in their own country, in a very captivating way.

5. Hikes, trips, trails, nature games. If you go to camp to take advantage of nature, it is a little silly to live just as if you were in the city. Special hikes to points of interest, trips of longer duration, nature trails, nature games add to the fun. The Crazy Critter Hike, for instance, provides for having groups go out to bring back interesting nature objects, telling the group a fabricated story about what the name is, what the object will do. Camera hikes (perhaps developing film at camp, if facilities are available), theme hikes such as a beeline hike (going in a straight line), book trails (reading a good book aloud after a hike into the woods) are suggestions.

6. Skill games, athletic games. If there is any objective at all for having campers take home these ideas, the plans for games may be mimeographed. Some simple games might be constructed at camp, or "game boards" marked on rough wood or scratched into the dirt or mimeographed, using coke bottle caps as markers.

   Such games as beanbag games, horseshoes, pitching washers, ball games, Sky Pie activities, Ring the Hook are samples.

7. Crafts, especially including nature crafts. Here you can take advantage of the setting by using native materials, making objects useful in camp and at home. (Don't forget, however, that the more native materials of the usual way of life may be tin cans and automobile tires, rather than pine needles and native clay!)

8. Listening to music, reading. The best camps, whatever their purpose, will see to it that some of the best music is available, to be heard, played, sung.

9. Spiritual refreshment and re-creation is a part of the programs of many camps. A "Green Temple" is often set aside as an area where the campers may go at will to meditate and worship in quiet. A good camp project might be to set up one.

10. In planning for camp activities which are enjoyable to do, don't forget work and service projects. Since recreation is more a matter of emotions than motions, a person with the spirit of fun and play can lead campers into a worth-while service or construction project during part of their hours and they will be happy doing it. Some camps start their season with such a work camp. Those attending usually think it's great because the fellowship of work, done in the spirit of play, *is* great.

Big Parties for Camp. Aside from the usual opening night get-acquainted party, many camps do not plan for another large all-camp affair because they do not know how to plan one. Here are some ideas, most of them worked out in detail in this book (see Index):

1. A Circus, involving the entire camp, featuring animals.
2. Mardi Gras, with parade, queens, celebrations.
3. Rodeo, with acts, side shows, "making a Western Movie," games.
4. County Fair, featuring free acts and side shows.
5. Dramatics, stunt, talent nights ("Hits in Skits").
6. Indoor Track Meet (even held outdoors, perhaps near the water).
7. Football Party (in this book—substituting Balloon Basketball or Question Baseball for the game if desired).

The Staff. At camp the staff needs some recreation on its own. However, it should mix with the campers in their fun times. Adults, particularly ministers, hold themselves back for various reasons. The planning committee should plan some affairs not too strenuous in which everyone can participate.

Often the staff introduction is done with a skit, such as "The Legend of Instant Postum," with each staff member wearing a sign as the narrator reads, walking across the stage and doing whatever is required of his role. This skit takes little preparation.

Adapted or improvised skits would be effective here, too. Young campers, especially, are highly interested in whether their staff are going to be "good Joes" or not. There's a "leveling effect" in skits.

The trend is for staff and campers to enjoy things together. Therefore, today's emphasis is more on co-operative activity between staff and campers than competitive between them (like the faculty-student baseball game of years back). The best relationship grows in the camp in which all persons (staff and campers alike) are regarded as growing people, always on the alert to find new ways of enjoying life together.

Rainy Day at Camp. When rain comes suddenly at camp, leaders often shudder and think of the bad hours that will come from having people cooped up until the rain is over.

It is best to anticipate rain as a definite part of the total camping program (unless you're in an area where there is no summer rain). Pre-preparation will make this much easier. Note some of the suggestions which indicate saving some equipment and activities especially for rainy days. (The large group may be broken down into several smaller ones.)

1. Special rainy day games kit or box. This equipment is to be brought out only when it rains.
2. Balloon games (as described in this book and others) with bright colors to drive gray away.
3. Puzzles, saved especially for rainy days.
4. Some simple, quick crafts especially for rainy times.
5. Active indoor games, relays, contests.
6. Playing mystery games, "send 'em out of the room" games.
7. Have Indoor Track Meet (see Index).
8. Bring out table games.
9. Have quiz show, perhaps boys against girls, or one group versus another.
10. Use one of large-group party ideas, like quickie Circus or Football Party, for life and action (materials having been gathered in advance).
11. Save your birthday celebrations until rainy days and then put on big one. (Everybody will want it to rain, then!)
12. Use some Sky Pie games. Teach some new ones.

13. Play Ping-pong Football, Balloon Basketball. (Several games could be going at same time if you have several ping-pong tables, several large balloons.)

14. Do some good group singing, learn new lively songs. Encourage campers to make up songs.

15. Play Camouflage (see Index).

16. Have indoor picnic for a meal, using all imagination possible (even with a few cut-out ants!).

17. Have "cook-in" instead of "cook-out," furnishing campers with precooked weiners to put on real or imaginary sticks. Have them toast marshmallows. Set atmosphere for imagination.

18. Use radio and TV if they are around. If campers would like such a program, tune in on ball game.

19. Storytelling, reading. Some of humorous material in this book and others might be read or told. Have continued story going around circle of campers (making sure circle is not too big).

20. Make up stunts, put them on. Allow campers to "take off" leaders, counselors.

21. Do charades.

22. Have string horse race or turtle race (see Index).

23. Play Ships (see Index). Use two sides of blackboard, or mimeographed sheets and have players all over, playing in pairs or in small teams.

24. Make paper-sack puppets, put on show. Or have show by some puppeteers who are in camp, presented for enjoyment of all.

25. Show movie or slides, especially one with outdoor scenes, lovely color, to cheer up spirits.

26. Have Christmas celebration. Campers might make gifts, exchange them. Sing carols.

INTERCULTURAL FUN

For a thing to be genuinely intercultural, there needs to be genuine interest first—interest in persons. If people are genuinely concerned, they will make long-time preparation and develop friendships with those of another cultural group. This may involve setting persons of Indian, Chinese, Negro groups to seek out friendly white groups; Spanish-American or Italian or Polish groups to select English-speaking groups as well as the reverse. The "majority group" become accustomed to thinking mistakenly that initiation for intercultural or interracial enjoyment must always come from them. The approach should be genuine and open—nobody likes to have people come to their group in a "We're going slumming" attitude.

The self-contained group misses richness of fellowship by not enjoying that of others different from themselves. (If they are not convinced of this, however, they had better *stay* self-contained!)

One of the best ways to do interchange is to enjoy food together. Many of the folk camps are having an entire evening devoted to the eating of foods, sharing of the cultural gems of a certain group. If that group customarily sits on the floor to eat, so do the campers. If a person of the nationality group is present (or many) there may be questions and answers. "Why do you Japanese sit on the floor?" "What is the basis of this custom?" (One from India once answered the "sacred cow" question by saying, "I understand that you in America have a special feeling for horses and do not eat their flesh. We do not eat that of the cow!") This could not take place except in an honest, informal setting. The questions should be not taunting but honest, and asked in a desire to understand.

Intercultural meetings will not necessarily make you "love everybody" of that group. It is easy to get a little sentimental about this. Genuine love is preceded by understanding and appreciation. It is "laughing with" instead of "laughing at." It involves coming to understand and appreciate people and peoples and customs without necessarily adopting those customs. Real appreciation takes time.

In learning songs, stories, dances from other cultural groups, it is more important to be sincere than to be correct. A Lithuanian appreciates your effort when you try to learn his material even though your pronunciation and style are off. (The writer will never forget the light in the eyes of an old man of Czech descent as he listened to a poor rendition of a Czech folk song—on a bus! His appreciation was not of the correctness but of the intent. (This is not to excuse sloppiness in attempting to "get it right.") An ethnic group may resent an outsider who, doing something in wrong style, thinks he's "just like a Mexican." The difference is whether you're appropriating it or sharing it. An American leader was very touched when, in a remote village in preparation for his coming, the folk had learned an English song which they sang in his honor. Its title was "Found a Peanut" and the villagers sang it for him in church!

A genuine festival will bring an interchange of ideas. It will be developed in the atmosphere of appreciation for each other—the treasures of nationality and cultural groups. Real intercultural effort may also involve asking some Negro folk to do a Swedish folk dance in demonstration, and the Swedes to sing spirituals with a bit of Swedish dialect. Otherwise an intercultural affair may be simply intra-cultural.

Many groups will have to have their intercultural fun secondhand. By using records and books and piano music and their best knowledge, they will enjoy these cultural gems. If so, try to explain the background for whatever is used. The "Fun and Festival" series of the Friendship Press gives good interpretations of material (see Bibliography), as do such books as the accompaniment book to *Lift Every Voice,* the accompaniment book to *Singing America,* and the like.

It is not necessary to be a folklorist to do a creditable job on a folk festival. An Alabama group annually uses the quadrangle of a small college to present a festival. Local groups work up some material, do their best on native costumes, and present their wares. Folk singing and general folk games are a part of their program.

Always it is interesting to learn a few words in another language, such as how to say "Hello," "How are you?" "Good-bye," "I love you." A person who speaks another language may get quick attention by teaching such short phrases as these.

FESTIVALS
(Regional—international—small, large)

Regional festivals such as strawberry festivals, and international folk festivals are becoming increasingly popular in community and city for large-group fun. Some of these affairs are held indoors, some outdoors. Some are annual, like the Asheville Rhododendron Festival; some are even triennial like the great St. Paul, Minnesota, Festival of the Nations. Others may be small ones sponsored by a Girl Scout troop or a school or church group.

It is good to have the purpose or purposes clear before going further. What is the festival to do? Acquaint those who take part and those who attend with past history of the area? Acquaint people from far around with the commercial products of the area, such as strawberries, oranges, tulips? Point up history, as the Ticonderoga Indian Pageant does? Help to interpret America as a land of many threads of cultural background? All are possible. Which is the group trying to accomplish?

Historical Festival. If this is decided upon, a writer should be engaged to create a script, bringing in a number of scenes of history, and using many of the folk of the community. Old settlers should be included, descendants of early families. Libraries and records should be checked. This kind of production should occupy several months in preparation and should call for large local participation. It should last for several days.

Flower or Fruit Festival. Usually such things as crowning a queen, having a parade with floats, having a big celebration in which demonstrations of singing and dancing take place are the order of the day. Sometimes athletic contests are held in connection. The particular flower or fruit of the region is the keynote.

International Festival Ideas. In celebration of U.N. Week or some other organizing time sponsored by school, church, or clubs, many groups have international festivals.

In them they feature song, story, game, poetry, dance, craft around the world. Often people from the countries foreign to North America participate.

Such affairs will feature these items:

1. A colorful Parade of the Nations, either in their own social rooms or perhaps down the main street of town, decorating floats in keeping. This is particularly true during U.N. Week.
2. Foods of the Nations. At St. Paul, for the Festival of the Nations, foods of different countries are served through a window or door in a housefront designed like a typical one of that country. The foods might be served at a banquet or as refreshments. (See foods section for recipes.)
3. Crafts Around the World. At Scarritt College where many international students are in attendance, this is a part of the annual U.N. party. Displays are set up around the edge of the

large social hall, and those attending the party are welcome to visit the booths and ask questions.

4. Play Around the World. This could be featured as part of the program itself, or in booths, displays, with figures and dolls representing the manner of play of the children, youth, and adults of different countries.

5. Courtship Around the World. A party involving international students in a college showed, in skit form, courtship as it is done in different parts of the world.

6. Films from Around the World. Film showings, during or preceding the festival, help to give atmosphere and to bring understanding of how the people in another part of the world live, work, play, worship.

7. Music Around the World. With recordings, solo singers, group singing this theme may be carried out. Usually music is a part of any world-minded program, whatever else is presented.

8. Dancing Around the World. If appropriate, demonstrations and group participation here give a picture of how people enjoy this form of recreation.

A Festival Program. Since the age, number, and condition of participation in festivals varies greatly, it is difficult to say just what should be done. Here is a pattern which might be modified to your situation.

I. The Pre-Program Features

International crafts, foods, dolls, products are displayed. Films shown. Music, live or recorded, played as background. Games shown.

II. The Festival

1. Parade of Nations. People carrying flags of many countries. Place them in positions of honor on stage or in front of group. Here some groups may plan an invocation.

2. Processional of festival folk, doing "Helston Furry Processional."

3. Demonstrations and performances, by folk singers, dancers, poets, craftsmen.

4. Group singing by all.

5. More demonstrations.

6. Participation by all in simple folk activities, such as singing games, folk games, with or without records.

7. Perhaps whole group seated together again for a closing story or two, singing, closing. (Religious groups may want to close with a prayer of brotherhood and benediction.)

(A script for a folk festival is found in *The Handbook of Skits and Stunts,* page 193. See Bibliography.)

Some Suggestions and Pointers for Folk Festivals

Out of the experience of many folk festivals have grown certain suggestions which will aid those who are trying a festival for the first time:

1. Practice what is done so that it will be well done. However, perfection is not so much the object as spontaneous fun. Well-covered-up mistakes may add more flavor to the affair than perfection. (One girl lost her skirt in the middle of a performance. She reached down, picked it up unabashed, held it in place until time to leave. She got thunderous applause.)

2. The keys to success are color, action, change of pace. There should be a good climax at the end. If the ending is on the stage, something involving every participant is good.

3. Keep the tempo moving. This does not mean that it won't slow down during a quiet solo performance. However, after the performance, have something planned to pick up speed again.

4. Capitalize on the experience of your group in foreign lands. This will help to keep them from seeming foreign.

5. Look for natural places to present such affairs. A denominational youth group in Birmingham uses a quadrangle on the Birmingham-Southern College campus, setting up booths and doing folk games on the green. One of the buildings has stairs leading to a second-floor entrance. The landing makes an ideal spot for the leader and public-address system.

6. Get a theme, but don't let it dominate completely. If there are worth-while features that do not fit the theme, they may still be used.

7. Pre-preparation of groups is good. It creates anticipation. The annual folk festival, held in April at Berea College, brings to-

gether young people who have practiced several months on the material to be used. They know it well.

8. Attend a smooth-operating festival to get ideas. One of the best of all is the Festival of the Nations at St. Paul, Minnesota, every third year. It involves as many as 8,000 participants, 10,000 spectators! Yet there are ideas in it for anyone producing a small festival.

9. U.N. Week makes an ideal time to have such an affair.

10. Provide some participation for everybody as part of the festival. Keep the part simple, very simple.

11. If held outdoors, and there is a place to go indoors, pre-plan what each person of the committee is to do if it rains. One is to take the records, two others the record player, six huskies are to move the piano indoors quickly. In this manner the festival can change location and equipment can be taken care of without losing time or without damage.

12. Any festival will benefit from the presence of people from other countries. In a small one, give every person who desires it the opportunity of talking with the performer or performers with different background.

13. Unusual musical instruments are particularly interesting for demonstrations, like the sittar from India, or the mbira from Africa.

14. Films from these countries may be shown in advance at a meeting of the group prior to the festival. Learning their songs may add interest too.

15. If stories are used, be sure to get the people seated reasonably close together and have the storyteller in a position where all may see and hear. Even recorded stories may be received well under these circumstances. The master of ceremonies should see to it that there is quiet, even if it is necessary to interrupt the storyteller and insist upon quiet.

16. The embassies of some countries will furnish information and pictures. Some airlines have travel posters for decorations.

17. Many localities are blessed with Indian-American talent for such a festival. Use it.

18. The National Travel Club, 50 West 57th Street, New York 19, N. Y., has beautiful films of many countries, available to its members. The cost of joining would not be greater than the

rent on one film, and the magazine, TRAVEL, comes with each membership. (See also Bibliography for companies that rent films.)

19. Specialists in folklore should be used, especially for leading or directing. These do not need to be professionals, but they do need to be proficient. Organizations such as the Y, Scouts, church groups may know such people, or you might write to your organization headquarters or to Michael Herman, Box 201, Flushing, New York, or to Lawton Harris, College of the Pacific, Stockton, California, for names.

20. Be sure to have nationality foods if at all possible. Arrange with people from the various countries to prepare food or at least supervise preparation so that it will have that "special flavor."

PUBLICITY FOR RECREATIONAL EVENTS

Telling 'em about a party or other recreational event is as important as planning a good one! The sky is the limit when it comes to using imagination for publicizing. Some suggestions are included here, one of the chief of which is to modify, change, adapt, "dream up" so that your group will come up with some real "doozies" to intrigue the people and make them come to whatever it is you're putting on—party, festival, circus, supper, money-raising affair, athletic contest:

Mailings. Postal cards, letters, booklets, fliers sent through the mail will attract some attention, especially if sent in more than one mailing. A postal card is a good advertising medium because you almost have to read it, even as you are throwing it away.

Handwritten mailings, personalized, are more effective than printed or mimeographed ones. Even a note in the margin helps to personalize it.

Cut out unusual shapes to mail in invitations: a lively witch, a grinning pumpkin, a cheerful heart, a lively Father Time, for the rhyming invitation that you will send.

Sometimes groups will have members address envelopes to themselves. Then when the invitation comes through the mail, they read it because the envelope is in their own handwriting.

Besides paper, such material as dried ears of corn, bolts and nuts tied with string, or a sucker, can be mailed. (The first might be an invitation to an African safari—see *Fun and Festival from Africa;* the second could bear, "Don't think we're nuts . . ."; and the third, "Don't be a sucker by staying away.")

Mailings, telegraph style, also draw attention.

Telephone. This is a fine method of publicizing because it is personal. If each person on the telephone committee will call a small number of folk, the experience can continue as a personal one. ("Each one call one" might be instituted. I call you, and give you the name of another person to call, and the name of a person for that person to call.)

The mystery element might be brought into telephoning, not telling who is calling, or assuming some famous or majestic name.

Bulletins, Bulletin Boards, Announcements. Most groups have bulletin boards where announcements and posters can be placed. (Make it mysterious—use several changes of announcement.) Announcements can be made in meetings, also in bulletins, newspapers.

It is much better in meetings to have a skit or stunt to present the idea than a mere speech. Use "teaser" ideas. Have folks walk through meeting places with signs (where appropriate) to advertise the coming event.

Get those who have bought tickets to wear badges (perhaps the ticket itself is a badge).

Signs on Cars, Drinking Fountains, Waste Baskets, Hanging from Ceiling. Go all out. Let them see word of the coming event everywhere they turn. People wearing tags will publicize it too.

Discs, Tape Recordings. Use them to broadcast the news. If not too expensive, mail out recorded discs as advertisers, teasers.

Poster Contest. This would stimulate interest, and the best posters (and worst ones too) could be displayed. Often stores in town will co-operate.

Radio, Television. Sometimes local radio, television will give publicity to coming affairs. If you use a skit, rehearse it, make it punchy, keep it brief.

"Commando." Have little groups in cars or on bicycles who are carrying announcements. They deliver them quickly, go on to the next place. Best done two by two.

Signs on Trees. In camps, on campuses, signs on trees can become a cue to the social affair.

Singing Commercials. Performed at meetings, over radio. A contest to see who can compose the best.

Clown with Signs. He strolls around at meetings, or stands on street corner. He may give out handbills, too.

Leaflets from a Plane. If legally OK, drop leaflets from a plane, with proper fanfare in newspaper, radio, TV.

Election of King and Queen. Name not revealed until the social affair.

Letter to the Editor. Write a letter to the editor of the paper, commending this as a worthy cause.

Pictures, Kodachromes. Display pictures taken at the last affair (or last year's). "This is the kind of fun they had last time." Take a set of colored slides for publicizing next year's affair.

Quick Sign Making. Tempera and show card colors are fine for signs, but very quick and attractive ones can be made from colored chalk on colored construction paper (large sheets). For quick signs, liquid shoe polish, brushed on with the dauber, are effective if rough.

THE MASTER OF CEREMONIES
(*See also the Toastmaster in Index*)

The master of ceremonies is the director of festivities. He or she has something of the same functions as the toastmaster, but may have broader responsibility.

Very likely the "MC" has been with the planning committee and has helped line up the program, acts, presentations, speakers. He is the one who keeps things moving, sees to it that program items are ready, that the performers get a good introduction, and that the program closes on time.

One of the best ways to show oneself an "amateur of ceremonies" instead of a master is to talk too much. Usually the people have come to hear the program, not the MC, so he is wise to keep his remarks brief.

The good master of ceremonies, like the toastmaster, will keep some humorous material at his disposal, either in his head or on cards, in notebooks. When appropriate, he brings out a pointed bit of humor.

If you are the MC, you will find it helpful to make out a timing sheet for the program. Reduce it to a card if you like. Try to know in advance how much time to allow for each item. Urge performers to stay within their time allotment.

In making presentations of persons, speakers or acts, say sincere, sensible things, perhaps with just a little flourish. Overelaborate statements and introductions may leave the audience feeling as people do at the county fair when they've eaten floss candy.

Have some "expander" items in the program which could be eliminated. Most programs run a third longer than anticipated— some of them twice as long. If you have some things which could be cut out, you can still end on time. Business meetings are particularly bad about taking more time than anticipated. (One speaker, whose time was taken completely, rose to say, "I was asked to give the address of the evening. I want you to have my address. It is 5847 Drexel Road, St. Louis." He sat down.)

If an item has had to be cut from the program, you may want to apologize for its omission and express appreciation for the graciousness of the performer in giving his consent to its deletion.

Decorations help to give atmosphere to a program, and it is always appropriate to have them. However, if they have not been arranged, do some "imaginary decorations."

Sometimes a Master of Ceremonies is supposed to play a role, such as the "Ringmaster," "President of the College," or some other role. You may need to spend some time to get a proper costume. Costume shops rent them for a nominal amount. At least improvise to keep within the theme idea. But do not call undue attention to yourself; you are the chairman, not the star performer.

Plan honor for those who deserve it. There is nothing more delightful to those who have worked long and hard than to have their work recognized. Depending on the occasion, have them stand for applause, for a lively song dedicated to them, perhaps for a gift. "Happy Birthday" is music in the ears of the most sophisticated, especially if it is a surprise, with candles.

Be kind to participants, especially if they are timid. The attitude of the audience toward the whole experience will be resting heavily on your relationship with your performers, as well as with them.

Plan more than you will use of humorous material and group singing, but be ready to condense. It is always good to have a number of possible items grouped in categories, if you yourself are to lead.

If a good many are to participate, have an understood signal for stopping folks. One group used a green, amber, and red light, in view of the participant but not the audience. When the amber came on, he had two more minutes; on the red he was to stop.

Building a Program. Change of pace, variety, balance, and also audience participation are important in programming. For this reason it is good for you as MC to begin with some "group starters" (see that section of the book), group singing, and the like. This "warms up" an audience, lets them get some of the fun of performing.

Start with some of the best items, presentations or acts. This is the technique of professionals. Use an interest catcher at the start.

Do the same at the end, closing with a climactic number on a climactic note. This means saving one of your best singers for the closing feature, having a song or two of rousing group singing, or getting the entire company of performers to do something.

Many masters of ceremonies like to end the program with a thought for the day. Groups with religious motivation may use spirituals, hymns, prayer, or sing The Lord's Prayer in unison, in closing. There should be a clean, clear dismissal of some sort.

The best master of ceremonies learns to "play the group by ear," sensing when they are restless (giving a breather, a stretcher, or opening windows), noting when they are happy and contented, and doing as nearly as he can what they want done.

Credit to those who have made the meeting possible is a "must," of course, including thanks for use of facilities, gratitude to planning committee and to the kitchen crew—especially if all this is volunteer labor.

ENDINGS FOR PROGRAMS

At the end of a recreation program, many groups want a quiet time of fellowship, thoughtfulness, consciousness of harmony, perhaps prayer. At least a climax is desirable.

The "ending" (sometimes called "signature") is used purposely to draw people back into a sense of togetherness after refreshments. Here are some of the things that have been used successfully:

Fellowship Circle. Since the circle formation is used so much it is appropriate to close that way. In the circle you can see everybody, and holding hands around the circle makes for a nice ending. Singing takes place, often leading from a lively song to a quiet one, to a hymn or spiritual and closing prayer.

Good Night, Ladies. In another mood, the group starts in a circle, but the leader breaks the circle (all the rest holding hands) and has everyone skip on the "Merrily We Roll Along." Repeat this two or three times, with "Farewell, Ladies" and "Sweet Dreams, Ladies" verses.

Seated, Quiet Singing. An appropriate setting for this is outdoors, around the campfire, on the steps of a building, or in the vesper kind of beauty spot.

Spiral Circle. A more formal kind of "ending" is sometimes used in which all are given candles to carry and they start in a circle, slowly drawing into a spiral, with song and words in that formation.

Closing with "The Lord's Prayer." Many groups close regularly by singing together Malotte's "Lord's Prayer." It is very impressive in an international gathering to have the Lord's Prayer spoken, each in his own tongue.

Story Reading, Telling. Starting with fun material, the group may sit in some natural rallying center for story reading or telling. Some Scripture passages are especially enjoyed in an outdoor setting like this.

Galilean Service. If near the water, some groups like to use that setting, having their performers come up in boats. Be sure that the boats are seaworthy, and that no one rocks or tips them.

Echo Singing. At a natural beauty spot in a summer conference setting it was discovered that one group, going to the point, could be heard across the water a half-mile by another group, if they stayed behind. The "ending" much enjoyed there, now, is to cross the lake and sing back and forth.

Start a Song. Sitting in near darkness, perhaps around a fire, the group—anybody in it—is invited to start a song. Sing one verse or stanza, then change to another song. Fun songs, love songs, folk songs, spirituals will likely be used. A designated person may close, saying, "One more song, and then we'll sing ———— ———— in closing."

What Have You Enjoyed Today? Often that question will be asked as the group is quiet and relaxed. The answer will be appreciated by the hard-working leadership. The mood for the closing is somewhat set by the remarks. (Sometimes, what would you like to have done differently, now?) This might bring some suggestions about the schedule or procedure, before a final closing.

A Presentation and Singing. At the end of the day after a fun period there is a nice lull in which a presentation can be made. Once a gift of an autoharp at such a time was given, and the receiver played the autoharp to accompany a song or two, before the closing.

Indoor Campfire. As well as the crepe-paper-over-electric-light-bulb kind, several candles grouped together in a safe manner can give the effect of a fire, without the heat of a fire.

Thought for the Night. A two-minute talk, centered around a single thought of uplift, will send folks away (in a camp, to bed) with a sense of completion.

Closing Centering Around a Person from Another Country or Racial Group. If this person conducts singing, it deepens the fellowship to have him lead.

Worship Service with a Theme. Such a service may be brief but very effective. A tendency in many groups is to overdo it, using too much material for folk who are tired and want to get home (or want to get refreshments). Be single-minded and brief!

FOODS AND REFRESHMENTS

Some planning committees for social affairs spend too much time on the refreshments. Many do not spend enough time and serve the same old things, over and over.

In the "finger foods" category there are many items that could be served, and for light refreshments, many other things. Here are some ideas:

"FINGER FOODS"

1. Apples
2. Bananas
3. Oranges, tangerines
4. Grapes
5. Raisins
6. Peaches
7. Pears
8. Popcorn, popcorn balls
9. Sandwiches
   toasted cheese

peanut butter
egg salad
hamburgers, hot dogs
10. Candy bars
11. Potato chips
12. Corn chips
13. Cheese curls
14. Pretzels
15. Pecans (shelled)
16. English walnuts
17. Peanuts
18. Cashews
19. Candy corn (for Hallowe'en)

20. Candy hearts (for Valentine's Day)
21. Marshmallows (for toasting)
22. Watermelon (outdoors)
23. Cantaloupe (outdoors)
24. Whole tomatoes (on picnic)
25. Stuffed celery
26. Carrots, radishes
27. "S'mores," a sandwich of two graham crackers, toasted marshmallow and ½ Hershey bar

OTHER IDEAS

28. Apple pie
29. Pumpkin pie (Thanksgiving)
30. Cherry pie (Washington's Birthday)
31. Blueberry pie (Highbrow Party)
32. Icebox pies (anytime)
33. Ice cream (molded for season)
34. Jello
35. Hot chili
36. Beans, cornbread (Hobo Party)
37. Waffles, bacon
38. Baked apples
39. Broiled orange, grapefruit (it's good!)
40. Fruit salad, whipped cream

41. Pear or peach salad (cloves for eyes, nose, mouth)
42. Hot drinks
coffee
chocolate (and marshmallow)
tea (and mint)
hot cider
spiced tea
43. Cold drinks
punch
lemonade
iced tea
Kool-aid
soft drinks
limeade
milk
chocolate milk
orangeade

Planning Parties

NOVELTY AND THE SURPRISE element are half the fun of a party. The clever party planner thinks up fresh ways of inviting guests and new approaches to old games as well as brand-new ones. In this chapter is a list of nearly 120 intriguing ideas which may spur the reader to concoct still more original ones around which to build a party. Here too we find some 35 suggestions for making brief social periods exciting. Then full details are given for parties on New Year's Day, Valentine's Day, Washington's Birthday, April Fool's Day, Hallowe'en, and Christmas, as well as for a Space Party, a Circus, a Football Party, and a One World Party.

IDEA STARTERS

Clock Watchers. Employees' party.

Lonesome Party. Get together and write to those in group who are away, also to anybody else who might be lonely.

Kaffee Klatsch. Coffee-and-talk affair, perhaps with a few acts, jokes.

Storytellers. Liar's Convention.

Movie Party. Go to one, return to group headquarters for refreshments and informal discussion of movie.

Walking Rehearsal. Play reading for small group.

Window Shopping Party. Give two or more groups one hour to go window shopping, return to meeting place to report adventures. Have quiz.

Round Trip. Short excursion on train or bus.

Prodigal Son. Someone who has been away returns.

Toy Patch. Repair toys before Christmas.

Sculptors. Small party for those interested in trying their hands with a little clay. Or, it might be work party to carve old plaster off prior to removing partition.

Better Half. You bring yours, couple games planned.

Gourmets. Something very unusual to eat, with table games. (Or something very lowbrow such as hot dogs.)

Park Party. Go to park for fun, eat picnic supper together.

Bible Party. Games come from Bible entirely. Play might be presented.

Sweet Potato. Tonette party. Learn to play Tonette.

Back at the Ranch Party. Western idea, garb, games, contests.

Psychiatrists' Convention. You fill in blanks.

Cabinet Makers. Build some cabinets needed in organization.

Dessert. Eat at home, but come for dessert, conversation, and games.

Mother Goose. Games come from that source.

Mere Maid's Party. For girls.

Neptune Party. Swimming party.

Garden Party. Home party idea.

Juke Box. Record party.

Photography. Make, develop pictures.

Nationality. Invite others. Do things from their lore. Swedes, Czechs, Italian, Chinese, Mexican, or whoever is in your community.

Let's Learn It. Anything.

Whittlin'. Learn to whittle, wood-carve.

Rod and Reel. Fishing trip.

Quiz. Feature quizzes, listen to TV programs.

River Boat. Go out on one.

Coffee Break. Enliven them with themes, posted. Jokes—embarrassing moments—acts.

Autoharp. Learn to play it.

Continued. Break party up in more than one section—part on one day, part on another.

Rodeo. Shoot the works. Acts, color.

Barnyard Frolic. Animal show, animal games.

Smorgasbord. Put on one.

Come As You Are. When telephoned, come as you were dressed.

Sloppy Joe. Dress-down party.

Knights of the Road. Tramp party.

Radio TV. Put on acts or go to studio.

Ocean Crossing. Ship party.

No School Today. For kids.

Table Games Party. Play 'em.

Old Mill. Find one, go to it, have storytelling, days of yore. Outdoor games.

Fireman's Shindig. Games, "rescues," and the like.

Tourists. For them, if appropriate.

Income Tax. They get together for mutual help.

Refrigerator. Raid it, freeze stuff.

Talent Night. Roundup of talent. Talent scouts.

Hobby Lobby. Hobby show, lobbying for hobbies.

Alpine Party. Climb real mountain.

Sightseeing for Fun. Group, family, or person could go; or this could be imaginary trip, or one with kodachrome slides, movie series, or lecturer.

Coffee Party. Serve coffee and dessert, play table games, do simple crafts, converse.

Trail Party. Drop confetti to mark trail. At end of trail have cookout, picnic meal, roast weiners, or storytellers convention, read aloud outdoors.

Back at the Ranch Party. Everything is Western—games, contests, food.

Street Fair. Another organizing idea like County Fair.

Indoor Picnic. All features of outdoor one, but held indoors, even in living room. Or Moonlight Picnic in yard, with Japanese lanterns for light.

FBI Roundup. Meet at regular place, go out and round up all erring members you can find, and have party. Send two "agents" to call on each one.

Fun-O-Rama. High-sounding name for carnival type of social affair.

Suppressed Desires Party. Come dressed appropriately for your suppressed desire (but wear something). Act out suppressed desires.

Beat the Clock, I've Got a Secret, and other shows can be reproduced with fun.

Record-Breaking Party. Bring your disliked records to party, and at proper time, break them with ceremony. (You might trade them, instead, for records you want.) This is just one feature of party.[1]

Disneyland. Reproduce some of features of Disneyland, like: Rocket Ship, Trip to Moon, Alice in Wonderland, Dwarfs, Frontierland, Stagecoach, Train Ride, Movies of Yesteryear, Penny Arcade, Space Patrol, 8-Dimensional Movies, Auto Race.

Bag (or Sack) Party. Bring paper sacks and use them for paper sack puppets, sack-bursting games, over heads for drawing faces, on feet as animal feet in acts.

Comic Characters Party. Everybody comes so dressed. Games appropriate.

Book Party. Read from books, book reviews, book games.

Tin Can Party. Craft things made from tin cans.

Dream It Up Party. After group gets there, they take time to think up what they are going to do.

Watermelon Social. Fun with watermelon eatin'. Have field and some "farmers" defending their melon plots with several melons wide apart. See if others can "steal" melons.

Higher Learning Party. For college crowd, fun items from college scene.

Chinatown Party. Go there for food, window shopping, perhaps visit to Chinese group

Easter Egg Hunt. For little ones.

Linoleum Party. For crawlers. At home on linoleum.

Tape Recorder Party. Record and play back.

Old South Party. Theme, decorations recapture past.

Back to the Salt Mines. Party for anybody or group returning to old grind.

Unbirthday Party. To honor somebody, but it isn't his (or her) birthday.

Copper Carnival. Penny carnival.

Folk Festival, with folk games, songs, crafts, arts.

Possum Hunt. Real one, or put cardboard ones in trees along trail and hunt 'em with flashlights.

Speedboat Party. Go for rides in one.

Chili Party. Mexican food, U.S. conversation and games.

March of Time Party. Put on things appropriate for A.D. 1, 1492, 1620, 1900, 2000.

Backward Party. Everything backward: "goodnight" on arrival, then refreshments; clothes worn backward.

Quiz Show. Patterned after radio, television quiz shows.

Old Settlers Festival. All-day affair with ceremonies, king-queen, stories, dinner on grounds.

Penny Walk. Do one (see Index).

Moonlight Hike. To certain point.

Vacation Party. Report on vacations with slides, pictures.

Gypsy Campfire. Gypsy acts.

Seasons Party. Celebrate all seasons and special days in one party.

Spooks. Hallowe'en title.

Pop's Concert. For or by father.

Nut Party. Play games with nuts, or go nuttin'.

Have a Heart Party. On Valentine's Day, guests do something for others.

Caroling. Go to those who need it.

Bicycle. Everybody cycles to some place for lunch. Play observation games.

Bookbinding. Repair library books of organization.

Re-creating Party. Paint, repair, or otherwise re-create.

Painting.

Watch-night.

Quilting. Get together and quilt.

"Yoo Hoo" Hike. Two parties, who signal to each other at intervals.

Celebrities. Honor famous people, use their names in quizzes.

Leap Year. Celebrate "girls' turn."

Jam Session. Get together for one.

Block Party. All those living on block get together for picnic and games and get acquainted.

Ring. Engagement. Play ring games.

Trip Camping. For fun.

Progressive Party. Go from one location to other for part of party or refreshments at each.

White Elephant. Bring your white elephants, auction them off, put money in club treasury.

Pickle Packin' Party. Just another name for picnic.

Gay 90's Party. Celebrating all music, games, and customs of "Gay 90's," even down to box social.

Flat Earth Party.[2] Using this theme (instead of "round the world") have things in four corners of room. Use square dances. Refreshments could be "flat."

Capsule Party. Fortunes, forfeits, acting out suggestions are contained in capsules. The party itself may be "shortie." Capsule relay: run up to chair, take capsule with water, run back and touch off next person in line.

TABLOID SOCIALS
(Social periods of 20-60 minutes for youth and adults)

There are more occasions in most groups for using a short social period of 20 minutes to an hour than for the 2½- to 3-hour party. Therefore, some suggestions are included for these fun periods such as those for men's and women's clubs, for after-meetings, including youth groups on Sunday nights, brief periods at school, part of a family night program, sometimes at home, dorm parties, student center.

The principle of this kind of social period is that it moves fairly fast in developing a sense of group spirit. Often the group is a small one. Use mixers if needed. If the group has been together, they may not be needed. Group singing is one of the most valuable tools for this kind of social time. The next best ally is probably the simple "chair game," and equipment games of the bean-bag-shuffleboard-ping-pong variety. Table games are also good, as is record listening.

Helps for most of these ideas below are found in this book (see Index):

1. Progressive Party, from house to house. This is mostly for exercise if time is limited.

2. Walk or ride to someone's home (or back yard) for fun with equipment games, refreshments.

3. Singing evening, with folk-song book, such collection as *357 Songs We Love to Sing,* spiritual collection, hymnal. Just singing for fun.

4. Quiz, of "What's My Line?" "Stop the Music," "Twenty Questions," "Battle of the Sexes" (male vs. female) type.

5. Creative writing, or use of other creative materials on tables, such as paints, clay, finger paints. Relax and see what you can do.

6. Puppet show. Either present one with puppets already made or else make some paper-sack puppets and put on brief show (divided into two or more groups).

7. Balloon Basketball Game. (See Index.) This may occupy most part of 20 minutes with fun. Build toward it a little, and have sides. Use frequent substitutions so that, if there are not too many people, everyone plays.

8. Quickie version of Football Party. It can be done in 45 minutes with enjoyment.

9. Bible Baseball or Question Baseball. (See Index.) Long-lasting game.

10. Charades. This is favorite of informal groups.

11. Skits, stunts. Pre-prepared, or divide up and let each of several groups present stunt ("Opera" stunt, like "Pirates and Penitence").

12. Situation drama. Same idea, but give each group a situation, to be worked out and presented.

13. Remembering shut-ins. Go singing to them, caroling in season, take along tape of group performance or of Sunday's sermon, or plan some other group activity for their enjoyment. Visit briefly and leave.

14. Story reading, storytelling. For brief, easygoing time have good storyteller, or someone who can read humorous material to do just that. Fireplace is ideal.

15. Birthday parties. They could be celebrated briefly and special surprises presented.

16. Letter writing. Get together around tables, eat popcorn or potato chips or apples, write letters to absent members of group, send cards to those who should receive them. Even make some original cards.

17. Equipment, table games evening. Around small tables, have number of games available of checkers, chess, Chinese checkers, Scrabble variety. Refreshments too, of course.

18. Big Trip. Someone who has been on trip shows his kodachromes to appreciative audience. Several could share vacation pictures in one sitting in this way, and you could get that

"postvacation" bragging worked off in short order. Could be called "The Picture Show." If there are several new babies in couples' group, this might be way of getting all this off at same time.

19. Travel movies or slides, professionally made and genuinely entertaining. Membership in National Travel Club, 50 W. 57th Street, New York 19, entitles holder to number of attractive free films.

20. Penny Walk. (See Index.)

21. Window shopping. For group not too large, in town, this can be relaxed fun. Go somewhere for refreshments.

22. Treasure Hunt. Over previously laid out course (indoors or outdoors) crowd, in small groups, looks for hidden treasure. This would not have so many clues as full-fledged 2-3 hour treasure hunt.

23. Concert. Either at group meeting place or in home, listen to some records. They could be long-hair, short-hair, comic records. Television or radio program might be sandwiched in.

24. Bull session. Get together over refreshments around small tables for "gab fest." There might be topic to start, but conversation quickly wanders.

25. Talent show. This would be briefer than full-fledged one. Several numbers could be presented now, and several this same time next month.

26. Campfire and fun. Fun consists of singing, informal stunts, joke telling, humorous material of other kinds, storytelling, dozing comfortably. Basket of apples passed about constitutes refreshments, perhaps. Campfires or hearth fires are good rallying centers.

27. Picnic, weiner roast. That would be all you'd have time for—no program.

28. Indoor Track Meet. This actually isn't very wild (see Index). It could be great fun.

29. Kaffee Klatsch. This is just another European name for coffee time, which could include anything for program or nothing. Perhaps table stunts, tricks with matches, puzzles could be used.

30. Prodigal Son Celebration. Member of group is back in town. You honor him with brief party.

31. Dessert Party. Someone invites group over home for dessert and fun.

32. White Elephant Party. Bring your white elephants and trade or auction them off. How did you get 'em in first place?

33. Chili Party (or any other food). If group is not too large, let them help prepare, or at least finish preparation. This could include hamburger fry, weiner roast or boil. One church group takes great delight in "potato fry." They wash, peel, fry and eat potatoes, night after night.

34. Most of theme party ideas could be reduced to "shortie party": New Year's, Valentine's, George Washington's Birthday, Fourth of July, St. Patrick's Day, Labor Day, Thanksgiving, Hallowe'en, Christmas. Certainly tables where refreshments are served can be fittingly decorated. Group could be asked to make hats of suitable style and wear them for atmosphere. One or two equipment games could be used, such as "horse racing game" adapted to theme. (Turkey race, cat race, and the like.)

35. Go to drugstore together.

VALENTINE PARTY
(*Ages 9 and over*)

Here are some possible titles: Land of Heart's Desire, Festival of Hearts, Cupid's Excursion, Hearty Party.

As in any party, decorations are important. Decorations could include hearts, red and white crepe paper streamers, comic valentines on the walls, aching, bleeding, broken hearts all over the place. Cupids, lacy decorations are appropriate.

Name tags are often heart-shaped, though they may use the "comic valentine" idea also. One party used a lei (Hawaiian style) of small hearts, placed around the necks of the guests.

Some organizations have the girls put on the party and bear the expense. Often it is better not to have people come in couples nor to plan all the games that way, since the number of folk coming will be uneven. Those without partners feel left out unless provision for them is made. Use musical and folk games in trios, those that allow "stealing partners" and the like.

For early comers, skill games such as Heart Darts (throwing darts at a heart-shaped cardboard target), Make an Original Valentine (from doilies, construction paper, scissors, paste, magazines, crayons, and other colors), or trying to flip a red-painted ping-pong ball from a coke bottle (which is dressed in Valentine garb).

Musical games are appropriate to start off with: a Hearty March (Grand March), a Hearty-Cake Polka (Patty-Cake), Cupid's Clap (The Clap Marlene), "A Toast to Cupid Who Is Brave and True." (By adapting slightly and changing titles, many folk and musical games would be appropriate.)

For group singing, use the heart songs, like "I Love You Truly," "Let Me Call You Sweetheart," "Tell Me Why," "Springtime in the Rockies," "Four-Leaf Clover," "Carolina Moon," "Harvest Moon." (Since most of these are somewhat sentimental, singing is usually used late in such a party.)

For getting partners, cut hearts in two, using unusual cuts that must be matched. Those whose hearts do match are partners.

Games for Valentine Party. Spin the Bottle becomes a spinning arrow, to determine in the seated circle (or circles in groups of over thirty) who has the biggest feet, broadest smile, loudest tie, best cupid's bow lips, brightest socks, heartiest laugh, greatest heartbreaker, who will marry first.

Whose Heart Did He Win? When leader calls out the name of one member of a famous couple, see who can supply the other name.

1. Adam	—Eve		12. Saul	—Ahinoam
2. Esau	—Judith		13. Jacob	—Rachel
3. Abraham	—Sarah		14. Joseph	—Mary
4. Ahasuerus	—Esther or Vashti		15. Boaz	—Ruth
5. Elimelech	—Naomi		16. Agrippa	—Bernice
6. Ananias	—Sapphira		17. Zacharias	—Elizabeth
7. Isaac	—Rebekah		18. Samson	—Delilah
8. Ahab	—Jezebel		19. Joseph	—Asenath
9. Moses	—Zipporah		20. Aquila	—Priscilla
10. Elkanah	—Hannah		21. David	—Michal and
11. Lamech	—Adah			Abigail

Clap Out Rhythm (of a love song). Divide into groups, each group claps out the rhythm of a love song for the others to guess.

Play games involving forfeits. (See Forfeits for ideas.) "Heavy, Heavy Hangs Over Thy Head" may be over the King or Queen of Hearts' Head.

The Shoe Game could be adapted to passing a number of appropriate objects, such as "hearts," "arrows."

In small groups or in couples, using magazines, have them clip and paste to compose love letters to be read.

Fish Game (see Index) could be adapted to having the people represent "famous lovers," and walk around when their names are called. Instead of "The ocean is stormy," say "The sea (of matrimony) is stormy."

Refreshments could include heart-shaped cakes or cookies, heart-centered ice cream, "Love Potion" of red fruit juice, and the like.

Singing heart songs makes for a good conclusion.

CHEERY CHERRY PARTY
(*Ages 9 and over*)

Here are some suggestions for a Washington's Birthday party that may be new to your group.

Group Starter. Give each guest a number. Divide into five teams. "General Washington" will ask each team to . . .

1. Find as many words as possible from George Washington.
2. Get all names of all persons present with black hair, blue ties, or whatever is decided upon.
3. Get all names of all people starting with M (for Martha) whether first or last name.
4. Find out who have birthdays during month of February.
5. Each group may be asked to present skit from Washington's life.

Chopping Down the Cherry Tree. Tell a story, the group standing in a circle. When the word "hatchet" is mentioned, each must drop to one knee. The last one to do so becomes It.

Shaking the Cherry Tree. While one person ("cherry tree") is blindfolded, others recite:

> Oh, here's a tree of cherries ripe,
> A tree both green and tall.
> We'll shake it now with all our might
> Until the cherries fall.

One person shakes tree gently, then, and tree tries to guess who shook him or her.

Reciting the Declaration of Independence. Box of candy to anybody who can do it!

Truth or Consequences. Ask several people (by number) to come forward, and ask them questions to which they must tell truth or pay consequences (see Forfeits and Consequences for ideas).

Musical Games. Patriotic names or "Early American" names can be given to them. Virginia Reel or Circle Virginia Reel would be appropriate.

Refreshments: Virginia ham sandwiches, United States Punch (cherry and pineapple juice, in blue cups). Drums can be made by baking cake in round cans, cutting slices 2 inches thick, cover with icing, decorate with red, white, and blue. Remove centers, fill with cherry ice cream.

KING APRIL'S BIRTHDAY
(An April Fool Party for older children, youth, adults)

Decorations could be in keeping with April—showers. (This would call for umbrellas, flowers. "Crazy" decorations would be appropriate. King April has throne.)

Each person is to bring April Fool surprise, like joy buzzer, end of thread through coat (running to spool of thread in pocket of wearer), drinking glass that leaks, "hot" chewing gum from novelty store.

Around room will be April Fool traps of various kinds, like object wired with electricity. Over some perfectly good chocolates is sign, "Have one." (They will leave them alone, probably, thinking there's something wrong.)

A Herald assembles Royal Court, calling for all to make way for King, give him Royal Welcome. He enters wearing rubber boots, colored raincoat as cape, indifferently made crown, umbrella as scepter. Beating of pans (and playing of improvised orchestra with combs) welcomes him. He sits on throne, holds out his scepter and blesses all, and calls on Jester to take charge.

ROYAL MARCH. Participants do grand march and other active and musical games, retitled appropriately.

ROYAL GAMES. Equipment games (with titles over them), retitled party games.

ROYAL MAGIC, STUNTS. Whatever has been prepared will be fun.

ROYAL MUSIC. Group singing or "Royal Band" playing. Musical gags would be appropriate.

ROYAL DRAMA. Skits, especially of foolish nature.

ROYAL FOOD. Refreshments.

ROYAL FINISH. Nice closing with songs, perhaps worship. This part to be serious.

HALLOWE'EN
(*Ages 9 to 90*)

> Shakespeare and his ghostly troupe
> Invite you to join their group.
> They'll tour the musty catacombs,
> And give you thrills to chill your bones.

Most of fun of traditional Hallowe'en party comes from effects: black cats, witches, scarecrows, ghosts, bats. Decorations are usually in keeping, along with painted graveyard scene on wall, dimly lit, spider webs, for instance.

Here are some suggestions for effects at Hallowe'en.

Reception. At door by person in ghostly costume with wet rubber glove. Dim lights. Guests are taken to Chamber of Horrors, perhaps through some passage where they must stoop, and are hit in face by "cobwebs" (thread or yarn suspended from ceiling).

Chamber of Horrors. Witch receives, gives swat with broom. Person made to taste Witches' Brew (Kool-aid fortified with powdered alum). Hand rail is charged with electricity. Floor is strewn with boxes, egg shells, corn stalks, balloons, "squeegy" things. Dim light reveals "corpse" on bed, which may move a bit. Face, dimly lighted, has eyes of eggshells, which suddenly light up in dark. Skeleton or skull is painted with phosphorescent paint. Strange noises, groans, grunts, hootings. Ghost on stilts. Beheading, with sight of axe slowly descending, groan, "spirit" led to next room. Several voices in mournful voice recite together, "Caught by witches, caught by witches."

Costumes. It is well to insist on having people wear costumes. Try to discover who is who. Contest for most interesting, most horrible, most original, may be held, judging made from Witch Parade, in which all join.

Death of Mr. Digger. This may be part of Chamber of Horrors, or in dimly lighted room. Story is told of death of Mr. Digger (substitute name) and his "parts" are passed around for all to feel: rubber glove with sand for hand, spools for spine, grapes for eyes, macaroni for windpipe, wet sponge for brains, calf's liver for liver, weiners for intestines.

Grand March, Musical Games. Done to ghostly music. Have people fly like bats, walk like ghosts, hoot like owls, screech like witches, groan, during Grand March, which may be soft dirge music. Retitle games, such as "Black Cat Mixer," "Witches' Schottische."

Active Games. Use relays, active games, with apples for objects to be passed, also games like Pass It On, Hot Potato (using apples).

Skill Games. Toss bean bags into Witches' Pot; throw darts at black cats; rework or retitle—and you have new game.

Music. Some 33⅓ rpm records played at 78 rpm sound very "witchy." One group played them slightly off center for effect (as witches were brewing their stuff behind sheet, in shadow picture). Then there was fortune teller looking into future, asking witches occasionally to brew up something.

Solos and special numbers in keeping would be good.

Apples, Doughnuts. Doughnuts or apples on strings, to be eaten with hands behind backs, or bobbing for apples, is fun. (These may be done by partners, too, two persons trying at a time.)

CHRISTMAS PARTY
(*Ages 9 to 90*)

Invitations might be done on miniature Christmas trees, Santas, stars. (Each is to bring gift, perhaps something he has made.)

When guests arrive, they make themselves name tags on appropriate material, such as construction paper, with crayons or new ball-point paints, in tubes. They also might be put to work to make for themselves special caps or other Christmas costumes. Each has bell to put on his cap.

Musical Games. Jingle Bells is a "natural," of course, to get started. Grand Marches can be done to Christmas music. Musical mixers can be retitled, such as Santa's Arches (for Musical Arches),

Christmas Conga (Schottische Conga), Kris Kringle Hop (Bunny Hop).

Games. Game of Telegram could be used. Have each person make out telegram beginning with letters in CHRISTMAS, or KRIS KRINGLE. See Star Tracing. Use Doodles, with people drawing Christmasy things. Drawing in Dark (draw Santa, his sleigh, his reindeer, a moon in sky).

Reindeer Racing Game (see Turtle Racing Game) would be fun. Also Bell Pass, Snow Modeling, Confetti Pictures (Christmas theme), Balloon Games. Pin the Pack on Santa's Back (old Pin the Tail on the Donkey, adapted). Don't use all—select some. Near end, play music, pass all presents around seated circle, and see who got what.

Songs. Carols and popular songs are always good at Christmas time, especially if around a fire. Turn room lights out with candles aglow instead of hearth fire. It gives warm glow. Close (after refreshments) with quiet carol, prayer for peace and good will.

SOME OTHER CHRISTMAS IDEAS

Here are some further ideas which will appeal to all ages:

Christmas Neighborhood Party. In homes in neighborhood, invite in neighbors or, in organizations, have series of home parties on same evening, in homes all over town.

Toy Repair Party. Bring and repair toys. This may extend over more than one session.

Craft Time for Christmas. See craft section for many craft ideas for Christmas. People come together and do simple crafts for Christmas presents. Especially good for children.

Holly Day Bazaar. Chester, Vermont, Baptist Church invited folk to come and buy gifts at St. Nick's Nook for their "holly-days": holly-woods, holly-dollys, holly-foods, holly-goods, holly-bibs. "Dine in the Holly Room from 5-7. Turkey, $1.25, Ham $1.00, Meat Balls 75¢." Another year it held Santa Claus Fair.

Ornament-Making Party.[3] Near Christmas time, student group in one college serves pot pies. After supper each student washes pie tin and cuts ornaments from it with scissors for group Christmas tree. They have colors of quick-drying paint, string, scotch tape, ribbon, nail polish.

Christmas Tree Lighting. Some groups like to have ceremony for lighting of Christmas tree, for home, group, or community.

Decorating Ingenuity. Chicken feeder or water trough, painted, makes interesting centerpiece. Poultry wire can be cut into bell shape, or formed into cornucopia. Beat with rotary beater 1 cup Ivory Snow and ½ cup water until fluffy, for snow. To "silver" objects, pour silver paint on top of water and submerge object, drawing it up slowly through paint. It will be coated with silver.

Christmas Caroling. Caroling party may be held, starting from church or other center, moving out to sing for families, shut-ins, children's homes, old people's homes, returning to get some coffee or chocolate after couple of hours.

Decorating Tree. This might be party for smaller group, either making decorations and decorating tree, or buying decorations and finishing job, singing while working.

See also Service Projects.

SPACE PARTY [4]
(*For older children, youth, adults*)

This "Space Party" was done in Methodist Youth Camp, Leesburg, Florida. (They do not have banquet during camp because excitement keeps young people from eating their food. Equivalent of banquet program is presented in another room.)

For atmosphere, advance announcements were made, "Listen to this important announcement," followed by slow speed tape played on recorder at fast speed so that voices were high, unintelligible. "Listen for further announcements" was followed by tape played on "rewind" so that it sounded like rocket ship.

At supper meeting leaders came in, dressed in "Space Costumes." One wore green bathing cap and green swim suit, and painted his entire body green. Another got two rubber false faces and had face front and back. They were brought in with "space ship" sound (rewind on tape recorder).

Decorations were "flying saucers" (two paper plates put together). Volley-balls, globes, were hung around to represent planets, some of them marked.

Games were renamed, like "The Flying Saucer Polka."

PLANS FOR A CIRCUS
(*All ages*)

One of the best affairs of all to use large numbers of people is an amateur circus. It may be elaborate or simple; rehearsed or almost spontaneous. Everybody can find something to do as animals, barkers, band members, ringmaster, sideshow operators, skill game operators.

It is important to have colorful atmosphere, circus music, lots of animals, big parade if possible. (Music may be recorded, but band is fixture, anyway.)

Very large circus might actually involve dozens and dozens of performers, while small one might involve 15-25.

With 45 minutes to one hour available, miniature improvised circus may be worked out, dividing crowd into five or six groups and assigning role to each one, such as band, animal act, side show. (This is particularly good in camps where people can run to cabins and get properties.)

Circus parade

Making the Animals. It is not hard to devise realistic-looking animals. Heads and necks are often formed of chicken wire, covered with cloth or newspaper or toweling dipped in paste like papier mâché, and painted when dry.

Paper sacks of various sizes, blankets, brooms, and shorter sticks are combined to make animal "raw material"; blanket to cover two players forming most animals; broom or stick for the neck, paper sacks for heads, and tied-on feet (especially for elephants) to make "footwork" look realistic. Belts or broad cords or ropes can become tails, rubber hose for elephant's nose. Newspapers are good for stuffing. Pajamas stuffed can be costume for many animals. Some can use wooden hoops.

The Ringmaster. He supervises all—acts, trainers, animals. Has top hat, cutaway or riding boots and pants and whip, whistle to "call the plays." He introduces acts and encourages applause at proper time. He may give "band" its cue to play or stop playing.

The Band. Improvised instruments are good. Band plays under direction of costumed director, and may itself be costumed. Records may be used for atmosphere.

Spectaculars for the Big Top

1. Cowboys and Indians, or rodeo procedure, with "trick riding" of stick horses or improvised "horses" made of two boys with blanket over them and fancy heads. Lassoing. "Last Roundup."
2. Mass dance—Spanish, Indian, and so on.
3. Trick riding acts by girls.
4. Chariot race, pulled by humans with human rider.
5. Bull fight, with all pageantry of bull fighting, using improvised bull.
6. Band parading, using combs, kazoos, clicking scissors, beating on wastebaskets.
7. Animal parade, elephants, each holding to tail of elephant ahead; lions in cages, bears dancing along on chains held by "keepers," and the like.

Animal Acts. Lions can roar, step up on stool as directed by trainer (armed with chair). Kangaroos can box. Elephants can count by pawing. Seals can balance balls or balloons on their noses, swim around. (This they would pantomime with their "flippers.") Trained dogs can climb or bark numerals. Peculiarly devised animals, like dragons, cattywampuses, can perform acts.

Clown Stunts

1. Run over by steam roller. Fashion steam roller from large cardboard boxes, and have it manned by clowns. It runs over clown (who gets up under it) and leaves his flattened clothes on floor.

2. High dive. Clown on high place is supposed to dive into bucket of water. He motions his assistant to right, to left, but never dives.

3. Tight rope act. With rope on ground or floor, clown on each end holding it, third clown does "tight rope act."

4. Surgery. Clown is knocked out. Other clowns pantomime trouble, get doctor (who may have his name on him, "Dr. Quack." He is a clown.)

   First test is to tickle him with feather (test his sense of humor).

   Next is to tickle bottom of feet. (Dead or alive?)

   Then step on him. (See if he's breathing.)

   Raise his hands. (He squirts water from his mouth.)

   Knock on his knees. (Test his IQ.)

   And any other tests that clowns can devise. Finally he gets up and goes off by himself.

5. Patent medicine act. Clown with umbrella under clothes, who can gain or lose weight on taking patent medicine by raising or lowering the umbrella.

6. Volunteer fire brigade. If safe to do it, use smoke pots, and child's wagon for the fire engine. Clowns are very inefficient. Fire engine could be made by old automobile stunt, with clown grasping ankles for each tire. Tire goes flat on way, must be fixed. Ladders, ladies' hose, other gags may be worked in.

7. Comic character clowns. Keep doing acts in keeping with their characters.

8. The filled auto stunt. Either real or imitation very small auto is driven up and many clowns get out—more than normally expected.

9. Operation stunt. This is done behind sheet, and garden hose (for intestines), cardboard knives, tin can are used. Punch line sometimes used: "A can, sir," holding one up.

10. Policeman stunt. Two clowns stage mock fight or holdup, are arrested by another. They take his stick from him and drive him off the scene.

11. Kiddy car clowns. They drive as in traffic, perhaps with policeman.

12. Clown juggler. He juggles some unlikely objects.

13. Trick shirt. Can be made or bought. The tail is 15 to 20 feet long, stuffed down in clown's pants. One clown grasps one shoulder of shirt, another the other, and they pull it over his head.

14. Other clown acts are things like looking for lost articles, finally finding them; chasing each other for cause or not; leap frog with variations; other athleticlike acts; playing silly musical instruments; handling a dangerous animal in casual manner. Also, lassoing, and strong man act (small clown carries off several weights which strong clown has hefted). Anything very small (like toy wagon) or of exaggerated size may be used by clowns. (They should not detract from other acts, but do theirs between times.)

15. Clown bull fight, with two clowns being bull (with blanket over them).

16. "Eats and sleeps under water." Clowns indicate by gestures and perhaps by signs, that this marvel eats and sleeps under water. They hold a glass or jar of water above him. (See also Side Show Ideas.)

Side Show Ideas

1. The Fat Lady—stuffed with pillows.
2. The Knife Eater—he eats with his knife.
3. Zaza, the Bearded Lady—with an obviously attached beard, even a mop.
4. Siamese Twins—two girls in one dress.
5. The Cancan—two tin cans.
6. Two-Headed Man—two heads coming from one coat (one might be painted balloon).
7. Snake Charmer—he works on human snake that wriggles about.
8. The Strong Man—lifts "heavy weights," with arms and teeth, bends hose.
9. Swimming Match—match swimming in water.
10. Water Color Exhibition—twenty glasses of colored water.
11. Headless, Hairless Dog—wiener.
12. Invisible Fish—bowl full of water.
13. For Men Only—display of toilet articles.

14. For Women Only—same. (Costs twice as much to get in wrong one.)
15. Headless Hydra—sponge.
16. Flying Red Bat—brickbat, suspended from ceiling.
17. Peep Show—mirror. (Or call it Monkey of North America.)
18. Palm Read—she drops mercurochrome in your palm.
19. Ancient Instrument of Punishment—worn slipper.
20. Bonaparte—two bones, apart.
21. Real Diamond Pin—dime and pin.
22. Drive Through the Wood—nail driven through wood.
23. Knight of the Bath—card marked "Saturday."
24. Cherry-Colored Cat—black cat.
25. Midget—child in grown-up clothing, or person with head and arms through a sheet, hands in some shoes resting on table.
26. Remains of Ancient Greece—candle holder, burnt candle.
27. Ruins of China—broken cup, saucer.
28. Watch on the Rhine—watch on an orange rind.
29. Unusual 25-Carat Ring—25 carrots, in ring.
30. Half Man, Half Woman—man side has hairy chest, sock, garter, man's shoe. Woman side has half wig, lipstick, eye shadow, earring, half dress, Nylon stocking, high heel shoe, bracelets.
31. Beauty and the Beast—girl dressed attractively; beast formed by two boys, blanket, special head. May be lion, tiger. It performs.
32. Bust of Blue Boy—pair of blue overalls, busted out at seat.
33. Bridle Scene—bridle on wall or chair.
34. Fatima, the Fan Dancer.
35. Northern Lights—have corner of room marked North, lights located there.
36. Total Eclipse—room goes completely dark.
37. The Wild Man—with savage face and tusks.
38. Horse with His Head Where His Tail Ought to Be—his tail is in the food end of manger.
39. Aladdin and His Lamp—fellow with sign on him, Al, "addin." His lamp is beside him.
40. Puppet Show—have short one.
41. Trip Around the World—take them around the "world" (globe) and have something to trip on.

42. The Giant—person with umbrella over head, who raises umbrella to become fat.
43. Birth of a Nation—chairs made up with blankets like pullman berth, with sign "Pullman" over them.
44. Tattooing—done with piece of ice, with victim not looking.

Concessions

1. Fortune teller—she actually tells fortunes.
2. Turkey shoot—darts thrown at target, marked for prizes.
3. Tossing objects into a barrel—free prizes for successful tosses.
4. Bowling—croquet balls, rolled at tenpins.
5. The grab bag—grab without looking.
6. Shooting gallery—with pop gun or water pistol.
7. Hit the clown—throw cotton balls at clown's face (or other soft object).
8. Grocery store—where you can buy objects.
9. Post office—where, for small fee, you can get lovely love letter.
10. Airplane ride—person is blindfolded after stepping on board, which is held by person on each end, lifted few inches off the floor. He has hand on head of person, who slowly goes into knee bend, giving impression of rising in air.
11. Almost any of the Skill and Equipment Games—see Index.

FOOTBALL PARTY
(*For youth and adults*)

Decorations. In the colors chosen for opposing teams—outlandish combinations such as violet and green, or red and orange.

Personnel. Each side needs 5 "players," captain, 2 to 5 substitutes, coach, waterboy, doctor, cheer leader, band (one for each side or one combined band), referee, scorekeeper, timekeeper. (The referee really directs the party.)

Refreshments. Hot dogs and lemonade or pop, or hot chocolate, popcorn, apples.

Some Equipment and Properties

1. Badges made from strips of crepe paper pinned behind small cardboard card, given to guests as they come. All who are not players become rooters.

2. Pennants for each side. (Triangular pieces of crepe paper pinned or pasted on small stick.)

3. Mimeographed sheets with songs and yells.

4. "Band instruments," including combs with tissue paper folded over them.

5. Buckets of water and towels for "water boys"; medicine case for doctor; watch or clock for timekeeper; whistle for referee, blankets for players on bench.

6. Large colored paper numbers (pasted on cardboard to make them stiffer) pinned on each player's back. Books in shoulders for padding.

7. Bean bag or other tossed object for football.

8. Diagram chalked on floor (approximately 6' x 4', like illustration.)

9. "Line of scrimmage" chalked about 10' from the playing field. Progress of ball indicated on scoreboard or blackboard.

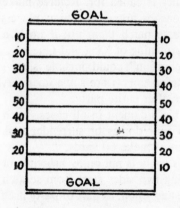

Description of Game (Reds vs. Blues)

1. Crowd arrives for football party, is divided into two sides, who choose nicknames and elect personnel mentioned above, if it has not been done in advance.

2. Each side has 20 to 30 minutes to get ready, including decorating, cheers, songs.

3. At signal, entire "Red" team gallops out in best football manner, warms up and exercises, facing "bleachers" of their side. Bleachers are chairs arranged in rows. Playing field (allow

10 to 12 foot width) is between the two sets of bleachers. "Reds" sit on their bench. "Blues" exercise, then sit, as Reds did.

4. Referee calls forth two captains for toss. He tosses coin. Winner plays first.

5. Each team, in rotation and within time limits, gets four pitches with ball. Game is played by pitching bean bag onto diagram. "Ball" starts on own 40-yard line as game opens and for second half.

6. Ball is put into play from behind "line of scrimmage" as players go into huddle, decide who will pitch it to diagram. Plays are to look like regular football, and regular rules are used where applicable. Quarters are best at 8 minutes, 6, 5, 4, as interest lags.

7. Spectators are seated in "bleachers," rows of chairs facing playing field. Referee is really director of party.

8. Much originality is called for. Referee makes up rules as he goes along; coaches argue with him; players get "hurt" and doctor and nurse patch them up; there is a snake dance at the half, and crowning of King and Queen.

9. "Victory Celebration" could include sing, group games, or folk games. Refreshments are sometimes served during game, and sometimes after entire party.

10. Referee uses his judgment in all cases. Each side must make touchdown in four downs or surrender ball. Therefore, first team to play must make 60 yards.

11. Sometimes this party is put on by bringing all materials necessary and having two sides start from scratch to name teams, choose queen, and so on, as part of party itself. Sometimes it is planned in advance.

ONE WORLD PARTY [5]
(*For older children, youth, adults*)

This "One World" idea was used outdoors by a group of 250 young people in a summer conference, and may have to be adapted if you use it. With some changes, it could be used indoors.

At first the idea was to have either an Airplane or a World Friendship Party. Instead, the ingenious committee said, "Let's put the two ideas together, and make it an outdoor party." They did, and this is the result.

Pilot Training. First there was the pilot training one afternoon. Then there were mimeographed tickets, distributed to each of 250 travelers. Flight assignments were made on tickets themselves. Passengers gathered at "port," where public address system had been set up. Here each pilot was given his "wings" by chairman in elaborate ceremony. Soon flights were called.

"Your Flight Is Ready." Voice of announcer called over speaker system, "Passengers holding space on Flight 1, please report to runway." All who held tickets for this flight went to runway, where their "trained pilot" awaited them at "plane." Outline of plane was made by two cotton strings, laid out like illustration. Pilot placed himself at head, at position of propeller. Each

(Outline of plane)

passenger was instructed to reach down, take hold of string, stand again, and hold on tight. (Appearance of group, then, was something like that of plane.)

"Pilot Jones, your runway is clear," said loud speaker. Pilot Jones then began to make noises like airplane engine (as per his instructions in training during afternoon) and all *ran* together down *run*way, to first stop.

Stops were made at "shows" depicting (either humorously or seriously) life in many countries around world. Other flights were called in similar manner, until all were soon "flying." Pilots had had their instructions as to order in which they were to make various shows.

"Gay Paree" represented France. It was special show devised by all-male cast. Boys put on what they called French Revue. India was represented by snake charmer. China was represented. Hawaii was presented by one of girls, dressed in grass skirt, singing Hawaiian songs. For Africa group did verse speaking arrangement of Vachel Lindsey's rhythmic poem, "The Congo." (This group was seated around fire like African natives.) Then there was The Valley of Nun (nobody there) and Shangri-la (refreshments). The group came together to "port" to sing international songs in closing.

Variations of this can be developed easily. Each "plane" might fly to a specific city—Moscow, Tokyo, London, Berlin, Rome, Prague, Sao Paulo, Mexico City. Then each group could work out a dramatization in keeping with the people who live in that city, and enact the playlet for the entire group. The plane could become a train or trolley. A group at Wilshire Church, Los Angeles, took a tour around town by projecting kodachrome scenes on cheesecloth in the background, and then putting on "acts" appropriate for that section of town. (Incidentally, they have frequent plays in the church. Audiences sit at card tables. When show is over, refreshments are served!)

NEW YEAR'S EVE PARTY—"Turn Over a New Leaf" [6]
(For youth and adults)

Planning to turn over a new leaf on January 1st? Come to
.... at 9:00 P.M., Dec. 31.
Bring along something you'd like to get rid of besides your
bad habits. Wrap it in mystery.

Hand each guest leaf-shaped tag with his name on one side and, on other, written resolution which he must put into effect at once at party. Suggestions: To talk about my heavy income tax whenever I can find anyone to listen to me; to speak affectionately to all girls during entire evening; to say "Sir" or "Ma'am" whenever spoken to; to count up to ten before answering any questions; to bow before addressing lady; to give pump-handle shake to all with whom I speak; to brag about my ancestors to everyone.

Give guests thirty beans apiece. Every time they are caught breaking their good resolutions they must pay penalty of one bean to the person who catches them in act. At close of evening the one with most beans might be presented with diploma of merit for keeping his resolutions.

Swap. Get out mysterious packages which have been brought and deposited on arrival in large box. Each takes package at random and starts to swap—using beans for money. Announce that special recognition will be given at end of game to one who has possession of largest package, smallest package, and one who collects most beans. Wrappings must not be removed until game ends. Package must be swapped each time to make sure that no one corners the booty, for each should have one package at end. To have most fun unwrapping, we suggest that all sit in circle, and one at time display his "swap."

Advice. Give each guest slip of paper on which is to be written bit of advice. Have the slips folded up and collected. After mixing them up, pass out to each, one at time. As each receives his slip, he will stand, state what he thinks of advice and what he intends to do about it, and then, and not until then, will he open slip and read aloud what is written there. Suppose John Jones has said advice is excellent and that he will carry it out to best of his ability; then he reads, "You should get up at 5:00 every morning and make Hungarian goulash for breakfast."

Father Time. Divide guests into teams of five to ten, depending on size of your group. Line up each team facing large sheet of paper on wall or screen. On chair beside paper place large black crayon, and number of slips of paper placed upside down, containing names of items to be drawn: two each of ears, eyes, arms, hands, and feet, robed body, nose, mouth, beard, hair, and name "Father Time." At signal each player runs up, takes slip, and draws feature named. Masterpieces of art resulting from this method will prove highly entertaining.

Resolutions. Give each guest slip of paper on which he will write resolution which he is making for 19—. No names are to be signed. When these are collected have them read for crowd to call out guess as to who wrote each one.

New Year's Greetings. With good march being played, get all into couples for grand march in circle. There should be one extra person at least who stands in center of circle. If there are enough men to make good number of couples, they should form marching circle, and all extra women should stand in center. Men march in outer circle, if they are smaller number. At each blow of whistle, inner circle reverses and marches in opposite direction. Outer circle always moves in same direction. When two circles are moving in opposite directions extra players get in line and march with inner circle. At blow of whistle inside circle again reverses and marches with outer circle. When they do this each person in inner circle tries to get partner. As each catches hands of partner (skating position), he greets other with "Hi, partner!" Outside circle does not slow up, but keeps moving in time to music. Again players without partners go to center. Use such songs as "O Susanna," "Polly Wolly Doodle," and "Old Zip Coon" for music.

This is time to lead marching circles past serving window for refreshments, or to places around long tables. The latter is particularly nice, for the time following fellowship of eating together might appropriately be spent singing, finally leading up to a high spiritual plane as midnight approaches. Many groups will want to have some special service in the sanctuary at this time; others may want simply to stand with bowed heads as clocks strike twelve, while someone reads:

"We have been joking together tonight about turning over a new leaf and making good resolutions, but let us be serious now as we pray:

Oh, make me glad, dear Lord, that every passing day
    Brings a clean page in thy book of life;
A chance to turn the blotted pages down
    And start again, refreshed for the great strife.

Teach me to turn each bitter fault and grief
    Into a lesson that may prove a guard
Against temptation, and the bitter foes
    That lie in wait and press the fighter hard.

Teach me to see the little joys of life,
    The beauty of the world each passing day;
Teach me wide sympathy and tenderness,
    That in the end I may most humbly say:

"There are some pages, Lord, both clean and white,
    Writ with good deeds, with sunshine, and with cheer;

That Thou may'st put into my eager hands
Thy book of days to make a better year."

AUTHOR UNKNOWN

Learn the song, "All Night, All Day," and use for closing.

10

Planning Banquet, Mealtime Fun

ONE OF THE GREATEST means of creating fellowship in the human race is the experience of eating together, particularly if the act can be made an enjoyable occasion through entertainment and fun. And this holds true whether the meal is a groaning banquet table or a supper of pancakes and sausage in somebody's big kitchen. However, when people are sitting beside each other who have not been previously acquainted, there can be awkward, uncomfortable times unless those in charge have thoughtfully provided icebreakers, as suggested in the later section on informal mealtime fun.

This chapter gives also tips for the toastmaster at a formal banquet. It lists with brief descriptions some thirty kinds of banquets that might be planned, and nine seasonal banquet briefs. Then there are detailed plans for seven other unusual banquets, and finally full suggestions for a mother-daughter and a father-son banquet.

THE TOASTMASTER
(*See also "Master of Ceremonies"*)

The toastmaster is the go-between chairman. He represents the group present in handling the program, he represents the planning committee and its ideas, and he is the one who may have a relationship to the kitchen about service details after the banquet has begun.

His job is to keep the affair moving in progressive, easy style. He is to know and introduce the performers, acquaint them with anything they need to know. The toastmaster should give all the performers such a background and build-up that each will feel at ease and be eager to do his best. (This rules out over- and under-emphasis on the personality, standing, and accomplishments of the performer.)

The toastmaster

The toastmaster keeps things pleasant with humorous remarks, jokes, even gags. Here too an overdose is not desirable. If such padding is not needed by him, even though he preplanned it, the best toastmaster will pass up his opportunity to shine in order to allow his performers to do it.

He not only introduces program people, but recognizes honored guests, making appropriate remarks as they are presented to the entire group. He spreads the limelight judiciously.

A toastmaster must deal with the timing and length of the program. It is his job to cut things short (not always a pleasant task) when they get too long. The guests should be able to leave saying, "I'm glad I came!"

Some General Suggestions to Toastmasters

1. Have the program worked out in advance, written on cards. Remarks too may be written on cards, to be placed aside when you are finished with them.
2. Prepare more "remarks" than you will need. Be ready for the unexpected. Consider in advance what you will do if the speaker or a main program performer does not show up.
3. You may have a bite or two in advance, only appearing to eat. A good many toastmasters cannot enjoy the meal, even if it be a good one, because of the coming responsibility.

4. Try to put yourself in the position of members of the group. Watch them carefully. Is the room too hot, too cold? Have it adjusted. Are they tired? Have a "stretcher" for them. (There are plenty in this book.)

5. Read the "mealtime fun" helps for some ideas for getting participation at the tables. After the invocation, for instance, ask the group to exchange humorous remarks with each other. Tell of a few you've heard. (See Chapter 13.)

6. Be prepared with several jokes that have a point related to the occasion. "Some of you know that our committee had considerable difficulty in getting this affair together. We had so many ups and downs that we felt like the elevator operator who muttered to himself, 'I'm not a man. I'm a yo-yo!' "

Sample Program. After the Invocation, you may want to warm up the group with some "group starter" idea or conversation stimulator. (If it is an athletic affair, have them tell the roughest time they ever had in a game.)

After the meal, ask the groups to share something that occurred at their table during the conversation (if the banquet is not too large). This is a good time for some group singing, toasts.

Take up items of business as quickly as possible. Entertainment and other program items come now—solos, quartets, acts.

Then comes the introduction of the speaker or the main event on the program.

Now is the time for honoring, awards, presentations, done with proper ceremony but not too much flourish.

End with a rousing patriotic song, group sing, hymn.

Religious groups will generally have a benediction. Dismissal may be otherwise with some fairly serious thought to take away with them: a thought for the day.

Stopping the Long-Winded. The greatest single problem of the toastmaster is keeping the affair within the time limits. This is particularly true of speakers. Here are a few suggestions that might work:

1. If you know the speaker well, you might say: "I know George Harper very well. We went to school together. He asked me

what he should speak about, and I suggested about 20 minutes. When I shake my watch, he is to quit."

2. Another way more delicate might be to say, "Some of our group must leave at 9 o'clock, Dr. Longwind, I happen to know, and they have told me they want to hear all of your speech. I'll notify you when you have five more minutes."

3. Pass the speaker a note, saying, "We must be through in five more minutes."

4. Perhaps with the help of some stooges (if your speaker is a notorious forgetter) lead an extra long applause, thank him, and move on.

5. Simply thank him (even though he is not through) when he has finished a soliloquy, and say pleasantly but firmly, "Our agreement was to be through by 9 o'clock, and we have reached that time. We want to thank Mr. or Mrs. So-and-so for this thought-provoking address, and we know you will want to come forward to talk with him/her."

No one likes to be rude, but you may be the only hope the group has of getting home before midnight. Remember that you are its representative! Do it graciously, but *do it!*

Wisdom for the Toastmaster. Some of these humorous little quips may sometime find a natural niche in the toastmaster's remarks.

A hair on the head is worth two in the brush.

The bigger a man's head gets, the easier it is to fill his shoes!

It isn't that happiness is absent—we just don't recognize its presence!

Try enlarging upon your blessings as you enlarge upon your troubles!

"We do not stop playing because we grow old. We grow old because we stop playing."—HERBERT SPENCER.

Wallflowers are the people left when the popular ones and their popular friends consort together.

Many a man who is a big bug at the office is little more than an insect when he gets home.

"The best way to cheer yourself is to try to cheer somebody else up."—MARK TWAIN.

It's not the hours you put into your work, but the work you put into your hours.

Don't waste time reflecting on missed opportunities. While reflecting you might miss some more!

Any old fish can float downstream. It takes a live fish to swim up.

Be kind to people as you climb the ladder of success—you may meet them again on the way down!

Three rules for avoiding criticism completely: (1) Say nothing, (2) do nothing, (3) be nothing.

For the courageous, each failure is a new starting point.

To be born a gentleman is an accident—to die one is an achievement.

It is not what we eat but what we digest that makes us strong.
It is not what we gain but what we save that makes us rich.
Not what we read but what we remember that makes us learned,
Not what we profess but what we practice that makes us religious.
                                                    —BACON

"Some children are on the streets at night because they are afraid to stay home alone." (STEWART CASE, Colorado).

When you point your finger at someone else's guilt or shortcomings, have you noticed that you have three fingers pointing at yourself?

"Men will argue for religion, fight for it, die for it, anything but live for it."—ANON.

You get ulcers more from what's eating on you than from what you eat.

The most underdeveloped territory in the world is right under your hat.

There are better ways of getting up in the world than hitting the ceiling!

SOME TYPES OF BANQUETS

If you are looking for an excuse to hold a banquet, perhaps some one of these nearly thirty types of banquets will give you one.

Brotherhood Banquet. In celebration of Brotherhood Week or for other purpose of fellowship.

Tribute Banquet. To someone who has achieved, served well, perhaps is retiring. Special songs for the person, special speeches, gifts, are in order.

TV Banquet. For program, several TV features could be imitated, such as quiz shows, news, comedy shows, variety presentations, hillbilly music.

Graduation Banquet. Complete with processional, high-class music, Last Will, Honor Graduates (who perform), Alma Mater.

Under the Big Top. This features circus, of course, with animal decorations, balloons, miniature tents at tables. Acts could perform there (if there is room) or in another spot or outdoors. Each table could be asked to decorate its own (from materials furnished) and to do circus act.

Melting Pot Banquet. Each table represents different country. At Colorado Women's College they plan this banquet months in advance, correspond with persons in those countries for ideas of climate, customs. Before banquet there is tour of the world. Program has international flavor—songs, games, stories.

Mother Goose Mother-Daughter Banquet. To give a little variation, use this theme with Mother Goose decorations and program features. Don't let it get too sentimental.

Gay 90's Banquet. Decorations, songs and program, dress are in keeping. Eat by lamplight. Singing waiters. Wear your costumes. More fun for older youth and mixed adult groups than for younger folk.

Transportation Banquet (Railroad Days, Airplane, Ox Cart to Flying Saucer, Ocean Cruise). Select program and decorations to fit. Costumes for leaders or table waiters could be in keeping with theme, such as trainman's garb.

Gourmet Banquet. Either serve fancy food and have highbrow program, or serve corned beef hash and have lowbrow program. Older groups more interested in this than school folk.

Rainbow Banquet. Decorate with all colors, including balloons. Songs like Over the Rainbow; have Pot of Gold Quiz.

Indoor Camping Banquet. Decorate tables appropriately, have camplike program.

Artists Banquet. Decorate with "artists" theme. For program have some artists perform. Let each person at table create work of art in paints, clay, crayolas, paper.

Musical March of Time. Program features music as it has been done through centuries, and how it will be done in A.D. 3,000.

Book Banquet. Each person comes representing book title. (One girl had miniature Venetian blind on her, for "Drapes of Lath.") Book characters from well-known works are represented in program. Have book quiz. A talk on values of reading, or how to enjoy book.

Kid Banquet. Everyone tries to recapture days of their youth.

Turnabout Banquet. Men come dressed as women, women as men. Both act their roles. "Battle of the Sexes" quiz.

Starvation Banquet. Short meal is served, money taken for world relief. Program may be lighthearted or serious.

Recognition Banquet. To honor some person, or to represent progress of group. Go back into history and bring things up to date.

Harvest Home Banquet. Have folk come dressed in old-fashioned clothes. Get them to make hats, bonnets when they come, from newspaper or colored paper. Cornucopias for tables.

Springtime Party. Features flowers, return of spring, "in the spring a young man's fancy turns to what the girls have been thinking of all winter."

Hobo Banquet. Decorations and food are in keeping. (Could be outdoor affair). Eat from tin cans, sing hobo songs, tell stories.

Dinner in —————— (You fill in blank). This banquet could take banqueteers to any part of globe, such as Alaska, Scandinavia, South Sea Islands, Australia.

Sadie Hawkins Banquet. At end of Sadie Hawkins day, or as special event—featuring all comic characters. Senior high school, older youth and young adults will like it.

Comic Characters Banquet. Broader than Sadie Hawkins, including any of comics. Skits represent comic characters. Each table might put on skit if there are not too many.

Gypsy Banquet. Decorations, atmosphere, songs, program are gypsyish.

Southern Plantation Banquet. Decorations, songs, program carry you back to ol' Virginny or Mississippy.

Doof and Nuf Banquet. "Food and fun" spelled backward—and banquet is that, served backward, people wear clothes backward, program is backward.

Organizational Banquet. Most organizations have banquet at some time to review achievements, celebrate milestone or progress, and to look ahead.

Decorations are usually in organization colors, motto on display, material of special emphasis at plates, program and speechifying directed toward furthering organizational purpose. Be sure to have some "table fun" along with serious stuff. Often a skit, some good group singing, humorous songs and performances send people away, glad they came.

SEASONAL BANQUET BRIEFS

Adam and Eve (New Year's Eve, that is). Banquet especially for couples, taking year in retrospect.

Rail Splitters Banquet. Decorations in keeping, and program too, in honor of Lincoln, "Honest Abe."

Cherry Tree Banquet. Cherries featured in decorations, George Washington in program.

Hearts and Hatchets Banquet. Combination of Valentine's and George Washington's Birthday in decorations and program.

Red, White and Blue Banquet. For Fourth of July.

Greenery Banquet. Everything green for St. Patrick's Day.

Turkey Tale Banquet. Especially for Thanksgiving.

Bright Star Banquet. For Christmas time. Be sure to use carols as part of program.

"Others' Day" Banquet. Some groups are declaring Thanksgiving as "Others' Day," and are doing for others at that time.

PLANS FOR SEVEN UNUSUAL BANQUETS

"Around the World Flight" Banquet. Seat belts are in seats. Decorations have colors of flags, planes. Stewardesses serve the meal. After the meal, the trip is made, via song, from country to country, using such a collection as *Lift Every Voice*. Group singing combined with solos and special numbers move the group from place to place. Films, filmstrips may be inserted to give flavor.

Decorate each table for a different country. One group had a Blarney Stone in a table for the O'Kellys, O'Gradys, and so on; windmills and tulips for Holland. Eskimos made of cleansing tissues stood in front of upturned cereal boxes for Alaska. Ming trees represented China and Japan. A tribe of Seminole Indians sat together at the table decorated with bow and arrows, tomahawks, buffalo skin. Egypt had a tall pyramid.

This banquet may be followed with a folk festival in another room.

Pirates' Aftermath.[1] Decorations were seaweed from green crepe paper; octopuses from newspaper and paste (small ones on the tables, big one on trunk from Davy Jones' locker). Whales made of construction paper (black). King Neptune wore beard made of mop. Around locker were "gold coins" (stones painted yellow). Davy Jones, toastmaster, wore skull and crossbones on chest and headpiece. The people were dressed as pirates. On the walls were sea monsters and hundreds of fish, cut and strung up, blown by fans.

The program included singing, games, and contests adapted in name, quiz, balloon, and other games.

Birthday Banquet. Give each person his "birthstone" ring material, and he makes ring himself, using pipe cleaners for bands, construction paper, and "glitter" (from stationery or paint store). Here is birthstone for each month:

January—garnet (deep red)
February—amethyst (purple)
March—aquamarine (pale green)
April—diamond (crystal)
May—emerald (deep green)
June—pearl (white)
July—ruby (red)

August—sardonyx (orange-red)
September—sapphire (blue)
October—opal (various colors)
November—topaz (yellow)
December—turquoise (blue-green)

Let guests talk about their rings, show to each other as conversation pieces. Each month may be asked to sit together and present something appropriate, with January forewarned that it is to have the invocation. Other features could take form of songs, stunts, performances, jokes, riddles.

After December, sing some Christmas carols. Little birthday present could be at each place, or have group swap presents.

Shining Stars Banquet (for athletes). Decorate with school colors and appropriate miniatures for football, basketball, baseball, track, with team nickname used prominently. If trophy has been won, have it ready to display (perhaps for first time).

Use outline of football or whatever ball is appropriate as shape of banquet program. Include in printed program menu and outline of program.

Save athletic jokes and cartoons, and place them around on tables for athletes to enjoy. Get them to tell, while eating, funniest thing that ever happened in a game. An invocation will precede the meal.

After the meal, have following features:

Welcome and response.

Music, perhaps including group singing.

Talks as appropriate by visiting speaker, coach, president or principal. If championship has been won, acknowledge this.

Skits, stunts (with laugh at some of things that have happened during past season) are good. Fellows (or girls) may enjoy "gags" of group starter variety. (These should precede any serious talk.) Magic, good puppet show, movies might be used.

Special music.

School song and, in some cases, benediction.

Our College Around the World. This was spring banquet of school whose students served around world. Program as printed read:

FELLOWSHIP (Greet your neighbor)

INVOCATION (The hymnic grace)

THE MEAL (Fresh food, canned dinner music)

WE SING TOGETHER (Music is the universal language)

FAMILY ALBUM (De-skeletonized, consisting of some of the fun and predictions that come at the end of every school year)

GARRETT AROUND THE WORLD (Some of the things that are being done by alumni)

THINGS THAT SHOULD HAVE BEEN SAID (but weren't until now—these were remarks of appreciation for student accomplishments and faculty labors)

GARRETT MEN'S CHOIR (Songs)
HYMN OF DEDICATION (By all)

"Over the Garden Fence" [2]

TABLE DECORATION: Flower or vegetable on each table, buried in dirt. Tables were Rakers, Sprinklers, Busy Bees, D.D.T.'ers, Carrots, Beets, Onions, Potatoes, Jack-in-the-Pulpits, Petunias, Daisies, Tulips, Weeders.

GRACE: Led by Jack-in-the-Pulpits

During meal each table contributes verse, song, or skit about what they are representing.

Sprinklers distribute milk and coffee, Busy Bees bring in food, Weeders carry out dirty dishes.

PROGRAM: Advice consists of their singing "Sweetly Sings the Donkey."

Song, "Mr. Rabbit" (see *Sing It Again*).

Group of four songs dealing with gardening.

So-called lecture by an authority on gardening as follows:

INTRODUCTION: "And now we present Miss Horty Culture from the *Onion*versity of *Seed*attle."

MISS HORTY CULTURE:

On the subject of gardening I couldn't be worse
So I'll speak to you in blank—er, garden verse.

When planting potatoes, cut them crosswise
And before covering them up, please close their eyes.

Try to plant your tomatoes all in a row
You'll find them lots easier to hoe, hoe, hoe.

Your watermelon vine by the gate you should stick
So that strangers passing by can take their pick.

Carrots, onions, and celery too—
Plant them together—they'll be ready for stew.

As far as squash and rutabagas go
It won't be far enough for me, I know.

Don't worry about weeds, just build a high fence
And plant many flowers—doesn't that make sense?

And for gardening advice, in prose or in rhyme,
I suggest that you get an authority next time.

Ye Olde Englishe Christmas Dinner. Here is the detailed description of a Christmas banquet that was very impressive:

SINGERS—enter from the hall, singing "It Came upon the Midnight Clear." March around center dining table, singing "Hark, the Herald Angels Sing." Are seated.

PAGES (soft music)—enter with wreaths and hang over fireplace. Trip out for garlands and fasten up. Hang mistletoe in center of room, then hide.

JESTER—comes running in, in most unusual manner, stubs toe and falls, jumps up, and announces the Lord and Lady. Jester says, "Yo! Ho! the Lord and Lady come!" and gesticulates in such a manner that the audience understands that it should rise. Runs back and forth joyously.

LORD AND LADY AND GUESTS (soft music)—pages enter, carrying candles. Lord and Lady follow. Two guests follow. March up one side of table and down the other, back to places. All are seated. Pages stand behind Lord.

READER: "It was an old English custom as far back as the Crusades to celebrate Christmas in this manner, especially at the Lord's Court. Part of the ceremony was the Yule Log. Everyone treated the log with great respect as it was dragged in, bowed to it as it passed. The log must burn all night, and then what was left must be kept very carefully, because it was supposed to guard the house during the year."

Advent of the Yule Log (soft music)

Pages march from the Lord's table to the entrance and return with the woodsmen dragging the log (Jester rides on the log). The Lord and his guests treat the log with great respect, bowing as it passes by and as the woodsmen place it on the fire and light it. (Woodsmen stand by the fireplace.)

READER: "A ceremony of great importance is that of bringing in the boar's head. It was usually on a silver dish and decorated with lemons and greens. It was carried into the hall accompanied by trumpets and lighted candles. The custom originated at Queen's College, Oxford, and it is still observed there."

Advent of the Boar's Head (soft music)

Pages retire and return with cook, bearing the boar's head on silver tray (decorated with greens). The cook sings the "Boar's Head Song" as he brings it in, places head on table and goes out main entrance.

READER: "One Christmas Charles II and his men went forth to hunt a stag. When they returned they piled logs in the fireplace that they might warm themselves and then have a feast. As they were all enjoying the huge loin of beef, King Charles knighted the beef. It is always served at a Christmas feast in England."

Advent of the Loin of Beef (soft music)

Pages retire. Re-enter beside cook bearing loin of beef. (Exit cook.) Lord rises and draws his sword and says, "Sir Loin, I dub thee knight!")

READER: "Sometimes the loin of beef was accompanied with a Yorkshire pudding, raisins and figs that make us think of the East, spices to remind us of the gifts of the Magi, sweets and fruits—the best of everything was placed on the platter. Then over it all was put a cover of pastry, on which a star is drawn, like that the wise men saw. They called it Christ's cradle."

Advent of the Plum Pudding (soft music)

Pages and cook enter as before.

READER: "When the cloth was removed, the cook brought in a huge silver vessel of rare and curious workmanship which he placed before the Lord. Its appearance was hailed with delight, being the wassail bowl so renowned in Christmas festivity. Having raised it to his lips with a hearty wish of Merry Christmas to all present, he sent it humming round the table for everyone to follow his example, pronouncing it the 'ancient fountain of good feeling' where all hearts met together."

Advent of the Wassail Bowl (soft music)

Pages and cook as before. Singers sing "Wassail Song" as cook enters. Lord rises, drinks from the bowl, and says, "I bid you all a merry, merry Christmas." Pages pass it to Lady and each guest.

CHRISTMAS DINNER—jester entertains by her wit and ridiculous things she makes others do and does herself. Singers and all guests sing carols at intervals during dinner—especially English ones.

MUMMER'S PLAY

ENGLISH FOLK DANCERS—followed by entire group participating in a folk dance.

TWO BANQUETS POPULAR WITH FAMILIES

Mother and Daughter Banquet. Favorite banquet idea is mother-daughter one. Other theme titles are sometimes used, such as "Hen-Chick" or "Cat-Kitten." Clever ideas should be devised to keep such an affair from getting too sentimental.

Use of skits and humor helps, also singing fun songs as well as sentimental songs. Little contests like mother and daughter who weigh least, who are youngest, mother with most daughters—all tend to keep program lighter.

Another idea would be to bring in some boys and men to perform for the program (and in exchange, girls and women will go to their father-son affair to perform).

Cute puppet shows, solos, trios, demonstrations of dances, slides, movies, may be used, as well as group singing, reading of humorous material such as boners or Colonel Stoopnagle's nonsense, will add fun. See also "Informal Mealtime Fun" in this chapter for ideas, especially for ideas like tongue twisters done at table between mother and daughter, or boners.

Most mother-daughter affairs like to end on a serious note, with a prayer. Try closing with the group singing Malotte's "The Lord's Prayer."

Father and Son Banquet. (Also called "Chip and Block" Banquet, "Dad-Lad," "Senior-Junior.") Many organizations like to get fathers and sons together, once a year, for a banquet. After the invocation there will be food and fellowship at the table. Jokes, easy puzzles may be conversation starters at the table.

Here are some ideas for the program:

1. Have contest to see what father-son combination have the biggest differential in waist measure.
2. Which father and son look least alike?

3. Which father and son have greatest total chest expansion?
4. Which is oldest father-son combination? Youngest? Tallest? Heaviest? (Have a set of scales at hand.)
5. Contest by tables (or between candles) to see which group of father-sons can name most father-son combinations in history and in the Bible.
6. Have talk by father (who might quote "A Father's Ten Commandments" given below), a response by son (or someone else's son). Don't let them get too sentimental. (Boy might point out that once a year is Father's Day, but every seven days it's Sunday.)
7. Quizzes are good for this group.
8. Skits and stunts, humorous readings like "What Is a Boy?" (which follows below) make good program features.
9. By all means have some good singing, both group singing by all and some special music, perhaps by a father and son.
10. A serious talk might be made about fathers or sons of the Bible, such as the Prodigal Son (Luke 15:11-19), the Loving Father (Luke 15:20-24), John 3:16.
11. Magicians and other entertainers, singers, puppeteers, movies, could be on program also.

Do not let program continue too long. It might be well to go to another room for some games between fathers and sons (see Men Only in Index).

WHAT IS A BOY?

BOYS COME in assorted sizes, weights, and colors. They are found everywhere—on top of, underneath, inside of, climbing on, swinging from, running around or jumping to. Mothers love them, little girls hate them, older sisters and brothers tolerate them, adults ignore them, and Heaven protects them. A boy is Truth with dirt on its face, Wisdom with bubble gum in its hair, and the Hope of the future with a frog in its pocket.

A boy has the appetite of a horse, the digestion of a sword swallower, the energy of a pocket-size atomic bomb, the curiosity of a cat, the lungs of a dictator, the imagination of a Paul Bunyan, the shyness of a violet, the audacity of a steel trap, the enthusiasm of a firecracker, and when he makes something he has five thumbs on each hand.

He likes ice cream, knives, saws, Christmas, comic books, the boy across the street, woods, water (in its natural habitat), large animals, Dad, trains, Saturday mornings, and fire engines. He is not much for Sunday School, company, schools, books without pictures, music lessons, neckties, barbers, girls, overcoats, adults, or bedtime.

Nobody else is so early to rise or so late to supper. Nobody else can cram into one pocket a rusty knife, a half-eaten apple, three feet of string, an empty Bull Durham sack, two gumdrops, six cents, a slingshot, a chunk of unknown substance, and a genuine supersonic code ring with a secret compartment.

A boy is a magical creature—you can lock him out of your workshop, but you can't lock him out of your heart. You can get him out of your study, but you can't get him out of your mind. Might as well give up—he is your captor, your jailer, your boss, and your master— a freckle-faced, pint-sized bundle of noise. But when you come home at night with only the shattered pieces of your hopes and dreams, he can mend them with two magic words—"Hi, Dad!" [3]

A FATHER'S TEN COMMANDMENTS
By Roy E. Dickerson

I. Thou shalt love thy son with all thy heart and hesitate not to show it. This is the first and great commandment.

II. Thou shalt not carry graven upon thy heart any love greater than this. Business, sports, pleasures shall all take secondary place, for God gave him to be a chum and pal unto thee.

III. Thou shalt not take the name of "Father" upon thee lightly, for God will not hold him guiltless who hath little regard for the responsibilities of Fatherhood.

IV. Remember thy son's portion of thy time and keep it sacred for his use. Many days shalt thou labor and do all manner of work to provide suitably for his needs, but in that portion of thy day which belongeth to him thou shalt not do any work, neither shalt thou bury thy nose in a book, betake thyself to the golf links or seek thine own pleasure otherwise.

V. Honor thy wife, my mother, for I, thy son, love her dearly and cannot admire, respect, and love thee if thou display not love toward her.

VI. Thou shalt counsel and advise with thy son in all things and share with him the secrets of thy heart.

VII. Thou shalt be firm in thy discipline, lest thy son stray away from the paths of righteousness for the lack of thy guiding hand. Not too tightly or too loosely shalt thou hold the rein of authority, but so that thy child shall recognize the wisdom of his father in life.

VIII. Thou shalt trust thy son and have patience with him for all his shortcomings, remembering that in thy boyhood others had so to do with thee.

IX. Thou shalt walk uprightly before all men, for thy child doth trust thee before all others. Moreover, if thou shalt shake his confidence in thee it will not be lightly regained.

X. Thou shalt not forget that thou wert once a boy, neither be unmindful that times have changed much since the days of thy youth.[4]

INFORMAL MEALTIME FUN
(*Luncheon club—camp—church supper*)

Here are some fun ideas to brighten the mealtime programs of groups in any situation short of a formal banquet.

Group Singing After Meals. Most people do not like to sing during meal, though they will sing between courses.

Decorating Own Table. If tables are assigned in advance, group may have much fun decorating its own table. Such materials as flame proof crepe paper, construction paper, balloons, colored straws, flowers, colored leaves, greenery such as evergreens and magnolia leaves or Spanish moss, cotton, candles, bowls of fruit for cornucopia, souvenirs from foreign lands, may be used. For place cards, such materials as cards, cut-outs, bits of leaves, bark, branches, feathers, felt, cork, cloth, postage stamps, beads, crayolas, construction paper, sprigs of pine, hemlock, or holly, lollypops, aluminum and other foils, milk bottle caps, cardboard tubing, paper plates, doilies, gumdrops, raisins, figs, dates, dried seeds (beans, rice, peas), alphabet spaghetti, paste, scissors. From whatever materials are furnished, each is to construct his own. Have them show their wares to their own table, neighboring tables.

Decorating to a Theme. Place cards, nut cups, centerpieces, and all the rest are in keeping. Assign several families to decorate for family affair. Much fun can be had with animal themes for tables.

Imaginary Decorations. As suggested for other social affairs, person blessed with vivid imagination might paint picture (mental, that is) of beautifully decorated table, groaning with good things to eat. (Then bring out bologna sandwiches!)

Group Starters, Conversation Starters. Right after the invocation, have everybody talk about same thing, such as an embarrassing moment, best joke they've heard recently, what can you do to reduce 10 pounds, tricks for managing children, biggest deception ever pulled on you, hardest thing you have to do.

Graces for the Table. Get members of group to collect some for group use. Perhaps also to be mimeographed to be taken home.

Jokes, Knock-Knocks, Humorous Material on the Table. At each person's plate have a joke, knock-knock, silly song title, or other humorous material. Have everyone read them aloud at their tables, select best to be read to entire group. (Gets multiple participation—good conversation starter.) Use boners in same way.

Tongue Twisters on cards. Same idea. See if you can say them three times, fast, to your neighbor.

Dividing into Groups. Often there will be 50 people seated at one long table. Candles may be used for dividers. Those between candles constitute group, or those between candle and end of table. Then these small groups can be asked to "make up something."

Doing a Skit, or Singing Commercial. These can be fun, if brief. (If the group is very large, table can do its skit for neighboring table and then neighboring table reciprocates.) Singing commercials for causes of group, or for St. Valentine, for Uncle Sam, or for Witches' Brew or Santa Claus can be composed and rendered. This brings group participations.

Puppeteers. After table has been cleared (if there is time) furnish each table with paper sacks, paper, paste, paints, crayons, and let them make puppets and put on little puppet show, either for entire group or for neighboring table. (In latter case, several presentations may be going at same time.)

Art Work. After tables are cleared, bring out some fun materials for those sitting there, such as piling straws, modeling clay, crayolas. Have brief show after meal is over, showing results of this creative activity.

Performances. Members of group who have rehearsed in advance present talent, skits and stunts, singing commercials, magic show, and the like.

Honoring. Table presents natural grouping for honoring member of group (or several) who have achieved, served, or have been recognized professionally, in unusual ways. Same is true of re-tiring from organization. Make it sincere, to the point, but don't let it get sloppy and maudlin. Sing "Jolly Good Fellow" to re-tiree, give him silly gift before big one. Try to make him feel that he is welcome to come back—that this is not good-bye for-ever.

Revolving Banquet.[5] Here is preplanned system for making socia-bility. At given signal, all those who have roses on their place cards, pick up water and napkin, and move to next position to their right, bearing rose place card. This idea is carried out twice more (adding coffee cup to moving process), with tulip place card people moving second time, and lily of valley place card people moving last time. Same could be done with numbers or other identification.

11

Planning Service and
Money-Raising Projects

Help thy brother's boat across and lo, thine own has reached the shore.—INDIAN PROVERB

LOSE YOURSELF in service to make others happy—and you find happiness yourself! In such efforts lie some of the best recreational opportunities. Many groups have discovered that any voluntary activity, chosen for one's "free-choosing time," is likely to have a recreational effect upon the person, whether it seems to be recreation or not. Two kinds of projects for fun of this nature are presented in this chapter with many suggestions for each—service and money raising.

MAKING SERVICE PROJECTS FUN

The fellowship of doing hard work to achieve a worth-while end often goes deeper than that of the usual party or social.

Work Camps. There is noticeable rise of popularity of week-end projects for youth, student, and young adult groups, and tremendous interest in regional, national, and overseas work camps in summer. Those attending often pay cost of their accommodations and transportation, work their heads off—and have fun doing it.

One such project, to clear up vacant lot for play area in New York City, was directed by a woman. The group of attractive young people was working side by side with a few youth from the community. A hardened-looking man watched them, day after day, fascinated.

Finally his curiosity got the best of him and he approached the lady with a half-whispered question, "Government project?" "No," she explained. "This is a Friends' Work Camp. They're Quakers, you know. These young people have volunteered their services." "You mean they don't get paid?" "No, they pay for coming here!" The man looked on in disbelief. "Well, I'll be switched!" he exclaimed. "Well, why don't you get a bulldozer to clear this?" "We can't afford it," she replied. "I'll have one here in the morning," said he, and he did, joining them and working throughout rest of project. Work camps do that for people—and they enjoy it. (The American Friends Service Committee, 20 S. 12th St., Philadelphia, Pa., has done much with this technique, as have many other denominational and faith groups.)

The Lord's Acre. Developed by Farmers Federation, Asheville, N. C., to put life and money into program of rural church, this plan is bringing spirit of work-fellowship to many small communities.

Based upon biblical customs, idea is simply for group to set aside plot of ground or head of livestock, and when yield comes, to dedicate income to use and purposes of church.

Recreational values come from working together, when groups and families take turns maintaining special area designated. One group set aside 40 acres for soy beans, and on appointed morning nearly 20 tractors were ready to begin plowing, after dedication service. (Rev. Dumont Clarke, Director of Religious Department of Farmers Federation, will be glad to share information. See Bibliography also.)

Time Tithers. This was name actually adopted by group of young adults, who gave tithe of their time to their leader to do any worth-while projects in community. Plenty of projects to work on were found. Dozens of people kept happily busy.

Visiting. Those in children's and old people's homes, detention homes, jail and penitentiary, are often lonely and would be cheered by visit. Groups often put on musical performances, do stunts, help with games and, if rules permit, take people out for rides, or to movies, concerts, ball games, plays, or opera.

Work Party or Slave Idea. Some groups do combination of work and money raising by hiring themselves out as "slaves" for one, two or more hours, weekdays or on Saturday, to do odd jobs, wash windows, mow lawns, wash cars, help with painting.

Pot Luck and Pay. Since people would have to eat at home anyway, they enjoy this money-raising idea. Every family brings along some food, and all enjoy fellowship. At end, then, all are asked to pay what it was worth, and the group's treasury benefits.

Helping, Cheering the Infirm. When people are sick, blind, bedridden, or house confined, there are many good turns that need to be done for them to make life happy. Some groups adopt such persons, particularly older folk, and read to them, do chores for them. On the other hand, some of these folk are able to do certain things, and it is an even better morale builder if group can think of ways to make them feel useful, such as helping with telephoning when long lists of people need to be reached, or making crafts at home to be sold and money used for good group purposes.

Parties for the Lonely. At group's own headquarters or meeting room, hold parties for orphan children, older folk, any others who might be lonely, especially because of institutional living. "Sponsors' Party."

Letter Writing in Groups. Have "letter writing party," to write letters, send cards to those who are away from community for long time, in college, in the army, on a job—anyone who would enjoy hearing from "folks at home." This activity, with incidental conversation and refreshments, makes satisfying evening.

Clothing Scavenger Hunt. Send people out in groups to gather clothing to be brought to central point, sorted, distributed to needy in community, or through such agency as Church World Service Center, New Windsor, Maryland.

Mother's Day for the Motherless. This would be nice time to have family or group adopt for one day child who is orphan, or who has no mother.

Adopting a Child for Christmas. Some groups sponsor having members adopt child for Christmas season. (Often this leads to permanent adoptions.)

Starvation Banquet. Meal much smaller than usual is served, presentation of world need of food is made, voluntary offering given.

Nonprofit relief food, Multi-Purpose Food, is available for such meals at low cost through 3-cent meal foundation, Meals for Millions, 115 West Seventh Street, Los Angeles 14, California. Menu might consist of soup, with Multi-Purpose Food added, green salad, Multi-Purpose muffins, and hot drink.

Others' Day. Suggested by little girl to Miss Florence Rose of Meals for Millions Foundation. Child reasoned that since we have "Father's Day" and "Mother's Day," we should have "Others' Day" too and do nice things for others. Thanksgiving has been suggested as season for this. Sacrificial Dinner. (Sometimes called "Starvation Banquet.")

Growing Flowers. Take them to sick, shut-ins. (This could be done as group or in small neighborhood groups, in manner of Lord's Acre plan.)

Hallowe'en Trick or Treat. Instead of usual "Trick or treat," collect money for U.N. Children's Fund and send to U.N. Children's Fund, United Nations Building, New York, N. Y.

Support of Orphans in Other Countries or Here. Many groups are doing this with regular contributions.

Helping Set Up Recreation Centers. Set up and equip them, especially in co-operation with Neighborhood Houses, city recreation department, or other agencies needing volunteer time.

Helping Harvest Perishable Crops. Often crops go to waste because there is not enough labor. Use vacation for this.

Working in Week-End Work Project. Many groups, on their week ends, help to rebuild, repair, paint, paper, make equipment and toys in community centers, small churches (city and rural); clear play areas and furnish leadership.

Collecting Parties, for Books, Shoes, Clothing, Food. Give articles to worthy groups in U. S. and abroad. Often such parties are held for orphan homes, old people's homes. Booth festival idea provides framework of display for these objects gathered by individual groups in church organization, with prizes for best-decorated booth. Program for afternoon is recreational.

Developing Fellowship Teams, Caravans. Many groups have teams going from their number to other groups who need leadership help, serving on Saturdays and Sundays, and during summer for several weeks. Pretraining and equipping these teams is highly desirable.

Presenting Plays, Play Readings on Problems. Excellent service project to start discussion on needed action (sometimes done over radio).

MAKING MONEY-RAISING PROJECTS FUN

Box Supper. Each girl makes box, boys or men bid on them, successful buyer eats with girl who prepared box, money goes to worthy cause.

Bake Sale. Sell or auction off baked goods. (Often people will turn them back to be sold again.)

Wishing Well. One group built wishing well around deep tin pan with brick blocks, trellis in front of it twined with paper flowers and vines. Money collected was used for relief.

White Elephant Sale. People bring their "white elephants" and sell them to each other, money going to treasury for "worthy purposes."

Charging Admissions for—

"County Fair"
"Circus"
Football Party
Concerts
Craft Fair
Hobby Show

Talent Night
Benefit Movie
For use of skating rink, bowling alley, swimming pool, excursion boat, motor boat, excursion train or bus, rental charge for facilities

Charging for Food, Services

Bazaars
Pancake Suppers or Breakfasts
Special Breakfast, such as at Easter (city-wide)
Baked Goods Sale
Watermelon Cutting
Seasonal meals, banquets, at holiday times
Ice Cream Social

Roving Photographer (sell the pictures he makes)
Baby Sitting Service, lawn mowing, window washing
Food stand at sales, public places
"Beauty Party." Girls give each other home permanents, donate money for service to club treasury.

Making and Selling Things

Selling books, magazines (like PARENTS' MAGAZINE, Bergenfield, N. J., or organizational magazines).

Sewing and selling. Have sewing meeting, sell what is made, such as aprons, pot holders.

Doing glass etching, raffia weaving, selling objects made.

Quilting—selling or auctioning quilt.

Making projects of tin cans at home or at meeting place, selling these projects. (Excellent ideas in *New Tin Can Projects,* pamphlet, Joseph J. Lukowitz, Bruce Publishing Co., Milwaukee, Wis.)

Making leather projects, selling, from such supplier as Larson Leather Co., 820 Tripp, Chicago, Ill.

Making "Glo-candles" of special paraffin. (Excellent booklet from Youth Department, 318 E. 10th, Kansas City, Mo., at 10 cents.)

Getting SPECIALTY SALESMAN'S MAGAZINES on news stands, find interesting things to sell, vending them at profit and putting money into treasury.

PROFITABLE HOBBIES, monthly magazine, lists ideas monthly for individuals and groups to make money. Modern Handcraft, Inc., Kansas City 11, Mo., has booklet, *178 Ways to Make Money at Home.*

Making and selling equipment games. (See that section, this book.)

"Seed Dollar Plan." Dollar is given to each person who will take it and make it earn other dollars, bringing in increase by stated time.

Hobby Shows, Craftsmen's Fairs, or Folk Festivals become good gatherings to use in selling objects made or donated by group or its good friends.

Collecting and Selling. Waste paper, neatly bundled and tied, can help earn money for organization. Likewise magazines (tied), coat hangers, even scrap metal.

"Chinese Auction." Goods or services are auctioned off. When person makes his opening bid, he gives it to roving collector immediately. Each person who raises bid pays amount of raise. If first person bids 25 cents, he puts that in. If next one raises it 10 cents, he pays 10 cents. Therefore, actual buyer may get service or object at rather nominal price.

PART FOUR

Materials

for

Fun

12

Group Starters

THE LEADER, OR THE COMMITTEE, in charge of a recreational event is concerned at the beginning of the program that it shall "get off to a good start." His chief desire is that a group spirit of friendliness and fellowship shall develop as quickly as possible. He therefore sizes up the situation and introduces the activities accordingly. He may be able to use what has been planned ahead of time, but if the situation requires it he adjusts and adapts, starting some activity more certain to bring the desired results under the circumstances.

In this chapter, Dreams, Tongue Twisters, and Your Horoscope provide starters for the leader to use with the group, one person at a time. The sections headed "Fun with Noises," "Stretchers," "Fun with Your Neighbor," and "Gags and Group Responses" give features or stunts in which the group, all at the same time, take part. "Feats and Puzzles" are entertainment features some of which can be done by one or two persons, some by leader and group, all with an element of mystery.[1]

TYPES OF ACTIVITIES

There are at least three types of activities that will be useful for the situations in which a leader is likely to find himself: absorbers, group starters, and "warmer-uppers."

Absorbers. At the beginning of a party to which people come straggling in over as much as a 30-minute period this kind of activity is one which can take on new people as they come, so that they can join in or "tack on" with a minimum of effort.

Illustrations are group singing, simple equipment games, telling or reading humorous material, trying physical can-you-do-this feats, easy folk games, mixers such as Patty Cake Polka, entertaining stunts like trying to flip a cork from the top of a soft-drink bottle or balancing on a bonga board, watching people learn or practice new dance steps, or watching a turtle race.

Group Starters. These are activities which begin to get the group spirit moving the instant they are used. They may be similar to "absorbers," but they have group-mindedness to more of a de-degree. Preparatory activities for a guest to take part in when he first arrives, like putting up the decorations, if it is a very informal party, helping to decorate a certain table, helping to present a puppet show, making a hat or costume or name tag for the party, to be worn later, are really group starters because they give him a sense of responsibility for the success of the party.

"Warmer-Uppers." These are group starters, too, but you assume that most of the guests are present and that now you can get busy warming up those present to a total group spirit. Group singing, an informal activity like Who Am I (trying to identify the label that is on one's own back by asking questions of many people) or identifying baby pictures of people who are present—these make the individuals present more group conscious.

Warmer-uppers may be nonsensical, they may involve exercisers, noise making, group singing, "gags," feats if the group is seated, or mixers and simple activities if the group is on its feet. "Aren't we having fun right away?" is the response the leadership hopes for.

Such activities as mixers (see Chapter 14), any of the group participation starters included in this book, conversation starters at the table, Group Fortune Telling, and "The King with a Terrible Temper" (in *Handy Stunts*), the "Wild West Weakling" (in *Skit Hits*), or "Clappertown" (in the *Fun Encyclopedia*), Stagnet or Fox, Gun, Hunter (see Index)—all these are good for warming up the group.

To get a group started informally, a leader needs to keep in mind, too, possible "rallying centers" (see Index) around which to build a group. For example, groups anywhere outdoors could be tossing a Sky Pie about (see Index), and wherever they are doing it, there is a "rallying center" which catches the interest and attention of others and draws them to the fun.

Humorous material should not be underestimated for its value in starting a group, whether it be gags, jokes, boners, read-aloud stories (if not too long), song titles to be guessed, or any of the other bits of fun with which people have been entertaining each other for centuries.

DREAMS

The leader reads following dreams aloud to group for fun. "How many have dreamed of ———?" He gets group to hold up hands. Then gives answer. Dreams may be used by handing out words and answers and having each member of group read answer on his slip.

Accounts (Bookkeeping). You have been thinking about income tax. Have you paid?

Ammunition. Good omen—for you, things will soon be booming.

Ants. Be careful when on picnics.

Baseball. Don't be afraid to *strike out* on a new venture.

Beggar. Go ahead and ask. You'll come out, all right.

Blossoms (Orange). You know what, don't you?

Broom (especially if new). Look out, if there's a new boss at your office.

Burns. Some dreams you don't like, but *this* is a *hot one!*

Camera. This is not so good—it means that you must be careful or you may be "taken."

Church. That's fine. But why don't you go in person?

Clams. Excellent. Remember that he never gets caught if he keeps his mouth shut.

Clover (especially rolling in). Good sign, unless you are making chains.

Confection. Wonderful. Something sweet is coming into your life.

Darning. All right, but watch your language.

Dirt. A political campaign will develop soon.

Duel. Be careful that your clothes don't clash.

Elevator. You are going up in the world (or down, one).

Fire Engine. If you're a married man, look out for the siren.

Fork (in the road). There are two ways to look at this dream.

Fright. Go and buy yourself some better cosmetics.

Gallows. Too independent. People want you to go hang.

Guitar. Keep strumming away and you'll get there.

Hammock. It's best not to try to lie out of it.

Handkerchief. Stop blowing quite so much.

Hurricane. You're blowing *far* too much.

Cyclone. Slow down—you're going around in circles.

Kettle. You must mend your ways, even if this makes you boil.

Mice. Although you're a big cheese, something's gnawing on you!

Mud. Same as dirt, but this political campaign will be during the rainy season.

Rake. Now's the time to start cleaning up.

Trees. Good sign, but be careful when walking under them in nesting season.

Zinc. You need to attend to some *miner* matter. (Perhaps it's the kitchen zinc.)

TONGUE TWISTERS

All "tongue twisters" are not really "tongue twisters." Some follow pattern of alliteration—beginning every word with same letter —which is not particularly hard to pronounce. To be difficult they don't have to be *long*. Tongue twisters are said *three times, fast*.

1. Bisquick, kiss quick!
2. She sells sea shells.
3. Six slippery, sliding snakes.
4. Fat friars fanning flames.
5. Great gilt gig whip.
6. Jack Jackson Zachary.
7. The judge jugged Judd.
8. This'll sift the thistle sifter!
9. Three terrible thieves.
10. Flat-fish fleets.
11. The zither sizzed.
12. Listless lisping.
13. The bank book blew back.
14. The girl with the green, gray geese.
15. Tim, the thin twin tinsmith.
16. Thirty-six sick theologs.
17. Strange strategic statistics.
18. Shoveling soft snow slowly.
19. Shabby stitches showing.
20. Plump Persian plum.

If you want to make your own, these represent hard combinations to say:

Sl and Sa, Se, Si, So, Su
Six—sick
Z and J
Jud—Jug
Strong Th followed by S or T, or Tl

Sw—Sm
Ch—Cl
Tw—Ta, Te, Ti, To, Tu
Pl and Pa, Pe, Pi, Po, Pu
Bl and Br
Gr and Ga, Ge, Gi, Go, Gu

How to Use

1. Just for fun, passing out slips with tongue twisters on them. See if you can say them to another person or small group.
2. At table, on back of place cards or on slips.
3. In "fun in small spaces" situation. Give out one, see if group can say them. Or have them turn to neighbor and try to say, three times.
4. As contest, to see which person or group is superior.

YOUR HOROSCOPE

Horoscopes may be used in several ways for fun: they may be read aloud to the group, delivered privately in sealed envelopes, or put in a penny arcade.

Jan. 20-Feb. 19. You are fond of the arts, have a good disposition, and are likely to be active in reform movements and progressive ideas.

Feb. 20-Mar. 21. Yours is a trustful, loving, sympathetic nature. You are most likely to succeed in a trade requiring skill, tact, and the ability to make the best of circumstances.

Mar. 22-Apr. 19. Natural leader, not easily discouraged. Have push and energy. Lover of justice and freedom. True friend!

Apr. 20-May 20. Gentle by nature when not abused, but stubborn when aroused. Practical, good organizer, sincere, trustworthy.

May 21-June 21. Experimental, given to investigation. Natural curiosity, bent toward research.

June 22-July 22. Fond of home and family, clever, saving, bent on making money. Responsive to kindness and praise. Know what public wants. Likely to succeed in merchandising.

July 23-Aug. 22. Thoughtful, generous. Frank, independent, forceful. Good-tempered yet high-strung; do not hold a grudge long.

Aug. 23-Sept. 23. Willing to risk savings in a deal with small chance to profit. Careful about details. Sometimes given to over-anxiety, but a good worker, a concerned leader.

Sept. 24-Oct. 23. Lover of justice. Will fight for liberty to the bitter end. Quick in decision and anger, yet easily won over. Fond of beauty in life and in art.

Oct. 24-Nov. 22. Exceedingly quick-witted, alert in speech and action, positive in expression of opinions. Keen judgment and mechanical skill likely.

Nov. 23-Dec. 21. Bright, hopeful, liberal, independent. Inclined to be sympathetic, loving. Likely to succeed in profession or commerce.

Dec. 22-Jan. 19. Serious, dignified. Ambitious and capable of long hours, hard work. Patient, kindly.

FUN WITH NOISES

Steam Engine in the Roundhouse (*five groups make the noises*). Once there was a little old engine in the roundhouse with the steam up. It was almost time to go to the station. It was on the track, steaming: (Group 1) "Cof'-fee, cof'-fee, cof'-fee."

The engineer pulled back the throttle a little, and it sounded like (Group 2) "fisssssh and chips, fissssssh and chips, fissssssh and chips." Soon it was going faster: (Group 3) "Meat and carrots, meat and carrots, meat and carrots." By now it was really high-balling down the track, and it said: (Group 4) "Cheese and crackers, cheese and crackers, cheese and crackers." Then the engineer pulled on the whistle cord: (Group 5) "Zoop! Zooooooooooop!"

The Frog Pond. Without telling them why, ask third of group (high voices) to say in falsetto, "Tomatoes, tomatoes, tomatoes, tomatoes."

A middle group say more slowly, "Potatoes, potatoes, potatoes, potatoes."

The lowest voices say very slowly, "Friiied bacon! Friiiied bacon! Friiiiied bacon!"

Big Sneeze. Group one says HISH. Group two says HASH. Group 3 says HOSH. Next, each group adds "ee" to end of its word, in order. Then they say them all together, in tremendous sneeze —to which proper answer of leader is, *"Gesundheit!"*

Hooray! System is announced. If right hand is raised, group is to respond, "Hooray!" If left hand is raised, it applauds violently. If both hands are raised, it does both. (Practice once.)

The leader then makes a few statements, not in keeping with response, like these: "The officers have just voted a $5 increase in dues." (Hooray!) "There will be no dessert tonight." (Applause!) "Knowing that you will enjoy it, the speaker is going to talk for two-and-a-half hours." (Hooray and applause.)

How They Clap. "Do you know how they clap at a painter's convention?" the leader asks, and demonstrates. (Making fingers on one hand loose, like bristles in a paint brush, he "brushes" them back and forth on palm of other hand, with clapping sound.)

"And at a barber's convention?" (Similarly, but making fingers stiff, he swipes them across palm of hand with an upward motion, first back side, then palm side, in imitation of stropping razor.)

"And the Boston tea clap?" (Three fingers, applauding lightly on side of hand.)

Wing Wing! Have group say "Wing" six times, fast. Near end, say, "He'wo!!" (for "hello," baby-talk style).

Group Response. Encourage group to respond immediately according to signal. As handkerchief is dropping, all are to do as you suggest, but when it hits floor, all must stop immediately whichever response they are making.

In this order, have them: (1) laugh, (2) cry, (3) yell, (4) applaud, (5) reverse: Wait till handkerchief hits floor, then do four above vigorously, in reverse order.

Football. Divide group into two teams—perhaps "Tigers" and "Lions." Leader stands where all can see, with hands extended in front of him (or her), a little lower than shoulder-high, palms down. Left hand is one indicating Tigers; right, Lions.

On toot from whistle, each team starts yelling, and leader marks their progress. If Tigers are louder than Lions, hand indicating that group rises; Lion hand lowers. Tigers continue yelling, but Lions must shift to booing. If Lion booing is loud enough, it can bring balance back and tip it over so that they are louder than Tigers, in which case Lions now yell and cheer, Tigers boo. If leader feels that enough noise has been made by one side to make a touchdown, both hands raised high in air and long blast on whistle indicates end of game.

Actually it is difficult to tell who is yelling louder, but this is wonderful to "warm up a group." They may stand if they wish.

Stagnet. (As reader reads, group responds to the emphasized words with all proper noises. They may be practiced in advance. Leader leads group in making noises, of course.)

The Miracle Broadcasting Company and all dependent affiliated stations present:

Stagnet! (*Dum, Dum-Dum Dum! Dum, Dum-Dum Dum! D-u-mmmm!*)

The story of high adventure in airships is absolutely true. Only the oil has been changed to protect the motors.

Our hero's name is JACK ARMSTRONG (*Hooray*) a 200 per cent all-American boy, and Texas space ranger. His partner's name is Saturday. Tonight they are on the rustling cattle detail.

At 10:02 the *telephone* rang. (*Brrrrrrr.*)

A *young girl's voice* was on the other end of the wire. *"Come quick to Bar B Q Ranch.* Rustlers are stealing our cattle."

Outside the *rain* was pouring in torrents. (*Shshshshshshsh.*) He emptied the torrents and rushed to the hangar where Saturday was spending Friday night *riveting* the plane. (*Rrrrrrrrrrrr.*)

"Hustle, Saturday, we've got to run down some rustlers," said *Jack Armstrong.* (*Hooray!*) "OK," said Saturday, "but I'll have to take along my riveting machine. (*Rrrrrrrrrrrr.*)

They jumped into the plane and started the *motors.* (*Arrrrr-rrrr.*) They taxied down the runway and took off, with the *motors* roaring. (*Arrrrrrrrr.*)

Outside the *rain* was getting worse. (*Shshshshshshsh.*) They checked the *props* (*Arrrrrrrrr*), but they were all there! Saturday was still busy *riveting* inside the plane. (*Rrrrrrrrrrrr.*)

Saturday asked, "What are we going to do?"

"Drop stink bombs on 'em and radio the sheriff," said our hero, *Jack Armstrong.* (*Hooray!*) "Then the sheriff can tell them by their smell!"

Right away they were over the ranch and saw the rustlers. Saturday heaved the first *smelly bomb* (*Whistle . . . P-Shew!*) and *another* (*Whistle . . . P-Shew!*) and a *third one* (*Whistle . . . P-Shew!*)

The rustlers ran out with their hands up (to their noses, that is) and Saturday and *Jack Armstrong* (*Hooray!*) made their way back to headquarters.

The *rain* was still pouring down (*Shshshshshshsh*) as they put the plane in the hangar, and cut off the *motors* (*Arrrrrrrrrrr*—let sound die out). Saturday went back to his *riveting* (*Rrrrrr-rrrrr*). Jack ate his hero cereal and went to sleep. This closed another case in the life of the 200 per cent all-American boy, JACK ARMSTRONG. (*Hooray!*)

FUN WITH MOTIONS

Row Sway. Seated in an auditorium, cross hands in front, take hands of neighbor on left or right. Slight pull of everyone with right hand causes entire row to sway, and same with left hand. Try it with one row starting to right, next behind going to left.

Clap Hello. Have everyone extend both hands directly to front, palms facing. Clap hands four times, slap thighs four times, stamp floor left, right, left, right. Repeat twice more, at end saying good and loud, "Hello."

"The Official." To greet or honor someone, many groups use this clap rhythm: 1-2-3-4, 1-2, 1-2, (Commas for pauses) 1-2-3-4, 1-2, 1-2, 1-2-3-4, 1-2-3-4, *1*. (At end, big ending clap.) If anyone has missed the rhythm, he starts over. "Cowboy version" is to do, during last two sets of 4 counts, long whoop as group is clapping 1-2-3-4, and tremendous whoop! at end.

Pat Head, Rub Tummy. Pat your head with one hand, rub stomach with other. Now reverse hands. (See how much harder it is?)

Change Seats. "In ten seconds after the signal, I shall expect you to be in your new seat. Those born in January, February, and March will be to my far left; April, May, June to left center; July, August, September to right center, and the rest to the right. When you move, get acquainted with your neighbors because I might call on you. Ready? Go!"

STRETCHERS

Let's Get Acquainted. "All right, let's get acquainted. Everybody stand up. Now shout out your name as loud as you can." (Wait for them to do it.) "Louder!" (They do it again.) "I couldn't quite hear." (They do it again.) "Fine—now, sit down!"

Exercises. Get all to stand and follow directions of this exercise:

Hands on your hips, hands on your knees,
Put them behind you, if you please!

Touch your shoulders, touch your nose,
Touch your ears, touch your toes,
Raise your hands high in the air,
At your sides; on your hair.
Raise your hands high as before,
While you clap, "ONE, TWO, THREE, FOUR."
My hands upon my head I place,
On my shoulders, on my face,
Then I raise them up on high,
Make my fingers quickly fly,
Put them out in front of me,
And gently clap them—ONE, TWO, THREE.

"Thank you—be seated." (This is a fine, quick rester.)

Correlation Exercises

1. Have group try grasping nose with right hand, right ear with left hand. Change. Continue changing with increasing speed.
2. Make circle with right arm; at same time, figure eight with right foot.
3. Starting with arms at sides, raise right hand shoulder high; then left hand. Right hand above head, then left hand. Move hands back down in same manner. Try several times.

O'Grady Says ... (Simon Says ...). The leader calls out command to group. If it is "O'Grady says ... stand up," all stand up. If only command "Stand up" is given, they are to stay still. Each does his own "bookkeeping" and sees who gets through with fewest errors.

Obey and Omit. Much like preceding test. Direction is given first, like "Nod your heads—Ooooooo-bey." (All nod heads.) If "Ooooooo-mit" is given, direction is not followed. (Sample acts: hop on foot, clap hands, turn around, mark time, shake hands with somebody.)

Birds Fly. Leader calls out names of birds or animals. If creature flies, group is supposed to make flying motions with hands. If creature does not fly, it remains still. On "Ducks fly" all would flap, but on "Horses fly" they would not.

Going with the Wind. As leader makes up sketchy story about traveler and mentions names of winds, people face that direction and do proper wind motion. *South Wind:* gentle waving motions.

East Wind: stronger motions. *North Wind:* violent motions and strong "ooooing" sound; *West Wind:* swing arms around freely. *Tornado:* turn around violently in place.

Three "Relays" (for group in auditorium)

HAND SQUEEZE. Everyone reaches sideward to grasp hands of people on left and right. On signal, person at end of each row at extreme right squeezes hand of person next to him. This squeeze is passed on from person to person until it reaches extreme left, then squeeze is returned in same way until it reaches original starter.

SHOULDER PINCH. Hands on shoulders or around waists of persons to left or right. A pinch or squeeze is passed from left to right down row, returned.

BACK SLAP. Everyone stands, faces right. Person at rear of line slaps person in front of him on back. This slap is passed up line to front, then everyone turns around and slap is back in other direction. "No one slaps until he has been slapped."

Chorus. Everyone extends hands forward in front, palms inward. On signal, everyone raises right arm up over head of person on his right and places hand on shoulder of that person. On second signal, do same with left arm over head of person on left. On third signal everybody squeezes! (When right arm is placed, everyone yells "Hip"; when left arm is placed, "Hip"; and a grand squeeze for "Hooray!")

I Went to Paris. Keep doing what you start until end. Leader says, "I went to Paris and bought a pair of shoes (*shuffle feet*), a pair of gloves (*open and close right fist*), an umbrella (*open and close left fist*), a hat (*nod head*), a pair of glasses (*blink eyelids*), and a set of false teeth (*open and close mouth*).

The Orchestra. While singing familiar song, leader is to play violin in pantomime. Rest are divided into groups, each assigned one instrument, such as trumpet, drums, trombone. Everybody plays his own instrument incessantly until leader shifts to his particular instrument. Then he must play violin. Fun is in quick shifts.

Clap to Rhythm. For an exerciser, stand and clap to rhythm of song, like "Coming 'Round the Mountain" or "Dixie" or "Yankee Doodle." Or tramp out rhythm, marching in place.

Friendly Handshake (standing). "This is a friendly meeting. Will you shake hands with your near neighbor?" "Now with another." "Now, let's all act together, once again. Everybody . . . turn around and shake hands with the person behind you!" (If all do it, there is no one there to shake with, of course.)

Fancy Handshakes (standing). "We want you to greet the folks near you tonight with special handshakes. Turn to a neighbor and shake hands:

1. Pump Handle Style. Pump up and down, exaggerated manner.
2. Fisherman's Style. Take another person's hand, let hands wiggle backward and forward on push-pull basis.
3. Model T Ford. Crank.
4. Paul Bunyan Style. Each person starts shaking hands in usual manner, but grasps own thumb with free hand, and both saw away. Yell "Timber" when tree is down.
5. "Hydramatic" Style. Hands just lie in each other without grip. Reason: "No clutch."
6. Milkmaid Style. One of the two interlaces fingers of both his or her hands, thumbs pointing up. Turn this combination upside down, exposing thumbs to "milkmaid," the other person, who hangs on and "milks."

FUN WITH YOUR NEIGHBOR

Face person next to you and do one or two of these stunts.

Fingers Up. Hold up fists at each other. On signal from leader (One, Two, Three, *Go!*), each will hold up as many fingers as he or she wishes. One who calls out first correct total of elevated fingers on all four hands gets one point. Play about five times.

Opposites. Decide which is to be the person, which the mirror. "Person" then faces "mirror," and "mirror" must "reflect back" what "person" does. Then shift roles.

Make 'em Yawn. Decide which will try first. Then that person keeps yawning, until he makes his neighbor yawn. Reverse it, if desired.

Make 'em Laugh. Same as "Make 'em yawn," except that you try to make your neighbor laugh.

GAGS AND GROUP RESPONSES

Who's Boss? Fold your hands together, in your lap. If left thumb is on top, you are dominant personality who tries to run things in your own home. (Try hands other way than "natural" way. It isn't so comfortable, is it?)

Scotchman's Money. Bend middle fingers of both hands down into palms, placing knuckles together to represent the roof. All other fingers are raised, with corresponding finger tips of both hands touching, and coin is placed between tips of ring fingers. "You can separate the Frenchman (little fingers), the German (thumbs), the American (forefingers), but you can't separate the Scotchman (ring fingers) from his money without raising the roof."

Mind Reading. Offer to read minds of any persons in entire group. Ask them if they'll give you dime if you can do it. (Keep trying until someone will answer "yes." Concentrate! Then announce to person that you've read his mind—he thinks you're not going to get that dime!)

How Many Birthdays You've Had. "I can tell you how many birthdays you've had," you say to an individual. "If I can, will you get me a coke?" When agreement is made, you indicate that he's had one birthday, and you're not sure how many anniversaries since then!

Palm Read. Get man volunteer to come forward for pretty girl to read his palm. She tells him several things, ending that he's somewhat of flirt, letting girl hold his hand in public like this!

Reading an Announcement (or Bulletin). Person comes in, hands leader paper. "Here's an announcement they asked me to read," says leader. Scans it hurriedly, hands it back to bearer, and says, "I've read it."

Getting Three Shirts from a Yard. While gathering is in progress, person comes through with some cloth goods. Leader says, "Hello, Bill, what you got there?"

"Got some material for my wife. She thinks she can get three shirts out of a yard." (*Leaves. Comes back later with three shirts.*) Leader: "Did your wife get these three shirts from a yard?" "No, but I did—out of my neighbor's (or name of someone present) yard."

Feed Bag. Performer comes through with feed bag. Leader says, "What do you have there?" "A feed bag. I gotta date." "You have a date? Why the feed bag then?" "Got a dinner date, and my girl eats like a horse." (*Leaves quickly.*)

Case to Court. Person comes through with soft-drink case. Leader asks, "What do you have that case for?" "Gonna take my case to court." (*He leaves. Comes back after an interval.*) Leader asks, "Well, how did you get along?" Person says, "You know I told you I was taking the case to court?" "Sure." "Didn't do any good. My girl wanted something softer to sit on." (*Leaves.*)

Another version of this has him with stepladder (taking case to higher court) and finally with three bottles (case was rejected, as three bottles do not make case).

Pronunciation. "How do you pronounce p-o-k-e? Say it three times!" Leader says it with group. "Poke, poke, poke."

"How do you pronounce f-o-l-k? "Folk, folk, folk."

"How do you pronounce the white of an egg?" (Usually it will be "Yolk, yolk, yolk.")

Facial Stretcher. Give large rubber band to each person taking part. Each puts it over head, around neck, with band starting on tip of nose. The object is to see who can get his band down over mouth and chin, and onto neck alone by using face muscles only.

Sight Tester. This is test of your sight. Fold your hands in your laps. Is your left thumb on top? Right thumb? Now, concentrate on top thumb. Concentrate. Slowly close your eyes. Are they shut tight? Dark, isn't it?

Little Red Band. Ask person, with small group around (such as at table) if he or she likes Russian music. Usually the answer is yes.

In which case, bring out red plastic band, from package of crackers or gum or cigarettes, and say, "Well, here's a little red band for you, then!"

Poke Your Fist Through a Ring. Can you poke your fist through a ring? (Hold a ring near your fist, then "poke" through it, to the elbow with a finger.)

Write Any Color. I have a pencil (or pen or chalk) here that will write any color. (Someone says, "purple," so you write p-u-r-p-l-e.)

Plane Landing. Stunt for two loud voices, Pilot and Control Tower, from different sides of room, out of sight. From Pilot's side of room, third person out of sight makes sound of airplane propellers. Group leader says, "I think I hear a plane overhead."

PILOT (*yelling loud*): "Pilot to control tower, pilot to control tower—I'm coming in. Give me landing instructions!"

CONTROL TOWER (*in loud monotone as if on microphone*): "Control tower to pilot, control tower to pilot—why are you yelling so loud?"

PILOT: "Pilot to control tower, pilot to control tower—I haven't got a radio!"

Prove That a Beehive Is a Bad Potato

A beehive is a bee holder, isn't it?
A beholder is a spectator. Right?
What is a specked 'tater but a bad 'tater?

Wire for Bill (*fill in name of person present*)! Knock on door, someone who is "in" on gag goes to door, apparently talks to person, takes yellow envelope, and announces, "Wire for Bill." When Bill comes forward, envelope is set aside, and under it is wire (strand, roll, spool—even wire coat hanger). (This gag could be introduction for birthday song for person.)

Beating Around the Bush

Person moves through group, patting several folk on head. "What are you doing?" he is asked. "Beating around the bush," is answer.

Mass Fortune Telling. Ask all people to look at their own hands, or to do as directed. In some cases person himself is to answer, in others his neighbor tells him. (There is another version of this in *Handy Stunts,* listed in Bibliography.)

1. Look into your hands. Do you have corns on your hands? How many do? You have been doing hard work.
   How many have no corns? You're too light for heavy work and too heavy for light work.
2. Look at your fingers. How many are long and slender? You are sensitive. Watch your temper.

How many are shorter, plumper? You are sensitive, too, but watch your *diet!*

3. How many of you boys (men) have a circle around your thumb? Be careful when hitch-hiking!

4. Now, do as I tell you: "Close fist, open hand, close fist, open hand, open hand, close fist. . . ." (Make it faster and faster.) *Hold it.* Just like that. How many have your fist closed? You're closefisted. Hand open? You're openhanded.

5. Look at your life line. That's the one that curves in the middle of your hand. Look at it closely! Well, that's it, all right, but I don't know anything about it, so we'll just Throw Out the Life Line!

6. Now, put your hand on top of your head. You are in touch with the biggest thing that keeps you from getting ahead!

7. Now touch your feet. You are a person of deep feeling, but for some I sense defeat!

8. Ask your neighbor: Do I have dark circles under my eyes? If you have that's a sign you've been traveling. Those bags are traveling bags.

9. Take a pencil or pen, hold it fourteen inches from your eyes. Open your eyes, close them, open them again. Do you see the point?

10. Reach into your pocketbook or billfold and take out a bill. Hold it between your finger and your thumb. Turn it over. Take your fingernail and make a mark down the middle the long way, and look at the bill. You have a marked attraction for the opposite sex!

11. Make bracelets by drawing your fist down toward your wrist. Look at the lower bracelet. How many have an unbroken line? You're level-headed. How many have a broken line? You go to pieces in a pinch.

    Now the upper line. How many have a broken line? Your eyes are bigger than your stomachs. An unbroken line? You have an unlimited capacity for food!

Little Girl, Little Girl, Look Out for That . . .

1. Cliff

    What clifffffffffffff? (Sound as if dropping over cliff.)

2. Clothesline.

What clothes line-ine-ine-ine?

3. Golf ball.

What golf balp? (Sound as if golf ball has just gone down throat.)

4. Revolving door.

What revolving door, revolving door, revolving door?

5. Mud puddle.

What mud puddle-duddle-duddle-duddle?

6. Washing machine?

What washing machine—machine—machine—machine?

(Action: Put knees together and do knee bend sideways, like dasher of washing machine.)

7. Quicksand. "What quick sluuup?" (Draw in breath quickly.)

8. Little girl on the bicycle, look out for that glass!

"What glasssssssssssss?"

Candy Store. Let's play candy store. "Here, take this string and hold on," says person starting this. "Now, let's get some others to hold on." When several are holding, it is explained that this is a "candy store" because here are some suckers on the line!

Spring. Gather to the front some people to be trees, birds, babbling brooks. Then ask for volunteer to be most important part, the hero. When he comes up, you have him run among trees. "Maybe the rest of you wonder how we know it is spring," you say. "That's easy. The sap is running!"

Book Ends. Get two volunteers to come forward and hold book by pressing their heads together with book between them. Ask if anybody can guess what this represents? (Two elephants playing book ends.)

Organ grinder. "You know, I used to play the organ, quite a while ago!"

"You did? Why did you stop?"

"Oh, the monkey died."

Paul Revere's Ride.[2] Write out slips containing all the numbered items in the following story, shuffle them, and distribute among the group. As the narrator reads the script, he calls for each number as he comes to it, making an obvious pause, at which time the person holding the slip of that number fills in the blank. Each member of a very small group may hold several slips. Here is the story:

THE STORY OF PAUL REVERE'S RIDE

In history, my friend, if your memory clicks, you will remember that it was 1776 when Paul Revere and his trusty horse ran through the Colonies to the Britains' remorse!

Now, life in the colonies was as dull as their axes, but old King George kept raising the taxes. But he didn't know what the colonists knew, that he'd (1. *Bit off more than he could chew*)!

One of his collectors said to a colonist lady, "Pay up your taxes and I don't mean maybe." She just replied, (2. *I can't give you anything but love, baby!*). Now the old king's agents were watching everybody—each Tom, Dick, Harry, and Sonia. As all in the American colonies knew (3. *The eyes of taxes were uponya*). But one of them once gave an answer to the Bureau of Eternal Revenue that made Old King George nearly bust. He said, (4. *You tell 'em, Pieface—'cause you've got the crust!*).

After this the King called up Cornwallis or somebody and said, "Let us send our navy to America with (5. *three sheets in the wind*)." Now, wind of this came to Paul Revere's wife. She was cooking away one day for dear life, when she thought of it all and she said to Paul, "Hark, I think that there is (6. *something rotten in Denmark!*). Isn't this the day that some smarties or smarty will irritate the town with the (7. *Boston Tea Party*)?"

"How do you know?" said Revere. "It's a mystery."

She said, "It's all in American history. Tonight is the night that Dick Tracy will perch up in the loft of the Old North Church, and down the streets of Boston your horse is to lurch!"

Now, Paul had been itching for a night out, so this was his chance. To make it seem convincing he protested, (8. *"Baby, it's cold outside!"*), but she told him to go anyway. He went right over to the home of his pal and started to explain. Tracy said, (9. *"I didn't get your drift! Snow again!"*). After Paul explained things carefully, he agreed to help in the loft at Old North Church if there were no (10. *bats in the belfry*).

So Paul mounted his steed and waited for the signal. Tracy heard a redcoat say, (11. *"Sit down, you're rocking the boat!"*) which told him they were coming by sea. He hung up a lantern and Paul Revere jumped on his horse, saying (12. *"Giddy-up, Napoleon, it looks like rain!"*). But being a jewelry man, he decided to change the horse's name, so he called out as he left town, (13. *"Heigh-ho, Silver. Away!"*).

As he rode he would cry out (14. *"To arms, to arms! The British are coming!"*). Benjamin Franklin thanked him and asked how he enjoyed the Boston Tea Party. He answered, (15. *"Good to the last drop"*).

As he passed the home of Marilyn Monroe he called, (14. *"To arms, to arms, the British are coming!"*).

By this time it was getting light on the Lexington Common. The men gathered around him in sixty seconds and were known as minute men. One said, (16. *"What's buzzin', cousin?"*). He told them (14. *"To arms, to arms! The British are coming!"*). Molly Pitcher wanted to know what the men should do, and he said, (17. *"Shoot them in the whites of their eyes."*)

The men crouched behind breastworks of sardine boxes and candy wrappers, and with cries of (18. *Remember the Alamo!*), (19. *Remember Pearl Harbor!*), (20. *Remember the Johnstown Flood!*), they let the British have it, and won a great victory.

Betsy Ross made them a new flag with red and white striped suspenders to match; the Pepsodent Company gave them a year's supply of toothpaste; and Paul rode back to a cold breakfast, a cold wife, and uttered this famous word in front of his cold house: (21. *"Whoa!"*).

Bible Story. (This is monologue, in which male actor imitates both Lot and Lot's wife. To represent Lot, he takes long marching steps, marking time in place, but for wife, he takes mincing steps, almost running to keep up with her husband, all in place. He talks in low voice for husband, falsetto for wife. Let group guess what it is, after performance is over.)

MAN: We've got to keep going ahead, we've got to keep marching forward.

WOMAN: Well, I don't understand it all, I just don't.

MAN: We have our orders. We're to leave the city and not look back.

WOMAN: I don't like to do it. I don't want our house burned up.

MAN: We were part of that wicked city. We deserve it.

WOMAN: Well, anyway, I'm glad Mrs. Methuselah's house is getting burned too.

MAN: You shouldn't talk about your neighbors like that.

WOMAN: Well, I don't like her. Did you bring my new hat?

MAN: I have more important things to think about than your hat!

WOMAN: It goes so well with this dress. Do you think we could take just a little peek backward?

MAN: You know what we are supposed to do. We're to leave town and *not* look back.

WOMAN: Not even one little teensy-weensy peek?

MAN: Not a look of any kind.

WOMAN: Couldn't we act as if we're going around a corner and accidentally look back?

MAN: You know you're not supposed to do that.

WOMAN: I think I will.

MAN: You'd better not!

WOMAN: Yes, I think I will.

MAN (*warning*): You'd . . . better . . . not! (*He walks along a bit in silence.*) . . . Are you there? . . . Are you there? . . . Are you there? (*Stops, then walks backward a few steps, licks finger, and without turning around, reaches finger behind him, apparently touches her, then tastes finger, nods solemnly.*)

FEATS AND PUZZLES
(*See also Physical Feats and Tricks in Chapter 17*)

Stand on Right Foot. With eyes closed, can you stand on tiptoes, then raise right foot?

Coin Grab. One player has coin in his hand, palm up. Other has his hand open, about 8 to 12 inches above hand of other. Object: to make top hand swoop down and grab coin from other hand before it can close on coin. (Coin holder has little chance.)

Breath Holding. Have legitimate test, seeing who can hold breath longest. Someone has almost won. Then in "finals," person takes deep breath, holds it awhile, takes balloon from pocket, blows breath into it, and "holds his breath" (in balloon) indefinitely.

Ice-Talking. Holding piece of ice in hand, player starts talking to his opponent. As long as he keeps talking he may hold ice, and his time is kept with stop watch. When he must give up talking, he hands to opponent who talks and holds ice.

Melt the Olive. Olive (or cherry or other small object) is frozen into ice cube. See who can melt cube with his hands first. (Using fingers to release olive not allowed.)

Touch Wrist. Can you press your hand forward and make your finger tips touch your wrist?

Six-Zero. Can you make figure six in air with your finger, zero with your toe at same time?

Thumb Rotation. Can you twirl one thumb clockwise, one counter-clockwise, at same time?

Clap Out Rhythm. Individual or group claps out rhythm of song for another individual or group to guess.

Whose Flag? International game is to line up flags of number of nations for people to guess (or to report on, if they know).

Handcuffed Couples. Tie one person's string to each wrist (the string is about 3 to 3½ inches long) and loop other person's string over that one before tying also to both wrists. Both are "handcuffed" to each other. The object: to get unhandcuffed without breaking string. (To get loose, put center of one of strings between wrist and loop of partner. They are still tied, but not looped to each other.)

Human Checkers. Six players are arranged on seven chairs, as Girls and Boys:

G G G O B B B
1 2 3   4 5 6

The object is to get them reversed, by moves and jumps in same order, on opposite sides of vacant chair. Solution: G3 moves right. B4 jumps her. B5 moves left. G3 jumps R. G2 jumps B4. G1 moves right. B4 jumps G1. B5 jumps G2. B6 jumps G3. G3 moves right one place. G2 jumps B6. G1 jumps B5. B5 moves left one place. B6 jumps G1. G1 moves right, and there you are.

No moves backward are permitted.

Identify. Mystery voices, owner unseen.

Mystery feet, they being only things seen (under sheet in doorway or under curtain of stage.)

Legs and feet (same idea).

Mystery person (made up to look and sound different, but known to group).

Advertising Slogans. (Read slogan—let group name product.)

Ask the man who owns one. Packard.

Be happy, go lucky. Lucky Strike.

Babies cry for it. Castoria.

They satisfy. Chesterfields.

Covers the earth. Sherwin-Williams.

His master's voice. RCA Victor.

The pause that refreshes. Coca-Cola.

More bounce to the ounce. Pepsi-Cola.

The breakfast of champions. Wheaties.

Snap, Crackle and Pop. Rice Krispies.

. . . For the Tummy. Tums.

57 Varieties. Heinz.

The skin you love to touch. Woodbury Soap.

Hasn't scratched yet. Bon Ami.

Candy mint with the hole. Life Savers.

Soap of beautiful women. Camay.

It likes you. 7-Up.

Wrinkle proof. Botany ties.

99 44/100% pure. Ivory Soap.

Time to re-tire. Fisk Tires.

From contented cows. Carnation Milk.

Chases dirt. Old Dutch Cleanser.

You can whip our cream, but you can't beat our milk! (Give name of a local dairy.)

This truck is driven by a blind man. (Give name of a local Venetian blind company.)

(Also use local slogans for firms that would not be known nationally, such as your community stores, laundries, bakeries.)

Puzzles

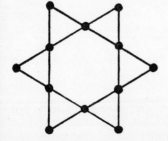
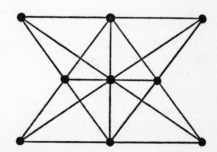

1. Place 12 checkers or coins in 6 rows, so as to have 4 in each row.
2. Make 10 rows of 3 with total of 9 coins or checkers.
3. Place 13 coins in 12 rows and have 3 coins in each row. (Use clock face, with coin in middle.)

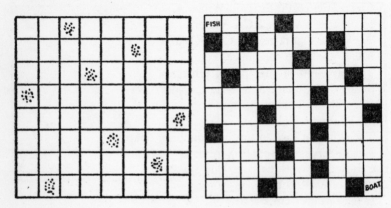

4. Eight-checkers puzzle. Place eight checkers on checkerboard, using all squares, so that no two checkers are in same line horizontally, vertically, or diagonally.
5. Fish-Boat Puzzle. Draw diagram like illustration and see who can get boat to fish in 10 moves or less. Starting in fish corner, see if it is possible to get to boat.

Picture Puzzles

Pictures of various kinds can be pasted on cardboard and cut up into odd shapes, to be put back together. Postcards are good for this, also larger pictures of group activity, taken in past.

Cardboard Puzzles

These two puzzles re-form into perfect squares. (Letters a, b, c, d represent midpoints in sides of squares.)

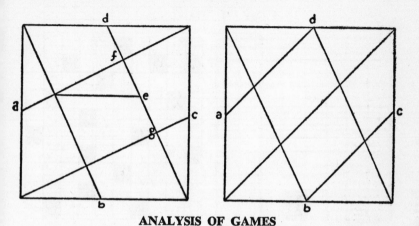

ANALYSIS OF GAMES

A check list follows which may prove useful to recreation leaders. It analyzes most of the games or entertainment items in this chapter, as to time required, type of entertainment, appropriate location, suitable occasion, and age interest.

	READ ALOUD	TIME REQUIRED	GROUP ABSORBER	NOISE	EXERCISER	AUDITORIUM	BANQUET, TABLE	SMALL PARTY	LARGE PARTY	CHILDREN	YOUTH	ADULTS	GAG	GROUP CO-OPERATION	INFORMAL (JUST STANDING AROUND)	INDIVIDUAL PERFORMER	FAMILY NIGHT
DREAMS	✓	10	✓			✓	✓	✓	✓		✓	✓		✓	✓	✓	
YOUR HOROSCOPE	✓	10-15				✓	✓	✓	✓		✓	✓			✓	✓	
STEAM ENGINE IN THE ROUNDHOUSE (FUN WITH NOISES)		5	✓	✓		✓	✓	✓	✓	✓	✓	✓		✓			✓
THE FROG POND		2		✓		✓	✓	✓	✓	✓	✓	✓		✓			
BIG SNEEZE		2	✓	✓		✓	✓	✓	✓	✓	✓	✓		✓			✓
CALLIOPE		5		✓		✓	✓	✓	✓	✓	✓	✓		✓	✓		✓
HOORAY		5		✓		✓	✓	✓	✓		✓	✓	✓	✓			✓
HOW THEY CLAP		1		✓		✓	✓	✓	✓		✓	✓	✓			✓	✓
WING, WING!		1		✓		✓	✓	✓	✓		✓	✓	✓	✓		✓	✓
GROUP RESPONSE		3		✓		✓	✓	✓	✓	✓	✓	✓		✓	✓		✓
FOOTBALL		5	✓	✓		✓	✓	✓	✓	✓	✓	✓		✓			✓
STAGNET	✓	8	✓	✓		✓	✓	✓	✓	✓	✓			✓			✓
ROW SWAY (FUN WITH MOTIONS)		1		✓	✓	✓	✓			✓	✓	✓		✓			✓
CLAP HELLO		5		✓		✓	✓	✓	✓	✓	✓	✓		✓			✓
"THE OFFICIAL"		3		✓		✓	✓	✓	✓	✓	✓	✓		✓			✓
PAT HEAD, RUB TUMMY		2				✓	✓	✓	✓	✓	✓	✓		✓	✓		✓
CHANGE SEATS		3				✓	✓		✓	✓	✓	✓		✓			✓
LET'S GET ACQUAINTED (STRETCHERS)		2	✓		✓	✓	✓		✓	✓	✓	✓		✓			✓
CORRELATION EXERCISES		3		✓	✓	✓	✓		✓	✓	✓	✓		✓			✓
O'GRADY SAYS		5	✓	✓	✓	✓	✓		✓	✓	✓	✓		✓			✓
OBEY AND OMIT		5	✓	✓	✓	✓	✓	✓	✓	✓	✓	✓		✓			✓
BIRDS FLY		5	✓			✓	✓	✓	✓	✓	✓	✓		✓			✓
GOING WITH THE WIND		5	✓	✓	✓	✓	✓		✓	✓	✓	✓		✓			✓
THREE RELAYS		5			✓	✓	✓		✓		✓	✓		✓			✓
I WENT TO PARIS	✓	3		✓	✓	✓	✓	✓	✓	✓	✓	✓		✓			✓
THE ORCHESTRA		3			✓	✓	✓	✓	✓	✓	✓	✓		✓			✓
CLAP TO RHYTHM		3	✓	✓	✓	✓	✓	✓	✓	✓	✓	✓		✓			✓
FRIENDLY HANDSHAKE		1	✓	✓	✓	✓	✓			✓	✓	✓	✓	✓			✓
FANCY HANDSHAKES		5	✓	✓	✓	✓	✓		✓	✓	✓	✓		✓			✓
FINGERS UP		3	✓	✓		✓	✓	✓	✓	✓	✓	✓		✓			✓
FOX, GUN, HUNTER		5		✓	✓	✓	✓	✓	✓	✓	✓	✓		✓			✓
WHO'S BOSS? (GAGS AND GROUP RESPONSES)		1				✓	✓	✓	✓		✓	✓		✓			✓
SCOTCHMAN'S MONEY		1				✓	✓	✓	✓		✓	✓	✓	✓	✓		✓
MIND READING		1				✓	✓		✓		✓	✓	✓	✓	✓	✓	✓
HOW MANY BIRTHDAYS YOU'VE HAD		1				✓	✓	✓	✓		✓	✓	✓			✓	✓
PALM READ		1				✓	✓		✓		✓	✓	✓				
READING AN ANNOUNCEMENT		1				✓	✓		✓		✓	✓	✓				
GETTING THREE SHIRTS FROM A YARD		1				✓	✓	✓	✓		✓	✓	✓				✓
FEED BAG		1				✓	✓	✓	✓		✓	✓	✓				
CASE TO COURT		1				✓	✓	✓	✓		✓	✓	✓				✓
PRONUNCIATION		1				✓	✓	✓	✓	✓	✓	✓	✓	✓	✓	✓	✓
FACIAL STRETCHER		1				✓	✓	✓	✓	✓	✓	✓		✓	✓	✓	✓

	READ ALOUD	TIME REQUIRED	GROUP ABSORBER	NOISE	EXERCISER	AUDITORIUM	BANQUET, TABLE	SMALL PARTY	LARGE PARTY	CHILDREN	YOUTH	ADULTS	GAG	GROUP COOPERATION	INFORMAL (JUST STANDING AROUND)	INDIVIDUAL PERFORMANCE	FAMILY NIGHT
SIGHT TESTER		1				✓	✓	✓	✓	✓	✓	✓	✓	✓			✓
LITTLE RED BAND		1	✓			✓	✓	✓	✓		✓	✓	✓		✓	✓	✓
POKE YOUR FIST THROUGH A RING		1	✓			✓	✓	✓	✓		✓	✓	✓		✓	✓	✓
WRITE ANY COLOR		1	✓					✓	✓		✓	✓	✓		✓	✓	✓
PLANE LANDING		1				✓	✓		✓		✓	✓	✓				
PROVE THAT A BEEHIVE IS A BAD POTATO		1	✓			✓	✓	✓	✓		✓	✓	✓		✓	✓	
WIRE FOR BILL _____!		1				✓	✓	✓	✓		✓	✓	✓				
BEATING AROUND THE BUSH		1	✓			✓	✓	✓	✓		✓	✓	✓		✓	✓	✓
MASS FORTUNE TELLING	✓	8	✓			✓	✓	✓	✓		✓	✓			✓		✓
LITTLE GIRL, LITTLE GIRL, LOOK OUT FOR THAT...		3	✓			✓	✓	✓	✓		✓	✓	✓		✓	✓	✓
BOOK ENDS		3				✓	✓	✓	✓		✓	✓	✓		✓		✓
ORGAN GRINDER		1				✓	✓	✓	✓		✓	✓	✓		✓		✓
PAUL REVERE'S RIDE		10				✓	✓	✓	✓		✓	✓					✓
BIBLE STORY	✓	3				✓	✓	✓	✓		✓	✓			✓	✓	✓
(FEATS AND PUZZLES) STAND ON RIGHT FOOT		1			✓	✓	✓	✓	✓		✓	✓		✓	✓	✓	✓
COIN GRAB		1			✓	✓	✓	✓	✓		✓	✓		✓	✓	✓	✓
BREATH HOLDING		1				✓	✓	✓	✓		✓	✓			✓		✓
ICE-TALKING		5	✓			✓	✓	✓	✓		✓	✓			✓		✓
MELT THE OLIVE		5				✓	✓	✓	✓		✓	✓			✓		✓
TOUCH WRIST		1				✓	✓	✓	✓	✓	✓	✓		✓	✓	✓	✓
SIX-ZERO		1				✓	✓	✓	✓	✓	✓	✓		✓	✓	✓	✓
THUMB ROTATION		1				✓	✓		✓	✓	✓	✓		✓	✓	✓	✓
WHOSE FLAG?		10				✓	✓	✓	✓	✓	✓	✓		✓			✓
ADVERTISING SLOGANS		10				✓	✓	✓	✓	✓	✓	✓		✓			✓
HANDCUFFED COUPLES		10	✓					✓	✓		✓	✓		✓			
HUMAN CHECKERS		10-20						✓	✓		✓	✓		✓			
IDENTIFY...		10-20						✓	✓		✓	✓		✓			
CLAP OUT RHYTHM		5	✓			✓	✓	✓	✓	✓	✓	✓		✓	✓		✓
PUZZLES		10-20					✓	✓	✓		✓	✓		✓			✓

13

Humor

THE GOOD RECREATION leader differentiates, of course, between humor and wit, and so he uses only that material which injures no one's feelings. In other words, humor laughs *with* people and is kindly; wit laughs *at* people and is unsportsmanlike. Such types of entertainment as ridicule, cynicism, sarcasm, fun at others' expense do not build group spirit. But there are many occasions when humor may be appropriately employed to lighten the atmosphere either briefly, as in conundrums and smart sayings, verbal gags, "daffynitions," and boners, or at greater length as in amusing stories based on an absurd situation, or a play on words, incongruities of time, parodies, or spoonerisms. Samples of all these types of humor are found in this chapter.

WHEN TO USE HUMOR

There are many recreational uses for humor, for the true spirit of good humor is that of fun and laughter. One leader says that humor is for the "lazy man's kit," since it takes so few muscles to smile or laugh!

1. Use humor just for fun as you talk in high school or college gatherings, men's or women's clubs, entertaining guests. Jokes? Read 'em aloud.
2. Speakers, toastmasters, masters of ceremonies find humor useful for relaxing a group or driving home a point.
3. Use on signs for trees or walls of a camp or institutional building or on a home bulletin board, especially pointed jokes, "daffynitions," or boners.

4. Make stand-up cards for the meal or banquet table, with a bit of humor on each. Have people read theirs to each other. Write a joke or a quip on the back of a place card; ask people to read theirs as a conversation starter.

5. Tell or read humorous material to fill in small gaps in programs. (Simply read one bit at a time, giving time for it to "soak in" and for the group to laugh.) Boners or short stories are especially good, but smart sayings or gags bring their fun, too.

6. Related jokes and smart sayings may be put together in combination to make skits, especially conversation between two persons. Many short skits are actually elaborated jokes.

7. In high school and college gatherings, especially freshman affairs, these can be used as conversation starters. To get partners, give boys the first halves of jokes, girls the second halves (the joke slips have been cut in two). To find a partner, find the other half of your joke!

8. In letter writing, especially to those who might be lonely—for instance, servicemen. Don't forget to save cartoons and send to them

CONUNDRUMS
(*Time: 1 to 10 minutes*)

Read these conundrums aloud to groups. If they can't answer, give the answer:

1. Figure this out. A man said, "How's your dog?" The other said, "I did." (He understood it as "house your dog.")

2. What is bought by the yard, but worn by the foot? (A rug.)

3. How can you carry water in a sieve? (Freeze it.)

4. What is the difference between a Northern Eskimo and a Southern Eskimo? (A Northern Eskimo says, "Glub-glub," but a Southern one says, "Glub-glub, you-all.")

5. Why do hens lay eggs only in the daytime? (Because at night they become roosters.)

6. What is the best way you know to preserve peaches? (Don't introduce them to good-looking young men.)

7. What is a go-getter? (A man out of gas, two miles from a filling station.)

8. Why did the chicken cross the road? (Because her boy friend was over there at the drugstore.)

9. What is a sheep after he is six years old? (Seven years old.)

10. Explain this situation: A train is on the track in Norway, with a Norwegian engineer, headed toward Sweden. A Swedish train is on the same track, with an intoxicated engineer, headed toward Norway. They both continue to their destinations, running on the same track. Why is there no wreck? (Because Norse is Norse, and Souse is Souse, and never the twain shall meet.)

11. But what if they should meet? (Twain weck.)

12. "Did you ever hear the story about the little red wagon?" "How does it go?"

13. "Have you time for a couple of dillies?" (you ask the group). "Sure," is the usual reply. "Okay, then. Dilly, dilly!"

14. Why was the little strawberry worried? (Because his mom and pop were in a jam.)

15. What is a good thing to lose? (A bad reputation.)

16. What turns green in the spring? (Christmas jewelry.)

17. How is racing a horse like eating an ice cream cone? (The more you lick each one the faster it goes.)

18. Can you add three 9's and make 10? (9 and 9/9.)

19. This is a sign in an English hotel. Can you figure it out? "Heresto pands pen dasoci al hou rinhar mlessmirt ha nd funlet friends hipre ign be just an dk indan devil sp eakof no ne." (Here stop and spend a social hour in harmless mirth and fun, let friendship reign, be just and kind, and evil speak of none.)

20. Did you ever see a: barn dance, horse fly, board walk, milk pail, house fly, lip stick, bottle neck, banana split . . . (Encourage group to fill in some more.)

21. What is a question that to answer truthfully, you cannot answer no? (What does y-e-s spell?)

22. Question that cannot be answered truthfully with "yes." (Are you asleep?)

23. A question to which you cannot answer "yes" or "no" without incriminating yourself. ("Have you stopped mistreating your family?")

24. In a luggage shop a man priced some luggage. "This size for

$20; this size for $10." The man said, "So do I." (Key: this sighs for $20!)

Bible Conundrums (Time: 1 to 10 minutes)

When was tennis mentioned in the Bible? (When David served in the courts of Saul.)

When were cigarettes first mentioned? (When Jezebel lit off on a camel.)

Who were the shortest and next-shortest people in the Bible? (Shortest was Bildad the shoe height.) (Next-shortest was Nehi-miah.)

When did Solomon make love to the Queen of Sheba? (When he fed her ambrosia and nectar.)

Why did Moses take *cheese* into the ark? (We don't know, but it should have been Noah, anyway.)

SMART SAYINGS
(*Time: 1 to 10 minutes*)

I said to the hostess on the plane, "How about stepping out?" She answered, "All right," and went to the side door, saying, "This way out."

One swallow does not make a swimmer.

The reason a dog has so many friends is that he wags his tail instead of his tongue.

Never slam the door on a fellow's puckered-up lips.

"What would you do if you had a million dollars?"
"Nothing."

Did you hear about the Texan who got engaged and gave his girl a diamond—mine?

Everybody wears a bathing suit in Atlantic City, but it's mostly a matter of form.

"Yes, ma'am, we ship out our fertilizer to the small towns to make them grow."

Men fall in love with women who ask questions they can answer!

"Do big ships like this sink very often, captain?"
"No, only once."

There are just two kinds of people who make foolish marriages —men and women.

VERBAL GAGS
(Time: 1 to 10 minutes)

Sometimes it's the verbal gag with a punch line that will unbend a stiff moment and pull the group together in a hearty laugh.

Have you ever heard these three special sneezes? Try them:
The suspicious sneeze—Whoisshe?
The chocolate sneeze—Hershey!
The hayfever toast—Here's looking atchoooo!

The train stopped with a jerk. (The jerk got off and the train went on.)

A thick-haired gent was bothering a bald one with remarks. The bald head replied, "The deader the wood, the longer the moss."

Sharp, and the world sharps with you; flat, and you flat alone!
(RUSSELL AMES COOK)

"What do you do for exercise?"
"Oh, I read mysteries and let my flesh crawl."

Did you hear of the fellow who holds the new record for staying under water? Twenty-one minutes! (Services tomorrow at 2:00.)

"What are you taking for your dyspepsia?"
"I don't know—make me an offer!"

"Guess I'll hit the hay," said the farmer, as he slid off the barn.

Say, have you heard about the new men's perfume direct from Texas? It's called Corral No. 5.

"DAFFYNITIONS"
(Time: 1 to 10 minutes)

This form of humor, usually based on the pun or sound of words, is generally popular in those circles in which people like to play with words. Children would generally not understand "daffynitions" well enough to enjoy them.

CYNIC. Article of kitchen equipment.

DECEIT. The place you sit.

ARREARS. What we listen with.

REPARTEE. An insult with its tuxedo on.

DIETING. Triumph of the mind over platter.

BACTERIA. The rear entrance of a cafeteria.

TRUE GENTLEMAN. When your husband holds open the door while you carry in the groceries.

BIGAMIST. A man who has made the same mistake twice.

DIVINE. What grapes grow on.

SADDLE. A big town in the State of Washington.

MINER. One who can make a living by going into the hole.

PILLAGE. What a doctor makes his living from.

INDISCREET. Where children should not play after school.

GRUDGE. Place to keep your auto.

ALARM CLOCK. Device for waking a childless household.

BATHING SUIT. Garment to help the girls outstrip one another on the beach.

PESSIMIST. One who looks through morose-colored glasses.

COOKBOOK. A volume with many stirring chapters.

GRAND JURY. Anyone that acquits you.

CEREAL. The stuff that heroes are made of.

DUCK. A chicken in snowshoes.

SKELETON. Bones with the people scraped off.

INSULATE. What you have to explain for getting.

HOSPITALITY. The art of making somebody feel at home when you wish they were.

FAME. What you get by dying at the right time.

PERPETUAL MOTION. Cow drinking her own milk.

HUG. Roundabout expression of affection.

CHILDISH GAME. One at which your wife beats you.

YARN. To open your mouth wide when sleepy.

SALT. The stuff that makes potatoes taste bad when you boil 'em and don't put any in.

BACHELOR. A fellow whose only ties are those that need cleaning.

CHIVALRY. The attitude of a man toward somebody else's wife.

SARONG. A dish towel gone high society.

ETIQUETTE. Knowing which hand to use when you put your napkin in your collar.

DARK AGES. Knight time.

GENIUS. The will to turn on your thoughts instead of TV.

SMALL TOWN. Where you can chat on the phone even when you get a wrong number.

BOSS. Man who gets to the office early when you're late.

OLD AGE. When it takes you longer to get over a good time than have it.

PINK TEAS. "Giggle-gaggle-gobble." (Oliver W. Holmes.)

TREE. A solid thing that stands in one place for 50 years and then suddenly jumps in front of a woman driver.

REINDEER. A horse with a TV antenna.

SWEETNESS AND LIGHT. What a proper girl tries to keep turned on when alone in living room with boy friend.

INTOXICATION. When you feel sophisticated but can't pronounce it.

TANGERINE. A loose-leaf orange.

TRANSPARENTS. Those that anybody can see through.

MIDDLE AGE. When the doctor stops calling you "old girl," and starts referring to you as "young lady."

OPERA. The only place where a man, stabbed in the back, sings instead of dying.

PERSONALITY. The ability to get along on banana oil instead of elbow grease.

MIDDLE AGE. When you look back to see that the mountain you've been climbing is only a molehill. (Or, when you can't eat your cake and have It too.)

SMALL TOWN. Where everybody knows everybody else's business and reads the papers only to see if they got caught at it.

BONERS
(*Time: 1 to 10 minutes*)

God's Own Country is Heaven.

A juvenile is what King Saul threw at David when he was playing the harp to him.

A man is an animal split halfway up and walks on the split end.

An octopus is a person who hopes for the best.

Acrimony, sometimes called holy, is another name for marriage.

A compliment is when you say something to another which he and we know is not true.

A Mayor is a he horse.

A monologue is a conversation between two people, such as husband and wife.

An optimist is a man who looks after your eyes, a pessimist looks after your feet.

A Senator is half horse and half man.

SOS is a musical term meaning same only softer.

"Laissez-faire" meant "Let the farmers pay the taxes."

Robinhood is a word like boyhood or girlhood, it means to feel like a robin and hop around.

A sirloin is the only article of clothing worn by Gandhi, the leader of India.

A spectre is a man who doesn't believe in things like Santa Claus.

An incinerator is a person who hints bad things instead of coming right out and telling you.

Maneuver is what they put on grass. We have maneuver on our lawn.

Queen Victoria was the only queen who sat on a thorn for sixty-three years.

Yom Kippur was a general in the Japanese army.

The clown in *As You Like It* was named Touchdown.

The proof that the witches in *Macbeth* were supernatural is that no one could eat what they cooked.

Some instruments used in an orchestra are: viles, cellars, trumpets, hornets, baboons, old boys, and bubble bases.

Write a sentence showing clearly the meaning of "posterity."
    He had a cat, but nothing else lived on his posterity.
    The man looked as if he had been reduced to posterity.
    Henry paid the fare because of his posterity.
    By his clothes he seemed a person of great posterity.
    The cat leaped about and then sat on its posterity.

There are three kinds of poetry—lyric, dramatic, and epidemic.

The theme of this poem is that Longfellow shot an arrow into the air, and many years afterward he found it in the heart of a friend.

Name three tragedies by Shakespeare.
    Macbeth, King Lear, and *Twelve Nights in a Bar Room.*

A poetic license is a license you get from the Post Office to keep poets. You get one also if you want to keep a dog. It costs two dollars and you call it a dog license.

First to thine own self be true,
Thou can'st then be false to any man.

Degrees of comparison of "Bad":
Bad: very sick: dead.

The feminine of bachelor is lady in waiting.

General Braddock was killed in the French and Indian war, he had three horses shot under him and a fourth went through his clothes.

Abraham Lincoln wrote the Gettysburg Address while traveling from Washington to Gettysburg on the back of an envelope.

Queen Elizabeth was a very wise, good queen, and so she never married.

The difference between a king and a president is that a king is the son of his father, but a president isn't.

Blockheads were the part cause of the War of 1812.

Martin Luther died a horrible death. He was excommunicated by a bull.

Watchword of the French Revolution: Liberty, Equality, and Maternity.

The Duck of Wellington won a big battle and when he finished he had one arm and one eye and he looked through the telescope with his blind eye and said it was all right and that is how he won the battle.

Horace Greeley was the worst defeated candidate ever elected.

The Spartan mother used to say to her son, "Return with your shield or pawn it."

The seats of Senators shall be vaccinated every six years.

The pilgrims landed at Plymouth Rock. They were greeted by the Indians who came running down the hill rolling their war hoops before them.

In Pittsburgh they manufacture iron, and steal.

The alimentary canal is located in the northern part of Indiana.

Where is the greater part of Europe?
In New York.

Manhattan Island was bought from the Indians for about $24 and now I don't suppose you could buy it for $500.

The original tribes of Central America were the Aztecs, the Cults, and the Morons.

An Indian reservation consists of a mile of land for every five square Indians.

Jacob, son of Isaac, stole his brother's birth mark.

Water is composed of two gins, Oxygin and Hydrogin. Oxygin is pure gin, Hydrogin is gin and water.

The difference between air and water is that air can be made wetter, but water cannot.

When you breathe you inspire. When you do not breathe you expire.

Why do we not raise the silk worm in the United States?
    We get our silk from the rayon. He is a larger animal and gives more silk.

A good milk cow can be told by her rudder.

Sea water has the formula CH_2O.

Explain the effect of heat and cold and give an illustration.
    Heat expands: in the summer the days are long.
    Cold contracts: in the winter the days are short.

What is an individual?
    An individual is a piece of people.

Inertia is when you go on after you stop and when you stop after you start.

Wampum is the money that Indians made with white men's scalps.

Buddha lived a normal life with a wife and family, and when he was thirty, left home in search of happiness.

Who were the Albigenses and where did they live?
    I don't know who they were nor where they lived, but whoever they were and wherever they lived, I wish them a Merry Christmas.

What are the two characteristic differences of the anatomy of the infant and the adult?
    The infant's anatomy is straight and narrow. The adult's is protruding and wider.

The food goes down the food pipe and the Efflougis shushes it off from going down the wind pipe.

To stop blood from flowing from a wound in the leg, wrap the leg around the body above the heart.

Often when people are drowned you can revise them by punching in their sides but not too hard. This is called resurrection.

They say music hath charms to soothe the savage beast, but I never noticed it had any effect on me.

Some men came to Jesus with a penny and he asked them, "Whose subscription is this?"

When my grandma lived in Germany she found a nest of snake's egges and she went there and hatched them. She hatched them with a hatchet.

When you want to kill a hog, you stab him in the aqueduct.

At the X mine, after sinking a shaft one hundred feet, they finally struck bed-pan.

Everybody should not try to do everything but should do one thing well. For instance cows can always give milk, but hens cannot do this. They prefer to lay eggs.[1]

THE LEGEND OF THE BLUE GNUS
(*Time: 5 minutes*)

Once upon a time, in the land of Zoos lived a pair of bright blue gnus. One was a cute girl gnu named Sue and the other was a boy, and his name was Hugh. Every day when they would meet, they would say something like this: "Yoo hoo, Hugh, you blue gnu you!" or "Yoo hoo, Sue, you cute gnu, you!"

Yes, Hugh loved Sue, and Sue loved Hugh, and they carried on like lovers do. They would get in the corner (just the two) and oh, how they would bill and coo! Hugh said to Sue one day, "I need yer. Let's go out and find the preacher!"

Well, they found the preacher, and had a wedding. He said, "Do you, Sue Gnu, love Hugh Gnu?" She replied, "Yes, of course I do." Hugh took the ring hidden in his hose, and put it in his new bride's nose. The wedding feast went on for hours, with all the guests eating up all the flowers. Oh, the gnuspapers were full of it the next day!

After the honeymoon Hugh went to work for the gnuspaper. Every day when he went to work Sue would smile at him and smirk, "Good-bye, Hugh, you blue gnu you." And of course he'd say, "Good-bye, Sue. Good-bye to you, you cute gnu, you!" Then he'd give her a great big kiss every day, he'd never miss.

Hugh had a very interesting job. At his work he worked hard every day, and to get his pay, he must have the cross-word puzzles call for "a three-lettered animal." Of course, this meant "gnu." Since three-lettered spaces are hard to fill, Hugh would usually fill the bill!

Back at home Hugh and Sue were happy gnus. "There is just one thing," Hugh often said, day by day since they were wed, "One thing that our love nest lacks. We need the patter of little feet! The love of

a child just can't be beat. We need the laughter of a tiny blue gnu!"
To that Sue said, "A little gnu or two."

Then an idea came to Hugh. "I know just what we can do! Let's
adopt a little blue gnu!"

"You are right," said Sue, "let's glance at the gnuspaper and see if
there's a chance!"

Both took the paper and they looked and looked, but all orphan
gnus just seemed to be booked. Nobody knew a tiny little gnu who
wanted to be adopted by some gnus—do you?

Sue and Hugh became discouraged. Gradually the two began to
fuss. (Gnus make noise, but of course they don't cuss.) Hugh would
say, "Foo to you, Sue! Foo-foo to you, you blue gnu you!"

Poor little Sue would cry, "Boo-hoo! Poo-poo to you, you old blue
gnu, you!"

Yes, their home was nice and neat, but it needed the patter of
little feet. They wanted the laughter of a little blue gnu to brighten
their present and their later years, too.

The problem soon took its toll at Hugh's work. It bothered him so
when he went to work that, though he worked as hard as a Turk,
there came a time (he just couldn't see how) when for three-lettered
animals in the puzzles they used the term, "a cow." This, of course,
made Hugh Gnu sad, and it also made him very mad.

He came home to his little place one night in a nasty mood, just
spoiling for a fight. He yanked the door open and he stalked right in,
making lots of noise as he went in. But then he took one look at Sue
and saw in her eyes a light that was new. Gone was the frown from
Sue's pretty brow. She looked so sweet and peaceful now. A happy
smile beamed on her face, and as she moved there was a new kind of
grace.

"Sue," was all that Hugh could say, "What has made you look this
way?"

She came over close, and he could see that she differed from the
way she used to be.

"Sh-h-h-h-h!" was all Sue said to Hugh. "Darling . . . I have gnus
for you!" [2]

"IT ALL STARTED WITH EUROPA"
(*Time: 10 minutes*)

Europe at the Beginning

The beginnings of Europe are shrouded in impenetrable myths. According to one of these, Europe was named after Europa, a girl who
rode around on a bull named Jupiter. The fact that Jupiter was actu-

ally not a bull but a god . . . gives us some indication of the uncertainty of those early days. All Europa knew was that it was transportation.

Except for lending her name, Europa had little to do with Western civilization. Some scholars, however, detect her influence on Far Western culture, notably the custom of riding the bull at rodeos and slinging it at dude ranches and Bar-B-Q's.

Europe is also called the Old Country, the Old World, and Where My People Came From. People who live in Europe are called Europeans until they emigrate to America, where they are called Foreigners.

GEOGRAPHY AND CLIMATE

Europe, like the rest of the Earth, was originally too hot to handle. It had no sooner cooled off than it was covered by ice as far as the eye could see, and even farther. The northernmost region was populated by Ice Men who carried ice picks and traveled in ice packs. It was generally agreed that what Europe needed was a good thaw, but while everybody talked about it, nobody did anything. Waiting for the ice to retreat to the north, a few inches a year, the Europeans grew increasingly impatient. They were eager to discover places like Norway and Sweden and to see their first Great Dane.

After the ice left, Europe was covered with dense forests, which first had to be cleared and later carefully preserved. The forests could hardly be seen because of the trees, and were full of fierce animals ready to spring, and fierce birds ready to chirp. Lakes, dug out by glaciers, provided our European ancestors with picturesque scenery and healthful spas. To these latter they went to take the baths, which they badly needed, and to recover from the gout, an ailment which it was as much fun to get as to get over.

In those days, which were extremely B.C., England was part of Europe, and Ireland, much to the disgust of the Irish, was part of England. Owing to the absence of the English Channel, channel swimming was virtually unknown.

Europe and Africa were still connected at Gibraltar, which was of no strategic importance and therefore not held by the British. Maps were very poor, and it was hard to distinguish Asia Minor from Asia Major and Asia Proper from Asia Improper. The largest region was the Unknown World, an area not yet Ripe for Conquest and Colonialization.

Prehistoric Man

According to Darwin, the first men hung from the branches of trees by their tails. It was not until much later that they discovered ropes and began to hang each other. For some reason, our ancestors' tails got shorter and shorter, and the fun gradually went out of swinging. Whether or not men descended from the monkeys, as soon as they lost their tails they descended from trees.

The earliest Europeans were Homo Sapiens, Neanderthal, and Cro-Magnon. The latter, because of his hyphenated name, was probably British. Little is known of these original men, except that Homo Sapiens was the brightest and Cro-Magnon had a long head. Nothing favorable has ever been said about Neanderthal, although his masculinity was unquestioned. He had the hairiest chest until Ernest Hemingway.

THE STONE AGE

After the Ice Age came the Stone Age. Stones had certain advantages over ice. For instance:

1. They were warmer, especially when left in the sun.
2. They didn't melt on the way home.
3. They gave employment to stone masons and made possible the naming of Stonewall Jackson.

On the other hand, they were inferior to ice in certain respects:

1. They were no good for iced drinks.
2. They were unsatisfactory for skating on.

Fortunately, stones were plentiful. Furthermore, there was little or no depreciation, and a used stone was as good as a brand-new one. Geology was in its infancy, and rock gardening was unknown.

LIFE IN THESE EARLY TIMES

We must not suppose that Europeans of the Stone Age felt thwarted by their failure to discover bronze and iron. Whittling away thoughtfully on stones, hunting wild beasts and women, they kept busy. The more energetic of them left no stone unturned.

Let us picture the daily life of one of our ancestors. Rising early, perhaps awakened by the dripping of water from a stalactite directly overhead, he makes his toilet by untangling his hair from his eyebrows and rubbing a small stone over his well-developed incisors, being careful to use an up-an-down stroke. He has a light breakfast of roots, berries, and raw mastodon meat, completely unaware that every mouthful is bursting with vitamins.

Putting the rumpled earth back into place, he makes his bed. This is woman's work, he thinks, and is reminded of his day's chores. He must find a double-breasted animal to skin for a new suit, and a woman to be his mate.

With a quick backward glance at his cave, and making a mental note to arch the top of his doorway a little, like his neighbor's, he is off on his appointed rounds. Avoiding the brontosauruses and the-sauruses, which are a bit large for his purpose, he searches out a saber-toothed tiger and removes the skin. Unless he has in mind military regalia, he also removes the saber.

The woman is a little more of a problem, but not much. Our ancestor has a poor posture, his forehead is repellent to those who prefer the intellectual type, and his teeth cry out for the attention of an orthodontist. But there is something exciting about the way he can beat a woman over the head with a club. He knows the right spot, just above the ears, and his blows have a certain manly authority about them. By mid-afternoon he has clubbed a smart-looking brunette into a swoon. Taking her silence to mean assent, he seizes her by the fore-lock, or anything handy, and drags her away. Whatever skin comes off along the road, he says to himself, will grow back.

As the shadows of late afternoon lengthen, our ancestor and his bride arrive home, unencumbered by rice or old shoes. He carries her over the threshold of the cave and tenderly drops her. The honeymoon is over. As soon as she regains consciousness, she assumes her wifely duties, cutting the tiger skin into long lapels and natural shoulders, preparing a supper of left-over mastodon meat, and enlarging the dug-out portion of the floor to make a double bed.

Little does our ancestor think, as he nestles his head into the clod that serves as his pillow, that in a few thousand years men will be urged to return to nature. He, although he does not appreciate his good fortune, is already there.

ARTS AND CRAFTS

Paintings were usually done right on the walls of caves, to save the expense of framing. Nude portraits were popular, especially those of deer and bison. But, since this was the dawn of civilization, the light was poor, and artists were unable to do their best work. They were scornfully called Primitives by those who knew nothing about art but knew what they liked. In terms of years, if not ability, Primitives must be considered the genuine Old Masters.

As the shapes and sizes of stones improved, craftsmen made spectacular advances in such fields as wood carving, meat carving, and murder.

We owe much to prehistoric man. It does not seem likely, however, that we can ever repay him.[3]

"IT ALL STARTED WITH COLUMBUS"
(*Time: 10 minutes*)

The Discovery of America

America was founded by Columbus in 1492. This is an easy date to remember because it rhymes with "ocean blue," which was the color of the Atlantic in those days. If he had sailed a year later the date would still be easy to remember because it would rhyme with "boundless sea."

Columbus fled to this country because of persecution by Ferdinand and Isabella, who refused to believe the world was round, even when Columbus showed them an egg. Ferdinand later became famous because he objected to bullfights and said he preferred to smell flowers if he had to smell anything. He was stung in the end by a bee.

Before Columbus reached America, which he named after a man called American Vesuvius, he cried "Ceylon! Ceylon!" because he wanted to see India, which was engraved on his heart, before he died. When he arrived, he cried again. This time he cried "Excelsior!" meaning "I have found it."

Columbus was mistaken in thinking he had reached India when actually he had not got even as far as Indiana. There is still a great deal of confusion about the East and the West. As Columbus discovered, if you go west long enough you find yourself in the east, and vice versa. The East and the West are kept apart by the Date Line, just as the North and South are kept apart by the Masons' Dixon Line. In the New World most of the eastern half of the country is called the Middle West, although it is known as the East by those who live in the Far West.

Columbus, who was as confused as anybody who has been at sea for a long time, called the first people he saw "Indians." It is not known what they called Columbus. His unfortunate error has been perpetuated through the centuries. The original Americans are still known as "Indians," while all manner of immigrants from England, Ireland, Angora, and Lichtenstein are referred to as "Americans."

Accompanied by his devoted followers, the Knights of Columbus, Columbus made several other voyages in search of India. Try as he might, however, he kept discovering America, and finally returned to Spain to die. He lived for a time in Madrid, but spent his last days in Disgrace.

A MINORITY OPINION

Some say it was not Columbus who discovered America but a man named Leaf Ericson. Leaf came from one of the Scandinavian countries with a shipload of people, all of whom were called Yon Yonson or Ole Olson or Big Swede, and went straight to Wisconsin, where he unloaded his passengers and went back for more.

On his next trip he went to Minnesota.

We know all this from some undecipherable remarks he made on a piece of stone. This stone has since become an utter rune.

FURTHER EXPLORATIONS

After Columbus proved the world was round, a great many people went around it. Marco Polo, who was one of the earlier explorers, had the misfortune to live several centuries before Columbus. Therefore, although he got around a good deal, he did not get completely around. He went far to the north, however, and is remembered for his discovery of the Polo regions.

The chief rivals in exploration were England and Spain. England had men like Cabot, who spoke only to a man named Lowell, and Sir Francis Drake, who had a singed beard and a ship called the Golden Behind.

Nor should we forget Sir Martin Fourflusher.

The struggle between England and Spain came to a climax in an epic sea battle off the Azores known as the Last Fight of the Revenge. In this decisive conflict, Sir Richard Grenville and Alfred Lord Tennyson proved conclusively that the lighter English warships could get more miles to the galleon.

England has ruled the waves ever since and has kept the sun from setting anywhere on her empire, thus providing a longer working day than in other countries.

STILL FURTHER EXPLORATIONS

Other explorers included Bilbo, Cabbage de Vaca, Cortez (known as the Stout, who traveled much in realms looking for gold), and Pantsy de Lion, a thirsty old man who was looking for a drinking fountain. He never found it, but he founded Florida, to which a great many thirsty old men have gone ever since.[4]

SHAKESPEARE EXPLAINED
(*Time: 12 minutes*)
Carrying On the System of Footnotes to a Silly Extreme

PERICLES
Act II, Scene 3

Enter first Lady-in-Waiting (flourish, hautboys and torches)
First Lady-in-Waiting—"What ho! Where is the music?"

Notes

1. Flourish: The stage direction here is obscure. Clarke claims it should read "flarish," thus changing the meaning of the passage to "flarish" (that is, the King's), but most authorities have agreed that it should remain "flourish," supplying the predicate which is to be flourished. There was at this time a custom in the country-side of England to flourish a mop as a signal to the passing vender of berries, signifying that in that particular household there was a consumer demand for berries, and this may have been meant in this instance. That Shakespeare was cognizant of this custom of flourishing the mop for berries is shown in a similar passage in the second part of King Henry IV, where he has the Third Page enter and say, "Flourish." Cf. also Hamlet, IV, 7:4.

2. hautboys: For the French "haut," meaning "high" and the Eng. "boys," meaning "boys." The word here is doubtless used in the sense of "high boys," indicating either that Shakespeare intended to convey the idea of spiritual distress on the part of the First Lady-in-Waiting or that he did not. Of this Rolfe says: "Here we have one of the chief indications of Shakespeare's knowledge of human nature, his remarkable insight into the petty foibles of this work-a-day world." Cf. T. N. 4:6, "Mine eye hath play'd the painter, and hath stell'd thy beauty's form in table of my heart."

3. and: A favorite conjunctive of Shakespeare's in referring to the need for a more adequate navy for England. Tauchnitz claims that it should be pronounced "und," stressing the anti-penult. This interpretation, however, has found disfavor among most commentators because of its limited significance. We find the same conjunctive in A. W. T. E. W. 6:7, "Steel-boned, unyielding and uncomplying virtue," and here there can be no doubt that Shakespeare means that if the King should consent to the marriage of his daughter the excuse of Stephano, offered in Act 2, would carry no weight.

4. torches: The interpolation of some foolish player and never the work of Shakespeare (Warb.). The critics of the last century have disputed whether or not this has been misspelled in the original, and should read "trochies" or "troches." This might well be since the introduction of tobacco into England at this time had wrought havoc with the speaking voices of the players, and we might well imagine that at the entrance of the First Lady-in-Waiting there might be perhaps one of the hautboys mentioned in the preceding passage bearing a box of "troches" or "trognies" for the actors to suck. Of this entrance Clarke remarks: "The

noble mixture of spirited firmness and womanly modesty, fine sense and true humility, clear sagacity and absence of conceit, passionate warmth and sensitive delicacy, generous love and self-diffidence with which Shakespeare has endowed this First Lady-in-Waiting renders her in our eyes one of the most admirable of his female characters." Cf. M. S. N. D. 8:9, "That solder'st close impossibilities and mak'st them kiss."

5. What—What.

6. ho! In conjunction with the preceding word doubtless means "What ho!" changed by Clarke to "what hoo!" In the original MS. it reads "What hi!" but this has been accredited to the tendency of the time to write "What hi" when "what ho" was meant. Techner alone maintains that it should read "What humpf!" Cf. Ham. 5:0, "High-ho!"

7. Where. The reading of the folio, retained by Johnson, the Cambridge editors and others, but it is not impossible that Shakespeare wrote "why," as Pope and others give it. This would make the passage read "Why the music?" instead of "Where is the music?" and would be a much more probable interpretation in view of the music of that time. Cf. George Ade. Fable No. 15, "Why the gunnysack?"

8. is—is not. That is, would not be.

9. the. Cf. Ham. 4:6. M. S. N. D. 3:5. A. W. T. E. W. 2:6. T. N. 1:3 and Macbeth 3:1, "that knits up the raveled sleeves of care."

10. music. Explained by Malone as "the art of making music" or "music that is made." If it has but one of these meanings we are inclined to think it is the first; and this seems to be favored by what precedes, "the music!" Cf. M. of V. 4:2, "The man that hath no music in himself."

The meaning of the whole passage seems to be that the First Lady-in-Waiting has entered, concomitant with a flourish, hautboys and torches and says, "What ho! Where is the music?" [5]

DER JACKASSERS UND DER ROPER
(*Time: 5 minutes*)

Der barnyarden insiden ben ein brownisch Jackasser mit ein shorten roper arounder-gehooken der necken. Also gehooken mit das roper ben ein whitisch Jackasser.

Der brownisch Jackasser ben wanten ein haystacker on der leften und der whitischer ben wanten ein haystacker on der righten. Mit snorten under grosser grunten-groanen der Jackassers ben tuggen und strainen und pawen der earthen mitout succeeden!

Finaller der dumkopfs ben gestoppen der pullen und obertalken ein schemer. Suddener, der Jackassers iss rushen aparten pellmellen mit breaknecken speeden! Ach! Der roper ben gebroken! Der neckers also ben gebroken.[6]

JOHANN HORNER
(Time: 5 minutes)

Der smallisch Johann Horner
  Ben gesitten in das corner
Der Yuletiden strudel gestauffen.
  Der thumber in-gesticken
  Und out-gepullen quicken
Mit burnen und blisters gepuffen!

Der oldisch rhymer ben claimen Johann iss outgepullen ein plum mit braggen, "Ach! Ich ben ein gooten boy!" Iss ein mistooker. Iss gooten youngischers ben gesitten in das corner? Nein. Johann ben ein littlisch schtunker und der fader und mutter ben outgaben der punishen. Ich ben gethinken iss better ein backwhacken. Und mitout strudel.[7]

THE TARE AND THE HORTOISE
(Time: 5 minutes)

Once a-time a pon, a big ray grabbit was faking a lot of mun of a tazy old lortoise for always slooving so moe-ly. "Oh, bosh!" tied the crortoise. "You just bait a wit! Why, I can fan so much ruster than you, my fine-frethered fend, that I shall inch you within a leat of your bife!" The labbit raffed, but the sere-toise was torious. "In that case," rehied the plare, inking his wye at a bander-sty, "let's sigh it and tree!"

So they finally decided to hire a fly sox to ket the source for them and to goot off the shun to rart the stace. It was a dright, bunny say, as a big grad cowthered and there were chowed leers as the two con-startents tested. Soon the hare was so har afed that he thought it was tie hime to take a right slest, so he day quietly lown on the croft gool sass and snarted to store. But the old, toe slortoise kept odding and odding plon and finally geached the roal. The croise of the nelling yowd hoke the weeping slare, and he duddenly sashed on, gossing the croal line several linits mayter.

And The Storal to This Mory Is: No matter how fast a rubbit can ran, he will never surtass a torpoise when it comes to wearing turtle-swecked netters.[8]

KELLING THE BAT
(*Time: 4 minutes*)

In a herten souse there lived a kye slat who just moted on dice. Every time the mice'd tie to have a good trime, the spat would coil it. So the mice decided to cold a hoart to fix it so they would know when the keeline was fumming so they could scamper safe to offty. "If you will allow ME to be Dean for a Quay," said a maidy louse, "I would suggest that there's buthing netter to warn us of the prat's a-coach than to bang a hell anound his reck." At first they leered chustilly, considering this a papital clan. "However, though," udded anather, "now that we're a-beed on the grell, who is the maive brouse who is going to cold the hat while we put it around the nat's keck?" But there was bro one naive enough to kell the bat.

And The Storal to This Mory Is: A small tell binkles and a large tell bowls, but what's the mifference if you're a douse? [9]

THE MYON AND THE LOUSE
(*Time: 4 minutes*)

Way back before Crossington delled the Washaware, a late big gryon was deeping peacefully in his slen, beaming of a dreef-steak, when he was awakened by a mee wouse, running fack and borth afoss his crace. Toozing his lemper, the gryon labbed the mittle louse by the nuff of the screck and was on the kerge of villing him. Moor little pouse! "Leaze, Mister Plyon," mide the crouse, "if you will only get me lo, I fomise praithfully to rekind you for your payness!" So the lierce fyon, who must have been a cub Scoy Bout in his dunger yaize, thought he would dee his daily good dude, and he set the frouse mee.

A couple of leeks waiter, this very lame syon got nangled up in a tet, and, though he was Bing of the Keasts (not to be confused with Craws Bingby) no one came to answer his rellowing boars. But, chear dildren, pay is the here-off: along comes the miny little touse, and, gnawing the topes with his reeth, he frees the shyon from his lackles! "Turn-affair is bout play!" meaks the squouse, and with that, he hurns on his teel and heats it for bome.

And The Storal to This Mory Is: Sometimes our bubbles are trig, and sometimes our smubbles are trawl, but if we TRAD no hubbles, how would we bleckognize our ressings? [10]

THE MUNTRY KAID AND HER PILKMAIL
(*Time: 4 minutes*)

Once on a dot August hay, a muvly laiden was walking slowly along a runtry code with a pilkmail balanced on her hurly kedd. (She carried it that way because the flop of her head was tat.) As she thudged along, she was trinking: "When I mell this silk, I shall have emuff nunny to buy deveral suzzen eggs at pryzant presses. (This was B.O. the 4 P.A.) Out of these eggs, allowing for feveral which may not be sertil,* will come about foo hundred and tifty chuffy young flicks. These chittle licks will grow into charge lickens and I can marry them to carket for the Trissmuss crade. Of course, in the Sooltide yeezon, scoaltry is pairce, so by the mollowing Fay I shall be able to dry myself a brand new bess. Now let's see . . . I think my bless shall be drew, to match the uller of my kyes, and I shall foe to the Gair, where all the fung yellows will part me for a wantner. But to each I shall say: 'Go feddle your pish!' "

And as she spoke thus to herself, she sauced her head tossily and off went the mail of pilk and grilled all over the spass. Mott a whess! Mott a careless whayden!

And The Storal to This Mory Is: Don't fount your cowls before they sheeve the lell.[11]

THE ROOGLE AND THE EASTER
(*Time: 4 minutes*)

Once upon a time a farmer owned a rupple of great big koosters who thought they were nuff as tales because someone told them they were Rimmuth Plocks. So every time they fast in the parmyard, they'd give each other the eye-vul E. They were obviously extremely bellous jerds. So one day they pined the proper saipers, and with the jessings of Mike Blacobs, they fought it out under the Roonsberry Queels.

For the sake of the awdies in our lady-ence, we shan't go into dorrible hee-tales, but when the fin was fightished, one dooster lay red. The one who FUN the wight flew up to the stoof of the raible, chuffed out his pest, and load so crowdly he could be heard wurteen miles a-thay. He might just as well have been in the stenter of a well-lighted sage, for a great awled beagle, who happened to by hying over-fled, tabbed the royzy nooster in his grallons and flew him to the mop of a high town-ten, where Isses Meagle made him into a fine dicken chinner for her houd pruzzband and all their eaggy baibles.

And The Storal to This Mory Is: Fide proeth before a gawl.[12]

THE PAG AT THE STOOL
(*Time: 5 minutes*)

A stursty thag went down to a quiet drool to pink. As he bent over to laist the delicious tickwid, he was terry much vaiken with his fine

* Her tuther had moaled her about the burrs and beeds.

anting spredlers, but when he took a lander at his geggs, which were skin and thrawny, he experienced a feeling of heffinite daitred.

While he stood there anting his likelers and laiting his heggs, he was attacked by a leerce fyon. But in the face which chollowed, he soon outdistanced the Bing of the Keasts, and he lept his keed as long as there was a lack of feeze and troaliage. But, coming fezzantly to a prorest, he was caught by his brantlers in the antches and the gryon labbed him in his cleeth and taws and shripped him half to reds. "Moe is wee!" stied the crag, with his brast leth, "I laited my himbs, which might have laived my sife; but the prorns of which I am so very howd have dooved my unprewing."

Stoor old pag! Lasty old nyon!

And The Storal to This Mory Is: What is mirth woast is often lallued veast. OR, if you anton to have happlers, you are stobably a prag; but if the saidies per-loo you, you are loutless a dyon.[13]

14

Mixers

THE PURPOSE OF MIXERS is to get people of a group acquainted with one another and to prevent those who already know each other well from staying in one small clique during the whole period. The more the individuals present circulate about the whole group, talk with others, and enter into activities with others, the more successful the event.

Name tags [1] are an important device toward accomplishing this purpose. Clever ones can be improvised by any group. The letters must be large enough for those without their glasses to see easily.

This chapter gives at least eight categories of mixers with several suggestions in each: Handshakers, Trading or Using Objects, Gamelike Mixers, Mixers Involving Names, No-Partner Mixers, Ways of Getting Partners, Couple Mixers, Dance Formation Mixers.

HANDSHAKERS

Lucky Shake, or Mysterious Stranger. No one knows who are distributors of prizes. Whoever happens to be tenth one to shake hands with one of them is given award.

Shake or Else. Certain types of handshakes are prescribed, and there are some "plainclothesmen" around to check and see that all are performing. "High-society style," "Wrestler who's lost his grip," "Sore-armed baseball pitcher," "Like an old friend you haven't seen in years," and the like. At musical signal group must change each time.

Bag Shake. Each person has paper sack on his hand for handshaking.

Handshaking Down the Aisle. Have two aisles of people, down which folks go, one at a time, shaking hands with right hand to persons on right, left hand to those on left, finally taking own place in line as he gets to foot of double-line.

Circle Handshake. Standing in circle, leader steps out, and with back to circle, shakes hands with person who was on his right, continuing all around circle. That person follows him as soon as leader goes to third person, and so on until all have shaken hands around circle. When each person comes back to his original place, he stops there and shakes hands with others as they come around circle. When leader gets back to his original place, all should have shaken hands with someone else, either as active handshaker or stationary one, staying in place. Finish by circling to music, swing partner (if playing by partners).

TRADING OR USING OBJECTS

Even or Odd. Each player has 10 or 15 beans. He walks up to someone and asks, "Even or odd?" (meaning number of beans he has in his closed hand). Person guesses. If he is right, he gets beans; if wrong, he pays like number of beans. See who gets most in given time.

Barter. Each player is given number of articles, such as beans, peas, small potatoes, hairpins, nuts, marbles, keys, buttons. During trading period he is to do as much trading as possible. See who has most articles at end, or place value in points on each of articles and see who has most points.

Color Barter. Same idea. Each has supply of colored squares. Trade during trading season. Colors are later assigned points, and winner is one with most points.

Numbers Mixer. Each person is given numeral big enough to be seen easily across room when pinned to him. Leader calls out certain numbers, such as 55. People organize themselves quickly to get several folk together whose number totals 55. Each gets bean for counter (or punch on his number). See who gets most. (Instead of sum, the numerals may stand in order to form given large figure, such as 13,947.)

Meal Mixer. Each person is given large, readable paper or card bearing name of food. At signal, people start out to get together complete meal of appetizer, meat, two vegetables, drink, dessert, salad.

Human Scavenger Hunt. Number of people present wear unusual clothes, mismatched sox, ring on wrong finger, and the like. Make list and have each person looking to see who is in that condition. At end see who found most. (Pencil and paper mixer.)

Who Is . . . Each person has list and writes down:

Girl with darkest hair   Woman with largest dimples
Boy with biggest feet   Girl with bluest eyes

Animal Hunt. Group is divided into several smaller ones, each with captain and animal name, such as bear, cow, horse, raccoon. Each animal is assigned color (such as red to cows) and at Go signal, they go out to search for "food," which consists of colored squares of paper. When player finds square, he calls with his animal noise and his captain hurries over either to claim square (if it is his) or to destroy it (if it is "enemy food").

At end of hunt, see which team has most squares.

Conversation System. Good for small group, especially on trip. Rule is that, having spoken to person, you cannot speak to that person again until you have spoken to everybody else.

Name Tag Rule. In conference wearing name tags, make rule that anyone caught without his tag will have to buy his catcher soft drink or pay some other penalty.

Rotation. On one-hour trip for 20 people, each person was numbered and had to change seats when signal was given. This meant that everybody sat with everyone else before trip was over.

Eating Buns. String rope between two trees and have hanging from it, at different heights, buns on string. Players must walk up to their buns, hands behind them, and eat them. With line jiggling, it is not too easy.

Reminiscence. Men have odd numbers pinned on them, girls have even numbers. Instructions are distributed to one or other in slips of paper: "Find No. 14 and tell what you did on the Fourth of July." "Look up No. 7 and tell of your most interesting adventure of the year," and so on.

Controlled Confusion.[2] Duplicate diagram shown and cut into six squares, passing them out evenly. Then get into groupings as called. Several assistants, equipped with paper punches, punch

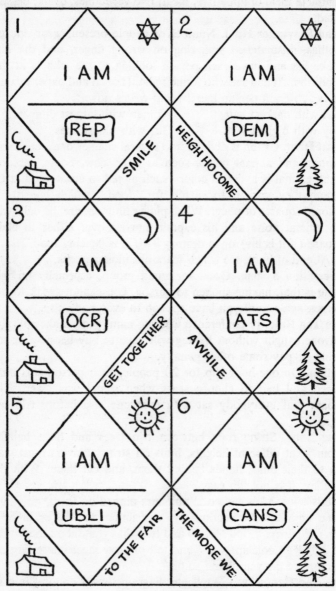

Controlled Confusion

holes in paper of each player who has the winning combination
—object, to see who has most punches. When players are in
groups, call for each group to search among itself for answers
to questions, such as these:

1. Highest number of pennies in group.
2. Largest number of Jims and Janes (or Bettys and Bobs).
3. Most people born outside of this city, or county, or state.
4. Three boys with longest feet.
5. The most buffalo nickels.
6. Girl with longest hair
7. Tallest girl or boy
8. Most wrist watches—or rings—brown shoes.
9. Most birthdays this month (be honest!)
10. Reddest sox, and so on.

Get them into groups of different sizes. Their cards will provide
in two groups: houses or trees; Republicans or Democrats; also
by their own last names in A to L, M to Z. (They will have
written their names on their own cards.)

Three groups: Divide by sun, moon, stars, or song titles.

Four groups: By their own birth months: January to March;
April to June; July to September; October to December.

Six groups: Use number in upper left-hand corner of their
square.

Face to Face. Persons stand facing partners. One extra one calls
out "Face to face," then "Back to back," and finally "All
change," whereupon they must get new partners, any extras doing same. Can be combined with fancy handshakes.

Another version has new partners get together, back to back.
Then directions are given: "You are a girl who has just seen a
mouse. Face to face!" (The girl must act out as directed.) Next
time, directions may be to boy, "You have just won a boxing
match," and so on.

GAMELIKE MIXERS

Basketball Mixer. Using bean bag or soft rubber ball, two teams
of five or more players are lined up, facing each other. (For
large groups, divide them into several "sets" like this.) The

captain of team A tosses ball or bean bag to team B. Whoever catches it holds it up. First player of team B must name person holding bean bag. For success: 2 points. For failure: 2 points to opposite team. Next, captain of team B tosses bag to team A, and first player of team B must identify.

Co-operative Spelling. Each person gets large card with letter of alphabet on it, also pin to put it on with. He also has card and pencil. He is to get together with other owners of letters to spell words. Writes those words on his card, rushes to spell other words. One with most words wins.

Hummer. Start out in pairs. On "GO" signal, each looks other in eye and starts humming. Continue until one has to take breath, which eliminates him. He must sit down. Other person finds another for elimination contest, and so on until one person is winner. (You can make other laugh, but cannot tickle him.) If there are those who spontaneously "want to take the winner on" at end, and you have time, let them do so.

Missing Persons Description. You have minute to get thoroughly acquainted with person who is your temporary partner. Everybody then separates. Leader calls on someone to describe person and see if all can guess who person was. Description should include: hair, eyes, size of nose, missing teeth, jewelry, color of shoes.

Draw Your Neighbor. Everyone is furnished with pencil and paper or crayon, to draw picture of his neighbor. Pictures are posted, and group try to recognize them.

MIXERS INVOLVING NAMES

The Borrow Game. Players are seated in circle. (In very large group there can be several circles.) Every other player is "odd." When piano plays chords, each person moves counterclockwise around circle as many positions as there were chords, and must introduce himself and borrow from that person some item.

Continue until players have accumulated three or four objects, when "REVERSE" is called out. Each must quickly return borrowed objects, thank donor, and sit down. Last one down pays forfeit.

Clock Mixer. To each person is given pencil and mimeographed large clock face, marked off into 12 pie-shaped segments. First fill in 12 divisions by having 12 persons autograph the section.

When finished, leader will call out: "Go to 5 o'clock and talk about hobbies (or favorite foods, or yourselves) for 30 seconds."

Second version of this involves handing mimeographed sheet to players, with instructions: 1:00—A stranger to you. 2:00—Same color hair as yours. Then procedure is as described above for making "dates" and talking.

Group Interviews. Superior "get acquainted" game. Around small circle (not more than 15, less if possible) have people introduce themselves, one at time, telling where they are from. Then *any person* in group may ask one just self-introduced *any questions* he chooses. (Person may decline to answer if he or she prefers.) Spend one or two minutes on each person and it will be surprising to see how much you can learn about that individual.

What's My Name? For steady group, small camp, or conference. At end of two or three days, announce that during day "What's my name?" will be played. Any person may walk up to another and say, "What's my name?" If he cannot give it, he must go with questioner to shoeshine booth and shine his shoes (or other forfeit or penalty).

It's a Nice Day. Sitting in circle (or circles) of not more than 15, first person says, to second person, "I, Bert Kessel, say it's a nice day." Second says to third, "Bert Kessel told me, Betty Watts, that it's a nice day." Third says to fourth: "Bert Kessel told Betty Watts who told me, Bob Peterson, that it's a nice day," and so on until all have been successful. (More than 15 makes this a slow, abominable game.)

My Name Is . . . Like game above. "His name is Bill Beatty, her name is Catherine Allen, my name is Warren Willis," and so on around circle. (If you get stuck, others may help you.)

Who Is This? On back of each person is pinned sheet of paper. You must first talk with person, get acquainted, then write remarks on his back. Later, these remarks are read aloud to see if person can be identified.

Introductions. Each person is to agree to introduce at least two members of group to each other, at least one of whom they do not know.

Collecting Autographs. Each person has sheet of paper and pencil. They are to get names and an additional description of 10 people (such as square, round, or oval face).

NO-PARTNER MIXERS
(See also singing games)

Longest Train. Get one or more persons out on floor and, when signal "Go" is given, see which one can form longest train by getting most people into his line, each with hands placed on shoulders of person ahead of him. Then do any of activities done in lines, like "I've Been Workin' on the Railroad," or Schottische Conga Line, without partners.

Shhhhh! Have everyone present say "Shhhhhhhh," getting all quiet. Then the leader takes someone's hand and says, "Come along," that person does same to another person, and so on until all are in.

Musical Arches ("Hawaiian London Bridge"). One couple make 2-handed arch over heads of circle of players who move under arch as long as music plays. When music stops, they catch whoever is under arch and that person stands behind one of arch makers. Music resumes, and when stopped again person who was caught forms arch with one caught earlier. Next time two players are caught in two arches, and so on until all people are in couples from this "arch" procedure.

Bunny Hop (Rabbit Conga). This one has its own music, but could be done to many polka tunes. A line forms behind head person, each person with hands at waist of one ahead.

Action: Each person in line hops with left foot, and at same time flings right foot out to side; then hops again and draws foot back (but not touching floor); repeat, making twice that foot has been extended out and drawn back. With left foot, do same action, same number of times. Now with both feet together hop forward one hop, backward one hop, then three quick hops forward, twice as fast.

Conga Polka, Schottische. Basic polka or schottische step can be used by groups in conga line.

Ten Pretty Girls (Conga Line), World of Fun Record No. M113. In regular single conga line, each person, with hands on shoulders of person ahead of him, or at waist of person ahead, raises left foot and puts his left toe ahead of normal position, then out to side of normal position, then steps behind right foot with left foot and puts weight on left foot, places right foot to right of normal position, and draws left foot to right one. Now he repeats same action, starting with right foot.

Next he takes four slow walking steps, followed by leaning backward with left foot extended forward (two counts), then backward (two counts), and a stamp-stamp-stamp (left foot, right foot, left foot) in place. Next time he starts with right foot, beginning from beginning.

A Circle Mixer. To march or polka music, group circles left in large circle. Stop music, get into groups by month of birthday, color of eyes, shoes, spectacle-wearers, or any others you devise. Play music between changes. Allow people to talk a little as they get into their groups. (In some cases, specify size of groups, for example, "Not more than five of those who wear glasses, or those who do not."

Get Acquainted Shout. Form circle without partners. Each person gets acquainted with person on each side of him. Ask all to shout out at same time name of person on their left; then on their right; then own name. Music starts, and group circles to left. While it is going, they are supposed to spot someone on opposite side of circle with whom they want to change places. When music stops, all rush for other spot across circle (a real mixer!) and process is repeated there, shouting names, then marching to music.

Introduction Circle. Leader introduces himself to person in circle who responds with his or her name, then continues to every fifth person around circle, introducing self. Each person who receives introduction then starts around circle *in opposite direction,* introducing himself or herself. Continue until number of introductions have been made, when leader calls out, "Everybody home." Last one back to place becomes leader next time, and introduction process is begun again.[3]

I've Been Workin' on the Railroad. This musical game requires no partners, and can be done in several styles. For family nights and children's groups, use it in choo-choo line, one person at head as engine, and rest with hands on shoulders or at waist of person ahead, as cars.

Sometimes it is done around circle, people with arms linked, two couples, side by side. May be done in trio form also, with center person moving forward after each horn blowing, to make it progressive.

Action: All sing "I've been workin' on the railroad" as they march along. Then they stop and place left heel out to left, bring it back to place, then right heel out, bring it back, and do two knee bends, as they sing line: "All the live-long day. Hey!" Continue with this pattern, marching on one line, doing the footwork on the second line, always with the "Hey!" on second knee bend. Exception: At end, instead of knee bends, do two toots on Dinah's horn, ("Dinah, blow your horn. Toot! Toot!") pulling an imaginary cord to toot horn. *Repeat as often as desired.*

Snake Dance. As lively march gets people in mood, ask them to clap, stand, then join in snake dance. Leader takes hand, then that person takes another, and soon everybody is in circle.

Come Along. This game is usually played in circle, standing. Leader holds out hand to someone and says, "Come along." That person takes another hand with "Come along." On signal, "Go home," all return to places, and It tries to get place.

To do this cumulatively, without people standing, explain briefly how it is played, and then proceed as in Snake Dance, above, until all are in who want to be in.

WAYS OF GETTING PARTNERS

Piecing Together Objects Torn or Cut Apart. Hearts, for Valentine's Day; hatchets, for Washington's Birthday; pumpkins, cats or witches, for Hallowe'en; leaves from old magazines; words of songs, proverbs, or jokes written on paper or cardboard. These are cut apart irregularly, half being given to men, half to girls. Partners are matched up.

Sing a Song. You will find another singing same song as you, or humming same tune.

Famous Combinations. (Cut them in half.)

Persons: Antony and Cleopatra; Columbus and Queen Isabella

Foods: Peaches and cream; salt and pepper; corned beef and cabbage; ham and eggs; bread and butter; liver and bacon

Same Trade. One girl and one boy (or man and woman) has each of several occupations on slip of paper. Each goes around trying to find partner who is acting out his occupation of bus driver, ditch digger, truck driver, log chopper, violinist, house painter, and so on. Several players will have same list of occupations on their slip as you do and will have chosen one of them. Find the person who has made same choice as you have made.

Blindfold Line. Girls stand in line. Men, blindfolded, walk down the line shaking hands until they decide on partner. They must decide as they go down—no turning back. Continue until all have partners.

Fishing for Partners. Each girl has her name on card, hole near its edge, floating in tub of water. Boys fish for partners with bent-pin fish hooks on strings.

COUPLE MIXERS

Don't just say "Get a partner" (unless the group is small, and know each other very, very well). Use some of these methods to get into groups.

Accumulation. While all are standing in circle, one person marches around inside circle as music plays. When music stops, this person gets partner from circle and marches, as music begins again. At next music stop, each of two get partners, making four people on inside. Continue marching with them; when music stops, each gets new partner, to make eight people in action. Continue until all are in circle.

"Circulation" Group Starter. Tell group that you want them to get some circulation in their feet. Ask them to rise, reach as high as possible, reach out in front as far as possible, reach out to each side. (Now turn up sound of very peppy march or polka record, or have it played on piano.) Ask them to start walking, around circle to left, then to right, then all girls or women to center and back; all men or boys to center, find a girl, swing her, and all promenade. (In some cases two girls will need to be partners.) Now you have them in couples.[4]

Clap Starter. In difficult situation such as gym, play good, rhythmic record and have people stand and clap. Continuing clapping, get men or boys to come to floor, then girls and women, who make ring around men and boys. Have two circles move in opposite directions until music stops. They are now facing their first partner. With simple routine line this may be done: "Forward and bow," "Right hand turn," "Left hand turn," "Both hands turn," "Swing," "Move on to the next girl," in manner of Virginia Reel.[5]

Musical Handshake. Two circles of equal numbers of people move in opposite directions (one inside other). When they stop, each person introduces himself to other, tells a little about self. (This is sometimes used as singing mixer with the action of Looby Loo but using circles as above. See Looby Loo in Index.)

Crazy Handshakes. Procedure as in Musical Handshake. After introducing each other, leader shows group how to do fancy handshakes:

1. MODEL T FORD. Shake hands by cranking laboriously.
2. PUMP-HANDLE STYLE. Each pumps other's hand vigorously.
3. FISHERMAN'S. Each makes hands very limp, wiggles them back and forth.
4. HYDRAMATIC. Each takes hands very limply. "No clutch."
5. PAUL BUNYAN. Clasp hands in regular fashion, take own thumb in left hand, and saw back and forth (still holding hands). When the tree is sawed down, yell "Timberrr!"
6. BOXER'S. Shake own hands, above head, in various directions, as if to crowd.
7. CHINESE. Shake own hand, bow three times.
8. BASEBALL. This is like "choosing up," using bat. One person starts by making fist, thumb up. Next person takes that thumb in his fist, thumb up. Continue until hands are stacked four high, then shake them up and down.
9. SHAKE LEFT HANDS ONLY.
10. SHAKE HANDS, SIDE TO SIDE, ONLY.
11. MILKMAID STYLE. Men or boys interlace own fingers, turn hands upside down, thumbs pointed down. Girls are to take hold, milkmaid style.
12. HAND SLAP. One person extends hands out, palms toward floor. Other extends hands, fingers together, palms up. Object: For one whose hands are below to slap back of hands of one whose hands are above, before that person can withdraw hands.

When he is successful, they shift roles. Play two or three times only in this formation.

O'Grady Starter. Play "O'Grady says" in usual fashion. That is, leader gives commands to group, who follow command if O'Grady said to do it, but remain motionless unless command is preceded by magic words, "O'Grady says . . ." Finally O'Grady says, "All boys to the middle of the room." Then "All girls make a circle around them, and all boys face the girls." Then they are in position for any circle partner game.

Go Between. Ask each man to go between two girls. Girl on his right is his partner, other goes to "lost and found" department in center. Then encourage others on sidelines to come and take a partner, or let "lost and founds" go out to take a partner for themselves, Sadie Hawkins style. Or they may couple up, two girls together, where necessary.[6]

Scatter Promenade. When group is in couples, call for them to circle four, any four. (This means any two couples getting together.) Then do one figure and call "Scatter Promenade," whereupon they must "promenade" to another couple anywhere and circle with them. (For suggestions of figures, see Chapter 21.) [7]

Partner Grab (when extras are present). While lively music plays, two circles (one inside other) move in opposite directions, boys or men in one circle, girls or women in other. When music stops, each person grabs nearest player as partner. Extras go to center of circle. When music starts again, they join proper line.[8]

My Name's Jane (mixer in trios). Get into groups of three, then promenade in three's around large circle. While marching to tune of "Goodnight, Ladies," outside ones in trios (farthest from center of circle) sing, "My name's —————." Next, inside circle (persons closest to center) respond, "My name's —————"; last, middle ones sing, "My name's —————." All sing "Let's go and meet the rest." Center person in each trio moves forward to join two players ahead. All skip or march forward singing "Merrily we roll along. . . ." Then the introduction process starts again. (Leader may ask outside circle to move forward instead of middle one, or inside one.) [9]

Easy March. Ask all to rise, take one step forward, right face, start marching. When they are on floor, have them join hands, circle left, circle right, march single file again. Then men step one step to inside of circle and march in opposite direction from ladies. When call comes to "Swing" they swing with next lady they meet, and march together counterclockwise.[10]

Nursery Rhymes. There are two circles, men's inside of women's (or boys' inside of girls'). Idea is to take nursery rhyme and say or sing it, one line to each person you meet, everyone acting out words where appropriate, such as "Jack Spratt" or "Little Miss Muffett."

Creative Mixer. Divide into small groups and give group several minutes to take song and work out action to it, mixer style.

Name March. All are sitting in circle, no vacant chairs. Person in center has names of all. Scrambles names, then picks names at random and reads them aloud. These people stand and march around, counterclockwise, inside circle of chairs as march music is played. When music stops suddenly everybody, including center person, rushes for chair. One left out becomes "It" in center.

"Big Wheel" Grand March. All people arriving are given, instead of their own names (or in addition), name of famous person in history, fiction, the Bible, politics, movies, radio, or television. They are in two circles, one inside other. When music plays, circles go in opposite directions. When it stops, the two are to carry on an appropriate conversation for character they are portraying.

Lucky Spots. As couples or as individuals, people move around room as music plays. When it stops, they stop. Lucky spot No. 1 is announced, and recognition given to lucky winner. Continue until all spots have been discovered.

Musical Arches. Players form single circle. Two persons make "London Bridge" arch. All march under arch as music plays. When it stops, whoever is under goes into circle. Next time, when person is under arch, he joins with first-caught person, and the two form arches. Continue catching people in each arch until all are in the circle.

Circle Four. To good, lively march music all players start marching in circle. When leader calls out, "Circle four," they must quickly get into fours and continue circling, until another number is called. If this is "Circle six" all six must break up and scatter to other circles. "Circle all" gets all in circle. Folks left out go to center until another call is given.

Hello Grand Right and Left. As music plays in circle of couples who know how to do grand right and left, they move about, greeting each person they meet with "hello," until they get to their partners on opposite side. There they bow to partner, continue beyond partner with more "hellos" until they meet again, where they promenade some more.

Same pattern may be used for "Good-bye" or "Good night."

Missionary Barrel. Each person is to come wearing some clothes he will not need beyond tonight. (They are to be given to some service agency that can use them.) As music plays, there are two circles, one inside other. Everybody marches around, and circles continue until all have seen clothes. When music stops, two persons facing each other must exchange as many clothes as they dare, and wear them for rest of evening.

Popularity. Circle of girls moves in one direction, circle of men or boys in other (inside first circle). When music plays, all march, single file. When it stops, girls try to find partner, ask his name, find out his good and bad qualities. When music starts again, circles start again.

Name Tag March. In meetings using name tags, each person takes off his tag, drops it on floor, toward center of circle. Then single circle moves to music about halfway around when the music stops. Each person is to pick up name tag and try to find its owner, get acquainted. Name may be shouted out.

Ten Little Handshakes

THE SONG: (Tune is Ten Little Indians)

> One little, two little, three little handshakes;
> Four little, five little, six little handshakes;
> Seven little, eight little, nine little handshakes;
> Ten little handshakes all.

FORMATION: Two circles, one inside other. They move slowly in opposite directions as people sing and walk along, shaking hands. On tenth handshake, give specially hearty one and get acquainted.

DANCE FORMATION MIXERS

Do-Si-Do Mixer. Using lively march, polka, or square dance music (all in circle):

1. All join hands and balance in (walk to center four steps and back). *Repeat.* (See "Glossary of Folk Dance Terms" in Chapter 21.)
2. Do-si-do with corner, do-si-do with partner (back to back).
3. Allemande left with corner, allemande right with partner.
4. Swing the corner and promenade.

Hello and Good-Bye (to march or Glow Worm, or Four Leaf Clover)

FORMATION: Double circle, men on inside. Circle faces counter-clockwise; man holds girl's left hand in his right hand.

ACTION: (1) Walk forward four steps. (2) Partners face each other, each walks backward four steps. (3) Each man now moves toward girl who was at his left, and she toward him. (4) These new partners join right hands and walk around each other with one complete turn. Now they are in promenade position, ready to move forward again.

NOTES: It is helpful to call out one-word or two-word description of action, as: (1) "Forward." (2) "Part" or "Apart." (3) "New Girl." (4) "Turn."

Irish Washerwoman Mixer

FORMATION: Single circle, facing in.

THE CALL: 1. "All join hands and into the middle,
2. With your big foot keep time to the fiddle,
3. When you get back, remember my call,
4. Swing on the corner and promenade all."

ACTION: 1. All walk to center four steps. 2. All stamp foot four counts. 3. All back to place four steps. 4. Swing corner once and promenade (16 counts in all for promenade).

Texas Schottische (World of Fun Record M102)

FORMATION: Double circle, facing counterclockwise. Man reaches across girl's shoulder to take her left hand in his, across his chest to take her hand in his.

ACTION: Each person takes step diagonally forward, slightly toward center with left foot; draws right foot up to left foot; steps again with left foot, pauses one count, to one measure of music. Now he does same with right foot leading, draws left foot to it, steps with right again, pauses.

Now he does four slow walking steps, left, right, left, right. Last, each person puts down left heel (count 1) then toe (count 2), and girl takes three quick walking steps, dropping right hand, going over to left side of man (pausing on count 4). Same action with right heel and toe and three more fast walking steps. She completes her turn, ending up at right of man who was behind her, with hands raised, ready for him to take her and begin again, with her left hand in his.

You say: "Left, slide, left and right, slide, right, and walk, walk, walk, walk. Heel and toe and walk, walk, walk. Heel and toe and walk, walk, walk."

VARIATIONS:

1. Instead of four slow walking steps, do eight fast running ones.
2. Do everything double time. (Instead of "heel and toe and," do heel-toe, heel-toe, and so on.)
3. Instead of passing girl back, keep her one time, send her back next.
4. Do opening steps like Ten Pretty Girls, up to "heel and toe and halfway round."
5. Partner-stealing version. As girl turns and faces halfway round, extra girls (who are on outside of circle) beat them to their partners. Those left out wait until next time. For men to steal, they stand in men's circle and receive girl as she comes back.

Jessie Polka (Any tempo polka record will do.)

FORMATION: Various. In couples, skating position; or without partners in conga line, or side by side, 3, 4 or more abreast. Step is same.

ACTION: With weight on right foot, point left heel forward, put it back in place. Shift weight to left foot and point right heel forward, bring it back to place, right toe backward, then bring it to place; shift weight to right foot and extend left foot forward, then bring it back diagonally in front of right foot with a fast sweeping motion; then lead with left foot for four polka steps. (Step with left, bring right foot to it, step with left again, pause; repeat same footwork, beginning with right foot.) Continue as long as desired.

Patty Cake Polka (World of Fun Record M107, "Little Brown Jug")

FORMATION: Double circle, men facing partners with their backs to center of circle, both with arms outstretched, hands joined.

ACTION: Starting with man's left, girl's right: touch heel to floor, then toe, then heel, then toe and do four slides around circle, counterclockwise. Repeat with opposite foot, coming back to place with same action.

PATTY CAKE: Partners face and clap right hands three times, left hands with each other three times, both hands three times, then slap knees three times. Hook right arms, walk around (or polka) and the man moves to next girl to his left (counterclockwise) to begin again.

Clap Marlene (adapted and simplified from Lili Marlene, "Susan's Gavotte," World of Fun Record M113)

FORMATION: Double circle of partners, men on inside, facing counterclockwise, inside hands joined.

ACTION:

1. Beginning with outside foot, take four walking steps forward, then partners face quickly and continue to slide four quick slides in same direction. Same action, back to place.
2. Clap own hands, then right on partner's right. Own hands, then left on partner's left; own, then both hands on partner's hands; clap own once again.
3. Link right arms and circle halfway around each other; left arms and back to place.
4. Repeat No. 2 exactly.
5. Link right arms, go all way around partner, man moves to next girl to his left, to begin from beginning.

Captain Jinks Mixer (World of Fun Record M103)

FORMATION: Single circle of partners, facing center.

ACTION:

1. Walk eight steps clockwise.
2. Walk eight steps, counterclockwise.
3. Four steps toward center and back, hands joined.
4. Swing corner person, who becomes new partner.

Jingle Bells Mixer

FORMATION: Couples in double circle, facing counterclockwise, inside hands joined.

ACTION: Eight walking steps forward, then eight steps backward. Four slides counterclockwise, then four back to place; then right shoulder do-si-do (back to back).

ON "JINGLE BELLS": On partner's hands, clap right hand three times, left three times, both five times, then link right arms, and go once completely around each other. *Repeat* Jingle Bells action, this time ending with man facing another girl, one to his left.

Circle Virginia Reel

FORMATION: Double circle, men with backs to center, facing partners, six feet separating them.

ACTION: (Calls are in quotation marks.)

1. "Forward and bow." Partners take three steps toward each other and bow or curtsey, back to place.
2. "Right hand swing." Raise right hand, join with partner, circle around each other, return to place.
3. "Left hand swing," "Both hands swing," "Right arm swing," "Left arm swing" all based on No. 2 with appropriate hands or arms used.
4. "Right halfway, left back." Swing around, right arms, halfway around; shift to left arm and return to place.
5. "Right shoulder, do-si-do." Partners advance toward each other, pass right shoulders, go around each other back to back, return to place.
6. "Left shoulder, do-si-do." Same, with left shoulder passing.

7. "Bow to the next girl." Each man advances to girl at his left and bows to her. Then begin with No. 2, above, and continue through No. 7, repeating as long as desired or until music ends.

Freeze. Novelty action. When music is stopped suddenly, each couple must freeze where they are and remain motionless. Those who move are eliminated. See who can last longest.[11]

Tray Mixer

FORMATION: Two lines, men and women, down length of room and close to one side of it. Two lines face three chairs. Leader sits in center chair, and first two persons in line of opposite sex to leader come and sit in chairs. He gives tray to one and polkas, schottisches, waltzes (whatever the music is) off with other one. That person holding tray goes to center chair, and two others come to sit in other chairs, with same procedure as at first. To stop game, stop tray passing.[12]

Good Night, Ladies

FORMATION: Double circle of partners, men on inside, women on outside, facing each other.

ACTION: As all sing, men bow low to their partners (who curtsey) as they sing first "Good night, ladies." Then men move to left to next lady for second "Good night, ladies," move third time for third "Good night, ladies," and fourth time "We're going to leave you now." Take this one for partner and skip or march around circle, promenade fashion. *Now repeat all action with verses* "Farewell, ladies," and "Sweet dreams, ladies." Emotion at parting is sometimes exaggerated for effect.

Following this action, many groups close with fellowship circle (all standing side by side, hands crossed in front, holding hands with those on either side) and sing quiet hymns, spirituals, and perhaps a prayer.

Standing Good Night Ladies. Group stand in circle, hands crossed in front and joined with neighbors on both sides. All bow low to left on first "Good night, ladies," to right on second one, toward middle on third. On "Merrily . . ." all wave joined hands up and down, gently.

Good Night Grand Right and Left

FORMATION: Single circle of partners, ready to say good night.
ACTION: As they go through Grand Right and Left figure, each person says, "Good night" to each person he or she meets, until meeting partner. Bow to partner, continue beyond with more good nights. Second time, swing partner and promenade as directed.

ANALYSIS OF GAMES

Again an analysis is provided for the recreation leader's use. It indicates by check mark details for most of the mixers described in this chapter such as whether a certain formation is required of the group, size of group for which the mixer is appropriate, whether it is to be played with partner or without, with music, what type of mixer, and so on.

No = NO FORMATION / II = LINES / O = CIRCLE	FORMATION	LEARNING NAMES	GETTING PARTNERS	CHANGING PARTNERS	WITH PARTNERS	WITHOUT PARTNERS	HAND SHAKING	SMALL GROUP	LARGE GROUP	WITH MUSIC	SINGING	MALES ONLY	FEMALES ONLY
(HANDSHAKERS) LUCKY SHAKE	No	✓				✓	✓		✓			✓	✓
SHAKE OR ELSE	No	✓				✓	✓		✓			✓	✓
BAG SHAKE	No	✓				✓	✓		✓			✓	✓
HANDSHAKING DOWN THE AISLE	II	✓				✓	✓		✓			✓	✓
CIRCLE HANDSHAKE	O					✓	✓		✓	✓		✓	✓
(TRADING OR USING OBJECTS) EVEN OR ODD	No					✓		✓	✓			✓	✓
BARTER	No					✓		✓	✓			✓	✓
COLOR BARTER	No					✓		✓	✓			✓	✓
NUMBERS MIXER	No					✓		✓	✓			✓	✓
MEAL MIXER	No					✓		✓				✓	✓
HUMAN SCAVENGER HUNT	No					✓		✓	✓			✓	✓
WHO IS	No					✓		✓	✓			✓	✓
ANIMAL HUNT	O's					✓		✓	✓			✓	✓
CONVERSATION SYSTEM						✓		✓				✓	✓
NAME TAG RULE						✓			✓			✓	✓
ROTATION	II					✓		✓				✓	✓
EATING BUNS	No					✓		✓				✓	✓
REMINISCENCE			✓		✓				✓			✓	✓
CONTROLLED CONFUSION	No								✓			✓	✓
FACE TO FACE	2's				✓				✓			✓	✓
(GAMELIKE MIXERS) BASKETBALL MIXER	II	✓							✓			✓	✓
CO-OPERATIVE SPELLING	No					✓			✓			✓	✓
HUMMER	2's				✓			✓	✓			✓	✓
MISSING PERSONS DESCRIPTION	2's	✓			✓			✓				✓	✓
DRAW YOUR NEIGHBOR	2s	✓			✓			✓				✓	✓
(MIXERS INVOLVING NAMES) THE BORROW GAME	O	✓			✓				✓			✓	✓
CLOCK MIXER	No	✓				✓							
GROUP INTERVIEW	O	✓				✓		✓	✓				
WHAT'S MY NAME	No	✓				✓		✓	✓			✓	✓
IT'S A NICE DAY	O	✓				✓		✓	✓			✓	✓
MY NAME IS...	O	✓				✓		✓	✓			✓	✓
WHO IS THIS?	No	✓				✓		✓	✓			✓	✓
INTRODUCTIONS	No	✓				✓		✓	✓			✓	✓
COLLECTING AUTOGRAPHS	No	✓				✓		✓	✓			✓	✓
(No = PARTNER MIXERS) LONGEST TRAIN	II					✓		✓	✓			✓	✓
SHHHHH!	No	✓				✓		✓	✓			✓	✓
MUSICAL ARCHIVES	II												
THE BUNNY HOP	I					✓		✓	✓	✓			✓
CONGA POLKA	I					✓		✓	✓	✓			✓
TEN PRETTY GIRLS	I					✓		✓	✓	✓	✓		✓
A CIRCLE MIXER	O					✓			✓	✓	✓		✓
GET ACQUAINTED SHOUT	O					✓	✓		✓		✓		✓
INTRODUCTION CIRCLE	O					✓	✓		✓				✓
I'VE BEEN WORKING ON THE RAILROAD	I					✓			✓				✓
SNAKE DANCE	I					✓		✓	✓				✓
COME ALONG	O					✓		✓	✓				✓

	FORMATION	LEARNING NAMES	GETTING PARTNERS	CHANGING PARTNERS	WITH PARTNERS	WITHOUT PARTNERS	HAND SHAKING	SMALL GROUP	LARGE GROUP	WITH MUSIC	SINGING	MALES ONLY	FEMALES ONLY
(WAYS OF GETTING PARTNERS)													
PIECING TOGETHER OBJECTS	No	✓	✓		✓				✓	✓			✓
SING A SONG	No	✓	✓		✓				✓	✓			✓
FAMOUS COMBINATION	No	✓	✓		✓				✓	✓			✓
SAME TRADE	No	✓	✓		✓				✓	✓			✓
BLINDFOLDED LINE	I		✓				✓		✓	✓			✓
FISHING FOR PARTNERS	No		✓				✓	✓	✓	✓			✓
(COUPLE MIXERS)													
ACCUMULATION	O		✓			✓			✓	✓			✓
"CIRCULATION" GROUP STARTER	O		✓			✓			✓	✓			✓
CLAP STARTER	O		✓			✓			✓	✓			✓
MUSICAL HANDSHAKE	O		✓	✓			✓		✓	✓			✓
CRAZY HANDSHAKES	O		✓	✓			✓		✓	✓		✓	✓
O'GRADY STARTER	II		✓			✓			✓			✓	✓
GO BETWEEN	O		✓			✓			✓	✓			✓
SCATTER PROMENADE	O			✓	✓				✓				✓
PARTNER GRAB	O		✓	✓					✓				✓
MY NAME'S JANE (3's)	O	✓	✓	✓					✓	✓	✓	✓	✓
EASY MARCH	O		✓			✓			✓	✓			✓
NURSERY RHYMES	O			✓		✓			✓	✓	✓		✓
CREATIVE MIXER	O					✓			✓		✓	✓	✓
NAME MARCH	O	✓				✓			✓	✓		✓	✓
BIG WHEEL GRAND MARCH	O			✓		✓			✓	✓		✓	✓
LUCKY SPOTS	No				✓	✓			✓	✓	✓	✓	✓
MUSICAL ARCHES	O		✓			✓			✓	✓		✓	✓
CIRCLE FOUR	O				✓	✓			✓	✓		✓	✓
HELLO GRAND RIGHT AND LEFT	O		✓			✓			✓	✓			✓
MISSIONARY BARREL	O			✓	✓		✓		✓	✓			✓
POPULARITY	O	✓	✓	✓			✓		✓	✓		✓	✓
NAME TAG MARCH	O	✓	✓	✓			✓		✓	✓		✓	✓
TEN LITTLE HANDSHAKES	O	✓		✓			✓		✓	✓		✓	✓
(DANCE FORMATION MIXERS)													
DO - SI - DO MIXER	O			✓	✓				✓	✓			✓
HELLO AND GOOD BYE	O			✓	✓				✓	✓	✓		✓
IRISH WASHERWOMAN MIXER	O			✓	✓				✓	✓	✓		✓
TEXAS SCHOTTISCHE	O			✓	✓			✓	✓	✓	✓		✓
JESSIE POLKA	I				✓	✓		✓	✓	✓			✓
PATTY CAKE POLKA	O			✓	✓					✓			✓
CLAP MARLENE	O			✓	✓					✓			✓
CAPTAIN JINX MIXER	O			✓	✓			✓	✓	✓	✓		✓
JINGLE BELLS MIXER	O			✓	✓			✓	✓	✓	✓		✓
CIRCLE VIRGINIA REEL	O			✓	✓			✓	✓	✓			✓
FREEZE	O				✓			✓	✓	✓			✓
TRAY MIXER	II				✓			✓	✓	✓			✓
GOOD NIGHT, LADIES	O			✓	✓			✓	✓	✓			✓
STANDING GOOD NIGHT LADIES	O				✓	✓		✓	✓	✓			✓
GOOD NIGHT GRAND RIGHT AND LEFT	O			✓	✓			✓	✓	✓			✓

15

Music

No one can experience beauty for me. It is a personal matter which I must experience for myself. As to what bounds it radiates in my own life and, breaking these bounds, touches other lives, is dependent upon how wholeheartedly I join in this quest.

Listen each day to some great music. In ten minutes you can hear one movement of a symphony by radio or phonograph, but listen intently. Give it your best listening. In absorbing the beauties of a great masterpiece you will find that there are areas in your consciousness that can be touched only by beauty. For your finest thoughts and ideals you are constantly drawing from these areas. They must be replenished.

Many of the tensions of these days can be released through music. In the welter of world emotions, the yearnings of the soul are still there. There is an ancient strength drawn from the accumulated energy and beauty of the ages, which possesses and repossesses us when we search for the beautiful. It may give to us and to many others that needed lift when times are dark. . . .

Music is the most democratic of the arts, especially when people sing together. Music, like all the arts, kindles the imagination and carries us down the roads of the past and over the highways of the present.[1]

THERE MAY BE A PROFESSIONAL SONG LEADER available to direct the group singing for some occasions, but there are many times when the recreation leader needs to do it himself. This chapter attempts to explain some of the simpler techniques of group singing under such headings as Functions of Group Singing, Preparation for Group Singing, When You Lead Group Singing, Uses of Music Other Than Group Singing, and Games with Music. Then there is also a whole section of words and melodies for Mealtime Prayers, Rounds, Nature Songs, Songs for Fun and Novelty, Motion Songs, and Spirituals.

Barber Shop Quartet?

FUNCTIONS OF GROUP SINGING

Of all the forces to unify a group, group singing is one of the best. It is usable in more varied situations than almost any other kind of recreational material. Here are some of its functions:

It loosens and livens a group. When people have just come together they need to sing out. (One recreation leader has the group stand up and sing one note as loud as it can, to warm itself up!) Singing is an almost sure cure for stiffness and uneasiness as a new group gets together. To a group whose members already know each other well, it gives a chance for expression. Then, too, in long meetings singing can furnish needed breathers or stretchers.

It expresses many kinds of feelings such as these: the spirit of play and the mood of nonsense; the spirit of fellowship, that group feeling of exuberance and of deep togetherness; nostalgia—the sweet looking-backward through rose-colored glasses; the spirit of love and affection toward each other, individuals, causes; dedication to group purposes.

It creates beauty, harmony; patriotism; empathy—the ability to feel into the situation of others, especially in folk songs or spirituals; the spirit of worship—love of God, gratitude to God, appreciation for God's creation.

It recognizes achievement or contributions to group life by members or others, as well as meritorious service, retirements ("Jolly

Good Fellow"); birthdays, weddings, anniversaries ("Happy Birthday"); presence of visitors ("We're Glad You're Here").

PREPARATION FOR GROUP SINGING

Most leaders have some system of keeping up with their songs. Some use looseleaf notebooks, others card files. Some leaders prepare a pasted-up notebook for an accompanist. Some select a good songbook and use almost entirely from it. It is well to get a supply of songbooks, but groups should be encouraged to learn the songs as quickly as possible. The most used and best loved songs are memorized.

Overplan—at least, be ready with more things than you will need. Have them listed in easy-to-see categories. Get there early to see that song sheets are in place, check the spot from which you are to lead singing. How does it feel? How shall you divide up for rounds or part singing? If a microphone is to be used, check your voice over it. (Sometimes too much treble will make the tone sharp.)

Practice with an advance group. A small group who happen to be around earlier may serve as a nucleus in introducing new songs.

Learn a lot of different types of songs. A book like this *Omnibus of Fun* is of necessity limited in the number of songs offered. If you are a leader, keep ahead of the group as much as you can.

Some leaders like to use a theme idea like Western songs, work songs, love songs. A little narrative may be woven in with song titles. (Detailed suggestions are given in the book *How to Lead Group Singing,* listed in the Bibliography.)

WHEN YOU LEAD GROUP SINGING

Here are some simple pointers that song leaders have learned from long experience and an explanation of the basic beats in directing.

1. Get your group into a singable mood. Cluster them as closely together as possible if they are spread out, and if they can be clustered without too much ado. Gathered around the piano, around the fire, on the steps of a building, on the pier, they are sitting close together. That in itself means better singing. A few humorous bits, a stretcher or group starter (see Chapter 12) may put the group in a better mood than they were when you "got them."

2. Face them pleasantly and start with one of your easier songs to sing. This is good practice, whether the singing is for fun or for religious expression. (If you are nervous, try the simple trick of rising on your toes, stretching. That relieves "mike" fright for some leaders and singers, too.[2])

3. Sing with the group. If you are using an accompanist, try to give clear signals for starting and for tempo. Whether you can "beat the time" or not, show as much animation as you can in your leadership. Do what comes naturally. (If you are a rank amateur, you may admit it, but don't dwell on it.)

4. Accompaniment is often needed. For some songs, accompaniment is essential. Besides the piano a portable or full-size organ, a guitar, autoharp, harmolin, ukulele, make interesting accompaniments, as well as violin, clarinet, recorder, and other instruments (even a musical whistle) for flavor. Many folk songs, however, sound better unaccompanied. Rounds, too, are better that way.

5. Move according to the plans you have decided will be good. If there is some "honoring" to be done, sing to the person. A good trick always is to ask, "How many have had birthdays in the past month?" Then have everybody else sing "Happy Birthday" to them.

6. Encourage the group to sing. Get them to sing loud. Then try something with harmony. (Merely to say, "Try harmony this time" on a song like "Stand the Storm," may bring wonderful harmony.) Even the monotones should be encouraged! Help the group to better their standard, but don't set it so high that it eliminates anyone. *Group singing is inclusive.*

7. Use phonograph records if they help. Folk songs may be learned in this manner.

8. Teach some songs if you like, but space them out with familiar songs. Use easy-to-teach ones at first.

9. Try to catch the wave-length of the group. "Play them by ear," listening to their enthusiasm (or the lack of it), watching expressions. Shift what you had preplanned, if necessary.

10. If you decide to take requests, jot several down and sing the most usable ones.[3] Sometimes people will request a song you do not know. Say, "If anyone here can lead it, I think it would

be fine to sing it." But say it sincerely and give the volunteer a chance if one does materialize.

11. Close in the proper mood for whatever is coming next on the program, for songs create moods. If the speaker is likely to start off with a lively joke, you will not want to end the song period with a quiet feeling. Keep the ending appropriate. Music makes wonderful fellowship closings for programs. (See Closings in Index.)

The Motions. Newcomers to the field of song leading should not worry too much about "the motions." However, it is good to know basic beats. (See also page 33, *How to Lead Group Singing*.)

Two-four time (2/4) is to be indicated with a down, up motion, one complete down-up motion to each measure. The speed and style of the motion will determine how the group sings.

Three-four time (3/4) is a triangle, with the motion down toward the waist (count one), out away from the body (count two), and up to the starting point (count three).

Four-four time (4/4) adds one beat. It is down (count one), in toward the middle of the body (count two), then out (count three), and up (count four).

Often fast 6/8 time will be beaten as 2/4 time. Occasionally 3/4 time, if sung fast, will be grouped, two measures together, and indicated in the same manner.

Outlining. The other major help to the new leader is outlining. That means, with the hand held parallel to floor or ground, indicating the level of the note as you go up and down the scale. With practice you can become very proficient at this. It is better in music the time of which is irregular, or in teaching a new song. Here you can show just where the note goes!

Practice before a mirror will show you how you appear to those you have been leading. There is no substitute for effort and repetition in becoming "good at leading the singing."

John Wesley's Singing Rules. The Wesleyan Revival in England in the 1700's was due largely to the spirited singing. Wesley laid down these rules:

1. Learn the rules.
2. Sing the hymns exactly as they are printed.

3. Sing all. See that you join with the congregation as freely as you can.
4. Sing lustily and with good courage. Beware of singing as if you are half-dead or half-asleep.
5. Sing in time. Whatever time is sung, be sure to keep with it.
6. Sing spiritually, above all. Have an eye to God in every word you sing. Attend strictly to the sense of what you sing.

USES OF MUSIC OTHER THAN GROUP SINGING

Singing is not the only way in which music can be used for recreational purposes, as is indicated by the types of musical entertainment which follow:

1. RHYTHM BANDS. Little children begin to learn rhythm and appreciation of music and harmony in these. Instruments can be improvised from bottles, sticks or sounding metal, or bought from music stores. Use good music.
2. BANDS. Many groups could sponsor band or orchestra to give expression to their members. Specialized groups like "uke" clubs or mandolin or guitar clubs could play for each other's entertainment.
3. RECORD-LISTENING. In this day of "hi-fi" enthusiasts, any music that has broad range is their "meat." That means that some of better compositions can be played on this equipment for more complete enjoyment. Take care about playing symphony and long-hair music for meals, however. Many people do not enjoy it. Lighter music is key here.
4. LEARNING AN INSTRUMENT EN MASSE. Such instruments as autoharp or guitar can be taught to number of folk at same time.
5. CREATIVE WRITING OF MUSIC. Mary Elizabeth McDonald, who arranged much of music for this book, has had great success with giving group 15 to 30 minutes to compose greeting song, grace for the table, or other specific assignment. (Even doing singing commercial is creative!)
6. TALENT NIGHT, when it encourages real talent, can be means of stimulating group members to develop skills with music instruments, including voice.
7. GOING TO CONCERTS AND OTHER MUSIC PRESENTATIONS will

also encourage group members to broaden their appreciation of music. Good music is not necessarily "long-hair."

8. SET UP A MUSIC COMMITTEE, if appropriate for your organization.

GAMES WITH MUSIC

Shoe Game

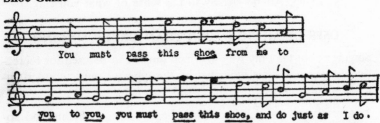

You must pass this shoe from me to you to you, you must pass this shoe, and do just as I do.

All sit in circle and sing, each player having one of his shoes off his foot, in front of him. Players pass shoes in rhythm, reaching to left and grasping shoe on off counts, and on strong beats (as indicated in music) passing shoe to next neighbor to the right. (In other words, on the words *pass, shoe, you, you, pass, shoe,* you are bumping shoe down for righthand neighbor.) On words "Do just what I do," hold onto the shoe, this time touching it down to right, left, and right, then as music starts from beginning, pass shoe on again. (Attributed to Brazil, Holland, and other countries.) Can be elimination game, but fun just to play to see who misses.

As table fun, pass spoon instead of shoe.

Get Up.[4] As music plays, players are seated in circle with extra in center. If extra is boy, he goes to girl and calls, "Get up," which she does quickly and he takes her seat. She rushes to boy and calls "Get up," and he does same. If music is stopped while boy is in center, point counts for girl and vice versa. Decide on point limit or time limit to win.

Name Six. Music plays as small object is passed around players. When music stops, person holding ball must name six objects beginning with letter called out by leader.

Broom Marching. As players march around room, one has broom for partner. When music stops, all must change partners. "Broom person" drops broom and gets into scramble. One left out marches with broom next time. (More than one broom could be used.)

Mother Goose Song. Divide larger group into smaller ones, each of which gets one minute to think up all nursery rhymes they can (not writing them down). All sing chorus, as indicated in the music, with letters, and then to same tune one group must sing one of its rhymes, such as "Hickory dickory dock." After they have completed their song, all join in chorus once again, and leader quickly (and unexpectedly) points to another group to sing. No group may sing rhyme that has been used before. May be used on elimination basis, gradually speeded up, but this is not necessary for fun.

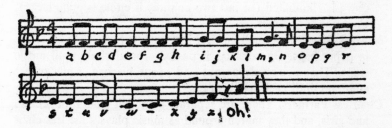

Going to Jerusalem. There is one less chair in row, alternating with seats facing front and back. Players march around as music plays. One is left out. Take away one chair and play music again. Continue until there is one player left.

This is partner-getting affair. First two people left out are partners, if of proper sex. At least boy gets first girl; girl gets first boy. Then they are ready for next partner activity. (If trios are desired, first three are in trio.)

Musical Men.[5] Boys make circle. Have them practice to see how far they can drop down on right knee. Have girls march around, looking them over. When music stops, boys drop on one knee (substitution for chair), and each girl must find knee. Girl left out is paired with boy who is removed (as in Going to Jerusalem for chairs) and they are partners.

Musical Girls. Same idea, with girls standing, one hand on hip, arms out alternately so that when music stops, each man has chance at every other arm, as in Going to Jerusalem. The man left out is paired with girl who is removed (like chair in preceding game). Continue on elimination basis.

Blocked Chairs. Similar game, chairs arranged as in Going to Jerusalem. When music stops, leader calls "Up" and each person tries to get back of chair. If "Down" is called, each person tries to sit in chair. Those left out step back. Instead of removing chairs, leader drops card on chair bearing words, "No seat." It can neither be sat in nor held onto. This means that players remaining have to walk by number of chairs they cannot use to find one that they can, as game nears end.

Squat. Marching in partners to music, boys are asked to "reverse march" making circles go in opposite directions. When music stops, each must find partner and squat (or stoop). Last couple down is eliminated (or last two or three if circle is quite large). Continue for winner.

Musical Pass. Some small musical instruments from dime store are in paper bags. One of bags is passed around circle until music stops. That person drops out and opens his bag, while others continue until each has instrument.

Chairless Partners. There are separate circles of chairs for fellows and girls, and they march around as music plays. One less chair in each circle than players. Boy and girl who are left out become partners for next activity, after eliminations are over.

AND NOW LET'S SING

The following 45 songs are selected for their functional values and given here because most are not found in any one collection, and some are new in print. We assume you will use a basic songbook (see Bibliography) for your broader repertoire. Because the music had to be set where it would fit on the page, the order of songs does not always follow the proper categories as listed. Most of the music has been arranged, and some written, by Miss McDonald.[6]

MEALTIME PRAYERS

Now Let Every Tongue
Thank You for This Lovely Day
Thank You for the World So Sweet
God Is Great

NOW LET EVERY TONGUE ADORE THEE

Bach

Now let ev- ery tongue a- dore Thee Let men with an- gels

sing be- fore Thee In praise to Thee for ev- er more

THANK YOU FOR THIS LOVELY DAY

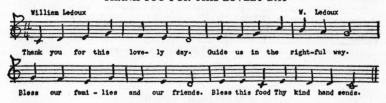

William Ledoux   W. Ledoux

Thank you for this love- ly day. Guide us in the right-ful way.

Bless our fami- lies and our friends. Bless this food Thy kind hand sends.

THANK YOU FOR THE WORLD SO SWEET

Thank you for the world so sweet, Thank you for the food we eat,

Thank you for the birds that sing, Thank you, God, for ev'- ry-thing

GOD IS GREAT

God is great and God is good, And we thank Him

for this food. By Thy hand have we been fed Give us, Lord our

dai- ly bread Give us, Lord, our dai- ly bread

ROUNDS

Echo Yodel
Allelujah
Dona Nobis Pacem
Alleluia
Shalom Chaverim
Let Us Sing Together

ECHO YODEL

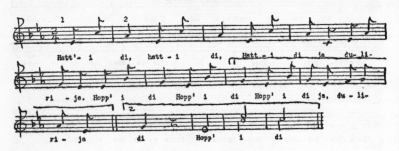

ALLELUJAH ROUND

DONA NOBIS PACEM

ALLELUIA

SHALOM CHAVERIM

* Succeeding voices enter here. May be sung in parts, up to eight.
(Pronounced: "Shallom chah-vay reem" "ch" as in German,
somewhat like the hard K in "keep")

PEACE I ASK OF THEE †

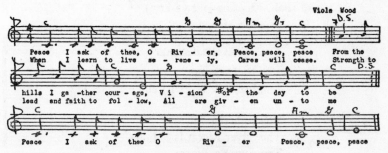

† Copright © 1941 by Janet Tobin. Used by permission.

LET US SING TOGETHER

This three-part round has been adapted from the Czech folk tune "Tancuj."

Here is an interesting Jewish version, using syncopation with an eighth rest preceding the first "Torah" in lines where the word appears two or three times. The numerals correspond to the above.

I. Torah, torah-torah,
   Torah, torah-torah,
   Torah T'sivah Lanoo Moshe. (To-rah tsee vah lahn-oo mo-sheh)

II. Torah torah, torah torah,
    Torah T'sivah Lanoo Moshe.

III. Morashah K'hilat Yakov (sing three times)
     (Mo-ra-shah, Kay hee-laht ya-kov)
     Torah T'sivah Lanoo Moshe.

NATURE SONGS

4-H Field Song
Land of the Silver Birch
Peace I Ask of Thee
The Ash Grove
The Silver Moon Is Shining
The Sun Be Warm

4-H FIELD SONG †

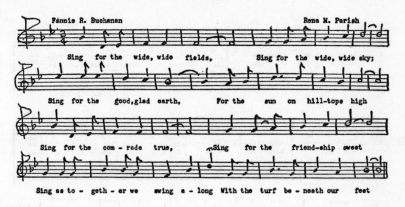

Fannie R. Buchanan   Rena M. Parish

Sing for the wide, wide fields, Sing for the wide, wide sky;

Sing for the good, glad earth, For the sun on hill-tops high

Sing for the com-rade true, Sing for the friend-ship sweet

Sing as to-geth-er we swing a-long With the turf be-neath our feet

LAND OF THE SILVER BIRCH

Boom-ba-de um boom Boom ba de um boom Land of the sil-ver birch

Home of the bea-ver Where still the migh-ty moose

Refrain:

Wan-ders at will. Blue lake and rock-y shore I will re-

turn once more Boom ba de um boom, Boom ba de um boom, Boom ba de um boom, Boom

2. Swift as the silver fish
   Canoe of birch bark,
   O'er mighty waterways,
   Carry me forth.
      Refrain

3. My heart grows sick for thee,
   Here on the lowlands,
   I will return to thee
   Hills of the North.
      Refrain

THE ASH GROVE

Welsh Folk Song

1. The ash grove how grace - ful, how plain - ly 'tis
When - ev - er the light - through it's branch - es - is

speak - ing the harp through it play - ing has lan - guage for me
break - ing, a host of kind fac - es is gaz - ing on me

The friends of my child-hood a - gain are be - fore me each

step wakes a mem 'ry as free - ly I roam; With

soft whis - pers la - den, its leaves rus - tle o're me, The

Ash - grove the ash - grove a - lone is my home.

THE SILVER MOON IS SHINING ‡

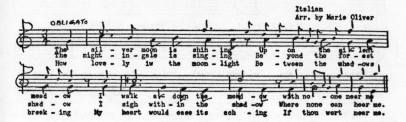

THE SUN BE WARM

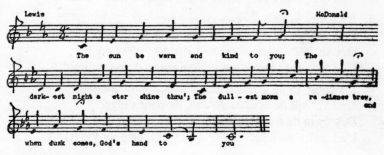

Nice at campfire closing

SONGS FOR FUN AND NOVELTY

It's Going to Be a Long Vinter
Old King Cole
Hi, Marsha Peter
Planting Rice
Old McDonald
Let's All Sing Like the Goldfish Sing
Down at the Station Saga
I Love My Rooster
Calliope Song
This Ol' Hammah

‡ From *Ten Folk Songs and Ballads*. Permission from E. C. Schirmer, Boston.

IT'S GOING TO BE A LONG VINTER

It's going to be a long vin-ter And vat vill de
boidies do den de poor t'ings? Dey'll fly to de barn, youse to
keep dere-selves varm, Und tuck der heads un-der dere vings, de poor t'ings

2. It's going to be a looooong springtime,
   And vat vill de boidies do den, de poor t'ings?
   Dey fly to de sky, youse to keep dereselves dry
   Und tuck dere heads under dere vings, de poor t'ings!

3. It's going to be a loooooooong sommer,
   Und vat vill de boidies do den, de poor t'ings?
   Dey sit in de pool, yoost to keep dereselves cool
   Und tuck dere heads under dere vings, de poor t'ings!

4. It's going to be a loooooooooooooooong autumn,
   Und vat vill de boidies do den, de poor t'ings?
   Dey fly in de trees, youse to sit in de breeze,
   Und tuck dere heads under dere vings, de poor t'ings!

(*As the song is sung, the word "long" gets longer and longer.*
De is pronounced "duh.")

HI, MARSHA PETER
(*Motion Song*)

Hi, Marsha Pe-ter, Hi, Marsha Paul Hi, Marsh-a
Pe-ter Hi Mar sha Paul Hi Marsha Pe-ter,
Hi Marsha Paul, Hi Mar sha Pe-ter, Mar sha Paul

The tune for this song is a variation of "Under the Spreading Chestnut Tree." The words are simply "Hi, Marsha Peter, Hi, Marsha Paul."

The fun comes from dropping words, one at a time, continuing to sing until only the "Hi" remains.

First drop Peter, then Paul, then Marsha.

Mrs. R. O. Bechtel,
Wakarusha, Indiana

OLD KING COLE

2. "Mulligan again today," said the private
3. "We want a ten day leave," said the captain
4. "Hold my horse by the head," said the major
5. "The army's gone to the dogs," said the gen'ral

DIRECTIONS: The players are divided into five sections. The entire group sings the first two lines of the song. The first section—representing the buglers—then rises and sings the chorus.

The song is repeated, the second section of players—representing the privates—rising and singing the second line. Immediately (in rhythm) the first section rises and sings the first line, and the entire group sings the chorus.

On the next repetition, the third section sings the third line, then the second group, then the first, then the chorus.

Continue through the 5th verse in this manner.

PLANTING RICE

Filipino Folk Song

Plant - ing rice is nev - er fun, Bent from morn 'till set of sun. Can - not stand, and can - not sit, Can-not rest for a lit-tle bit. Plant- ing rice is no fun; Bent from morn 'till set of sun; Can - not stand; can- not sit; can- not rest for a lit - tle bit

CHANT

Divide into two groups, one singing the background chant, "Planting, Planting," the other sings the words. Sing twice through, continuing the "Planting" chant beyond the end, then fading out.

OLD MC DONALD (SYMPHONIC STYLE)

Use regular verses of Ol' McDonald Had a Farm (with chick, duck, wife—"gimme," daughter—"smack-smack").

Next have the entire group follow directions. "Don't get ahead," "don't get behind." Then direct slowly, holding out "farm," and singing "E-i-e-i-o" with great feeling. "And on this farm he had some chicks!" (Cut off short.) "E-i-e-i-o" again with feeling. Then softly, "with a chick-chick here, a chick-chick there, here chick, there chick, everywhere chick-chick!" (Sharp cut-off.) Softer: "Old McDonald had a farm" (very slow, soft, in harmony); "E-I" (softer); "E-I" (yet softer); "OOOOO" (very, very soft).

Follow with a lively song.

LET'S ALL SING LIKE THE GOLDFISH SING
Tune: "Let's All Sing Like the Birdies"

Let's all sing like the goldfish sing,
O OO OO *   (Repeat all)
Let's all sing like the goldfish sing
To keep the seaweed green!
If there's one thing I wissssssshhhhhh
It's to sing like a fishhhhhhhhhhhhhhhh!
O OO OO *

DOWN AT THE STATION SAGA

Roy Severance and others have worked on this old favorite to bring some variety to it.

1. Down at the station early in the morning
   See the little puff-a-billies all in a row,
   See the engine driver turn a little handle:
   Whoo—whoo—; choo-choo; off they go.

(Make the motions of turning handle, and pulling whistle cord)

2. Down by the seashore, early in the morning,
   See the little steamboats all in a row,
   See the little sailor turn the little handle:
   "Whoop, whoop, whoop, whoop"—Off they go!

(Whistle sound, each a pitch higher)

3. Down by the seashore early in the morning
   See the little submarines all in a row,
   See the little sailor turn a little handle,
   Burble (Finger lips to make sound of gurgling water)
   Off they go!

* Make a kissing sound, lips pursed as when saying "prunes."

4. Down in the kitchen early in the morning,
   See the little doughnuts lying in a row,
   Hear the percolator, perk a little coffee
   Dunk, dunk (Make soup eater sounds)
   Down they go!

5. Down at the airport, early in the morning,
   See the little airplanes all in a row,
   See the little pilots turn the little handles,
   Arrrrrrrrrrr! (Sound of plane motors)
   Off they go!

6. Down by the ranch house, early in the morning
   See the little horses standing all in a row,
   See all the cowboys saddle up the horses,
   Weeeeeeeee (Whinney sound)
   Off they go!

7. Down at the drugstore, early in the evening,
   See the little hep-cats sitting in a row,
   See the little soda-jerk jerk the little sodas!
   Slurp, Slurp, Boop, Boop Down they go!

CALLIOPE SONG

Oh, haw, haw; Oh, haw, haw   Tweed-le dee dee   Um, paw paw

1. Divide into four groups, each of three singing the parts above.
   Bring these in one at a time.
   Then a fourth group or soloist sings a song in 3/4 time like
   "Daisy, Daisy," or "Where, Oh Where Has My Little Dog
   Gone?" or "The More We Get Together."

2. A variation is to have the "orchestra" sing
     (1st group): Um-pah-pah
     (2nd group): Um-tsss-tsss (sound of steam)
     (3rd group): Um-tweedle-dee, um-tweedle-dee (falsetto)

I LOVE MY ROOSTER

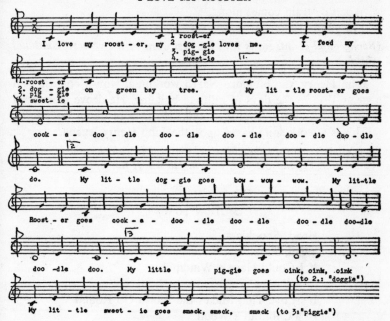

Start at the beginning each time, but skip down below to the appropriate number, working way back through the numerals.

THIS OL' HAMMAH

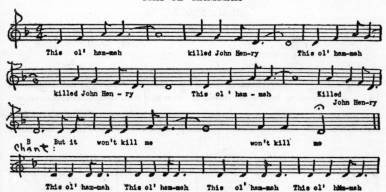

2. This ol' hammah shines like silver (repeat three times)
   But it rings like gold, rings like gold.

3. Gonna lay mah head on the railroad track (repeat three times)
   When de train comes along,
   I'm gonna snatch it back.

(*Background chant: starts with the first word of the verses—continues through song*)

John Henry, the fabulous Negro workman, won a contest with a steam drill in the days of railroad building. He drove more steel than the drill, but overworked and died as a result of his efforts.

This is a work song based upon the John Henry legend.

(*It is effective to start the chant before the solo voices come in, also to continue it beyond the end, tapering to a soft hum.*)

MOTION SONGS

Head, Shoulders
Head, Shoulders, Knees, and Toes
If I Could Have a Windmill
Musikanter
It's Love That Makes the World Go Round
In a Cabin in a Wood
Six Little Ducks
My Bonnie

HEAD, SHOULDERS
(*Exercise Song*)

Tune: Mulberry Bush

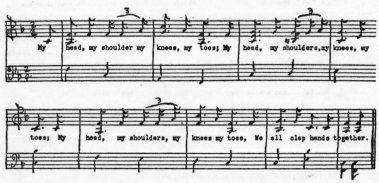

Directions for both of these songs:

1. Touch the part of the anatomy mentioned, when mentioned.
2. Repeat song leaving off words (one at a time) and just do motion.

HEAD, SHOULDERS, KNEES AND TOES [7]

Tune: Tavern in the Town

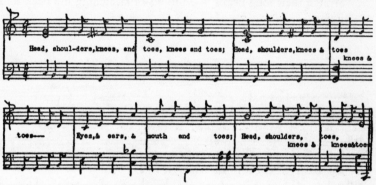

IF I COULD HAVE A WINDMILL

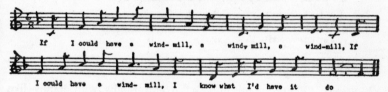

2. I'd make it pump the water, the water, the water
   I'd make it pump the water, Up from the river below.

3. And then I'd dig a duck pond, a duck pond, a duck pond
   And then I'd dig a duck pond, For the ducks and geese to swim.

4. The ducks would make their wings flap
         their wings flap, their wings flap
   The ducks would make their wings flap
         And then they would go quack, quack.

5. The geese would stretch their long necks,
         their long necks, their long necks,
   The geese would stretch their long necks
         And then they would go sss, ss. (Hiss)

DIRECTIONS:

1. "Windmill"—Arms move up and down like a windmill
2. "Make it pump"—Motions of pumping tire with old style foot pump
3. "Dig a duck pond"—Motions of shoveling
4. "Make their wings flap"—Arms flapping at sides
5. "Stretch their long necks"—Motions of stretching the neck and hissing

MUSIKANTER

1. VIOLA. Motion is as if playing a violin.

2. PIANO. "Plank, plank, plank." (Slap thighs with hands like playing a piano. Then do "viola.")

3. TRUMPETER. "Rat-ta-tat-a, Rat-tat-tat" (Act as if playing the trumpet, then play "piano" and "viola.")

4. FIFE (pronounced "fifuh"). Play in falsetto, "fee-fee-fee" in imitation of fife, then do trumpeter, piano, viola.

5. CYMBALS. "Clank-clank-clank," hitting hands together like clanking cymbals. Then play fife, trumpet, piano, viola.

6. DUDELSACH (pronounced "doodle sock"). This is a bagpipe, played by squeezing sides with arms. (Also by making an "ah" sound, and hitting the throat with the hand.) Then play cymbals, fife, trumpet, piano, viola.

IT'S LOVE THAT MAKES THE WORLD GO ROUND

FORMATION: People sitting with arms ready to place on shoulders of those on both sides, then sway (making ocean waves) when chorus is sung.

IN A CABIN IN A WOOD

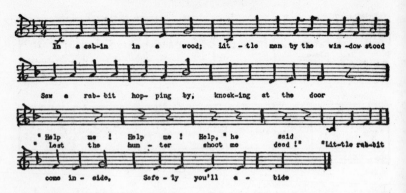

In a cab-in in a wood; Lit - tle man by the win -dow stood

Saw a rab- bit hop- ping by; knock-ing at the door

"Help me ! Help me ! Help, " he said
"Lest the hun - ter shoot me dead !" "Lit-tle rab-bit

come in - side, Safe - ly you'll a - bide

MOTIONS:

"Cabin"—form a pointed roof with fingers of both hands together

"window"—hold hands up, palms in beside face, as if looking out window (or shade eyes with hand)

"rabbit"—make a V of forefinger and middle finger, and in slow rhythm four times motion along as if a rabbit were hopping

"knocking"—knock slowly four times.

"Help me"—in high falsetto voice, throw both hands high into the air, rising somewhat from the chair

"Lest the hunters shoot . . ."—eight shots as if from a tommy gun

"Little rabbit come inside"—motion with beckoning forefinger, four times

"Safely you'll abide"—stroke the rabbit.

(Leave off one phrase at a time, but do the motion just the same. This can be done beginning with either the first phrase—or the last.)

SIX LITTLE DUCKS

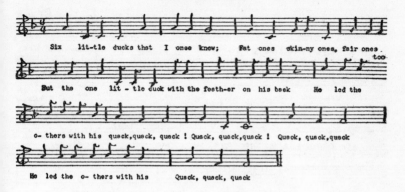

Six lit-tle ducks that I once knew; Fat ones skin-ny ones, fair ones too.

But the one lit-tle duck with the feath-er on his back He led the

o-thers with his quack,quack, quack! Quack, quack,quack! Quack, quack,quack

He led the o-thers with his Quack, quack, quack

2. Down to the river they would go,
   Wibble, Wabble, Wibble, Wabble to and fro

3. Home from the river they would come
   Wibble, Wabble, Wibble, Wabble, Ho-hum-hum

(*This motion song is especially for children, three and above.*)

MOTIONS:

Motion with fingers for "six"

"Fat ones, skinny ones," motion with both hands for fat, skinny

"There were two" (two fingers)

"But the one" (one finger)

"with the feather on his back" (put hands together—behind you to motion for feather)

"quacks" (motion with both hands together at base of palm, making motions as if quacking)

"river" (motion for river running). Do this each time.

"wibble-wabble" (hands on hips, wibble-wabble yourself)

MY BONNIE
(*Motion Song*)

MOTIONS: My (point to self) Bonnie (outline her picture, both hands) lies (hands to side of head as if sleeping) over (make motions with hands indicating over) the ocean (ripple motion with fingers); oh (form letter with thumb and forefinger) bring (palms up, making motions with fingers toward you) back (reach over shoulder, touch own back) my (point to self) Bonnie (draw her picture again) to (hold up two fingers) me (to self again).

OTHER VERSES:

2. My Bonnie looked into the gas tank
   The height of its contents to see
   She lighted a match to assist her
   Oh bring back my Bonnie to me.

3. My Bonnie's complexion is lovely,
   Her face is beauteous to see
   One day she got caught in a rainstorm
   Oh bring back my Bonnie to me.

SPIRITUALS

Stand the Storm
Let Us Break Bread Together
My Lord's Writing All the Time
I Never Felt Such Love
Kum Ba Yah
Gwine to Ride Up in the Chariot
Rock-a My Soul
He's Got the Whole World in His Hand
All Night, All Day
Do Lord Remember Me
Hallelu

STAND THE STORM

Other words frequently used

1. Same as above
2. My ship is on the ocean

3. We're headed for the harbor
4. King Jesus is the Captain
5. We're making for the Kingdom

Julius Scott teaches all four parts of the chorus to a group in two or three minutes, total! The effect is electric, for they do not realize usually that it is so easy to have nice harmony.

LET US BREAK BREAD TOGETHER

MY LORD'S WRITING ALL THE TIME

Oh He sees all you do, He hears all you say My Lord's

writ-ing all the time 1. Come down, come down, my Lord, come down
2. When I was down in Egypt's land

My Lord's writ-ing all the time. And I take me up to wear the crown
heard some talk of pro-mised land

My Lord's writ-ing all the time.

3. O Christians, you had better pray
   For Satan's round you every day.

4. King Jesus rides in the middle of the air
   He's calling sinners from everywhere.

(This spiritual is also sung in the major key—play in the key of A: 3 sharps)

I NEVER FELT SUCH LOVE

I ne-ver felt such love in my soul be-
I ne-ver heard a man speak like this man be-

fore; I ne-ver felt such love in my soul before; I ne-ver heard a man speak like this man be-

fore; All the days of my life ev-er since I been
fore; All the days of my life, ev-er since I been

born I ne-ver felt such love in my soul be-fore
born, I ne-ver heard a man speak like this man before

KUM BA YAH *

African (Angola)

Kum ba yah, my Lord, Kum ba yah Kum ba yah, my Lord, Kum ba
Some-one's cry-ing, Lord, Kum ba yah Some-one's cry-ing, Lord, Kum ba

ya. Kum ba yah, my Lord, Kum ba yah Oh Lord, Kum ba yah
ya. Some-one's cry-ing, Lord, Kum ba yah - Oh Lord, Kum ba yah

(PRONOUNCED: "Koom-bah-yah"—Translation "Come by Here.")

3. Someone's singing, Lord, Kum ba yah!

4. Someone's praying, Lord, Kum ba yah!

* Copyright 1955 by Co-operative Recreation Service, Delaware, Ohio. Used by permission.

GWINE TO RIDE UP IN THE CHARIOT

3. Gwine to meet my massa Jesus

4. Gwine to walk and talk with Jesus

ROCK-A MY SOUL

TO DIVIDE: Have one group sing part one; while the other, at the same time, starts with part two.

HE'S GOT THE WHOLE WORLD IN HIS HAND

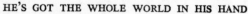

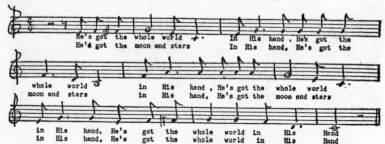

3. He's got the little bitty babies in His hand
     (repeat 3 times)
   He's got the whole world in His hand

4. He's got you and me in His hand (etc.)

5. He's got the whole world in His hand

ALL NIGHT, ALL DAY

3. If I die before I wake,
   Angels watchin' over me, my Lord,
   Pray the Lord my soul to take,
   Angels watchin' over me

   Repeat 1

4. Keep me safely through the night
   Angels watching over me, my Lord,
   Wake me with the morning light
   Angels watchin' over me.

   Repeat 1

DO LORD REMEMBER ME

2. When I'm in trouble—Do remember me

3. When I'm dying—Do remember me

4. When this world's on fire—Do remember me.

(This spiritual is sometimes "jazzed up"—hardly appropriate for the words of the thief on the cross, spoken to Christ! It is better to sing it with dignity)

HALLELU

Hal-le-lu, Hal-le-lu, Hal-le-lu, Hal-le-lu-jah, Praise ye the Lord. Praise ye the Lord, Hal-le-lu-jah Praise ye the Lord, Hal-le-lu-jah, Praise ye the Lord, Hal-le-lujah Praise ye the Lord

16

Dramatics

PLAYING ROLES OTHER THAN one's own is great fun. Sometimes it is both an escape and a release. Besides being fun, any form of dramatics—Shakespearean or the briefest of skits—offers a chance for self-expression, and the slightest role may be of more value to a shy person than the lead part to the most articulate member of the group.

This chapter opens with a discussion of Drama as Recreation, stressing especially the pleasure of reading plays aloud, and goes on to supply many bits and pieces for informal dramatics under the headings of Skits and Stunts, Seventy-five Brief Stunt and Skit Ideas, Settings for Stunt Nights, Other Quickies, Stunts Using a Narrator, Production Skits, and Puppets.

DRAMA AS RECREATION [1]

The use of drama as recreation is as old as ancient history, and as young as your three-year-old "playing circus" under the pear tree in the back yard. It seems to be part of man's native impulse to live more than one life. He can do this best by pretending to be someone else. This kind of fun may be as impulsive as the undirected play of childhood or as elaborate as a symphonic drama developed by a Paul Green in some historic community. To present a play for the public is to enlist the co-operation of a group for a period of not less than three weeks, to secure the offices of a competent director, to discover and exploit the skills of designers, builders, painters, and seamstresses, as well as players, and to cope with the myriad details of budget and bills. This elaborate process does not spell recreation except for a special few who find great satisfaction in such a project. For the purposes of this book let us suggest a few approaches to the drama which do not demand such elaborate preparation.

Informal Play Reading. One of the most popular forms of dramatic entertainment is informal play reading. This is primarily a form of social recreation and should not be regarded as an art production. For a successful play reading, one had better invite a small group, not more than six couples, all of the same approximate age and interests. The host or hostess for the occasion assumes the temporary role of director. He makes sure that the room where the play reading is to be held is orderly, comfortable, and well lighted. He provides cool water or fruit juice and plenty of glasses. He does not invite readers to eat a covered dish supper *before* the reading. That might come later. He chooses, cuts, and casts the play.

How does he choose the play? Well, for the first attempt he will probably select a one-act play. If the group reading the play is new at this process he will probably choose a comedy. (Actually, it is harder to read comedy than heavy drama, but it sounds like more fun when you issue the invitation.) There are many ways of choosing a good play. Your standards will be influenced by the group participating. In his pamphlet, How to Write the Religious One Act Play, Dr. Fred Eastman has suggested a list of questions by which the inexperienced playwright can check the quality of his work. The answers to these questions make an excellent standard by which a one-act play, either secular or sacred, can be judged.[2]

Two tests of a good one-act play are always related to characterization and language. Are the characters believable? Are they three-dimensional? Do you believe that they existed before the play began, and have they a future beyond the final curtain? Are you interested in them? Are your sympathies engaged?

Merely to reproduce the language of our times in complete phonographic detail is no guarantee of a play's realistic content. To select the colorful and significant phrase is the work of a real artist. Dr. Eastman's list of questions will help you to eliminate many modern plays. It is equally true that a liberal sprinkling of "thee's and thou's" will not assure literary merit of a biblical drama. To invite a group to read a play suggests automatically that the play must be worth reading.

A second responsibility belongs to the host or leader of a play-reading group. He must make all necessary cuts and deletions. In church and youth groups it is the custom to omit profanity and the vulgarities with which too many contemporary scripts are larded. A good play will usually survive such cuts. If your group is purely social it may be permissible to retain questionable language when it specifically relates to the character.

Another reason for cutting may be the length of the play. If your group plans to read a three-act play it may be wise for the narrator to condense certain scenes in the interests of time.

A third obligation of the leader of a play-reading group is to cast the play. I like to do this casting well before the arrival of my guests. I write the name of a guest on a slip of paper, and after it indicate the two or three roles which he will read. Take it for granted that your guests will read. But if there is one member of the group who expresses himself as definitely reluctant, do not use pressure. The time will come when he too will want to read. Perhaps he will act as research man for your group; bringing you interesting reviews and criticisms of your play which he has clipped from newspapers and magazines. I remember a play reading of Christopher Fry's "A Sleep of Prisoners," [8] which was made enormously interesting by a collection of newspaper reviews gathered from English and American sources by "the silent" member of our group.

Be sure that you do not ask one person to read too many roles. You might keep the size of your group in mind as you select your plays.

The success of an informal play reading depends to some extent on the comfort of your readers. Do not ask more than two persons to share a book. This brings up the question of where to find copies of plays. Usually one-act plays may be bought inexpensively, and the collection of copies can be added to your church, school, or club library. There are several anthologies of plays which you might care to purchase in some quantities. Their titles are given in the Bibliography. Books may be borrowed from state and state university libraries under certain circumstances. Do not overlook the full-length plays published in THEATER ARTS MONTHLY. Occasional one-act plays of religious content are sometimes printed in MOTIVE MAGAZINE, HIGH CALL, and other denominational youth magazines. PLAYS, a monthly magazine for young people from the third grade to the eighth grade, was still being published at the date of this writing.

It is wise in a play reading to appoint one person to act as narrator. This individual will read all stage "business." This refers to the italicized stage directions for actual movement of actors. Of course, no one will read such directions as *"laughingly," "softly," "fiercely."* Such directions must be indicated by the character as he reads. It is possible even in an informal selection to characterize vividly. You are reading at sight, but a little experience will soon make it possible for you to suggest the age, temperament, and emotion of the character you are "playing." It is important that all readers try to give performances even in a first reading.

After the play is over there is a tendency to waste a good deal of time in mutual congratulations. This is fun, but does not justify the repetition of play reading as a recreational project. Make sure that someone also knows how to lead a discussion about the merits of the play. Now is the time for food if you plan to serve refreshments. I have known groups to remain until a weary hostess sent them home, so earnestly were they discussing the content of the play they had read.

Formal Play Reading. This technique of reading a play has become very popular in the last few years. Our busy lives make it impossible for many of us to participate in a full-length dramatic production. But the formal play reading offers an interesting outlet for our creative imaginations with a minimum of mechanical effort. The formal play reading differs from the informal in its motives. It takes into consideration the audience. Therefore, it makes some demands upon the competent direction. The play should be cast with one person reading each role. Occasionally one person may read a group of very brief roles such as servants or mob. At least two rehearsals are necessary for such a performance.

Seating the readers is an important part of a formal play reading. They should be grouped along one side of a long narrow table.

Each reader is provided with a straight back chair and a copy of the play. Lighting should reach the readers' faces, as well as their books. Players in the same scene should be seated near each other. As a player "enters" the scene he sits up, holding his book on the edge of the table. As he "exits" he relaxes, sitting back away from the table. But players who are "off stage" must be careful not to move restlessly, less they detract attention from the scene being played.

Some people provide their formal play readers with full costume and make-up, though such elaborate details are usually reserved for the walking rehearsal. A few essential items of costume (a shawl for grandma, a straw hat for the farmer, and a pair of black-rimmed glasses on a ribbon for the professor) will be sufficient to suggest the character which you are reading. The narrator is a very important person in the cast of a formal play ring. It is he who introduces the players and "sets the stage" in the imaginations of the audience. In such a reading, vocal projection and well-defined characterization are imperative.

The Walking Rehearsal. The walking rehearsal is an extension of the formal play reading. Now the players leave their chairs and play the play. But no attempt is made to memorize all the lines of the play. At first glance this may seem an easy way out for the drama chairman in any group. Actually it is sometimes more difficult to walk while holding a book than to memorize the role. In a walking rehearsal it is advisable to provide the players with paper-backed play books. Each player underlines his stage business and checks his own lines clearly on the margin of the pages. The back is folded and held in the free hand as a single page. It is surprising how quickly these books "disappear" as we watch the play.

Just as the audience for a walking rehearsal accepts the convention of the book-in-hand performance so does it create its own stage setting. Two chairs back to back with a three-foot space between them becomes a doorway. Three chairs close together and facing the same direction become a sofa. Single straight-back chairs may represent objects as widely different as a tree, a throne, or a gun emplacement. In a walking rehearsal no attempt is made to provide realistic properties. Tea cups, newspapers, books, fans, or telephones are imagined. Some skill in the art of pantomime is required.

It might be fun sometime to experiment with a walking rehearsal in-the-round. This style of playing places the audience in a circle around a central playing space. Exits and entrances are made through aisles. The advantages of audience intimacy, empathy, and clear projection more than overbalance the problems of sight lines and shadows. Where nonprofessional players are reading from books while they walk and act, the advantages of the arena style are self-evident.

In the walking rehearsal the narrator should be seen only between the acts. His function is now largely absorbed by the acting participants.

The obvious extension of the walking rehearsal is the full-length production of a play. None of the informal techniques described above can ever rival the satisfaction of being part of a produced play. No director willingly sacrifices the thrill of holding the reins on the complexities of a full production in exchange for the easy rehearsals schedule of a play reading. Of the writing of books about dramatic production there is no end. This is not the place to go into elaborate detail. The Bibliography at the end of the book suggests sources of information.

If the reader feels burdened by the complexities of using a great art form for recreation he may wish to turn his attention to a few simple dramatic games. These "actor games" are amusing for use at meetings of the drama club. But they also obviously help to improve the quality of the actor.

The Memory Game. This is a good mixer for a drama group. The leader announces his name and the fact that he prepares to test the group on their ability to memorize. He introduces another member of the group and together they walk to the next "victim." The first victim says, "My name is Mary So and So, and this is Mr. Blank (*naming the leader*). Who are you?" The new person gives his name, turns to his "victim," and says, "My name is John Long and these are Miss Mary So and So and Mr. Blank. Who are you?" Thus each new person joins the chain, moving to a next victim. By the end of the game the last player may have to remember as many as fifteen or twenty names in sequence. Don't prolong this game; it is just an introduction.

In the Manner of the Word. This game, a favorite of actors, has been gleefully immortalized in Noel Coward's comedy, "Hay Fever." One person is chosen to be "It" and leaves the room. While he is out the rest of the group select a vivid and vigorous adverb. Suggested adverbs might be coyly, brazenly, tragically, stupidly, awkwardly, or violently. Now "It" returns; he says to some member of the group, "Play the piano," "Sing a song," "Propose to Mary Ann," or "Eat your dinner." "In the Manner of the Word," this often makes heavy demands on the acting skill of the victims. "It" keeps at it until he discovers the word chosen.

The Game. This old favorite is a variation of Charades and has many names and styles. The writer has used it extensively with drama groups. Two sides are chosen and one chooses a phrase, book title, name of a play, or a song. From the opposite team a leader is selected. He is told the selected phrase and he must act it for his own team without resorting to any words or physical properties. A code is agreed on for such small words as "a," "the," "this," and for such essential punctuation as quotation marks.

Pantomime. Groups who are already well acquainted sometimes enjoy testing their skill on single exercises in pantomime. Here are a few that test imagination and skill:

a. Wrap a small jewel box first in gift wrapping and then for mailing.

b. Cut a soft lemon pie into six equal sections and serve them to members of the group. (Don't forget the crumbs!)

c. Take an excited puppy for a walk on his leash.

d. Board a crowded bus with a week-end armload of groceries.

e. Watch a parade on a hot day and try to identify a particular person.

f. Enter a dark movie theater after a picture has started; find your way to a seat in the middle of the row; at the same time watching the unfolding of a romantic love scene on the screen.

Many more situations will occur to you as you experiment with the art of pantomime.

Building a Scene. Now let's extend our imaginative skill in the direction of characterization. Let each of three persons in a group choose either a character or a place. Choose two players; they are apprised of the choice. It might work like this:

a. "Mary, you are to be a very fat, middle-age woman who has never left the farm."

b. "Dave, you are to be a homesick sailor on a brief shore leave."

c. "The place you meet is a hot-dog stand at Coney Island; you will proceed from there."

From this mixture of characters and places the participants are given five minutes to build a scene. What would she do? What would he say? Other simple situations will occur to you for exploration.

It is out of such situations that drama is made. Perhaps some of the more advanced members of your group would like to experiment with making a play. This is not precisely a recreational project as the term is conventionally used. But if recreation is conceived as a relaxing and refreshing experience, then the renewal of play making certainly belongs.

Drama is an art, and great plays are usually written by great artists working alone in agonizing solitude. This statement, however, does not preclude the creation of plays which serve an immediate purpose and make no claims to profundity. To make such a play, you need an adult group—eight or ten people is the limit—and a patient leader. At your first meeting you will talk; you will consider topics, and situations, but not plots. You see, a plot is a result. At your very first meeting you had better appoint a secretary who can take down your conversation in shorthand. It may take you two or three meetings to find a topic. I remember watching such a group in a summer camp situation. The members were young adults. For the first week of daily meetings they apparently produced nothing. They walked about the camp with glazed expressions, and if an outsider intruded with a question concerning food or swimming it took these budding playwrights a few seconds to reorient themselves to the mundane. But all this time their discussions and their arguments were producing results. At last they agreed to place the chief character, a pampered, self-righteous church member, at the scene of an automobile accident which he had caused by his own selfishness and neglect of traffic courtesy. There were results: a young woman was injured for life; a boy lost his glorified concept of his father's infallibility, a budding romance was ruined; a humbled old man knelt at an altar and prayed for the first time since his boyhood. You see these writers had probed deeply and a conflict had been revealed. Out of it a plot was developed. Dialogue was as inevitable as the development of the characters around the central theme. The whole project took nine meetings, but none who participated will ever forget the enriching experience.

The kind of play making above indicated is only slightly related to the spontaneous play making of young children. In this situation adults dealt at an adult level with an adult theme. The play developed in children's dramatics is usually the dramatization of an already existing story. Again the books in this field are legion. Several are listed in the Bibliography.

Drama is fun; even the long-term creation of a drama can be fun. But the best dramatic fun usually requires preparation and some skill. Not everyone has time to memorize the leading role in a three-act play, or to help in the creation of an original script. But to be briefly touched by the wings of imagination is to know the experience of recreation at one of its finest levels.

SKITS AND STUNTS

Whether they will admit it or not, most people like to play-act. Skits and stunts can give them that opportunity.

With very young children play is imitative in a dramatic way. They enact the roles of adults in playing house, cooking, sweeping, even in correcting dolls or pets. They assume the roles of animals. With imagination they turn boxes into stoves, cloths into gold curtains, a draped card table into a cave. This quality of imagination is sometimes called "childfulness."

In adults this quality may be crusted over, but it can be rediscovered. When it is, life is refreshed. Adults can become tables, chairs, telephones, swinging doors, and so can young people. The meek become the mighty in skits, and the mighty, meek. A bathrobe becomes regal, and a towel properly draped represents the finest of gold cloth.

Informal skits and stunts feature the players and their ingenuity. That's why they are so much fun, both for participant and viewer. Many of them take large casts, which is good. The more participants the merrier. Fun, not perfection, is usually the object.

Uses Other Than Entertaining. Some informal drama may be more serious in nature. Skits, humorous or serious, may be used to present group thinking or club problems. They are often used as springboards for discussion, giving the gist of the problem in the skit and allowing the group to "take it from there" under the guidance of a discussion leader. (Some of the plays of the National Association for Mental Health take this approach. See Bibliography.)

Skits of a serious nature may be used for honoring an individual. Sometimes "role playing" in an improvised, informal manner, is done before the group. Each person has a role, such as the minister in a situation where there has been conflict over the details of the new church kitchen; the head of the women's group who wants certain things done, and so on. Each of these persons plays a role, but not from a script. They have a general idea of what they want to present. Then the group may take over from there. (Role switching, with members of the group playing parts of leaders and vice versa, if carefully and skillfully used, can bring good results, sometimes healing conflict.)

Shadow plays, done behind a sheet or other transparent object with a strong light behind the players, can be either humorous or serious. The properties (objects used) are often made of cardboard and held close to the sheet. The opening in a door is good for this.

Puppetry is really a form of informal dramatics, and can be quite creative, when the group make their puppets and present their own play. This will be discussed in more detail at the end of the chapter.

Creative and Canned Dramatics. The greater value in this field is achieved through creating original material. However, in many situations there is not time enough. In some situations the "end product" (the skit itself) must be reasonably good. Here is the place for the prewritten (and perhaps preprepared) skit. It can still be spontaneous. Modifications can help to make it creative. There are times when a well-worked-out skit or stunt is what is called for, not a hit-or-miss effort to try to create something good.

In using created skits, the members of a group begin to learn form. They get possibilities in mind. When it is time to use a starter to create their own plot, they are better able to do it. However, don't wait. When there is time to "make up one," give them the chance to do it, in groups of not more than ten. (If more than four groups "report back" with skits, it is likely to be tiresome.)

Skit Starters. Not only are ideas good "skit starters" but *single words* or *names of persons* can start the idea wheels going. The plan is usually to divide into small groups, give each group one idea-starter word, and let them work out from there. They must have not less than 15 minutes. Do not try this unless there is more than 30 minutes available for the whole effort. Some words or names will suggest immediately what is to be done. Others will take more thought.

ONE WORD		PERSONS	
Election	Bargain	George Washington	Abraham Lincoln
Crash	Thunder	Sir Walter Raleigh	Aladdin
Tailspin	Witch	Napoleon	Winston Churchill
Nectar	Villain	Pocahontas	Buffalo Bill
Mysterious	Telescope	Roy Rogers	Davy Crockett
Cellar	Calamity	Davy Jones	Man in the Moon
Cave	Cobra	Christopher Columbus	Babe Ruth

ONE WORD		PERSONS	
Mausoleum	Diabolical	Joshua	Noah
Fortune	Hanged	Shakespeare	EdgarAllen Poe
Key	Lantern	Benjamin Franklin	St. Nick
Lighthouse	Octopus	Uncle Sam	St. Valentine
Poison	Pirate	Eisenhower	Caesar
Spear	Smoke	Cleopatra	Clark Gable

Age, 12 up . . . Cast, 4-6 . . . Prep., ½ hr. . . . Length, 2-4 min.

SETTINGS FOR STUNT NIGHTS

A theme to tie together stunt nights is valuable, although every single act may not be completely appropriate. Decorations and the role of the master of ceremonies are set by the theme. For school-days—it's teacher; school picnic—principal. Showboat—captain. Plantation—owner. Telecast—master of ceremonies. Wedding reception—bride's mother. Camp—director. Campus—president. Football—referee or captain. Circus—ringmaster. Newspaper idea —editor. Comic strip—cartoonist. Toy shop—owner. Jungle—lion. Police—captain. Funzapoppin'—nut comedian. Here are also a few worked out in more detail:

The Magic Carpet. Carpet is in view of group. With lights dim or out, there are whistling and mysterious sounds. Group is whisked with words, skits, slides, and films from one spot to other.

Round the World Stratosphere Flight. With chairs set up like those of plane or rocket, noises help illusion that group is traveling, as in The Magic Carpet.

Department Store Sale. Signs "Special on watch dogs—jewelry department." "Shirts 79¢—They won't last long at this price." "Ladies' Bathing Suits ½ off." "Bathrobes slashed."

Medicine Show. Years ago medicine shows set up little platform and had "acts"—singers, dancers, comic routines. In between, there was sale of medicines (and other products) including testimonials.

Living at Camp. Follows campers through day with rising bell or bugle (campers getting up, fixing or prettying up, counselors shaving). One side of stage might represent girls' section; other, the boys'.

Morning dip (toe in water); breakfast scene with latecomers.

Morning interest groups of exaggerated title and content. Noon meal followed by rest hour (some snoring, some cheating), afternoon hiking, interest groups or games, evening program or campfire, going to bed. Roles of leaders may be played by campers and vice versa.

This Is Your Life. As surprise, do scenes from life of well-known leader or other individual. Write or call home, get surprise relative into camp. (Or do it burlesque style with "incidents" that never really happened to the person. Master of ceremonies gets highly emotional because of greatness of person portrayed.)

Stunt, Talent Night. Planning committee should make sure material is interesting and varied.

The Village Store. People come into store to exchange ideas with storekeeper. Stunts may be presented in this setting.

The Seashore. On beach all these stunt things are happening, perhaps group rehearsing for show.

TV Variety Show. This setting would permit any variety of stunts, talents.

SEVENTY-FIVE BRIEF STUNT AND SKIT IDEAS

1. **The Wishing Machine.** Whatever you wish for, the machine gives you.
   (Age, 8 . . . Cast, 3-10 . . . Prep., 30-60 min. . . . Length, 5-10 min.)

2. **Camper's Heaven.** Whatever he wants, comes true in Camper's Heaven.
   (Age, 8 up . . . Cast, 5-100 . . . Prep., 30-60 min. . . . Length, 5-20 min.)

3. **Crystal Gazer.** Tells fortunes, holds hands, drops ice down back.
   (Age, 10 up . . . Cast, 2 . . . Prep., 10-30 min. . . . Length, 5-10 min.)

4. **Fountain of Youth.** Those who come to drink of it, are completely rejuvenated—some too much.
   (Age, 21 up . . . Cast, 5-15 . . . Prep., 10-30 min. . . . Length, 5-10 min.)

5. **Talking Animals.** They say some interesting things about people present.

(Age, 8 up . . . Cast, 3-10 . . . Prep., 20-60 min., Length, 5-15 min.)

6. **Reliving History.** Columbus, Pilgrims, Caesar, Bunker Hill, Paul Revere, Franklin and Electricity.
   (Age, 8 up . . . Cast, 5-10 . . . Prep., 20 min.-2 hrs. . . . Length, 5-10 min.)

7. **Panning the Leaders.** A take-off on ways of leadership.
   (Age, 12 up . . . Cast, 5-40 . . . Prep., 20 min.-2 hrs. . . . Length, 5-30 min.)

8. **Convention of the Artists of the Centuries.** Likewise musicians, writers.
   (Age, 12 up . . . Cast, 6-20 . . . Prep., 20 min.-2 hrs. . . . Length, 10-30 min.)

9. **Scene in a Toy Shop.** The toys come alive.
   (Age, 6 up . . . Cast, 5-20 . . . Prep., 20-30 min. . . . Length, 5-15 min.)

10. **Scene in the Automat.** Machines won't give out right food.
    (Age, 12 up . . . Cast, 5-10 . . . Prep., 20-40 min. . . . Length, 5-10 min.)

11. **Small-Town Telephone Operator.** In action.
    (Age, 12 up . . . Cast, 1 . . . Prep., 20-60 min. . . . Length, 5-10 min.)

12. **The Mind Reader.** He has some obvious tips.
    (Age, 12 up . . . Cast, 2 . . . Prep., 20 min.-2 hrs. . . . Length, 5-10 min.)

13. **1880 Style Show.** Or of any other year or kind.
    (Age, 12 up . . . Cast, 10-50 . . . Prep., 1-5 hrs. . . . Length, 10-30 min.)

14. **Womanless Wedding.** Old stunt, performed by males.
    (Age, 12 up . . . Cast, 10-20 . . . Prep., 1-5 hrs. . . . Length, 10-20 min.)

15. **Walking, Talking, Singing, Dancing Dolls.** They're human, almost!
    (Age, 8-12 . . . Cast, 5-15 . . . Prep., 20 min.-1 hr. . . . Length, 5-10 min.)

16. **No Smoke!** On bus, little old lady tries to get man to put out his cigar without success. Finally she takes out scissors, snips off end. Looks triumphantly ahead as he glares.

(Age, young adult up . . . Cast, 2 . . . Prep., 10-20 min. . . . Length, 3-5 min.)

17. **The Silent Movie.** Comedy, Western or drama. Chest heaves, elaborate motions.

(Age, 12 up . . . Cast, 5-20 . . . Prep., 30-60 min. . . . Length, 5-15 min.)

18. **Bull Fight.** Bull may be one or two players, draped and with cardboard or papier-mâché head. The matador wants a smoke. Bull gives him some Bull Durham. Matador shakes hands with bull and calls it a day.

(Age, 12 up . . . Cast, 4-10 . . . Prep., 20-40 min. . . . Length, 5-15 min.)

19. **Well Read.** Several people, one at a time, try to read man's paper on the bus.

Age, young adult up . . . Cast, 4-5 . . . Prep., 20-40 min. . . . Length, 5 min.)

20. **Acting Out . . .**

advertising slogans   songs   familiar sayings
jokes   ballads   familiar titles

(Age, 12 up . . . Cast, varies . . . Prep., Varies . . . Length, varies)

21. **Comic Characters Skit.** Make characterizations true to life.

(Age, 8 up . . . Cast, 3-12 . . . Prep., 20-60 min. . . . Length, 5-15 min.)

22. **Pantomiming Dramatic Stories.** Try Bluebeard, Little Red Riding Hood, Cinderella. No words spoken.

(Age, 8 up . . . Cast, 5-25 . . . Prep., 20 min.-2 hrs. . . . Length, 5-15 min.)

23. **Western Movie.** Do a Western picture in several scenes, if needed.

(Age, 8 up . . . Cast, 5-25 . . . Prep., 30-60 min. . . . Length, 10-15 min.)

24. **Stiff Neck.** One at a time people come in, look upward. "What are you looking at?" they ask each other; no one seems to know, until first one is asked. "Just have a stiff neck," he says.

(Age, 8 up . . . Cast, 4-6 . . . Prep., 5 min. . . . Length, 3 min.)

25. **The New Paris Styles.** Modeled for females by males, of course.

(Age, 12 upward . . . Cast, 6-15 . . . Prep., 30-60 min. . . .
Length, 5-15 min.)

26. **The Perch on the Old North Church.** The story of Paul
Revere, enacted with flourish.
(Age, 12 up . . . Cast, 6-8 . . . Prep., 20-60 min. . . . Length,
5-15 min.)

27. **Paper Sack Drama.** Each group is given paper sack with six
unrelated objects in it, like inkwell, comb, key, dagger, tooth,
balloon. They are to work all these articles into a stunt and
present it in turn.
(Age, 8 up . . . Cast, varied . . . Prep., 15 min. . . . Length,
3-5 min., each)

28. **Park Bench Warmer.** Man wants to sleep there. Finally gets
rid of people who are in his way by scratching.
(Age, 12 up . . . Cast, 4 . . . Prep., 10-20 min. . . . Length,
5 min.)

29. **Boston Tea Party.** Put on with flourishes in imitation of original. Ladies, of course, are known as Boston tea bags.
(Age, 12 up . . . Cast, 6-12 . . . Prep., 10-20 min. . . . Length,
5-10 min.)

30. **Ghost Minuet.** Hallowe'en minuet with some of folks of past
taking part, like George and Martha Washington, Napoleon
and Josephine.
(Age, 8 up . . . Cast, 4-16 . . . Prep., 30-60 min. . . . Length,
3-10 min.)

31. **Fire Alarm at Midnight.** Gives chance for heroics for men.
(Age, 8 up . . . Cast, 8-15 . . . Prep., 10-20 . . . Length, 5
min.)

32. **Superman (or Mighty Mouse) Rides Again.** Complete with
cape.
(Age, 8 up . . . Cast, 5-15 . . . Prep., 10-30 min. . . . Length,
5-10 min.)

33. **Rip Van Winkle Returns.** They show him what has been going on.
(Age, 8 up . . . Cast, 5-15 . . . Prep., 20-60 min. . . . Length,
5-15 min.)

34. **The Last Roundup.** Sad Western tale.
(Age, 8 up . . . Cast, 5-15 . . . Prep., 20-60 min. . . . Length,
5-15 min.)

35. **Romeo and Juliet, Mountain Style.** Romeo is of Sheets family, Juliet of Pillows family. Villain is Percy Covers. In end, Sheets and Pillows decide not to let Covers come between lovers.

(Age, 12 up . . . Cast, 5-15 . . . Prep., 30-60 min. . . . Length, 5-15 min.) ⁴

36. **A Night on the Police Prowl Car.** "Calling all cars." Have several silly things happen, using names of members of group.

(Age, 12 up . . . Cast, 3-15 . . . Prep., 30-60 min. . . . Length, 5-10 min.)

37. **Occupational Skits.** Showing scenes in lives of G men, TV and movies stars, ball players, circus clowns, waiters and customers, firemen, policemen, engineers.

(Age, 8 up . . . Cast, 3-15 . . . Prep., 20-60 min. . . . Length, 5-10 min. each)

38. **Shakespeare Up to Date.** Modern versions of Shakespeare themes.

(Age, 12 up . . . Cast, 5-20 . . . Prep., 30 min.-5 hrs. . . . Length, 5-10 min.)

39. **Life in a Bee Colony.** Busy bees are buzzing at all kinds of jobs, even at other people's business.

(Age, 8 up . . . Cast, 5-20 . . . Prep., 20-60 min. . . . Length, 5-10 min.)

40. **Xylophone Stunt.** Musician makes music by beating lightly on top of head of some lined-up players, each of whom gives out a certain sound. (For organ, he presses on their outstretched hands. "Peda-phone"—he pokes their feet with short broomstick. "Glass-o-phone"—he tinkles on glasses with spoon. "Gramma-phone"—his performers are grandmas.)

(Age, 8 up . . . Cast, 5-10 . . . Prep., 10-15 min. . . . Length, 3-5 min.)

41. **Embarrassing Moments.** Examples—Opera singer starts to warble, discovers laryngitis . . . Man's wife overhears him giving "line" to girl on phone . . . Walking in squeaky shoes . . . After train has left station, girl discovers self on wrong train . . . Cop bawls out man who proves to be big shot on police force.

(Age, 12 up . . . Cast, 5-15 . . . Prep., 10-60 min. . . . Length, 5-10 min.)

42. **No Fishing.** Three fellows are on park bench. Two are panto-

miming fishing, third is not participating. Policeman asks what they're doing. "Fishing," says third one, "is what they think they're doing." "Why, there's no fishing here!" says policeman. "Okay, then," says third one and rows away, pantomiming.

(Age, 12 up . . . Cast, 4 . . . Prep., 10 min. . . . Length, 5 min.)

43. Trees. While serious mood is established, person is talked into doing solo. It is announced as "Trees." The accompanist plays a very serious introduction. Singer stands thoughtfully, then suddenly shouts at top of voice, "Timberrrrr!"—and walks away.

(Age, 12 up . . . Cast, 2 . . . Prep., 5 min. . . . Length, 2 min.)

44. The Lost Sheep. Same idea. The solo is "Baaaaaa!"

(Age, 12 up . . . Cast, 2 . . . Prep., 5 min. . . . Length, 2 min.)

45. A la Spike Jones. Divide into two, three or four groups. Each group prepares song and renders it in manner of Spike Jones.

(Age, 12 up . . . Cast, 6-8 . . . Prep., 10 min. . . . Length, 2-5 min.)

46. One-Man Band. In this musical gag, several musicians come in, carrying cases, open them up, and give all the instruments to fellow—who is one-man band. They are singers, and together they produce some music.

(Age, 8 up . . . Cast, 5-8 . . . Prep., 10-15 min. . . . Length, 5 min.)

47. Silent Orchestra. Orchestra, in pantomime, tunes up. Conductor, in pantomime, gives directions, signals, "pep" talk. Then orchestra plays song with great feeling and much help from director, for appreciation of audience. Solos, trios, quartets can be worked in. If actors do well, interest can be sustained for some time. At end, director bows, but waves the plaudits modestly to orchestra, who bow low.

(Age, 8 up . . . Cast, 10-50 . . . Prep., 10-60 min. . . . Length, 5-10 min.)

48. Several Kinds of Bands. Plumbers' Band—plays on plumbers' tools . . . Kitchen Band—plays on kitchen utensils . . . Robber Band—plays on rubber bands (Robin Hood and his Robber Band).

Age, 8 up . . . Cast, 5-15 . . . Prep., 10-30 min. . . . Length,
5 min.)

49. **Misunderstanding.** Have girl get under table on which another
person is standing. What word does this represent?
(Age, 12 up . . . Cast, 2 . . . Prep., 10 min. . . . Length, 3
min.)

50. **The Trial.** Bring loud costume worn by member of group to
trial. Hurts people's eyes, is too expensive, and other accusa-
tions.
(Age, 12 up . . . Cast, 2-5 . . . Prep., 10 min. . . . Length,
5-10 min.)

51. **Twisted Title.** Have a group dramatize "I Dream of Brownie
with the Light Blue Jeans" and see if rest can guess correct
song title.
(Age, 12 up . . . Cast, 5-10 . . . Prep., 10-20 min. . . . Length,
5 min.)

52. **At Home with the Range.** Have group dramatize Cinderella,
using "At Home with the Range" as title.
(Age, 12 up . . . Cast, 5-10 . . . Prep., 10-60 min. . . . Length,
5-10 min.)

53. **Talking Animals.** Have animal act or show, with each actor
saying only a few words, in manner of animal he is portraying.
(Age, 8 up . . . Cast, 5-10 . . . Prep., 10-60 min. . . . Length,
5-10 min.)

54. **Then and Now.** A setting idea for skits in two scenes. How
they used to dress . . . How men used to treat their wives
(and now) . . . How he used to court her (and now) . . . How
she used to give him something he wanted for his birthday
(and now—a black eye).
(Age, 12 up . . . Cast, 2-10 . . . Prep., 10-60 min. . . . Length,
3-5 min.)

55. **Tragic Pantomime** (in five scenes). Turn lights on and off to
show scenes:

1. He gives her flower with a flourish—she accepts grace-
fully.
2. He kneels, begs her hand—she acknowledges.
3. Jealous lover appears—challenges to duel.

4. Our hero duels, loses, dies.

5. She jumps off cliff (table or chair).

(Age, 12 up . . . Cast, 3 . . . Prep., 10-60 min. . . . Length, 5-10 min.)

56. **Love Is Like That.** Scene: Living room. "He" is courting "She." Little brother is listening. Conversation centers around whether "She" loves "He." "He" says he loves her. She says she likes him a little. He wants her to say she likes him a lot . . . and so on. Kid brother breaks in from behind divan, "For Pete's sake, tell him you love him. I gotta go to bed right away."

(Age, 8 up . . . Cast, 3 . . . Prep., 10-20 min. . . . Length, 5 min.)

57. **Make Up a Soap Opera.** Divide into two or more groups and have each group take time to compose, ready to present, a soap opera.

(Age, 12 up . . . Cast, 3-6, each group . . . Prep., 15 min. . . . Length, 3-5 min.)

58. **Make Up a Horse Opera.** Same thing, with a Western.

(Age, 8 up . . . Cast, 3-8 each group . . . Prep., 15 min. . . . Length, 3-5 min.)

59. **Do a Fairy Tale or Mother Goose Story.** Same idea.

(Age, 8 up . . . Cast, 3-8 each group . . . Prep., 15 min. . . . Length, 3-5 min.)

60. **Lying (a Gag).** Fellow comes in, all butchered up and bandaged. (Group leader is "in" on stunt.) Injured man tells about seeing a man from Mars, riding in on flying saucer, and about how he and two friends (whose names are known to group) worked the man over. "Where's John?" asks group leader. "Lying in the woods." "Where's Pete?" "Lying about ten feet away from John." "Where were you?" "Oh, lying about the way I am now."

(Age, 12 up . . . Cast, 2 . . . Prep., 5 min. . . . Length, 2-3 min.)

61. **The Panel Quiz Show.** Panel of men and women (or boys and girls) are chosen to discuss some subject such as What Should a Husband Do Around the House, What's Wrong with the Girls of Today, or When Was the War of 1812 Fought? The

audience responds by screaming RIGHT or WRONG as points are made, or by applause and booing.
(Age, 12 up . . . Cast, 4-8 . . . Prep., 10-60 min. . . . Length, 5-15 min.)

(Note: The following 8 stunts are situations in two scenes each.)

62. **(a) Man goes to doctor** in far-away resort community. That doctor says, "Go home to your own doctor, who knows you best." (b) He goes home, only to have that doctor tell him that rest at (first resort place) is what he needs.

63. **Why is it** that (a) it's a tough job to give youngsters even pleasant medicine, but (b) they'll take anything in the medicine cabinet when mama's away?

64. **(a) When a man borrows money,** it's strictly in a quiet whisper, but (b) when he pays it back it's done with a great flourish.

65. **(a) He brings home books** from college for the vacation period, but (b) does he study them? Of course not. (Show what he does.)

66. **(a) He's the one** who came into the meeting late, but (b) he's the one who insists that we quit on time.

67. **(a) The boss sits there** all day long, doing nothing, and the stenographer wants something to do and asks him, but (b) about 4:30 he comes to life and gives enough dictation to last a week, blaming his secretary if she can't finish the letters.

68. **(a) They encourage him** to go to the boss for a raise, but (b) when he gets it, what do they say?

69. **When they are trying** to put on the dog, who should drop in but their lowbrow relatives! Loud and funny with strong perfume!
(Age, 12 up . . . Cast, 2-10 . . . Prep., 10-60 min. . . . Length, 3-5 min.)

70. **Rest Cure.** Victim is sent home for this purpose. He (or she) is interrupted by wife (or husband), children, neighbors, police, robbers.
(Age, 8 up . . . Cast, 5-10 . . . Prep., 10-60 min. . . . Length, 5-10 min.)

71. **Tombstone Revue.** Each one answers how he got there. (Hallowe'en Special.)

   (Age, 12 up . . . Cast, 5-10 . . . Prep., 10-60 min. . . . Length, 5-10 min.)

72. **The Truth Balloon.** Someone at side of stage indicates that he has here magic truth balloon which blows up every time lie is told. Scene involves people who are lying to each other, like man or youth who got in late or woman caught in a "social situation."

   (Age, 8 up . . . Cast, 2-10 . . . Prep., 10-20 min. . . . Length, 5-10 min.)

73. **What's Wrong Here, or Believe It or Not.** This can be used in several ways. Have each group think up situation, dramatize it for all, for example: (1) Man forcing money on his wife. (2) Little boy washing behind his ears voluntarily, or complaining that his nap was interrupted. (3) Woman who has been married 25 years, telling her husband how perfect he is.

   (Age, 12 up . . . Cast, 3-15 . . . Prep., 10-15 min. . . . Length, 3-5 min.)

74. **Living Pictures** (one-shot pictures with captions). Posed for audience to guess, like single-picture cartoons.

   (Age, 12 up . . . Cast, 3-5 . . . Prep., 10-60 min. . . . Length, 2-3 min.)

75. **Movie Contract.** Divide into groups. Each group is supposed to try to put on the best movie, Hollywood style, and win contract. Are given limited time to work up stunt. (As an ending it might be announced that _____ (famous movie actor) has been awarded contract.

   (Age, 12 up . . . Cast, 3-8 each group . . . Prep., 15-60 min. . . . Length, 3-5 min.)

OTHER QUICKIES

Abdominal Exercise [5]

"M.C.": Here's a pair that has always said they'd never let anything come between them. Well, we'll see about that! I'll start by putting this shoebox between you. The cover against your tummy; the bottom against his. Now, you both press on it. Here on the table are eleven more shoeboxes. Your problem is simply to wedge them in between yourselves, like the first one, until you have twelve in a straight line. You may use your hands, of course. Now, press with your stomachs and start adding boxes. You have 50 seconds to BEAT THE CLOCK!

(Age, 12 up . . . Cast, 3 . . . Prep., 10-60 min. . . . Length, 3 min.)

Stamp on the Schnozz [6]

"M.C.": I'm going to give this fellow a postage stamp—and ask him to get rid of it. Sounds too simple, doesn't it? Well, maybe not. Now, all we do is lick the stamp, like this—and paste it firmly on the end of your nose—like this. Now, when I say "go" —I want you to get that stamp off, without touching it. How? Simply blow at your nose until it falls off. You have 35 seconds to BEAT THE CLOCK! Ready—go!

(Age, 8 up . . . Cast, 2 . . . Prep., 10-20 min. . . . Length, 3 min.)

Basketball Dribble [7]

Needed: Peach basket with a dozen pins taped around the rim; six blown-up balloons with ½ cup of water in each; rubber sheet. A rain-loving pair.

"M.C.": You know, friends—there's more than one way to make a basketball dribble. You'll see. Sir, please stand over here, on the rubber sheet, and hold this peach basket—which is rimmed with pins—about chest level. That's fine. Girl friend stands over here, about eight feet away. Good! Now these balloons are weighted with enough water so you can play basketball. To BEAT THE CLOCK, you must "sink" three—without breaking them—in 40 seconds! Fire away!

(Age, 8 up . . . Cast, 3 . . . Prep., 20-30 min. . . . Length, 3 min.)

Lilliputian Basketball [8]

Needed: A small tea strainer; five or six ping-pong balls. An athletic pair.

"M.C.": Somebody got the idea for this game from reading Gulliver's Travels. If the Lilliputians played basketball, he figured, they'd probably use what I have here—a little tea strainer and a few ping-pong balls. Now, we'll stand the gentleman here, and shove the handle of this tea strainer in his mouth. The lady stands over here—and takes these ping-pong balls. She's going to bounce them to her mate, and he'll have to catch two of them in the strainer in 45 seconds to BEAT THE CLOCK! Think he can do it? Let's find out—go!

(Age, 8 up . . . Cast, 3 . . . Prep., 10-30 min. . . . Length, 3 min.)

Medical Progress

Scene: A doctor's office. The doctor and a patient.

PATIENT: Well, Dr. Grossman, here I am again.

DOCTOR: What's bothering you now, Mr. Chilblain?

PATIENT: My stomach is troubling me again.

DOCTOR: That's too bad. We'll check you. (*Starts to do so.*)

PATIENT: Doctor, they certainly are making terrific strides in medicine now.

DOCTOR: That's right.

PATIENT: Why can't some of these miracles cure me?

DOCTOR: They can, if they cure what you've got.

PATIENT: I guess that's true. Well, what do you say?

DOCTOR: Do you get hungry at night?

PATIENT: Sure. Awfully hungry!

DOCTOR: All right, then, you eat a hearty meal before going to bed.

PATIENT: But doctor, a month ago you told me not to eat *anything* before going to bed!

DOCTOR: I did, did I? Well, now, that just goes to show you what progress medical science has made in the last month!

(Age, 12 up . . . Cast, 2 . . . Prep., 5-10 min. . . . Length, 2 min.)

Sea Hazards

Scene: The deck of a ship. Captain pacing back and forth.

CAPTAIN: This is the lousiest crew I've ever shipped out with. If I ever get this boat into harbor, I'm going to resign. (*Screams down the hatch.*) Who's down there?

VOICE FROM BELOW: Will, sir!

CAPTAIN (*screaming*): What are you doing?

WILL: Nothing, sir.

CAPTAIN (*tears his hair*): Ahhhhh! Tom there?

WILL: Yes, sir.

CAPTAIN (*very loud*): What are you doing, Tom?

TOM: Helping Will, sir.

CAPTAIN (*going berserk*): Ahhhhhhh! (*Throws hands over head, gives up, jumps overboard.*)

(Age, 12 up . . . Cast, 3 . . . Prep., 10 min. . . . Length, 2 min.)

How to Get Peace

Scene: A train. Two women are arguing, other passengers are outdone. Porter.

FIRST WOMAN: I don't care what you say, it's just too stuffy in here.

SECOND: Well, it's too cold to have the window open.

FIRST: All right, let's call the porter. (*Does so.*)

SECOND: Porter, we want you to settle a difference for us.

PORTER: Well, ma'am, I don't know . . .

FIRST: She wants to keep that window closed. It's so stuffy in here I'm going to suffocate.

SECOND: If that window is open, I am sure I'll catch cold and die.

PORTER (*stands scratching head, perplexed*): Well, I doan' know . . .

IRATE GENTLEMAN: I'll tell you how. First open the window. That will kill one of them. Then shut it and that will kill the other. Then the rest of us can have some peace. (*Reads paper angrily.*)

(Age, 12 up . . . Cast, 4 . . . Prep., 10-20 min. . . . Length, 3 min.)

Ask Him

Scene: Courtroom. Attorney is examining a witness. The jury is listening.

ATTORNEY: What is your work?

BOY: Oh, I don't work much.

ATTORNEY: Do you ever work?

BOY: Ummm . . . when I cain't git out of it.

A: Did you ever earn as much as $10 in a week?

B: Maybe a couple of times.

A: Is your father on a payroll?

B: Nope.

A: Is he shiftless and good-for-nothing too? Is that true?

B: Don't know. You ask him. He's settin' right there in the jury box.

(Age, 12 up ... Cast, 2 ... Prep., 10 min. .... Length, 1 min.)

Two Chances

Characters: Optimist
              Pessimist

PESSIMIST: It's all up. I've been exposed to the flu and everything goes so hard with me.

OPTIMIST: Cheer up! You have two chances. You may get the germ and you may not.

PESSIMIST: Yes.

OPTIMIST: And if you get the germ, you have two chances. You may get the disease and you may not.

PESSIMIST: Yes.

OPTIMIST: And if you get the disease, you have two chances. You may die and you may not.

PESSIMIST: And if you die—well, you still have two chances.

(Age, 8 up ... Cast, 2 ... Prep., 10 min. .... Length, 1 min.)

The Lower Is Higher

Two men.   Time: Two minutes.

Characters: Traveler
              Ticket Agent

Action:

TRAVELER: Let me have sleeping accommodations on the train to Albany.

AGENT (*after a pause which shows his utter indifference as to whether the Traveler travels or not*): For a single passenger?

TRAVELER: No, I'm married, but I'm not taking anybody with me. A single shelf will answer.

AGENT: Upper or lower?

TRAVELER: What's the difference?

AGENT: A difference of $1.80. Our prices to Albany are $7.20 and

$9.00. You understand, of course, the lower is higher than the upper. The higher price is for the lower berth. If you want it lower, you'll have to go higher. We sell the upper lower than the lower. It used not to be so, but we found everybody wanted the lower. In other words, the higher the fewer.

TRAVELER (*interrupting*): Why do they all prefer the lower?

AGENT: On account of its convenience. Most persons don't like the upper, although it's lower, on account of its being higher, and because when you occupy an upper you have to get up to go to bed, and then get down when you get up. I would advise you to take the lower, although it's higher than the other, for the reason I have stated, that the upper is lower than the lower because it is higher. You can have the lower if you pay higher; but if you are willing to go higher it will be lower.

TRAVELER: Never mind! I'll ride in the day coach!

(Age, 12 up . . . Cast, 2 . . . Prep., 10 min. . . . Length, 2 min.)

It Was a Nail

MRS. SMITH (*enters hall of schoolhouse, carrying hammer, very excited; speaks loudly*): "Where is Miss Thompson? Where is Miss Thompson?"

MISS THOMPSON (*opening door of her room and looking out into hall sees woman and hammer, yells and slams door shut*): Oh! Oh!

PRINCIPAL (*coming into hall*): "Now! Now! Quiet down! Just step into my office and let's quietly talk things over."

MRS. SMITH (*still loudly*): "No fear. I've come here to use this hammer, and I'm going to use it. My Johnny's got the seat right out of his pants."

PRINCIPAL (*bewildered*): "But surely, Miss Thompson did not do that!"

MRS. SMITH (*emphatically*): "No, and I'm not blaming anybody, but I'm going to knock that nail down."

(CURTAIN)

(Age, 12 up . . . Cast, 3 . . . Prep., 10 min. . . . Length, 2 min.)

Creation Schoolroom Nonsense

"Shem, how much is 4 and 4?"

"Nine."

"No, no. Can't you tell me?"

"No."

"Can you, Adam?"

"What?"

"Adam!"

"What?"

"Can you add 'em?"

"I can't add 'em till you tell me what!"

"Is Cain able?"

"Of course not. His brother is Abel."

"But why isn't Cain able?"

"Because they can't both be Abel."

"I don't see why not."

"Well, if Cain is Abel, then his brother wouldn't be Abel. Aren't you able to see that?"

"No, I'm not Abel!"

"I know you're not. You're Shem!"

"Yes, but even if I'm Shem, I can't see why Cain isn't able!"

CURTAIN

English Dialect Skit

(Take-off on a Noel Coward type of thing . . . in the Beatrice Lillie manner. . . .)

Two characters: Reginald and Cynthia.

CYNTHIA (*looking out the window when Reginald enters*): Reginald!

REGINALD: Cynthia!

CYNTHIA: Back?

REGINALD: Yes.

CYNTHIA: So soon?

REGINALD: Yes, Cynthia, we must talk . . .

CYNTHIA: I know.

REGINALD: You mean . . .

CYNTHIA: Quite.

REGINALD: I'm leaving.

CYNTHIA: Oh . . . so? (*pause*) Pamela?

REGINALD: No.

CYNTHIA: Mary?

REGINALD: No.

CYNTHIA: Cecily?

REGINALD: PRE-cisely (*strong emphasis on "pre-"*)

CYNTHIA: Oh, tonight?

REGINALD: Tonight!

CYNTHIA: I see.

REGINALD: I'm glad. Hmmmm and you?

CYNTHIA: I'm off too.

REGINALD: Oh?

CYNTHIA: So.

REGINALD: Algy?

CYNTHIA: No.

REGINALD: Gerry?

CYNTHIA: No.

REGINALD: John?

CYNTHIA: No.

REGINALD: Leslie?

CYNTHIA: PRE-cisely.

REGINALD: Well, cheerio.

CYNTHIA: Cheerio.

   (*Someone plays chopsticks—Reginald enters again.*)

REGINALD: Cynthia, our tune.

CYNTHIA: Oh, love me?

REGINALD: Terribly.

CYNTHIA: Want me?

REGINALD: Frightfully.

CYNTHIA: Marry me?

REGINALD: Instantly!

CYNTHIA: Oh, Reggie, you've been a brick through the whole ugly mess.

No More Accidents [9]

SCENE: A taxicab on an icy day. (*You can improvise one from chairs.*)

CAB DRIVER: Lady, this is a slippery day.

PASSENGER: Yes, I'm so worried. I'm not accustomed to this ice.

DRIVER: Worst I've seen it in about 20 years!

PASSENGER: Have you been driving that long?

DRIVER: Man and boy, I've been behind the wheel!

PASSENGER: Well, I can breathe easier, then.

DRIVER: I've driven on ice plenty before. Ooops! (*Swerves. She does too, of course.*) Don't you worry, lady, I ain't goin' to the hospital again.

PASSENGER: You've been in the hospital? (*Worried.*)

DRIVER: Spent 18 months in one overseas.

PASSENGER: My, that's too bad. You must have been seriously wounded to stay in the hospital that long.

DRIVER: Oh no, ma'am. Never got a scratch! I was a mental case! (*Continues driving fiendishly for*

BLACKOUT

"Peculiarity"

SCENE: Man reading newspaper. Person enters.

MAN: Hello there, Bill!

PERSON: Hello y-y-yourself, Ray.

MAN: Do you *always* stutter?

PERSON: N-n-no. Only when I t-t-talk.

MAN: How come you stutter?

PERSON: It's my p-p-peculiarity. Everyb-b-body has s-s-some p-p-peculiarity.

MAN: Oh yeah? I haven't got any.

PERSON: D-d-don't you s-s-stir your c-c-coffee with your r-r-right hand?

MAN: Yes, of course.

PERSON: See? That's *your* p-p-peculiarity. Most p-p-people use a s-s-spoon! (*Exits triumphantly.*)

Scene at the Art Gallery: This is solo stunt, in pantomime. Actor has long overcoat on coat hanger, with soft hat balanced on top. With this costume hung over his shoulders and head he comes in, keeping his back to audience, and crouching low so as to give effect of very short man.

He pauses before picture on wall, with his face very close to it. Then he moves about foot along wall and appears to study another picture. Keeping at same height, he moves along entire width of the wall. Then he straightens up about 10 inches (with little hop) and studies pictures on next level, moving along with small jumps. At end of row he again straightens up a notch, and again studies row of pictures at that level. He continues thus, simply by moving up coat and hat with one hand.

STUNTS USING A NARRATOR

Tale of Whoa! [10]

NARRATOR: Shhhh! Lend me your ears. (*Someone hands him some big cardboard ears.*) I have a tale to unfold (*unfolds a real tail*).

Once there was a man—what a man. John was his name. (*He comes by.*) There was a woman—and what a woman! Marsha was her name. (*She comes out.*) When they were very young they bumped into each other (*do so*).

He looked back. She shyly beckoned, and he flew to her side. (*Makes flying motions with hands.*) He said, "My heart beets for you." (*Takes beets from a sack.*) "Do you carrot all for me?" (*Pulls out some carrots.*) She said, "Lettuce go steady." (*Each takes some lettuce and walks steady.*)

Here was a fine match (*they take out a match*). A new flame of romance was begun (*strike the match*).

He wooed her—she wooed him. (*"John!" "Marsha." "John." "Marsha."*) Soon they would be wed! (*Shine a red light on both.*) They went to the preacher (*a person with a sign on*) and soon the knot was tied. (*He ropes them together*). They were hitched! Right away she gave him orders, which he called Marsha Law!

Time passed. (*Person with a sign, "Time," passed.*) Came the event of a lifetime. John paced the floor. Then he heard a cry . . . and another . . . and another . . . and another . . . and another! (*Five cries, one at a time.*) When John discovered that he had five in a row, he called out excitely . . . *"Bingoooo!"* He shouted the news from every corner! (*He goes to the four corners of the room and from each one shouts "The News."*) Marsha brings in her little bundles (*five dolls*). John looks, then racks his brains! (*Knocks them on hatrack.*) What to do? In vain he tries to shoulder his new responsibilities. (*Tries to put the dolls on his shoulder, but there are too many.*) He beats his fists on his chest (*beats on a chest*) and mops his brow (*with a dish mop*). Perspiration rolls down his face in beads. (*From his handkerchief beads fall to the floor.*)

Marsha meanwhile is busy flitting here and there. (*She is spraying with a flit gun.*) There is a sound at the door (*person with sign "Sound"*). A government official sweeps into the room (*with a broom*). He brings the case against them. (*Presses suitcase against both.*) "You do not raise your children properly," he says.

Marsha is puzzled. "Like other mothers, I raise my children on a bottle," she says. (*Raises each one on a large ginger ale bottle.*) "I usually rock them to sleep." (*Conks each one on head with a rock.*)

The government man says, "Let me lay my cards on the table." *He brings out packs of them.*) "I will spread the whole idea before you." (*Spreads a blanket on which are the words "Whole Idea."*) John gradually becomes wrapped up in the whole idea. (*Lies on the blanket, wraps himself.*) Marsha refuses to see the light. (*Official flashes flashlight in her face but she closes her eyes.*) "Do not take my children from me," she says. "Let me appeal to you!" (*She peels a banana, holds it to him. He takes it, removes the banana, hands back the peel*). "I'm sorry. Your appeal is fruitless," he says. He is so final that she begins to smell defeat. (*Sniffs.*)

John begins to knit his brows (*with knitting needles*). Then his face lights up (*with a flashlight*) and darkens (*light out*). He reaches out to press her hand (*he has an iron*) but she is wringing her hands (*with a bell or a wringer*). John takes on a paned expression (*through a glass pane*).

Now John and the agent chew the rag. (*Do so.*) "Perhaps you are not as bad as I thought," said the agent. I will withdraw my suit. (*Takes one from his suitcase.*) Let us sew up the deal. (*Sews up the blanket.*) For the time being I will leave. (*Person with sign, "Time Being" comes in with gun, makes him leave.*) "Goodbye," call John and Martha. "And nuts to you." (*They grab a sack and throw peanuts broadside to the audience. Leave.*)

NARRATOR: Thank you for listening, friends. This is the end of the tale. (*Pulls out tail, points to its end, bows, leaves.*)

(Age, 12 up . . . Cast, 7 . . . Prep., 30-60 min. . . . Length, 10-15 min.)

Pilgrims Land on Steamboat Rock [11]

NARRATOR: It was a long way to _____ (*name of community*) for the pilgrims. They had the Atlantic, the Great Lakes, and the _____ (*local river*) and _____ (*local river*) rivers to cross. Finally one looked from the look-out and said . . .

JOHN STEWART: Look out the look-out. Land ahead. We will call it _____ (*insert name of local landmark*).

PRISCILLA WELLS: Land! What a sight. All the way over, the only thing I could keep on my stomach was my hands.

JOHN: I wouldn't say I was seasick—but I sure hated to yawn!

PRISCILLA: John Stewart, you know I told you to take some seasick pills along.

JOHN: Nothing doing, I got sick enough without taking pills.

PRISCILLA: Hush, here comes Rev. Randall. Hello, Reverend. We're almost on land.

REV.: I knew we were almost to land because things are getting better. Better buttons in the collection plate!

JOHN: Why, here come Mert and Mary Steiner.

REV.: Hello, Mert. Say, I was sorry for your wife in church this morning when she had that terrific attack of coughing and everyone turned to look at her.

MERT: Oh, you didn't need to worry about that. She was wearing a new spring hat.

MARY: Now, is that any way to talk? We've just been married a year.

PRISCILLA: Yes, I can tell you're a married man all right. No holes in your stockings.

MERT: Yep, one of the first things my wife taught me how to do was to mend them!

PRISCILLA: Well, Mary, I suppose we'll set up housekeeping here in _____ (*community*) now.

MARY: Yes. Say, Prissy, I hear you and John are going to be married.

JOHN: Yep, I want a wife. I always say that a wife is a woman who will stick by you in all the trouble you wouldn't have gotten into if you hadn't married her in the first place!

PRISCILLA: And we're not going to live with our folks either.

MARY: Why not?

PRISCILLA: They're still living with their folks.

NARRATOR: And so the pilgrims came and settled here at
_____ (*community*). Our community had begun.

(Age, 12 up . . . Cast, 6 . . . Prep., 15-30 min. . . . Length, 4 min.)

Front Stage Life [12]

ANNOUNCER: The Makers of Guzzle-Guzzle Soda Pop bring you "Front Stage Life," the story of a poor simple country boy who married the rich and famous Mary Moron. Our hero is the inscrutable, insurmountable, scrupulous Harry Kerry.

But first a word from our sponsor:

SPONSOR: Have you tried Guzzle-Guzzle Soda Pop? Guzzle-Guzzle Soda Pop is the only soda pop guaranteed not to make you (*word censored*). But if you do (*word censored again*) you'll enjoy again and again its five delicious flavors—chocolate, strawberry, raspberry, lemon, and lime! Guzzle-Guzzle is a treat *and* a treatment! It contains antihistamines, anticlusterines, coagulating fluid and soap! (The soap makes *this* a soap opera!) Eminent throat specialists say not one case of throat irritation from drinking Guzzle-Guzzle. And remember

When your bottles get down to four
That's the time to buy some more.

ANNOUNCER: Some more what?

SPONSOR: Guzzle-Guzzle! Get yourself a year's supply *today!*

ANNOUNCER: Now, our story: "Front Stage Life" and the true-to-life story of Harry Kerry and his talented wife Mary Moron. Yesterday you remember Harry and Mary were traveling in the wilds of Africa. Harry had just, barehanded, strangled a wolf that was after his wife, Mary, and today as we join them—

HARRY: You know, dear, when we were hunting today, a big animal shot past me.

MARY: Reindeer?

HARRY: It just poured . . . But through the rain I saw this big elephant coming—so I went out and shot it in my pajamas.

MARY: But darling, how did it get in your pajamas?

HARRY: I don't know—it must have parachuted in. After today I'm not going to wear pajamas any longer.

MARY: Why not?

HARRY: They're long enough.

MARY: I forgot to tell you. Our friend, _____ (*fill in blank*) is going to be married. They want us to come to her shower!

HARRY: Count on me—I'll bring the soap!

MARY: Ah, weddings! Our wedding. I don't think you love me like you did. You loved me more when we were engaged, I know.

HARRY: To tell you the truth, dear, I never cared too much for married women.

(*Dog barks*)

MARY: Is that our new dog?

HARRY: Yes, it's a bloodhound. Here, Oscar.

MARY: It doesn't look like a bloodhound.

HARRY: Come here and bleed for the lady, Oscar . . . I paid a hundred dollars for that dog. Part bloodhound and part bull!

MARY: What part is bull?

HARRY: The part about the 100 dollars.

ANNOUNCER: Meanwhile as our happy family talks over the affairs of the day a certain beautiful woman named Boots is on her way to the Kerry home. Mary Kerry has gone to dancing school . . . and as our scene opens Harry is all alone.

HARRY: I am so lonely here. Mary's all right, but . . .

BOOTS: Well, here I am, darling! Kiss me . . .

(SMACK—*from a distance*)

BOOTS: Where did you learn to kiss like that?

HARRY: I used to be a bugler in the Boy Scouts.

BOOTS: But you must stop now. My lips are meant for another.

HARRY: All right, hold still and I'll give you another now!

(SMACK)

HARRY: Darling, there's something I must tell you. I want you for my wife.

BOOTS: That's sweet of you, but what would *your wife* want me for?

ANNOUNCER: So . . . it looks like *Boots* for Harry! Tune in tomorrow when Mary returns. You'll get a kick out of this! Follow "Front Stage Life" tomorrow!

SPONSOR: In the meantime, friends, remember Guzzle-Guzzle, the original Soda Pop of Champions, ideal for babies, mealtime specialty for presidents!

ANNOUNCER: And don't forget to be with us in the future at the same time for another adventure (Chapter one million 96) in the life of Harry Kerry and Mary Moron in "Front Stage Life." (Age, 12 up . . . Cast, 5 . . . Prep., 10-30 min. . . . Length, 8 min.)

The Night Before Christmas [13]

The narrator reads as the actors act this out on an improvised stage. Some effects from behind the scenes are necessary.

NARRATOR:

'Twas the night before Christmas, and all through the house
Not a creature was stirring (they didn't have any spoons)
Not even a mouse (he didn't have one, either)!
The stockings were hung by the chimmey with CARE (*a sign*)
In hopes that St. Nicholas soon would be there.

The children were snestled all bug in their neds . . .
   . . . were bestled all nug in their sneds . . .
   . . . were nestled all snug in their beds
While visions of sugar plums exercised in their heads.
And Ma in her kerchief and I in my cap (*two girls dressed as Ma and Pa come out and get in bed*)
Had just settled our brains (and we use that loosely) for a long winter's nap.

When out on the lawn there arose such a clatter (*dead silence*).
When out on the lawn there arose such a clatter (*more silence, Narrator speaks louder*)
When out on the lawn there arose such a clatter! (*Scream. Bedlam breaks loose backstage.*)
I sprang from my bed (*Pa gets up, stretches, yawns, moseys over to the window*) to see what was the matter.
Away to the window I flew like a flash (*moves slowly*)
Tore open the shutter (*tears a paper shutter*) and threw up the sash (*throws a sash into the air*).

The moon on the breast of the new-fallen snow (*crash on "fallen"*)

Gave a luster of midday to objects below,

When what to my wandering eyes should appear (*Pa does a "Junior Birdman" act: makes spectacle-like circles with forefinger and thumb, turns them upside down, and places so his eyes look through the circles, palms toward forehead.*)

But a miniature sleigh and eight tiny sparkle-darlings (reindeer, that is).

With a little old driver so lively and quick

I knew in a moment it must be St. Nick.

He whistled and shouted and called them "by name" (*backstage voices call out "By name," "By name," "By name!"*)

Now Dasher, Now Dancer, now Prancer and Vicks,

On Comet, on Cupid, on Donder, on Energine, Old Dutch and Ajax! (*Person backstage says, "What have those last ones to do with this?" Narrator replies: "Oh, we're just trying to make a cleaning."*)

Now dash away, dash away, dash away, dash away (*from backstage comes the cry, "Broken record"*), dash away all!

As I drew in my head and was turning around,

Down the chimney St. Nicholas came with a bound. (*He crawls slowly out of the fireplace.*)

He was dressed all in fur from his head to his foot (*cotton fur, dirty*).

His eyes how they twinkled, his dimples. How? Merry?

The stump of his pipe (Oh, I can't read that here . . .)

And the smoke (Oh, no, not that either . . .)

He was chubby and plump (*he is thin as a rail*) a right jolly old elf,

And I laughed when I saw him (*Pa laughs*). My wool underwear tickled.

A wink of his eye (what a flirt!) and a hist of his twead ("twist of his head")

Soon gave me to know I had nothing to dread.

He spoke not a word (the main reason women can't be Santa Claus) but went straight to his work,

And filled all the stockin's and turned with a jerk (*person with sign, "Jerk" comes out. Santa turns around with him*).

Up the chimney he rose, to his team gave a whistle (I could
have used it in my stocking)
And away they all flew like the down of a thistle.
But I heard him exclaim, ere he drove out of sight: (*All people
backstage yell together*)
"Merry Christmas to all, and to all a good night!"
(Age, 12 up . . . Cast, 5 . . . Prep., 30-60 min. . . . Length,
8-10 min.)

Pirates and Penitence [14]

A Pantomime Skit

Time and Place: Time is early 18th century when pirates in-
fested West Indian waters. Setting has ocean at back right-stage,
village at left back, and beach at right and center-front. Placards
may indicate setting. Arrange stage so that action on each side is
apparently unseen by other side.

CHARACTERS:

THE NARRATOR, probably an adult	PIRATE CREW, one to six
THE PIRATE CAPTAIN	NATIVES, two to six
THE MATE	THE WITCH DOCTOR

Costuming and Properties: Pirates may wear old shirts and discarded pants, cut ragged at the bottom; they have dirty faces, and
at least one, a black eyepatch. For accessories, use bandanna or
folded-paper hats, boots, cardboard cutlasses tucked in large-
buckled belts, and paper earrings. The captain's hat might be more
elaborate; he has pistol as well as cutlass, carries an empty sack
somewhere, and flourishes a bottle of coke. The natives may wear
shorts, with crepe paper grass skirts over them, stocking feet,
blackened faces and fuzzy hair-do's. One has a tom-tom; the others
might have shields and spears. The witch doctor is made up with
watercolor, or wears a grotesque mask. He will need a sharpened
stick and a rag doll that resembles a pirate. Additional properties
are shovels, a large trunk or box, and treasures to fill the sack.

Pantomime: You can have a lot of fun working out details. General suggestions are given at the right of each stanza. It may be
necessary for the narrator to pause midway, or at the end of some
stanzas, if the action is long or noisy.

As the curtain opens, the pirates enter from right (minus the MATE), carrying the chest and shovels, while the captain waves his cutlass in one hand and the bottle in the other. They sing a simple tune, or chant in unison: (As *loudly* as possible!)

HIDE YOUR GOLD, 'CAUSE HERE WE COME

The NARRATOR takes over:

Once there were some pirates,
 Who spied a tropic isle;
Dropped their anchor in the bay
 To come ashore a while.
They planned to hide the loot
 From a recent kidnap job,
For a rainy day when they'd run
  short
 Of vessels they could rob.

Action: PIRATES put down chest and begin digging at right front. CAPTAIN goes to center front and relaxes, enjoying his bottle.

Soon after their arrival,
 The mate returned from town;
Brought surprising news
 Of an edict from the Crown:
A pardon to all buccaneers
 Who'd promptly quit the sea,
Or the penalty of hanging
 If they stuck with piracy.

MATE hails PIRATES as he enters from right. They stop digging and listen. He gestures, indicating spurning the sea, and being hanged.

The men were sick of treasure—
 They had no chance to spend it;
And ending on the gallows
 Hadn't much to recommend it.
So the mate approached the
  captain.
 Said the crew were all inclined
To grab the King's kind offer,
 before he changed his mind.

PIRATES talk over the offer, nod in agreement. MATE and PIRATES go to CAPTAIN. MATE converses with him.

The pirate Captain, furious,
 Seized him by the throat;
Drew his pistol, roared and
  cursed,
 In terms we durst not quote,

CAPTAIN grows livid. Jumps up and down. With cutlass in hand and pistol in another, ranges

So fiercely he attacked his men,
  A weapon in each hand,
That one by one, he laid them out,
  Defenseless, on the sand.

"As long as I'm alive," he cried,
  "I'll sail the Seven Seas,
A-sacking and a-plundering,
  As wicked as I please!
Get up, ye sniveling cowards!
  Or ye'll take a permanent nap;
Go back to your digging—
  AND BE SURE YE MAKE
  A MAP!"

Then he skulked through the
    jungle
  Till he reached a native village,
And finding it deserted,
  Undertook a little pillage.
He ransacked each abode,
  Not a single one he missed;
E'en the jewels of the temple
Filled his hot and sticky fist!

The natives soon returned,
  Saw their temple and their
    huts—
Bellowed the West Indian
  Equivalent of "NUTS!"
They beat upon their tom-toms,
  Danced their savage-est,
Vowed to get revenge
  On their uninvited guest.

They'd seen the black-flagged
    vessel
  At anchor in the sound;
They found a pirate's earring
  Lying on the ground.
One of them suggested
  A raid with poison arrows;
Another argued this approach
  Was strictly for the sparrows.

through the group of PIRATES and
knocks them all down.

CAPTAIN stands over bodies with
foot on the chest of one of them
and declaims fiercely, waving cutlass. Steps back, gestures them to
rise, points to treasure chest,
starts off to left, comes back as
afterthought on line about map.

CAPTAIN creeps stealthily across
stage to left rear. Goes in and out
of huts, tossing out things and
putting others in his bag. Then
sneaks away again, back to the
pirates.

NATIVES enter left, observe their
dwellings, and react violently.
Just after "NUTS!" they let out
one yell, then begin war dance.

At end of dance they get together
and confer. One picks up earring
and holds it for others to see.
One pantomimes shooting with
bow and arrows. Another waves
this idea away.

The method he endorsed
  Was the magic art of voodoo,
In which you harm your enemies,
  With a doll that you probe into.
'Twas then agreed, they'd find a man
  Who could do voodoo hoodoo;
The problem still confronting them
  Was which witch doctor knew.

They go into another huddle, while the second pantomimes his idea, sticking pins into imaginary doll, NATIVES nod in enthusiastic agreement, then march up and down, hands behind backs, trying to think.

Conveniently, one happened by
  And he knew voodoo, too;
They specified the knave he should
  Do voodoo hoodoo to.
He quickly shaped a doll of wax,
  Attired in pirates' rig.
And muttering incantations,
  Seized a sharpened twig.

WITCH DOCTOR enters in their midst. They surround him and wave their hands, explaining what he should do. He pantomimes action indicated in stanza.

Meanwhile the pirate Captain
  Joined his comrades on the shore;
Ordered them to hide the loot
  He'd added to their store.
But suddenly he felt a pain
  Of terrible degree;
It smote him in the hand, the foot,
  Then stabbed into his knee.

During preceding three stanzas, PIRATES should not detract from NATIVES' actions. They might finish burying the chest, then all take a nap. With this stanza CAPTAIN rises, orders them to work, then registers pain.

The doll grew full of punctures—
  The shoulder, then the crown,
The middle of the back,
  And points much lower down.
At last the mystic doctor
  Invoked his final play:
He pricked a very curious spot—
  The place the CONSCIENCE lay!

CAPTAIN gives a fresh start at each new stab of pain. WITCH DOCTOR has been poking the doll, starting in the preceding stanza, and continues, sticking it in the indicated locations. Let the final stab be near the heart.

The Captain's face contorted,
　He gave an awful start,
Fell down upon his knees,
　Put his hand upon his heart.
"My friends," he cried, "my
　　malady
Has taken a strange course;
This agony I'm feeling
　Is oddly like remorse.

CAPTAIN follows lines of stanza. PIRATES, who have been watching in amazement, come close to him as he speaks.

"The cut-throat life of piracy,
　In which I've been so active,
For some peculiar reason, now,
　Seems highly unattractive.
No longer do I question
　Your wish to quit the sea,
For a try at honest labor and
　Respectability."

CAPTAIN rises, talks to his men, hangs his head in shame, then nods to show he agrees with them. They jump around with joy.

The witch doctor put down the
　　doll,
　Satisfaction on his face;
The crew beset their Captain
　With many a crude embrace.
"To former victims," promised
　he,
　"We'll tender back their booty;
And henceforth we'll live happily,
　As men who do their duty."

WITCH DOCTOR, PIRATES, and CAPTAIN pantomime as indicated. NATIVES creep forward to left front, and on hearing the CAPTAIN'S promise, join the PIRATES. Everybody is very happy!

As they return the treasures to the NATIVES, *the* PIRATES *sing!*

"Here's your gems, your golden plate:
We don't want it now, 'cause we're going straight!"

(CURTAIN)

(Age, 21 up ... Cast, 7-15 ... Prep., 1-2 hrs. ... Length 20-40 min.)

PRODUCTION SKITS

Old King Cole [15]

As the musician plays some stately and dignified air on the piano, two pages walk down the aisle of the auditorium to the stage where they blow their trumpets to announce Old King Cole and his attendants.

Down the aisle comes his Majesty, followed by his train bearers, attendants, entertainers, and members of the court. The jester dances along with, or ahead of, the King who is much amused at the antics of the Fool.

With much business and dignity the King mounts his throne on the stage, the court arranged in a semicircle around the throne facing the audience. Some fan his excellency with towels. One tells him a funny story. When he laughs he shakes all over, for he is a jolly old soul. (He wears a pair of boxing gloves and holds a rolling pin in his hand for a scepter.) Three attendants carry in, with much effort, a three-hundred-pound weight (a cardboard box painted black with white letters indicating the weight). The King comes down from his throne and lifts the weight. He is delighted with his strength. With a grand air he calls for his pipe. A servant dashes in with a cigarette on a tray, gives it to the King and lights it with a lighter.

Five attendants bring in a five-hundred-pound weight, the King repeats the weight-lifting business, this time with greater effort. General delight when he succeeds. With another grand gesture he calls for his bowl. A servant, wearing a white apron, rushes in with a mug of cold tea. His majesty consumes the contents at a single draught.

Seven attendants bring in a seven-hundred-pound weight, the King removes his royal robe and tries to lift the weight without success. With a still greater air of grandeur he calls for his fiddlers three. Fiddlers rush on and tune up their musical instruments, a ukulele, a bass viol, and a trombone.

The King and the attendants sit, as the musicians (the piano player) play the "Volga Boatman." At the end of the first strain the King gives a great heave on the weight, the attendants heaving with him without touching the weight. On the second strain, the same business is repeated with even greater effort. On the third strain, which is a trifle longer than the other two, everyone gets set for the final heave. The jester realizes that a national crisis is at hand, and prepares to act accordingly. He pulls a long pin from his garment and, on the final heave, jabs the King with a vicious thrust. The King responds by throwing the weight across stage into the arms of an attendant who catches it and falls to the floor with the weight on top.

A Terrible Ghost Story

Players are seated about room or in large circle. Leader will divide group into various characters and tell them what kind of noise to make.

CHARACTERS	*NOISE*	CHARACTERS	*NOISE*
Timid Young Girl	Sob or scream	Old, Old Woman	Cracked laugh
Large Black Cat	Meow	Black Snake	Hisses
A Tall Man	Groan	Yellow Dog	Howl, Bark
Black Crow	Ca-Caw	Black Bats	Squeak
Bogie Man	Booooooo!!	Ghost	All together

The story is read slowly by the leader and each time one of the names is mentioned, the players who represent that character must make the noise indicated. (*Turn lights low.*)

The story: "On a dark and stormy night in October, a stage coach rumbled along a country road. In it a TIMID YOUNG GIRL bounced up and down on the hard cushions and gazed, frightened, out into the darkness. Suddenly the coach stopped and in stepped an OLD, OLD WOMAN. From under one arm peered a BLACK CAT and around the other twined a BLACK SNAKE. "Hoity, toity! a TIMID YOUNG GIRL traveling alone tonight?" she exclaimed with a hideous grin. "Let me tell your fortune, my pretty dear." Toward the YOUNG GIRL the OLD, OLD WOMAN stretched a bony arm, while the BLACK CAT arched his back and growled and the BLACK SNAKE watched with beady eyes. "No, no," cried the YOUNG GIRL, shrinking into a corner. At that moment, the door was thrown open violently and in rushed a TALL MAN in a long raincoat. His face was hidden by a drooping hat. He said, "Allow me." He gently pushed between the YOUNG GIRL and the OLD, OLD WOMAN. "Allow me," said the OLD, OLD WOMAN and three times pointed her fingers at the TALL MAN. A YELLOW DOG howled from under the seat, the BLACK CAT meowed again, and the BLACK SNAKE hissed. On the window sill a BLACK CROW lighted and croaked most dismally, and into the coach flew four BLACK BATS and beat their wings into the face of the YOUNG GIRL, while through each window peered the grotesque face of a BOGIE MAN. Nearer to the OLD, OLD WOMAN bent the TALL MAN, fixed on the OLD, OLD WOMAN two startling eyes, and pushed back his hat. With a shriek, the OLD, OLD WOMAN

springs to the door, followed by her BLACK CAT, howling YELLOW DOG, BLACK SNAKE, four BLACK BATS and the BLACK CROW. In the coach the TIMID YOUNG GIRL has fainted, for under the hat of the TALL MAN was the ghastly countenance of _____.
(*Fill in with name of someone present.*)

PUPPETS [16]

Puppets can be made from all sorts of things—everything from scrap paper, paper sacks, stockings, to corncobs, plaster, papier mâché, wallpaper cleaner, plastic wood, wood, sponge rubber, cork, or what have you? Below are some of the easier ones.

Bag Puppets. Crumple piece of newspaper. Stuff it into paper bag. Crumple bag around paper ball, and tie with string. Open part of bag is skirt. Cut out some arms. Paste them in place. Take three or four layers of newspapers and cut to make good wig. Curl strips of paper with your scissors. Paste in place on head. Color inside sack (skirt). Now you have a puppet. Same can be done with crepe paper.

"Susie" Stocking Puppet. All you need is sock, wad of cotton, an 8-inch stick, 2 small weights (nuts), string, paints, crayons, needle, and thread. Tie wad of cotton to top of stick. Pull sock over ball, so that toe part fits over ball. Tie in place. Cut off sock. Paint face so that eyes are in middle of head. Top half you will need for forehead and hair. Make hair out of yarn, raveled bits of knitting, shavings, cornsilk, chore girl. Make dress, sewing it securely to neck of puppet. Make hands by placing small wad of cotton and small weight in piece of material. Tie and fasten to arms of dress. Hold stick in your hand under dress. Now you can make "Susie" act as you want her to.

"Carol" Corncob Puppet. Find dry corncob. Take off husks, and put them in water a little while. Take kernels off cob. This bare cob is your puppet's body. Tie husks in place with piece of string, rubber band, heavy thread or ribbon, leaving about three inches of butt end of cob exposed for face. This is the dress. Corn kernels stuck in place with stick pins (especially colored kernels) make good eyes, nose, and mouth. Hair can be made out of cornsilk, or husks. Trim hair with chicken feathers.

Finger Puppets. Tear sheet of newspaper into little pieces, and drop pieces into pan of water to soak. Cut piece of cardboard 3 or 4 inches long and 3 inches wide. Roll and tie it on index finger. Crumple newspaper ball and tie with string. Poke little hole in ball for cardboard tube to stick in. Smooth paste over ball. Cover with bits of soaked paper. Add layers of paste and paper until ball is smooth. Roll little balls of paper—one for nose, two for eyes, and one for chin. Place balls to fit character of your puppet. Hold each ball, one at a time, on face, fasten securely with paste and pieces of soaked paper over and around them. Cut out dress and sew, having long sleeves, sewed shut at ends. Fasten securely to neck of head.

Stick first finger in cardboard tube in head and thumb, and second finger in sleeves of dress. This will enable you to work your puppet. Face is painted on, and hair can be made similar to methods above.

Marionettes. Good Marionette heads have exaggerated features. It enables audience to recognize character quickly. Heads can be made in variety of methods.

Sock Head: Stuff toe of sock with rags or cotton. Tie, use yarn, crayons, or paints for features.

Sawdust Head: Mix 2 cups sawdust, 1 cup plaster of Paris, ½ cup wallpaper paste, 2 cups water. This makes three puppet heads. Model your heads. You can use shiny buttons or marbles for eyes. You can add wire earrings, paper hats, yarn or paper hair while mixture is soft.

Papier Mâché Head: Tear 4 double sheets of newspaper into bits. Cover with boiling water. Knead well. Squeeze off water. Add 1 cup of paste. Makes 2 heads.

Plastic Wood Head: Buy can of plastic wood at hardware store. Model it into character you want.

Wallpaper Cleaner Head for Marionette: Use wooden block a little smaller than size of head you wish for your puppet. Put in screweyes where ears should be and at neck. Now cover block with cleaner and model face and back of head. Shape deep eye sockets even with screweyes. Make nose and cheeks, chin, and eyebrows stick out. Press buttons or marbles into eye sockets for eyes. Yarn, paper, string, or rags, can be struck in for hair before cleaner dries. Let head dry for two or three days. Then paint mouth and cheeks.

Wigs for your Marionettes can be made from rags; toe of sock slit along edges; chore boy; colored paper, curled or straight; rope, twine, or cord; corn silk; leather scraps; felt; cotton, raffia; wood shavings; paint; aluminum foil, cellophane strips; or artificial hair.

Hands: Hands can be made of any of mixtures above, but should have small weight buried within them and screweye imbedded at top for attaching to body.

Feet: Likewise feet can be modeled from any of mixtures above, and weighted a little bit more than hands. Little blocks of wood painted and weighted will also serve purpose. A screweye again must be inserted at top for attaching to rest of body.

Bodies: Bodies can be made of wood, cork, spools, or sewn from cloth and stuffed. Bodies should be jointed or sewn for bending at top of arm, elbow, waist, knee. Hands, feet, and head are attached by means of screweyes. Strings are attached at ears, hands, and back of waist on one bar, and at knees with smaller separate bar.

Dress as for a doll, making clothes large enough to permit easy movement. Clothes need not be fancy for good-looking puppets.

Knee Dolls.[17] These performing dolls can be used as chorus girl stunt or by one person.

First, player's knees are painted to look like faces, then rest of leg is dressed like chorus girl or midget, with black stocking on lower part to black it out. Legs and arms are made of stuffed stockings, fastened by rubber bands under doll's dress (which is secured on in some such manner). Yarn wig tied above knee gives added effectiveness.

Strings, marionette-like, are tied to ends of arms, which come through holes in crepe paper dress (or of other material). The "puppet-teers" may stand or sit. Putting flashlight on this performance at night gives startling effect. (Blanket, held just above knees, blocks out performer's body and gives added realism.)

17

Quiet Games

FOR THE USER'S CONVENIENCE, the more than 300 games and ideas in this long chapter have been grouped in certain categories which give a clue to the situations to which they are best adapted. The sixteen kinds, with the number of items under each given in parentheses (actually there are even further variations within some of these items), are listed as follows:

Games for Preschool Children	(9)	Games with Proverbs	(6)
Quiet Games for Circles or Small Groups	(30)	Creative, Improvising Games	(17)
One-Less-Seat Games	(16)	Fun with Art Materials	(26)
Games, Standing or Walking	(26)	Magazine Games	(7)
Cumulative Games	(10)	Blindfold Games	(7)
Passing Games	(6)	Balloon Games	(14)
Mystery, Puzzler, and Accomplice Games	(49)	Forfeits or Consequences	(8)
		Novel or Quiet Relays and Races	(32)
		Physical Feats and Stunts	(25)

It will be noted that the games in this chapter are relatively quiet ones by comparison with the vigorous, active games of Chapter 20.

GAMES FOR PRESCHOOL CHILDREN

There are activities for young children in other sections, such as equipment games, crafts. Here are some miscellaneous ideas.

Tepee, Tent. Use tripod, card table, tree branch, and throw sheet or blanket over it for children to play "Indian."

Bubbles. Children love to blow bubbles from soapy water (with few drops of ammonia or glycerin added for strength). You can buy bubbles.

Two Little Bluebirds. Paste little pieces of paper on forefingers, place them on table. "Two little bluebirds sitting on a fence. One named Jack and one named Jill!" (Indicate which is which.) "Fly away, Jack." (Throw it over your shoulder, replace with middle finger on table.) "Fly away, Jill." (Same.) "Come back, Jack." (Put hand up to shoulder once more, but this time place forefinger on table again.) "Come back, Jill." (Same idea.)

Pinning the Tail on the Donkey. This old party favorite of having children blindfolded and trying to pin tail on donkey can be adapted seasonally to: pin cherry on tree, pin mouth on Jack-o'-lantern, pin beard on Santa.

"Did You Ever See a Farmer"? Sing, having farmer do his chores of digging, sowing, driving tractor.

Imitating Animals. Little children like to make noises of animals, later to act out animals in action.

Marching. To music, even two small children can amuse themselves marching, especially if adult will help them get mental image of themselves doing some grand thing.

Water Play. Little children like to play and mess in water, to pour, splash it on each other, whether outdoors or in bathtub. Little boats can be made of English walnut halves with toothpick as mast, triangular piece of paper as sail.

Hunting. Hide objects, let children hunt for them. Give hints if necessary.

GAMES FOR CIRCLES OR SMALL GROUPS

These games, many of which can be played around a table, are mostly the kind which challenges the player to be quick on the trigger—with a maximum of mental alertness and a minimum of physical energy to be expended.

Alphabet Verses. Divide into small groups. Each group is to find verse of Bible beginning with all letters of alphabet it can, in 10 to 15 minutes, and report back.

(Age, 9 up . . . Groups, 3-10 each . . . Time, 20 min.)

Cackleberry [1]

Seated in small circle, best not over 10 players, each one takes a motion which can be done easily, repeated in rhythm four times. All check with each other to see that there is no duplication. Sample motions: pat head, clap hands, flip ear, pull nose.

Then they practice chant: CACKLEBERRY, CACKLEBERRY, CACKLEBERRY, NOW! (There are several versions, like Checkerberry.) Now they put this chant together with their motions, for practice.

The object is to look at person at your left, make your motion four times, then shift to motion your left hand neighbor is doing, every fourth time. In other words, after the word NOW in the chant, you change to the motion your left-hand neighbor has just been doing. If this is done accurately, each person gets back his own motion in as many changes as there are people in the circle. Good table game.

(Age, 9 up . . . Group, 5-10 . . . Time, 10 min.)

Rainbow Game

Colors of rainbow are, of course, red, orange, yellow, green, blue, indigo, violet. Starting around circle, first person names something red, next one something orange, next yellow, and so on. If you miss, stand behind your chair. See who can stay in longest.

(Age, 6 up . . . Group, 5-30 . . . Time, 10-15 min.)

Stick Rhythm

Any number of players are seated in circle on floor, six to twelve preferable. Four round smooth sticks, about 14 inches long and ¾ inch thick are passed to right around circle in slow waltz rhythm of piano or recorded music.

Two persons beside each other hold stick in each hand. Counting one, two, three to music, bring sticks down to floor on "one," toss stick in right hand to person on right on "two," and toss stick in left hand on "three." Sticks are caught in corresponding hands of next person; for example, first stick is tossed and caught in right hand and second stick is tossed and caught in left hand.

(Age, 9 up . . . Size of group, 5-10 . . . Time, 15-30 min.)

Air, Land, Water, Fire. "It" tosses into lap of player knotted handkerchief or other object and calls "Air," "Land," "Water," or

"Fire," counts to 10 quickly. Receiving player must name a dweller of the element named (remaining silent for "fire") before count of 10 or become It.

(Age, 9 up . . . Group, 5-30 . . . Time, 10 min.)

Snip. Similar game. "It" spells a three-letter word, like "Dog" or "Cat" and pronounces it, then counts to say 12. The person whom he indicates in the circle must give a word beginning with each of those letters or be It.

(Age, 9 up . . . Group, 8-20 . . . Time, 10 min.)

Bird, Beast, Fish. Similar, also. On challenge, player must name "bird," "beast" or "fish" before count of 10 or become It.

(Age, 9 up . . . Group, 8-30 . . . Time, 10 min.)

Shopping. "I'm going to Columbus. What can I buy?" says It, quickly counting to 10, having indicated player in circle who is to answer. That person must answer with something beginning with "C," first letter of city.

(Age, 9 up . . . Group, 8-30 . . . Time, 10 min.)

Dutch Band. Each player in circle is assigned instrument to play in pantomime, such as fiddle, trombone, trumpet. Several may be playing same instrument. Leader signals play by putting his thumbs in ears and waggling fingers, whereupon all play their instruments. If he shifts to any instrument, however, those players must waggle fingers as he did. If he catches someone making mistake, he changes places, and that person becomes new band leader.

(Age, 9 up . . . Group, any size . . . Time, 5-10 min.)

Fun with Numbers:

Take any number, for example, 50

Double it	100
Add any even number	42
	142
Take half	71
	71
Subtract original	50
	21

You simply double answer and you will arrive at half the number that was added (42).

(Age, 9 up . . . Group, any size . . . Time, 10 min.)

This Is My Nose. Seated in circle with It in center, player points to his eye and says, "This is my nose." Before he counts 10, person who is approached must put his finger on his nose and say, "This is my eye," or else become It.

(Age, 6 up . . . Group, 5-30 . . . Time, 10 min.)

We Don't Like Peas. Each person is to try to find something that you do like, as you question them around circle. You like pears, apples, turnips, because all contain letter "P." Gradually players will get it. (Other letters, such as "B's," "T's" may be used.)

(Age, 9 up . . . Group, 5-30 . . . Time, 10-15 min.)

Fox, Gun, Hunter.[2] Gun (represented by aiming) kills fox. Fox (wiggle thumbs in ears) can outrun hunter, and Hunter (represented by folded arms) can shoot gun. Thus each is superior to one other. Leader calls signal, "One, Two, Three, GO!" and action begins. Here are three uses of game.

1. Two players face each other. This could be in dozens or hundreds of "twos" around auditorium, in meeting, or at table. On signal, "Go!" each immediately represents one of three. See who gets point for that time.

2. Two teams, often one of boys or men, one of girls or women, play. Each team gets into huddle and decides which of three entire group will represent. Two teams then line up. Leader gives starting signal, "One, two, three, GO!" and on "Go" entire team represents its chosen symbol to opposite. Play for 5-7-9 times. Ties do not count as a time.

3. Leader walks around circle of not over 25 players, makes one of signs quickly to one person, who before count of ten must return superior one, or become It.

   In all cases it is good to have group practice symbols several times. Sometimes it is good for leader to represent one (such as gun) and have group quickly do superior one back to him.

   (Age, 6 up . . . Group, 5-30 . . . Time, 10-15 min.)

Laughing Hyenas. In two teams, one group is "tops," one "bottoms," as plate is spun in full view of them. When spun plate lands, bottom up, "bottoms" laugh heartily, others are silent. If top side is up, "tops" laugh. Any player laughing out of turn joins other team.

(Age, preschool up . . . Group, 5-50 . . . Time, 5-10 min.)

Heavyweights and Lightweights. Divide into several groups, giving each a pair of bathroom scales. See which group can get the 2-4-6-8 heaviest, or lightest people. (No turning back of scales!)

(Age, 9 up . . . Group, 5-20 . . . Time, 10 min.)

Roman Numeral Flash Cards. Make large numeral cards with Roman numerals on them. Hold them up one at a time. Person who calls correct number first gets card. See who gets most cards. May be played in sides; side getting most cards, wins.

(Age, 9 up . . . Group, any size . . . Time, 10 min.)

Letter Cards (Flash Cards). Have complete set of large cards (quick way is to make them with liquid black shoe polish) and use them in any one of following ways:

1. Tell story, hold up letter, and ask for name of city, car, famous person, beginning with that letter. Weave into story. Whoever speaks first holds letter. Person or side getting most, wins.

2. "See who can name something you would find in grocery store beginning with this letter." (Then hold it up.)

3. Similar idea, seeing who can name Bible persons, places, events beginning with letters you display, one at a time.

4. Or call for names of any of the following beginning with letter held up by leader:

Vegetables	Rivers
Names of athletes	Minerals
Scientists	Flowers
Book titles	Fish
Characters from Shakespeare	Trees
Books of the Bible	Birds
Actors	Animals
Authors	What you find in a garage
Presidents, Kings or Queens	Musical terms
Lakes or seas	Nature objects

(Age, 6 up . . . Group, any size . . . Time, 10 min.)

Hidden Bible Verses. Parts of ten Bible verses are hidden around room, only two or three words to each slip of paper. Hunt for them as couples or teams, to see who can piece together total list of ten most correctly.

(Age, 9 up . . . Group, 5-50 . . . Time, 10 min.)

Room Scavenger Hunt. Divide into teams. Each has list of several items (up to ten) hidden around room, or in building or close by. Each list is different, and no team may take any object except those on its own list. See who gets most complete list.

(Age, 9 up . . . Group, 3-10 . . . Time, 10-20 min.)

Camouflage. Divide into couples. Each is to take trip through room or building to discover ten items listed which are in plain sight but camouflaged by naturalness of place where located, such as red comb on red divan, brown penny on brown window sill, gold ring on lampshade ball. When person or couple discovers object, they make only mental note for time being, lest they give its location away to others. (Excellent game for getting people acquainted with rooms, buildings, facilities, in schools, camps, churches, or community centers.)

(Age, 9 up . . . Group, 2 each . . . Time, 15-20 min.)

Elephant (and variations). Group of not over 30, seated in circle. "It" in center suddenly points to any person, who must make trunk with both fists. Persons on each side of him must make elephant ears by cupping hands and placing at his ears. Last one to do his job becomes It.

Many groups improvise their variations like these:

RABBIT. Middle one eats carrot, side people form ears.

DONKEY. Same, except that middle one brays, nods head.

EARLY BIRD. Center one puts finger in mouth, side people form wings.

DUCK. Center person makes bill with both hands, others peck at him with fingers.

SPIRIT OF '76. Center one pantomimes holding flag; one at his left beats drum, one at his right plays fife.

FIRECRACKER (involving five players). Center person says SSSSSSSS. One on each side says BOOOOM. One on each side of Booms holds hand over BOOM's ear to keep out noise.

BANDIT. Center one raises both hands, and persons on each side raise the hand closest to center one.

Or for a Bridal Party:

BRIDE: Center person holds bouquet; one on each side makes half crown.

GROOM. Center one puts ring on fingers. Side ones hold him up.

USHER. Center one paints car; sides offer arm to center person.

MAID OF HONOR. Center one catches bouquet; sides throw rice.

MUSIC. Center one sings solo in pantomime; sides play organ.

(Age, 6 up . . . Group, 8-30 . . . Time, 10 min.)

Rhythm. Numbered players are seated in circle, with marked "Head" and "Foot," No. 1 at head to start. Principle is to keep in rhythm.

All at same time SLAP legs with both hands, CLAP hands, and first player calls his own number (at same time SNAPPING fingers on left hand) then calls number of another player, such as 6, at same time with SNAP of fingers of right hand. Rhythm is continued, with No. 6 calling own number on left-hand snap, another number for right-hand snap. Continue until one player breaks rhythm. He or she goes to foot, all others seated below that player move one position toward head. Each player takes number of chair, rather than keeping same number all the time.

(Age, 9 up . . . Group, 10-30 . . . Time, 10-15 min.)

"California Game." [8] Another version of Rhythm calls for two slaps on legs, two claps, one snap of right fingers, pause, and then word given. (On snap of right fingers, word is given, such as "egg," and after pause, number of a player is called, such as 12.) Rhythm is continued, and on snap of right fingers, No. 12 must give word beginning with last letter of previous word, "egg," which might be "gum," then calls another number, on snap of left fingers. Words may not be repeated. Other counting is as in Rhythm.

(Age, 9 up . . . Group, 5-30 . . . Time, 10-15 min.)

Indian Rhythm. Around small circle, such as table, each person chooses two-word Indian name. All introduce themselves around circle at least twice, so that names become familiar. At start, rhythm is begun by four slow, steady beats on table or on own legs, whereupon starting player gives own name, like "Red Cloud" and name of another person, "Running Deer." Then after four more beats, Running Deer gives own name and another. In this there is no penalty for missing. It is fun to see if you can maintain rhythm. Faster way to play is to eliminate interval of four beats, tossing names back and forth fast.

(Age, 6 up . . . Group, 8-20 . . . Time, 10 min.)

Football Game. Large circle is chalked on floor and players sit with their feet right up to circle. There are two teams, divided by line across center of circle. Object is to kick football (or other ball) outside circle across center line, into opponent's territory. Such a successful kick calls for one point. Game is 10-15 points. Make your own rules as needed.

(Age, 9 up . . . Group, 10-30 . . . Time, 10-15 min.)

Simon Says. Players sit in circle, or if played in schoolroom, sit at their respective desks. Each player makes a fist of each hand with thumb extended. One is chosen for leader, whom others follow.

Leader says, "Simon says, 'Thumbs up!' " whereupon he places his own fists before him with thumbs upward. Players must all do likewise. Leader then says, "Simon says, 'Thumbs down!' " whereupon he turns his own hands over so that tips of thumbs point down, others imitating him.

He may then say, "Simon says, 'Thumbs wiggle-waggle!' " whereupon he places his fists before him with thumbs upward and moves thumbs sideways, players imitating him.

If at any time leader omits words "Simon says," and goes through movements simply with words, "Thumbs up," "Thumbs down," or "Wiggle-waggle," players must keep their hands still and not imitate his movements. Any player imitating him under these circumstances must either pay forfeit or become leader, or both, as may be decided on beforehand.

(Age, 6 up . . . Group, any size . . . Time, 5-10 min.)

Gossip. Seated in small circle, one player whispers to neighbor that "Jim was seen coming in a few nights ago under suspicious circumstances at 3:00 A.M." Neighbor then relays the gossip around circle. Fun comes in comparing original statement with what got around circle. (This may be made seasonal: "There's a story abroad that George Washington really didn't cut down a cherry tree.")

(Age, 9 up . . . Group, 10-30 . . . Time, 5-10 min.)

Spin the Bottle. As players sit in circle, they spin bottle in middle of circle, first asking it question which can be answered by pointing. Bottle points to proper one to answer question, like "Who is the prettiest?" Bottle can also point to folks to do stunts, tasks.

(Age, preschool, up . . . Size of Group, 5-20 . . . Time, 5-10 min.)

Human Tic-Tac-Toe. In large circle of 20 or more players place nine chairs in middle, three in row, three rows, as in Tic-tac-toe. There are two teams and each captain of each team, one at a time, sends one of his players out to sit in certain chair. Object is to get three of your team in a row, as in Tic-tac-toe.

Rhythmic Spelling.[4] Best in circle of not more than 20 players. All may participate simultaneously, or may be single individuals.

In spelling word, player hops simultaneously with both feet off floor to represent consonant, and with one foot raised to represent vowel. Words with interesting rhythms have repeated letters, like Tennessee, Mississippi. It is fun for all, simultaneously, to hop and spell words such as those indicated.

Another version of this is to have people spell out their names, then tell something about themselves, as get-acquainted activity.

Another is to have them spell out word for others to guess. Similarly it could be guessing game with hidden object of seasonal significance, like clock (New Year's), heart (Valentine's), flag (Independence Day), gobbler (Thanksgiving).

(Age, 6 up . . . Size of Group, 5-30 . . . Time, 5-15 min.)

"ONE-LESS-SEAT" GAMES

In nearly all these games there is one less chair in the circle than there are players, and there is a leader or starter person (or couple) whose object is to get a seat (or else to exchange places with someone in the circle).

Fruit Basket (basic game). Each person sitting in circle bears name of some fruit. When leader calls names of two fruits, they must change and he tries to get seat. Signal for all to change is: "Fruit basket upset," whereupon all change, and leader tries to get seat.

(Age, preschool up . . . Group, 5-15 . . . Time, 10 min.)

Numbers Change. See Fruit Basket. Same idea except that persons are numbered instead of named as fruits.

(Age, 9 up . . . Group, 5-15 . . . Time, 10 min.)

Blowout. Similar to Fruit Basket, except that players are named parts of an automobile, and they fall in line behind leader until he calls "blowout," when all try for seat, including leader. "Traffic cop" is signal for all to change. Similar titles are found in Stagecoach, Taxicab, Post Office.

(Age, preschool up . . . Group, 5-15 . . . Time, 10 min.)

Poorhouse. This is a couple version of same idea, where there is a couple sitting in "poorhouse" (two chairs apart from others) and other couples are numbered. When "poorhouse" couple call numbers of two other couples, all try to get seats, couple remaining going to poorhouse.

(Age, 6 up . . . Group, 8-50 . . . Time, 10 min.)

Danish Fish Game. Similar to "Blowout" in that "It" couple walks around room, where couples are sitting with their chairs facing in random directions, and calls off names of fishes. (Couples secretly choose names of fishes for themselves.) When their name is called, they fall in line and march behind lead couple. Signal for return to seats is, "The ocean is stormy." Since there is one less pair of seats than players, last couple is It. (Signal for all to move: "The ocean is calm.")

(Age, preschool up . . . Group, 10-50 . . . Time, 10 min.)

Honeymoon Express.[5] Based on similar idea, this game calls for chairs arranged like a train, with couples seated together, each couple having state as destination which they have chosen secretly. "It" couple start out (in role of conductor and trainman) calling off names of states, and couples get off train to join in march around train. Signal for "Everybody march" is "Niagara Falls," and that for reboarding is "All aboard." Last couple is It for next try.

(Age, 6 up . . . Group, 10-50 . . . Time, 10 min.)

Drop the Keys (mixer). Leader greets player seated in circle by exchanging names with him or her, and the two start in opposite directions around circle, speaking to every fourth or fifth player, who in turn does same thing. When several are on their feet, leader suddenly drops bunch of keys, and all rush for places. Last one is It next time, taking keys.

(Age, 6 up . . . Group, 10-50 . . . Time, 10 min.)

Follow Me. "It" greets person seated in circle with "Follow me." Player does. Continue until several are in line, then call "Go home," and last one home starts next time.

(Age, preschool up . . . Group, 10-100 . . . Time, 10 min.)

Come Along. Same as "Follow Me," except that person says, "Come along" and takes him by hand. Then that person says to another, "Come along," and so on.

(Age, preschool up . . . Group, 10-100 . . . Time, 10 min.)

Rose Garden. Players are numbered off by fours around circle, named "Red Roses," "White Roses," "Pink Roses," "Ramblers." "It" calls for two kinds to change places and he tries to get seat in process.

(Age, 6 up . . . Group, 5-30 . . . Time, 10 min.)

How Do You Like Your Neighbor? Players ask names of those seated on both sides of them in circle. (If they do not know each other well, number off.) "It" in center says to player, "How do you like your neighbors?" "Fine," he says, whereupon all change seats and It tries to get seat. If, however, he says, "I don't like 'em," then he is asked to designate whom he'd like to have for neighbors. His present neighbors and those he has named (or numbers called) must change places and It tries for seat. Last one is It.

(Age, 9 up . . . Group, 5-30 . . . Time, 10 min.)

Who Are Your Neighbors? (mixer). This version calls for person challenged to give names for his neighbors, or else become It. Then It proceeds as above.

(Age, 6 up . . . Group, 5-30 . . . Time, 10 min.)

Hot Potato (also called "Hot Towel," "Hot Rag," "Hot Handkerchief"). Object such as handkerchief is passed from one to another around circle, seated very close together. Whoever lets It get object becomes It, or whoever touched it last before It recovers. Object may be ball, piece of sponge, or any other object. It may be passed or thrown.

(Age, preschool up . . . Group, 8-30 . . . Time, 10 min.)

Swat. "It," with rolled-up newspaper in hand, walks around circle of seated players, eventually strikes one with "swatter," rushes and places swatter on stool or bench in center of circle. As the struck player tries to get swatter and swat It, It tries to get the vacated seat before he can be swatted. If swatter rolls off bench, It must replace it, even though this puts him in danger of getting swatted. If It gets vacant chair without being swatted, the loser becomes It.

Rag Tag. Similar game, using knotted rag. May be schoolroom game. "It" strikes seated player, places towel on desk of another, and then runs down aisle, around room, around last row of seats, and into vacated seat of one who is now chasing him. If he gets back without being swatted, he sits, and new one is It.

(Age, 6 up . . . Group, 10-40 . . . Time, 10 min.)

Bird Game. Each chair is named for bird. When kind of bird is called by leader for which your chair is labeled, you clap hands. Then when leader calls out, "Fly, bird, fly," you fly to chair vacated by another bird, taking on that new bird name. Leader may try to get place (in which case one left out becomes leader). If leader fails, he continues as It.

(Age, 6 up . . . Group 5-20 . . . Time, 10 min.)

Scoot (also called "Ocean Wave"). Players are seated in strong chairs in circle with one vacant chair. When center player says, "Scoot right," all must protect chair to their right by scooting into it when it is vacant. On "Scoot left" they move to left. "It" tries to get into chair, and one responsible becomes It.

(Age, 6 up . . . Group, 8-30 . . . Time, 10 min.)

GAMES, STANDING OR WALKING

Bell Pass. Players stand in circle, hands behind them, and pass bell (or other noise maker) around behind their backs. "It" tries to guess who has bell, and when successful that person becomes It.

(Age, preschool up . . . Group, 10-30 . . . Time, 10 min.)

"I Say Stoop." Players stand in circle, leader in center. Leader says, "I say stoop!" and stoops, and all must do same. If he says, "I say stand," and stoops, all must remain motionless. Can be used on elimination basis, or just for fun.

(Age, 6 up . . . Group, 10-30 . . . Time, 10 min.)

Pass Left. Standing in circle, players are passing around two objects, several persons apart, trying to make rear one catch up with other. Leader calls, "Pass left" (if object is going to right), and they must shift. If any person gets both objects at same time, he is out, also if he happens to drop one. Or just play for fun.

(Age, 9 up . . . Group, 10-30 . . . Time, 10 min.)

Follow the Leader. Players are seated to start, but join him as he beckons. When he has several followers, they play "follow the leader," doing as he does. When signal is given, all rush for seats, and the one left out is leader. (Music could stop as signal, or leader could clap hands or shout "Go home.")

(Age, 6 up . . . Group, 10-50 . . . Time, 10 min.)

Opposite. Each player is holding handkerchief or corner of napkin, standing in circle. When leader calls, "Hold fast," all are to drop it. If he calls, "Drop it," they are to hold fast.

(Age, 9 up . . . Group, any size . . . Time, 5-10 min.)

Cracking Nuts. One or more "nuts" are in inside of circle formed by players, holding hands. The "crackers" are outside circle with rolled newspapers. Nuts are cracked by reaching over hands of circle and swatting them. When cracked, nut exchanges places with cracker. After a while, shift and get others in circle to become nuts or crackers.

(Age, 6 up . . . Group, 10-30 . . . Time, 10 min.)

Squirrel in the Tree. Players stand around room, two holding hands and a third in middle of their little circle, as the nut. There are two or more squirrels who are trying to get nuts. On called signal by squirrel, "Nuts," all must change trees, and each squirrel tries to get tree too. Those left out become chasers, and one or all will give signal, "Nuts!" for a change.

(Age, 6 up . . . Groups, 3 each . . . Time, 5-10 min.)

Swat the Fly.[6] Players stand in close circle, hands behind them, extra It in center. One player starts passing swatter (rolled newspaper or soft bedroom slipper) around outside circle. When center person has back turned, some player slyly swats him and quickly passes swatter on. If caught, player goes to center to exchange places with It.

(Age, 6 up . . . Group, 10-30 . . . Time, 10 min.)

Western Union. This game, "Telegram," is played with group standing in circle, hands joined, an It in center. Jim Flynn, in circle, says, "I'm going to send a telegram to Mary ———," who is on opposite side of circle. She holds up her hand. "It" turns his back until Jim says, "Go," whereupon It tries to see "current" as it is passed from one to other by squeezing hands. (If person receives squeeze from left, he passes it on with his right.) "It" must discover through whom current is passing before "message" gets to Mary or be It again. Whoever is caught becomes It, otherwise.

(Age, 6 up . . . Group, 10-30 . . . Time, 10 min.)

Electricity. Similar game except that "shock" is sent around circle constantly until It finally catches someone.

(Age, 6 up . . . Group, 10-30 . . . Time, 10 min.)

Pocketbook Game.[7] Divide into several small groups (four to eight players each). After "Go" signal they are to empty pocketbooks, pockets, and other possessions to see what they can get to represent every letter of alphabet, A to Z. Some may even run out to their cars to get objects.

(Age, 18 up . . . Group, 4-8 . . . Time, 10-15 min.)

Indoor Scavenger Hunt. Played in several groups (can be large) equidistant from leader, who is in center with piano bench or table upon which "loot" may be placed. Each group chooses runner who will bring to leader whatever is called for. First one with correct object wins point for his team. Start simple and get harder. Sample objects:

Man's belt	Girl's anklet	Bobby pin
Girl's glove	Boy's undershirt	1928 penny
Key ring	Black shoestring	Chip of nail polish

(Age, 9 up . . . Groups, 5-30 each . . . Time, 10 min.)

Bird, Fish, Animal. Divided as in Indoor Scavenger Hunt, each team sends representative to center, who must return and act out bird, fish, or animal for his team. First team guessing by shouting out name gets a point. Send different runner each time.

(Age, 9 up . . . Groups, 5-30 each . . . Time, 10 min.)

Run and Draw. Similar to Bird, Fish, Animal except that when person returns to his group, he must use pencil and paper to draw whatever he has been assigned, which might be simple like "catfish," or harder like "an automobile transmission," "a burned-out light bulb," "justice," or such words. No writing can take place. The person may nod or shake head to indicate "Yes" or "No."

(Age, 9 up . . . Groups, 5-30 each . . . Time, 10 min.)

Shoe Scramble. All of one sex remove shoes, place in center of floor. Those of other sex mix them up and, at signal, scramble for proper shoes begins. Now repeat for opposite sex. First one with own shoes on and laced up, wins. (If there are many shoes without laces, skip lacing.)

(Age, preschool up . . . Group, 5-100 . . . Time 10 min.)

Feather Race. Who can blow his feather to finish line first?

(Age, preschool up . . . Group, 2 at least . . . Time, 10 min.)

Bean Bag Shuffle Board. Use sliding bean bags instead of pucks in shuffleboard.

(Age, 6 . . . Group, 2-4 . . . Time, 10-60 min.)

Button Snap. Lanes 10 to 12″ wide are chalked on floor. Object: all players start on signal, snapping by pressing edge of button, trying to get to finish line first.

(Age, 6 up . . . Group, 5-10 . . . Time, 10 min.)

Candle Bowling. Arrange candles in lines of 1, 2, 3, and 4 as in bowling, near edge of table (with brown paper underneath to catch drippings). Stack books up so that player's chin is at right height to blow out candles. Each player gets two blows, as in bowling. If two tables are going, one can be used while other is being relighted. (Be careful of fire.)

(Age, 6 up . . . Group, 4-12 . . . Time, 10-45 min.)

Table Hockey. This ping-pong blow game can have four teams on rectangular table. Each is lined up at table's edge. One team starts blowing ping-pong ball, across table. A point is counted against team for allowing ball to roll off their edge.

(Age, 6 up . . . Group, 8-24 . . . Time, 10-20 min.)

Group Ping-Pong. Players form circles at two ends of ping-pong table, one player holding paddle on each end of table. One serves, lays down paddle, other knocks it back, lays down paddle. Next person in line must pick up paddle and hit ball back. Can be elimination (out if you miss) or played just for fun. Sometimes single circle goes around entire table.

(Age, 6 up . . . Groups, 5-10 each . . . Time, 10-20 min.)

Ping-Pong Dodge Ball. Played as in regular dodge ball.

Chain Spelling. Two teams play. First team spells out name of word, and first player of other team must spell word in same category (such as cities, proper names, grocery items) beginning with last letter of first team's word before count of 10, or lose a point. First player might spell out NEW YORK. Whereupon first player of other team must spell KANSAS CITY (or some other beginning with K). May be played around table. (Age, 9 up . . . Groups, 5-30 each . . . Time, 10-30 min.)

Dumb Crambo. There are two groups. One leaves room, other chooses verb, such as "eat." They send word to those outside that their verb rhymes with "heat." This team then figures out answer, comes inside and acts it out. If it is right, players inside clap; if not, they shake their heads. Continue until hidden word is detected, then shift roles, inside team going outside, and inside team choosing verb.

(Age, 9 up . . . Groups, 5-30 each . . . Time, 15-30 min.)

Occupational Wheel of Fortune. Large wheel with pointer is ready. It contains number of occupations. Player spins it until it stops and then acts out occupation for others to guess. (If group is divided into teams, he might return to his team and tell it, and have entire team act out occupation for others to guess.)

(Age, 9 up . . . Group, any size; 1 player . . . Time, 10-30 min.)

Turtle Racing Game. Outlines of two or more turtles are cut from heavy cardboard, hole punched through head and strong string 20 feet or longer slipped through. String is tied to chair or table leg, just as high as turtle's length, so that his "hind legs" can touch floor. Hole in his head is large enough that animal slips on string easily.

At "Go" signal, all turtles start racing by having their masters start them on string from point farthest from chair leg. When master pulls or jiggles string and thus helps turtle's feet to touch the floor or ground, it can move up to goal. Some races have turtles go up and back.

This game may be made seasonal by using a cut-out appropriate for season, like Easter bunny, turkey, black cat, for Easter, Thanksgiving, Hallowe'en, or it may be used as horse race.

(Age, 9 up . . . Group, 2-5 . . . Time, 10-30 min.)

CUMULATIVE GAMES

These are the games that keep "adding on." Besides being fun, many of them are good memory drills.

Do This and Add Something. In circle of not more than 20 people, leader starts with action, such as tapping foot. Person to his right does leader's action, then adds one of his own, perhaps waving hand. Continue until all have done the action. In group larger than 20, divide into at least two groups.

(Age, 6 up . . . Group, 8-20 . . . Time, 5-10 min.)

Aunt Sally Went Shopping.[8] (May be done as performance stunt with five players who come up front, or in group of not more than 20.)

"My Aunt Sally went shopping and guess what she bought?" leader says. "What?" is answer. "A pencil sharpener." Whereupon each person must act it out, down the line, for his neighbor, and each action is continued for duration.

Other things she bought:

> Electric milker (milking motion)
> Some bubble gum (chewing)
> New bicycle (motion with feet)
> Spring seat (bounce up and down)
> Cuckoo clock (say, "Cuckoo, cuckoo")
> Spinning wheel (rock back and forth).

As large group activity, entire group begin to do action as soon as they are told or shown, making this suitable for auditorium and table use.

(Age, 6 up . . . Group, 5-20 . . . Time, 5-10 min.)

Auntie from Borneo.[9] Using tune, "Bury Me Not on the Lone Prairie," leader sings first phrase, with group following in repetition, and so on through song. An action, once started, continues throughout.

Song: "My aunt came back from Borneo. The fan she brought goes to and fro." (Fan with right hand.) "My aunt came back from old Algiers. She brought to me a pair of shears." (Make cutting motion with first and second fingers of left hand.) "My aunt came back from Ararat. She brought to me a sailor hat." (Nod head.) "My aunt came back from Burma fair. She brought to me a rocking chair." (Add motion of rocking chair.) "My aunt came back from Kalamazoo. She brought to me, some gum to chew." (Chewing motion.)

(Age, 6 up . . . Group, any size . . . Time, 5-10 min.)

Ha Ha. With players seated in circle or around table, one player says, "Ha." Second one says, "Ha ha," and third, "Ha, ha, ha." Each one adds one more "Ha" than previous one did. No one must laugh. If so, extract forfeit, have them drop out, or just start over and see who laughs least.

(Age, 9 up . . . Group, 8-20 . . . Time, 5 min.)

Quaker Meeting. Quakers are noted for their silence and solemnity. Groups in circle of not more than 20, preferably less. The leader solemnly taps person on his right on knee, lightly. Tap passes around circle. Then tap on cheek, or nose, or ear, or head goes around circle in same manner. No one must smile or laugh.

(Age, 9 up . . . Group, 8-20 . . . Time, 10 min.)

I'm Going to London . . . Seated around circle of up to 25 players, one player starts, saying "I'm going to London, and I'll take with me an apple." Next person adds something beginning with "B" and so on. This is effective as game played when person from group is leaving for another town to work or live. Substitute that town for "London."

(Age, 6 up . . . Group, 8-25 . . . Time, 10 min.)

Count to 30. As players sit in circle, they try to count to 30, using certain rules. Instead of saying 7, 17, 27, etc. player places hands together, palms facing. Instead of saying any multiple of 7, put hands together, knuckles together, palms facing away from each other. Also, after any of these symbols has been given, the count reverses direction around circle, going back in other direction. If there is a miss, group starts over from some position across circle from where miss takes place. Trickiest combination is 27 (palms facing) and 28 (a multiple), with directions reversing at same time.

(Age, 9 up . . . Group, 8-30 . . . Time, 10-30 min.)

Buzz, Fizz. Same game as "Count to 30" except that word "Buzz" is substituted for 7, 17, 27, and the like, and "Fizz" for multiples. Reverse as above.

(Age, 9 up . . . Group, 8-30 . . . Time, 10-30 min.)

One Frog. Players seated in circle, one person leads, saying "One frog." Next person to his left says, "One head," next one, "Two eyes," next, "Four legs," next, "Petunk," and next "In the puddle." Then double each: "Two frogs," "Two heads," "Four eyes," "Eight legs," "Petunk, petunk," "In the puddle, in the puddle." Continue to see how high the group can get. After a miss, start over again.

(Age, 9 up . . . Group, 8-30 . . . Time, 5-10 min.)

Geography. One person in seated circle names geographical item: city, state, country, river, mountain; second person must give word beginning with last letter of first person's word. So on around circle. For missing: pay forfeit, drop out, or have mark chalked against you, whichever is agreed upon.

(Age, 9 up . . . Group, 8-30 . . . Time, 5-10 min.)

PASSING GAMES

In these games, players are seated in a circle, passing an object. Large groups can be divided into smaller circles, and the game played simultaneously in all the circles.

A What? There are several versions of this game. One is to start an object around circle to left saying, "This is a dog." Next person says, "A what?" Starter says, "A dog." Object is then passed to next person with same procedure, but "A what?" question is always relayed back to starter, who in turn gives answer, which is relayed back around circle, gradually repeated a number of times.

Simultaneous with starting dog to left, he starts "cat" to right, with same procedure.

Popular version is to have a several-word description, like "A freshly baked peach pie" and "A jar of watermelon pickles," or "This is a shawl with a long fringe" and "This is a pair of galoshes, slightly worn but wearable." (Longer the line, smaller the circle should be to enjoy it.)

In any version fun comes when signals for "dog" and "cat" or others begin to cross each other halfway around circle, and players do not know which way to turn for "A what?"

(Age, 9 up . . . Group, 8-20 . . . Time, 10-15 min.)

Numbers Race. Two or more competing circles of same number of players are passing object around circle. Designate winning number of times object is to pass, such as six. Each time object goes by first person he counts aloud, "One," "Two," etc. After six complete revolutions, first one through, wins.

(Age, 9 up . . . Group, 8-20 . . . Time, 10 min.)

Pass It On. As music plays, object is passed around circle, counterclockwise. When music stops, whoever is caught must, next time he receives object, pass it under left leg, then pass it on. If caught second time, he adds: Pass it around neck, then passes it on. If caught third time, adds: Pass under right leg. For a fourth time adds: Stand up. For a fifth, adds: Sit down. (Also called "Musical Ball.")

(Age, 6 up . . . Group, 8-30 . . . Time, 5-10 min.)

Circle Poison. Similar game. If caught once, raise right hand. Twice, right hand and right leg. Three times, add: raise left leg. Four times: raise both hands, both legs, and then pass object past you.

(Age, 6 up . . . Group, 8-30 . . . Time, 5-10 min.)

Musical Hats. As music plays, three hats are being passed around circle. Each person must try on hat, then pass it on, as it comes by him. When music stops, whoever has on hat pays forfeit, counts point against himself, or is eliminated.

(Age, 6 up . . . Group, 5-20 . . . Time, 5-15 min.)

Pass the Question. Folded piece of paper is passed around circle quickly. Whoever has it when music stops must answer question on slip. Then another question is passed around circle.

(Age, 9 up . . . Group, 5-30 . . . Time, 5-15 min.)

MYSTERY, PUZZLER, AND ACCOMPLICE GAMES

In these types of games, something is hidden. It may be a concrete object, or it may be a bit of information, a fact, a certain action, or a certain arrangement. The mind is challenged to solve the mystery or find the answer to the problem.

In the following group of MYSTERY GAMES, "It" does not know the solution, but the group does—or sometimes It does know, and the group does not.

Who Am I? Each person has pinned on his back name of famous person. By asking questions that can be answered "Yes" or "No" he is to find out who he is.

(Age, 6 up . . . Group, 5-100 . . . Time, 10 min.)

What Am I? Same idea, except that each person is a What instead of being a Who.

(Age, 6 up . . . Group, 5-100 . . . Time, 10 min.)

Who Left the Room? While It is out of room, someone else leaves. His job when he comes back is to figure out who left room.

(Age, 6 up . . . Group, 10-25 . . . Time, 10 min.)

I Have an Idea (also called Compliments and Slams). Group chooses object while It is out of room. When he returns, player says, "I have an Idea." "How's that?" asks It. "Just like you." "How?" asks It, again. "Green," says player. (Object chosen was leaf on plant.) Here It may take one guess, then receive other clues. If he prefers, he does not have to guess, but never gets but one guess at a time. Continue until It has discovered object. Person who gave last clue now goes out.

(Age, 9 up . . . Group, 10-50 . . . Time, 10-20 min.)

Teakettle. In this one, action is chosen, and when It returns to room, he uses word, "Teakettle" instead of action, like "Would you teakettle alone?" Answers must be yes or no. Continue until action is discovered.

(Age, 9 up . . . Group, 5-25 . . . Time, 10-20 min.)

Find the Leader. When It returns to room and goes to center of circle he finds people doing something. His job is to find person who is leading them in what they are doing, for when any change comes, leader must indicate it. When It catches leader, another person goes out.

(Age, 6 up . . . Group, 10-25 . . . Time, 10 min.)

How, When, Where. When It returns he finds that group has selected noun, like word "trip." He asks any person three questions: "How do you like it?" "When do you like it?" "Where do you like it?" Answer might be, "Ever so much," "Whenever the opportunity presents itself," "Anywhere in the U. S. or abroad." Continue until It has guessed. Sometimes words with double meanings are chosen, like bear, bare.

(Age, 9 up . . . Group, 10-25 . . . Time, 10 min.)

Bronx Cheer, Organ Grinder Man, Magic Music, Clap Hot and

Cold, Beat the Pan. These are all same basic game. When It returns from being out, something has been chosen for him to do, such as play piano. He is directed by these signals:

1. Clapping when he is going right, booing when he is going wrong.
2. Singing Organ Grinder Man, louder when he's close or ready to do it, softer when he's far away.
3. Playing piano or clapping and singing any song, louder and softer.
4. Clapping loud when he's close or "hot," softer or very softly when he's far away.
5. Tin pan is beat upon, louder when close, softer when away. One person beats pan.

(Age, preschool up . . . Group, 10-100 . . . Time, 10 min.)

Chain Reaction. While three persons are out of room, act is figured out, like changing tire, changing baby, washing elephant, taking down screens. One person is chosen to act this out for No. 1, who comes into room, and watches. Then No. 1 acts out what he thinks it is for No. 2, and No. 2 acts out what he thinks it is for No. 3. Then group tells them what was hidden action.

(Age, 9 up . . . Group, 10-100 . . . Time, 15-20 min.)

Your Predicament. Group figures out predicament for person who is out. "It" has privilege, on returning, of asking anybody in room what they would do in his place, which they must answer. If predicament were that he has date with two girls by mistake, answer might be, "I'd get sick," or "I'd try to reason with them."

(Age, 12 up . . . Group, 10-25 . . . Time, 10-20 min.)

Pretzel (Chinese Puzzle).[10] If group is large, divide into smaller ones of ten who form circles. Each one sends one of its number out of room. Leader then helps those remaining to wind and twist, scramble, and so on without letting go their hands. Object: for person sent away to return and unscramble mess by telling which person will step over, duck under, twist, turn. No turning loose of hands!

(Age, 9 up . . . Group, 10-25 . . . Time, 10-20 min.)

Statue. When It returns, he finds group all in poses. They are representing some famous person, and he is to guess who it is. Another way of playing would be for him to point to a player, who would go into his version of pose of that individual.

(Age, 9 up . . . Group, 5-50 . . . Time, 10 min.)

Animal Crackers. Each person in group of 25 or less, has animal cracker, and is to describe animal, one clue at a time, to see if others can guess what his animal is.

(Age, 6 up . . . Group, 5-25 . . . Time, 10 min.)

Bible Characters. Each person chooses Bible character and describes him, sentence at a time, allowing others to guess.

(Age, 9 up . . . Group, 5-20 . . . Time, 10 min.)

What Book of the Bible? Leader describes something that took place, and game is to see who can get correct book in which occasion was recorded. May be done from memory, or with Bibles.

(Age, 9 up . . . Group, 5-20 . . . Time, 10 min.)

I'm Thinking of a Word. Player starts off in group of up to 50, seated in circle: "I'm thinking of a word that rhymes with light." Others must guess by acting out word, like "sight," "might." They say, "Is it . . . ?" then act out word they think it is. Whoever guesses correctly becomes It for next time.

(Age, 6 up . . . Group, 5-100 . . . Time, 10 min.)

Imaginary I Spy (Dwarf Hide-and-Go-Seek). Player thinks of object in special location, such as the light overhead, and answers questions "Yes" or "No" from group until they discover where he has hidden it. Two may hide object at same time. Person who discovers where, becomes It.

(Age, preschool up . . . Group, any size . . . Time, 10 min.)

Twenty Questions. Same principle. Jim Flynn's automobile is thing Mary Alice Jones is thinking of, and he will answer questions (up to 20) "Yes" or "No." Sometimes played as "Vegetable-Animal-Mineral," and sometimes person who is It will reveal which of the three the object is. (House would be vegetable or mineral depending on whether it were wood or brick, in construction.) If group has not discovered in 20 questions, person who is It can try again, after telling them what object was.

(Age, 9 up . . . Group, 3-100 . . . Time, 10 min.)

Telephone Conversation. All participate in twos, each pair given five minutes to plan telephone conversation between two persons well known to group (either local folk or national or historical characters). Two designated to talk are indicated when leader hands them two toy telephones, or reasonably exact facsimiles. One person then goes across room and they talk back and forth. Object: for others to guess by their conversation who is being impersonated, on each end of "telephone." It could be such combinations as Jack Benny and Alexander the Great." (Age, 9 up . . . Group, 5-50 . . . Time, 10-20 min.)

Running Indians. As group sits and waits, five members run through and out door. Then, in a minute, they run through again, rearranged in order. Object: to put them back in proper order. This can be done by small groups observing, or as individuals. Indians may have Indian names on them for identification, especially in group who do not know each other very well —White Cloud, Running Deer, and the like.
(Age, 9 up . . . Group, 5-20 . . . Time, 10 min.)

Then here is a small group of PUZZLERS just as a sample of the many others that leaders can devise or find in other books.

Guess:
Number of beans, peas, or buttons in jar
Weight of dictionary in pounds and ounces
Length of ball of cord
Number of seeds in any kind of fruit
Number of words on page (magazine or newspaper)
Number of potatoes or apples in basket
(Age, 9 up . . . Group, any size)

Guess What. Hidden word or words are spelled out by articles displayed in order, like: SOUPY (soap, orange, union suit, peeling, yesterday's date).
(Age, 9 up . . . Group, any size)

Mystery Boxes. Several objects are in boxes of different sizes. People try to decide by rattle, sound and weight, what's in box.
(Age, 9 up . . . Group, any size)

Mystery Bags. In cloth bags (size of bean bag) insert articles, as above, and sew so that no one may see. Then let them feel to see if they can detect what hidden objects are. Number the bags.
(Age, 9 up . . . Group, 5-50)

Match Removal. Pair of players try, each attempting to force opponent to take last match. Matches are in three groups: 5, 4, 3. Up to all matches may be taken from any group at a turn, but not from more than one group at a turn. Toothpicks, sections of soda straws make good counters.
(Age, 9 up . . . Group, 2 . . . Time, 5-15 min.)

Sixteen Matches. In row are 16 matches. Two play. Players may pick up 1, 2, or 3 at a time. See who can make opponent take last match.
(Age, 9 up . . . Group, 2 . . . Time, 5-15 min.)

And finally there are ACCOMPLICE GAMES in which the leader and a confederate are in cahoots, unknown to the other players. There is always a "system" and the point is for the group to "figure out the system." It is customary to let anyone who thinks he has the "system" try his luck.

Usually the group chooses some object to be indicated to the confederate by the leader.

Object Guessing. When confederate returns, he is to indicate chosen object which is merely pointed to by leader.

Objects are placed on chairs which are numbered, 1, 2, 3, 4, 5, left to right, by unwritten, unspoken understanding. If leader points to chair No. 1 first time, that would be correct one. Likewise, to point second to that on chair No. 2, point to No. 3, third. If he points to any other chair, that is, of course, not correct one.
(Age, 9 up . . . Group, 6-100 . . . Time, 10 min.)

Spoon Photography. While confederate is out of room, picture is taken with spoon. Confederate names person, for leader is sitting in same position as one whose "picture" was taken.
(Age, 9 up . . . Group, 6-50 . . . Time, 10 min.)

Turkey Gobbler. While accomplice is out of room, small object, the "turkey," is given to one of players, seated in circle on floor. Leader sits cross-legged, foot pointing to side of circle where "turkey" is hidden. As accomplice goes around listening to everybody's hands to hear turkey, he looks at leader, who wiggles toe slightly when he comes to right person. To make this seasonal, let hidden object be clock (New Year's), beating heart

(Valentine's), firecracker (Fourth of July), music box (Christmas).

(Age, 9 up . . . Group, 6-50 . . . Time, 10 min.)

Name the Number. Group picks number, and when confederate returns to room, leader calls off: "44, 16, 10, 8, 6, 10." Accomplice says immediately, "32," which is correct. His clue: first numeral, 4, of the first number, tells him which numeral is significant, and second number, also 4, tells him what to multiply that fourth number by, giving him 4×8 or 32.

(Age, 12 up . . . Group, any size . . . Time, 10-30 min.)

Writing a Number with Matches. Actual number is number of fingers placed unobtrusively on edge of table after arranging matches (or toothpicks, pieces of soda straws) in geometric shapes. Each time you change number, change arrangement. Gradually make it more obvious until some catch on. You may have one or more accomplices who are "in the know." After "writing" number with matches, tell group what number is.

(Age, 9 up . . . Group, 3-15 . . . Time, 10-30 min.)

Tom Thumb. When confederate returns to name chosen object from three, he finds leader giving him cue with hands—if right thumb is over left, it indicates article to right; if left is on top, to left; if both are parallel, to center.

(Age, 9 up . . . Group, 5-50 . . . Time, 10-15 min.)

Chop Sticks. As leader crosses chopsticks in middle of room, confederate can tell which question will be the answer by noting that first stick is placed to represent 12 o'clock on clock face, and other will have head at o'clock hour which represents proper question, such as 4:00 o'clock, fourth question.

(Age, 9 up . . . Group, 5-50 . . . Time, 10 min.)

Number Guessing.[11] When confederate leaves room, group chooses number from 1 to 156. After number is selected, leader places three coins on floor representing that number. Confederate is called back, he studies it, and gives number without hesitation.

Key is face of clock, with dime representing center, nickel and quarter, the hour marking positions. Numeral on which quarter rests is squared (multiplied by itself), and numeral on which nickel rests is added or subtracted from squared number. (If nickel is head up, add; if tails up, subtract.)

(Age, 12 up . . . Group, 5-50 . . . Time, 10 min.)

Magic Writing (also called Mysterious Writing, Chinese Writing, Magic Cane). While confederate is out, group chooses word to be written to that person by leader. Word is transmitted by first letters of all sentences spoken by leader for consonants, and by tapping out vowels, one tap for A, two for E, three for I, four for O, and five for U. Color can be added by using dim lights, "oriental tones," and mysterious motions that mean nothing with cane, yardstick, or wand, or even "mystic pencil," or flashlight, or magic rope.

(Age, 9 up . . . Group, 5-50 . . . Time, 10-15 min.)

Golly Golly. Variation of Magic Writing in that names of famous people are used and fingers denote vowels. Group chooses name of famous person and some associated phrase may be spelled out, for instance, Babe Ruth might be spelled "King of Swat." [12]

(Age, 9 up . . . Group, 5-50 . . . Time, 10-15 min.)

Reading Temples. This can be very mysterious in appearance, and may be presented as "hypnotism." When accomplice returns to room, having been sent out and verb chosen, leader communicates to him in these ways:

1. Accomplice puts his hand on temples of leader, and leader says, "You must tell us the word." Then leader, by biting teeth together, gives signal, and accomplice counts. He bites 19-9-13-7 times, with pauses in between, to spell out word "Sing." Muscles at temples flex every time leader bites, so it is easy to count.

2. Accomplice may be seated in chair and "hypnotized" by having leader pass soothing motions across his forehead. Really, he is spelling out, as above, word, with accomplice going through alphabet with him, as 19 strokes for S, 9 for I, 13 for N, and 7 for G. (A short-cut may be used by having extra long stroke to represent five counts. It may go from middle of forehead back to ears, where short stroke goes only to temples.) "Hypnotized" person then sings in dazed fashion, and many will believe in "spell."

(Age, 9 up . . . Group, 5-100 . . . Time, 10-20 min.)

Who Did It? Accomplice and another person who does not know stunt are picked to take positions on floor with sheet or blanket over them. It is explained that entire group will stand in circle around them and will take turns touching either one or other of two under sheet. As soon as one is touched, they both uncover their faces and attempt to pick out person touching them. Accomplice has a yardstick alongside of him, and throughout entire procedure does all the hitting. After being hit number of times, victim is replaced by substitute and is shown how stunt has been done.

(Age, 9 up . . . Group, 10-50 . . . Time, 10 min.)

Legs. When accomplice returns, he can identify immediately object chosen by group in his absence, when questioned by leader, because it is next object mentioned by leader after something that has legs.

(Age, 9 up . . . Group, 10-50 . . . Time, 10-20 min.)

Which Panel? There are four panels on door. When leader calls accomplice back, he indicates which one by number of words he uses, like "Come on back in" for fourth panel.

(Age, 9 up . . . Group, 5-50 . . . Time, 10 min.)

Which Article? (Also called Jamboree.) Accomplice gets his signal as he leaves: leader unobtrusively puts fingers on door jamb to indicate which question in order, such as third, will contain correct answer. Group chooses article, and confederate says "No" until third question, or whatever one was indicated.

(Age, 9 up . . . Group, 5-50 . . . Time, 10 min.)

Nine Books. Confederate re-enters room to tell group which of nine books it chose, arranged in three rows of three, as in illustration.

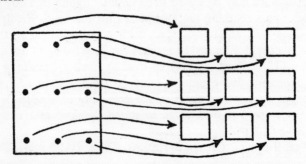

Leader touches spot on first book which indicates location of correct book.

(Age, 9 up . . . Group, 5-25 . . . Time, 10 min.)

Black Magic. Leader indicates chosen object to assistant by next thing pointed to after something black.

(Age, 9 up . . . Group, 5-50 . . . Time, 10 min.)

Red, White, Blue Magic. Same as black magic, but with more colors.

Power. All are sitting in circle and two persons move around in mystic manner making magic gestures. One asks other if he has the power yet. Trick comes when first person speaks after one of mystics says, "Power, power, power, come hither, power!" One mystic leaves room and other shakes hands with person who spoke. Naturally when the one who left returns, he can shake hands with same person.

(Age, 9 up . . . Group, 5-50 . . . Time, 10 min.)

In Cahoots. Same idea as Power. Accomplice places left hand on right shoulder of leader and follows around room while leader says, "The Magic Circle now begins" . . . and continues until some person speaks. Leader says to accomplice, "Are you in cahoots?" (meaning Did you notice who spoke?) and he says, "Yes, I'm in cahoots," and leaves room. Then leader gives small object to person who spoke, and accomplice can, of course, come in and identify who has object. (If accomplice did not note who spoke, he says, "No, I'm not in cahoots.")

(Age, 9 up . . . Group, 5-25 . . . Time, 10 min.)

Time and Place. One individual goes out of room while group decides on city, hour, and minute. For example: Cincinnati, Ohio, 2:30 P.M. Partner, upon return of first person, recites list of cities and immediately is told by one who was out of room correct time and place. Technique is as follows: first, hour is given by name or names of cities in four time zones: Eastern time, 1, 2, 3; Central time, 4, 5, 6; Mountain time, 7, 8, 9; Pacific time 10, 11, 12. Person would say then, two cities in Eastern zone, e.g. Boston, Mass., and Philadelphia, Pa., and then shift to another time zone to give minutes. Letters with which next two cities begin designate minutes.

0 1 2 3 4 5 6 7 8 9

a b c d e f g h i j   Thus could be used Denver, Colo., and Albany, New York. The next city designates either A.M. or P.M. Any city beginning with letters A-M stands for A.M. and between N and Z for P.M. For example: person might say Reno,

Nevada. Name of city following any combination of three cities beginning with San or New is correct one.

When individual returns to room his partner could say, Boston, Mass., Philadelphia, Pa., Denver, Colo., Albany, N.Y., Reno, Nevada, New Haven, San Francisco, New York, Cincinnati, Des Moines and correct answer of 2:30 P.M. Cincinnati would be given immediately.

(Age, 12 up . . . Group, 3-25 . . . Time, 10-20 min.)

No, Nope. Accomplice leaves, object is selected by group, accomplice returns. Leader continues to point out wrong objects as long as reply is "Nope," but when accomplice shifts to "No" he means for leader next time to point to correct one, in which case he or she will say, "That's it."

(Age, 9 up . . . Group, 5-50 . . . Time, 10-20 min.)

Concentration. Accomplice leaves, and leader gets someone in group to write out sentence. Accomplice is to write same thing. Group writes, "Birds of a feather flock together." When accomplice returns, leader asks if he is ready. "Yes." "All concentrate, then, while he writes." They are supposed to be doing it. Accomplice writes out, "The same thing."

(Age, 9 up . . . Group, 5-100 . . . Time, 5 min.)

GAMES WITH PROVERBS

There are many uses for proverbs. They can be dramatized, used for quizzes, in games, or even for a partner-getting device (cut them in two, let the two partners hunt for each other). Here are a hundred proverbs with which you can devise all kinds of entertainment.

1. Half a loaf is better than no bread.
2. Blood is thicker than water.
3. The early bird catches the worm.
4. Beggars cannot be choosers.
5. Beauty is skin deep.
6. It takes two to make a bargain.
7. April showers bring May flowers.
8. A watched pot never boils.
9. Too many cooks spoil the broth.
10. A fool and his money are soon parted.
11. Actions speak louder than words.

12. A guilty conscience needs no accuser.
13. Brevity is the soul of wit.
14. Don't cry over spilled milk.
15. Everybody's business is nobody's business.
16. Clothes don't make the man.
17. Better be safe than sorry.
18. Practice makes perfect.
19. A bird in the hand is worth two in the bush.
20. Every dog has his day.
21. Two heads are better than one.
22. Make hay while the sun shines.
23. A barking dog never bites.
24. Misery loves company.
25. As the twig is bent, so the tree is inclined.
26. Like father, like son.
27. Spare the rod and spoil the child.
28. Children should be seen and not heard.
29. Let sleeping dogs lie.
30. There's no fool like an old fool.
31. You can't teach an old dog new tricks.
32. One man's meat is another man's poison.
33. Turn about is fair play.
34. Familiarity breeds contempt.
35. Where there's smoke, there's fire.
36. Laugh and grow fat.
37. A little learning is a dangerous thing.
38. You can't have your cake and eat it too.
39. Don't look a gift horse in the mouth.
40. Easy come, easy go.
41. Experience is the best teacher.
42. If wishes were horses, beggars would ride.
43. Still water runs deep.
44. Don't put off until tomorrow what you can do today.
45. Virtue is its own reward.
46. Practice what you preach.
47. The proof of the pudding is in the eating.
48. Don't count your chickens before they're hatched.
49. If at first you don't succeed, try, try again.
50. A miss is as good as a mile.
51. The empty wagon rattles the loudest.
52. Birds of a feather flock together.
53. A rotten apple spoils the whole barrel.

54. A new broom sweeps clean.
55. A penny saved is a penny earned.
56. After the storm comes the calm.
57. Circumstances alter cases.
58. Better late than never.
59. It is too late to lock the barn after the horse is gone.
60. Better to have an empty purse than an empty head.
61. It is never too late to learn.
62. Marry in haste and repent at leisure.
63. The road to hell is paved with good intentions.
64. Honesty is the best policy.
65. A stitch in time saves nine.
66. God helps those who help themselves.
67. Be sure you're right, then go ahead.
68. It's easier said than done.
69. It's an ill wind that blows nobody good.
70. Time and tide wait for no man.
71. Jack of all trades—master of none.
72. Nothing succeeds like success.
73. Every rose has its thorn.
74. Silence is golden.
75. All's fair in love and war.
76. People who live in glass houses shouldn't throw stones.
77. Every cloud has a silver lining.
78. All good things must come to an end.
79. Nothing ventured, nothing gained.
80. Where there's a will, there's a way.
81. You can lead a horse to water, but you can't make him drink.
82. Forewarned is forearmed.
83. Health is better than wealth.
84. He who dances must pay the fiddler.
85. There are two sides to every question.
86. Necessity is the mother of invention.
87. It never rains but that it pours.
88. "It's the hit dog that hollers."
89. Two wrongs don't make a right.
90. A man is known by the company he keeps.
91. Out of sight, out of mind.
92. All that glitters is not gold.
93. It takes a thief to catch a thief.
94. Absence makes the heart grow fonder.
95. Rome wasn't built in a day.

96. Forewarned is forearmed.
97. Curiosity killed the cat.
98. A friend in need is a friend indeed.
99. An apple a day keeps the doctor away.
100. Don't put all your eggs in one basket.

Translated Proverbs. In small groups of two to four players, take proverbs and step them up to highbrow language. Let them read their work of art to others. Samples: "The humidity is not comparative, but it is absolute." (It never rains but that it pours.) "Accelerated execution produces faulty results." (Haste makes waste.)

What Is the Proverb? While It is out of room, a proverb is chosen. On his return he asks any player any question he wishes, and that player, in his answer, must use at least one word of proverb. Continue until he guesses, then another leaves room.

Shouting Proverbs. Divide into 2 to 6 groups. (They may be large.) Each thinks of proverb and every person takes one word of proverb, such as "Every dog has his day." "Signal caller" stands in front of group performing, and gives signal, "ONE, TWO, THREE, *GO!*" On word "Go," each person shouts his word as loud as he can, blending his voice with others. Object: for any of others to detect what proverb is. (This one works well if each group performs in same location in which it "thought up" its proverb.) Others may gather around very closely to listen, but must not block view of "signal caller." Any person may call "Again" and proverb is performed again, until finally it is detected.

(Age, 9 up . . . Group, 5-30 . . . Time, 15-20 min.)

Singing Proverbs. If there is difficulty in solving hidden proverb with shouting, group may be asked to sing its proverb, each person doing his one word to familiar tune like "Jingle Bells," with "signal caller" or someone else starting it. This makes it easier for guessers. May be played as separate game.

(Age, 9 up . . . Group, 5-30 . . . Time, 15-20 min.)

Hidden Proverbs. On blackboard are marked lines for each word in familiar saying, like "IIIII II I IIIIIII IIIII IIIIIIII" for "Birds of a feather flock together." The group are then to work proverb out (1) individually or (2) in small groups, seeing who gets it first.

(Age, 9 up . . . Group, 3-100 . . . Time, 10 min.)

Twisted Proverbs. Divided into groups of 3 to 10, they take familiar proverbs and come up with some twisted ones, like "Too
many cooks spoil the clock" or "All's fair as the Romans do."
Another angle is to modify proverbs: "You can't eat your cake
and have *It* too!"

(Age, 12 up . . . Group, 3-10 . . . Time, 10 min.)

CREATIVE, IMPROVISING GAMES

In the following games, persons or groups are to improvise and
then show what they have worked out. In some cases they will do
it together. These games are different, a little more challenging.

Buckets. Seated in circle, group learns that each person is to pantomime bucket on floor in front of him. Each person, without
talking and in turn, shows how high bucket is, what its other
dimensions are, its shape, whether it has handle. After all have
described their buckets in pantomime, they pantomime contents,
then, one at a time, showing, by way they take it out, what it is
(or way they let, say, "beans" run through their hands). Others
may be asked to guess what is in bucket.

(Age, 9 up . . . Group, 8-15 . . . Time, 10 min.)

What's Wrong with This? In groups of 5 to 10, present stunt and
let others figure out what is wrong in situation. This might be
done in serious vein, like having someone committing a social
error such as introducing man to woman.

It might be done in nonsense, like bride and groom skipping
lively down aisle. (What's wrong? Groom is already married.)
Three large people are trying to get under umbrella. (It isn't
raining.)

Another angle: just simple turn-about, having characters
dramatize unexpected, like youngster refusing cookies (might
spoil his meal), wife saying that she didn't mind husband's
being late for dinner—she knows he had some things to go
over with his new secretary. What a pretty, intelligent girl . . .,
and so on.

(Age, 9 up . . . Group, 5-10 . . . Time, 10 min.)

Fireside Freud. For small group, older youth and older adults,
only. Each person has pencil and paper and is given starter

word, like "embarrassment." Each person is asked to write for two minutes, all the words that come into his mind in way of association, one after other, in column.

These are handed to "Dr. Freud," who takes them and gives silly psychoanalysis of word-association. Person doing this needs to be clever, yet tactful, so as not to hurt feelings.

(Age, 18 up . . . Group, 5-15 . . . Time, 15-25 min.)

The Big Sale. Divide larger group into smaller ones of 3 to 6 players to think up funny signs for Big Sale, and let them read their signs after five or ten minutes. Samples: "Men's shirts 69¢ and they won't last long at this price." "Ladies' bathing suits, ⅓ off." They could also work on mottoes for complaint department, work out special combinations to be featured.

(Age, 12 up . . . Group, 3-6 . . . Time, 10-20 min.)

Historical Telegram. Two or more groups are working on historical telegram. When all finish, they read their telegram for others to guess who sent it, and perhaps to whom it was sent.

(Age, 9 up . . . Group, 2-8 . . . Time, 10-20 min.)

Conjugating (New Style). In small groups of 2 to 6 players, work out some funny conjugations and read them aloud, such as: "I am thrifty, you are close, he is an old tightwad." "I am not at all bad-looking, you are plain, he (or she) is a hag." Or reverse it and give "nasty" first, ordinary second, nice last.

(Age, 9 up . . . Group, 2-6 . . . Time, 15-25 min.)

Concentration. In center of small circle stands individual whom all are touching. They are all looking toward one person in circle. If concentration is hard enough, center person will have tendency to fall toward person to whom all are looking!

(Age, 12 up . . . Group, 8-10 . . . Time, 5-10 min.)

Discovery. In small groups, examine any volume of accumulated knowledge, like dictionary, Bible, volumes of encyclopedia, World Book, Book of Knowledge, and after 10 to 15 minutes, have each group tell some of interesting things they discovered that they hadn't known before.

(Age, 6 up . . . Group, 3-8 . . . Time, 10-25 min.)

Cliché. In small groups, think up all the clichés or redundancies you can, and read list aloud. They might take form of series of those obvious statements, like "You're not back, are you?"

"You didn't get burned, did you?" "I didn't step on your toe, did I?" Additional fun could come from acting them out.

(Age, 18 up . . . Group, 3-10 . . . Time, 15-25 min.)

Alibis. Leader tells of some incident that happened just before the meeting, gives exact time, and calls on different people to give their alibis as to where they were. (Pie was stolen from refreshment supply, for example.) Then have group vote on who was probably guilty.

(Age, 12 up . . . Group, 3-25 . . . Time, 15-25 min.)

Brainstorming. Business and industry are using this creative system, so why not for fun? In small groups of 3 to 10 persons, you simply take problem and think it through from all angles, sometimes coming up with some colossal ideas. One group took a few minutes to think up all the recreational things they could do, and were amazed that list totaled 75 items! Such subjects as "How could we raise some needed money?" or "What could we do for fun for next six months in our group?" might bring some truly workable answers. It's fun, too.

(Age, 12 up . . . Group, 3-10 . . . Time, 15-60 min.)

Organized "Gripe Session." Divided into groups of 5 to 8 persons, just turn loose and gripe—girls about boys, men about women, and vice versa. Anybody may gripe about school, lessons, work, bosses. If done in spirit of good fun, it may help to get rid of some steam. (Once in group of high school folk we did this. Girls griped about boys who didn't bathe and use deodorants. Boy quickly called attention to male gripe: girls who wear too much cheap perfume.) It is always important to lead such a session toward positive conclusion. "What can be done about it?" is necessary question.

(Age, 9 up . . . Groups, 5-8 each . . . Time, 10-20 min.)

New Year's Resolutions (in April). Write out your resolutions, give them to member of group such as secretary, and open them about April 1 to see how well resolutions were kept.

(Age, 9 up . . . Groups, any size . . . Time, 10 min.)

Poetry Club. Select short piece of light poetry and make enough copies for each person to have one. Then number off in group until 10 or 12 people have numbers. They are, when their number is called, to stand and read their poetry in manner indicated.

1. A train announcer
2. Somebody without teeth
3. A small child
4. A first-class gossip
5. With a lisp
6. With a stammer
7. A forgetful fourth-grader
8. A Shakespearean actor-r-r
9. In old elocution style
10. As a mellow-voiced radio or TV announcer

(Age, 9 up . . . Group, 10-12 . . . Time, 15-20 min.)

Who's Who? [13] Players sit in pairs, with chairs so arranged that you can see who are partners. Each player starts by exchanging names with his partner. Bob becomes Betty and Betty, Bob, for instance. Leader calls for two persons to change places, and he tries to get seat. Persons who change are not real ones, but ones currently carrying these names. If leader gets a seat, one left out becomes It, still bearing assumed name he or she had. Each time a person sits, he exchanges names with partner in other seat. At end, have several people do characterization of person whose name they had when game ended.

(Age, 12 up . . . Groups, 2 each . . . Time, 15-20 min.)

Putting Puns into a Sentence. Divide into groups and see who can make sentence containing most puns.

(Age, 12 up . . . Groups, 3-5 each . . . Time, 10-20 min.)

Creative Writing. Divide into groups and let each one try its hand at "ad" writing, singing commercials, composing grace for table, writing limerick or serious piece of poetry. Display works of art or have them read.

(Age, 12 up . . . Groups, 2-5 each . . . Time, 10-30 min.)

FUN WITH ART MATERIALS

Paper, paints, crayolas, finger paints, water colors, and the like can furnish many enjoyable hours both for children and for youth and adults. Many of these activities, very informal in the arts and crafts line, can be done with little advance preparation. Some can be used for early comers at parties.

Making Name Tag. At affairs where this is needed, name tags may be made from slips of paper or cardboard, decorated gaily with crayolas, wax pencils. It is important that name can be read for some distance away. Have table (or several tables for large crowd) at which each may take some time to make his own.

Wooden name tags are popular. They may be decorated with wax pencils, with new ball-point decorators' colors, or by wood-burning needles. Colorful yarn, used through holes, makes it easy to hang this one around neck. By distributing yarn carefully, groups may be formed automatically by color of yarn.

(Age, 6 up . . . Group, 1 . . . Time, 10-20 min.)

Self-Expression. As people arrive at party, have some "art tables" equipped with materials: paper hat materials, paper sack puppet materials, sculpture with apples, pears, or potatoes, or soap or modeling clay. "See what you can do" may be followed by "See what I made."

(Age, 6 up . . . Group, 1 . . . Time, 15-30 min.)

Art Exhibit. Divide into groups of 3 to 6 persons, give them scissors, paper, crayons, pins, and have them make children's cut-outs, to be displayed later.

(Age, preschool up . . . Groups, 3-6 each . . . Time, 15-60 min.)

Silhouettes. Get early comers to have their silhouettes made. Put sheets of paper on wall and have someone shine a bright light close enough to his profile to cast shadow on paper. Outline with crayon or charcoal. Display.

(Age, 9 up . . . Group, 1 . . . Time, 15-25 min.)

Making Own Favors, Place Cards. With materials, such as paste, scissors, construction paper, feathers, cork, felt, raisins, marsh-mallows, each person is given opportunity to make his own favor or place card. Or make place cards or favors for another person. (Here is opportunity to make something nice for older person or bedridden individual.)

(Age, preschool up . . . Group, 1 . . . Time, 10-30 min.)

Abstractions and Concretions.[14] Use sheet of pastel-colored paper and box of crayons (24-color box is good). First person uses one color and draws any line or enclosure, avoiding making it look too much like any object. Next person takes a color and draws an addition. Change colors when changing turns. Result is interesting for any age, any situation. Good family game.

(Age, 12 up . . . Group, 1 . . . Time, 10-60 min.)

Colors. Have enough sets and jars of paints for all to try their hand at a "paint job," either to do as "just for fun" or to make Christmas card, favors, and the like.

(Age, preschool up . . . Group, 1 . . . Time, 10-60 min.)

Paper Fashions. Divide into small groups, each electing girl as model. Boys or men in group must design and make costume with newspapers, pins, scissors. Girls may advise but not help.
(Age, 9 up . . . Groups, 5-15 each . . . Time, 15-25 min.)

Blindfolded Drawing. Each person trying is blindfolded and led to his sheet of paper on wall (or blackboard). There he draws some object as directed (animal, landscape, person).
(Age, 6 up . . . Group, 1 . . . Time, 15-25 min.)

Self-Portrait. With paper bag on his head, each person draws, with crayon, eyes, one at a time, ears, nose, mouth, eyebrow, cheeks.
(Age, preschool up . . . Group, 1 . . . Time, 5-20 min.)

Initial Portraits.[15] Put initials on paper (or on blackboard or floor, or in sand). Then draw face, working in letters. Children will watch leader draw pictures from their initials for long periods. Also for one or two persons who like to "doodle."
(Age, 6 up . . . Group, 1 . . . Time, 5-20 min.)

Pinhole Pictures. Each person has several grains of rice to drop on his drawing sheet. He punches hole in paper with pin where each grain lay, then draws picture including all these points.
(Age, 6 up . . . Group, 1 . . . Time, 5-15 min.)

Chinese English.[16] This is fun in itself, also interesting way to write invitations for "around the world affairs" or for posters. It can be made to be read "top down" or "bottom up."
(Age, 9 up . . . Group, 1 . . . Time, 5-20 min.)

THIS IS CHINESE ENGLISH

ITS FUN TO TRY AND

WITH A LITTLE PRACTICE

ANYONE CAN DO IT.

Star Tracing.[17] Duplicate number of double stars, outer of which is about 6 inches from point to point, and inner one an inch smaller, tip to tip, as illustrated. Place mirror about an inch from point of star. Object is to try to trace within lines of double

Star Tracing

star, between inner and outer stars. Several mirrors permit several star tracings to go on at same time. Excellent as guests arrive at party.

(Age, 9 up . . . Group, 1 . . . Time, 5-15 min.)

Doodles

1. Give everyone slips of paper and pencil (or crayons) and encourage them to doodle. Pass doodles around table, display them on wall, perhaps judge them for best.
2. Another version is best as blackboard game, in sight of all. One person starts by drawing line of some sort, perhaps irreg-

ular or wavy, on board. Whoever has an idea may come forward, take chalk, complete it into picture, then erase and start another "doodle."
(Age, 9 up . . . Group, 1 . . . Time, 5-15 min.)

Blot Drawing. Each person makes ink blot on his paper, folding it while ink is still wet, then completes it into picture as directed by leader: cow, plane, Superman, bird, person. Display results.
(Age, 9 up . . . Group, 1 . . . Time, 5-15 min.)

Drawing in the Dark. Each person has paper and pencil (or crayons) and large sheet of paper. Explain that since so many are bashful about drawing when people are looking, you are having them draw in the dark. Give assignment and tell in order what parts to draw, like a house, then windows, then chimney, smoke coming from chimney.
(Age, 6 up . . . Group, 1 . . . Time, 5-10 min.)

Illustrated Music. As tunes are played on piano, one or more "illustrators" work at blackboard to draw appropriate pictures for titles, such as "Home on the Range." May be contest with two or more drawing.
(Age, 9 up . . . Group, any size . . . Time, 20-30 min.)

Editing a Paper. Dividing larger crowd into smaller groups, each is given assignment in editing paper, like sports, household hints, society, comics, want ads, front page, editorials, and the like. After 15 to 30 minutes, each presents its version of the news.
(Age, 9 up . . . Groups, 3-8 each . . . Time, 30-40 min.)

Magazine Autobiography. Provide materials, scissors, paste, notebook paper and cover, magazines, for each person to make up tongue-in-cheek notebook, "The Life and Works of _____ _____," to be shown to others after 30 to 45 minutes of preparation. Angles might be: "First Photo," "Childhood," "Aim in Life," "Greatest Enjoyment," "Biggest Mistake," "Best Friend," "My Travels," "My Hobby," "My Finish." All illustrations are to be clipped from magazines.
(Age, 9 up . . . Group, 3-8 . . . Time, 30-45 min.)

Mother Goose Commercial. In small groups, redo Mother Goose in manner of today's commercials, including singing.
(Age, 6 up . . . Group, 2-8 . . . Time, 30 min.)

Snow Modeling (winter game). Provide dishpan of clean snow for each small group from which they are to model some interesting figures and display them, in about 15 to 20 minutes.

(Age, 6 up . . . Group, 3-5 . . . Time, 15-20 min.)

What Is It? Arrange on several tables odds and ends: needles, pins, corks, cotton, glue, nuts, prunes, pickles, pine cones. On center table are three resting places: pan with sawdust, bird cage, and bowl of water.

People are to make strange creatures with these materials and display them. They are then placed in proper place, whether bird, beast or fish, for others to see.

(Age, 6 up . . . Group, 1 . . . Time, 15-30 min.)

Confetti Pictures. Have enough paste and confetti for each person to make some "futurist" pictures and display them, with appropriate names.

(Age, 6 up . . . Group, 1 . . . Time, 15-30 min.)

Thread Sketching. Each person gets piece of white cloth and plenty of black thread. Idea is to sketch interesting picture with black thread. Scissors are available in case of error. Finished products are displayed gallery style. Some might be cartoons, some landscapes.

(Age, 6 up . . . Group, 1 . . . Time, 15-30 min.)

Make a Hat. Seasonal party idea. With colored paper, cloth, scissors, pins, and ornaments, either have small team make hat for one of its members, or have everybody make one, appropriate for party theme.

(Age, 6 up . . . Group, 1 . . . Time, 15-30 min.)

MAGAZINE GAMES

With scissors, paste, and imagination, individuals and groups can have a lot of fun with old magazines. Children can cut and paste into scrapbooks those things which interest them. Adults often enjoy doing this, too.

Here are some other suggestions for the use of magazines that are partylike.

Scavenger Hunt. As in regular scavenger hunt, each group is given list of things to hunt for, to be found in perhaps 10 or 15 minutes. Whoever has most nearly complete list, wins. (Divide larger group down into groups of three or four each.)

Story. Each group is given magazine, and is to write story, using clippings from features, stories, ads, or anything else found in magazine. (Done in groups of three or four.)

Love Letters. See who can take their magazine and compose with clippings and explanations a good, mushy love letter. (Groups of three or four.)

Other Letters. Same idea as Love Letters, but letters to the President, to an enemy, to Santa, to St. Valentine, to Uncle Sam, to a Witch, and others.

Magazine Covers. Let small groups work with water colors, paper, crayons, scissors, paste, and other materials to create magazine cover. Alternate: to pose in tableau form, a magazine cover.

Magazine Costumes. Find costume in magazine, then dress one of members of group in that style, using sheets from magazine.

Make Up Your Own. Give out magazines to small groups and let them make up their own magazine game.

(Age, 9 up . . . Group, 2-6 . . . Time, 15-30 min.)

BLINDFOLD GAMES

Blindman's Buff. Players circle around blindfolded blind man, singing verse of a song. They stop at end. "Blind man" points stick at someone in circle and asks him to "bark like a dog," or use his voice in some other way. The player does so, disguising voice. If blind man can still detect who it was, they change places.

(Age, preschool up . . . Group, 8-50 . . . Time, 10 min.)

Bell Tag. All players are blindfolded except bellboy (or girl), who rings bell as he or she moves around. Others try to catch her or him. If successful, they change places.

(Age, preschool up . . . Group, 5-40 . . . Time, 10 min.)

Tight Rope Walker (Blindfolded). Stretch rope on floor, and one at a time blindfold contestants and let them see who can walk farthest on rope.

(Age, 6 up . . . Group, 1 at a time . . . Time, 10 min.)

Pillow Fight (Blindfolded). Each of two blindfolded persons is given pillow, with instructions to hit the other. They are started from opposite ends of room. Unknown to them, third person has a pillow, and pelts them before they get to each other. He goes from one to the other.

(Age, 6 up . . . Group, 2 . . . Time, 10 min.)

Pickup. Blindfold a person, get him to pick up handful of coins or other objects that have been dropped to floor.

(Age, 9 up . . . Group, 1 . . . Time, 10 min.)

Blindfold Walk. Blindfold several players and send them across room. Idea is not to (1) ring any of bells that are hung from ceiling, (2) step on egg shells that are on floor, (3) bump into furniture that is in the way.

(Sometimes these things will be removed, and those watching will get delight from seeing contestants try to dodge what is not there.)

(Age, 6 up . . . Group, 5-10 . . . Time, 10 min.)

Blindfold Fortunes. Certain things are symbolic of fortunes. Load up table with number of these things, have blindfolded players walk up one at a time and place finger down on object. This automatically tells fortune, for example:

coins (for wealth)	toy plane (take a trip)
ring (for marriage)	pile of dirt (farming)
dolls (for number of children)	top (spinster)

(Age, 6 up . . . Group, any size . . . Time, 15-20 min.)

BALLOON GAMES

Besides lending color and gaiety to any party, there are many games that can be played with balloons—in fact, just about all the games for which you would ordinarily use a ball.

Balloon Dart. Fill balloons with gas, tie them to furniture or other anchors so that they float. Give players darts and have them throw darts in turn, to puncture balloons.

Hot Air. Give each person balloon. With all starting at same time, see who can blow his balloon up to bursting point first. Or, do it in pairs, and continue as elimination contest. (Loser drops out.)

Balloon Defense. Have group choose partners and tie balloon to girl's ankle. She and her partner, working together, try to defend her balloon from being stepped on, but to burst others' balloons at same time. (Can be played singly.)

Balloon Relays

1. Each person kicks balloon up to line or goal, then breaks it by stamping on it.
2. Each person bats balloon with paddle to goal, then breaks it by hugging it.
3. Each person runs to goal with balloon between knees, then sits down on balloon on chair at goal to break it before returning.
4. Each person blows balloon to goal line, then sits on it to break it before returning.
5. Pass small balloon under chin down the line to end of relay line. First one through, wins. (If one breaks, head person must blow up and start another balloon.)
6. Seated in long line, each player must run around head of his line, back to his seat, blow up his balloon and sit on it to burst it, before next player down line from him can run. Several lines of equal numbers are competing.

Balloon Sweep. Each team of five or six has balloon, some spares, and broom, and its members stand in circle. At signal, first player with broom sweeps balloon around circle and back to place, then next one does same. If team breaks balloon it must blow up another and tie it.

Balloon Squeeze. Two or more married couples are competing. They blow up balloon, tie it or hold it, put it between them, and squeeze until it breaks. (Could be used as relay of husband-wife pairs.)

(Age, 18 up . . . Groups, 2 each . . . Time, 5-10 min.)

Wastebasket Basketball. Played like regular basketball, except that there is no dribbling (balloon is passed or batted) and that goal is wastebasket, carried by team member, who must stand in place but can move around to help "ball" in. Devise your own rules.

(Age, 9 up . . . Groups, 4-10 each . . . Time, 10-20 min.)

Creative Activity with Balloons. Divide large group into several small ones, 3 to 6 persons. Give each group eight or ten balloons and some scotch tape. Let group make something to be shown to other groups in about 15 minutes. Animals are usually made, but try other things, too. Let preschool children try it.

Balloon Tail. Each person has balloon either under belt, fastened on back, or tied to string around waist and hanging down in back. Object: to protect your "balloon tail" but at same time to break other balloons.

(Age, 6 up . . . Group, any size . . . Time, 5-10 min.)

Balloon Hockey. Each wall is designated as goal for team. Play with two teams, each person equipped with cardboard fan to fan or bat balloon. Object: to knock balloons so as to hit goal of other team and make point. One or several may be put into play at "midfield" at same time. One team may knock red, other team blue, balloons.

Balloon Volleyball. Players are sitting in chairs with string stretched between as net. Outside lines are indicated, as in volleyball. No player may get up out of seat; otherwise play as in regular volleyball. Object: to score point by knocking balloon in such manner that it touches floor on opponent's side, inside line. Set your own total point score for winning.

(Age, 9 up . . . Groups, 4-10 each . . . Time, 10-20 min.)

Balloon Dodge Ball. In fairly small circles (so that balloon can actually be thrown at players) play dodge ball with balloons.

(Age, 6 up . . . Groups, 8-15 each . . . Time, 5-10 min.)

Balloon Basketball. Five players are sitting in chairs in two lines facing each other, with "goalie" sitting in chair at end of setup. Lines are close enough that feet of opposing players may touch. Each team will bat balloon to its own right to its human goalie, who is holding his arms in circle. Goalie may bend or contort in any way except leave chair. No other player may leave chair.

Game is started by having "referee" toss balloon into air in middle of two lines. Successful goal is two points. Set time limit in beginning, such as 6 or 10 minutes. Substitutions may be used. Cheers from sidelines may be organized, and teams even named. May be played at cleared table, with 4 to 5 players on side and goalie at each end, with referee for each table.

(Age, 9 up . . . Groups, 4-6 each . . . Time, 10-30 min.)

Balloon Headball. A string as net is tied about 5½ feet high, and players play on both side of net in teams. Serving is by hitting ball over net with head, and playing as in volleyball. It is a foul to hit ball with hands, although you might permit hitting with shoulders, if agreed in advance. String may be raised or lowered, depending on ability of players.

(Age, 6 up . . . Groups, 5-10 each . . . Time, 10 min.)

FORFEITS OR CONSEQUENCES

A number of games call for the possibility of forfeits. Generally they are simple individual stunts which could be done without idea of forfeit for group amusement.

Imitations

1. Three barnyard noises
2. Jack-in-the-box
3. Monkey eating bananas
4. A back-seat driver
5. A ballet dancer in action
6. A mule braying
7. An opera singer
8. A child giving first recitation
9. A tightrope walker
10. An organ grinder's monkey
11. An umpire
12. Three bird calls
13. A photographer taking pictures
14. Paul Revere
15. A shadow boxer
16. A radio or TV announcer
17. A dog chasing a cat
18. Imitate a cat chased by a dog
19. A TV comedian, tell who it is
20. A Western hero's horse
21. Someone taking a shower
22. A politician, warming up
23. A trick dog
24. A soap salesman selling new soap
25. A Hollywood producer
26. A truant officer, going after someone present
27. A barker at a circus or carnival
28. Two Shakespeare or Dickens characters
29. Some unknown celebrity (Let group guess who you are.)
30. The Statue of Liberty

Speeches

1. Three nice compliments about yourself
2. The political situation
3. The plight of the farmer
4. Flowery compliments to three persons present
5. A funny story
6. A Mother Goose rhyme
7. A speech without words, only lip movements
8. The three books you would want to take with you on a desert island
9. The three "big shots" you'd like to know most
10. Your pet peeve
11. An exploit to brag about
12. Counting as far as you can in a breath
13. Your funniest joke—without smiling
14. Why you like your hobby (golf, sewing, girls . . .)
15. Answer truthfully two questions put to you
16. "The ideal boy" or "The ideal girl" (or husband/wife)
17. Where you'd like to spend your vacation and why
18. How to make a tossed salad (if a male is asked)
19. How to fix the flooded carburetor on a car (if a female is asked)
20. "What's wrong with this club, church, school, firm" (Choose one.)
21. Reciting "Mary Had a Little Lamb"
22. Reciting anything you know from Shakespeare
23. Reciting something from the Bible
24. Prognosticating the future: telling about some of the people present
25. Giving this yell twice: Owha tagoo Siam

Actions

1. Laugh, cry, whistle and sing in four corners of the room.
2. Kneel to three persons, smiling as you do it.
3. Hop like a grasshopper.
4. Yawn until somebody else does.
5. Do some acrobatic act.
6. March like a tin soldier.
7. Whirl around with an imaginary partner.
8. Dance a jig.
9. Crawl across the floor.
10. Find somebody who isn't ticklish.
11. Sing like a popular male star; or female star.
12. Tell the fortune of someone by palm reading.

13. Give a hen's triumphant cry that she's laid an egg.
14. Give the rooster's claim for part credit.
15. Leave the room with two legs, come back with six (a chair or small table).

Heavy, Heavy Hangs Over Thy Head. If forfeits are used as such, an article is demanded from each person losing out in game. (Sometimes game is made hard to get forfeit item from everyone.) There is a judge, over whose head article is hung (without his seeing it). "Heavy, heavy hangs over thy head," says official. "Fine or superfine?" asks judge. "Fine," says helper, meaning that it is boy's item. Whereupon judge pronounces what is to be done. (The preceding lists would be of help in prompting his imagination. However, it is easy to make forfeits seasonal. For New Year's, speech on My Resolutions; for Valentine's, on Love; for Hallowe'en, on Witches.)

Color Forfeits or Stunts. During refreshments, pass around candies of different colors, and get one or more persons for each color to do stunt.

Stir the Broth. First player says, "I will stir the broth if (name of someone present) will recite the Gettysburg Address." If he won't, he must stir the broth. (You may actually have some "broth" to stir.) Person stirring does not stop until he finds someone who will *not* do as requested.

(Age, 9 up . . . Group, 1 at a time . . . Time, 10-20 min.)

The Sack Society. Initiates are sent from room. Those remaining have large sacks for their heads with "eye holes" and "nose holes."

One initiate at a time is brought in and seated in middle of room. He is to thread needle while holding one foot outstretched by candle light in dark room. To make it a little tougher, leader will hold one hand over contestant's eye (hand has lamp black on it). When needle is threaded, contestant gets a sack. At end all have sacks, and lights are turned on. All new members see each other with black eyes. (Here somewhere should be a place for the gag: "Shopping bag?" "No, just looking.")

(Age, 9 up . . . Group, 1 at a time . . . Time, 15-20 min.)

The Fortune. With appropriate costume and lighting and smells, person is brought in to confront great fortuneteller, seated in front of him. Great seer shines light on subject and starts his speech: "My frrriend, I see you looking for great joy and happiness which will come in time. In the future, the near future, however, I see that dame fortune is cold to your attempts. Even now she is lowering the boom. . . ." (An assistant quickly puts an ice-filled cloth sack on back of neck of person, who, if properly surprised, may make a little noise!)

(Age, 9 up . . . Group, 10-20 . . . Time, 15-20 min.)

NOVEL OR QUIET RELAYS AND RACES

Many of these relays can be performed in circles instead of lines, particularly those which involve passing an article. This enables everyone to see how his team is doing and enjoy the actions of his teammates. When a team has completed its action everyone yells or stands up.[18]

Crazee Man Walk
Age: 10 up

EQUIPMENT: Each team provided with potato (or orange or ball) and book.

FORMATION: Teams in file formation; turning point, 15 feet in front of each team.

DIRECTIONS: First player puts potato between his knees and book on his head. Without using his hands he moves to turning point and back, tagging second man. Action is repeated until all finish. Peculiar waddling gait attained by performers is great cause of merriment. Sometimes chain is added which has to be twirled on right index finger.

Orange Passing
Age: 8 up

EQUIPMENT: Orange, apple, ball, or grapefruit for each team.

FORMATION: Teams in file or circle formation.

DIRECTIONS: On signal to start, first player puts orange under his chin, and without using his hands passes it to second player who takes it with his chin, and without use of his hands. Orange is passed down line in this manner. If dropped, can be retrieved by hand, but must be passed on by person dropping it. First team to complete passing, wins.

Raisin Relay

Age: 8 up

EQUIPMENT: Saucer of raisins for each team and toothpick for each player.

FORMATION: Teams in file or circle formation. First player in each team has saucer of raisins, and each player has toothpick.

DIRECTIONS: On signal, leader spears three raisins on his toothpick and feeds them to next person in line. Leader then passes saucer to second person who spears three raisins and feeds them to third in line. Continue until all are finished.

Hand Clasp Relay

Age: 8 up

EQUIPMENT: From three to six peanuts (or marbles or stones) for each team.

FORMATION: Teams in file or circle formation. Each player grasps his teammate's right wrist with his left hand. The peanuts are placed on desk or chair in front of first player.

DIRECTIONS: At signal, first player picks up peanuts, one at a time, and passes them down line as rapidly as possible; last player puts them on chair beside him. In similar manner, peanuts are then passed back up lines so that they will be in their original positions at end of game. If peanut is dropped, it must be picked up without unclasping hands. Team that first passes all peanuts down and back, wins relay.

VARIATION: Instead of clasping wrists, place hands palm to palm, interlacing fingers.

Tennis Ball Relay for Couples

Age: 10 up

EQUIPMENT: Tennis ball, orange, or apple for each team.

FORMATION: Teams divided into couples according to height or sex (depends on age!). Pop bottle for each team is placed on table corner or small stand.

DIRECTIONS: First couple face each other and place both hands on each other's shoulders. Tennis ball is placed between two foreheads and held there without using hands while couple walks to pop bottle and gently balances ball on small end of bottle. As soon as ball is resting securely they grab ball and run with it to next couple in line. If ball is dropped, couple dropping it must start over again from beginning line.

Kick the Stick Relay

Age: 6 up

EQUIPMENT: Crooked stick about 12 inches long for each team.

FORMATION: Teams in file formation with stick in front of each team.

DIRECTIONS: First player kicks stick to turning point and back, leaving it in front of next player, who repeats action. Sticks are to be pushed along ground, not kicked up into air. Line finishing first is winner.

Egg Relay

Age: 12 up

EQUIPMENT: One egg for each team; tablespoon for each player.

FORMATION: Teams in circle or file formation. Good table game. Each member holds tablespoon in his mouth.

DIRECTIONS: Object is to pass egg down line by tilting head with spoon in mouth. (Boil eggs, but don't let players know it.)

Post Card March Relay

Age: 10 up

EQUIPMENT: Post card, alphabet card, or calling card for each team.

FORMATION: Team in file formation.

DIRECTIONS: First player puts post card between his nose and upper lip and marches to turning point and back. He exchanges card with second player without using hands, and action is continued until all have finished.

Clodhopper Race

Age: 10 up

EQUIPMENT: Dozen or so little pieces of paper for each team.

FORMATION: One player from each team, preferably one with biggest feet, is chosen and blindfolded. Rest of team forms circle and scatters pieces of paper on floor.

DIRECTIONS: On signal to start, blindfolded players must try to step on each piece of paper in his circle. He is directed by his group only in what they say to him. They cannot touch him, or move themselves. First one to step on every single piece of paper is winner.

Gossip Relay

Age: 8 up

FORMATION: Teams in file or circle formation.

DIRECTIONS: Sentence is whispered to first player of each team, and he whispers it to next person in line, who passes it to next. So it goes on to last players, who run to leader and tell what they heard. The team finishing first with most correct message wins, but final messages are usually more entertaining than competition among the teams.

Gobble Relay

Age: 10 up

EQUIPMENT: Each team is provided with box or basket containing number of edible items wrapped in waxed paper—one for each member of team.

FORMATION: Table with baskets of food is equidistant from all teams. Chair is placed next to each team's basket.

DIRECTIONS: At signal, first member rushes to table, picks up article of food, sits in chair, raises feet off ground, unwraps package, eats food, says "Thank you," and returns to his team. This is continued until all have eaten. Contestant must keep feet off floor while eating. Half fun is in watching hesitation in choosing of packages. Good food items are apples, crackers, gumdrops, popcorn, taffy.

Capsule Relay or Race

Age: 15 up

EQUIPMENT: Paper cups of water and empty capsule for each team member.

FORMATION: Teams in file or circle formation.

DIRECTIONS: First member tries to swallow capsule as quickly as possible. Upon accomplishment, second man is tagged. Continue until all finish. Expressions on people's faces as they try to swallow capsule quickly cause much hilarity.

Stepping Stone Relay

Age: 11 up

EQUIPMENT: Two bricks, or similar objects, for each team.

FORMATION: Teams in single file.

DIRECTIONS: First man in each line puts one brick out, steps on it, puts other down, and steps on it. Then he reaches back, gets first, and places it on in front. Thus, he continues across course and back. Second man walks on bricks same way; and gives to number three. This continues until all are through.

VARIATIONS: Use folded newspaper, footstools, chairs, or boxes.

Pushing Peanuts (Ping-pong Balls)

Age: 8 up

EQUIPMENT: Peanuts or ping-pong balls.

FORMATION: Players line up on hands and knees.

DIRECTIONS: Players push peanuts with their noses.

VARIATIONS: Use toothpick or pencil held in teeth to push peanuts. Potatoes may sometimes be used for peanuts.

Hobble Relay

Age: 10 up

EQUIPMENT: Rubber band cut from inner tube, about four inches long for each team.

FORMATION: Teams in file formation. Turning point in front of each team.

DIRECTIONS: At signal, first player in each line slips rubber band over both feet up to ankles. He then hobbles to goal and returns, giving band to next player, and so on. Players must walk; they cannot jump or work band up on legs. Peculiar waddle motion is laugh provoker for other players and audience.

Suitcase Race

Age: 12 up

EQUIPMENT: Each contestant has suitcase and umbrella. In suitcase are hat, coat, gloves, and any other clothing desired; contents should, however, be uniform.

DIRECTIONS: At signal, all contestants run to goal, open suitcases, put on clothes, close suitcases, open umbrellas, and run to starting point.

Match Box Relay

Age: 10 up

EQUIPMENT: Covers off penny boxes of matches.

FORMATION: File formation or circle.

DIRECTIONS: Place match box cover over end of first player's nose. On "go" he "passes" box to nose of second player without using hands. When dropped, box may be picked up, however. Continue down line until every person's nose has been fitted.

Cracker Whistle Race

Age: 8 up

EQUIPMENT: Ordinary soda crackers (or any type cracker).

FORMATION: Two teams of equal number in parallel lines facing each other.

DIRECTIONS: Each player has cracker. First players eat crackers, and as soon as they finish eating they whistle. As soon as they whistle, second players begin. Player cannot begin until after preceding player has whistled.

Penny Push

Age: 8 up

EQUIPMENT: Yardstick, two chairs (or other level supports for yardstick), toothpicks (or soda straws) for each person, and one penny for each team. (Each team has yardstick, chairs.)

FORMATION: File formation.

DIRECTIONS: Split groups so that one person can push penny up yardstick, and another person pushes it back. Pennies are pushed with straw or toothpick clenched in teeth. Continue until all have finished.

Soda Straw and Bean Contest

Age: 9 up

EQUIPMENT: Soda straw for each player and one container full of beans.

FORMATION: File or circle formation.

DIRECTIONS: Place beans in one container. Suck on soda straw and try to move beans one at a time to empty container.

Eggshell Relay

Age: 10 up

EQUIPMENT: Eggshell with its contents removed (or a ping-pong ball) for each team. Also a fan or 10 x 12-inch cutout of stiff cardboard for each team.

FORMATION: Each team in file facing turning point some 20 feet away. This turning point can be soda bottle, rock, book, or any other object indicated.

DIRECTIONS: First player of team puts eggshell on ground and begins to fan it with his fan. He drives it around turning point and returns to his starting position. He then hands fan to second player who repeats procedures. This is continued until last man finishes. Players are not permitted to kick or touch eggshell in any way.

Candle Blow and Light Relay

Age: 9 up

EQUIPMENT: Candle and matches.

FORMATION: File.

DIRECTIONS: First runner goes to candle, strikes match and lights candle, then runs back and touches second runner. Second runner blows out candle, relights it and returns to teammates. This continues until all the team have completed their turn.

Candle Race

Age: 9 up

EQUIPMENT: Candle and matches.

FORMATION: File.

DIRECTIONS: First runner of each team lights candle, carries it to touch point, and returns to home base where he gives it to next runner. If candle goes out, runner must return home, light candle and repeat course. First team having all runners finish course, wins.

VARIATION: Use this as shuttle relay.

Apple Race (Book)

Age: 9 up

EQUIPMENT: Apple, book, or similar object for each team.

FORMATION: File formation with touch line 20 feet away.

DIRECTIONS: First player puts apple on head and walks to touch line and back to starting line. He then gives apple to second player, and so on down line. If apple is dropped, it must be picked up and placed back on head.

Writing or Drawing Relay

Age: 10 up

EQUIPMENT: Chalkboard and chalk for each team.

FORMATION: Players of each team in single file.

DIRECTIONS: First player runs to chalkboard and writes word on board. Each player continues this action. Object is to have completed, readable sentence after last player has finished. Correctness and speed are both required in this relay.

VARIATION: Each player draws line, attempting to create picture. Sometimes two turns are allowed in order for picture to be completed.

Pillowcase Relay

Age: 9 up

EQUIPMENT: Pillow and case for each team.

FORMATION: Members of each team lined up, single file.

DIRECTIONS: On signal, first player takes pillow out of case and then puts it back. He passes it to second player who does same. First line through, wins.

Baby Bottle Race

Age: 12 up

EQUIPMENT: Baby bottle of milk with new, enlarged hole, nipple for each person.

FORMATION: Each team in single file.

DIRECTIONS: Contestant kneels, with hands behind him while teammate holds bottle. Put only a little milk in each bottle. Contestants run in turn to chair, where bottle is held, put on fresh nipple, suck bottle, return to line, and tag teammate.

"Pop" Races (Balloons or Paper Sacks)

Age: 10 up

EQUIPMENT: Balloon or paper sack for each person; chair for each team.

FORMATION: Each team in single file.

DIRECTIONS: First man runs to chair 20 feet from home, blows balloon or sack, and pops it by sitting on it. He then runs back and tags next man. Bags must be popped before leaving chair.

VARIATION: Have each team seated in chairs or on ground. First player runs around chair and back to place, blows up balloon or sack, and then sits on it. Second player can't start until balloon is popped.

Alphabet Relay

No: 12-10   Age: 12 up

EQUIPMENT: Set of cards for each team.

FORMATION: Teams grouped equidistant from spelling area.

DIRECTIONS: Each player has one or more cards. Words are called out by leader, and players with appropriate letters dash into position at other end of room to form word. First team finishing, gets a point. Double letters are represented by swinging card from side to side.

VARIATIONS: Call word, teams spell it out backwards.

Split Affinities: Leader calls out affinities omitting last word. Players dash into place to spell it out.

EXAMPLES: Adam & _____ (Eve)

Alpha & _____ (Omega)

Fair & _____ (Warmer)

Bread & _____ (Butter)

Half & _____ (Half)

Soap & _____ (Water)

Thunder & _____ (Lightening)

Assault & _____ (Battery)

Numbers "Racket"

No: 20-60   Age: 12 up

EQUIPMENT: Use cards about 4 x 6 inches with numbers up to 25, or for smaller groups just to 10.

FORMATION: Teams with each player holding number card.

DIRECTIONS: Leader calls out number. Since each team has identical numbers, team to first send up persons with cards totaling number, wins point. For wrong answer deduct two points from score.

VARIATION: Award point to side sending up largest number of cards to total number.

Mock Track and Field Meet. Advance publicity helps build up enthusiasm for this occasion. If possible, divide into sides in advance, making certain that there are equal numbers of boys and girls on each team, and allow each group to elect captains. Give each team list of events and let them assign various players to specific events. However, don't tell true nature of event.

If group is extremely large, provide roles on each team for cheerleaders, bands, doctor and nurse, homecoming "king" and "queen" (usually boy is the "queen" and girl is the "king"). Try to get everyone in the act. Encourage cheerleaders and team captains to keep enthusiasm high.

Two types of track meets are presented. One is for indoors, campfire, and rainy-day activity. Other is outdoor version incorporating more activity. Both will provide great fun for any group. As example, suggested number of participants from each team is presented for each event.

Indoor Events (may also be used outdoors):

50-Yard Dash: (Request fastest boy on each team.) First to thread needle and take 50 stitches on piece of cloth, wins.

Javelin Throw: (Boy and girl from each team.) Throw soda straw or feather for distance. Variation: Throw for accuracy at large bullseye drawn on floor.

Obstacle Relay: (Four boys and four girls from each team.) See directions for Human Croquet Relay in Active Games sections. Let teammates not running be wickets.

Discus Throw: (One boy and girl from each team.) Sail paper plate or powder puff as far as possible.

Hurdles: (One girl from each team.) Peanuts in shell sprinkled along each course. Peanuts must be shelled and eaten as they are picked up.

Standing Broad Grin: (Boy and girl from each team.) Measure grins and allow one boy and one girl as winners. Prize is lemon or ripe persimmon.

Boarding House Reach: (Boy from each team.) Measure armspread from fingertip to fingertip.

440 Yard Relay: (Two boys and two girls from each team.)

Push penny across yardstick with toothpick held in teeth. Run it relay fashion.

High Jump: (One boy and girl from each team.) Contestants with hands tied behind backs jump for suspended doughnut. Tie doughnuts 6 inches over head of each participant.

Hammer Throw: (One boy and one girl from each team.) Inflate paper bag and tie with string 3 feet long. Contestants hold loose end of string, whirl bag around head, and throw.

Shot Put: (One boy and girl from each team.) Contestants throw balloon or ball of cotton as far as possible. Variation: Contestant singing highest note, wins.

Mile Relay: (Four boys and four girls from each team.) Each team has ball of twine. First man holds end of string and unwraps ball, passing it around himself once. He then passes it to next player and so on down line. Last man begins to rewind string and starts it back up line. First team to rewrap ball of twine, wins.

Low Jump: (Two girls and two boys from each team.) Contestants pass under string without touching. Start at 3 feet and work down. Touching string disqualifies contestant. It is a surprise how low some can get!

Two-Mile Race: (Boy with biggest feet from each team.) Contestants heel and toe around course. First one to complete the circuit, wins.

Tug of War: (One player from each team paired with one from another team.) String 3 feet long with marshmallow in the middle. Contestant holds one end in his mouth. First one to chew up string and reach marshmallow, wins.

Marathon Race: (All players from each team.) Give each one peanut. They then push peanut across room with their noses.

Refreshment Time: Everyone participates. Don't forget this event.

Outdoor Field Day (Use also indoor events ideas.)

Relays and races suggested here incorporate much activity with minimum of skill. Boys and girls, when used in equal numbers on teams, can enjoy and participate in these activities together. Points can be awarded and running score kept for competing teams. Allow 5 points for first-place finish and three, two, and one for second, third, and fourth-place finishes. Since much enthusiasm is generated in these events, leader should limit number of events in which players enter in order that all will have equal participation. Playing area should be marked off in advance and loudspeaker secured if possible. Events suggested for this Field Day are described in active game section of this book.

Wheelbarrow Relay: (Equal number of boys and girls from each team.)

Sack Race: (Equal number of boys and girls from each team.)

Egg Throw for Distance: (Couples from each team.)

Girls' 50 Yard Dash: (Any number.)

Boys' 100 Yard Dash: (Any number.)

Dizzy Izzy Relay: (Equal number of boys and girls from each team.)

Centipede Race: (Equal number of boys and girls from each team, girls riding boys' backs.)

Backward Three-Legged Race: (Couples from each team.)

Medley Relay: (Four boys and four girls from each team.) Example: First player duckwalks 50 feet down course, tags next; second player crabwalks back; third player on hands and knees pushes ball with nose; fourth player puts ball between knees and returns to starting area: fifth and sixth players pick up seventh and carry her, chariot style, 25 yards down course; seventh player gets off and runs 75 yards down course; eighth player (anchor man) runs 100 yards back to finish line. (It is suggested that first, fifth, sixth, and eighth players be boys in this relay.)

PHYSICAL FEATS AND STUNTS

These games and contests involve one or two persons. Some are tests of strength and agility. Others are merely stunts for laughs. All can be used effectively in campfire settings, as "breathers" between strenuous activity, or as a series of small group fun.

Rolling Pin Throw

Age: 10 up

EQUIPMENT: Dummy husband made of odds and ends.

DIRECTIONS: Seat dummy in chair or tie him to pole. From a throwing line about 20 feet away, women contestants take turns in throwing rolling pin at dummy. Each is allowed five or more throws. Every solid hit scores one point.

VARIATIONS: May be derived by using different dummies and throwing objects other than rolling pin.

Egg-Throwing Contest

Age: 11 up

EQUIPMENT: Eggs.

FORMATION: Players lined up in row, side by side, partners in similar row, facing them, three feet away.

DIRECTIONS: Players in first row are given one egg each. On signal, they throw eggs to their partners. Receivers take one step back and return egg to their partners. Throwing continues, each time one of partners stepping back, until championship is awarded to partner who can throw greatest distance without breaking egg. Best record we have heard of is 85 feet!

Handcuff Puzzler

Age: 11 up

EQUIPMENT: Length of rope for each couple.

FORMATION: Couples.

DIRECTIONS: Tie ropes so that each has ends of rope looped around own wrists, but with rope passed behind rope of other so that the two players are linked together. Problem: to separate couples so that they are free from one another.

ANSWER: Slip middle loop of one under wrist loop of opposite.

Napkin or Handkerchief Stunt (Rope could be used.)

Age: 10 up

PROBLEM: To tie napkin into knot without letting go of either end.

ANSWER: Fold arms over chest, lean over table, and grab both ends of handkerchief or rope. Then unfold arms, thus leaving knot.

Apple Bobbing

Age: 8 up

EQUIPMENT: Tub of water with apples floating in it.

FORMATION: Teams.

DIRECTIONS: Contestants kneel with hands behind back and try to bring apple out with their teeth.

VARIATION: Apple Biting.

DIRECTIONS: Apples tied with string to links or door casing or standards over head. Height of apple adjusted to contestant. Contestant should barely reach apple when on tiptoes. First one to get bite wins.

Indian Hand Wrestle

Age: 8 up

FORMATION: Players stand with wide-legged stance, outside of right feet together, and grasping right hands. (This is reversed when done lefthanded.)

DIRECTIONS: On signal they jerk, pull, shove with right hand and wrist, trying to force opponent off balance. Object is to get opponent to move either foot. Left hand cannot be used, and cannot touch ground.

Pull-Up Contest

Age: 9 up

FORMATION: Contestants sit on ground facing each other. Knees are straight, and feet are braced flat against opponents' feet.

DIRECTIONS: Each grasps strong stick between them (over toes) and tries to pull his opponent to him. If contestant bends his knees, he forfeits.

Blind Monkeys

Age: 10 up

EQUIPMENT: Blindfold and bag of peanuts for each couple.

FORMATION: Couples.

DIRECTIONS: Couples are blindfolded and given peanuts. Man shells them and feeds them to his partner. Winner is group that eats most peanuts first.

Stone, Paper, Scissors

Age: 11 up

FORMATION: Pairs, opponents facing one another.

DIRECTIONS: Leader counts "1, 2, 3," and on "3" the players bring hands forward from behind backs. Each player has his hands in position for stone, paper, or scissors. Stone is clenched fist, paper is open palm, scissors is a V formed by middle and index fingers. Stone beats scissors, paper beats stone, and scissors beat paper. Keep count of winnings and play until one person has won 5 times.

VARIATIONS: Play with two sides: have quarterback for each group who signals what sign will be used. On 3, both sides flash their sign.

Rabbit, Hunter, Gun or Fox, Hunter, Gun played in similar fashion. Rabbit sign made by placing a hand behind each ear to represent rabbit ears; gun sign made by aiming hands and fingers; hunter represented by standing with hands crossed over chest.

Hand Slap

Age: 11 up

FORMATION: Couples.

DIRECTIONS: One of couple has his hands extended palms down. Other person has palms up, underneath hands of first person.

OBJECT: Person underneath tries to slap hands of person on top by quickly withdrawing them and striking hands on top before they are withdrawn. If person on bottom fails, person on top gets to change and become hitter.

Hand Push

Age: 11 up

FORMATION: Two players face each other arms length apart. Arms are extended, palm out.

DIRECTIONS: Players, on signal to begin, hit palms together, pushing, until one player loses his balance. Object is to make opponent move one or both feet. It is not permitted to strike body or arms. Only hands are hit.

Chinese Get-Up

Age: 6 up

FORMATION: Two players sit back to back with arms folded.
DIRECTIONS: Each player tries to get up by pushing against other.
VARIATION: Try same contest with arms locked.

Indian Leg Wrestle

Age: 8 up

FORMATION: Contestants lie side by side with feet in opposite directions. Adjacent arms are locked.
DIRECTIONS: On signal, adjacent legs are raised and locked at knee. Object is to force opponent over by bringing his knee back so that he must roll over.

Over the Toe Jump

Age: 12 up

FORMATION: Stunt. Player stands on right foot and holds left toe by the right hand.
DIRECTIONS: Player springs off his right foot and tries to jump over the arch formed by his left leg and right arm. Several times are usually needed before balance is attained. Dropping toe by hand does not count in successful jump.

Stick Acrobatics

Age: 12 up

FORMATION: Stunt. Player holds 3-foot stick behind his back with palms forward.
DIRECTIONS: Player brings stick over his head to position in front of his body without losing grip on stick. Lowers stick and steps over it from front with right foot. Continues, head first, raising left hand over head and passing stick over back. Now lifts left foot off floor and steps backward through stick. This can be repeated by starting backward and going backward through routine. Stick must always be held by both hands, but they can slide slightly to shorten or lengthen stick.

Cossack Dance

Age: 12 up

FORMATION: Stunt. Player in deep knee bend or squat position with arms folded on chest.

DIRECTIONS: Player hops on his right foot and extends his left foot forward with heel touching floor. He hops on right foot again and brings left leg back to original position. This is repeated with other foot. After gaining proficiency, legs may be interchanged on a single hop. Also they may be extended sideways, or backward. Clapping hands or suitable music adds to performance of this stunt.

Knee Dip

Age: 10 up

FORMATION: Player stands on foot and grasps other foot behind back with opposite hand.

DIRECTIONS: Squat on one leg and touch bent knee to ground, and stand up again. Do this in one movement.

One-Legged Knee Bend

Age: 10 up

FORMATION: Player stands on one leg with other leg straight forward.

DIRECTIONS: Player goes down into a squatting position by bending supporting leg and comes up again and repeats with other leg.

Tip Up

Age: 10 up

FORMATION: Player assumes squat position with hands on floor between knees.

DIRECTIONS: Player tilts body forward. Knees are pressed against elbows. Weight is on hands as feet come off floor. Player tries to maintain balanced position as long as possible without falling forward or allowing feet to touch floor.

Bulldog Pull

Age: 10 up

FORMATION: Two players on all fours, facing each other, with heads close together. Belt, strap, or rope is looped around heads of both players.

DIRECTIONS: Each player tries to pull other forward a few feet. If either ducks his head and allows strap to be pulled off, he loses round. Two out of three trials determine winner.

Jump the Stick

Age: 12 up

FORMATION: Stunt. Player holds stick in front of his body, with palms facing back.

DIRECTIONS: Player jumps up high, bends and tucks legs, at same time pulling stick under feet. This stunt can also be done by starting with stick in rear.

Tractor Pull

Age: 10 up

FORMATION: Two larger persons are competing tractors; get on hands and knees and face opposite directions. Two smaller persons get atop tractors (one on each "tractor"), facing in directions of their tractors.

DIRECTIONS: Holding on with his legs, each rider reaches both hands back to grip hands of his opponent. When pull is made, the rider who is unseated loses.

Toe Tilt

Age: 10 up

FORMATION: Two players sit on floor or ground facing each other with knees bent, feet flat on ground, and arms clasped around their legs. Under knees and over arms of each is a wand or broomstick.

DIRECTIONS: At signal, each player tries to lift with his toes feet of his opponent. One who succeeds compels his opponent to lose his balance and roll over on his back.

Rooster Fight

Age: 9 up

FORMATION: Two players stand in a circle drawn about 6 feet in diameter. Each puts his right hand behind his back, clasps his left foot with it, and then grips his right arm with his left hand behind his back.

DIRECTIONS: Players hop toward one another trying to force each other out of circle. If player lets go of foot or arm, or steps out of circle, he loses.

VARIATION: Players may fold arms over chests, grasp own elbows, instead of position above.

Chicken Fight

Age: 9 up

FORMATION: Two players stand in circle drawn about 8 feet in diameter. They stoop and grasp their own ankles.

DIRECTIONS: Players try to push each other out of circle or off balance. Player who leaves circle, releases either hand, or touches ground with any part of his body other than his feet, loses contest.

18

Contests and Quizzes

THE FIRST SECTION of this chapter offers some 26 Little Contests that are mostly "just for fun," though there are five or six more serious competitions among them. The 17 Pencil and Paper Games and Quizzes and their variations will provide good entertainment for rainy days at camp or for quiet times. "How's Your IQ?" gives an excellent chance for young adults to discover their own approximate intelligence without the self-conscious strain of a real IQ test. And finally in the last section is an opportunity to convert an honest-to-goodness vocabulary measurement into a game contest.

LITTLE CONTESTS

Eating Cracker. Contestant puts it in his mouth and must eat it without using hands.

Rolling Lemon with Pencil. A specified distance.

Rooster. Each of two contestants has colored ribbon on his back. Object: by twisting and turning, to see other's color and identify it correctly.

Touch. Leader tells teams that they must "Go and touch iron, or door, or 9-paned window . . ." First team to do this and get back to place gets point.

Black Contest. Give each person black hat or other black object that has been covered (unknown to him) with powdered charcoal. Stick many pins in it. Object: for players to remove pins with their teeth. (Seat them so that they won't see each other.)

Sewing. From several groups, have each send out volunteer boy and girl. Girls are supplied with needles, thread, patch. Object: to be first to sew patch on boy's trousers.

Blind Throw. Selected contestants toss bean bags into bucket hidden so that aim is to be taken only by looking into mirror.

Paper Cup on a String. Hole has been punched in bottom of paper cup for each one playing game, and string inserted, tied on both ends to make it taut. Object: On GO signal, each player is to blow cup to other end of string.

Alliterations. Divide crowd into threes, each with captain. Letter is given (such as H) and other two must pantomime to their captain words that begin with that letter. The captain calls them aloud and counts them on his fingers. No words are spoken. Group with largest number of words is asked to give its words. (Other good letters are E and N.)

Spelling Contest—spelling words backward. One giving out words should have words spelled backward on sheet before him.

Chain Spelling. One player spells word, then next one sitting around circle must spell word beginning with first player's ending letter in specified time (5 to 20 seconds) or drop out. (If preferred, count one mark against him.) See who has fewest marks at end.

Newspaper Race. Each contestant has newspaper for each foot. After starting signal, he must walk up to goal and back, stepping only on papers. (Magazines or anything else can be used.) First one back, wins. May be done as relay.

Out-Talking. Two players are up before group; object of each is to out-argue other in specified period of time. They may be assigned a subject, or each may choose his own, or wander. Applause judges the better contestant. Also may be done by limiting contestants to using letters of alphabet, spoken as words, with great feeling.

Scissors Race. Take strips of adding machine paper (or other) 10 feet long, one for each contestant. He has pair of shears. Object: to cut along the 10-foot length in shortest time and be winner.

Pinning Tail on Donkey. Figure of donkey is on wall. Players, one by one, are blindfolded and try to pin tail, handed them, on donkey. (Can be adapted to other animals and themes.)

Lightning Vocabulary. Two teams compete. Leader gives out letter of alphabet, and one player of Team A gives to scorekeeper all words he can think of that begin with that letter. Then Team B has a word namer.

Needle-Threading Contest. See how long it takes men contestants to thread needle.

Guessing. . . . Seeds in bottle, yarn on spool, apples in basket, beans in glass jar, and so on.

Finding Bible Verses. Have two teams, with Bibles for each. Announce verse of Scripture. First one finding and reading it gets a point.

Bible Word Hunt. Give out some familiar words (like water, well, vine, heavens, fishes) that occur in Bible to players, all of whom have copy. First one reading verse containing that word gets point.

Spelling Bee. Divide into two teams and give out words for spelling bee. Either have folks drop out, or count point against them for words missed. See which team has highest score. (On elimination basis, see who has most people standing at end.)

Hog-Calling Contest. Indoors or outdoors, have several compete. To end it, have someone announce dinner, or ring bell.

Pronunciation Contest. Select number of words to be pronounced, inserting some that are tricky. Those who miss may either be eliminated, or may have point counted against them. Best played in two teams, each person getting chance in order to pronounce. Leader gives word first to one team then other, spelling it or writing it on board, or handing it on card to person. Have good dictionary handy, in case someone contests your statement.

Question Baseball. Put chairs for nine players in regular baseball formation. At each base is extra chair for batter and runners, also chair for the umpire back of pitcher.

One team takes place in field; other is on sidelines except batter, who comes to place beside catcher. Pitcher fires question to batter, who answers if he knows it. If not, batter can toss question to any fielder, such as "first base." If that person cannot answer correctly, batter goes to first base. Umpire rules on any matter of interpretation, but prompting is not allowed. Run is made when "base runner" has been to first, second, third, and home bases. Three outs are allowed. Play for any number of innings, but don't let it drag out.

Here are some questions that might be used, but each team should be free to make up its own questions:

1. How many players required in a baseball team? (Nine)

2. When was the "Man-O-War" born? (1917)

3. What has six legs and catches flies? (Outfield of baseball team)

4. Name three sets of married words. (Man and wife, bread and butter, cup and saucer, knife and fork, black and white)

5. Are the Great Lakes fresh water or salt water? (Fresh water)

6. What is the difference between a penny and a new dime? (Nine cents)

7. What trade does the sun follow? (Tanner)

8. What trade does the preacher follow at weddings? (Joiner)

9. Why is a dog who bites his tail a good manager? (Because he is making both ends meet)

10. Why is U the jolliest letter? (It is in the midst of fun)

11. What foreign fruit is on a penny? (Date)

12. What is the keynote of good nature? (B natural)

13. Of what trade is the sun in May? Mason (May sun)

14. What is filled every morning and emptied every night except once a year when it is filled at night and emptied in the morning? (A stocking)

15. Why are fish considered well educated? (Generally in schools)

16. Why does a horse eat in an odd way? (He eats best when he hasn't a bit in his mouth)

17. When a boy falls in the water what is the first thing he does? (He gets wet)

18. In story land who fell off the wall? (Humpty Dumpty)

19. What is full of holes and still holds water? (A sponge)

Baby Dressing Contest. Bring out a doll, diaper, and safety pins for each male contestant and on signal have him try to get his diaper on first.

Memory Selection Challenge. Two teams are used. One team names its first contestant. The other team thinks up lines of a familiar quotation, song, Bible verse, and that person must identify it or quote some more from same work. If successful, he gets point for his team. If not, other team gets point. Then reverse process.

PENCIL AND PAPER GAMES AND QUIZZES

Bible Association Quiz.[1] This may be done as pencil and paper game or as "group information" quiz. In latter case association phrase is read out to see who can remember correct answer first.

1. The face of an angel	Stephen
2. Burning bush	Moses
3. Handwriting on the wall	Daniel
4. Locusts and wild honey	John the Baptist
5. Coat of many colors	Joseph
6. Fat king in a summer parlor	Eglon
7. A leper as white as snow	Gehazi, Elisha's servant
8. Jawbone of an ass	Samson
9. Blinding light on the road to Damascus	Paul
10. Ark of gopher wood	Noah
11. Chariot of fire	Elijah
12. Fiery furnace	Shadrach, Meshach, and Abednego
13. Five loaves and two fishes	Jesus
14. Ladder reaching to heaven	Jacob
15. King's cupbearer	Nehemiah
16. Pillar of salt	Lot's wife
17. Walls of Jericho	Joshua
18. Receipt of custom	Matthew
19. Blossoming rod	Aaron
20. Five smooth stones and a sling	David
21. Long hair in the branches of an oak tree	Absalom
22. Sycamore tree	Zaccheus
23. Gourd vine	Jonah
24. Firebrands to foxes' tails	Samson
25. Trumpets and pitchers	Gideon

26. Boils from head to toe	Job
27. Vision on a housetop	Peter
28. Juniper tree	Elijah
29. Fast driving	Jehu
30. Valley of dry bones	Ezekiel

Are These Bible Characters?

1. St. Francis (no)	11. Ham (yes)
2. St. Peter (yes)	12. St. Patrick (no)
3. Queen of Sheba (yes)	13. Caesar (yes)
4. Cleopatra (no)	14. Aladdin (no)
5. Philemon (yes)	15. Miriam (yes)
6. Helen of Troy (no)	16. Shylock (no)
7. Lady MacBeth (no)	17. Mark Twain (no)
8. Levi (yes)	18. Pontius Pilate (yes)
9. Socrates (no)	19. King Vidor (no)
10. Jezebel (yes)	20. Freud? (no)

Bible Questions

1. What man in the Bible lived the longest? (Methuselah)
2. What man suffered from boils? (Job)
3. Who was the strong man of the Bible? (Sampson)
4. Who was known as "the beloved disciple?" (John)
5. What person lost his head over a dancing girl? (John the Baptist)
6. Who tried to walk on the Sea of Galilee? (Peter)
7. Who climbed a sycamore tree to try to see Jesus? (Zaccheus)
8. Who is known as the writer of Psalms? (David)
9. What was the group who asked, "Come over and help us?" (Macedonians)
10. Who was David's favorite friend? (Jonathan)
11. Who almost offered his son as a sacrifice? (Abraham)
12. Who threw a javelin at David? (King Saul)
13. What is the last word in the Bible? (Amen)
14. How many books are there in the New Testament? (27)
15. Who betrayed Jesus? (Judas)
16. How many lepers thanked Jesus for healing him? (One)
17. Why did Joseph's brothers go to Egypt? (To get food)
18. Why did Mary and Joseph take Jesus to Egypt? (To prevent Herod from killing him)

19. Where did Noah's Ark land? (Mt. Ararat)
20. Into what body of water does the Jordan River flow? (Dead Sea)
21. What is the shortest verse in the Bible? ("Jesus wept")
22. What woman of the Bible would be appropriate on your table? (Lot's wife—pillar of salt)
22. What were the ten girls of the Bible who ran out of oil called? (Foolish virgins)
23. How many books in the Bible? (66)
24. Did Jesus write any part of the Bible? (No)
25. What is the longest river in the Bible? (Nile)
26. Who saw the "handwriting on the wall?" (Nebuchadnezzar)
27. What Psalm begins with these words, "The Lord is my shepherd"? (Ps. 23)
28. Name three or more birds appearing in the Bible. (Hen, sparrow, partridge, raven, doves, eagle, cock, swallow)
29. Who was Barabbas? (A revolutionary released instead of Jesus)
30. How old was Jesus when he talked to the doctors in the Temple? (12)
31. How old at his crucifixion? (33)
32. What did Joseph do for a living? (Carpenter)
33. What was the name of the helper of Moses? (Aaron)
34. Name the two sons of Isaac. (Jacob and Esau)
35. What were the gifts of the Wise Men? (Gold, frankincense and myrrh)
36. Who blamed his sin on a woman? (Adam)
37. Where does "Cleanliness is next to godliness" appear? (In John Wesley's sayings)
38. What was the sin of the Prodigal Son? (Riotous living)
39. Who was exiled to the Isle of Patmos? (John)
40. Who inherited the mantle of Elijah? (Elisha)
41. Did Daniel kill a giant with a slingshot? (No; David)
42. What book of the Bible is really a census? (Numbers)
43. Who led the Hebrews after Moses died? (Joshua)
44. Who wrestled with an angel? (Jacob)
45. What food did Jesus use to feed the 5,000? (Loaves and fishes)
46. Are the books of the Bible arranged in order of writing? (No)

47. What animal was killed when the Prodigal Son got home? (Fatted calf)
48. Which four books of the Bible are called the Gospels? (Matthew, Mark, Luke, and John)
49. What man was put into a den of lions? (Daniel)
50. Why do the Jews celebrate the Passover? (Deliverance from the plague of death to first-born while in Egypt)

Baby Contest. Have players bring or send baby pictures, which are posted for all to see, numbered. Each person has pencil and paper to guess whose picture each one is.

Next, have a contest with categories. Which is the prettiest? Which is the most improved since baby days? Which has had a relapse?

Question Football. An equal number of contestants from each team (or from boys and girls) are sent to front of room where questioner is. Each is given pencil and paper.

There is a linesman for each team. He brings slip of paper on which answer of question is written to referee, who gives out question. If both teams answer correctly, there is no gain. If one team misses, but other gets it, they make a 10-yard gain. (Harder questions may have greater value.)

Each contestant will have his turn at questions in rotation. He must not be coached by his team. Cheering is encouraged.

Quarters are several questions long, number getting fewer as game progresses.

Team scores by advancing ball over opponent's goal line. Extra point may be made by answering bonus question correctly.

Some Cliché Similes. Group stands in row. Leader calls off similes rapidly down the line, omitting last word. Anyone who can't supply correct word drops out. (Or use as pencil and paper game, with last word omitted, of course.)

As thin as a . . . rail.	As hard as a . . . rock.
As fat as a . . . pig.	As clean as a . . . whistle.
As brave as a . . . lion.	As blind as a . . . bat.
As stiff as a . . . poker.	As round as an . . . orange.
As deep as a . . . well.	As dead as a . . . door nail.
As bitter as . . . gall.	As bright as a . . . dollar.

As ugly as . . . sin.
As proud as a . . . peacock.
As sly as a . . . fox.
As clear as . . . crystal.
As spry as a . . . cat.

As fair as a . . . lily.
As flat as a . . . pancake.
As neat as a . . . pin.
As pure as an . . . angel.

State Abbreviation Quiz

1. What state is to cut grass? (Mo.)
2. What state is a father? (Pa.)
3. What state is a church function? (Mass.)
4. What state was important to Noah? (Ark.)
5. What state thinks of itself? (Me.)
6. What state is an exclamation? (O.)
7. What state is a number? (Tenn.)
8. What state doesn't feel so good? (Ill.)
9. What state reminds of Monday morning activity? (Wash.)
10. What state is an unmarried girl? (Miss.)
11. What state is a doctor? (Md.)
12. What state is a musical note? (La.)
13. What state finds its men nicknamed for its abbreviation? (Tex.)
14. What state has a nickname like an Oriental deity? (Ala.)
15. What state is raw metal? (Ore.)

Do You Know People? See how you come out on this true-false test:

1. Crow's-foot wrinkles at outer corners of the eyes show sense of humor.
2. Fat people are always good-natured.
3. People with cold hands are affectionate in disposition.
4. Anybody who doesn't look you in the eye is not honest.
5. If you learn slowly, you'll remember it better than if you were a fast learner.
6. Redheads are more temperamental than other folk.
7. Long and slender hands mean you're artistic.
8. Thin, tight lips indicate a miser, or at least one who is secretive.
9. A jutting chin denotes strong will power; a weak will power is indicated by a receding chin.

10. A high forehead indicates high brain power.
    (ALL ARE FALSE.)

Check Your Knowledge (Quiz)

1. Dandruff causes baldness. (False)
2. Tight hats cause baldness. (True)
3. Coated tongues indicate stomach upset. (False)
4. Overwork causes nervous breakdown. (False. Tension and emotional strain may, however.)
5. Drinking six or eight glasses of water a day brings good health. (False. Doctors now say this may be harmful.)
6. Mixing fish and milk can cause acute indigestion. (False)
7. "Feed a cold and starve a fever." (False. It's better to do the reverse.)
8. Everybody needs eight hours of sleep. (False. Some people require less than others.)

Flower Show. Have many flowers or plants on display, numbered. Give each guest pencil and paper and see who can identify most flowers without consulting anybody else. (Could be done in couples.)

Pantomiming Trees. Have these pantomimes presented for group and see how many can get name of tree represented. (Each person has pencil and paper. These tableaux may be presented with flourish. "Number ONE!!")

DATE. One or more persons, anxiously looking at calendar.

PALM. Gypsy scene.

ELDER. Person dressed and acting like old man.

BEECH. Child with pail of sand and shovel.

PINE. Girl with very sad expression on her face.

SPRUCE. Youth nattily dressed.

FIR. Girl with fur scarf, muff.

ASH. Woman with apron, dust pan, carrying ashes.

PEAR. Boy and girl walking together, hand in hand.

RUBBER. Person dressed in rubber raincoat and boots.

Indian Code [2] (especially for the young). This code is made with Indian signs and symbols. It is not real Indian writing, but these signs come from Indians. Have the code and message mimeographed and give each child a copy, with pencil. See who translates the message first.

HERE IS THE CODE:

HERE IS A MESSAGE TO TRANSLATE

A = ᶾ   N = ⩕
B = ⦃   O = +
C = ◊   P = ⑥
D = ⊙   Q = ⊕
E = ⩎   R = ∧
F = ✳   S = ▽
G = △   T = ⌐
H = ▣   U = ◖
I = ℂ   V = ◻
J = ◊   W = ◈
K = ﺵ   X = ⩑
L = Ɔ   Y = ⊕
M = ◈   Z = ∨

Old Art Museum.[3] Each person has pencil and paper and 15 minutes to examine this great exhibit, displayed on several long tables and numbered differently from list below. He places exhibit number beside description.

EXHIBIT NO.

1. Two Performing Dogs. (Hot dogs)
2. The Swimming Match. (Match floating in water)
3. Eighteen-Piece Band. (Rubber band in 18 pieces)
4. Vanity Fair. (Mirror)
5. Out for the Night. (Candle)
6. The Lost Scent. (Empty perfume bottle)
7. The Perfect Foot. (Ruler)
8. Ruins in China. (Broken crockery)
9. The Fancy Ball. (A gaily decorated ball)
10. A Body of Water in Asia. (A black C)

11. Family Jars. (Fruit jars)
12. The Sweets of Childhood. (Candy)
13. The Milky Way. (Milky Way candy bar)
14. Kids at Rest. (Two kid gloves)
15. Lot's Wife. (Salt)
16. A Candidate. (Candy date)
17. An Absorbing Subject. (Blotter)
18. True to the Core. (Apple core)
19. A Drive in the Wood. (Board with nail)
20. We Part to Meet Again. (Shears)
21. My Own Native Land. (Some dirt)
22. A Wayworn Traveler. (Old shoe)
23. The Light of Other Days. (Kerosene lamp)
24. A Policeman. (A copper)
25. An Acrobat. (Tumbler)
26. A Commentator. (A common 'tater)
27. The Flower of the Family. (Flour)
28. Springtime. (Spring water in glass)
29. Darkness That Is Felt. (Black felt)
30. In for a Scrape. (Dirty dish)
31. Eve Before the Fall. (Calendar, September 20)
32. A Picture in Greece. (Photo, in grease)
33. The One-Eyed Monster. (Darning needle)
34. A Tale of the Sea. (A letter C with tail)
35. Something to Adore. (Padlock)
36. A Pair of Slippers. (Banana peels)
37. Rock of Ages. (Miniature cradle)
38. Crossing the Styx. (Sticks crossed)
39. The Tutor. (A horn)
40. Greatest Bet Ever. (Alpha-bet)
41. Common Sense. (5¢)
42. The Black Friar. (Black frying pan)
43. Old Ironsides (An iron)
44. Cause of the Revolution. (Crank for a mechanical phonograph)

Bible Art. Divide into groups of 5 to 10 persons. Give each player pencil and paper. A representative from each group is sent to leader, who tells these representatives name of person or place or event in Bible. Representatives dash back to their groups and try to make their groups understand by drawing (not writing) the word or words given. This person may nod "Yes" or shake head "No" only. First group wins round. Change representatives every time.

Song Identification. Each player has pencil, paper, and list of number of places, in U. S. and abroad, and is to write down title of song recalled by that place, or more than one song. See who gets most. Sample places: New York (Sidewalks of New York); Tennessee, (Tennessee Waltz).

Testing the Senses.[4] This game testing five senses requires some equipment in advance.

SIGHT: Arrange 20 or more articles in large carton open at top. Let each one look in for 30 seconds, then write down all he saw. (Simple everyday things like key, pencil, toothpick, match, penny, button, nail, screw, and so on.)

HEARING: Identify noises made behind curtain or in other room; such as sawing wood, filing on metal, musical saw, ripping cloth, crumpling paper, scratching stone, rubbing crystal glass, rasping wood, and the like.

SMELL: Arrange vials containing common household things like wood alcohol, gasoline, kerosene, turpentine, camphor, vanilla, lemon extract, citronella. After smelling all these scents, few can tell gasoline from vanilla.

TOUCH: Have carton with hole in side to insert arm. Feel articles in carton: key, coins of various values, putty, glass, wood, cloth, and so on. Blind folk are especially keen in this sense.

TASTE: Not so easily tried out, since players are likely to identify by smell rather than by taste. Might have them hold nose and lay piece of apple or onion on tongue to identify.

Map Games. (An opaque projector may be used in some of these games to show the picture on the screen for all to see.)

1. Cut out outlines of states or countries from black paper, paste on bulletin board or big sheet of white cardboard, and let contestants see if they can identify outlines. Excellent for international emphasis.
2. Prepare outline of U.S. with states drawn in and numbered,

but not named. Give 10 to 15 minutes for people to write in names of states. (Also could be done with countries.)

3. Cut out of road maps circular or square pieces, about an inch across and number them. See if players can identify them—for example, "Where are you in No. 1?" About a dozen pieces make a good game.

4. Give each small group (2 to 5 persons) road map and trip to take. Let them figure out shortest way to get there, announcing it and distance.

5. A child whose father travels on business a great deal could follow his father's trips on road map with toy auto. Toy boat could be used if father travels by river, lake, or sea.[5]

6. Figure out some map surprises and hold quiz, using questions like these:

Which is farther south—the tip of Florida or Mexico?

Is Los Angeles north or south of Jacksonville, Florida?

7. Giving several groups detailed road maps, tell them to look for oddest-named towns and report their lists. Or towns with persons' names, perhaps girls' names.

8. Pass out maps and let group itself figure out some map games!

Try This One for Size.[6] Do you have trouble remembering your shoe or neck sizes? If so, this quiz will really baffle you. But don't stop here. Try your talents on identifying the sizes of various articles which you see or handle every day. Listed here are 25 different sizes and types. Each matches an article in the right-hand column. Link them up and check your score. Get 20 correct and win a sizable victory. Less than 12 right should send you running for the yardstick. (Answers are found in footnote 6.)

1. 2 x4	A. Flashlight
2. 7½	B. Umbrella
3. 18	C. Radio
4. 6.70-15	D. Shoes
5. 6d	E. Watch
6. 11 oz.	F. Motor
7. 60 watt	G. Lumber
8. 16 rib	H. Baby clothes
9. 35 mm	I. Auto tire
10. 4 hp	J. Gold
11. 30 amps	K. Drinking glass

12.	50	L.	Rake
13.	3 cell	M.	Women's hose
14.	6 months	N.	Hat
15.	8A	O.	Rifle
16.	32-30	P.	Typing paper
17.	15^2-33	Q.	Screen
18.	8½ x 11	R.	Fuse plug
19.	5 tube	S.	Trousers
20.	16 mesh	T.	Light bulb
21.	51 gauge	U.	Movie film
22.	14K	V.	Thread
23.	30-06	W.	Dress
24.	18 tine	X.	Shirt
25.	21 jewel	Y.	Nails

HOW'S YOUR IQ?

Here is a quick and easy way for testing intelligence:

Your IQ—High or Low? *

We all wonder how intelligent we are, and how our intelligence stacks up against the next fellow's. That is why we are so eager to test ourselves on quiz programs and on the innumerable vocabulary tests, puzzles, and the like which are presented to us daily.

The following test was designed by one of America's leading psychologists and should give your intelligence with the smallest possible margin of error. The same expert has also compiled the average IQ's of Americans by professions and occupational groups. You will be interested to compare your IQ with his tables to see where you stand.

There are 55 problems in this four-part test. You have 20 minutes to do the test with a pencil: stop working when the time is up. If you hit a snag on a single problem, do not use a disproportionate amount of time for it: go on to the next problem. You may, if time permits, return to the puzzling problem later on.

* This section is an article reprinted by permission from CORONET Magazine, August, 1955.

PART I

INSTRUCTIONS: A series of simple arithmetic problems follows. Do them as rapidly as you can. Circle the letter preceding the correct answer.

1. How many pencils can you buy for 75¢ at the rate of 2 for 5¢?
   a. 10   b. 20   c. 30   d. 35

2. A salesman sold 80 sweaters in five days. The first day he sold 18 sweaters, the second day 12 sweaters, the third day 20 sweaters, the fourth day 16 sweaters. How many sweaters did he sell the last day?
   a. 11   b. 12   c. 18   d. 14

3. If 3½ yards of ribbon cost 21 cents, what will 5½ yards cost?
   a. 32¢   b. 33¢   c. $3.30   d. 50¢

4. A jeweler bought some diamond rings for $800. He sold them for $1000, making $40 on each ring. How many rings were there?
   a. 10   b. 5   c. 3   d. 6

5. A ship has supplies to last her crew of 500 men 6 months. How many months would it last for 1,000 men?
   a. 8 mos.   b. 3 mos.   c. 4 mos.   d. 6 mos.

6. If a car goes 100 yards in 10 seconds, how many feet does it go in one-fifth second?
   a. 6 ft.   b. 9 ft.   c. 12 ft.   d. 2 ft.

7. Every time Johnny drops a quarter in his bank his mother drops in 3 quarters. If Johnny has $48 in his bank, how much of it did he alone save?
   a. $16   b. $18   c. $12   d. $36

8. A grocer buys an equal number of jars of two kinds of jam. He sells 5/6 of one kind and 7/8 of the other. What fraction of the total number of jars is unsold?
   a. 1/7   b. 7/48   c. 2/7   d. 1/4   e. 13/40

9. A tractor goes 5 miles per hour in low gear and 10 miles per hour in high gear. How long will it take to travel a stretch of road 50 miles long if it goes 2/5 of the way in low gear?
   a. 4   b. 7   c. 9   d. 12

10. We have a three-piece toy train consisting of an engine, passenger car, and caboose. The engine is 3 inches long; the caboose is as long as the engine plus ½ of the length of the

	1	2	3	4			
1.	Go	—come	buy	—a. money	b. sell	c. return	d. books
2.	Sky	—blue	grass	—a. big	b. green	c. pretty	d. cold
3.	Shoe	—foot	hat	—a. nose	b. head	c. shirt	d. coat
4.	Boat	—water	ski	—a. winter	b. sport	c. snow	d. fun
5.	Dec.	—Jan.	last	—a. Jan.	b. Mon.	c. first	d. month
6.	State	—governor	army	—a. marines	b. soldier	c. general	d. corporal
7.	Leg	—knee	arm	—a. thigh	b. elbow	c. shoulder	d. ankle
8.	Body	—food	engine	—a. wheels	b. smoke	c. fuel	d. move
9.	Palace	—king	kennel	—a. man	b. dog	c. chair	d. prince
10.	Bird	—nest	man	—a. fly	b. home	c. sleep	d. live
11.	Hope	—despair	happiness	—a. joy	b. sadness	c. fun	d. pleasure
12.	Dismal	—cheerful	dark	—a. moon	b. night	c. bright	d. sad
13.	Winter	—summer	cold	—a. freeze	b. warm	c. damp	d. January
14.	Bench	—wood	axe	—a. cutting	b. chair	c. steel	d. hatchet
15.	Begin	—establish	end	—a. slavery	b. wrong	c. start	d. abolish
16.	Wheat	—granary	books	—a. desk	b. library	c. paper	d. teacher
17.	Cold	—ice	heat	—a. lightning	b. warm	c. coat	d. steam
18.	Moon	—earth	earth	—a. ground	b. Mars	c. heaven	d. sun
19.	Throne	—queen	chain	—a. bonds	b. slave	c. link	d. medicine
20.	History	—authority	fiction	—a. perception	b. novel	c. imagination	d. news

passenger car; the passenger is as long as the engine and caboose together. How many inches long is the train?

a. 5 b. 16 c. 20 d. 24

PART II

INSTRUCTIONS: In each row on p. 413, words in Column 1 are somehow related to the words in Column 2. The words in Column 3 have the same relationship with one of the words in Column 4. Circle the letter before that word which properly establishes this relationship.

PART III

INSTRUCTIONS: In each line below, find the rule by which Fig. 1 is changed to make Fig. 2. Applying this rule to Fig. 3, select the resulting figure from the four choices at the right. Circle the letter with the correct choice.

PART IV

INSTRUCTIONS: The numbers in each series below proceed according to some rule. For each series you are to find the next number, circling the letter preceding that answer.

1. 9 9 8 8 7 7   a) 6; b) 7; c) 8; d) 9.
2. 10 15 20 25 30 35   a) 30; b) 35; c) 40; d) 45.
3. 8 11 14 17 20 23   a) 20; b) 18; c) 26; d) 22.
4. 10 8 11 9 12 10   a) 13; b) 12; c) 11; d) 10.
5. 1 7 2 7 3 7   a) 4; b) 5; c) 6; d) 7.

6. 1 4 1 6 1 8	a) 10; b) 8; c) 4; d) 1.
7. 6 9 11 14 16 19	a) 19; b) 20; c) 21; d) 22.
8. 16 17 19 20 22 23	a) 18; b) 20; c) 24; d) 25.
9. 12 16 13 17 14 18	a) 15; b) 19; c) 18; d) 17.
10. 3 5 8 10 11 13	a) 14; b) 15; c) 16; d) 17.
11. 20 17 15 14 11 9	a) 8; b) 21; c) 14; d) 7.
12. 81 27 9 3 1 ⅓	a) ⅓; b) 1/9; c) 0; d) 3.
13. 16 17 15 18 14 19	a) 20; b) 11; c) 12; d) 13.
14. 1 4 9 16 25 36	a) 28; b) 38; c) 49; d) 52.
15. 29 28 26 23 19 14	a) 11; b) 8; c) 15; d) 22.

ANSWERS

INSTRUCTIONS: Compare your answers with these correct answers, counting the number you have right. Then determine your IQ from the Scoring Chart and compare it with the Professional and Occupational Groups tables.

PART I: 1 c; 2 d; 3 b; 4 b; 5 b; 6 a; 7 c; 8 b; 9 b; 10 d.

PART II: 1 b; 2 b; 3 b; 4 c; 5 c; 6 c; 7 b; 8 c; 9 b; 10 b; 11 b; 12 c; 13 b; 14 c; 15 d; 16 b; 17 d; 18 d; 19 b; 20 c.

PART III: 1 c; 2 c; 3 d; 4 d; 5 c; 6 b; 7 a; 8 a; 9 d; 10 c.

PART IV: 1 a; 2 c; 3 c; 4 a; 5 a; 6 d; 7 c; 8 d; 9 a; 10 c; 11 a; 12 b; 13 d; 14 c; 15 b.

SCORING CHART

Number Right___54___

Test Score	Equivalent IQ	Verbal Description
51—55	140—above	Very superior
45—50	120—139	Superior
30—44	110—119	High average
20—29	90—109	Average
below 20	80—89	Low average

AVERAGE IQ BY PROFESSION

Profession	Average IQ
Doctor, lawyer, accountant, engineer	125—130
Dentist, teacher, draftsman, stenographer	120—125
Radio repairman, salesman	115—119
Manager, retail store; toolmaker	110—114
Sales clerk	105—109

Butcher, plumber, carpenter, auto mechanic	100—104
Truck driver	95—99
Farmhand, miner	90—94
Teamster	85—89

AVERAGE IQ OF OCCUPATIONAL GROUPS

Occupational Level	Average IQ
Professional	115
Managerial	108
Clerical	104
Skilled	99
Semiskilled	97

MEASURING YOUR VOCABULARY

Haven't you often wondered how much of a vocabulary you really have? Here is an interesting device for measuring it which can be made into a contest if you can supply each player a mimeographed sheet of these groups of words with instructions.

How Big Is Your Vō kăb′yə lěr′ı?[†]

(The more you improve it, the greater the success you are likely to achieve.)

BY ROBERT P. WEEKS

Surveys by the Johnson O'Connor Research Foundation indicate that an exact and extensive vocabulary is more likely to accompany success than any other single characteristic so far isolated and measured.

Does this mean that those who do not possess extensive vocabularies are destined to remain in the lower ranks? Definitely not.

Your IQ and your fingerprints are with you for life—but not your vocabulary. Once you become aware that it is limited, you can greatly expand it. But first, you must get some idea of its size.

The average five-year-old knows at least 3,000 words; by age

[†] Reprinted from CORONET Magazine, April, 1955, by permission.

ten, he knows some 5,000; and by 14 he has doubled that number. The average high school graduate has a vocabulary of at least 15,000 words, the college graduate from 20,000 to 30,000; and if he goes into law or medicine, his vocabulary will jump several thousand more.

The words in the following list are placed in four groups according to the frequency with which they appear in general reading material.[7] Group 1 contains words that appear from ten to eighteen times per million words. There are some 2,000 words in this group.

A person knowing at least seven of the ten words in Group 1 is very likely to know most of the 4,000 words that appear more frequently than 18 times per million. He can be said, therefore, to have a vocabulary of at least 6,000 words.

Group II contains words that appear from four to nine times per million words. There are approximately 4,000 words in this group. A person knowing at least seven of these has a vocabulary of at least 10,000 words.

Group III contains words that the average high school graduate should know. They appear from two to three times per million words. A person who knows seven or more of these is likely to have a vocabulary consisting of at least 14,000 words.

The words that appear least frequently are in Group IV. Anyone knowing at least seven of them probably has a vocabulary of almost 20,000 words.

Give yourself this test and discover how large your vocabulary is. Look at the italicized word carefully, then check the word or phrase that comes closest to defining it.

GROUP I

1. *scope:* patch, range, newsbeat, fancy shop.
2. *bellow:* beneath, hollow, grunt, roar.
3. *lance:* spear, shield, helmet, dagger.
4. *particle:* tiny piece, monocle, portion, gem.
5. *obstacle:* cutting tool, in the way, carriage, old-fashioned.
6. *unique:* one wing, light blue, unequaled, friendly.
7. *cherish:* charred, blemish, value highly, obey.
8. *parson:* minister, individual, clerk, teacher.
9. *wither:* accompany, lose freshness, recover, glow.
10. *meteor:* singer, bullfighter, stream, shooting star.

Group II

1. *prudent:* careful, insulting, brainy, gay.
2. *obstruct:* vague, to hunt, to hinder, to cover.
3. *reservoir:* cabinet, wallet, mud hut, storage place.
4. *magnify:* double, make larger, reverse, shorten.
5. *tedious:* tiresome, repetitious, watery, difficult.
6. *scrutinize:* examine closely, twist, waste, test.
7. *posterity:* depression, the future, antiquity, good times.
8. *fang:* snare, trap, long tooth, capture.
9. *juvenile:* immoral, common, youthful, occasional.
10. *czar:* Russian emperor, catarrh, prince, cart.

Group III

1. *deft:* silly, nimble, confused, secret.
2. *philanthropist:* fake, benevolent person, musician, wise man.
3. *torrid:* scorching, ugly, this way, frightening.
4. *tenure:* beginner, holding, singer, tyro.
5. *analogy:* study of birds, distance, correspondence, fiasco.
6. *incite:* provoke, penetrate, anger, placate.
7. *dubious:* peevish, doubtful, penurious, double.
8. *harangue:* witch, Moslem church, abuse, windy speech.
9. *lank:* barrier, lean, curly, stout.
10. *plausible:* true, apparently true, practical, false.

Group IV

1. *criterion:* standard, Roman official, winged staff, vessel.
2. *trite:* hackneyed, scrapple, tested, distilled.
3. *recalcitrant:* level, rocklike, stubbornly opposed, repetitious.
4. *tacit:* bitter, pungent, mendacious, silent.
5. *culpable:* versatile, blameworthy, fey, responsive.
6. *noxious:* otiose, pernicious, boring, rude.
7. *flume:* vapor, artificial channel, membrane, sear.
8. *stigmatize:* invalidate, distort, corrupt, disgrace.
9. *pied:* variegated, intoxicated, mercenary, skilled.
10. *winsome:* coiled, charming, sympathetic, dainty.

ANSWERS

GROUP I

1. *scope:* range
2. *bellow:* roar
3. *lance:* spear
4. *particle:* tiny piece
5. *obstacle:* in the way
6. *unique:* unequaled
7. *cherish:* value highly
8. *parson:* minister
9. *wither:* lose freshness
10. *meteor:* shooting star

GROUP II

1. *prudent:* careful
2. *obstruct:* to hinder
3. *reservoir:* storage place
4. *magnify:* make larger
5. *tedious:* tiresome
6. *scrutinize:* examine closely
7. *posterity:* the future
8. *fang:* long tooth
9. *juvenile:* youthful
10. *czar:* Russian emperor

GROUP III

1. *deft:* nimble
2. *philanthropist:* benevolent person
3. *torrid:* scorching
4. *tenure:* holding
5. *analogy:* correspondence
6. *incite:* provoke
7. *dubious:* doubtful
8. *harangue:* windy speech
9. *lank:* lean
10. *plausible:* apparently true

GROUP IV

1. *criterion:* standard
2. *trite:* hackneyed
3. *recalcitrant:* stubbornly opposed
4. *tacit:* silent
5. *culpable:* blameworthy
6. *noxious:* pernicious
7. *flume:* artificial channel
8. *stigmatize:* disgrace
9. *pied:* variegated
10. *winsome:* charming

19

Equipment and Skill Games

ONE OF THE BEST OF "group absorbers," equipment games should form an important part of the repertoire of most groups. Such games as ping-pong, shuffleboard, basketball goal shooting are fairly common. A few ball games are familiar. Here are some games which can be assembled easily, many of them made of scrap or waste materials, and nearly all from very inexpensive materials. In the dozens of possible games described, you should be able to find many suitable for your situation.

These games perform a fine function in occupying folk as they first arrive. Pick out ten or fifteen of them, have them around the walls. (Sometimes they are used as special features in carnivals staged by clubs, schools, or churches.)

Simple skill games make wonderful family night activities, whether rolling, tossing, sliding or bouncing kinds. Families might be encouraged to make some of these games.

Picnics are "naturals" for equipment games, if that kind of fun is needed. Notice how easily some of the tossing games could be rigged up. (Of course, the old standby, horseshoes or quoits, may be added.) Washer tossing is inexpensive and satisfying. Rainy day at camp calls for bringing out a number of skill games, such as these, to see who can do it the best. Set players to improvising new games.

One of the more interesting of the new inventions is the Sky Pie,[1] a flying disc of soft plastic. For indoors or outdoors it is a game property that encourages players to improvise. Many games, such as end ball, softball, basketball, may be played with it. Sky Pie floats in the water, so it can be used for water fun, too.

TOSSING GAMES

Probably the most popular games in the simple skill category are those that involve tossing at, into, or through something. Work up your own game and make your own rules!

Here are some of the most popular articles to toss:

1. Bean bags
2. Balls, marbles
3. Quoits (fruit jar rubbers, rope rings, quoits made of hose, even cardboard hoops or barrel hoops)
4. Rubber heels
5. Discs like checkers, linoleum discs, metal washers, curtain rings
6. Feathers, darts
7. Even stones, seeds, fruit, or vegetables
8. Horseshoes, shoes
9. Clothespins (usually dropped)
10. Things difficult to toss any distance, like feathers, toothpicks, soda straws, balls of cotton, corks, cards, paper plates, envelopes

These objects are tossed *into* following receptacles:

1. Tin cans of various sizes
2. Cake pans
3. Wide-mouthed bottles
4. Egg cartons (with sections numbered for points)
5. Cups
6. Barrels
7. Holes in ground
8. Holes in bean bag board, or side of box, usually numbered for points, smaller, harder holes bearing higher points
9. Basketball goal

They are also tossed *onto*—

1. Targets like archery target, targets on floor
2. Squares, each having different value depending on how hard it is to hit

They are tossed *at*—

1. Archerylike targets (for darts)
2. Special boards having special values, like dart baseball

In tossing games, you may make your own rules of the game, your own combination of objects to be tossed, what they're to be tossed *into* or *onto*.

Washer Tossing. Like horseshoes, in many ways. Holes in ground (or tin cans) are 10 to 20 feet apart (depending on ability of players). Some count washers in hole three points; some five. Usually game is played to 21. Washer on washer in hole cancels. Closest washers of same color (washers have been painted) count one each. It is customary to pitch from two to four washers, alternating in turn.

Small tin cans nailed onto wide boards are used for washer tossing indoors. Some craftsmen are skillful enough to set cans *into* boards, flush with edge of board so that washers can slide in!

Make your own rules, your own points, your own distances. Here is an opportunity to create something of your own!

Games with Fruit Jar Rubbers

1. Drive nails in board and number value of each nail. Give each person five fruit jar rubbers to toss from distance of 6 to 10 feet.
2. Dodo is a version of this. One nail or hook is called Dodo and counts off. All others are valued as numbered. Play to total score of 50 or whatever is agreed upon in advance.
3. Use fingers upon which to toss rubbers. Two partners, standing six feet apart, are competing with another couple in same fashion. Each person tosses five rubbers to his partner's fingers, and counts one point for each successful try. Then partner tosses the five back. Game may be played to see who gets 25 or 50 points first, or who has best score in specified number of total tosses (between team members) like 30, 50.
4. Spring clothespins are fastened on side of box or bucket, with value of each pin written on it. Players toss fruit jar rubbers to try to ring clothespins.
5. Played in partners, one person holds up clothespin, and other

tries to toss fruit jar rubbers onto clothespin, with partner helping. Score as in No. 3.

6. Turn chair upside down and toss fruit jar rubbers at legs from 6 to 10 feet back. One point for each successful toss.

7. Several soft-drink bottles are lined up. Object: to toss fruit jar rubbers onto necks of bottles from 6 to 10 feet back.

Quoit Tossing (any kind of hoops, rope rings)

1. Turn chair upside down and toss rope rings at legs, points counted for successful tries, such as 10. Cardboard rings cut from oatmeal boxes will do.

2. Toss quoits over soft-drink bottles or milk bottles, count points for successes.

3. Put clothespins on cardboard box. Count points for successful ringers.

4. Quoit Golf. Make nine pegs by sawing off lengths of broom handles and nailing them onto boards as bases. Set these out as if on golf course and count against each player number of tosses necessary to make rounds. (No toss can be made from less than 3 feet away.)

Tossing Larger Balls. Games have been devised for tossing volleyballs, basketballs, footballs, softballs, such as these:

1. Baseball throw into barrel, or through barrel hoop.

2. Football throw for accuracy, distance. (Same with other balls.)

3. Bouncing volleyball, basketball into can, wastebasket, barrel.

4. Basketball free throws—see who gets most out of 10 tries.

5. Toss or throw any of these balls for certain line or spot, such as nearest to base.

Tossing Paper Plates

1. Toss or sail for distance. See who can toss farthest.

2. Toss or sail plates through barrel hoop or wire ring, suspended from ceiling, door. Count points for each successful try.

3. Toss or sail through Christmas wreath, large heart, turkey outline made of wire, pumpkin outline made of wire or other seasonal device.

4. Toss or sail paper plates into wastebasket, or through basket-ball goal.

Tossing Checkers, Corks, Pebbles, Marbles, Curtain Rings, Milk Bottle or Coke Caps, Small Wooden Cubes

1. Toss specified number (5 to 10) into small end of megaphone.
2. Toss into a No. 10 tin can from 10 to 15 feet back.
3. Toss into flower pots, each one marked for score, from 8 to 15 feet back.
4. Toss into muffin tins, with each hole marked for points. (In case of cube, count points for marking on each side: 5, 10, 15, 20, 25, 30—or 1 to 6).
5. Toss into a cake pan with center hole, scoring five points for hitting in pan, 25 points if hit hole, from 8 to 10 feet back.
6. Tossing into egg carton, with each hole numbered for points, like 2, 3, 5. Count total score after tossing 25 times, or devise your own system.
7. Make cardboard diagram one foot square or larger, with the mystic 15 on it. Each player gets points in keeping with where their marker stops. (Marbles are not suitable for this.) If anyone gets exactly 15, it doubles score.
8. Suspend horseshoe 6 to 8 feet away from line and let contestants try to toss through horseshoe.
9. Suspend 8-inch hoop from door or ceiling and then within the hoop suspend bell. Object: From distance of 6 to 8 feet, to toss an object through hoop without ringing bell. For each success, 5 to 10 points. (A ping-pong ball is good for this.)
10. Throw rocks at fence posts. Point for each hit.
11. From 20 feet back, toss objects into barrel, counting points for each success.
12. Toss into box through holes in side. Place number value on each hole. Play for highest score in 10 tosses, or to specified score, such as 50.
13. Draw diagram as indicated. Toss flat discs (checkers, milk bottle caps, coke caps). Bull's eye doubles, triangle halves score, corner diamonds cancel score, up to point it was hit. Take 10 trials.

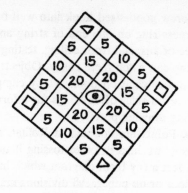

14. Toss into cans of different sizes, one set inside the other, with highest points for hitting smallest cans.
15. Make hoops of different sizes from wire or wood strips and place point value on each one. Toss objects into hoops, counting points as indicated. Stand 6 to 12 feet away.

Match Darts. Make three darts by cutting heads from matches, slitting one end so that piece of folded paper about 2½ inches square can be slipped in. Force large sewing needle into other end. (Feather might be substituted for paper.)

Target as shown is 15 to 18 inches in diameter on outside.

Players stand 8 feet away, and each tries to hit bulls eye, counting whatever score he makes.

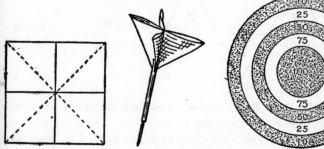

Piercing the Hoop. Suspend barrel hoop from tree and let players throw fishing pole or its equivalent through hoop. Each one gets three to five tries. Start from about 15 feet back, gradually go farther back to encourage more skill.

Ring the Hook. Screw good-sized hook into wall or tree. Put curtain ring or harness ring on one end of string and tie other end in branch of tree or suspend from ceiling, testing length to hook to make sure ring can catch there easily. Object: to stand back, swing ring up and catch it on hook. Many camps have several of them in trees or on sides of buildings for informal play. (This game has amazing drawing power!)

Roman Star Toss. Points are counted in Roman numerals, Bean bags, rubber heels, washers or other tossing items may be used. Line is about 6 feet away from diagram which has been chalked or marked on floor or on paper. All divisions must be somewhat larger than whatever is tossed. Anything touching line does not count. Each player tosses in rotation. Predetermine total points to win, but make rule that no player may win with first toss. (That is, if 500 is winning score, player may not win by tossing D or an M.)

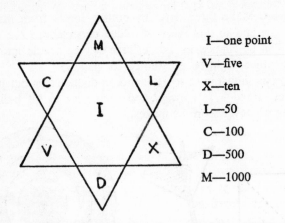

I—one point
V—five
X—ten
L—50
C—100
D—500
M—1000

How to Make Bean Bag Boards. These may be simple or more complex. Here is one example.

Make board 2 feet wide, 2½ to 3 feet long. Cut holes as illustrated. Eyes are 7 × 5 inches, mouth is 10 × 4 inches, base of triangle 8 inches. Place board against building or give it hinged prop.

Players stand 10 to 15 feet back of board. Each has 5 bean bags (or other specified number). See who gets most in five pitches, or play to certain score, such as 100. May be played on team basis, each person pitching one bag.

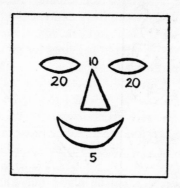

Games with Bean Bags or Rubber Heels

KITCHEN GOLF. With kitchen utensils placed in zigzag fashion around room or outdoor space, play in couples or by individuals. Each has bean bags to toss into these utensils, keeping score. As soon as one couple has finished with first hole, another starts.

TARGET GAME. Toss bean bags at target on floor, each player getting specified number of tosses, such as three, in rotation. Play to specified score to win like 25, 50, or 100.

500. Players are in sixes, each having bean bag. Target is made with center circle of 1 foot, next circle 1½ feet, next one 2½ feet, outside one 3½ feet, and all is enclosed in 7-foot square. Players toss from line 10 to 20 feet back (depending on skill and age). Object: to be first to make perfect score of exactly 500 with six bean bags.

Rules: Bean bags resting on line are tossed again, those making score are left in place. Captain of either team has privilege of returning any bean bag not making sufficient score. At end, an exact score of 500 must be recorded to win.

BEAN BAG TOSS. Using target similar to No. 3, have players toss and keep individual scores. See who gets highest total in five tosses, ten tosses.

BEAN BAG SHUFFLEBOARD. With bean bags or rubber heels, toss or slide on shuffleboard court, counting as in shuffleboard.

Bean Bag Golf [2]

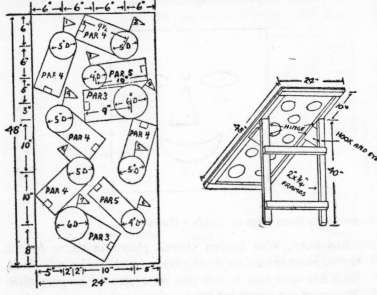

OBJECT: Using bean bags, to get around nine-hole golf course in fewest number of throws or strokes. Par for course is 36. You cannot toss more than par for any hole. If you have not holed out, you take par for your score for that hole. Entire group playing move from hole to hole, as in golf.

Bean Bag Basketball. Five players are on team, each one shooting from goal line edge of diagram (chalked on floor or otherwise marked). First player tosses bean bag and gets what diagram indicates. If he hits "Side shoots again," next player in line takes over toss and he goes to foot of his line. If he makes goal he keeps shooting. When player has finished his turn he goes to foot of his line, and other side takes over.

If bean bag lands midway on line, player shoots again; otherwise it counts for side on which most of bag lies.

On "free shots," player gets free tosses, then shoots again. Only thing on diagram that counts in "free shots" is a goal, which counts one point for each success. (Regular goal is 2 points.)

Play for specified length of time, such as 5-minute quarters. More players than five on team can be used. Also in large room, several games could be going at same time.

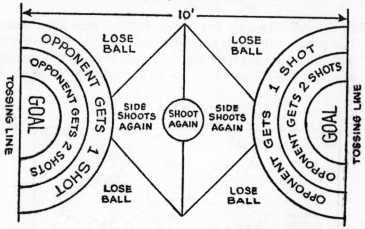

Bean Bag Baseball.[3] Play with two teams. Each batter continues to toss bean bags until out or on base. Regular baseball rules apply.

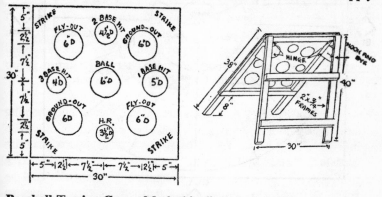

Baseball Tossing Game. Mark this diagram on floor:

HOME RUN	TRIPLE	DOUBLE	WALK
FLY OUT	STRIKE OUT	FOUL OUT	3 BAGGER
WALK	DOUBLE	WALK	HOME RUN
SINGLE	OUT	DOUBLE	OUT

Toss onto diagram metal washers, rubber heels, or bean bags. Two teams play. Each player tosses, in turn, until on base or out. Rules are as in baseball.

Dart Baseball. There are two teams. "Batting" team tosses darts, first player until he gets on base or out. Same rules as baseball, with teams changing sides after three outs. Play as many innings as are desirable. Darts can be bought at sporting goods stores.

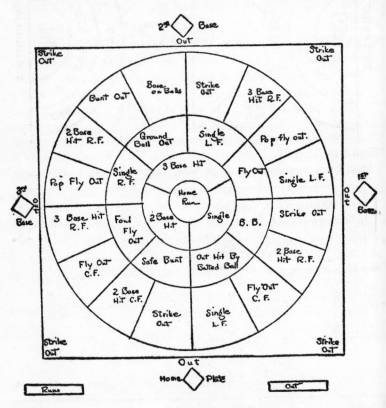

Seasonal Tossing Games.[4] Using rubber heels, bean bags, or other things to toss, draw diagram on floor in keeping with season, such as the following:

THANKSGIVING (draw outline of turkey): breast, score of 20; leg, 10; wing, 5; neck, 5.

HALLOWE'EN (draw jack-o-lantern): nose, 20; eyes, 15 each; mouth, 10; ears, 5 each.

CHRISTMAS: small star in center, with larger ones surrounding. Largest score in center.

ROLLING GAMES

There are innumerable miniature games that can be played with golf, ping-pong, and small rubber balls, or with marbles. Some are in imitation of standard games such as golf, dodge ball, hockey, polo.

Clock Golf. Played in circle, 15 to 40 feet in diameter, with positions numbered, 1 to 12, around circumference like clock face. Hole into which to putt is placed anywhere in circle. It is wide and deep enough for ball used.

Golf or hockey sticks or even knotted tree branches are used to putt ball, which may be golf ball or rubber ball about that size. Each player plays around clock, trying to do it in smallest number of strokes.

Obstacle Golf. This small-space game uses tin cans, bent tin tunnels, mounds, trenches, soil pipe. Holes are laid out as in regular golf, with tin cans 4 inches in diameter sunk in ground (holes in bottom to let water through in case of rain). Instead of smooth course these obstacles are deliberately planned. Object is to get around course in fewest strokes.

Marble Dodging Game.[5] Object is to get as many as possible in

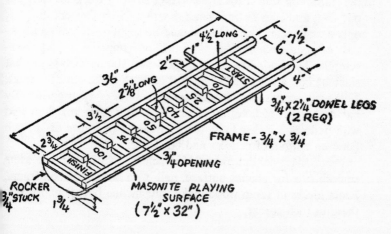

high-point stalls before one sneaks through to finish. Ten marbles are used.

Game is played by placing all marbles in section marked "start." Player takes track by handles, raises it slightly, turns it back and forth on rocker to get marbles to roll through narrow openings into spaces with progressively higher point value.

When marble slips through to finish line, place game down on its legs immediately and tally score. Then next player takes his turn.

Table Polo

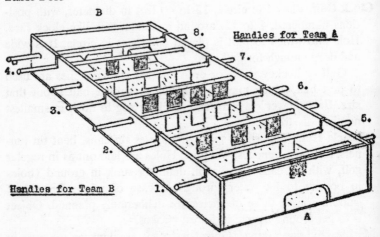

DIRECTIONS FOR CONSTRUCTING: Using ¾-inch thick lumber, cut out sides and ends of box as per diagram. Note slots cut in sides, only *four* to side. These slots should be slightly wider than thickness of paddle material so as to facilitate removal of paddle assemblies by turning paddles upward and sliding out. Note that sides of box are cut in ⅜ inch at ends to make stronger joint. This way, screws can be used on both sides of each corner. By having bottom of holes on sides 3⅛ inches from box floor and with paddles 3 inches long, there would be clearance of ⅛ inch between bottom of paddles and box floor.

From Masonite cut piece 21½ inches × 48 inches and using smooth side for playing surface, nail it on bottom of box frame. From pieces of scrap wood make four incline boards and fasten these in each corner.

Using discarded mop or broom handles and Masonite scrap, make eight paddle assemblies—two of each of four shown. Sheet metal $\frac{1}{32}$ inch thick may be used instead of Masonite. Note that paddle goes all way up through handle and is fastened with glue and small bolts.

"Stops" are necessary on two paddle assemblies with only one paddle because their movement is restricted by corner incline boards. "Stops" are optional on other paddle assemblies, but if used, should be fastened to handles so that paddles just miss touching side walls. "Stops" can easily be removed to facilitate removal of paddle assemblies from box.

Thoroughly sand game box and equipment before either varnishing, staining, or painting.

DIRECTIONS FOR PLAYING: There are two teams with 2 to 4 players on each team. One team stand on one side of box and play paddle assemblies 1, 2, 3, 4. They have as their goal end B. Second team stand on opposite side and play paddle assemblies 5, 6, 7, 8, and have end A as their goal. Goal for any team is always to players' left. A ping-pong ball is used and paddles are players. Game starts with ball thrown into middle of box between paddle assemblies with four paddles.

Object of game is for each team to get ball through their goal, at same time preventing their opponents from doing same thing and scoring. Each ball going through opening at either end scores one point. Any arbitrary number of points decided upon by teams can constitute game. If ball is hit out of box, it is tossed into center of box, and play is resumed.

To make game faster when from 4 to 8 people are playing, two balls are used at same time. However, team must get *both*

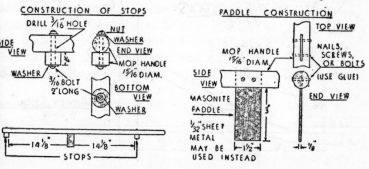

balls through their goal before point is scored. If both teams get one ball each, no point is scored.

Basket Hockey. Two to four persons can play with this board on table. Using hockey sticks they attempt to drive marble through their opponent's goal, up and around and into basket.

Marble is put into play by dropping in center of playing field.

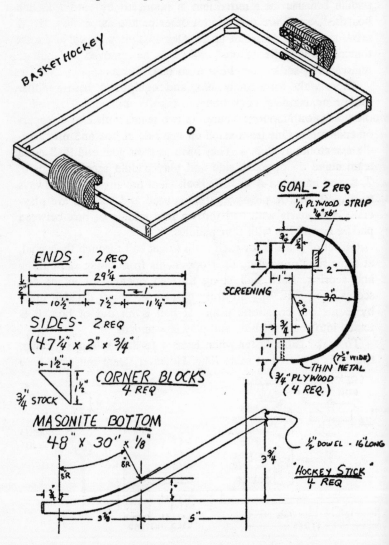

CONSTRUCTION: Build frame with ends and side pieces; note overlapping joints. Attach Masonite bottom, smooth side up, to frame and add corner blocks.

Goals are constructed by tacking thin sheet of tin to two ¾-inch plywood sides as shown. Insert ¼-inch plywood strip and nail. Wire screening is fastened to front to form basket. Basket goals can then be inserted into openings at each end until metal is flush with Masonite bottom. Holes can be drilled through frame at each prong of goals, and nails used to hold the goals more firmly to frame.

Hockey sticks are ½-inch dowels steamed and bent into shape. Make form for bending sticks before steaming, and then after steaming let stick remain on form until dry. A five-quart oil can with approximately 1-inch diameter hole in top will serve for steaming. Add ½ inch of water to can and heat on stove to boiling; place stick in can and let steam for 10 minutes or more.

Rolling Games with Simpler Equipment

1. Little children like to roll a ball back and forth with other children or adults, sitting on floor.
2. Rolling ball into can or series of cans, counting points for successful tries is fun for children and older folk. (Balls from small golf size to large size, with cans in proportion.)
3. Set three milk bottles up with few inches between them. Try to roll ball or marbles between bottles without clinking. Points for successful tries.
4. Cut holes larger than marbles in side of cigar box and turn box upside down, as shown. Each player shoots or rolls marbles into holes from appropriate distance away.

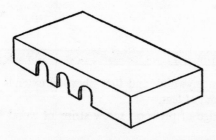

5. Roll small ball up flap of egg carton, into carton. Points counted for successful tries, with different squares having different point values.

6. MINIATURE BOWLING. Buy set of small tenpins at specialty store and use small rubber balls to knock them down by rolling, scoring as in regular bowling. (Another version is to suspend ball on string in doorway, set up pins there, pull ball back and let it swing on string, knocking down pins.)

7. Cardboard milk cartons are good tenpins, if ball large enough to knock them over is used. (Also blocks of wood or tenpins, tin cans.)

8. Marble bowling is accomplished by using large nails or spikes, sitting on their heads, as tenpins, and scoring as in regular tenpins.

9. GOLF. Try putting into cans set up at end of room. See how many times you can hit can in five tries, or make own rules.

10. GOOFY GOLF. Lay out course outdoors, use hockey sticks and small rubber ball, play as in regular golf.

11. CORK GOLF. Shape coat hanger into putter and use cork. Hole is chalked or otherwise marked at other end of room. See who can "hole out" in fewest strokes.

12. AUTOMOBILE RACE. Lay out course on floor or table, marking numbered areas within last 12 inches. Push toy autos down speedway into scoring area. Object may be (1) to get them to stop closest to finish line, or (2) to get cars to race across finish line first.

13. TABLE LEAF BOWLING [6] Use a 3½- to 4-foot table leaf for alley. To bottom side of table leaf screw piece of ¼ inch plywood which is about 6 inches wider than leaf so that leaf is

centered on plywood, and that plywood extends 5 inches beyond one end of leaf.

Around edge of plywood screw strips of wood ¾ inch thick

and 2 inches high to form gutters. Next, screw together two pieces of ¼-inch plywood about 12 inches long and 2 inches wide to form V-shaped trough down which to roll balls. This trough should be cut at slant at one end so that it will rest on alley at a 45° angle. Finally, paint spots at other end of alley to represent position of pins. Use wooden pins bought from toy or "dime-store," and three wooden balls. Score as in tenpins.

DROPPING, BOUNCING, AND PUSHING GAMES

Besides the scores of tossing and rolling games that require simple equipment there are many games in which a ball or a disc is dropped or bounced into a container, or pushed around a charted area.

Dropping Clothespins, Nuts, Pebbles, Coins

1. Dropping clothespins into milk bottles from back of chair, counting points for number out of five pins dropped that go in.
2. Same, but each pin has value marked on its head. Score points by checking heads of successful pins. Head of certain color, such as red, might double score.
3. Drop pin, one from each shoulder, from nose, and from each eye, bending over milk bottle. Count points for successful tries.
4. Same idea as above, but using nuts or coins.
5. Drop five coins into fishbowl half-filled with water, containing small glass. Count one point for each coin going into bowl, five points for those going into glass.

Bouncing Games

1. Bounce ball from distance of 6 to 10 feet, into wastebasket or box of similar size. Count points for each success. Try two bounces and in!
2. Bounce ball (up to tennis ball size) on floor, off wall, and catch it in funnel.
3. Bounce ball over back of chair and into wastebasket or box, or bucket.
4. Bounce ping-pong ball on table and into egg carton.
5. Cut 6-inch holes in large piece of canvas and mount it perpendicular to ground. Players bounce tennis ball (or other small ball) on ground and through holes, each of which is marked for points (5, 10, 15, 25, and so on).

Maze.[7] Maze is home-made skill game, incorporating shooting of caroms with three-foot long ⅜-inch dowel rod, and it can be played by 2 to 8 persons. (Carom here is a wooden disc flipped with finger.)

Board is 3 × 4 feet with ½-inch square molding (glued and nailed securely) around edge and along all heavy lines. (See diagram.) Hazards are painted in red. Advances are painted in green.

MAZE

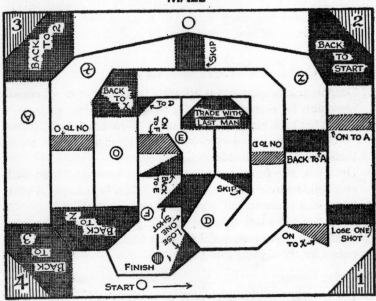

Color Code: Blue ▦ Green ▨ Red ■

Object of game is to shoot your caroms into each corner pocket (1, 2, 3, and 4) and then continue shooting through maze area until carom is upon blue-finish circle. First player to do so is winner.

Additional materials needed: a different colored or marked carom for each participant. Cues (⅜-inch dowel rod) for each player or every other player. (If there are not enough cues to go around, players can trade back and forth, since they play in turn.)

Rules:

1. Determine by lot shooting order (take turns).
2. First shot is from Start Circle toward corner pocket 1. (Each time corner pocket is scored, shooter immediately gets another shot from pocket opening toward next objective.)
3. Carom must be completely on a color. (Color shows all way around before directions of markings can be followed.)
4. A player may not shoot backward to earn advance or to interfere with opponent. He may shoot back to try to make corner pocket.
5. As soon as carom stops on green advance, carom is moved to designated area.
6. If carom stops on red hazard, it remains until its next turn. Then it is played from its designated area.
7. A carom that jumps over partition is returned to spot from which it was shot; and next player continues.
8. If a carom rests too near partition for good shooting, it may be moved out to width of cue.
9. Opponents' caroms are not to be removed from board to facilitate shooting. They too become hazards, to be shot around or hit.
10. "Trade with Last Man" means to trade positions with person farthest from finish circle.

HINTS: Before difficult hazards, Back to Start, Back to Z, Back to 3, Back to X, and Trade with Last Man, it is often wise to shoot for advances and play cautiously. In rest of maze, play with boldness. Study angles of partitions and plan how to carom. It is often better to "lose one shot" than "trade with last man."

Regulation Shuffleboard. Diagram is painted or drawn on floor. (It can be set in asphalt tile.) Regulation disc is 6 inches in diameter, 1 inch thick. Pusher (shovel) is about 5 feet long.

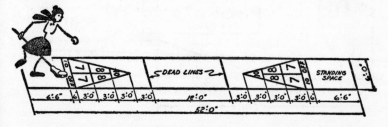

If two players play, each takes turns pushing his discs from standing space. (Discs are of two different colors for easy scoring.) No disc on lines counts. Game is to 50 points.

If doubles are played, one partner is at each end of court. In all cases, player with larger score pushes first.

Deck Shuffleboard. This type is for smaller spaces. Diagram can be chalked on floor. (One leader carries a 1- × 3-foot piece of ply-

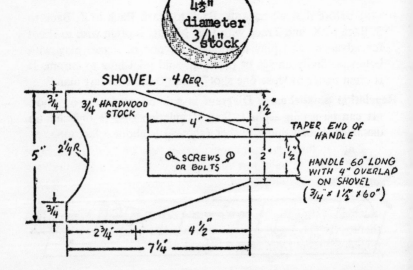

wood, and a rounded-end 1- × 3-foot piece, and quickly marks diagram and numerals on floor.) Broomsticks can be used for pusher handles, and discs are usually smaller than regulation.

Draw line 10 to 12 feet back from diagram. Play from 10 plus side.

Road Block.[8] For two players, each holding twenty-six squares, $2'' \times 2''$, of colored cardboard, red for one player, yellow for the other. Note how the squares are marked, and that a different number of each of the five types of squares are marked as indicated, each player having 8 "corners," 11 "though roads," and so on.

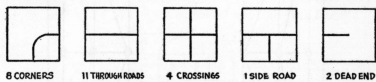

8 CORNERS   11 THROUGH ROADS   4 CROSSINGS   1 SIDE ROAD   2 DEAD END

One player leads off. They play alternately. The object is to get 10 squares in a forward direction to win. (Side moves or backward moves do not count on the total of 10.) A player may, in turn, either play on his own "highway system" (offense) or on his opponent's to block him (defense). The latter may be done by placing a dead-end block to stop opponent's forward progress. Opponent must then start at a crossing or back behind the beginning, going in the other direction (which will now be considered "forward" for him). If in doubt, agree on your own rules.

Corner blocks may be used to turn opponent's line of progress into stopping place, as shown:

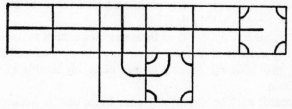

Marble Trap. This game can be played by two, three, or four, persons. Object of game is to "trap" opponents' marbles. Each has six marbles of a color.

Play: In turn, place one marble at a time on board, with hope of being able to have row of three of your color, while preventing others from doing same.

When any player succeeds in placing three marbles, of his color, in a straight row he has succeeded in making a "trap" and thereby is privileged to take one marble from each of his opponents, except from closed trap.

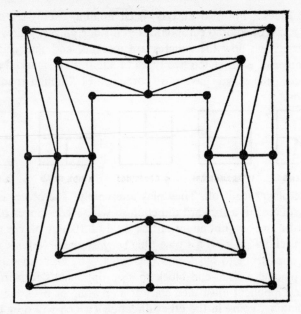

After all marbles have been placed on board they may be moved from one hole to next only in straight lines.

When player has but three marbles left he is privileged to "jump" his marble to any place on board (he does not have to follow lines as others do).

Persons having less than three marbles cannot make a "trap," so they are out of game. "Traps" may be opened and closed at will, providing opponent does not place his marble in strategic position.

Boards may be almost any size. Lines can be burned in with an iron.

Racing Game.[9] Get piece of brown wrapping paper, 3 × 7 feet. With crayon, mark out race track similar to sketch. Track should be wide enough for three or four toy cars to stand side by side.

Mark numbers, 1 to 6, on sides of a block or cube. Let each player, in turn, roll block to see how many spaces to move his car. If he stops on space with written directions, he must follow these directions. Driver of car with bumper touching finish line first, wins. Continue to see who comes in for other positions.

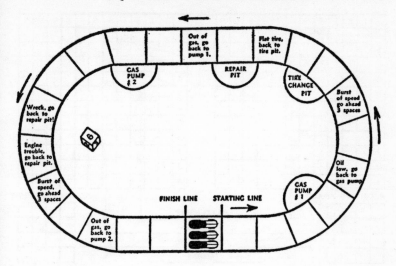

Battleship [10]

PLAYERS: Two persons or group. Each group has form similar to one above.

Each player or side locates his ships on receiving board—1 Battleship (four squares), 1 Cruiser (three squares), 2 Destroyers (2 squares each), 4 Mines (one square each). Player is not allowed to see location of opponent's ships. Ships are located by circling proper number of squares in pencil. Ships may be located horizontally, vertically or diagonally.

Each player—playing in rotation—fires volley of seven shots at his opponent's ships. "Volley" consists of calling out to opponent, say, "B-7"; opponent marks this on his chart. Next might be "J-2," and so on. Shooter also keeps record on his chart, showing spots he shot on round 1 by placing figure 1 in all spots toward which he shoots. This consists simply of calling out numbers of spots where he thinks his opponent's equipment is located. These shots he records on sending board while his opponent records on receiving board. He must call letter and number of each square at which he fires.

Number 1 player places his seven shots and then asks his opponent, "Did I hit anything?" Player Number 2 must answer truthfully, but he does not tell where hit scored. He simply says,

RECEIVING BOARD

SENDING BOARD

BATTLESHIP

CRUISER

DESTROYER

MINES

"Yes, you hit my battleship once. Nothing else." Then number 2 player shoots in same manner.

When a ship goes down, that player loses that many shots at his opponent ships—3 for Battleship, 2 for Cruiser, and 1 each for Destroyers. When mine is hit, firing player loses any remaining shots in that particular salvo. Player is not defeated until all his ships are sunk.

Outdoor Tetherball. Pole 10 feet high has rope or strong cord (7½ feet long) fastened at top, and ball of tennis-ball size or larger on other end of rope or cord. Line is marked on pole 6 feet high. Two play. Object: to wind ball around pole, make it touch above line.

Table Tether Ball (for two players) [11]

CONSTRUCTION: Bore hole through center of board to fit mop handle. Attach two brackets with bolts to board. Insert handle and bolt. Attach screw eye to top of handle. Tie string to eye with ball on other end.

Rules: Each person uses a paddle. Ball is put in play by one player serving; he hits it with the idea of winding the string around the pole above stripe. Server may choose direction in which he desires to wind string. Opponent tries to hit ball back

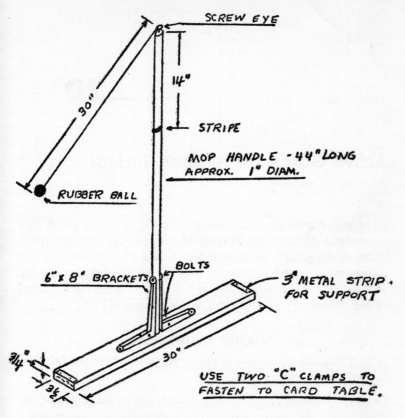

and wind it in opposite direction. Player fouls when he winds string around his paddle. Penalty for foul is free hit by opponent. If he can wind string around pole above stripe in one unimpeded stroke, he scores point. Players set score; anywhere from 5 to 15 points make game.

20

Active Games—Outdoor, Indoor

HERE ARE FOUND DESCRIPTIONS of over 130 games in which any-where from eight or ten to forty or fifty players may take part. Many of the games are possible for the age of 6 on upward. The collection seems to fall naturally into five main categories: Games with Sides (13), Races and Relays (39), Tag Games (42), Games of the Athletic Type (20), and Water Games (17).[1]

GAMES WITH SIDES

Rabbit Hunting (Variation of Dodge Ball)

No: 10-40   All ages

EQUIPMENT: Gymnasium or playground; one or more basketballs.

FORMATION: One hunter for every ten people; players scattered about playing area.

DIRECTIONS: Hunter takes ball and starts "shooting" "rabbits." That is, he tries to hit those who are playing. When player is hit he immediately falls down and is dead. Last to be hit is winner and next hunter. Players must hit below waist.

Lost Patrol

No: 20-80   Age: 9-12

FORMATION: Teams of equal numbers.

DIRECTIONS: Goal and signal station are established. Group is divided into two teams, Searchers and Lost Patrol. Two captains are selected. Captain of Lost Patrol hides his team in one place. He returns to signal station and signals searchers to begin hunt.

Their captain directs search. Lost Patrol captain remains at signal station and, by means of previously agreed-upon signals, keeps his team informed of whereabouts of searchers. When searchers are at safe distance, he signals his patrol to return to goal as quickly as possible, by shouting "Lost Patrol." Searchers chase Lost Patrol. Whichever team reaches goal first, wins. Winning team then becomes Lost Patrol.

Hanker Fight

No: 2-40   Age: 9 up

FORMATION: Equal teams.

DIRECTIONS: This is particular favorite with boys. Each player inserts handkerchief in his hip pocket, so that it extends out about two inches. If he has no hip pocket, handkerchief is tucked in shorts or trousers at waist. At signal, each attempts to pull out other's handkerchief and protect his own. All tactics are fair except unnecessary roughness. Losers must retire to sideline. Team with most "scalps" wins.

Balloon Battle Royal

No: 6-8   Age: 10 up

EQUIPMENT: Inflated balloons and string.

DIRECTIONS: Tie one balloon to waist of each of six or eight players, balloon being tied in front. At signal, they all go after each other's balloons, and survivor wins. As soon as player's balloon is burst, he withdraws. Have one troup after another compete until all who desire have entered. Then bring winners together to determine champion.

VARIATION: Tie balloon to player's ankle. Let players try to stamp on balloons and burst them.

Broom Hockey

No: 10-30   Age: 9 up

EQUIPMENT: Two chairs for goals, two brooms or broomsticks, one old rag.

FORMATION: Two teams taking part sit facing each other in two long equal lines, broomsticks lie on two chairs on each end, and rag in middle. Teams are numbered from opposite ends.

DIRECTIONS: Leader calls number and players from each team with that number pick up broomsticks and try to push rag under opposite chair. When one succeeds a goal is counted for his side. Upon occasion of both players' progress being checked, stalemate ensues, and sticks and rags are returned to their original position. No points are given and new numbers are called.

What's Your Trade?

No: 10-50   Age: 9 up

FORMATION: Players divided into two teams, each standing on their home line. Home lines are about 40 feet apart.

DIRECTIONS: Team No. 1 approaches Team No. 2, who are standing on their home line. Team No. 1 says, "We're taking a trip." Team No. 2 says, "Where are you going?" No. 1, "To Arabee." No. 2, "What's your trade?" No. 1, "Watch and see." Then team members begin to act out their trade. When member of Team No. 2 calls out right answer, all No. 1 members turn and run for their home line. Team No. 2 members try to catch them. Players that are caught return with No. 2 and become part of their team. Each team alternates in choosing a trade and being chasers.

Crows and Cranes

No: 10-50   Age: 8 up

FORMATION: Divide players into two equal sides, one named "Crows," other "Cranes." Stand in line fairly close to each other. Each has home line about 20 feet from beginning line.

DIRECTIONS: When leader calls out "Crows," side called Crows must run for their home line with Cranes trying to catch them. If tagged before reaching home, player must join other side. Leader mixes up sides by calling out "Crrrrrrr" before indicating which he will call. Also throw in words like cracker or crunch.

VARIATIONS: Sol and Sombra, a South American game; Black and White in which leader flips disk and whichever side's color is up must run with other chasing; True and False in which Trues must run if statement is true; Odds and Evens in which leader gives out number; if it is even, that side runs. He can also give out two numbers and total must be added to see which side runs.

Steal the Bacon (Snatch the Handkerchief)

No: 10-30   Age: 9 up

FORMATION: Two lines about 15 feet apart. Equal number of players. Each line numbered from left to right, facing each other. Handkerchief or other article is in center in small circle.

DIRECTIONS: Leader calls out number, and players whose number was called come out. Object is to snatch handkerchief and to get back to line without being tapped. Two points for this. If tagged, one point goes to side who prevented stealing handkerchief. Other numbers may be called if stalemate comes. Handkerchief may be passed to teammate who has also been called out.

Stealing Sticks

No: 10-40   Age: 9 up

EQUIPMENT: Sticks for each team.

FORMATION: Ground is divided into two equal fields, each having equal number of sticks placed in pile at opposite extreme sides. If sticks are not available, caps or handkerchiefs will do. Players divided into two equal groups, and each group occupies territory with its respective pile of sticks.

DIRECTIONS: Players of one side invade territory of other to steal their sticks. Any player reaching enemy's goal, without being touched by player of enemy side, may take one stick back to his own goal and may not be touched on return trip. If tagged in enemy's ground however, while attempting to steal stick, player remains prisoner in goal of enemy until tagged by one of his own side. As player cannot release prisoner and steal stick at same time, neither can prisoner take stick with him upon release. Neither prisoner nor his rescuer may be tagged on their return home. The game is up when one side captures all sticks.

Capture the Flag (Prisoners' Base)

No: 20-200   Age: 9 up

FORMATION: May be used in limited area, or it can cover whole campgrounds or woods area. There is dividing line or zone which separates home territory for two sides; each side has prison area which is same distance from dividing line as others.

DIRECTIONS: Each side hangs a flag (handkerchief, bandana, tie or rag on a stick) on their territory. Flag must be visible from 50 feet away, and no defenders can hide within 50 feet of it. At signal to begin, both sides deploy their men. Some run into enemy's territory and try to discover and capture flag. Others serve as defenders. If one is tagged and captured (this must be agreed on in beginning—such as 3 quick taps in succession) in enemy territory, he is taken to prison. He can be rescued only when one of his members breaks through and tags him. Both get "free passage" home. Game ends either when all of one side is captured, or when enemy's flag is captured and brought safely back to home side.

Cavalry Battle Royal

No: 10-20   Age: 9 up

FORMATION: One man is horse and another is rider (usually smaller of the two). Rider wraps legs around body of horse and holds on to neck and shoulders with one arm. Horse holds legs of rider.

DIRECTIONS: On signal, two sides clash, each rider tries to jerk off opposing rider. When rider is pulled off horse, or else both horse and rider are knocked down, then they must retire from contest. Always play on soft turf or in water.

VARIATION: Use bands on arms—when he is jerked off player must retire. This can be used as dual game with only two horses and riders opposing each other.

Pass Fast

No: 10-40   Age: 10 up

EQUIPMENT: A ball or bean bag (something to pitch and catch).

FORMATION: Two teams, aligned parallel and facing each other 15 feet apart.

DIRECTIONS: Ball or similar article is passed back and forth from one team to other, working from head to foot and back. Music is played during passing. If music stops while one team holds article, other team scores point, and vice versa. Play until a certain number of points is attained.

RELAYS AND RACES

The first 21 of these 39 relays and races require no properties. The Sack Race Relay and those following it need some simple equipment.

Touch and Back

Age: 6 up

FORMATION: Teams seated in file formation.

DIRECTIONS: Leader names something in sight; this may be indefinite, as wood, iron, or water; or it may be specific object, as garage door, certain tree, or player (who tries to run away from rest). Leader may give further directions, such as "Hop on the right foot." Each line sets out to touch object and return to place. Line first regaining its original position, wins race.

VARIATION: Forty Ways to Get There. Players may hop, jump, skip, roll, carry each other; but no one is to duplicate mode of transportation used by teammate.

Automobile Relay

Age: 6 up

FORMATION: Teams of eight standing in file formation numbered from head to foot. Each team names itself for an automobile. Goal is fifteen feet away.

DIRECTIONS: This is played like relay race with following variations: No. 1 has flat right tire, so he hops on his right foot. No. 2 has flat left tire and hops on his left foot. No. 3 can go only in reverse so he goes backward. No. 4 has water in gas and he goes two steps forward, one step backward. No. 5 must be cranked every fourth step. He stops and cranks himself. No. 6 won't go, so No. 7 pushes him. No. 8 runs fine. Team reaching home first, wins game.

File Relay

Age: 6 up

FORMATION: Teams seated in file formation; may be on ground, in desks or chairs. Players are numbered consecutively in each file, starting with front.

DIRECTIONS: Leader calls number, and players with that number in each file get up on right side, run around foot of file, up around head and back to their seats. Numbers should be called at random, and should be continued until all numbers have been called. Row which gets its players back in place first, the greatest number of times, wins.

Human Over and Under

Age: 8 up

FORMATION: Players line up single file about 10 yards apart. First stands erect with feet well apart, second bends over in leap frog position, and so on down line.

DIRECTIONS: At signal to go, last player in line crawls between legs of player in front of him, over next player, under next, over next, until he has gotten to front of line. He then takes his position (astride or leapfrog) in front of line. As soon as first player is in position, second player from rear repeats action. This continues until all players have gone "over and under" and are in their original order.

Torpedo

Age: 12 up

FORMATION: Players form two double rows, with odd one left over for each double row. Players in each row, or double row, hold hands firmly.

DIRECTIONS: Odd player for each row, beginning at one end, falls on hands (or platform, formed by players holding hands) of first four players. They, together, swing him forward, depositing him as far down line as possible. In this manner he is passed on to end of line; line wins which gets its man, or torpedo, through first.

Back-to-Back Race

Age: 9 up

FORMATION: Two players pair off. They are placed back to back with their arms linked (or tied at waist). Touch line is some distance from starting line, 25 yards.

DIRECTIONS: On word "Go," players with arms linked, back to back, run to touch line. One is running forward, and other backward. When touch line is reached, teams start back toward home. Person who was running forward is running backward.

VARIATION: Use as relay.

Wheelbarrow Relay
Age: 11 up

FORMATION: Each team has players in pairs behind home line. Touch line is about 30 or 40 feet away.

DIRECTIONS: On signal, to get ready, one player gets down on his hands and knees. Second man then grabs his legs below knees and lifts up, much as one would do to a wheelbarrow. Man on ground keeps his legs stiff. On "Go," couple starts toward touch line, man on ground walking on his hands, and other holding his legs and pushing him along. When touch line is reached, players exchange positions and return home. Next couple is tagged, and so on until one team wins.

Horse and Rider Race
Age: 10 up

FORMATION: Players pair off, one is "horse," other is "rider." Rider jumps on horse's back.

DIRECTIONS: With rider on horse's back they run a certain distance, change places, and run back to finish line.

VARIATIONS: Use as relay. Also good for water games. Mule and Rider Race. This is slower as mule is on all fours with rider on his back.

Skin the Snake Race
Age: 8 up

FORMATION: Two or more teams from 5 to 10 players in single file. Each player stoops over, putting his right hand between his legs and grasps left hand of person behind him.

DIRECTIONS: On "Go," last man lies down on his back, putting his feet between legs of man in front of him. Line walks backward, straddling prone bodies of their teammates, each player lying down in turn. When all have passed over him, last man gets up and pulls next man up as he backs over players lying down. This continues until all are "home" in their original positions.

Circle Relay
Age: 6 up

EQUIPMENT: Players may sit in chairs, but not necessarily.

FORMATION: Teams of equal number sit in circles.

DIRECTIONS: First man gets up and runs around circle. (May walk, hop, skip to music.) When he sits in his old place, person on his left gets up and goes around circle. This is continued until last person has finished the round.

VARIATION: Group seated on ground in tight circle back to back with legs spread wide, alongside legs of persons next to them. First person gets up and hops around circle between legs of teammates and back to place. Continue on around until all have made round.

Weaving Relay

Age: 8 up

FORMATION: Teams in small circles facing center.

DIRECTIONS: Tallest player starts walking to left on word "Go," passing in front of first player, behind next and so on around circle. He returns to place and tags player on his left who starts walking left and repeats action. Team finishing first, wins.

Hand Shaking Relay

Age: 6 up

FORMATION: Teams in file formation. Teams are paired, with heads of each team facing each other.

DIRECTIONS: First player runs across room and shakes hands with everyone in opposite line. He returns and tags second player, who repeats action. Continue action until entire team finishes.

VARIATIONS: Different types of handshakes may be used for each member of team. These are explained elsewhere in book.

Slow Freight Relay

Age: 7 up

FORMATION: Teams in file formation with turning point 12 feet in front of each line.

DIRECTIONS: Players of each team pair off. Numbers 1 and 2 face each other and then squat, extend legs, and sit upon each other's feet. They try to progress forward to turning point by bending knees and lifting partner off floor. When turning point is reached, players reverse directions and return to their team. Players 3 and 4 repeat action. This is continued until all players have finished.

Centipede Race

Age: 12 up

FORMATION: Players are divided into teams of 10 or 12. Half the teams are "crawlers" and other half are "riders." ("Riders" are the lighter members.) Finish line is 40 feet in front of teams.

DIRECTIONS: "Crawlers" line up in single file. They bend over and put their heads between legs of man in front and grasp his knees with both hands. First "crawler" is head of centipede and will call cadence. When "crawlers" are steady, "riders" mount and lock their legs around waist of "crawlers." Now, centipede is formed. On starting signal, head man calls cadence and "crawlers" move to it: left, right, left, right. Cadence will have to be increased if centipede falls behind others. If "crawlers" become disjoined or "rider" falls off, centipede must stop and reform. This race is one of most popular of all.

Measuring Worm Relay

Age: 8 up

FORMATION: Players divide into teams. Each team in single file facing turning point 10 feet away. First player of each team is on hands and toes, with body extended in straight line.

DIRECTIONS: Arms remain stationary and legs fully extended without body-sag throughout action. On starting, player takes very tiny steps until his feet reach his hands. Once feet are in position, he walks forward on his hands until his body is once more straight and fully extended. He repeats this until he returns and tags second player. At no time is body allowed to sag. Continue with all players until each has completed action.

Bicycle Relay

Age: 6 up

FORMATION: Teams number off by threes. Nos. 1 and 3 join single hands. No. 2 straddles joined hands.

DIRECTIONS: Upon signal, first threesomes run to goal and back and tag next threesome. If hand holds are broken, the "bicycle" must tour course again.

Antelope Race

Age: 6 up

FORMATION: Teams in file formation; players with hands clasped around waists of players in front. Turning point some 50 feet in front of each team.

DIRECTIONS: At signal "Go," teams run to goal designated, and then return. Race is won by antelope who has all its players across finishing line first. Team is disqualified if players lose their grip.

Tunnel Relay

Age: 6 up

FORMATION: Teams in file formation.

DIRECTIONS: Players in each line standing with legs apart. At signal, last player begins to crawl through "tunnel" to head of line. As soon as he has started, next player follows. First line whose members all have crawled through, wins race.

Under the Arch

Age: 8 up

FORMATION: Teams of equal length facing forward in file formation. Players are numbered consecutively from head to foot.

DIRECTIONS: Leader calls two consecutive numbers, for example: 4 and 5. Immediately Nos. 4 and 5 of each team turn sideways to face each other and form arch by raising both arms. Players behind them then run in single file under arch, swing around, and return to their original position again. At same time players in front of arch run to rear, join on to end of file, follow it through arch and take their original positions. Game is over when every player is standing in his original position. First team wins. Leader calls numbers at random but always consecutive numbers. Point out that running is always from back to front under arch.

Thread the Needle

Age: 8 up

FORMATION: Teams in file formation. Each line numbers off consecutively and joins hands.

DIRECTIONS: Leader calls off two numbers (as 6-7, 10-11, or 1-2.) Those two players raise joined hands and step apart from each other. Lines led by ends come down in front and quickly pass through arched opening made by two players and return to place. Two players dishrag into place to complete movement. First line returning to original position, wins. Continue calling other combinations.

Human Croquet Race
Age: 10 up

EQUIPMENT: None.

FORMATION: Nine players are wickets; they stand with feet apart at their field positions. Group is divided into teams of five players each, numbered 1 to 5.

DIRECTIONS: When signal is given, Team A starts player No. 1 at head stake. As soon as he has crawled through all wickets and is back at starting point, player No. 2 follows. Team B starts player No. 1 at lower stake at same time that Team A starts at head stake. Winner of first game, A or B, plays winner of second team, C or D, and so on for championship.

Sack Race Relay
Age: 8 up

EQUIPMENT: Burlap bag for each team.

FORMATION: Teams in file formation. Turning point 25 feet in front of each team.

DIRECTIONS: First player gets into sack feet first and hops to turning point and back. He hops out of sack and gives it to second player who repeats action, and so on until all finish.

Three-Legged Race
Age: 8 up

EQUIPMENT: A belt or 2-foot strip of clothesline for each pair of contestants.

FORMATION: Pairs of contestants with their inside legs tied at ankles placed on starting line. Finish line is some 60 feet away.

DIRECTIONS: At signal, pairs of contestants race to finish line.

VARIATION: Have couples race *backward*. Confusion and collisions result.

Bean Bag Relay

No: 2 or more teams   Age: 8 up

EQUIPMENT: Bean bags or similar objects.

FORMATION: Players of each team in single file. Bean bag or similar object is placed in small circle short distance in front of team.

DIRECTIONS: First player of each team runs to circle, picks up bean bag, and returns to team. He hands bean bag to second player who runs to circle, places bean bag in it and returns, tagging third player. This is continued until last man finishes. Bean bags must be placed entirely within circle before player is allowed to continue.

Soccer Relay

Age: 10 up

EQUIPMENT: Soccer balls or large playground balls.

FORMATION: Teams lined up in file formation. First player of each team has ball. Thirty feet in front of each team is turning line.

DIRECTIONS: At signal, first players place ball on ground and kick it to turning line and back. After reaching their team, they return ball to second player, who places it on ground and continues relay. This continues until first player is back at head of line.

Hippodrome Race

Age: 10 up

EQUIPMENT: Four small carts or "chariots," long colored ribbons, stakes.

FORMATION: Broad circular course is laid out with stakes. Drivers are seated in chariots, holding reins of colored ribbons, and are pulled around course by two "horses."

DIRECTIONS: Race is three times around course, and colors are green, blue, red, and white—ancient Hippodrome colors.

Siamese Centipede Race

Age: 8 up

EQUIPMENT: A 10-foot pole for each team.

FORMATION: Six people form team and get astride 10-foot pole—three facing forward and three backward.

DIRECTIONS: At signal, each "centipede" races to goal, and without turning around, returns to starting place. Team to return first without mishaps is winner.

Hurdle Relay (Broomstick Relay)

Age: 11 up

EQUIPMENT: Each group has broomstick, or straight stick.

FORMATION: Divide into equal groups. Line up in single file.

DIRECTIONS: Players 1 and 2 hold broomstick on each end. Keeping it close to ground they run down line of players, each jumping it in turn. As soon as end of line is reached, No. 1 stays there, and No. 2 goes back with the broomstick to No. 3 at head of line. No. 2 and No. 3 come down line this time. This continues until No. 1 is back at head of line.

Dizzy Izzy Relay (Twister)

Age: 9 up

EQUIPMENT: Baseball bat, umbrella, cane or straight stick; one for each team.

FORMATION: Equal size groups in single file. Stick or other object is placed about 50 feet from starting place of group.

DIRECTIONS: First players run forward, place hands on top of stick, then bend over and put their heads on their hands. They keep their feet firmly on ground and, without straightening up, walk around stick five or six times. A counter will count for each so that they will know when to go. Player then staggers back and tags next player, who goes down and repeats action of first. Continue until all finish. Warning: Place human buffers at danger points, for contestants cannot run in straight line after turning.

Kangaroo Relay

Age: 12 up

EQUIPMENT: Ball for each team.

FORMATION: Teams line up in single file with several feet between players in line.

DIRECTIONS: Players hold ball between knees and skip to next person.

VARIATION: Pick up single ball from pile with knees and drop in basket. Must hop with knees together like a bunny.

Barrel Hoop Relay (Lariat Loop)

Age: 8 up

EQUIPMENT: 4 hoops for each team.

FORMATION: Teams in single file.

DIRECTIONS: First man takes hoop, steps into it, pulls it up over his body and head, and passes it to second man. First man immediately picks up second hoop and does same. This continues all way to finish. Last man in turn puts it over his head first this time, and hoops travel back to first man. First group with all four hoops back, wins.

VARIATIONS: Use inner tubes or rope loops.

Toad Frog Relay

Age: 10 up

FORMATION: Teams in file formation with turning point some 15 feet in front of each line.

DIRECTIONS: First player of each team assumes squat position. At starting signal, he reaches forward with his hands and places them on floor. Keeping hands in place, he leans forward and brings feet up, with legs outside arms. This action is repeated as he hops forward to turning point and returns to his team. Other players repeat the action in turn.

Elephant Walk

Age: 10 up

FORMATION: Stunt or file relay. Player No. 1 locks legs around No. 2 and bends backward. No. 1 crawls between legs of No. 2 and grasps back of his ankles. No. 2 leans forward and places both hands on floor.

DIRECTIONS: From this position they attempt to walk forward to goal and return. No. 1 must raise his body to keep from dragging. Rest of team pair off and run doing their turn. This relay is always good for much merriment from onlookers and participants.

Crabwalk Relay

Age: 10 up

FORMATION: Players of each team in single file. Turning point is 15 feet in front of each team.

DIRECTIONS: First player of each team assumes squat position, leans backward toward turning point, and puts both hands on ground. Back is raised, and weight is supported equally by arms and legs. Player walks face up in this position to turning point and back. Rest of players continue action in turn. Faster progress is made when right hand and foot move together.

Rowboat Relay

Age: 10 up

FORMATION: Players of each team paired off in single file with turning point 15 feet in front of each line.

DIRECTIONS: First and second players sit down, one behind other, with their backs to turning point. Player No. 1 puts his feet in lap of No. 2 and locks his ankles. They crabwalk backward toward turning point, with No. 2 using both his hands and feet and No. 1 using his hands. Upon reaching turning point, they return to their team in backward position by merely changing their direction. Other players continue action until all finish.

Crow Hop Relay

Age: 7 up

FORMATION: Players of each team in single file.

DIRECTIONS: First player grabs his ankles with arms outside knees, walks to turning point and returns. Second player repeats his action; and so on until last player has finished.

VARIATION: Duck Waddle Relay.

Directions: Same formation. Players sit on their heels in deep knee bend with hands on hips. They walk or waddle to turning point and return, tagging second player. This action is repeated until all complete relay.

Potato Spear Relay

Age: 11 up

EQUIPMENT: One fork for each team and one potato for each player.

FORMATION: Teams in single file. Potatoes line up at distance from starting line.

DIRECTIONS: First man takes fork, runs to potato, spears it with fork, returns to starting line and puts it in basket or sack. Second man takes fork. Action is repeated until last man finishes. At no time may hand touch potato. If potato is dropped, it must be speared again with fork.

VARIATIONS: (a) Each member of team provided with fork, sharp stick. On signal, first man spears potato and passes it to second man, who must spear it without using hands and pass it on. First team through, wins.

(b) The Rodeo.

EQUIPMENT: Potatoes, boxes, sharpened stick, and broomstick pony for each participant. (Larger team members can be used as horses. Watch spurring!)

FORMATION: Teams in single file; members mounted on horses (stick or human); row of 4 potatoes per team at some distance from team; box near team.

DIRECTIONS: Give each cowboy sharpened stick. Riders and ponies gallop down to their first potato, spear it with stick, and convey potato back to their box. Then they gallop back for next potato, and so on until all potatoes are reposing in their own boxes. Hands cannot be used.

Running Relays

2 or more teams   Age: 8 up

EQUIPMENT: Bean bags, balls, handkerchiefs—anything to use for baton.

FORMATION: Teams in single file (usually).

Track Relay (Base running).

FORMATION: Use softball diamond or else mark off square field with tenpins or pop bottles. Place teams at each corner.

DIRECTIONS: At signal, first player runs around square and returns home, handing bean bag to second player. Continue until last man finishes. If player misses base or runs inside tenpin, he must repeat run.

VARIATIONS: (a) Rope Jumping Relay.

DIRECTIONS: Each player must jump rope around course.

(b) Run, Toss, and Catch Relay.

FORMATION: Each team lined in single file short distance from rope (or net) stretched between two trees (or posts). This rope should be about 10 feet off ground.

DIRECTIONS: First player runs to rope, throws bean bag (or ball) over, catches it, and returns to line. Second man takes ball and repeats action. This continues until all finish. Should player not throw ball over rope or not catch it, he must repeat action until successfully completed.

Bean Bag Circle Toss Relay

Age: 8 up

EQUIPMENT: Bean bags or similar objects which can be thrown.

FORMATION: Teams in file formation. Circle 3 or 4 feet in diameter is drawn 15 feet or so in front of each file.

DIRECTIONS: First player of each team throws bean bag and tries to make it land in circle. If he misses, bean bag must be retrieved and he must try again. After successful throw, player runs to circle, recovers bean bag, and returns to his team where he gives it to next player. This continues until last player finishes. Accuracy plays as important a part as speed in this relay.

TAG GAMES

Tag games are favorites of all who can run. A minimum of directions, adaptability to any space, and much activity combine to make these ideal for the elementary age. However, older youth also enjoy these and adults have played with much enjoyment Squirrel Cage, Vis-à-Vis, Bronco Busting, Old Plug, Scoot. The leader need only look with his age group in mind to discover interesting activity for all ages.

These games are called "Tag" or "It" games since one or more players are selected to be the chasers while the rest are the hiders or runners. There are several basic formations which apply to most of the games. For ease in learning and application while teaching we shall list the games under several categories.

CIRCLE "IT" GAMES

Number Call

No: 8-30   Age: 8 up

EQUIPMENT: Blindfold (for leader).

FORMATION: Players sitting in chairs in circle with It in center. Players are numbered. "It" in center of circle is blindfolded.

DIRECTIONS: "It" calls from two to four numbers, and players must change seats. "It" tries to tag players. They move quietly, trying to exchange places and slip by It without being caught—dodging when tagged at. If caught, player exchanges places with It.

Open Market

No: 8-30   Age: 8 up

FORMATION: One player is It in center of circle.

DIRECTIONS: All other players are given names of things that are commonly sold at city markets, such as hogs, sheep, chickens, turkeys, grain, hay, fruits. To make game more lively, several players may have one name. Center player calls out, "Sheep, hay, and turkeys change!" at which all of that name scramble to change places. "It" also tries to get seat. One left without seat takes the center and becomes It. When It calls, "Open market," everybody changes.

Scoot

No: 10-50   Age: 8 up

FORMATION: Players seated in circle of sturdy chairs. One chair is vacant. "It" stands in center.

DIRECTION: "It" calls out, "Scoot right," and person who is sitting on left of vacant chair quickly slides into it, and so on around circle, each person going to his right. "It" tries to sit in vacant chair. If successful, person who was supposed to slide into chair becomes "It." "It" can call out any time, "Scoot left," and the circle must change direction of scooting.

VARIATION: Have several vacant chairs with same number of people being It.

Bull in the Ring

No: 10-30   Age: 6 up

FORMATION: Players in circle. One player, the "Bull," in center.

DIRECTIONS: Good for youngsters. Players form ring around "bull" holding hands. "Bull" tries to break through by rushing, lunging or pulling. He cannot duck under. If he escapes, players chase him. Whoever catches him becomes bull in turn.

VARIATION: Whoever lets bull escape, becomes It or "Bull."

Frog in the Sea

No: 12-40   Age: 8 up

EQUIPMENT: Outdoor yard or large room or shallow water.

FORMATION: Players form circle around five "frogs" who sit with their feet crossed, tailor-fashion.

DIRECTIONS: The players in circle skip (if on land) and walk (if in water) close to frogs and back, repeating the words: "Frog in the sea, can't catch me." Frogs try to tag any player without rising or uncrossing their feet. If player is tagged, he changes places with frog, and frog joins circle.

VARIATION: Player tagged may sit in circle with frogs instead of changing places. Game continues until there is one player untagged.

Sewing Up the Gap

No: 10-50   Age: 6 up

FORMATION: Players form circle. Two persons are chosen: one, the "Chaser"; the other, It.

DIRECTIONS: Object is to tag other person *before* he can sew up all gaps between other players. This is done by person being chased, It, weaving in and out among players of circle. "It" passes between two players, they sew up gap by joining hands. Person being chased wants to close all gaps with himself on inside and chaser on outside at close of game. If It is tagged by chaser, roles are reversed.

Cat and Rat (Use any animals' names.)

No: 10-40   Age: 8 up

FORMATION: Players in circle. Two players are chosen to be Cat and Rat.

DIRECTIONS: Rat is inside circle and says, "I am the Rat." Cat (use two if you want) is outside circle of players and says, "I am the Cat and I will catch you." "If you can," says Rat. Players help Rat by letting him pass under their arches freely as he dodges around, but they try to hinder Cat or cats. When Cat catches Rat others take their places.

Circle Tag (Bamboo Tag)

No: 10-25. Age: 8 up

FORMATION: Players in circle. "It" stands in center.

DIRECTIONS: Bean bag (or any other object) is passed from person to person around circle. "It" tries to tag person who has object. Players must receive object when it is offered. Players may first pass object in one direction and then another to fool It. When player is tagged with object, he becomes It.

Who's the Leader

No: 10-40 Age: 8 up

FORMATION: Group standing or sitting in circle.

DIRECTIONS: One player is elected It and goes out. Group then elects leader who will lead them in action, such as clapping hands, patting heads, rubbing stomachs, twirling thumbs. Leader changes from one action to another, and rest of group follows as quickly as it can. When leader is finally discovered by It, new one is selected to be It, and game continues.

Drop the Handkerchief

No: 10-40 Age: 8 up

FORMATION: Players in circle. "It" moves around outside with handkerchief or rag.

DIRECTIONS: "It" drops handkerchief and continues around circle. When discovered by person behind whom it was dropped, handkerchief is picked up and chase is given. If It succeeds in circling around and reaching player's position where handkerchief was dropped without being tagged, he exchanges places with tagged player. Game continues with new It.

VARIATION: May also be played to music with players walking in time to it. When music stops they stop; when speeded up or slowed down players react accordingly.

Flying Dutchman

No: 12-40 Age: 8 up

FORMATION: Players form ring by couples. Couples hold hands.

DIRECTIONS: One couple is It. "It" walks around outside of circle.

Directly they slap hands of one couple and start running around circle in direction they are going. Other couple starts in opposite direction. Couples hold hands as they run. First couple back to vacant place, wins. Other couple then is It and begins new round.

VARIATION: When couples meet as they race around circle, have them each stop and shake hands; or recite proverb or nursery rhyme; or do stunt such as kneeling on one knee, or putting finger over head and twirling around three times.

Swat Tag

No: 8-30   Age: 8 up

FORMATION: Similar to Drop the Handkerchief. Players (can use couples as in Flying Dutchman with two swatters) form circle and put hands behind back. All look straight ahead.

DIRECTIONS: "It" circles around outside of circle and directly places a swatter (folded newspaper, a bag or stocking filled with sawdust or old rags) in hands of player. Player then begins beating player on his right with swatter, trying to hit him on seat. He chases player around circle and back to original position. Player with swatter then becomes It and continues action.

VARIATION: Couples—partners face counterclockwise—use two newspapers.

Three Deep

No: 12-40   Age: 8 up

FORMATION: Players stand in double circle with one player standing directly behind player in inner circle. "Chaser" is on inside of circle, and one who is "It" stands outside.

DIRECTIONS: "Chaser" attempts to tag It. "It" may run or dodge around circle for as long as he or she wants, but if tagged, the players exchange places, and person who was It becomes "chaser" and vice-versa. "It" may get someone else to be It by managing to get into circle without being tagged and standing in front of any players who are standing two deep. The person who was on outside of circle then would be player who would become It. Action would continue then with new player as It until "chaser" succeeded in tagging him or he managed to stand three deep.

VARIATION: Whip the Donkey.

DIRECTIONS: Form as in Three Deep, although if space permits, four or five in file is better. Groups remain well apart all facing center, and with arms around waist and firmly holding player immediately in front. Two players remain out; one, Driver who has whip; other is extra tail. Each group is Donkey with head and tail (front and rear players respectively.) Player who is extra tail tries to hook on to tail of donkey. Donkeys try to keep Extra Tail from annexing himself by swinging around. Extra Tail, with Driver in pursuit, tries to secure Donkey. If he succeeds, head of that group must then become Extra Tail, while former Extra Tail grabs whip and gives chase.

Fire on the Mountain

No: 12-30   Age: 8 up

FORMATION: Two circles. Boys stand behind their partners who are girls. "It" (or Its—may be spare boys, or girls, or both) stands in middle.

DIRECTIONS: "It" calls out, "Fire on the mountain, Run sheep, run." Everybody holds up hands and circles; boys counterclockwise, girls clockwise. Soon It calls out, "Fire is out." "Its" try to get partners as all the rest are doing same. Whoever is left out becomes leader.

Old Plug

No: 12-40   Age: 9 up

EQUIPMENT: Volleyball, playground ball, or tennis ball.

FORMATION: Players stand in circle using ball. Four players are in center of circle, each with arms around one ahead.

DIRECTIONS: Players in circle pass ball around and throw at Old Plug, rear person. He can be hit only on "rear." Old Plug tries to keep his head toward ball. Person who hits Old Plug becomes head man, and tail man retires to circle.

Center Base

No: 10-30   Age: 7 up

EQUIPMENT: Playground or volleyball.

FORMATION: Players standing about five feet apart, in circle. One player is in center of circle with ball. This player is It.

DIRECTIONS: Player who is in center throws ball to another in circle and runs out of circle. Player who catches ball runs to center, places ball on ground and starts chasing first player. If first player can return to ball without being tagged, he may be It again. However, if he is tagged, he must take his place in circle, and second player becomes It.

Circle Out Ball

No: 20-50   Age: 10 up

EQUIPMENT: Large rubber playground ball or volleyball.

FORMATION: Players standing in circle with arms crossed over chest with ball in middle.

DIRECTIONS: Man in center tries to roll ball through legs of players in circle. Players cannot move their feet, but must attempt to block ball with their knees by twisting and bending their legs. Arms must remain folded over chests during game. Player who allows ball to pass between his legs will exchange places with person in center, and game continues.

Spoke Tag

No: 20-60   Age: 9 up

FORMATION: One player is It. The rest form several files of equal number of players with heads of these lines meeting in common center. (Files of players converging in center resemble spokes of wheel.)

DIRECTIONS: "It" goes around rim of wheel and tags last player in line. This player tags one in front of him, and tag is passed along until whole line knows it is to move. As soon as player sees that his line has been touched, he may tag person in front of him, whether he has been tagged or not. Then players chase It around outside and try not to be last one back in line. Last player to return to his line is It for next time. Fun in this game is in keeping watch to make quick start and also in trying to pass those in front on way around circle. "It" may also change directions, causing whole line to reverse its directions in running around outside.

SCATTERED CHASE GAMES

These tag games have no specific formation for the players. "It" chases and attempts to tag players before they reach a base or assume some position which insures a brief immunity. Upon being tagged or hit a player becomes It. Several players may be Its at the same time, depending upon the size of the group or the type of game.

Tag Games

No: 8-40   Age: 6 up

FORMATION: One or more persons chosen It (depending on size of group). Rest of players scattered in playing area.

DIRECTIONS: In these tag games, unless otherwise specified, there is an It who may touch any player he chooses after starting signal. Player is safe if he fulfills certain conditions.

Squat Tag: To be safe, player must squat to keep from being tagged.

Sole Mate Tag: To be safe, player must have his shoe sole touching sole of another.

Ankle Tag: Here he must be touching his own ankle with his hand to be safe.

Cross Tag: When It is chasing another player, third player can run between them. Then It must chase this player, instead.

Chinese Tag: When It tags another player, tagged player becomes It and must hold spot where he was tagged.

Back-to-Back Tag: Players are safe from It if standing back to back with another.

Hindu Tag: Players are safe when on their knees bowing down with foreheads touching ground.

Base Dodge Ball

No: 8-30   Age: 8 up

EQUIPMENT: Playground ball and some objects for bases.

FORMATION: All players standing on bases, scattered at random, with exception of one who has ball and is It.

DIRECTIONS: Players signal to one another and try to exchange bases; player who is It tries to hit them with ball when they run between bases. If he succeeds, player who was hit becomes It. "It" may also steal someone's base if it is vacated. That person would then take ball and become It.

Elbow Tag
Age: 12 up

FORMATION: Couples, with elbows linked, scattered around with outside hands on hips. One player is It, and another the chaser.

DIRECTIONS: "It" is chasing another person who may at any time "hook on" to outside elbow of any player. When he does this, other person of couple becomes It. If chaser tags person he is chasing, they reverse roles. With large crowds use more than one It and chaser.

Statue
No: 6-30   Age: 6 up

FORMATION: Players stand in couples informally about ground.

DIRECTIONS: Couples take hands and, at a signal whistle from leader, they swing each other around. At a second signal, which should be given before they get dizzy, they stop instantly, each player becoming statue by maintaining pose of movement he was in when whistle blew. Hands should be released when signal to stop is given. Leader announces best statue, and then gives signal for another one.

Sardines
No: 8-50   Age: 6 up

FORMATION: One player hides; others come together in informal group.

DIRECTIONS: Players count to 100. When counting is finished, they set out to hunt. When player finds hider, he secretly joins him, hiding from rest of group. This continues until all players are hidden with original hider and are "packed in like sardines." When last hunter discovers spot, game starts over, first finder becoming hider.

I Spy
No: 8-40   Age: 6 up

DIRECTIONS: Good for children. "It" shuts eyes and counts to one hundred. Others go hide. "It" shouts, "Here I come, ready or not. All around base are It. "It" then tries to find hiders. On seeing one he shouts, "I see Johnny," and tries to beat hider back to base. "It" must call out correctly name of person hiding, or he doesn't have to move and thus be caught. First one caught is It next time.

VARIATION: Kick the Can—Can is base. If hider gets home first he kicks can and "It" must recover can and put it back before he can look for others.

Squirrel in the Cage

No: 15-200   Age: 6 up

FORMATION: Cage formed by having two or three people holding hands in little circle. "Squirrels" stand in center of circle. Several "Its" are spotted around.

DIRECTIONS: At signal, all "squirrels" must change cages. "It" tries to get into cage. Those who fail become It. Occasionally shift, so that you have new set of squirrels.

Back to Back (Vis-à-Vis or Icebreaker)

No: 10-200   Age: 6-12

FORMATION: Players paired at random with one or more Its.

DIRECTIONS: All players paired except one, two, or more, depending on size of group. One of unpaired players acts as leader and gives commands which others follow, such as "Knee to Knee," "Nose to Nose," "Thumb to Thumb." Sooner or later he calls "Vis-à-Vis" and all must find new partner and stand back to back with him. Odd players also try to get new partners. Players left out become odd men and one acts as leader in calling out commands. When it is used as get-acquainted game, have players turn around, shake hands, and exchange names.

Pussy Wants a Corner

No: 5-20   Age: 6-9

EQUIPMENT: Objects for bases, such as chalk marks, stones, bean bags.

FORMATION: Each player stands on base, scattered at random with exception of "Pussy" (It).

DIRECTIONS: "It" moves around saying, "Pussy wants a corner." Players try to exchange bases without Pussy's taking their place. If Pussy does beat player to his base, then that player becomes Pussy. Sometimes leader may call "All change bases." Then all players must exchange bases. Player left without base becomes Pussy.

VARIATION: Moving Day.

DIRECTIONS: Players in lines, exchanging places constantly. "Renter" tries to occupy position when player leaves to exchange with another. All must move when leader cries "Moving Day."

Lame Fox

No: 10-40   Age: 8 up

FORMATION: One player is fox and is in his den. Other players are chickens and are scattered around area.

DIRECTIONS: Chickens move near den and tease fox to come out, saying, "Lame fox, lame fox! Can't catch me!" Fox moves out at an opportune time and tries to tag as many chickens as possible. Fox can take only three running steps upon leaving his den and hereafter is restricted to hopping on one foot. However, he is allowed to change feet upon tiring. Players tagged must retire to fox's den and await his return. They become new foxes and, upon signal from first fox, help in tagging chickens when they approach den again. Last chicken caught becomes first lame fox in new game.

Spud

No: 8-25   Age: 9 up

EQUIPMENT: Use playground ball, volleyball, or tennis ball.

FORMATION: Players scattered around playing area. Leader has ball.

DIRECTIONS: Leader bounces ball and calls out name of player. (Players can also be numbered and call out numbers.) Leader throws ball. "It," the player whose name was called out, recovers ball and attempts to hit another player. Each miss counts a "spud." "It" must recover ball and throw again. Three "spuds" and It must suffer some penalty, or else be put out of the game. When someone is hit by ball he becomes It and must chase after other players.

Old Man Stick

No: 10-50   Age: 7 up

FORMATION: All the players except one (It) are scattered over the ground.

DIRECTIONS: "It" throws a stick as far as he can, and calls the name of a player. The player whose name is called runs and gets the stick, and immediately starts a chase to touch others with the stick. Anyone touched becomes a helper to catch others in the chase, but such ones must be caught and held until Old Man Stick can come and touch them. One caught may make a get-a-way before touched, if he can. When all have been touched, the game starts over, with Old Man Stick throwing the stick and calling the name of another It.

Fish and Net

No: 12-40   Age: 6 up

FORMATION: Five players represent the "Net"; the remaining players, the "Fish," go to the far end of the playing area.

DIRECTIONS: The players representing the Net clasp hands, and on the signal, "Swim, fish, swim," the Net attempts to surround as many fish as possible. If the Net is broken all Fish are allowed to escape. All players caught become part of the Net and the play continues. The last five persons to be caught serve as the Net during the next game. On the signal, "Swim, fish, swim," all players except Net cross from one playing area to other.

Old Mean Cat

No: 10-40   Age: 6 up

FORMATION: Several players are Mice and each chooses a place for his hole. (Indoors, it may be the corner of a room, under a table, or behind a chair. Outdoors, it may be a tree, stone, or fence corner.)

DIRECTIONS: Mice assemble in a ring in the middle of the play space. The other players, the Cats, are scattered around. The leader calls, "Cats are hungry," which is the signal for the Mice to scamper to their holes, chased by the Cats. Those caught exchange places with the Cats.

ZONE TAG GAMES

The tag games described here involve a safety zone in which the players rest. On signal, they must advance into hostile territory where they can be tagged by It, therefore becoming the helpers of It. The players attempt to run across this zone and reach the opposite safety zone or else return to their original safe zone.

Pom-Pom Pullaway

No: 12-50   Age: 7 up

FORMATION: Two lines about 50 feet apart are drawn or designated. All players stand behind one of lines, except one player who is It.

DIRECTIONS: "It stands in center and shouts, "Pom-Pom Pullaway! If you don't come I'll pull you away." At this signal, all players must leave their safety zone and run across to opposite line. "It" tries to tag as many as possible before they reach safety line. Those tagged join It in center and help on next call. Game continues until all are caught. First one caught is It next time.

VARIATION: Fish in the Ocean.

DIRECTIONS: Same as Pom-Pom Pullaway. Different rhyme. "It" shouts, "Fish in the Ocean, Fish in the Sea; Don't get the notion, You'll get by me." When several are caught, they form net and scoop up runners. If net breaks, all get away that trip.

Old Man, Old Man

No: 10-50   Age: 7 up

FORMATION: Line is drawn near each end of ground. Back of one line is Old Man; back of other, rest of players.

DIRECTIONS: Players advance near Old Man's line and say: "Old man, old man, what's the matter with you?" Old Man replies, "The moon's gone down, and I've lost my shoe." At this, players put forward a foot and begin asking, "Is this it? Is this it?" Old Man moves up and down line as if he were examining their shoes, but cannot come nearer than three feet to line, players being three feet other side. Presently he calls, "My shoe, my shoe," Whereupon visiting players flee for their own line, Old Man chasing. Any touched in chase join Old Man, and become his confederates. Game is up when all have been caught.

Ham, Backbone, Spare Ribs, Bacon!

No: 10-50   Age: 9 up

FORMATION: Line is drawn across each end of ground. In space between, one player who is It takes his stand. The other players stand back of lines, same number at each end.

DIRECTIONS: Player in center space calls, "Ham, backbone, spare ribs, bacon!" Word "bacon" is signal for other players to run to opposite field, center player trying to catch them. Any caught remain in center and become catchers with one who is It. Point in play is that no one may run except on word "bacon" and this must be called by original It. He may call, "Ham, backbone, spare ribs," or just "Backbone," but the run can be made only on word "bacon." Other helpers whom he has caught may make whatever calls they wish, but *run must be made only on the call of one who is It*. Anyone starting on wrong call is counted caught and goes to center to help catch.

Go Home

No: 10-50   Age: 6-12

FORMATION: Players all standing at one of two goal lines, with It in center.

DIRECTIONS: "It" calls, "Go home, go home," and players must run for opposite goal line. Any tagged or taking excessive time in reaching opposite goal become Its helpers.

TAG GAMES OF DEFINITE PATTERNS

Streets and Alleys

No: 15-50   Age: 8 up

FORMATION: Two players are chosen to be runner and chaser. All other players, in rows facing front of room, stand in parallel lines with arms outstretched so as to touch hands on either side of them. This makes series of aisles or streets.

DIRECTIONS: When leader blows his whistle, or calls, "Change," players (keeping their arms outstretched) make quarter turn to right. That makes new aisles. Neither runner nor chaser may break through column, nor duck under. Each time leader blows his whistle, there is quarter turn to right. Fun of game consists in sudden changes that leader calls. When runner is caught, new players are selected to take places of chaser and runner.

VARIATION: When runner tires he may stop in front of player who will then take his place. Chaser is allowed to do same thing. In large crowds several chasers and runners may be used.

Chase the Fox

No: 10-50   Age: 7 up

FORMATION: One player is fox and another is hound. Other players stand in two parallel lines, those in each line standing one behind another. Fox is head of one line, and hound the other.

DIRECTIONS: At signal to start, fox runs, winding in and out around members of his line until he reaches bottom, when he turns and comes up other line in like manner. Fox does not have to run between each two players, but may skip any he wishes and choose his own track. Hound must follow exact track of fox. Should he "get off the track," he must go back to place where he lost it and take it up again. If fox gets back to head of second line before hound catches him, he is in "free" and takes his place at foot of line, hunter becoming fox. Should he be caught, he becomes hunter, original hunter going to foot of line of fox. Head member of line becomes fox.

Bronco Busting

No: 20-150   Age: 9 up

FORMATION: Scattered lines of four players with their arms clasped around waist of player in front. Several single players (Bronco Busters) move among them.

DIRECTIONS: Single player attempts to hook on to rear man of four players (the Bronco). They attempt to prevent this by twisting, turning, running, without breaking their arm clasps. If Bronco Buster is successful in grasping Bronco, leader of file must leave and look for another Bronco to grab onto. Bronco or line having most of its original members is winner.

Chair Tag

No: 10-40   Age: 6 up

FORMATION: Group is seated in several lines on substantial chairs or in regular desks in schoolroom. One person is chaser and another is It.

DIRECTIONS: "It" tries to elude chaser and take place of someone by sitting on edge of chair and pushing sitter off. Player then becomes It. If It is tagged, chasing is reversed. This is fast game, if It moves rapidly from one chair to another without running too long.

Fox and Geese, or Wheel Tag

No: 8-30   Age: 6 up

FORMATION: Mark level surface with illustration shown. Chairs, lines, string may be used.

DIRECTIONS: Fox, who is It, chases others, trying to tag someone. All must run in paths of spoke, hub, or rim. Geese may jump across paths, but fox cannot. Failure to stay in paths or to be tagged, makes that person It next time. The hub (center) is safe but can be occupied by only one at a time. Last one in takes possession and all others must leave. Fox cannot tag across paths.

X—The Hub is safe for *one* player at a time.

GAMES OF THE ATHLETIC TYPE

BALL GAMES AND SPORTS OF LOW ORGANIZATION

The games presented here have as their primary aim the fun of the group and fellowship involved. In these low-organized games individuals of all experience may participate upon an equal basis. Competition is minimized. In its stead, total group participation is encouraged. These games, while employing simple rules and requiring a minimum of equipment, are attractive to young and old alike. Picnics, outings, parties, scout groups, students, church camps, and assemblies can all use this type of activity to good advantage.

End Zone Ball

No: 8-30   Age: 8 up

EQUIPMENT: Rubber playground or volleyball. (Football can sometimes be used for passing and catching practice.)

FORMATION: Field approximately 30 × 60 feet, divided by a middle line. At each end of field is zone 3 feet wide across width of field. Several players, depending upon number of sides, occupy this end zone. The opposing team also places same number of players in end zone and others in large zone. (If there were nine players to a team, three might occupy the 3-foot end zone and the other six the large zone. See diagram.)

END ZONE BALL COURT

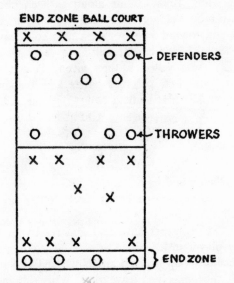

DIRECTIONS: One side puts ball into play. They try to pass or roll ball to their teammates in end zone. If teammate gains possession of ball without taking more than one foot out of end zone he scores point. If ball goes over end zone or is intercepted, opponents take over. Some of players in large zone must be defenders of their goal and try to interrupt opponents' throws. Upon interrupting, they throw quickly to teammates closer to middle line who are passers. There, players in turn try to throw or roll ball to teammates in end zone. From time to time, positions should be exchanged so that all players will have chance to throw, catch, and defend. Practically any number can play. In large groups two balls can be used. Only rule necessary is that players are not allowed to cross middle line.

Stop Ball

No: 12-40   Age: 9 up

EQUIPMENT: Any rubber ball.

FORMATION: Two teams of equal numbers. One team scattered over playing area. Other team stands in line with player holding ball.

DIRECTIONS: First player bats ball into air and begins running around his team. Team counts aloud as each circuit is completed. Player on fielding team retrieves ball, and rest of his teammates run toward him. As soon as whole team is in line, they yell "Stop!" Number of complete revolutions by batter before "Stop" was yelled is then given. Teams now reverse roles, player with ball becomes batter and runner, and other team disperses in order to field ball. Continue as long as wind lasts!

Circle Dodge Ball

No: 12-50   Age: 9 up

EQUIPMENT: Playground ball.

FORMATION: Two sides; one forms circle, other takes scattered positions within circle.

DIRECTIONS: Circle players have ball and try to hit those inside circle. Any player inside circle who is hit, takes place in ring. Those of inside group may do anything they wish to evade ball except that they may not leave ring. When all inside players have been hit, two groups exchange places.

Double Zone Dodge Ball

No: 8-60   Age: 8 up

EQUIPMENT: One playground ball.

FORMATION: One third of "A" team in zone at end of field. One third of "B" team on other end of field in their zone. Field is divided in center. Rest of "A" team is on opposite side of division from third of their team. Same with "B" team.

DIRECTIONS: Each team has a ball. "A" players try to hit "B" players next to division. Same with "B" team. Players in end zones can't be hit. When player of team in dodge zone is hit, he must change sides and move into other dodge zone.

Diagram of a Double Zone DODGE BALL COURT

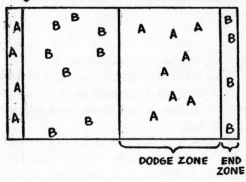

DODGE ZONE   END ZONE

Kick Goal

No: 10-50   Age: 10 up

EQUIPMENT: Volleyball, soccer ball, or other playground ball.

POSITION: Two teams facing each other, with boundary lines indicating middle of field, side lines, and opposite goals.

DIRECTIONS: One team puts ball in play. It attempts to kick it across opposite goal. Other team attempts to block it and kick it back. Teams cannot cross middle line. Ball must not be touched with hands or it counts as goal for other side. Point is counted only when ball crosses goal line below the belt. Other team gets to put ball in play after a goal.

VARIATION: Arrange two teams in circle, each occupying one half of circle. Try to kick ball through circle on opponents' side. Captains may roam in center. All other players are limited to one step. Ball cannot be kicked above waist high or touched by hands.

Sponge Ball

No: 2-20   Age: 10 up

EQUIPMENT: Large sponge ball formed by cutting from large car sponge. Net (badminton, volleyball) or rope with streamers.

Paddles (ping-pong, paddle tennis) or rackets (badminton or tennis), for each player. (Paddles and rackets can be eliminated and game played by hand.)

DIRECTIONS: Game is played like volleyball, with sponge hit by paddles or hands. Sponge ball is very light and remains in air much longer than ordinary balls. All ages will enjoy playing this.

Forceback
No: 2-40   Age: 10 up

EQUIPMENT: Bean bag, any type of ball, or football.

FORMATION: Two teams with goal at each end of field. Length of playing area depends on equipment being used. Football would require goals from 50 to 100 yards; bean bag would require from 50 to 100 feet.

DIRECTIONS: Teams try to throw or kick ball over opponents' line. Each team is allowed one kick or throw with players rotating their turns. Ball is kicked or thrown back toward opponents' line from point of its being touched. When caught, player is allowed three running steps toward opponent's line. Ball must go over line on fly to be scored as goal. Balls caught behind line are brought to lines to be kicked or thrown.

Hand Hockey
No: 8-30   Age: 10 up

EQUIPMENT: One playground, soccer, or volleyball.

FORMATION: Two teams aligned on their side of court facing offensive goals. (A 10-foot marked area in middle of goal line.)

DIRECTIONS: Object is for team to bat ball over goal line between goal posts and defend its own goal. When ball is rolled out and game begins, players attempt to push, roll, or bat ball with open hand toward their goal. No player can hit ball twice in succession. Referees should prevent unnecessary roughness.

Four-Square Ball
No: 4-20   Age: 12 up

EQUIPMENT: One volleyball; one ruled square 14 × 14 feet divided into four equal parts.

FORMATION: One man in each square and line of players outside of playing area.

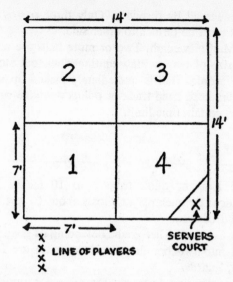

DIRECTIONS: Server starts action by dropping ball in his square and hitting to opposite square (diagonal; No. 2 court). Ball is kept in play by each man hitting ball into another square.

RULES: Ball must bounce before it is hit. Player cannot hit ball straight back to square from which it just came. Player must not guide ball, but must hit it with either or both hands. Player must have both feet in his square when hitting ball. Slamming ball is not allowed. Ball that hits line is counted a miss. When player misses he drops to end of waiting line. First man in waiting line drops to square No. 1. Rotation is toward server's court (No. 4). Object of game is to rotate around until player becomes server and to remain in as long as one can without missing. This is a fast game and a very attractive one for youngsters and adults alike.

Newcomb

No: 4-40   Age: 10 up

EQUIPMENT: Playground ball or volleyball with net.

FORMATION: Two teams with two or more on a side.

DIRECTIONS: Rules are same as in volleyball with following exceptions: Ball is thrown instead of batted; ball must be caught by player, but immediately thrown to teammate or back over net; ball is served by throwing. Only three passes are allowed before ball must be thrown to other side.

VARIATION: Mad Newcomb. Two or more balls are used, depending upon size of teams. Play continues without stopping when points are scored. Ball is immediately picked up and put into play. Scorers need keep track of points and give running score. Play within certain time limit.

Floor Hockey

No: 8-20   Age: 10 up

EQUIPMENT: Ring or quoit from 6 to 10 inches in diameter. Wooden sticks for each player. Goals about 10 feet wide marked at each end of area.

FORMATION: Each team has goalie defending its goal. Playing area is divided into two parallels. Half the team are forwards and other half, guards.

DIRECTIONS: Opposing forwards scramble for quoit when it is tossed out. One maintaining possession carries it toward his goal with opponents' guards defending. Stick is inserted in quoit and pushed along floor. Quoit must be in contact with floor at all times. When passed to teammate, it must not leave surface. If this occurs, opposing team gets quoit out of bounds. Object is for either team to score goal by sliding quoit across goal line between markers. Guards attempt to steal quoit or intercept passes and in turn get quoit to their forwards. Blocking, tripping, or other rough play is not allowed. Whenever opponents both

FLOOR HOCKEY COURT

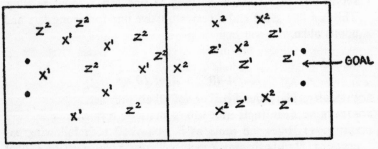

X^1 — Guards of X Team   Z^1 — Guards of Z Team
X^2 — Forwards of X Team   Z^2 — Forwards of Z Team

have their stick in quoit and neither can secure possession, referee stops the action, lines opponents up facing each other, and rolls quoit between them. Play continues as before. Team scoring greater number of goals wins.

VARIATION: When playing outdoors on field, rubber ball can be substituted for quoit. Old brooms with all except 6 or 8 inches of straw cut off make excellent sticks.

Keep It Up

No: 6-30   Ages: 10 up

EQUIPMENT: Volleyball or playground ball.

FORMATION: Players in circle with one in center.

DIRECTIONS: Player in center bats ball into air and counts one. Other players continue to bat ball, trying to keep it in air. Center player counts each tap aloud. Object of game is to see how many times group can hit ball into air before missing. Catching or hitting twice in succession by player is not allowed. Center player is allowed to hit ball and can direct it to that section of circle which had little action. Simpleness of game does not hurt its effectiveness. Especially effective when there is insufficient time for organized games.

Bowling on the Green

No: 2-20   Age: 10 up

EQUIPMENT: Golf ball and croquet balls.

DIRECTIONS: Roll golf ball to serve as mark; then roll croquet balls as close to golf ball as you can. Closest ball scores, or closest team balls if more than one ball of team is closest.

Three in a Hole

No: 5-20   Age: 12 up

EQUIPMENT: Ball (golf ball, chips, or rocks) and a stick.

FORMATION: Players are in circle, each player having hole which may be small circle or hole made by turning around on heel.

DIRECTIONS: All balls are tossed to center of ring described by holes of players. At signal, each player scrambles to get three balls in his hole. Balls cannot be touched except with stick. Any ball knocked beyond previously determined boundary must be returned. No player may knock ball from hole of another. One who first gets three balls in his hole, wins.

Hop Golf

No: 4-20   Age: 12 up

EQUIPMENT: Rubber playground balls; any desired number of greens, preferably nine.

FORMATION: Center ring several feet in diameter is made in center of play space. Greens are arranged around this circle at equal or unequal distances. A "cup" is in center of each green; this may be smaller ring about 1 foot in diameter.

DIRECTIONS: Player may never stand on both feet while on green or on tee. To start off, player goes to center ring and "drives" off from "tee." After putting ball in one cup, he goes back to "tee," "drives off," puts ball in another cup, and so on until he has put ball in each cup. In order to hit ball, he must stand on one foot and kick or hit ball toward desired green. If he is about to lose balance, he may jump out of circle and put both feet down, but if he puts both feet down within circle, he must start over. Player wins who makes all cups with fewest strokes.

Miniature Golf Course

No: 2-36   Age: 12 up

EQUIPMENT: Some old golf balls or small rubber balls. Old golf putters, croquet mallets, walking sticks.

FORMATION: Place nine coffee cans into ground in various grassy spots on lawn or field.

DIRECTIONS: Play as you would golf. Object is to make each hole in as few strokes as possible. Total your score at end of round of 9 holes. Low score wins.

NOTE: Lots of family fun as well as enjoyment with friends may be attained by such a course in one's yard. Small sand traps, water hazards, uncut grass (for roughs) add to game.

GAMES OF SOFTBALL VARIETY

Kickball

No: 8-40   Age: 9 up

EQUIPMENT: Rubber ball, 8 or more inches in diameter; 4 soda pop bottles or tenpins for bases.

FORMATION: Pop bottles laid out similar to a softball diamond, 35 feet between bases.

DIRECTIONS: Similar to beat ball. Pitcher bowls ball toward home plate and tries to knock over pop bottle there. Batter standing beside bottle tries to kick ball into fair territory. If ball knocks bottle down, or kicker upsets bottle while trying to kick ball, batter is out. On kicking fair ball, kicker circles bases. Fielders throw ball to first baseman (who knocks bottle over by tagging it with ball). Relay goes around bases (second, third, and home), each baseman in turn knocking over bottle. If ball beats runner to any base and bottle is knocked over, runner is out. Any fly ball that is caught also constitutes an out.

Safety Zone Ball

No: 10-60   Age: 10 up

EQUIPMENT: Rubber playground or volleyball.

FORMATION: Two teams, one fielding, the other batting. Two lines, approximately 100 feet apart and parallel. One is home base line, other is safety zone line.

DIRECTIONS: Fielding team scatters around playing area between two lines. (In case of long ball hitters, some fielders can play farther past safety zone line.) Batting team forms line behind first batter and will continue to bat in this order throughout game. Pitcher stands about 15 feet from home base line and pitches softly underhand to batter at this line. Batter tries to hit pitch with his hand into fair territory (any area on fielders' side of home base line). If he succeeds, he then has choice of running to safety zone or else awaiting more opportune moment. If he chooses to run, he tries to avoid being hit by ball which fielders will retrieve and throw at him. If batter decides not to chance running at this time, he may move to any point behind home base line and run later on any fair hit by teammate. Upon reaching safety zone, runner still has choice of returning on any hit which he thinks will provide good chance for him to reach home base line unscathed. Run is counted only when runner returns safely across home base line. Fielder must not run after he gains possession of ball. (He cannot chase runner.) Rather, if he is out of position and will not have good chance to hit runner, he should pass it to teammate who is closer to path of runner. This game encourages teamwork and much passing. Consequently, all players get to participate frequently. Runner who is hit by ball while running between home base line and safety zone line is out. Any fly ball caught also constitutes an out. Three outs retire a side. Inning is completed after both sides have batted. Any number of innings can be played. Try this game. Both young and old love it.

Sockaball

No: 12-30   Age: 10 up

EQUIPMENT: Softball and bat. Any fielders' equipment available. Four bases.

FORMATION: Ball field similar to softball diamond; 60 feet between bases. Two teams, from 6 to 15 on each side.

DIRECTIONS: Rules of game similar to softball. However, there is one big change. Each team has its pitcher throwing to its own batters. Hence it becomes batters' and fielders' game, which for less skilled and inexperienced is much more fun. Pitcher does not field, so there can be no bunting. And due to slowness of pitching, stealing is not allowed. In all other respects, game is same as softball. Scores are surprisingly low. Fielders back against fences and make many a spectacular catch. Try it once.

Lyle Ball

No: 10-40   Age: 10 up

EQUIPMENT: Softball bat, rubber ball 8 to 12 inches in diameter, and four bases.

FORMATION: Bases 45 to 50 feet apart laid out similar to a softball diamond. Two teams from 5 to 20 on a side.

DIRECTIONS: Similar to Sockaball. However, when mixed groups of boys and girls are playing, have boys bat opposite from their normal way. (Left-handers bat right-handed, and vice-versa.) Pitchers throw rubber ball underhanded to batters of their side, placing ball wherever they ask for it. No gloves are needed with playground ball. This type of game is good when ground is unsuitable for softball (such as beach, rocky ground, or pavement). As in Sockaball, no stealing is allowed; also, no bunting.

Beat Ball

No: 8-30   Age: 10 up

EQUIPMENT: Rubber ball 6 to 8 inches in diameter, sacks for bases.

FORMATION: Two teams of any number, one batting, other in field. Fielding team has pitcher, catcher, infielders, and outfielders. Four bases (sacks) are laid out similar to softball field; 35 feet between bases.

DIRECTIONS: Batter hits easy pitch and begins to circle bases. He is not allowed to remain on base but must run home. Fielders must field ball and throw it in turn to second, third, and home. Ball must make circuit but if it beats runner to any base he is out. Any fly ball caught is also an out.

WATER GAMES AND CONTESTS

One of the most popular recreational activities is swimming, yet few leaders take full advantage of this. Many people will not respond to a water carnival idea because they consider themselves poor swimmers. Actually, many people can be turned away from this area of recreation. Therefore, the leader needs to bring the activity down to the reach of all. Confidence will come and encouragement from the familiarity of playing in water will cause a person to more readily attempt new skills. Activities that are enjoyable, yet which may be participated in by both the skilled and the unskilled, are the ones to select. Many games which are played on land can be adapted to a water version and can be played in a wading area. Cavalry Battle Royal, Beatball, Steal the Bacon, relays, folk games and dances, and countless others are very adaptable.

Team of Horses

No: 8-20   Age: 8 up

(Deep Water Version)

EQUIPMENT: Long rope and inner tube for each team.

FORMATION: Each team has driver who sits in inner tube and gives directions. Rope is tied to inner tube, and equal number of players from each team grab hold and become horses.

DIRECTIONS: At starting signal, horses begin to pull inner tube and driver by swimming any stroke. However, one hand must be in contact with rope at all times. Driver gives "horses" needed directions. First team which goes around turning point and returns to finish line, wins.

(Shallow Water Version)

Instead of swimming, allow "horses" to run in waist-deep water. Caution them to hold on to rope at all times.

Water Football
Age: 9-18

EQUIPMENT: Any floating ball.

FORMATION: Two teams scattered over playing area.

DIRECTIONS: Referee tosses ball up between two players, basketball style. Each team then tries to get ball over opponents' goal by passing or carrying ball over goal. When touchdown is made, change ends of pool if in pool having a deep end.

Swim Tag
Age: 9 up

EQUIPMENT: Waterfront or pool.

FORMATION: Players line up at one end of swimming area; one player is It. "It" stands alone in middle of area.

DIRECTIONS: "It" shouts, "Watch the shark!" All try to swim across to other side without being tagged. "It" tags as many players as possible as they swim across designated area. All those tagged join It, and game continues until all are tagged.

Heave the Ring Buoy
Age: 9 up

EQUIPMENT: Ring buoys.

FORMATION: Group is divided into teams. Captains remain on one pier; teams line up on opposite pier.

DIRECTIONS: Number ones dive in; captains throw out buoys and pull in their teammates. Number twos dive in and, in turn, are pulled in by number ones. Number threes are pulled in by number twos, and so on.

Lighted Candle Relay
Age: 12 up

EQUIPMENT: Candles, one for each team.

FORMATION: Teams.

DIRECTIONS: Contestants have lighted candles at start. Upon signal, they proceed to finish line by swimming or wading. Winner is first person who reaches goal with lighted candle.

Balloon Push

Age: 12 up

EQUIPMENT: One balloon for each contestant (ball can be used); pool or waterfront.

FORMATION: Entrants line up at one end of pool.

DIRECTIONS: Entrants, at signal, push inflated balloons with their faces toward goal. Contestants using their hands are eliminated.

Inner Tube Race

Age: 9 up

EQUIPMENT: One inner tube for each contestant; waterfront or pool.

FORMATION: Contestants, in inner tubes, line up at end of pool.

DIRECTIONS: Each contestant sits in inner tube with his legs and arms outside. Race may be run by using arms only or arms and legs, doing reverse flutter kick.

Underwater Balloon Blowing

Age: 9 up

EQUIPMENT: One 8-inch balloon for each contestant; pool or waterfront.

FORMATION: Players scattered around area.

DIRECTIONS: On agreed signal, all submerge and blow up balloons. First one to come up with fully inflated balloon, or one with largest balloon, is winner.

VARIATION: Proceed as above, but have objective of being first one to eat banana, or something similar.

Pan Race

Age: 12 up

EQUIPMENT: One deep pie pan for each contestant; pool or waterfront.

FORMATION: Players line up at one end of pool.

DIRECTIONS: Contestants push pie pans with their face, chin, mouth, or nose. Swimming must be smooth to avoid sinking pan with wash or splash.

Sharks and Minnows

Age: 12 up

EQUIPMENT: Shallow pool.

FORMATION: Circle of players; one player is shark; one is minnow.

DIRECTIONS: Shark chases minnow; circle helps minnows and hinders shark.

Crabs and Crayfish

Age: 12 up

EQUIPMENT: Pool or waterfront; two goals.

FORMATION: Two teams lined up, one at each end of pool; one team is called "Crabs," other, "Crayfish."

DIRECTIONS: Leader calls "Swim." When two teams are close together, he then calls "Crabs" or "Cr-r-rayfish." If leader calls "Crabs," Crabs run or swim back to goal with Crayfish chasing them. All tagged join other side.

Tug of War

Age: 9 up

EQUIPMENT: Waterfront or pool; line about twenty feet in length.

FORMATION: Group is divided into two teams.

DIRECTIONS: Each team grasps rope, one on either end of middle mark. Each team, using shallow arm pull and scissor kick, tries to tug rope to its side.

Block-Gathering Contest

Age: 12 up

EQUIPMENT: A large number of wooden blocks, painted white, yellow, or orange; pool or waterfront.

FORMATION: Blocks scattered on water 15 yards from edge; players lined up at edge of pool.

DIRECTIONS: On given signal, all contestants start to gather as many blocks as they can in one minute and then return to starting line where blocks are counted to determine winner.

Jackstone Diving

Age: 12 up

EQUIPMENT: A large number of jackstones; pool of shallow water.

FORMATION: Jackstones scattered over area of shallow water.

DIRECTIONS: Players submerge and see who can gather most jack-stones in two minutes.

Umbrella Race

Age: 12 up

EQUIPMENT: One umbrella for each contestant; pool or waterfront.
FORMATION: Swimmers line up at end of pool.
DIRECTIONS: Each contestant has open umbrella which he holds over himself while swimming.

Duck Race

Age: 12 up

EQUIPMENT: Two pie tins for each player; swimming pool.
FORMATION: Players line up at end of pool.
DIRECTIONS: Each swimmer holds two pie tins in his hands while swimming 25 yards.

Candle Race in Water

Age: 12 up

EQUIPMENT: Candle and matches.
TYPE: Race or Relay.
FORMATION: Shuttle or file formation in water.
DIRECTIONS: First player strikes match, lights candle, and runs to start where he gives candle to second player. Second player blows out candle, lights candle with match and repeats actions of first player. Continue until all players have participated.

21

Folk Games—American, Other Nationality

For many centuries the folk peoples of the world have been composing and enjoying rhythmic activities in social groups. We are proud to include some of these treasures, as well as some new mixers, in this chapter.

In some of them man has acted out his work or scenes from his daily life that involved playing or courting. In the pioneer days of the United States the settlers took familiar tunes and made up a form of singing game now known the world around as the "play party game." Families would gather into a barn from miles around, have a sort of indoor picnic supper, and have fun until the late hours, sometimes all night long. As the children would drop off to sleep they would be put to bed on benches, in baskets, in the hay, while the older folk continued with their fun. (These occasions were few and far between, so everybody made the most of them.)

European peoples have had festivals for centuries, and many of these happy activities formed the basis of the festival, along with song, story, crafts. "Helston Furry Processional," included here, is an excellent example of the festive processional. (See "Festivals" in Index.)

HOW TO MAKE FOLK GAMES FUN FOR ALL

In modern days, as in former days, these folk games and dances are used for sociability and fun. They are designed to give the

494

young people, and older ones too, an opportunity for wholesome social expression together. They have earned the approval of many church groups. (If your church does not approve, it is better to use some other form of activity, since there is great breadth of possibility in social recreation.)

Some of these activities will help the leader get folks on their feet. Included also are some games not requiring partners. Another interesting form, the Grand March, allows the boys and men to get into one line, the girls and women into another, and to have their partners furnished to them. This is good, in that the timid don't have to ask someone to be their partners.

Some pointers for making a program of folk games and dances successful may be useful at this place in the chapter:

1. Put down more ideas than you will use. List them in categories, like "no partners," "simple, single circle," "mixers." (A mixer is one in which the players change partners.)
2. Use some "name calling" folk games in situations where it seems appropriate.
3. Ofttimes it will be necessary to use formations of 3's instead of 2's, in order to prevent leaving someone out. If there are many more girls than boys, or boys than girls, this can prove to be a lifesaver. Improvise!
4. Explain some background of the folk game, if you know any, and if time permits. However, since each of these activities should stand on its own feet for values, this interpretation is not absolutely necessary.
5. Changing the pattern for variety and balance will help. After a grand march which leads into a circle and one or two circle activities, you might shift to one done in line formation, or in squares, or in trios, either around the circle or in free formation.
6. Learn how to get people into groups of different sizes. ("Developing Groupness," Chapter 2.)
7. Have a workable "get quiet" signal. (See "General Aids to Leaders," Chapter 2.)
8. A good public-address record player is essential, if records are to be used. (Piano and singing are effective, too.) Be sure to get a record player, if you can afford it, with a slow-fast vari-

able regulator on the turntable, such as is found in some models of Califone, Newcomb, David Bogen, Rek-o-kut, Garrard. (This means that instead of 3 or 4 set speeds, such as 45 rpm or 78 rpm, you can vary the speed up and down from set speeds.) The reason is that records need to be slowed for learners, older folk, young children.

9. Plan ahead for the figures, leading one into the other. In a grand march you can end up in lines of 4, 8, 16, 32, or in a single or double circle.

10. There are several ways of getting into formations with ease that you can try:

a. To move from a double line (men in one line, girls in another) into a circle, have each person shake hands with the one facing him or her. Have each girl shake hands with the next man down the line from her, also holding her partner's hand. Then head man can lead this joined-hand line out into a circle. There you can call out, "Circle left, circle right, to the center and back" for a little activity in a single circle. If a double circle is desired, have each player swing his partner and promenade.

b. To move from a double circle to a line, break the circle at the foot of the room and have a couple march up the center of the room, the others following. This makes a long line out of a circle.

c. To get into groups of 3's or other odd number (especially when you have such a mixture of folks that "boy-girl" doesn't mean much), call out numbers and have the large group form smaller numbers as you indicate, like "five," then "seven," and finally "three." (Chords on the piano are even better.) Then get any trios having too many boys (or girls) to trade with another trio close by.

d. To form squares from a circle of couples, call out: "Now two couples circle up together—to make circles of four people. Now put your four together with another four to make eight." Then have them shape up their squares.

e. To go from trios to couples, have two trios get together to form six. Then ask each six to form three couples. (If a set of six close by has more of the lesser sex, an exchange can be made.) This often means that girls must be partners of girls.

11. Identify those girl-boys. Sometimes girls must take the part of boys when couple folk games are played. If these girls can wear painters' caps or men's hats, or chefs' caps they are detected more easily. Some systems have girls wearing bows in hair, "boys" wearing bow ties made extra large. Others have the girl-boys wear slacks. It seems easiest to see something on top of the head.

12. Teach figures progressively. Use something that teaches grand right and left, another figure for right and left through, and a third that demonstrates ladies' chain. Then all are ready for something that combines all three.

13. Start with *group* needs, not your own personal preferences as the leader. You should be ahead of them somewhat in ability and taste, but remember: they are the springboard, not you. (Those who shoot over the heads of others are not superior to them—they're just poor shots.)

14. Practice on an experimental group. This is always helpful, in order to get the patterns firmly in mind.

Of the circle formations given in this chapter, all are easy to learn except Swing on the Corner and Dr Gantzlig, which are medium hard. The Virginia Reel and the Ninepin Reel are the only ones of the line formations that are hard to do. Older folk would be able to do Ach Ja, Come, Let Us Be Joyful, The Wheat, and Gustav's Skol. If played to slow tempo, Oh! Susanna, Sally Down the Alley, Betsy Liner, and the Virginia Reel can be done by them. The Bear Went over the Mountain, The Thief, Pop! Goes the Weasel, Jibidi, Jibida, and Troika are apt to make them out of breath.

A GLOSSARY OF FOLK DANCE TERMS

There are certain special terms used in reels and square dances which both caller and players need to understand. Here are the most frequently used ones:

ALLEMANDE LEFT. Man takes left hand of girl at his left in his left hand and walks once around her as she walks around him. Each returns to original place. (Usually followed by Grand Right and Left, but not always.)

BALANCE. Here are three ways (and there are others):

1. Bow (man) or curtsy (woman).
2. Two small steps backward away from partner, two forward. Often followed by a swing.
3. Point right toe over in front of left (count 1), back in place (count 2), point left toe in front of right (count 3), and in place (count 4). (Sometimes done with a hop.)

BALANCE HOME. Return home and bow to partner.

BREAK AND SWING. Turn hands loose, swing your partner with a waist swing.

CIRCLE LEFT, CIRCLE RIGHT. Entire group join hands and circle around in direction indicated, either clockwise or counterclockwise.

CLOCKWISE. Direction to your left as you face center.

COUNTERCLOCKWISE. Direction to your right as you face center.

DOUBLE CIRCLE. Couples in circle, ready to march counterclockwise; man has lady at his right.

ELBOW SWING. Partners (or couple) hook elbows and walk around each other once.

FOOT COUPLE. If first couple is active, foot couple is third couple. In other words, it is couple opposite active one.

FOURTH COUPLE. Couple to left of first couple and opposite second couple. Third couple is opposite first couple.

GRAND RIGHT AND LEFT ("Grand Chain"). Partners face, join right hands; men move counterclockwise and ladies move clockwise. Partners pass right shoulders, join left hand with next person around circle and pass this person on left side, weaving in and out, right and left, as they move around circle.

HEAD OF THE HALL. The end nearest music.

HEAD COUPLE. Couple with backs to music (usually most experienced).

HOME POSITION. The original position of each. When changing, man's position is "home."

HONORS ALL (also called "Address" or "Salute Partners, Salute Corners," or "Honors Right and Honors Left"). Man bows, woman curtsies, first to partner, then to corner.

INSIDE RING. Path a couple follows when they promenade around set inside other three couples.

LADIES' CHAIN. With two couples facing each other, ladies cross to opposite places, giving right hands to each other as they pass, and left hands to opposite men, who place right arm around girls' waists and turn with them, counterclockwise, in place, ending with girls facing original position. Repeat same crossover and turn action back to place. (To assist turning, girls often make little "saddle" with right hand placed at waist, palm out, with man putting his right hand in hers as they turn.)

OPPOSITE. Person standing opposite you across set.

OUT TO THE RIGHT. Lead-off man, or couple, goes to couple next on right and executes there whatever is called.

PROMENADE. (1) To march in couples with lady at man's right, hands clasped in skating position. Man is on inside of circle as they move about. (2) Cross shoulder position. Man reaches across girl's shoulder to take her right hand in his; he does same with left hands. (3) In New England squares: men place right arms around partners' waists (girls put left hands on men's right shoulders) and men form left-hand star, marching around to place.

RIGHT AND LEFT THROUGH AND RIGHT AND LEFT BACK. Couple faces another couple. Each person gives right hand to person opposite, passing on to that person's position. Each lady gives left hand to her partner when they are in opposite position, and he turns her completely around to face back to original place; return to place, giving right hand across again, and turn with left hands as before. Same as Right and Left.

SIDE TWO COUPLES. Second and fourth couples in square.

SWING (or TURN). Western style: man extends left arm and supports lady's right hand in his left hand. She places left hand on his right shoulder or upper arm; his right arm is around her waist. They stand off center, and with light walking steps circle around each other in place, moving clockwise.

TWO-STEP. "Step, together, step, hesitate." Step on right foot to side with right, bring left foot to right and take weight, then step to right on right foot again. Repeat starting with left. (Also done in forward direction or turning.)

HOW TO DO A POLKA OR A SCHOTTISCHE

There are many variations of the polka, but essentially it is done either in open position or closed position.

The Polka

POSITION: Shoulder-waist or waltz.

ACTION: As partners face, man makes little spring with right foot, at same time, sliding to left with left foot, draws right foot to it, steps left again with left foot, slight rest (to music of one measure, or 4 counts). The girl does comparable thing. Spring is actually a hop-turn, with couple turning clockwise as they turn. (It takes two complete polka steps to make complete turn.) Of course, next time, he leads off with other foot.

To teach more simply to group, have all stand in circle. Everybody goes in same direction while learning. Have them step to left with left foot; slide right foot to left foot; step left with left foot again; pause. Then step to right with right foot, slide left foot to it; step right again, pause. *Step, slide, step; and step, slide, step,* etc. Then, in place of the *"and,"* where there is a pause, have them learn to include hop. After that, try to put hop in first in measure instead of last. Next, let them try it with partner, going very, very slowly at first. (Slow down piano or record player.)

The Schottische. Partners stand side by side, using skating position or this one: girl has left hand on boy's shoulder, he has his arm around her waist. In Scandinavia, she has her free hand on top of his, at her waist, and he has free hand on her hip.

ACTION: Starting usually with outside foot (man's left, girl's right), they move around circle, counterclockwise, with three running steps, and a hop (*step, step, step-hop*), and repeat with inside foot. (2) Next, *step-hop, step-hop, step-hop, step-hop.* (Four *step-hops,* beginning with man's left, woman's right.) Sometimes this is done with partners facing, joining both hands or using shoulder-waist, and turning around each other with the step-hops. Sometimes it is done forward, moving on around circle.

(See directions for Texas Scottische for two in Chapter 14.)

A Western Schottische

POSITION: Partners stand side by side, man has right arm around partner's waist, girl has left hand on man's right shoulder.

ACTION:

1. Do two complete schottisches forward (*step, step, step-hop; step, step, step-hop; step-hop, step-hop, step-hop, step-hop*).
2. Similar, but on step-hops, each person turns self, man to his left, and lady to her right, both finishing face to face using four step-hops.
3. Third figure involves two *step, step, step-hops* forward, then to do in place; the couple "rock forward" with a step-hop forward on outside foot (at same time taking weight off inside foot) and then rock backward (on inside foot, taking weight off outside foot). *Repeat Rocking.* These actions take same music as four step-hops. Then repeat all: *step, step, step-hop; step, step, step-hop; rock forward and backward and forward and back.*

CIRCLE FOLK GAMES

Some of the following circle games are done with partners, and some without. Still others are played in trios, usually with a man between two ladies.

The Bear Went over the Mountain (musical game—action from Danish Seven Jumps)

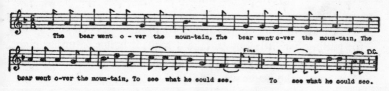

FORMATION: Single circle. Partners not necessary.

ACTION:

1. (a) Group joins hands and moves to left, singing lustily, "The bear went over the mountain." (b) On "To see what he could see," players halt. (c) On second "To see what he could see," lift right knee pointing uplifted foot toward center. (d) On third, "To see what he could see," lift left knee in same manner.
2. (a) Group moves to left, singing as before. (b) Stop as above.

(c) and (d) Repeat movements above. (e) Repeat last "To see what he could see," while kneeling on right knee.

3. Repeat a, b, c, d, e, and add f: kneeling on left knee.
4. Add placing right elbow on floor and resting chin on right hand.
5. Add shift to left elbow and left hand.
6. Add resting chin in both hands, elbows on floor.
7. Add touching head to floor.

The game ends with circle moving to left singing to end of song.

Looby Loo (English Singing Game)

An English mother was supposed to have devised this system for getting her little boy to take a bath, it being Saturday night. He put himself in, part at a time, and soon he was immersed! (Sometimes the water was cold!)

FORMATION: Circle without partners.
THE SONG (*Chorus*):

> Here we come, Looby Loo, here we come, Looby light,
> Here we come, Looby Loo, all on a Saturday night.

1. I put my right hand in, I take my right hand out,
   I give my right hand a shake, shake, shake, and turn myself
   about.
   (*chorus again*)

2. I put my left hand in . . . (etc.)
3. I put my right foot in . . .
4. I put my left foot in . . .
5. I put my head all in . . .
6. I put my whole self in . . .

ACTION: Circle left on chorus, every time. In keeping with words, then, extend right hand into center, withdraw it, shake it vigorously, and turn self completely about. At end, to "put whole self in," jump in, jump out, shake self, turn self about.

Mazoo (children's singing game from Kentucky mountains) [1]

THE WORDS:

1. Go wash your tiny windows, Mazoo, Mazoo,
   Go wash your tiny windows, my Susy-Anna-Sue.
2. Go face your tiny partner, Mazoo, Mazoo,
   Go face your tiny partner, my Susy-Anna-Sue.
3. Now let me see you hustle, Mazoo, Mazoo,
   Now let me see you hustle, my Susy-Anna-Sue.

ACTION:

1. As players stand in circle (no partners) one player goes around making face-washing motions (window-washing) in faces of players he wants to "wash."
2. On this verse he selects partner and stands in front of him or her.
3. The two do jig step to each other if they can, otherwise hop in place. To jig: put left foot down and do step-hop on it; at same

time, swing right foot around behind left, step-hopping on it then. Continue action, alternating with left foot, then right. (For step-hop, simply put foot down on count "one and" and hop on it "two and.")

4. Start song again, this time with two players who jigged to each other going around. Continue until all are in circle. (Good for family nights.)

The Thief (Norwegian) [2]

FORMATION: Single circle of partners, an extra in center, the "thief."

ACTION: Thief slides sideways diagonally across circle and steals partner from someone in circle. He takes both of her hands and brings her back to his place. Player whose partner was stolen immediately goes diagonally opposite his position to steal another. Continue as long as desired.

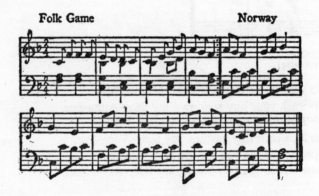

Folk Game   Norway

"Thief, yes, thief, that is your name,
  For you stole my little friend;
  But I hope to get another,
  Hope to get one soon again.
  I believe, tra, la, la,
  I believe, tra, la, la,
  I believe, tra, la, la,
  Tra, la, la, la, la, la."

Oh! Susanna

I came to Al-a-bam-a wid my ban-jo on my knee, I'm
rained all night de day I left, De weath-er it was dry, De
gwine to Lou'-si-an-a, my true love for to see It
sun so hot I froze to death, Su-san-na don't you
cry. Oh! Su-san-na, oh, don't you cry for me, For I'm
gwine to Lou' si-an-a wid my ban-jo on my knee.

FORMATION: Single circle, by partners, all facing center.

ACTION:

1. Ladies walk four times to center, and back to place.
2. Men the same.
3. Grand right and left. Partners join right hands and pass each other by right shoulders, men moving counterclockwise, ladies clockwise. Continue in same direction, alternately taking left and right hands, weaving in and out. Counting original partner, as No. 1, each will take seventh person he meets as his new partner.
4. On chorus, each man gets new partner and, joining hands in skating position, they promenade counterclockwise. Come into single circle at end, and repeat as often as desired. (Drop the grand right and left for children. Plan it for older adults.)

Goin' Down to Cairo (pronounced Ká ro). (American Play Party Game.)

Go-ing down to Cai-ro, Good-bye and a bye bye,

Go-ing down to Cai-ro, Good-bye Li-za Jane;

Black them boots and make them shine, Good-bye and a bye bye,

Black them boots and make them shine, Good-bye Li-za Jane.

FORMATION: Single circle of six couples (could be a little smaller or larger).

ACTION:

1. On first verse, all promenade single file, counterclockwise, girl in the lead.
2. At beginning of second verse, start grand right and left, with girl first turning toward her partner. When man gets back to his partner at end of grand right and left he swings her once around, and continues around until he has swung all girls, ending with his partner, whom he swings twice around. Start again from beginning.

Old Brass Wagon (American Play Party Game)

THE SONG:

1. Circle to the left, the old brass wagon (3 times)
   You're the one, my darlin'.
2. Swing, oh, swing, the old brass wagon,
   You're the one, my darlin'
3. Promenade home, in the old brass wagon (3 times and then
   last line).
4. Shaddish * all around the old brass wagon. . .
5. Break and swing, the old brass wagon . . .
6. Promenade around the old brass wagon . . .

FORMATION: Single circle of partners, facing center.

ACTION: On No. 1, above, circle left. On 2, swing partner. On 3,
promenade with partner. On 4, do a grand right and left (see "A
Glossary of Folk-Dance Terms" if not familiar with term). On
5, swing person you meet on word "Break." This is your new
partner. On 6, promenade with new partner.

Sally Down the Alley [3]

FORMATION: Couples stand facing in double circle, boys with backs
to center, both hands joined with partner to form two-hand arch.

THE SONG:

1. Here comes Sally down the alley, down the alley, down the
   alley,
   Here comes Sally down the alley, down in Alabama.
2. Hand on the shoulder and promenade (3 times), down in
   Alabama.
3. Swing that lady at your back (3 times), down in Alabama.

* Means schottische, but that step is not used.

ACTION:

1. Extra girls start down "alley" under arches, with skip or gallop step as group sings. Just before "hand on the shoulder" line, these extra girls stop beside their chosen new partner. (The girls thus left without partner wait their turn next time, going to center of circle.)

2. All the rest put right hand on left shoulder of person ahead to form single circle, as they sing "hand on the shoulder and promenade, down in Alabama."

3. "Swing that lady at your back." Man turns around to swing girl who was behind him. Repeat from beginning as often as desired. (If extras are boys, words "Here comes Sammy" are used.)

Pop! Goes the Weasel!

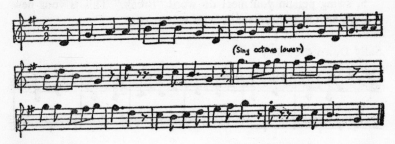

(Sing octave lower)

THE SONG:

A penny for a spool of thread,	The monkey chased the weasel,
A penny for a needle,	The monkey thought 'twas all
That's the way my money goes,	in fun . . .
Pop! Goes the Weasel!	Pop! Goes the Weasel!
All around the vinegar jug,	

FORMATION: One large circle of smaller circles of 2 couples each. Each boy has his partner at his right.

ACTION:

1. Little circles of 4 persons circle left four steps; circle right four steps.

2. Holding hands, they take two steps toward center of little circle (left, right) and two steps back (raising hands high as they get into center).

3. Pop! Goes the Weasel! The couples facing clockwise make arch with joined hands and pop other couple underneath arch and on to next. In this way, each advances to meet another couple. *Repeat same action with couple you meet.*

Another Version Done in Trios:

FORMATION: Threes, shaped like triangle, holding hands. Odd one is behind. Skip forward, and on "Pop!" they pop odd person up to next trio.

Swing on the Corner (Tennessee Play Party Game)

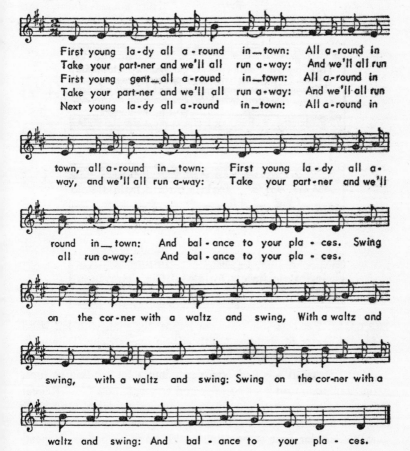

First young la-dy all a-round in town: All a-round in
Take your part-ner and we'll all run a-way: And we'll all run
First young gent all a-round in town: All a-round in
Take your part-ner and we'll all run a-way: And we'll all run
Next young la-dy all a-round in town: All a-round in

town, all a-round in town: First young la-dy all a-
way, and we'll all run a-way: Take your part-ner and we'll

round in town: And bal-ance to your pla-ces. Swing
all run a-way: And bal-ance to your pla-ces.

on the cor-ner with a waltz and swing, With a waltz and

swing, with a waltz and swing: Swing on the cor-ner with a

waltz and swing: And bal-ance to your pla-ces.

FORMATION: Circle of about six couples, facing center.

ACTION: A "first young lady," previously chosen, moves around inside circle, getting back home in time for "balance in your places." This is simply full walking step toward center (left, right) and backward to place (left, right).

On words, "Swing on the corner," man turns corner with left hand, partner with right, and both get into position to do "balance in your places," which is really balance to center.

"Take your partner" signals promenade, counterclockwise, stopping in time to "balance in your places."

Gents then follow similar procedure to that of "young ladies."

Ach Ja (German)

When my fa-ther and my moth-er Go a-jour-ney-ing to the fair;
What__ if they have no mon-ey They're as rich as an-y there.
Wenn der Va-ter und die Mut-ter In die kirch-weih ge-hen,
Und__ hab-en wir kein Geld, So__ hab'n die an-der Leut.'

Ach ja! Ach ja! Tra la la, tra la la, tra la la la la la la la, Tra la la, tra la la, Tra la la la la la la, Ach ja! Ach ja!

THE GAME: Partners join adjacent hands, the man with left hand toward center of circle and with girl on man's right. They walk to right around circle four slow steps; partners then face each other, release hands and bow very simply by bending at hips, on "Ja," then turn back to back and bow again on "Ja." Repeat from beginning.

CHORUS: Partners face each other, join hands and side-step to man's left for four steps. Finish with bows as before. Repeat, moving in opposite direction. Then each man moves forward and takes next girl as partner, and whole dance is repeated.

Jibidi, Jibida (French)   Folk Dancer Record MH 1044

NOTE: usually done with singing. Just sing la-la-la-la for first part, and for second, everybody sings:

> "Jibidi, jibida, tra la la la la la la la,
> Jibidi, jibida, tra la la la la la la!"

These are simply nonsense syllables (pronounced "zhee-bee-dee, zhee-bee-dah").

FORMATION: Circle of partners, hands joined low.

1. Facing center, all move sideways to left starting with left foot. Step on left to side, bring right foot next to it, step on left to side, bring right foot next to it. Swing left foot forward and back (bending right knee) and stamp lightly in place on left foot. *Repeat all.*
2. Still facing center, spring on right foot and at same time place left heel forward. Pause. Spring on left foot, place right heel forward. Pause. Then do four of these changes, twice as fast, as you sing the chorus. *Repeat* all of 2.
3. Same as 1.
4. Same as 2, but facing partner and, as you extend foot toward partner, extend and shake corresponding finger at partner.

Dr (pronounced Drrr) **Gzatzlig** (Swiss)
         Folk Dancer Record MH 1114

FORMATION: Couples, partners facing with man's back to center of circle.

CHORUS: Man puts his right arm around girl's waist, her left hand on his shoulder. He takes her right hand in his left, and at start flips their joined hands forward stiffly, as if pointing to couple ahead, and they take four slow side steps counterclockwise.

Now he flips their joined hands toward them, taking two side steps clockwise, then flips hands forward toward next couple again, and they take two side steps counterclockwise.

All this action is repeated, except starting clockwise with four side steps, then two counterclockwise, two clockwise. (The arm flipping is a part of each change.) *Repeat all.* (This is only time that chorus is done twice.)

PART 1: Still in same position, partners open up into side-by-side position and face counterclockwise. Starting with man's left, girl's right foot, do heel and toe and step-together-step, and without dropping hands, face other way, starting with man's right, lady's left and do same step in clockwise direction. Now both turn clockwise with four very slow step-together-steps (two-step), moving around big circle counterclockwise. *Repeat Part 1.*

CHORUS: Do it once completely, but do not repeat.

PART 2: (a) Face partner in single circle formation so that girl has back against line of direction, facing clockwise. (Man is counterclockwise.) Man folds hands on chest, girl has hands on hips. Both take schottische step sideways toward center (man to left with Left, Right, Left, hop on Left; girl to right with a Right, Left, Right, hop on Right). Then both move away from center with similar schottische step.

Now girl starts backward around circle, turning to her own right (clockwise), starting with her right foot, for four easy step-hops, while at same time man goes forward with four step-hops (starting with left foot) without turning around. *Repeat all of Part 2(a).*

(b) Now take right hands and do same action as 2(a), except that you hold hands in process and girl turns under joined right hands. This includes repeat.

There is enough music to do it once through again, remembering that first time, chorus is done twice.

Texas Schottische for Three [4]

FORMATION: A line of three, one man between two ladies, all facing to right around circle (counterclockwise). Man takes outside hands of ladies; they join hands behind him, shoulder high.

ACTION:

Measures 1-4: Exactly as in Measures 1-4 of twosome version, all beginning with left foot.

Measures 5-6: All place left heels forward, then back, touching toes (now ladies release inside hands). While man takes three steps back, he pulls ladies around to face him—ladies taking three steps to turn halfway around.

Measures 7-8: Repeat heel and toe step with right feet, then all three (with slight pull of hands to give a little "send off") take three steps straight ahead, man passing between his own ladies to join hands with next two ladies ahead; two ladies, taking hands of next man behind their own.

Jingle Bells Trio (Mixer)

FORMATION: Trios, arms linked, all facing counterclockwise around big circle. May be equipped with jingle bells.

ACTION:

1. Trot forward eight steps, backward eight steps.
2. All face center, join hands into three circles. Each takes eight good slides around and back: middle circle going counterclockwise and other two moving clockwise.
3. On Jingle Bells chorus: center person faces one closest to center and slaps right hand on right, 3 times, left on left, 3 times, and both, 5 times. Then links right arm, goes around that person, and left arm and around other one in his trio. Repeat same action, but with person farthest from center and, instead of left arm to inside person, moves ahead to next trio to begin from beginning.

Chimes of Dunkirk (in 3's)   World of Fun Record M105

FORMATION: Sets of threes, around large circle, one person with back to center, and two facing center.

ACTION: Clap three times, pause. Stamp three times, pause. Join hands and circle three, once around to left, ending as they started.

Now person with back to center of circle balances to person on his or her left (takes right hand in right hand, steps forward on right foot and puts weight on it; backward on left foot and takes weight; repeats), then same action to one on his right. Then circle three once around, and active one moves to next position to left.

Red River Valley (in 3's) [5]   World of Fun Record M104

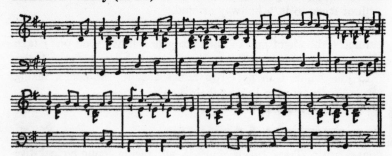

FORMATION: Trios, arms linked, each facing another trio around large circle. Ideally a man in the center, girl on each arm, but any combination is all right. Person on left of center person is one "in the valley"; and one on right, "Red River girl" (or man).

THE WORDS TO THE SONG (everybody sings):

1. Now you lead right on down the valley,
   And you circle to the left and to the right,
   And you swing your girl in the valley,
   And you swing your Red River girl.

2. Then you lead right on down the valley,
   And you circle to the left and to the right,
   Now the girls make a wheel in the valley,
   And the boys do-si-do so polite.

3. And you lead right on down the valley,
   And you circle to the left and to the right,
   And you lose your girl in the valley,
   And you lose your Red River girl.

ACTION: To "lead down the valley" each trio links arms, moves to own right around the trio they were facing, and comes face to face with another trio. They join hands with them and circle 4 steps to the left, and to the right 4 steps. (This precedes each figure.)

1. Center person swings the one at the left, then the one at the right.

2. Girls make a right-hand star and walk around once. Boys do a regular do-si-do.

3. On "lose," the "girls in the valley" exchange places; so do the "Red River girls."

Key words for the changes: *"SWING," "WHEEL," "LOSE."*

Troika (Russian)   World of Fun Record M105

FORMATION: Trios around large circle, man in center, girl on each side of him. (Usually in formations done in trios, any three persons may form group—as one male, two females, or three men, or any other combination.)

ACTION:

Figure 1. With light running steps, trios move forward around circle, sixteen steps. They stop in place, and center person raises left hand to make arch with person on his left. Right person goes through arch, center one turning under own hand. Then he makes an arch with person on left, and person on right goes underneath arch, center person again turning under own arm. (Similar to Crested Hen)

Figure 2. The trio now join hands into small circle and, continuing running steps, circle to left, 12 running steps, ending with a stamp, stamp, stamp (pause); then circle right 12 steps, stamp again. If progression is desired, center person may move to trio ahead during last three stamps.

Come, Let Us Be Joyful (German)   World of Fun Record M102

FORMATION: Trios, facing each other, around large circle. Five or six feet separate trios. Usually one man in center, girl on each side of him.

ACTION:

1. Hands held shoulder high, each trio advances toward opposite one 3 steps, making little dip on fourth count, retires to places. *Repeat.*
2. Elbow swing. Link right arms with girl on right and skip around, left arm at left and swing around. Girl who is inactive may skip around in little circle by herself.
3. Advance and retire at first. Then advance again, this time dropping hands and passing through opposite trio (passing right shoulders with person you are facing) to meet another trio advancing from other direction.

THE SONG.

Come, let us be joyful, while life is bright and gay,
Come, gather its roses, ere they fade away.
Oh, don't you worry and don't you fret,

There's lots of life in the old world yet,
We'll take the rose, the thorn forget,
And go on our way rejoicing.

LINE GAMES

Instead of in a circle, many folk dances are set up in a line formation. Several of these are based on the Virginia Reel, directions
for which are given in this section.

Helston Furry Processional (English)

NOTE: This little schottische processional is often used to introduce
a folk festival. It is a traditional May Day dance. Participants
often bring in sprigs of green, celebrating the return of spring.
FORMATION: Long line of couples, numbered alternately 1 and 2.
ACTION: Line moves forward with schottische step. (Step, step,
step-hop; step, step, step-hop; step-hop; step-hop; step-hop.)
The steps are little light running steps. For step-hop, take a
step, then a short hop in the same foot, to count of 1, 2; 1, 2.
Music A is sufficient for four schottisches as described.

Next is a right-hand star. Continuing schottische step, form
right-hand star, and move around with schottische step. (To
form star, man No. 1 gives right hand to girl No. 2, and man
No. 2 gives his right hand to girl No. 2.) Music B is sufficient
for two schottisches with right-hand star. As Music B is repeated, shift to left hands across and do a *left-hand star,* returning to place.

Alabama Gal (Southern Play Party Game)

World of Fun Record M111

THE SONG:

1. Come through in a hurry, Come through in a hurry,
   Come through in a hurry, Alabama Gal.
2. I don't know how, how, I don't know how, how
   I don't know how, how, Alabama Gal.
3. I showed you how, how, I showed you how, how
   I showed you how, how, Alabama Gal.
4. Ain't I rock candy? Ain't I rock candy?
   Ain't I rock candy? Alabama Gal.

FORMATION: Longways line, Virginia Reel style, men in one line, women in other. Difference from ordinary Virginia Reel is that as many as 20 couples or so can be in same "set." About 6 feet of distance is necessary between lines.

ACTION:

1. Head couple join hands (man's right and girl's left) and go down center of set toward foot for "Come through in a hurry" repeated. For third "Come through in a hurry" they return to the head, reel a time and a half, then start *reeling* down line as other verses are sung. (To do reel: partners link right arms, turn half way around, then give left arm to persons in line— man going to girls' line, girl to man's line. Then return to partner with right-arm link again.)
2. Next couple starts down center in like fashion *after* "rock candy" verse. They go down the set only as far as other couple, then they return to head and start reeling down toward foot. Each couple continues until it has been head couple and has reeled clear down line to foot. This particular version was learned in Florida. We have run across several variations, all of them stemming from Virginia Reel longways formation.

Betsy Liner (a singing version of the Virginia Reel)

World of Fun M112

THE SONG (Tune: Ten Little Indians)

1. Bow down, Old Betsy Liner (3 times)
   You're the one, my darlin'.
2. Right-hand swing, Old Betsy Liner . . .
   You're the one, my darlin'.
3. Left-hand swing . . .
4. Both hands swing . . .
5. Shake that right foot, git on around 'er, . . .
6. Shake that left foot, git on around 'er . . .
7. Slide 'er up and down, Old Betsy Liner . . .
8. Boy wouldn't swing, I wouldn't have 'im . . .
   (Alternating with "Girl wouldn't swing and I wouldn't have 'er . . .")
9. Moon and stars, shinin' too . . .

FORMATION: Two lines, men in one, girls in other, facing. About six feet between lines, 5 to 6 couples in a "set" (Virginia Reel style)

ACTION: (See numerals above)

1. Head lady, foot gent, forward and bow, retire to place. Then head gent, foot lady do same.
2. Head lady, foot gent advance, take right hands, and turn around each other. Same action for head gent, foot lady.
3. Similar action, using left hand.
4. Similar action, using both hands, turning clockwise.
5. Do-si-do is "back to back." Each person folds arms, advances toward other, passes around other without turning around, back to back, and backs up to place. This time pass right shoulders.
6. Similar action, but with left shoulder for do-si-do.
7. Head couple join both hands, gallop sideways to foot and return with same sliding step to head. There they link right arms and turn around one and a half times, man going to girl's line, girl to man's line, each offering left arm to line as they start to reel down line.

8. For Swing verses, head couple reel to foot. For reel, players link right arm with partner in center of set, give left arm to those on side, turn halfway around, back to partner in center, alternating all way down line. At foot, link right arm with partner once again, turn one and a half times, come back to head, ready to lead lines to foot. While this is done, two verses, "Boy wouldn't swing . . ." and "Girl wouldn't swing," are sung alternately.

9. Each head couple leads line in march to foot of line. There they make two-hand arch (join both hands, raise them high) and all other couples pass under arch, move toward head. This now leaves second couple at head. *Repeat until all couples have been in head position.*

Virginia Reel (Family Style)   World of Fun Record M103
Irish Washerwoman

FORMATION: Longways position, men in one line, women in other. As they face head of room, girls are at right of their partners. About six feet between lines.

ACTION:

1. All go forward toward other line, back to place.
2. All swing with right hand.
3. All swing with left hand.
4. All swing with both hands.
5. Do-si-do, right shoulders.
6. Do-si-do, left shoulders.
7. Reeling (as described in Betsy Liner). When head couple are at foot, all swing partners and start over again, until all have been in head position. (Note that head couple in this version do not return to head to lead their lines to foot.)

The Duke of York

Oh, the no-ble Duke of York, He had ten thou-sand men; He marched them up to the top of the hill and marched them down a-gain.

2

Oh, when they were up, they were up;
And when they were down, they were down,
And when they were only half way up,
They were neither up nor down.

3

Oh, a-hunting we will go; a-hunting we will go.
We'll catch a little fox, and put him in a box,
And never let him go.

FORMATION: Two lines, partners facing each other.
ACTION: While all players sing first verse, head couple promenade to foot of set and back to head, inside hands joined.

On second verse, first couple join hands and swing rapidly down middle to foot where they remain and make an arch.

During third verse, second couple lead their respective lines down outside and up through arch made by first couple. As partners meet, they join hands and return to position.

New head couple repeat game.

The Wheat (Czech)

FORMATION: Trios. Man in center, girl on each side of him is ideal. Any combination of three may be used.

ACTION: "An old man in Czechoslovakia put down his bag of wheat and went inside the tavern to get something to drink. Some bad boys put some pigeons in his bag. When he returned and started off with his burden, they shouted from a safe distance, "Let those pigeons out, old man." [6]

1. All march forward, 16 walking steps, bent over as if carrying heavy burden.
2. *Arming.* Center person links right arm with right arm of person at his right and skips around, then left arm with person on left and skips around each other. *Repeat.* Center one moves up to next trip. (*Begin over.*)

THE WORDS: "From the fields there came a farmer, on his back a
bag of bran;
And those bad boys shouted at him, "Let those
pigeons out, old man."

CHORUS:

"Let those pigeons out, old man," (*repeat*)
And those bad boys shouted at him,
"Let those pigeons out, old man."

Ninepin Reel (English)
World of Fun Record M109 (Good Humor)
Folkraft 1209 (Cumberland Square)

FORMATION: Square set. Extra man, "Ninepin," is in center.
ACTION:

1. Head and foot couples join hands and slide across beyond each other's positions eight counts and back to place; side couples do same.
2. Head and foot couples join hands and do skipping circle left around ninepin for eight counts; circle right back to place, and sides same.
3. Ninepin swings ladies, first, then second, then third, then fourth (four counts for each). As their partners are swung, men go to center.
4. With polka step, five men in center polka left, each trying to get partner. One left out is new Ninepin.

Gustav's Skol (Swedish)   World of Fun Record M108

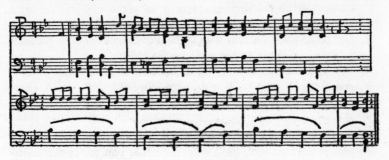

FORMATION: Square set of four couples, about 8 feet square, head couples facing music or with their backs to it; side couples at sides of head couples.

ACTION:

1. Head couples advance toward each other, retire to place, pledging toast to King Gustav, singing "A toast we pledge to Gustav, who is brave and true," and repeating words. Side couples do same, sing same.

2. Now side couples make arch with joined hands, free hands on hips. Head couples advance toward each other, shift partners, go through arch on own side of square, drop hands with temporary partner, look through peek hole (formed by hand on hip of side person) and go back to place. Then head couples make arch, free hand on hip, and side couples do same action. (Music is "Tralala" for chorus, sung.)

Stealing Partners. This game is fun because of "partner stealing." In order to steal partner, player stands near peek hole of player whose place he or she wants to take. Then stealing player simply gets to partner first, joins both hands, and skips around in place. Person who was "cut out" then goes out to get partner in same manner. It is permissible for couple to steal entire vacated space.

CALLING SQUARES

Some groups like to do squares. You too can call! It isn't hard, but it does take practice. Here are some tips for learners:

1. Use calls in this book; also get some of the good books recommended in the Bibliography.

2. Learn the call thoroughly. Start with a very simple one.

3. Get some good records with calls (see record section, Bibliography) and listen to the style of the callers.

4. Try out your ability on an experimental group who understand that it may be laborious to work the call out. A complete set of four couples is best. There is no short-cut for actually trying your calls with a group.

5. When you have one or two calls ready, try them on a regular group, perhaps with the explanation that you are in the learning stage.

6. A hand card helps at first, a "calling card." (Calls on a blackboard or other "dummy sheet" in plain view of you—and perhaps of nobody else—are equally good.)

7. All good callers call for the slower sets, making the fast ones mark time until the others catch up. (If some sets "don't get it," have some of the "smart ones" help them—or help them, yourself.)

8. A good technique practice is to (a) talk it, (b) walk it, (c) do it!

9. Just as you will in your learning (if you're a starting caller) begin with the simple, work toward the more complex.

10. Tape-record your calls, play them back to yourself to see how you sound to others.

11. Take a course now and then. City recreation departments often sponsor them, and so do other groups.

12. There are some teaching records of special value, such as those by Ed Durlacher.

13. Select music with marked rhythm. Try to keep that sense of rhythm in your voice. Tune your voice to the music.

14. Test your music in advance for suitability with that particular call.

15. Call clearly. It is better for the starting caller to leave fancy words alone until he gets his voice coming through clearly. Use as much treble as the room can stand, for additional sharpness, when using a public address system.

16. A public address system with a slow-fast regulator is valuable in square dance calling.

The Pattern. Though square dancing, at first a rural community activity, is getting urbanized or citified and therefore more complex, the simple calls are enjoyed by most groups, and the pattern for quadrilles is fairly standard.

There will be these types of calls:

1. *An opening,* beginning, "warmer upper" or introductory call. (It goes by these names and others.)
2. *The "change call"* that usually gives the square its title.
3. *Breaks* interspersed after a completed phase of the change call, such as a complete visit of the couple around the set.
4. *An ending,* which may be simple or more complex with several parts.

The construction of the "big circle" square, done in many parts of the South, is fairly similar in that there is an opening, a succession of change calls, and often a closing promenade, or a spiral.

In quadrilles there are several types of calls, such as these, besides "hash" calls which combine a number of kinds:

1. The single visitor type. One person visits around the set, usually returns to partner after each visit.
2. Visiting couple. A couple visit around the set, moving counterclockwise.
3. Simultaneous calls. In these, all move at the same time, or at least all men or women move at the same time.
4. Split the ring. Head couple go to the foot couple and between them, "split the ring." The pattern varies greatly after that.

Calling is done either in prompting style (short phrases to give directions), rhyming or patter (every syllable is filled with words, sensible or otherwise), and singing. Music for most square dancing is in 2/4 or 6/8 time, although there are some interesting ones in 3/4 time.

Square dancing has its own terminology. See the glossary for those terms that do not sound familiar.

For the best sociability, musical mixers and simple folk dances and singing games should be included in any large-group parties.

Some Introductions to Square Dances

1. Honors right; honors left. (Bow to partner, then to corner.)
   All join hands and circle left, (Do as directed.)
   Break and swing and promenade all. (As directed.)

2. It's allemande left with your left hand, (Give left hand to left hand of lady at left, walk around her and back to place; then grand right and left; promenade.)
   Right to your partner and a right and left grand,
   Meet your honey and promenade. (See Glossary.)

3. Everybody balance and everybody swing, (Bow, swing partner.)
   Left allemande and right hands grand, (As directed. See Glossary.)
   Meet your partner and promenade eight (Meet partner, promenade to home position.)
   Till you come straight.

4. All join hands and circle to the South (Join hands, circle left.)
   Let a little sunshine in your mouth
   It's the other way back in the same old track (Reverse, circle right.)
   Make those feet go wickety-wack
   Now you're home and now you swing (Swing in home position.)
   Promenade, go round the ring. (Promenade, end at home.)

Whirligig and Cheat [7] (square dance)

Any breakdown tune.
Introduction . . . anything you like.
   First man out to the right of the ring.
   That right-hand lady with your right hand around.
   Then back to your own and the left hand around.
   To the opposite lady by the right hand around.
   Then back to your own and the left hand around.

Your left-hand lady with the right hand around.
And back to your own by the left hand around.
Then that *one* man cheat or swing
Anywhere in the hall or the ring.
Then run back home and swing your own.
Don't get caught a-cheatin' your own.

Repeat entire figure with first and second men active.
Repeat entire figure with first, second, and third men active.
Repeat entire dance with all men active, and then with all ladies active.

Ending Calls, Closing Calls

1. Promenade a mile Indian file,
   Just let me remind you
   To turn right back in the same old track
   And swing that gal behind you.

   (All promenade single file, lady in lead. Man turns back, swings girl behind him. Continue three more times to get back to partner, "Now I am through and so are you.")

2. Swing, swing, everybody swing.
   Swing that gal across the hall,
   Now your own, but don't you fall
   And promenade, promenade!

   (All swing.)
   (Man goes over to girl opposite him and swings her. Returns to own to swing and promenade back home.)

3. Same as No. 2 above in "Some Introductions."

4. Balance to your corner all.
   Swing that girl across the hall.
   Leave her alone and swing your own
   Promenade eight and you know where
   Take her out and give her air.

   (Bow to corner.)
   (One you face across set.)
   (Go home, swing.)

   (Promenade, then to seats.)
   (Substitution: "Promenade around, two by two. I am through and so are you." Same action.)

Haymaker's Jig (Contra) [8]   Suggested records:
MH 5002, MH 1072, MH 1073

FORMATION: Longways line of couples, numbered, men with partners at right. Odd-numbered couples exchange places.

1, 3, 5, couples active.

Cross over before dance starts.

ACTION:

"Swing the one below." Men swing next girl below. "Actives swing partners in center. Down the center four in line" (take along the ones you swung). March down center of set, two couples side by side. "Same way back to place." Turn and come back to place.

"Two ladies chain." (See Glossary.) Couples 1 & 2, 3 & 4, and so on.

Timber Salvage Reel   Record

FORMATION:

1, 3, 5, and so on, couples active

Cross over before dance starts

ACTION:

Do-si-do the one below.

Active couples do-si-do partners

Active couples balance and swing partners.

Down the center, same way back, cast off.

Right-hand star with next couple.

Left-hand star back to place.

Old Number Nine   Folk Dancer Record by

The Call: [9]   same title

1. First couple to the right and you *balance* there so light
2. Then you circle to the left just once around.
3. Separate, go round that couple, and between that same old couple
4. And couple one, you swing there all alone.
5. Now the lady go round the lady and the gent go round the gent
6. And both couples swing there with your Jane
7. Then the ladies half-chain over and you turn them twice around
8. And active couple lead on down the lane.
9. You form a *right-hand star* and go round the way you are

10. Then you *left-hand star,* go back the other way
11. Separate, go round that couple, and between that same old couple
12. And couple one, you swing there all alone.
13. Now the gent goes round the lady and the lady goes round the gent
14. And both couples swing there with your Jane
15. Then the ladies half-chain over and you turn them twice around
16. And the active couple lead on down the lane.

Repeat with fourth couple.

The Action:

1. First couple goes to No. 2 and does hop balance.
2. Circle left.
3. Couple No. 1 separates, going behind other couple. Return to position and
4. Swing
5. Couple goes between No. 2, girl around girl, man around man.
6. Both couples swing in home position.
7. Ladies half-chain.
8. Active couple move to No. 3.
9, 10. Star formations.
11-16 same as 5-8. Beginning with 9, do all with couple 4.

Then next couple leads out, and so on, until all have led.

Bouquet Waltz Square (Square music at moderate tempo) [10]

Select an introduction:

CALL:

a. First lady to the couple on the right, and three around they go.
b. On to the next and the little boy follows.
c. Three by three in a bouquet waltz,
d. On to the next and the little boy follows.
e. Three by three in a bouquet waltz.
f. Get that couple over there,
g. Four by four across the floor.

Repeat for second, third, and fourth couples.
Select your own closing call.

EXPLANATION:

a. First lady goes to couple on right (couple No. 2) and circles three. Gentleman stays home.

b. First lady leaves and goes on to couple No. 3 and they circle three. Head gentleman goes to couple No. 2 and they also circle three.

c. These two small circles of three now circle around each other (counterclockwise) and return to their places. Small circles are moving to left and move around each other in counterclockwise movement.

d. Now first lady goes on to couple No. 4, and first gentleman follows on to couple No. 3. These begin to circle left.

e. These two circles move around each other and back to their places as in (c).

f. First gentleman joins his partner at No. 4 couple. No. 2 and No. 3 couples also join and circle four together.

g. Now these circles with two couples in each duplicate the action in (c) and (e), turning around each other and returning to their starting positions.

This is repeated for second, third, and fourth couples.

Balance Across (from Madison County, Alabama) [11]

1. Balance across to the opposite lady, take her by the right hand; take your partner by the left and promenade the girl behind you.

2. Oh, that girl, that pretty little girl, the girl I left behind me; with the laughing eyes and the yellow curls, the girl I left behind me.

FIGURES: Square for four couples.

1. Top and bottom couple meet. Each man swings opposite lady with right hands coming back immediately to swing his partner with left hands. Then each man (top and foot men) takes side lady (who was on his left in square), and each side gent steps to inside of set and takes top and bottom ladies as previous swing is being finished. All face counterclockwise in set ready to . . .

2. . . . promenade around once, counterclockwise, to men's places. Top and bottom couples repeat this figure, promenading new girl each time, until original partners meet again.

Repeat these figures with side couples doing "balance across."

Texas Star

Use your own introduction.   Good, lively ¾ music

1. Ladies to the center and back to the bar
2. Gents to the center with a right-hand star
   Back with the left, and there you are.
3. Meet your honey and pass her by
   Take that next gal on the fly.
4. Gents swing out, and ladies swing in
   Make that Texas star again
5. Ladies swing out, and gents swing in
6. Now everybody break and swing.
   And promenade around the ring.

   (*Repeat 3 times*)

   Work out your own closing call.

1. Ladies take two steps toward center of square, turn around, return to place.
2. Men form right-hand star, go about once around, change to left-hand star.
3. Passing partner, take next girl around waist.
4. Men break hands, make full turn around, leaving girls in to make star.
5. Girls break as men did, men make star.
6. Drop hands, all swing, and
7. Promenade.

Grand Square [12]   World of Fun Record M110

FORMATION: Square set of four couples, men with partners at their right.

ACTION: Head couples are those with backs to music or facing it. Sides are at their left and their right. (Never turn your back to a person in Grand Square.)

GRAND SQUARE CHORUS: Simultaneously, couples in side positions face each other and walk backward 4 counts to corner of square, while two head couples walk from their position to middle of set in 4 counts. Now side persons walk forward 4 counts to meet their new partners, while head couples are walking backward 4 counts. Now sides walk forward with new partners, while heads are backing away from new partners (4 counts); all complete square, returning to original position for last 4 counts, retracing steps.

All now do a reverse Grand Square, with sides coming forward first while heads are parting from original partners.

1. Right and Left Through (see Glossary): Head couples do it first (8 counts), then side couples, with this exception: head couples stay in other position until sides have gone across. Then heads return to place (8 counts), and sides return to place (8 counts). Now do Grand Square and reverse Grand Square.

2. Ladies' Chain (see Glossary): Heads do it (8 counts), then sides, head lady remaining in opposite position until side lady has chained across. Then heads return to place, sides return to place, followed by Grand Square and reverse Grand Square.

3. Grand Chain: Men (right arm around girl's waist) swing into center to form girl's right-hand star, men remaining in place. In star formation girls go to opposite man, who swings them around with left hands joined, right arm around girl's waist, and back into left-hand star, which girls use to get back to original partner, who swings them similarly in place. Now do Grand Square and reverse Grand Square.

4. Circle, Promenade: Entire square circle left (clockwise) and promenade for end of music.

Cast Off Six

Select your own introduction.

1. First couple balance, first couple swing
2. Down the center and split the ring
   The lady goes right and the gent goes left
3. Swing when you meet at the head and the feet
   The side four the same
4. Down the center as you did before
5. Down the center and cut away four
   The lady goes right and the gent goes wrong
6. Swing when you meet at the head and the feet
   The side four the same.
7. Down the center as you used to do
   Down the center and cut away two

8. The lady goes gee and the gent goes haw
   And everybody swing.
9. Allemande left with your left hand
   Right to your partner, right and left grand
   Promenade eight when you get straight.

   (Repeat three times)

ACTION:

1. First couple bows, swings, move toward couple No. 3.
2. Go between them, coming back to home position.
3. All swing.
4. Go down center.
5. Separate, girl turns right and goes between man of couple 3, girl of couple 2, back to place; man is turning left and going between man of couple 4, girl of couple 3. Head couple return to place.
6. All swing.
7, 8. Same, best girl goes between couple 2, man between couple 4.
9. See Glossary if necessary.

Opposite with Right-Hand Round

Use your own introduction.

1. First and third couples forward and back,
2. Forward again in the same old track,
3. Your opposite lady with the right hand round.
4. Left to your own as she comes round.
5. Corners all with a right hand round,
6. Left to your own as she comes round.
7. Twirl your corner as she comes down.
8. Promenade around the town.

Repeat again for first and third couples, then do for second and fourth twice. At the end each person has original partner back.

Use your own closing.

1. Couples 1 and 3 advance toward each other, retire to places.
2. Come forward again and

3. Each man turns other man's partner with right hand,
4. Own with left hand,
5. Goes to corner position (from his home position) and turns that girl with right hand,
6. Turns his own with left hand.
7. Swings corner and
8. Promenade.

Ol' Arkansaw

Use any introduction.

1. First lady out to the right and circle three
2. Now swing your maw,
3. And then your paw,
4. And don't forget ol' A-r-kan-sawwwwww!
5. On to the next and (repeat 2, 3, 4, for third and fourth couples), then:
6. Home you are and everybody swing.
7. Allemande left with your left hand,
   Right to your partner and a right and left grand,
   Meet your honey and promenade.
8. Repeat all for the next three ladies, in order.

1. First lady goes to couple 2, circles once.
2. Swings girl,
3. Swings man,
4. Returns to own partner and swings.
5. As directed.
6. Now all swing in home position.
7, 8. See Glossary if needed.

Shoot the Goose (Any 2/4 music)

Use your own introduction.

1. First couple balance and swing
2. Lady go right, gent go left
3. Circle 3 and don't turn loose
   It's halfway 'round and shoot the goose
   And swing in the center.
4. Lady lead on and gent follow up

Circle 3 and don't turn loose
It's halfway 'round and shoot the goose
And swing in the center.

5. Repeat once more—then everybody swing.
6. Repeat 1, 2, 3 for couple No. 2, No. 3, and No. 4.

1. First couple bow and swing.
2. Girl goes to couple No. 2, man to No. 4.
3. They circle halfway round, then their respective couples "pop" them toward center where they swing.
4. Now girl goes to couple No. 3, man to No. 2, and action is repeated.
5. Girl goes to No. 4, man to No. 3, and all is repeated.
6. Repeat action for No. 2, girl going to No. 3 and man to No. 1, and so on.

Northern Lights (Canadian) [13]

Music: Little Brown Jug   World of Fun Record M107

THE SINGING CALL (using no opening or closing call):

1. First couple out to the couple at your right.
2. Have a good look at the Northern Lights.
3. Into the igloo by the door, while you clap. One, Two, Three, Four.
4. Out of the igloo, into the ring, Give your partner a great big swing . . .
   Swing and swing and swing and swing, Swing around, yes, everybody swing.
   On to the couple at your right . . . and so on.

ACTION:

1. Numbering is counterclockwise. First couple go over and face Couple No. 2,
2. They shade their eyes and look over each other's heads in amazement, the lights are so beautiful.
3. Couple No. 2 join adjacent hands and make an arch. No. 1 enter and stand without turning around, then clap four times.
4. They now turn around and come out of the igloo into the center of the square. Swing in the center and move on to the next couple.

5. Each couple continues around the square, in rotation, goes home, then another couple starts out until all have completed action.

Square Calls in a Circle (Any "square" music)

FORMATION: Large circle of couples, each man with partner at his right, and with one couple facing other. "Stationary" couple faces center of circle, and active couple have backs to center of circle. Active couple progresses to its left.

NOTE: This formation helps handle odd numbers (not exactly enough for square sets) and also proves to be simple teaching technique. (Square dances are done in circles in some sections of country.) Any visiting couple calls can be used in this fashion.

SOME CALLS:

1. Around that couple and take a little peek,
   Back to the center and swing your sweet (*or shake your feet*)
   Around that couple and peek once more
   Back to the center and everybody swing. (*or swing all four*)
   On to the next.
2. Rights across and "How do you do?"
   Left hand back and "How are you?"
   Swing the corner lady,
   And now your own sweet honey baby.
   And on to the next.
3. The ladies whirl . . . and the gents all whirl . . .
   And don't forget the butterfly whirl!

ACTION:

1. Couples with backs to center are active ones, and should follow calls. They drop hands, look around behind couple they are facing for a little peek, man going around girl, and girl around man. Return to center, swing partner. Peek again, swing again.
2. The two couples form right-hand star, call out "How do you do?"
   Left-hand star, and loud, "How are you?"
   Swing corner, swing partner.
3. With arms to sides, each person, as directed, does whirl in place, left shoulder leading. For Butterfly Whirl, all whirl with hands

in air. (*Any "Visiting Couple" call can be used in this arrangement, like Birdie in a Cage, Shoot That Pretty Girl, Chase the Squirrel.*)

Birdie in the Cage

Use any opening call.

CALL:

1. First couple balance and swing. Lead right out to the couple on the right.
2. Birdie (lady) in the cage, and three hands 'round.
3. Birdie hop out, and crow (gent) hop in. Join your hands and circle again.
4. Crow hop out, give the birdie a swing.
5. On to the next (repeat 2-5 for couples 3 and 4), except that after last couple you say, "Home you go, and everybody swing."

Call 1 to 5 for couples 2, 3 and 4.

Use Ending.

1. First couple bow, swing, go over to No. 2.
2. Girl gets in middle, and they circle around her.
3. She rejoins circle, but her partner goes to middle (often saying "Caw! Caw!")
4. Man rejoins circle, then each swings partner.
5. Moves on to next.

GRAND MARCH FIGURES

There are many possibilities for figures in Grand Marches. Most of those listed below come from other folk games, so you could look to the folk games you know for other possible figures.

It is well for the first two couples to know the routine, also to have a person leading at the head, and a helper at the foot of the line, to keep things moving properly.

Any good march, or any music suitable for squares, is all right. (See Index for list of tunes for Grand Marches.) If it would be too tiring for your group to go through all this, select only the figures you like.[14]

1. *March in 2's.* Two lines form, ladies on left side of hall, men on right, as they face head. Head person of each line marches

to center of head-side of room, and takes partner from other line, walks down center, turning left at foot, marching around hall, and eventually up center to head of hall.

2. *Promenade in couples* around room and draw in couples who wish to take part. They "tack on" to line.

3. *Ladies stand in line,* one in back of other on one side of room; gentlemen stand on opposite side in same formation. Lines march toward each other, passing with ladies on inside and gentlemen on outside. They meet at opposite end of hall, and march up center in twos.

4. *Players come down center of room in twos and separate,* couples alternately turning one to right, other to left. They countermarch in twos. When they meet again at other end of room, inside line of group at leader's left continues marching on inside, and outside marches between couple of other line. Same figures may be worked out in fours.

5. *Three and One*. March up center in fours; separate, three to left and one to right. Single line on right, and triple line on left march around hall until they meet again, when they come up center in fours. Separate, three to right and one to left, and march around room as above, coming back in fours.

6. *London Bridge*. For easy convenience we are calling lead couple Tom and Mary; second couple (who are in the march line right behind them), Joe and Sally. As couples reach head of room, Tom and Mary turn to left and Joe and Sally, to right. Couples alternate this way, all down line, and march down sides of room to foot, where they meet. Tom and Mary form 2-hand arch and lead their line over heads of Joe and Sally's line, who go under 2-hand arch tunnels which Tom and Mary's line have formed. When they meet again, they reverse, and Joe and Sally's line form arch, others going under.

7. *Over and Under*. When two lines meet again, coming from opposite sides of room at foot, they do over and under. Tom and Mary form 1-hand arch, and Joe and Sally go under it. Then both couples continue in same direction in which they started, alternating with making arch, and ducking under arch, with couples they approach. This is over-and-under figure of "Waves of Tory." This can be repeated if desired, when lines meet again.

8. *Zigzag.* Tom and Mary link adjacent arms, and so do Joe and Sally (and so do each of couples in their lines). They do "grand right and left" without taking hands. Tom and Mary veer to right, Joe and Sally to left, and they pass shoulders, continuing around circle, like doing grand right and left, but moving as couple, and not taking hands.

9. *Arches.* At center of foot, couples meet and come up center of hall singly. When head couple gets to head of hall, they form 2-hand arch and stand. All others come through arch and form arch, around sides of room. When they have finished, all step back one step.

10. *Face-to-Face Slide.* Head couple join both hands, outstretched at sides, and slide through alleyway formed by other couples, who have stepped back. Second couple follows, and others continue until all have done so.

11. *Back-to-Back Slide.* After all have finished other slide, head couple then turn back to back, join hands outstretched at sides, and slide sideways down "alley."

12. *Promenade.* Head couple link arms and promenade through lane (alley).

13. *Up by 2's, 4's, 8's.* All march around room until head couple can lead line up from foot toward head once more. Then they alternate (as in opening directions for Tunnel) head couple going to left, second couple to right, third to left, and so on. Come up from foot by 4's, then by 8's, and if desired by 16's.

14. *Serpentine.* Lines stand still in place. Lead couple turns and goes between first and second line. When last person in first line passes first person in second line, they join hands and follow, until all are in.

15. *Spiral.* Leader leads line in a spiral formation, walking clockwise in wide circle and closing in gradually. Arriving at center, he reverses and walks between lines of spiral, so unwinding and bringing line out into large circle.

16. *In and Out.* Joining hands in large single circle, all can go to center and back two or three times. Some like to shout as they go in.

17. *Grand Right and Left.* Each person faces his partner in single circle and does *grand right and left* (see Glossary) either until he meets partner, or until signal is given to march.

18. *Changing Partners.* All promenade around circle, men on in-side, counterclockwise direction. All mark time. Have each man march forward 5 girls (counting own partner as No. 1) and take her for new partner, promenading again when he gets her. Likewise with girls, having them go forward 3 men, perhaps.

19. *"Funny Marching."* Promenading around circle, they can be asked to run (double time), do slow motion, hop, limp, skip, fly, shake hands, trot like horse, hop like clown, lumber like elephant, tiptoe, sing and clap, clap hands over head, behind, turn around while marching—or do polka, waltz, or schottische steps.

20. *Each woman has a hat.* She puts it on table, men march by tables, pick hat up, put hat on. Women then come to men wearing hats and march. (Or women might receive hats from table appropriate to occasion—Leap Year, Valentine, Sadie Hawkins—or perhaps uniform hats, for women or men.) You must find, as partner, person whose name is inside hat.

21. *Walk That Queen's Highway* (Not over 50 couples). Prom-enading in circle, lady of first couple drops partner's hand and turns back to right, walking in opposite direction on out-side of circle. All other ladies promenade in order behind lead lady, men continuing to circle. Lead man meets circle of women led by leading lady. He nods to her, continues on. Next time they meet, lead couple swings once, promenades on. Following couples in order swing once, promenade.

22. *Walk That King's Highway.* Starts from promenading circle. Man of first couple drops partner's hands, passes behind her to outside of circle, turns back to right and walks in opposite direction, meeting and swinging in as in Queen's Highway.

23. *Formations from the Grand March.* End grand march with group in proper formation for next game. If it is "Sally Down the Alley," you might want to end with back-to-back slide. If it is single circle, end with circle at end of spiral. If square sets of 4 couples, have group come up from foot by 2's, 4's, 8's, then form circles (which are ready to do squares). If first one is to be in a line (as in "Waves of Tory"), have them come up in lines. Relays can be used at end of grand march by having them come up in 8's or 16's and face side of room.

22

Nature Activities

THIS CHAPTER IS NOT only a reminder to those who already have been initiated into the world of nature and have found that all sorts of fascinating entertainment and recreation await discovery in the out of doors. It is also a stimulus to others who have not been acquainted with outdoor pleasures and mysteries to try some of the projects suggested here.

Whether it be picnics or hikes, recipes for cook-outs or for beautifying the campfire, games to play on outings and field trips or compass and measurement games, how to make a treasure trail or hold a nature scavenger hunt, games and contests of woodcraft or observation games to play on the homecoming bus—there are briefly written ideas on all these subjects and more that will start you on a new world of exploration, with fun as the outcome.

PICNICS AND OUTINGS

Everyone welcomes the opportunity to get out into the open air and relax for a time. Whether it be at the beach or in the mountains, in the back yard or in the great open spaces, there can be fun. Families, church groups, school classes, 4-H clubs and other youth groups are all eager participants.

Picnic or Outing Committee Responsibilities. For a group to derive the maximum pleasure from any picnic or outing there need to be at least two or three persons who love the out of doors to serve as a planning committee for the event. Such a committee may decide on the location or destination of the outing and on the type of activities—whether it shall be a Field Day, Outdoor Folk Festival, Water Carnival, Derby Day, or whether the recreation shall be of an informal nature. The kind of activity is dependent upon the purpose of the event and upon the location. If transportation is required, such as cars or bus, the committee makes the arrangements. The committee, of course, will have made sure that there is a plentiful supply of food on hand. And when the event is over, the committee reminds the group of their responsibility to others for leaving the picnic area in as clean a condition as is possible and for making a final check-up on garbage disposal and on campfires.

Hiking. Sometimes the best transportation to an outing is the two legs. Groups have often enjoyed following Treasure Trails to the hidden destination and discovering the picnic supper. (See "Nature Treasure Trails" in this chapter.) Those who have laid the trails will have just as much fun as those who hunt for the clues. Novelty hikes are fun as a means of getting to the picnic area. For instance, in a *Beeline Hike* the hikers must take a compass bearing and follow it to their destination. Objects in their path must be climbed over or under, or pushed through. This one requires perseverance! However, food and fun at the end of the trail are rewarding. A *Zigzag Hike* is similar to the Beeline Hike, but a changing compass course must be followed. In a *Heads or Tails Hike* one person flips a coin at the junction of each trail or road or street to determine a new direction. You can end up in some unexpected places. *Hike Out, Hayride Back* is a fine combination, for after a good hike, games, picnic or cook-out, it is very nice to settle down on the old wagon and sing your way back home. More modern methods of transportation would involve trucks, bicycles, buses and automobiles. No matter what methods are used, the group should take every possible safety precaution. If the trip is very long, a caravan should be organized with planned stops along the route. Safety cannot be overstressed.

Food: Covered dish suppers, pot luck suppers, planned picnic menu, cook-outs (see section on Cook-outs), box suppers are possibilities for picnic refreshments.

Games and Activities: The group might wish to have some theme as previously suggested. In that case the games would carry out that theme. A Field Day (see Mock Field Day in Index) or Folk Festival might be desired. However, theme or not, the recreation leader must be able to handle a large group in an outdoor situation. For that reason, the activities should be those which can be organized quickly and in which both young and old, men and women can participate. The section on Low Organized Games in Chapter 20 and on Novel or Quiet Relays and Races in Chapter 17 are recommended for this purpose. The age and interest of the group are the chief criteria for choosing the activities. It is important to choose some good mixer for use at the beginning of the recreation period which will serve to loosen up the crowd both physically and mentally. From there on anything can happen. Some self-explanatory ideas that might be used are hand puppet or shadow puppet shows, singing contests, talent nights (or days), Lil Abner Days, folk festivals, dramatics, charades, small group competitions, campfires, storytelling, nature hikes and activities, star studying, ceremonial campfires (firelighting, legend, Indian costumes).

DAY CAMPING

What's It All About? Actually day camping is what the name implies—camping during the day. All the activities of a regular camp are provided with the exception of sleeping overnight. Cooking meals, hiking, wading in a brook, building a camp home, getting acquainted with birds and insects—these are only a portion of the activities carried on over a period of a week or so.

WHO ATTENDS? Generally, children from eight to fourteen are the ones who participate.

WHAT AGENCIES PROVIDE THESE CAMPS? Any agencies such as churches, Scouts, YM and YWCA's, schools, civic clubs, city park commissions, or private individuals may plan and conduct day camps.

WHAT IS THE PURPOSE? Day camps provide a chance for youngsters to be out of doors where groups may learn to live happily together, to live simply, and to know and appreciate their environment. Many youths who might never be able to attend a resident camp are afforded the opportunity for small-group living in a camping situation. Democratic procedures involved in planning and working together contribute toward deepening relationships and a growing interest and concern for each other and common goals. The concurrent development of resources and the growth in appreciation of the out of doors encourages better social adjustment.

Day Camp Program: Objectives of a day camp might include acquisition of new skills, gains in physical health and social development, increased understanding of both individuals and groups, and appreciation of Nature and the out of doors. These goals may be attained through a variety of means. However, there are several requirements which must be met that will determine the degree of success in reaching these objectives:

LEADERSHIP. Basically, the program is determined by the capabilities of the leadership. A person who enjoys creative work with children in the out of doors is to be desired. Sources for this type of leader might be the elementary schools, high schools, scout and other youth organizations, church youth workers, college students of high character, and persons who have a hobby or known ability in natural sciences.

SITE. The ideal location might be described as one which is healthful, safe, and rich in natural beauties. It should be free from hazards such as cliffs, swamps, and deep swift running water. Poison ivy, poison sumac, and poison oak should not be present. The one fundamental necessity is a safe and adequate supply of drinking water. Seclusion and necessary space for activities are to be desired.

FACILITIES. Separate toilet facilities should be provided for both sexes. A large central building for shelter and rainy day activities is also needed.

HEALTH AND SAFETY. Each camper should have a thorough medical examination within two weeks of the beginning of camp. The camp should provide ample insurance coverage and a safe method of transportation to and from camp. Staff members need to be well trained in first aid, and adequate equipment should be available. A careful method of waterfront control must be established and adhered to. Instructions regarding the use of knives, axes, and other camp tools should be given campers early. A relaxed schedule is to be desired. Campers should be allowed plenty of rest between strenuous activities, since it is known that fatigue causes the greatest number of accidents.

PRECAMP TRAINING. This is the most important phase once the leadership and site have been chosen. A three- or four-day training period is necessary. Specialists in various areas may be secured to serve as resource leaders. If the staff can divide into small groups of six or eight and participate in the same group processes involving democratic procedures and cooperative planning that the campers will follow, they will be better prepared. Wholehearted participation is necessary for an understanding of small-group living. From this will stem discussions and methods of motivation, counseling, and group leadership. The site should be examined, and a general idea of its possibilities gleaned. The staff should decide on general goals and objectives as well as some specific plans, remembering, however, that the campers will be allowed to plan and carry out within their small units as much of the program as possible.

Program Activities: Activities that can best be carried on out of doors would take precedence over others in all planning. This would be the chief criterion for determining program possibilities. Other criteria need be decided by the staff (and later the campers) in light of the facilities, site, and leadership available as well as the needs of the campers. From this thinking would emerge a general philosophy of the group that would inculcate the objectives of the camp and the campers' relationship to them. All other portions of the program would follow naturally.

SINGING. A good way to begin and end the day. All types of songs are available—hiking songs, work songs, quiet songs, worship hymns.

SITE BUILDING. Each small group builds its home for the camp period. The campsite is chosen, and resting places, storage space, equipment, fireplaces, totem poles, logs are decided upon and prepared.

HOUSEKEEPING. Daily duties which are necessary for camp life. Wood gatherers, water carriers, cooks, clean-uppers, log keepers, beach combers are jobs which can be rotated from day to day.

CAMPCRAFT. This includes the skills necessary for good camping:

care and use of knife, axe, saw, and spade; knot tying, lashing, fire building, outdoor cooking; care of tents; making of simple equipment; hiking preparations, sack packing. A relationship of true skill to lifelong hobbies might be explained, as use of knife in woodcarving. Specific references to outdoor cooking and fire-building may be found in the section on cook-outs.

HIKING AND EXPLORATIONS. This is a good group-planning activity. Clothing, equipment, objective routes, food must all be decided. Nature observations and games involving plants, trees, birds, insects, rocks, are very interesting to the campers. Insure interesting and adequate rest periods along the way.

NATURAL SCIENCES. Campers enjoy leaf prints; plaster casts of tracks; nature quests; weather bureaus; nature trails; conservation studies, soil erosion control; cutting of hiking trails. The great out of doors is all around; it is better to include nature in all activities than to set it aside for one class during the day.

DRAMATICS. Informal dramatics and impromptu acting out of stories, charades, and songs are much a part of the days' activities. The dramatization of local legends and pageants, and the construction and use of simple puppets make good contributions to the general camp meetings and other special events.

GAMES. A wide variety of games is needed; quiet games, active games, nature games, campcraft contests, hikes and trails, stalking games, campfire activities. These games should involve simple equipment at the most. Sports and other games that are more suitable for the playground have no use in a camping situation.

ARTS AND CRAFTS. There are ample opportunities for these in an outdoor program. Activities that require little expense and that will increase one's appreciation of the out of doors are the ones to be used as a natural part of the program. Sketching; unit log decoration; hand and shadow puppets; clay modeling; dyes made from barks, roots, and berries; basketry; wood carving; pine cone figures; flint and tinder fire acts; bracelets and beads from nuts and seeds—these are suggestions for natural arts and crafts.

PARENTS' DAY. Parents will enjoy taking part in a day's activities toward the end of camp. It is better not to prepare any extravagant presentation. Rather, a demonstration of daily activities, campcrafts, natural arts and crafts, waterfront activities are indicative of a camper's growth and acquisition of skills.

COOK-OUTS

Cooking on an outdoor fire is an enjoyable activity for young and old alike—from the youngster learning to toast his sandwich over a fire to the grizzled veteran of many an outdoor meal grilling his fresh caught bass to the tune of popping "hushpuppies" and sizzling French fries. The inexperienced yearn to learn, and the old hands love to teach the knack of outdoor cooking. The experience of planning the details and sharing the work adds to the enjoyment and develops a wholesome fellowship within the group.

Laying the fire: There are several types which can be used for cooking purposes. Remember when building the fire to (1) use dry tinder and small wood, (2) place the twigs and tinder close together so that the blaze will kindle larger pieces, (3) lay the larger pieces partially off the ground so that the air can come in below and be drawn up through the fire.

Hunter's Fire: Stones may be used instead of green logs. Level off the tops of the logs with an axe. Place the logs about 6 inches apart at one end and 18 inches apart at the other. Scrape a trench between the logs and lay your fire. Crisscross twigs and small logs in teepee style so that air can come up through them. Allow your wood (preferably hard wood) to burn into a large bed of coals. Sticks and logs that are split burn more quickly.

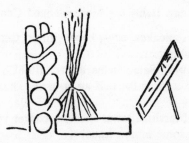

Reflector Fire: A fire laid close to a dirt bank, or against some large flat stones will serve the purpose of the type illustrated. Heat will be reflected from the logs (stones or dirt bank) to the pan which is tilted. This fire is especially good for baking purposes.

Tin Can Stove: Cut a door (4 × 5 inches) in the bottom of a gallon or No. 10 tin can. Cut another opening close to the top for the smoke to escape and several other vents in the bottom. The

fire needs to be replenished periodically. Charcoal may be used very successfully. This type is used for quick-cooking foods and frying.

Planning for Cooking: The menus selected must depend upon (1) the age and experience of the group, (2) the time allowed for cooking, and (3) the cost and availability of the food. The planning should allow everyone an opportunity to cook some item, and each person should meet with some success. There will be real enjoyment in learning new skills as the cooking becomes progressively more difficult.

Simple Methods and Items for Inexperienced Cooks

TIN CAN STOVE: Pancakes, eggs, bacon, toast, thin steaks, French toast, and hamburgers.

ON-A-ROCK COOKING: Same items above. Build a fire over a flat rock and keep burning for half an hour. Rake off coals and put on the food.

STICK COOKING: Marshmallows, wieners, cheese bobs (bacon and cheese), toast, some-mores, kabobs.

FOIL COOKING: Baked potatoes; corn; tomatoes; apples; steaks; ground beef mixed with chopped onions, carrots, potatoes, and celery; fish with sliced onions, carrots, potatoes, and bacon. (Wet articles slightly before enclosing with tin foil. Turn only once.)

BROILER STICKS: (Weave green sticks into a tennis-racketlike contraption): Tender cuts of meat, hamburger patties, bacon, toast, fish steaks, chicken (cut up), pork chops.

BAKING IN HOT COALS: Potatoes, apples, corn on the cob (wrapped in husks), sweet potatoes, stew-in-a-can.

ONE-POT MEALS: Stew, soup, hot chocolate, chile con carne.

The inexperienced should take along vegetables such as carrots, celery, and lettuce in order that a balanced meal may be provided without requiring the cooking of a large number of items.

Here are some campfire recipes that may be new to many hikers or picnickers:

EGGS ON A STICK: Pick tiny hole in each end of egg and run thin green stick through holes. Place on forks over coals. Cook about 10 minutes, turning several times.

EGGS IN ORANGE HALVES (or onion halves): Split large orange and scrape out fruit. Break egg in orange half and place in coals. Cook about 5 minutes. Same procedure is followed when using onion halves.

KABOBS: Cut beef or lamb into one-inch squares. Cut onion lengthwise through middle and separate leaves. Quarter tomatoes and slice cucumbers, potatoes, and green peppers. Cut bacon into three-inch strips. String these articles alternately on long green stick. Broil next to coals, turning repeatedly. Lay portions on buns or baked bread when done.

CHEESE BOBS: Cut cheese in two-inch cubes. Wrap slice of bacon around cheese and place on sharp green stick. Place on roll or bread twist when done.

STEAKS ON THE COALS: Steaks about one inch thick. Work Wesson Oil over meat. Do not salt. Place on hot bed of coals. Turn once after 6 minutes. When done, brush off ashes; salt, and enjoy real steak.

CHICKEN (OR FISH) IN THE CLAY: Rub thin clay paste into feathers of cleaned but unplucked chicken. Then enclose chicken in clay pack about one inch thick. Place in coals and bake for two hours. Continue to add to fire so that hot bed of coals is maintained. When clay is cracked, feathers will come off with clay shell. Fish may be cooked in same manner.

BREAD TWIST: Dough for twist may be made right in ready mix

box. Just add small amount of water and stir until dough has formed. Shape into long rope and twist around stick. Place on forked sticks close over coals and turn occasionally.

NATURE GAMES FOR HIKES AND FIELD TRIPS

The material from here to the end of this chapter was written by Reynold E. Carlson especially for *The Omnibus of Fun*.

Sentinel (any age, any number of players). Hikers walk single file. The one in the lead is the "sentinel." He finds a tree, flower, rock, or other interesting object which he can positively identify. He stops. Every hiker passing by must either whisper the "password" (name of the object) correctly to him or else go to the end of the line. The leading hiker becomes the new "sentinel," while the old "sentinel" takes his place behind those who answered correctly but in front of those who answered incorrectly. The object of the game is to keep as near the head of the line as possible and to become "sentinel" as often as possible.

This is a good game to add interest to a long homeward journey. It slows the group down, makes them forget sore feet, yet carries them toward their destination.

Variation: The same person may serve constantly as the leader. The object of the game in this case is to keep as near the head of the line as possible.

Observation Field Trip (adjustable to any age, any number). Hikers are given a list of things to look for or do on the trip. They write answers to their questions on sheets of paper; and the answers are discussed on their return.

Variation: A simple list of things to find may be given to the hikers as they start out. These may include such things as a blue flower, a toad, an eight-legged animal, an acorn cup.

Sounds. Hikers, while resting, may sit quietly and write down the sounds that they hear in a limited period of time, such as five minutes. The longest list wins. The sounds included might be bird calls, water, wind in the trees, a woodpecker pecking.

"I Spy" (young children, about 5 to 8 years of age; any number). On a trip with young children, the leader may say, "I spy a robin." All children who see the robin may squat; the rest remain standing. Then the leader either points out the robin or asks one of the squatting children to do so. The group continues the trip until another object of interest is seen.

Nature Scouting. Hikers setting out on a trip are told that they are to serve as scouts and to find something interesting in nature during the hike. They will report what they see at an evening campfire or other meeting.

Look-Listen Trip. A list of things to see or hear on the trip may be given to the hikers as they start out. A sample of this kind of trip follows:

How many of the following can you identify through listening?

( ) Crow   ( ) Running water
( ) Sparrow   ( ) Wind in the tree tops
( ) Blue jay   ( ) Cow
( ) Cardinal (Does the cardinal   ( ) Horse
    have more than one song?)   ( ) Cricket

How many of the following things can you see?

( ) Sparrow (Does the sparrow   ( ) Beech tree
    walk, run, or hop?)   ( ) Maple tree
( ) Starling (Does the starling   ( ) Walnut treet
    walk, run, or hop?)   ( ) Granite
( ) Turkey buzzard   ( ) Shale as part of "bed rock"
( ) Elm tree

Fish Descriptions. The leader names a variety of fish and sees who can describe it; or the leader describes a fish and sees who can tell what fish it is.

Flower Show. See which hiker can bring in the greatest variety of wild flowers. Provide books in order that unfamiliar species may be looked up. Give points for the correct names of each specimen.

Geology. Divide into groups. See which can bring in the best variety of rock formations. A hunt of this kind will surprise many whose attention has not been called to geological features of their community.

Horticulture. See which hiker can find the greatest variety of plants. Provide books in order that unfamiliar species may be looked up. Give points for the correct name of each specimen.

Tree Race. Allow time for hunting and investigating trees. Bring in samples of leaves, bark, fruit, nuts, wood of various trees. Arrange displays for all trees in the vicinity of the camp.

Bird Descriptions. While resting during a hike, see who can imitate the call or song of the most birds. Have someone give a description of a bird, and let the others guess what bird he describes. Describe birds seen along the trail, and ask who saw it, what kind of flight it had, shape and size of beak, and other questions.

Bird Habits. Give the name of a well-known bird in the locality and see how many interesting things can be told about it. Recognition should be given the person telling the most things about the greatest number of birds.

Bird Hunt. Divide group into teams. Give them a limited time in which to return to camp. See which group can find the most birds.

Bird Nest Hunt. Divide players into groups and send in different directions for a specified time. See which group can find the most bird nests. See who can tell to what kind of bird each belongs.

Freaks of Nature. Pieces of wood can be found resembling animals, fish, inanimate objects, friends. Polish and shellac or wax. Mount on blocks of wood in some cases. These make good centerpieces, table or desk decorations. Old rocks or stones resembling many strange things can be found. They make good desk weights and arouse curiosity among your friends.

Wood Collection. Cut selections from different trees. Place small screw eyes in top and hang in a row. Make letter openers with various specimens. Reveals both grain of the wood and also the bark of each kind of tree.

See What I See. This is a game to play when hikers are resting. They gather in a circle. One says, "See what I see when I see a _____" (naming some natural object which he can see, like a white pine, a piece of quartz, a beetle), at the same time pointing to the object. The player to his right repeats what the first player has said and adds an object of his own. The process continues around the circle, each person repeating the previous objects and adding a new one. A player is eliminated if he fails to name a new object or to name the objects in correct order.

Zoo or Museum Observation Games. Visits to zoos and museums may often be made more pleasurable and more meaningful if challenging questions are given, the answers to which are obtainable from observation or from information given on labels. Here is a sample of such a game. Each child was given a mimeographed sheet containing the following:

A WILD ANIMAL HUNT AT THE ZOO

You are going to hunt wild animals with a pencil. Shoot straight and keep track of your shots. A hunter needs keen eyes.

HUNT FOR THE WAPITI.

1. Why don't all these wapiti have antlers? _____
2. What country did the wapiti come from? _____

HUNT FOR THE ANIMAL WE SEE ON OUR NICKELS.

1. Which part of the back stands higher on this animal—the front or the rear? _____

HUNT FOR THE LLAMA.

1. How many toes has the llama? _____
(The llama spits at people who annoy him. Don't let it be you.)

HUNT FOR THE BADGER.

1. Does the badger walk with both heel and toe on the ground? _____
_____

2. Do you? _____

GO 'COON HUNTING.

1. Why does the raccoon like running water? _____
2. Are his hind feet and his front feet shaped alike? _____
3. Are yours? _____
4. What mark on the raccoon gives him the name "the highwayman"?
_____

5. Can he shell a peanut? _____

HUNT FOR THE ANIMAL WITH THE SKIN YOU'D LEAST LOVE TO TOUCH.

1. Does he have spines on his tail as well as on his body? _____
2. Is he a fast-moving creature? _____
3. Can he raise his quills? _____
4. Which are more dangerous, the long or short quills? _____
5. Can he throw his quills? _____

HUNT FOR THE "KING OF BEASTS."

1. Which of these beasts have manes? _____
2. Can you see this animal's claws? _____
3. Does he have whiskers like a cat? _____
4. Does he walk flat on his feet or on tiptoe? _____
5. How many cubs does this mother beast have? _____

HUNT FOR THE ANIMALS THAT GOLDILOCKS VISITED.

1. Can you see his claws? _____
2. Does he have as many toes on each foot as you do? _____
3. Can he stand up? _____
4. When he walks, do his toes point inward, straight ahead, or outward? _____

HUNT FOR THE ANIMAL WITH THE LONGEST NOSE IN THE ZOO.

1. Can this animal shell a peanut? _____
2. Why do you suppose his hind leg lacks the bend common in other animals? _____
3. Can he jump? _____
4. An Indian elephant has ordinary-sized ears. An African elephant has enormous spreading ears. Which elephant is this? _____
5. What would happen to the elephant if he did not have a trunk?
   _____

HUNT FOR THE DUCKS IN THE BIRD CAGE. (CROWS ARE HERE, TOO.)

1. Draw a duck's foot. _____
2. Draw a crow's foot (not the kind we have around our eyes!)
   _____
3. Why is the duck's foot better for the duck? _____

HUNT FOR THE ANIMAL MOST FAMOUS FOR HIS ABILITY TO GO FOR A LONG TIME WITHOUT DRINKING WATER.

1. How many humps does he have? _____
2. Do all camels have the same number of humps? _____
3. How many toes does he have? _____
4. Does he have eyelids? _____
5. Does he have eyelashes? _____
6. Of what use are the thick callus pads on his knees and breasts?

HUNT FOR THE ANIMAL THAT SUPPLIES OUR VENISON. (When you hunt them this way, you don't need a license and you don't have to worry about the hunting season.)

1. Do the antlers look different from the horns of cattle? _____
2. In what way? _____

YOUR HUNTING EXPEDITION IS OVER, SO COME TO THE ELEPHANT BUILDING AND WE SHALL COMPARE OUR GAME BAGS.

NATURE TREASURE TRAILS

Here are some tips on setting up nature treasure trails or treasure hunts:

1. It is a good idea for the treasure hunters to go in small groups of two or three.
2. Hunters should be reminded to leave notes where they found them for the benefit of later hunters. Groups may be sent out at different times, and the last group sent out should be asked to pick up the notes so that the area—park, forest, or wherever it is—will not be littered.
3. It is helpful to outline roughly in advance the boundaries of the treasure hunt area so that no one will get lost.
4. The prize may be something the whole group will enjoy. It may be "buried" at the last spot; or a refreshment stand may be set up at this end of the trail.
5. In a nature treasure hunt, the clues given may be of two types: those that depend upon a knowledge of nature or those that depend primarily on the powers of observation. Both types of clues may be used; but if the group has not had much nature work, it is best to stick to clues which depend primarily on observation.
6. The treasure hunt may be of any length, but usually from six to twelve locations, in which notes giving clues to the next location are hidden, are enough.
7. It is sometimes helpful to lay the nature trail backward, laying the last note first, so as to avoid having to retrace steps.

Clues may read somewhat like this: "Go upstream about 100 feet until you find a willow tree. There you will find the next note"; "Nearby is a tree with smooth gray bark on which someone has carved his initials. Look for your next clue there."

Variations: a. *Problem Treasure Hunt.* On each note is a problem which must be answered correctly from observation before the next note can be found. For example, a note might read: "If this pine tree has five needles to a bunch, the next note is in a hollow log fifty feet to your west. If it has three needles to a bunch, the next note is on a maple tree midway between here and the stream." Players who choose the wrong answer may find a note at the described spot reading, "What are you doing here? Go the other way," or "Sorry. Wrong choice."

b. *Secret Number*. Each note may contain a secret number. The winners in the treasure hunt (there may be several winners) are those whose numbers from all the notes equal, when added together, the number which the leader has on a slip in his pocket. For example, a note might read: "Your secret number for this clue is 10. The next note will be found on a black walnut tree near the gate." The finding of the secret number may also depend upon solving a problem, such as, "Your secret number equals the number of legs on an insect." The advantage of this form of treasure hunt is that a player or group of players must find every note in order to win and cannot skip notes by following groups who are ahead.

NATURE SCAVENGER HUNTS

Nature scavenger hunts are easily organized and lots of fun for small or large groups. Here are some tips on setting them up:

1. It is usually more fun for two or three to work together than to work singly.
2. Each group of participants is given an identical list of things to secure. These should all be objects which can be taken without damage to the area. They may include objects easy to find and hard to find, so that no one will be discouraged yet no one will finish too soon.
3. A few "teasers" might be included, such as "something no one has ever seen before" (players might break open a rock to expose an inner surface for this one); or "the leaf of a tree named for something left after a fire" (ash).
4. Each team is given a large bag into which to place the articles collected.
5. A definite time limit should be set before the players start. This may be from about fifteen minutes to an hour, depending on the age of the participants and the length of the list of ob-

jects. At the end of the time, all players return to the starting point. Speed is not considered in determining the winners.

6. If the group consists of young children, a space limit should also be set so that no one will get lost.

A sample scavenger hunt follows:

Bring as many of the following items as you can in the allotted time. Bring *fallen* leaves and seeds as much as possible (rather than breaking them off trees and plants).

1. A palmately-compound leaf. (No poison ivy, please!)
2. A needle from a tree that dresses up (spruce).
3. A fossil shell.
4. A flower that is half a fine fellow and half a fierce feline (dandelion).
5. A piece of stone named for a sour fruit (limestone).
6. All is not cactus that pricks. Bring spines from

       a. hawthorne
       b. honey locust
       c. prickly ash

7. A mineral harder than steel.
8. The fruit of the shagbark hickory.
9. Tail feathers of a blackbird.
10. A pine cone.
11. A four-winged insect.
12. An elm leaf.
13. A pinnately-compound leaf

Variation: *Alphabet Scavenger Hunt*. The players bring in objects beginning with different letters of the alphabet, each team being responsible for certain letters. For example, Group I may bring in objects beginning with A, B, C, D, and E, and may bring such things as acorns, buttercups, cones, dogwood leaves, and elderberries.

COMPASS AND MEASUREMENT GAMES

The object of these games is to develop an ability to judge distances and understand compass directions.

How Big Is an Acre? The players are divided into groups of four persons each. These four stand so that they form what they believe to be the four corners of a square acre of land. The group closest to the correct measurement wins. The varying notions of the size of an acre often prove both amusing and revealing.

How Long Is a Foot? Players are asked to stand at distances of 100 feet, 200 feet, and so on, from the starting point. The player nearest the correct distance wins.

Square Play. Before starting, each player should measure his stride by seeing how many steps he takes in a precisely measured distance of 100 feet. Each player needs a compass.

The game starts along a straight stretch of road. Each player walks at a 90-degree angle from the road for 400 feet, turns left 90 degrees and walks another 400 feet, turns left 90 degrees and again walks 400 feet. By this time he should be back on the road 400 feet from the starting point. Here he places a stake, possibly with an identifying flag attached. The player nearest the correct, accurately measured distance is the winner.

Judging Distances. At an outlook (a mountain top or a fire station, for example) the group attempts to judge distances of various points of interest. These are checked against the map for accuracy.

Orienteering. Orienteering, a sport introduced into the United States from Sweden in 1946, involves the use of the map and compass in unknown territory. Its chief element is traveling from one designated spot to another (control points) by means of the map and compass. The sport is described in detail in *The Sport of Orienteering*, by Stig Hedenstrom and Bjorn Kjellstrom.[1]

Compass Consequences. Each player has a compass and knows the length of his stride. The players are given a compass bearing (for example, 212 degrees) and are told to walk in that direction for 100 feet. The player nearest the correct point wins.

WOODCRAFT GAMES AND CONTESTS

Hare and Hounds. One player, the "hare," is given ten or fifteen minutes' start over the hounds. He lays a trail as described below. The hounds follow the trail and try to catch the hare. When they see him, the hounds may give chase and the hare may stop laying a trail. It is wise to restrict the area and the time allotted to this game.

Laying the trail: Trails may be laid by dropping corn, popcorn, beans, acorns, or leaves of a particular species. Paper or other litter should not be used.

Trail signs, such as one rock on top of another ("duck on a rock"), bent twigs, and bunched grass, may be used (see illustration). Blazes on trees should be avoided.

TRAIL SIGNS and THEIR MEANINGS

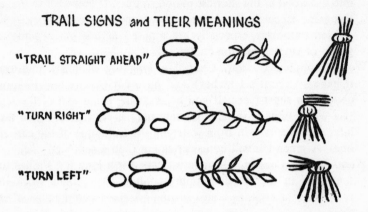

"TRAIL STRAIGHT AHEAD"

"TURN RIGHT"

"TURN LEFT"

Tracks may be made with tracking irons if desired. These are made by means of iron placed on the end of a stick and used to make impressions in the ground. The iron may be in the shape of an animal track or other sign.

Fire-Building Contest. Fire-building contests may have several forms. Here are two:

1. Each contestant is given two matches. He must gather tinder and kindling and start the fire without paper. The fire must burn for two minutes.

2. A string is strung about twelve inches above the place where the fires are to be built. Another one is strung about eighteen inches above the area. Contestants may not pile their kindling and fuel higher than the lower string. Contestants are allowed a specified time (such as 10 minutes) to lay their fires before applying matches. The winner is the one whose fire burns the higher string first.

Water-Boiling Contest. Each contestant is given a cupful of water in a tin can. The winner is the one who can build a fire and boil the water first.

Variation: A teaspoonful of soap powder or detergent may be added to the water to make it foam over the top of the can when the water starts to boil.

Nail-Driving Contest. Each contestant is given five nails, a piece of wood, and a hammer. The winner is the one who drives his nails into the wood in the shortest period of time. If you wish to make this game especially hard, use well-seasoned oak or hickory.

Men onlookers especially are amused at this game when a group of women are the contestants.

Wood-Chopping Contest. Choose a long log of fairly uniform thickness (about six inches) and have each contestant in turn chop off a short piece. If you begin at the small end of the log you will restore to the first contestants the advantage which the later contestants gain from watching the technique of the earlier ones. A green log will be easier to cut than a seasoned one.

Wood-Sawing Contest. This contest calls for a long log similar to that used in the wood-chopping contest. Contestants work in turn, using a buck saw and sawing off slabs about two inches thick.

Log-Rolling Contest. A log eight to ten feet long and twelve inches or so thick is needed. A contestant stands on each end and endeavors to get his opponent to lose his footing by turning the log with his feet. The game may be played in water by good swimmers. The winner challenges all comers.

Paul Bunyan Day. A "Paul Bunyan Field Day" may be set up by organizing the group into competitive teams and having a number of woodcraft contests. Winners in each contest get points for their teams.

Ceremonial Campfire Lightings. Ceremonial campfires have long been an experience of beauty and feeling when handled effectively. Among Scouts and campers most vivid recollections are those moments around the campfires where games, singing, storytelling, and the quietness of Taps all blended into the perfect evening. The key to those well-planned programs oftentimes is in the lighting of the fire. Here are listed some of the favorites of groups through the years.

Spontaneous Fire (Use Chemicals). A mystifying and beautiful stunt. After the group has gathered around an unlit council ring, suddenly, at the command of the leader the fire starts.

EQUIPMENT: Wood, shavings, kerosene, matches, potassium chlorate, sugar, sulphuric acid, string, and a bottle

DIRECTIONS:

1. Build council-type fire. In inside, set up small shavings in wigwam fashion. Put kerosene around wood and kindling.
2. Prepare a mixture of equal parts of potassium chlorate and sugar. Mix thoroughly and spread this mixture on the kindling.
3. Concentrated sulphuric acid (less than an ounce) is placed in a bottle. A string is tied to the top. When the signal is given, the string is pulled, tipping over the bottle so that it is poured on the mixture. There is a slight explosion and the shavings burst into flame.

WARNING: Keep people away from the fire, for the acid spatters and will make holes in clothing.

Fire by Friction

EQUIPMENT: Leather thong, bow, and a hardwood drill, base plank about ½ inch thick

DIRECTIONS: There should be a hole already begun so that drilling will be easier. Loop thong around drill, press hard on top of drill and work bow very fast. Have tinder under base plank and on the side. When spark catches flow, add tinder.

Flint and Steel Fire

EQUIPMENT: Piece of old file and sharp edge of a piece of flint or stone, small nest of tinder, large prepared fire

DIRECTIONS: Strike edge of rock with steel. Try to knock shower of sparks on a small nest of tinder. When spark lands and catches, pick up nest and blow. Add more tinder and then stick to large prepared fire. Use Indian costumes and motif throughout evening; makes a fine beginning.

TINDER: Some bark of cedar, when very dry is the best. Charred, thin cloth also can be used.

Fire from Heaven

EQUIPMENT: Campfire with opening on one side, kindling, kerosene, stake, wire, cloth

DIRECTIONS: Saturate kindling with kerosene. Drive stake into ground in middle of fire. Stretch wire from there to a tree or bank close by. Never let wire be less than a 40-degree angle to the ground. Have a boy hidden in foliage, with a ball of excelsior or rag soaked with kerosene. This ball is wrapped with wire and is hooked over and tied loosely around the wire leading from the tree to the fire. (The tree-fire wire should be blackened so that it isn't visible.) At a signal, the boy lights the ball and lets it slide down the wire. This fits in well with the Indian type of fire. Use legends for introduction.

WARNING: Do not let campers sit directly under the wire as the ball might slip off the wire.

OUTDOOR NATURE GAMES FOR SMALL AREAS

Fetch It. The players make two or more parallel lines, and each line numbers off. The leader says, "I want a ————" (naming a leaf, rock, cone, or other natural object nearby which may be taken without injury to the area). "Number—will fetch it." The person on each team with the given number must find the object and bring it to the leader. The first one doing so wins a point for his team.

Tree Tag. Players are safe from "It" only when they are touching a tree of a particular kind (as maple, pine, elm). This is a "game way" to teach new species of trees. The kind of tree may be changed from time to time.

Plants and Animals. Two teams form parallel lines, facing each other. A safety zone is located about twenty feet behind each team. One team is named "plants"; the other, "animals." The leader calls out the name of a plant or animal. If a plant, the animals chase the plants to their safety zone; if an animal, the plants do the chasing. Captured players join the opposing team. The game ends when all players on one team are captured by the other.

Variation: This can be played as a "true and false" tag, with the leader calling out true or false statements about natural history. If true, the false team chases the true; and vice versa.

Find It. The leader collects, ahead of time, leaves, minerals, flowers, ferns, insects, mushrooms and places them on a table. The group is divided into two or more teams, with each person numbered. The leader describes something on the table, then calls a number. Players with that number dash for the object. The one bringing the object first to the leader wins a point for his team.

Flash Cards. The leader briefly shows a picture card of a bird or animal. The person first calling out its name is given the card to hold. The one having the most cards at the end of the game wins. (The Audubon bird cards are very good for this game; or pictures from other sources may be cut out and pasted on cards.)

Did You See? One player exhibits an object or a picture (birds, animals, fish, and so on) for a few seconds and then covers it. The remaining players are to answer his questions about it, such as its color, markings, shape.

Variation: The object remains in full view of all the players but one, who is to turn his back to it and answer questions. This way of playing can be very funny to the group.

Name Me. The leader scatters interesting natural objects, such as birds' nests, leaves, rocks, insects on tables about the room and numbers them. Each player is given a piece of paper and a pencil. He tries to guess the names of the objects. The winner is the one with the most correct names.

Nature Categories. Each player has a sheet of paper which he divides into six columns. He heads each column with a letter from the word N A T U R E. The leader calls one of the letters and a category of nature (such as trees, flowers, fish, rocks, birds). The players must fill the column with the names of things in that category which begin with the required letter. For example, if the leader calls "N" and "birds," the players might write "nuthatch," "nighthawk," or "nightingale." A player receives one point for each item listed, plus an extra point if he is the only player listing it.

Aviary.[2] Here's a chance to learn of new birds. At least 53 birds' names may be found in this game.

The "aviary" holding all these feathered friends is divided into 49 pens. You may enter through any pen and travel from pen to pen in *any* direction without skipping. (For 8 names you will have to use the same letter twice in succession.) As you find each bird, write its name on this sheet.

Surely you can see the JAY at the top of the center column. Can you find 3 other members of his family? Can you discover 3 extinct birds? Which ones are tropical? Which ones have you

D	O	T	Y	N	M	T
U	O	R	A	E	L	O
K	C	U	J	B	U	I
U	A	N	I	H	S	G
L	R	E	T	R	D	A
W	E	G	K	I	P	N
H	O	T	L	A	R	E

observed in nature? You may consult bird books or museums for help. Try to learn something distinctive about each bird you find.

OBSERVATION GAMES FOR BUS OR AUTO

There is often a good deal of time used in going to and from day camps in buses—time which can be enjoyably and profitably used. Games might be played in the morning, when wits are fresh, and songs sung on the return in the evening, when it is time to relax.

The games which follow were considered a regular part of a day camp program on the trip to camp. The games were mimeographed and a copy given to each child on the morning bus trip. They can be adapted to any environment.

Observation Game I (Observation Lotto)

Each child is given a card like the one at top of next page.

On seeing an object named on his card, the child puts an X in the appropriate square. The first child to fill a row of X's horizontally, vertically, or diagonally, calls "Lotto." The game may be continued until someone fills all the squares and calls "Lotto" again.

A RABBIT	WILD MUSTARD	BIRD HOUSE	ROBIN
STREAM OR RIVER	BIRD-FEEDING TABLE	FLOCK OF SPARROWS	REFORESTATION PROJECT
PINE TREE	SQUIRREL	BIRD BATH	ERODED LAND
BLACKBIRD	OAK TREE	ROAD SIGN READING "DEER CROSSING"	VULTURE

Variation: Each child's card may be somewhat different. In this case, he calls aloud when he sees an object named on his card, and all players having that object on their cards fill their squares with X's. Otherwise the game is as described above.

OBSERVATION GAME II

Check (x) the things you see on the way to camp by bus.

Farm products
Corn
Soy beans
Fruit trees

Farm animals
Cow
Horse
Pig
Sheep

Signs
"Deer Crossing"
"Rest Park"

Birds
Cardinal
Turkey buzzard
Robin

Trees
Elm
Maple
Pine
Cedar

Pets
Dog
Cat

Flowers
Yucca
Daisy
Queen Anne's Lace
Blue bonnets

Interesting Spots
Limestone quarry
Gravel pit
Cemetery
Sawmill

(Your secret! What is the most unusual thing you saw on your trip? Do not let anyone else know. You will have a chance to tell about it after you reach camp. Keep it a secret until then!)

23

Hobbies and Crafts

WHEN WE STARTED TO COMPILE this book we intended to make two separate chapters of Hobbies and of Crafts, for they were written by different authors, but the subjects are so closely related that it seems appropriate to make them two sections of one chapter. An interest in crafts very frequently generates interest in hobbies, and conversely.

HOBBIES*

A hobby is an activity entirely apart from one's gainful employment which one does with enthusiasm during his spare time for the pure joy of doing it. Enthusiasm is the key word. Lacking is the feeling of duty, hurry or responsibility. Hobbies are unhurried, pleasurable living among one's native enthusiasms.

THE VALUES OF HOBBIES

Our lives are full of activities, but it would be good to stop occasionally and inquire of oneself just how many things we do purely for joy. Often we realize the importance of recreational release, but let ourselves drift into a round of unpleasurable duties—and then wonder why we are ill-tempered or uncommonly fatigued. For this reason, it is good to schedule some regular time each week to indulge in one's own particular hobby—and it may be completely different from hobbies of other members of the family. It is usu-

---

* By Dr. George Steinman, Abilene, Texas.

ally more fun to enjoy one's hobby with someone of like enthusiasm, so one should be on the lookout for hobby-mates who would understand and encourage one's own interests.

There are many reasons why a person needs a hobby, or hobbies, but the most apparent one is for good health. In ancient times, a physician would prescribe the game of chess for its curative powers, and the game would be bought in an apothecary shop. Even then doctors realized that forgetting one's self in pleasurable activity had its reward in improved health. Today when the pressures of living so mightily result in men with ulcers, "businessmen's stomach," and the dreaded heart diseases, doctors urge patients to let up, and to release tensions by relaxing with a hobby. One can easily draw a parallel between King Midas and some of our ambitious, money-covetous men, who discover sometimes too late that acquiring gold too avidly has in it the kiss of death. But men are not the only ones needing recreational release. Doctors who minister to "disorders of women" find that the most common ailment of mothers of young children is a feeling of fatigue, brought about not so much from the myriad duties she must perform, but from pure boredom and monotony. Many doctors now prescribe one or two evenings away from home (at least for one-hour stretches) each week, a time when the wife and mother can leave the children with the baby sitter and get out with her husband for recreation. Many recommend taking off one afternoon a week to get away to some enjoyable play activity. Women can't always get away, however, so it is good to have an around-home hobby, also. One woman gardener confesses: "I have dug many a trouble into the soil and seen many a joy spring therefrom."

Hobbies are taken for granted in therapy for the handicapped. The saddest sights are the people stricken by some physical handicap in their later years, those caught without a hobby when they need it most, those who feel they are too old to learn something new. Without some joy in life, such persons degenerate physically, mentally, and also socially. A happy soul draws friends; an empty life repels them. We would probably admire the foresight of one woman who, looking forward to the years when her eyesight might fail, committed to memory large portions of the Bible so that her favorite selections might always be with her. It would be good to have a storehouse of hobbies to draw upon in case of some handicapping injury or illness, or to turn to full time at time of retirement.

Beside health benefits of hobbies, there are personality-enrichment rewards. "The craftsman does more than build things; he builds himself." They draw one from isolation into companionable ways and give a sense of achievement, confidence, and satisfaction that enriches personality. They keep us from becoming bores or, as Luccock describes it, from being "headache-giving people."

Another bonus from cultivating hobbies is mental stimulation. Expansion of the areas of awareness can be the greatest of delights. It is an interesting thing to witness people who are exposed to their first attempts at art—at drawing what they see. It is not unusual to hear them exclaim, "Why, I never really *saw* things before!" Stamp collecting is mentally stimulating, and through it many have increased their knowledge of history, symbolism, mythology, and have acquired many other interesting facts. Many a self-made man becomes very successful, not from learning he got at school, but from learning he got from following his love of reading. Hobbies can become international bridges to an appreciation of art, crafts, cookery, music, literature, and mode of living in other lands.

What of moneymaking hobbies? Often a man's second string turns out to be his best one, and it becomes his vocation. There are plus and minus factors in this. It cannot be denied that if one can get paid for time pursuing a specialized interest, it erases that feeling of guilt that one sometimes feels when indulging in play. However, if pressure of making money causes the activity to be less appealing or desirable, some analyzing is in order. We must remind ourselves that there is no sin in doing some things for one's own personal enjoyment—in fact, it is a sign of a well-ordered life. Thus, if making a hobby "profitable" tinges its enjoyment, one must either drop the desire to make money in connection with the hobby, or use it as a money-making, enjoyable activity and develop other hobbies for recreation. One should always have several projects in mind that would be fascinating to explore if there came the chance and the time. But, as Calkins in his excellent booklet *Care and Feeding of Hobby Horses* cautions, ". . . don't get 'hobby' mixed with 'fad.' Hobby is what you do because you want to, and 'fad' is what you do because other people do it."

TYPES OF HOBBIES

Leisure-time diversions fall into four classes: collecting, doing, creating, and learning.

Hobby Collecting. An interest in accumulating certain items seems to be universal, though it may only manifest itself in one's reluctance to throw something away—for instance, buttons, magazine articles, scrap lumber. When we get really bit by the collecting bug, however, life takes on added interest; things are saved and acquired because of their color, shape, design, composition, history, age, or rarity.

Hobby Doing. All games and sports, and square dancing, folk and ballroom dancing would be classed as "doing" hobbies. Swimming, boating, hiking, piloting a small plane, bicycling, taking trips, skating would all belong in this category. Playing an instrument or singing would be such a hobby, or table games such as chess or Scrabble.

Hobby Creating. Possibly the most rewarding is this sort of hobby. As one art teacher told her class, "We are all made in the image of our Creator; therefore, it is within each of us to be able to create." It is a fundamental drive. Arts and crafts of all kinds are a result of this urge to create. It is possible that the early pioneers, for whom we feel pity because they had to work so hard, actually had rich, challenging lives. If you have ever tried building a house, weaving cloth, braiding rugs, making furniture, embroidering pillowcases and scarves, you will remember the glow of pride from doing such artful work yourself. There is a deep, encompassing satisfaction from painting an acceptable picture (at least acceptable to you), making jewelry, forming puppets or dolls, turning commonplace materials into things of beauty and usefulness.

Hobby Learning. Learning is fun, if you don't feel you *have* to learn, and if you are studying something which is of vital interest to you. Reading is one of the most common ways of learning, and it is always a fascination to spend time in a library reading about topics of interest. It is fun to clip articles of special interest as one reads the daily newspaper or a magazine, then to put them in scrapbooks or in files. Museums are dedicated to the furthering of learning, and they often have speakers and show films of interest to hobbyists. Collecting fossils, rocks, and minerals is an excellent learning hobby, for it can be done in groups, and requires hiking in the outdoors, and thus combines several types of hobbies into one. Studying stars with a telescope is becoming a favorite hobby. Experiments in chemistry are usually fascinating to boys. The list is endless of things people enjoy learning about, and in the process of learning, minds continue to be alert and interesting.

SOME HOBBY LISTS

Several suggestions of hobbies will be given, but of course it is a mere beginning of possibilities. One must search one's own inclinations before choosing something for a hobby, and one must decide whether the hobby should be related to one's own customary occupation or quite different in nature. And if a hobby turns out to be wrong for someone, he must feel free to look around for another.

Some Suggested Hobbies for Boys

Coins
Stamps
Tricks
Puzzles
Pets
Marbles
Pencils
Model air planes
Homemade games
Knot tying

Indian lore and
    relics
Cowboy lore and
    brands
Lariat twirling
Miniature horses
Fossils
Freaks of nature
Minerals and rocks
Chemistry

Insects
Soils
Camping
Pen pals
Match covers
Astronomy and star
    lore
Archery
School pennants
    and stickers

Some Suggested Hobbies for Girls

Buttons
Costume dolls
Post cards
Puppets
Autographs
Miniature vases
Papier-mâché figures
    and masks

Finger painting
Shellcraft
Butterflies
Salt and pepper sets
Bird lore
Records
Felt craft
Spatter printing

Bottles
Bandannas, scarves
Folk games and
    stories
Scrapbooks for
    jokes, cats, dogs,
    babies, poems

Some Suggested Hobbies for Men

Sports
Bowling
Boating
Mountain climbing
Novel coin banks
Ham radio
Hospital visitation
Aviation, gliding
Deep sea fishing
Big game hunting

Wood Carving
Antique nut
  crackers
Quail hatching
Campaign relics
Antique locks and
  keys
Firearms and
  powder horns
Rare books

Hi-fi music
Bee keeping
Chess
Canes
Gems
Meteorites
Tall tales
Boys' work
Scientific
  research

Some Suggested Hobbies for Women

Hooked rugs
Homemade dolls
Wild flower garden
  or scrapbook
Jewelry making
Art
Music
Little Theater
Girl Scouting
Driftwood art
Ceramics

Creative writing
Growing orchids
Genealogy
Textile decoration
  (stencil or block
  print)
Lamp shades
Leathercraft
Collecting bells, old
  glass, samplers
Horseback riding

Golf
Swimming
Skating
Folk dancing
Hiking
Badminton

Job-Related Hobby Suggestions for Religious Workers

Devotional classics
Prayer manuals
Hymnals
Bibles
Bible lore
Christian symbols
Clipping library
Rosaries
The Madonna in
  art and legend

Negro poetry and
  spirituals
Wood carvings
Costume dolls
  of Bible people
Paired animal
  figurines
Wedding ring boxes
Church flower
  arrangements

Worship file
Simulated stained
  glass windows
Chapel garden
Camping

SUGGESTIONS FOR A HOBBY PROGRAM

Set up an educational program concerning the values in such a
  program.
Stage a hobby show for all ages.

Equip a game room for the use of various groups.

Equip a craftshop open to members either regularly or at several seasons during the year.

Distribute a hobby interest finder, then follow up with a hobby night program of groups with various hobbies.

Promote leisure-time activities such as Open Houses, Religious Dramas, Hymn Festivals, Hikes, Picnics, Religious Films, Hobby Demonstrations.

Place craft and hobby books in the group's library.

Build picture files for Christian education.

Collect items for a Missionary Museum, to use during vacation schools and for special study groups.

Send a delegate to a recreation workshop for help in building a program.

Sponsor a recreation workshop.

Enlist local hobbyists: 4-H club workers, Home Demonstration agents, shop workers, teachers of art, drama, home economics, museum directors.

Start hobby clubs for older adults.

Investigate the hobby helps one may order from The Superintendent of Documents, Washington 25, D. C.

HOW TO GET THE MOST OUT OF YOUR HOBBY

1. Assemble a library about it. "Hobby horses need books in their saddle bags."
2. Compile a scrapbook for further background.
3. Keep a catalogue of your collection: donors, dates, prices paid, significant facts.
4. Find a hobby mate to enjoy hobby with you.
5. Find adequate cases or places for exhibit.

SOME HOBBY POSTER SUGGESTIONS

"CIVILIZATION MAY BE CALLED THE SUM OF THE HOBBIES OF INDIVIDUALS AND THEIR ACCEPTANCE BY THE HERD."

"THE WHOLE SECRET OF LIFE IS TO BE INTERESTED IN ONE THING PROFOUNDLY AND IN A THOUSAND OTHER THINGS WELL."

—HUGH WALPOLE

HOBBIES HELP TO PROVIDE
  RESTFUL WORK
  BUSY LEISURE
  PRODUCTIVE IDLENESS
  VARIETY TO OUR DAYS
  OLD-AGE HAPPINESS INSURANCE

"THE GREATEST PEOPLE OF THE FUTURE IS GOING TO BE THE PEOPLE WHICH USES ITS LEISURE BEST."
—L. P. JACKS

HOBBY ADVENTURES
  WITHOUT MONEY AND
  WITHOUT LEAVING HOME:
    THROUGH BOOKS,
    THROUGH NATURE,
    IN GARDENS,
    IN MUSIC,
      WITH ARTS AND CRAFTS,
      IN PERSONALITIES ABOUT US.

HAVE YOU TRIED
  THE HOBBY WAY
  TO HAPPINESS?

"THE INTERESTING PEOPLE ARE THE INTERESTED PEOPLE."
—WILLIAM LYON PHELPS

KINDS OF HOBBIES
  DOING THINGS
  MAKING THINGS
  COLLECTING THINGS
  LEARNING THINGS

SOME HOBBY VALUES
  ENTERTAINMENT
  ESCAPE FROM MONOTONY
  HEALTH
  PERSONALITY DEVELOPMENT
  INTELLECTUAL DEVELOPMENT
  CHARACTER DEVELOPMENT
  GLOBAL OUTLOOK
  JOY IN THE COMMONPLACE

SERVICE TO SOCIETY
VOCATIONAL GUIDANCE
RELIGIOUS GUIDANCE
PRESERVATION OF OUR AMERICAN WAY OF LIFE

INEXPENSIVE HOBBIES
NATURE STUDY
SCRAPBOOKS
PICTURE COLLECTIONS
CLIPPING LIBRARY
DRIFTWOOD
READING
GARDENING
KINDS OF PAPER
BOTTLES
SCRAPCRAFT
STORYTELLING

CRAFTS

To make a thing of beauty or usefulness with one's own hands is recreation of a special sort. It is within each of us to be able to create beauty if we honestly and perseveringly try. The history of mankind is revealed not through written records but through the efforts of those in each civilization who have created articles of beauty. We feel the greatest respect for those forebears of ours (and even some of our contemporaries) who fashioned all their articles of civilized living with their own hands and imaginations, and we especially admire those who took the second step and made them well-proportioned and lovely in design. Occasionally some of us feel a stir of unrest when we realize how dependent we are upon factories for our every need. There is deep satisfaction in learning basic survival crafts—articles from clay mud, baskets from native willows, grasses, or corn shucks; bows and arrows from materials at hand, spinning and weaving of cloth, and things made of leather. Lester Griswold in his book *Handicraft* does a magnificent job of illustrating processes involved in fashioning primal articles.

The most common handcrafts are those used to beautify our homes, or adorn our bodies, those used in teaching, or those used for quick, satisfying entertainment. Since we are limited in what we can include in a single chapter, we shall describe a few simple crafts, and in more detail we shall give numerous "scrapcraft" suggestions written by the editors of PACK-O-FUN Magazine. We shall give pointers for a craft program, then we shall list handcraft projects and give names of handcraft companies who can supply you with material and directions for each project. Write to these companies for a free catalogue, and allow plenty of time after an order is placed before you plan to use the material. Summertime is the busiest time for handcraft companies, so do early planning and order two months in advance if at all possible. It is good to get your materials early so that leaders have ample opportunity to experiment with them and to make samples. It is only through doing that a leader can acquire the knowledge and experience necessary for teaching.

BEGINNING A CRAFT PROGRAM

If you are at a loss about starting handcrafts in your church, community, club, Teen Town, you would do well to print or mimeograph a number of Interest Indicators such as at least one church [1] we know of has done. One side of the card gives spaces for Name, Address, Phone, Occupation, and Age Group. It gives opportunity for a person to circle the day of the week on which the activity would be most welcome; also one specifies whether morning, afternoon, or evening would be most convenient. Blanks are left for listing hobbies and skills, and for experiences which are related. The other side of the card headed "WHAT IS YOUR RECREATION QUOTIENT?" lists a great variety of activities followed by three columns "Interested," "Would Do," and "Could Lead," which they are to check according to interest. These cards are given to all members and newcomers, and the information on them has helped the church to work out a yearly program including arts, crafts, drama, literature, music, outdoor recreation, social recreation, and sports.

If you have the interest and the leadership, there can be a year-round program of handcrafts. Many groups, however, have found it most helpful to make it a seasonal project—especially welcome before Christmas and during the summer. One church in Pennsylvania began a craft program for junior age children during the church hour, requiring the parents to attend church in order to enroll their children in the program; it increased church attendance 500 per cent.

SUCCESS TO YOUR HANDCRAFT PROGRAM! [2]

1. Each person should go home at the end of the first session with a sense of achievement, and some tangible evidence of his best endeavors. This means the beginning project must be simple and dramatic, and something a person might be glad to possess. One cannot expect the newcomer in handcrafts to be ready to begin a long involved process with its culmination in some distant future.

2. Have a number of samples on display, but encourage creativity. Remember that the more creative a project is, the more pleased will be its creator. For those, however, who lack confidence enough to create their own designs, have a variety of examples or suggestions.

3. Explain directions carefully, going through the process before them. For detailed work, one might briefly summarize the steps involved, then take each step at a time—first showing the group, then letting them go through it. Let them help each other; sharing and helpfulness are character products reaped from group handcrafts.

4. Compliment any special points of merit, and let criticism come from the worker—perhaps with leading questions such as "Are you happy with your work as it now stands?" or "Is there any part of your work you feel might be improved?" or "Get back from your work and look at it. Is it in good proportion and design? Do the colors go well together?"

5. Separate groups according to age level, if possible. Children get discouraged if their work is not so polished as that of their elders. There is no need to separate boys from girls, men from women; quite often interests overlap and a girl should not feel ashamed if she longs to do woodworking, nor should a

man feel abashed if he has a hankering to do cooking or shell-craft.

6. It is good to charge for materials used in order to encourage necessary respect for the cost involved. Charge 10 per cent extra over cost of materials sold to cover loss and waste. Figure postage as part of actual cost of materials.

7. Have at least one instructor for each fifteen persons, another person for finances, and another for distributing materials.

8. Handcraft room or rooms should be situated so that noise will not bother others. It is good to have it readily accessible, so participants do not have to go through a labyrinth of halls and steps to find it. It should be a room that won't be desecrated by a crushed crayon on the floor, a charcoal smudge on the wall, or a table accidentally scratched by a slipping knife. However, craftsmen should do all within their power to keep it neat and well cared for.

9. An hour's time of actual work is the minimum to do an adequate job. Most craft programs allow fifteen minutes to get materials, an hour for working, and fifteen minutes for cleanup. (Cut working time to 20 minutes for small children, ages 6 to 10. Adults can work with enjoyment for two or three hours, except for "golden agers" who might tire if not limited to an hour and a half.)

10. Don't conduct too many projects at once. It is better to start with one medium for everyone, unless the group can be divided and extra instructors can go with each group. The teacher must not allow for more variety of instruction than he is capable of giving in the time allotted.

11. Have fun with the group.

SIMPLE CRAFTS FOR TEACHING AND FOR RECREATION

Paper Modeling is one of the simplest of methods of making figures, puppets, dishes, ornamental boxes, toys. The main ingredients are narrow strips of newspaper and either starch, wallpaper paste, or paste made of flour and water. Newspaper strips may be torn along a ruler edge to make them fairly straight. Procedure for figures of people or animals: Wad balls of newspaper around a rough skeleton of wire; dip strips of newspaper into starch or paste, then slide between second and third fingers to remove excess starch; wrap around the wadded paper, shaping as you go. Sometimes it is not even necessary to have the wire armature if the figure is stocky—such as a pig or turtle—for the wads of paper will be sufficient base. After several layers of strips have been pasted around the figure, set it in a warm place to dry. Then paint with poster or tempera paints. Extremely attractive animals may be made this way; one first-grade teacher made a large giraffe, big enough for the children to sit on it (which required a wooden frame for the armature). Small animals, decorated with gay folk designs, are very colorful.

Bowls or baskets may be made by modeling paper strips across the bottom of an inverted bowl, after greasing it thoroughly with vaseline. The first strips applied should be wet with water only, but the rest should be pasted on. Trim edges while still damp. After drying, remove it from bowl and paint. Ribbons may be taped on for basket handles.

Papier-mâché is useful in making relief maps, figures, and wastebaskets, in covering boxes to put them into many uses, and for any project requiring a modeling material. Materials needed are newspapers, water, and thick flour-and-water paste. Crumple newspaper and soak overnight, then tear into small pieces and squeeze almost dry. Add flour-and-water paste to paper mixture until it is a thick, modeling consistency, then shape into whatever purpose you need. As in paper modeling, if forming over an object, such as metal wastebasket or china dish, grease the mold with vaseline before applying the papier-mâché. Let dry in warm place until dry, then paint. In making relief maps, trace outline of land upon blue paper (which is to be the oceans, rivers, and other waterways). Place paper in glassed picture frame, then shape papier-mâché into land masses atop the glass.

Salt Maps or Salt and Flour Modeling have many teaching uses and are extremely easy to do. For modeling it is preferable to heat the salt and flour before adding water, but for maps it is not necessary. Ingredients: twice as much salt as flour, enough water to form a dough, food coloring. Procedure: stir salt and flour over heat until thoroughly hot; add water and stir until doughlike. Separate into several containers and give each container a few drops of different food color and mix well. This makes a pleasant modeling material for making decorative flowers, birds, leaves, butterflies, boats, people.

Pipe cleaners of varied colors can be twisted into miniature figures. These are purchased from a drugstore or dime store. Crepe paper clothes can be twisted or taped onto the figures.

Sand Pictures. Stir food coloring into small jars of sand. Draw design on paper, then apply glue to all parts to be of a particular color. Sprinkle sand upon glue. After one color is set in glue, and the glue has dried, shake off excess sand. Then apply glue for the next color.

Shadow boxes are attractive ways to display nature materials. Secure a deep picture frame with cardboard backing. Cement your picture onto the cardboard. Flowers and leaves and grass may be dipped in wax or paraffin (melted over boiling water) or may be pressed in a book until dry and flat, then cemented into the picture. Landscapes with real sand, pebbles, and diminutive plants may be made; or seascapes using real shells and dried seahorses. Cigar boxes could be used by removing the lid and using papier-mâché or the salt and flour "clay" to give the putty-like slant around the inside of the frame.[3]

Clay figurines may be preserved by dipping them in melted crayons or wax, then allowed to harden.

Potato printing can be very attractive. Slice off the end of a potato in order to have a flat surface. Cut away the potato around a design, keeping in mind that the part not cut away will be what does the printing. Use indelible stamp pads, or brush indelible ink across the printing surface before applying it to paper or cloth. This is a very easy method of doing block printing.

Pastel chalk pictures are extremely attractive, but easy to do. Get special paper and the pastel chalks from an art dealer or craft store. Draw picture, then practice shading in lighter and darker areas by rubbing finger over such areas, sometimes applying another color by rubbing finger over chalk and then passing it over place to be darkened. A small bit of chamois skin, which can be bought in most auto supply stores or drugstores, makes an excellent eraser. When picture is completed, spray it with a shellac fixative which also is bought at an art supply store or stationery shop.

Crayoned Tapestries. Crayons are an easy medium to use in cloth decoration. Children enjoy drawing heavily upon a lightweight cotton material, coloring in figures as darkly as possible, then pressing with a hot iron on the opposite side of the material. This causes the crayon wax to penetrate the material. A picture like this, fringed at two sides, makes a creditable wall decoration. Camp curtains, dresser scarves, and the like may be decorated this way, also.

Finger painting is a gooey art medium enjoyed by all ages. Finger paints and paper may be purchased from art and craft stores, but you can make your own. Make a thick, cooked starch, either with laundry starch, wallpaper paste, or plain flour and cold water stirred gradually into boiling water. A few drops of oil of wintergreen or oil of cloves from the drugstore will keep the starch from souring if you wish to save it for another day. Pour starch in several containers, then add color, as desired.

"Gold" or "silver" crosses from tin cans [4] are truly beautiful when done carefully. Use cans opened with rotary-type opener. For a beaten silver cross, use ordinary cans rubbed with steel wool; those with "gold" linings will give the effect of bronze or brass.

Mark top and bottom of can into four equal divisions, using tape measure, to be sure each arm area will be the same. In order that the arms of the cross shall taper toward the center, mark off a space of one-half inch or more *within* the marks at each side at the *bottom* of the can. Draw lines of cross on can, using a ruler, with the four arms touching each other at the *top* of the can, angling toward the center or *bottom* of the can. Using light cotton gloves for protection, cut out the cross with tinner's shears, purchased inexpensively at a hardware store. It will take a bit of pressure to cut through the rim at the top, and one must be sure to *let up* on the pressure the instant the rim has been severed, or it will spoil your cutting of the thinner tin. Do *not* cut along an entire line at one cutting, but cut a little down each line, going around several times before the bottom of the can is reached. Flatten the four arms, leaving the four sharp triangles sticking up. Trim off the dark seam, cutting closely along each side and twisting out with pliers. In order that each section between the arms of the cross shall appear the same, *cut out similar pieces* of tin in the middle of the other triangular areas and twist out. Cut again a line down the middle of the eight upright pieces that remain, not touching the flattened arms of the cross. With screwdriver, pliers, or pencil, *roll* the narrow strips of tin to the circular rim of the bottom of can. This gives ornamentation around the center of the can. One might instead cut these into pointed triangles, suggesting rays from the center of the cross.

For beaten effects, pound back of metal with ball peen hammer (one with a rounded end). Different effects are achieved by beating part of each arm and leaving part of each one smooth. At the center, one may leave the circle smooth, or tamp lightly with nail and small hammer. Religious symbols such as I H S or CHI RHO may be tamped in. In case bending of the arms caused the center to get slightly squared, tap *lightly* on the bottom rim with a hammer, forcing it back into a circle. Sharp edges may be dulled with steel wool, then wash the cross, dry well, and paint with clear lacquer to prevent tarnishing or rubbing.

Crosses can be hung by suspending a small wire across back, but for best effect, hang the cross against a dossal or wall hanging of velour or velvet. Greek crosses have arms of the same length, but the familiar Latin cross has the three upper arms shortened.

SCRAPCRAFT
By John and Edna Clapper

There is nothing quite so rewarding as the magic of turning "throw-aways" into clever, useful articles. Though we can't possibly, within this one chapter, include every type of material or all the projects feasible for even one such item as tin cans, we should like to give you a few starters to show how worth while scrapcraft can be. It is a particularly satisfying subject to leaders whose budgets are low, yet whose children like to make gifts, toys, party favors, decorations and other things that are truly acceptable in the adult world.

The extent to which any of the items are finished and decorated will depend largely on the age of the children. The suggestions given are the simplest, since most of the projects have been designed for children in the 7-to-12-year age group. However, if you have some teen-agers with real creative instincts and lots of ingenuity, they will probably be capable of adding the fine finished details necessary to turn their handicraft into true creative art—or possibly even a money-making venture. The illustrations on the two-page spread are indicated by corresponding numbers in parentheses in the text.

PLASTICS

One of the most common "throw-aways" these days is plastic material. Everything, from torn shower curtains, tablecloths, and leaky beach balls down to the numerous vegetable bags you get, is usable.

Beach Bag. The leaky beach balls can readily be converted, without any complicated patterns, into beach bags and make-up capes. For the beach bag, cut off about ⅓ of the ball. On the remaining piece, turn down the top edge twice as if hemming. This gives a double thickness of plastic in which to punch holes and insert eyelets (available in most dime and variety stores). Finally, add a drawstring through the holes along the top. This bag will conveniently carry a swim suit, towel, cap, and a few other accessories. (1)

Make-Up Cape. The roundness of the beach ball makes it fit nicely over the shoulders to become a make-up cape especially handy for the popular home permanents. You can get two such capes from one beach ball if it is not too badly damaged. Cut the ball in half right around the middle. Then cut an opening up the front and around the circle at the top of the ball for the neck. At the neck, put a snap fastener through several thicknesses of plastic for reinforcement. Several snap fasteners will make it adjustable for small fry as well as Mother and older sister. (2)

Picnic Kit. Large pieces of plastic can, of course, be sewed into small bags and cases for marbles, glasses, compacts, and so on; they can also be used in sheets for place mats, doilies, and other protective covers. Perhaps the best suggestion we have seen is this plastic picnic kit which converts into a tablecloth. In the center of the plastic, sew on pockets of the same material for paper plates, cups, spoons, forks and knives with Mystik tape. Double-fold the side edges in over the pockets; then double-fold the ends in the same way, and make tape handles over the top fold. You will find this a convenient way to carry all your table settings in one simple package, and eyes will really pop when your kit opens to become a tablecloth with the table almost set! All your friends will want one like it. (3)

TIN CANS

Before you cast your tin cans into the rubbish, better take another look, because they have wonderful possibilities. Books have been written about this craft alone, and, though many of the projects require soldering and shaping, there are still many, many very satisfying things to make without the use of any tools at all.

Sewing Kit. Sewing kits can be devised from almost any container, but this one made from the pretty plaid "Scotch" brand cellophane tape cans is so compact and useful, you'll wonder why you didn't think of it yourself. The large can, which is 5 inches across and just the height of a spool of thread, you will probably have to get from some office. The two smaller ones (one for buttons and the other for pins) are 2½ inches across and can be found in homes that use a tape dispenser. Glue one of the small cans, for buttons, to the inside center of the large can and arrange spools of thread around it. Glue the other small can to the top of the large cover and fill it with pins. To the top of one of the small covers, make and glue on a small pin cushion. A little paint around the edges, and your gift is ready for Mother, appropriate at any time of the year. (4)

Wishing Well Planter. Coffee cans should be easy to get, and you will be amazed at the cute gifts you can make from them. This wishing well planter is very popular with the youngsters and is very much appreciated by flower lovers. The roof is made from two pieces of wood with a cross bar at each end. Two side posts form supports. The can and the roof are wrapped with cord and shellacked ready for assembling and planting. (5)

Pouch Bag. A coffee can also can be made into a unique pouch style purse. Line the can inside and on the bottom with felt. Take five of Daddy's old ties and cut off both ends at an angle. Glue these ten pieces to the side of the coffee can near the top, wrap the outside with cord, and shellac. For a drawstring, punch holes several inches down on the ties and insert eyelets (available at most dime and variety stores) so that the drawstring

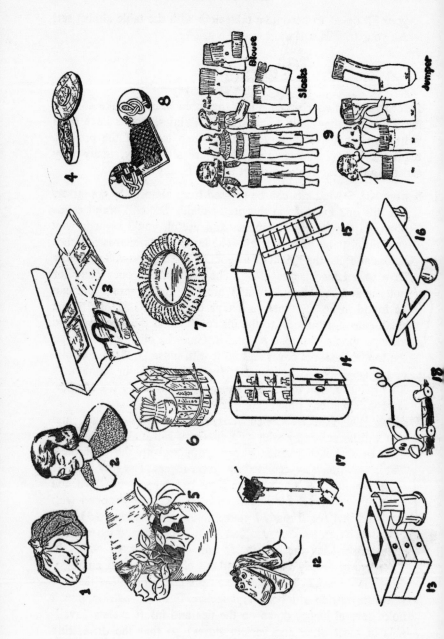

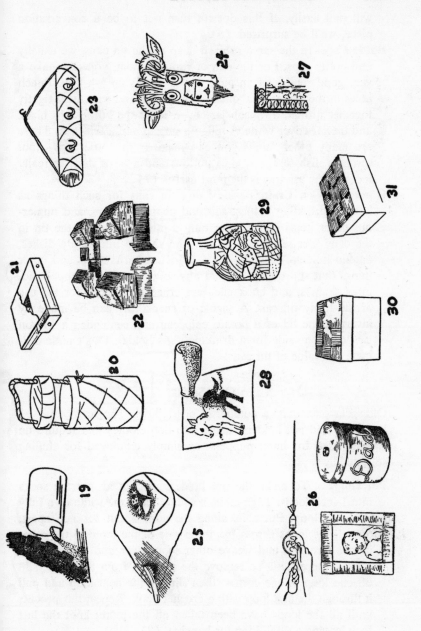

will pull easily. If this doesn't turn out to be a conversation piece, we'll be surprised. (6)

Bottle Caps. In the same rubbish heap as the tin cans, we usually find bottle caps. For the den or rumpus room, you can make a very good replica of an auto tire to use as an ash tray. Punch holes in the center of about 50 bottle caps and wire them tightly together around a Mason jar cover. Paint the bottle caps black and the jar cover white or gilt. Be sure to add a felt base. There are many other things you can make from bottle caps—foot scrapers, fish scrapers, club buttons and awards, but we really feel that the ash tray is the most useful. (7)

Other Tin Can Craft. Beside using tin cans for such things as banks, sprinkling bottles, salt and pepper shakers, and numerous other items that require only a little decorating, the tin in the cans themselves can be cut and shaped into candy dishes, napkin holders, letter openers, Christmas ornaments and other things that still do not require any soldering. Metal-tapped pictures, frames, and book ends are other suggestions for the use of the lowly tin can. A picnic or snack tray can be made by inverting the lid of a potato chip can and cementing a Mason jar lid to one side for a drinking glass holder. Don't underestimate the value of tin cans!

OLD SOCKS

Old socks offer quite a number of possibilities. They can be woven into mats and pot holders; made into doll clothes that require no sewing; used for hand puppets; or simply employed for stuffing soft, cuddly toys.

Pot Holders. To make the pot holders mentioned, cut the socks into 1-inch loops. Then make a square loom the width of a fully stretched loop. Put nails along the edge about ½ inch apart. Stretch the loops across from one side of the loom to the other in one direction and weave other loops over and under in the opposite direction. To remove the weaving from the loom, slip off one loop in one corner, then slip off the next loop and pull it through the first loop with a crochet hook. Repeat this process until all the loops have been taken off the loom; knot the last loop leaving a small loop for hanging. (8)

Doll Clothes. The doll clothes that require no sewing make a wonderful rainy afternoon pastime for little girls. To help you get started, we shall tell you how to make a blouse, a jumper, and a pair of pants. After you have accomplished these few items, you should have no trouble designing your own snowsuits, skirts, halters, playsuits, and a whole wardrobe for your little doll, including a few perky little hats. The idea basically is to take advantage of the elastic tops of the socks. Sizes are not given here, but you can dress everything from little storybook dolls to the large "Toni" dolls, depending on the socks you have available.

To make a long-sleeved blouse, you will need to cut the tops off of three ribbed socks such as the ones many girls wear these days. Cut a loop about 1 inch wide from the top of one and save. In that same sock, cut armholes about 2 inches down from the top. Slip this sock over the doll's head and arms and turn down the top for a turtleneck collar. Fold each of the other socks in half and slip them up over the arms for the sleeves. Then take the 1-inch loop from the first sock and slip it around the arms and across the back of the doll to hold the sleeves in place. For short sleeves, omit the extra pieces from the second sock.

To make the jumper, use an elastic top sock. Cut off the toe. Just below the elastic top, cut along the back of the sock and down the sides to the heel, removing the heel also. Slit the sock along the center of the front from the elastic band halfway down the sock. To assemble the jumper, slip the skirt thus made over the feet of the doll up to the arms. Then push the doll's head through the slit and turn just the elastic back down over her head and arms to the waist. Adjust the jumper so that it is neat and trim with its own snug elastic waist band.

Yes, you can even make a pair of pants from two elastic-top socks (one for each leg) without any sewing. For long pants, cut the socks off just above the heel. Cut a small slit, just large enough for one leg, right along the elastic. To put the pants on, you put on only one sock at a time. Slip the elastic over both legs and then just one leg through the slit. When assembled, you have two elastic bands at the waist, with one sock around each leg. The bottoms of the pants can be gathered together with a rubber band, another elastic top doubled over or wound with thread and then boots slipped onto the doll's feet. For shorts, either cut off the legs or roll up the pants for cuffs. (9, 10, 11)

Puppets. Hand puppets afford hours and hours of pleasure for the youngsters. From old socks, you can make one in a jiffy, and with the cost almost negligible, you can make them by the dozens. For the mouth opening of the puppet, cut around the toe of the sock and down the side of the foot from the toe almost to the heel. Turn the sock inside out and sew a piece of red material the size and shape of the opening for the mouth. Cut a piece of cardboard the same as the mouth piece and fold it in half. Turn the sock right side out and slip the folded cardboard down into the mouth. Sew on button eyes, buckle nose, and yarn hair. Slip the sock over your hand with the thumb in the lower jaw and the rest of the fingers in the top of the mouth. A variety of characters can be created by changing the details such as the size and shape of the mouth opening, position of the eyes and nose, or different hair-dos and kinds of hats perched on the top of the head. (12)

CARDBOARD BOXES

Everyone certainly has many boxes around that can be transformed into toys, doll furniture, many, many gifts items, or used for model construction, card table dioramas and matched storage boxes.

Doll Furniture. Let's make a few simple pieces of doll furniture first. Round up six of the penny matchboxes for a desk. Put paper fasteners in the ends for drawer pulls; glue together three high for each end of the desk. Across the top glue a piece of cardboard. In the center of the desk, add a miniature blotter. For the chair, glue a cardboard back to the top of a spool, and paint. For a corner cabinet, use a small Easter egg carton. Cut out the top half of the lid of the carton for open shelves, and leave the bottom of the carton as is for doors. Paint to match your décor. For the bedroom, make a set of bunk beds from some small pill boxes using sucker sticks for the corner posts; add a small ladder made from cardboard and toothpicks. A table for the dining room, kitchen, or porch can be made by gluing a piece of cardboard to the top of two sets of crossed clothespins. The bench is cardboard glued to spool legs. Sofas and such can be made with more elaborate cutting and shaping, plus a little padding with scraps of material. There are many other possibilities, but just these few items will give your little girl a lot of things to play with, and even more important, the satisfaction and fun of making them. For larger-sized furnishings, use cigar boxes and regular egg cartons. (14, 15, 16)

Other Toys and Gifts. Two long cigarette cartons taped together with a pocket mirror at each end will make a wonderful periscope, the very thing to stimulate the fabulous imaginations of any child. More practical and quite realistic is the piggy bank made from an old salt box. Pull the pouring spout out for the pig's snout; add thumbtack eyes, spool legs, a pipe cleaner tail. Paint, and make a slit along the back of the pig for regular "deposits." The salt box can also be put to very, very good use for any adult that drives a car. Fill the box with thoroughly dried sand and keep it in the back of the car for a Handy Sandy, should you get stuck on ice or snow in the winter. As a gift, you could decorate with wall paper and add an appropriate verse on the side of the box. (17, 18, 19)

Certainly there is someone on your list who would like a knitting bag. Cover an oatmeal box with wallpaper and attach a cord from the sides of the box up through the cover. Other boxes can be covered and divided with partitions for hankies, gloves, hosiery, and sundry odds and ends. If someone in your family needs to take medicines regularly or likes to carry aspirin, why not decorate a small box just for his exclusive use? (20)

Match Boxes. Four match boxes take on a new look if arranged in a square with one box opening out on each side of the square. Cut 2 squares of cardboard that will fit the top of this arrangement; trim and decorate the two pieces and glue them to the top and bottom. It will be pretty enough for Mother to have in the living room on the coffee table handy for guests; then, when the boxes have been emptied, they can be used for storing small items like paper clips, thumbtacks, stamps and pins. (21)

Corrugated Cardboard. Closely associated with boxes is corrugated cardboard material. Aside from the decorative possibilities of corrugated cardboard, there are hundreds of practical applications, such as using it for holding small nuts and screws when making minor repairs, or for lining up beads ready for stringing. The corrugations also lend themselves to holding such items as chalk for music rules or soda straws in varying lengths for a home-made pipe organ. One of the most interesting uses is that of building realistic models of log cabins, block houses, forts and stockade fences. A holder for small tools, pencils and brushes can be made by rolling up a piece of corrugated cardboard about three feet long, tapered from 5 inches at one end to about 2 inches at the other. Tape the end so that it won't unroll, and put your small implements into the corrugations. (22)

Cardboard Rolls. By decorating cardboard rolls with wallpaper, crepe paper, painting or other camouflaging, you can make imitation candles, fire crackers or logs. You can use them for party favors, napkin rings, pot holder racks, holders for soda straws, and even puppet heads—just to name a few things. Most of these items are self-explanatory. We might add that the pot holder rack is first covered with wallpaper, then cup hooks are screwed on for holding the pot holders, and a cord is strung through the roll for hanging. The little puppet heads are made by covering a roll with plain paper. The ears and nose are cut as "stand-out" features, and the eyes, mouth, and perhaps a moustache are painted on. You will also have to sew a dress or shirt to the bottom of the cardboard roll to cover your hand when you make the puppet perform. (23, 24)

DECORATING

It would be easy to write another whole chapter on the possibilities and varieties of decorating, without even touching on the endless designs you can obtain by painting or by covering with common materials like wallpaper, oilcloth, or other scrap material. Perhaps, however, the following will introduce you to some new techniques and ideas.

Spatter Painting. For this technique you will need a stencil for your design, and either an old toothbrush and piece of screen wire, or an old spray gun. Pin your stencil in place on your project and spatter around the design by rubbing the toothbrush (which has been dipped into ink or paint) across the screen. Carefully remove the stencil when you have sprayed sufficiently.

In many instances, you will want to thin the paint for better results. This method is best for things like napkins, gift cards, and program covers. If airplane dope or oil paints are used, you can also work on cloth materials and metal trays. (25)

Crepe Paper Raffia. To make your crepe paper raffia, you will need to borrow Dad's hand drill. Cut strips 1 to 2 inches wide from the end of a roll of crepe paper. Put one end of the crepe paper into the chuck of the drill and have someone hold the other end off at a distance while you turn the handle on the drill until you have a firm, twisted cord. Your raffia substitute can be used for lamp shades, woven mats, knotted and braided belts; or wrapped around jars, cans, and cardboard rolls for a great variety of colorful gifts. (26)

Beads, Buttons, Seeds, and the Like. There is no particular technique in using these materials, but they deserve to be mentioned among novel ideas for decorating. An arrangement glued to the cover of a box or to a plate for the purpose of a wall hanging is very effective. A use for larger seeds (cherry, apricot, peach) is to glue them around the edge of an old frame and gild it, giving an antique finish. Crushed eggshells also can be adapted to this method of antiquing. (27)

Colored Sand. Ordinary sand can be colored or tinted very easily with vegetable coloring. Put a little sand in a small jar. Add a few drops of the coloring and shake well. When thoroughly dry, it is ready for use. To "paint" a picture with the sand, first trace the outlines onto the surface of your object. Spread ordinary glue onto the areas that are to be all one color. Sprinkle your sand and let it set for a few minutes before you shake off the excess. (Be sure to save the surplus sand for later use.) Repeat this process with another color. When the picture is completed, give it a coat or two of shellac. You can make some very interesting, almost 3-D effects with this method of painting. It also makes a very unusual way to decorate jars and boxes. (28)

Small Scraps. Perhaps you have only small pieces of such things as colored paper, wallpaper, or paint samples. If you're a real saver, you can even make use of these little bits. Paste them in a planned geometric design or helter-skelter (patchwork fashion) on jars, boxes, or scrapbook covers. The little pieces can also be rolled or cut into confetti, and glued on. Another idea is to use the scraps to form pictures; pasting the different little pieces on for flowers, windows, roofs, and such in scenes; and for the skirts, shirts, pants, hats and such, for the people in the pictures. (29)

Corrugated Paper. Corrugated paper is both useful and decorative. If you will take advantage of the lines of the corrugations, you can create some surprising geometric designs. Cut the corrugated paper into strips and triangles, and then rearrange the pieces for the effect you want to create before pasting them onto your project. You can use this idea for decorating box covers, scrapbook covers, wastebaskets and many other things. (30)

Burnt Matches. Probably the most startling of all decorative suggestions is this one using the burnt matches. By cutting them to various lengths and letting the burnt ends of the matches form your designs, you will be amazed by the endless effects you can create. After laying them out and planning your design, glue them to the surface of cans, boxes, jars, and all sorts of things. When glued in place and dry, give them a coat of shellac. (31)

It is obvious that we have omitted many worth-while materials like scrap lumber, leatherette, fabrics, pipe cleaners, spools, and toothpicks, just to name a few. However, we hope we have opened your eyes to this new field of "Fun on a Shoestring" as we like to call it. Once you have become an addict (and that may not be so exaggerated as you think), you will find yourself seeing possibilities in almost everything that you are about to toss away. Then, when your friends admire your latest costume jewelry, you can reply, "My necklace? Oh, that's just the cantaloupe seeds from last Sunday's breakfast!"

CRAFT PROJECTS AND SOURCES OF PROJECT MATERIALS

Numbers given below refer to handcraft supply houses listed by number on the following pages.[5]

ALUMINUM, 4, 5, 7, 8, 10, 11, 13, 14, 16, 17, 18, 19, 24, 25, 26, 28, 34, 35
ART SUPPLIES, 2, 3, 4, 5, 7, 9, 12, 13, 14, 18, 25, 32, 37, 47, 48, 49, 50
BEADS, 34
BEADS, Coralite, 26
BRACELETS, 10, 14, 24, 26, 29, 32, 34, 49
BOOK ENDS, 26, 34
BURNING NEEDLE, 26, 34
BRAIDERS, 26, 34
CALENDARS, 26, 34
CANDLES, Order information and materials from Youth Dept., Consumers
    Co-operative Association, 318 E. 10th, Kansas City, Missouri.
CERAMICS, 10, 32, 49
CLAY, 2, 3, 4, 12, 17, 19, 32, 49, 50
CHINA, GLASS PAINT, 3, 5, 7, 8, 15, 17, 18, 19, 24, 25, 32, 50
COPPER, 4, 5, 7, 10, 11, 13, 16, 17, 18, 19, 24, 25, 26, 28, 29, 32, 49, 50
CORK, 7, 10, 12, 13, 17, 18, 24, 25, 26, 34, 39, 47, 49, 50
DESIGNS, 26, 34
EARRINGS (Metal), See Jewelry
            (Shell), See Shellcraft
FELT, 4, 7, 11, 13, 14, 18, 20, 25, 26, 29, 34, 49, 50
FINGER PAINTS, 2, 4, 7, 9, 11, 12, 13, 19, 32, 34, 49, 50
FOOTSTOOLS, 19, 26, 34
FRAMES, Picture, 34
GIMP, LUSTRO-LACE, 7, 11, 14, 19, 25, 26, 34, 47
GLASS ETCHING, 4, 7, 10, 11, 12, 14, 17, 19, 34, 37, 49, 50
INDIAN CRAFTS, 19, 34
JEWELRY, Wire, 4, 19, 34
JEWELRY, Stone, 19
JEWELRY, Enameled, 2, 4, 34
LAMP SHADES, 4, 34
LANYARDS, 26, 34
LEATHER, 1, 4, 5, 10, 11, 13, 14, 17, 18, 19, 23, 24, 25, 29, 31, 32, 34,
    36, 49, 50
LINOLEUM BLOCKS, 3, 4, 10, 11, 12, 13, 17, 18, 19, 24, 25, 32, 49, 50
LOOMS, 4, 7, 11, 18, 26, 49
LUSTRO-LACE (See Gimp)
METAL, Modeling, 4, 26 (also companies under Aluminum, Copper)
METAL DISCS for trays and dishes (See Aluminum, Copper)
METAL JEWELRY (See Jewelry)
MODEL KITS, 11, 46
MOLDS, RUBBER, 19, 34
NAME PLATES, 26
PAPER WEIGHTS, 34
PICTURE FRAMES (See Frames)

PIPE CLEANERS, 6, 7, 17, 20, 24, 25
PLASTIC, 4, 10, 13, 18, 19, 24, 30, 40, 41, 43, 49, 50
POTTERY EQUIPMENT, 2, 4, 10, 32, 49
RAFFIA, 7, 12, 17, 25, 32
REED BASKETRY, 4, 7, 11, 25, 49
SHELLCRAFT, 4, 7, 10, 11, 13, 18, 21, 24, 27, 29, 38, 44, 45, 49
STENCIL PAINTING, 2, 3, 4, 10, 11, 14, 17, 18, 24, 25, 32, 33, 40, 47, 49, 50
SHOE BUTTONS, 19, 34
SPAN-TYPE LIQUID PLASTIC, 4, 34
TILES, 7, 27, 34
WEAVING (See Looms)
WOOD PROJECTS, 4, 7, 10, 11, 19, 25, 26, 32, 34, 39, 47, 50, 59

This list is not intended to be complete, but does give an idea of places near you. You may have a local supply store which handles many of these items.

SOME HANDCRAFT SUPPLY COMPANIES

1. ACE LEATHER CO., Inc.
5065 W. Eleventh St.
Indianapolis 24, Ind.
2. AMERICAN ART CLAY CO.
(AMACO)
4717 W. 16th St.
Indianapolis, Ind.
3. AMERICAN CRAYON CO.
1706 Hayes Ave.
Sandusky, Ohio
4. AMERICAN HANDICRAFT
CO., Inc.
12 East 41st St.
New York 17, N. Y.
or
45-49 S. Harrison St.
East Orange, N. J.
5. AMERICAN HANDICRAFTS
CO.
3091 Wilshire Blvd.
Los Angeles, Calif.
6. AMERICAN PIPE CLEANER
CO.
Norwood, Mass.
7. AMERICAN REEDCRAFT
CORP.
83 Beekman St.
New York, N. Y.
8. EDITH BARKER'S STUDIOS
Bowman Field
Louisville 5, Ky.

9. BINNEY AND SMITH CO.
Dallas, Texas
10. BUFFALO HOBBY HAVEN
Buffalo 12, N. Y.
11. BURGESS HANDICRAFT
STORES
182 N. Wabash Ave.
Chicago 1, Ill.
12. CENTRAL SCHOOL SUPPLY
311 W. Main St.
Louisville, Ky.
13. CHICAGO CRAFTS SERVICE
509 North LaSalle
Chicago 10, Ill.
14. CLEVELAND CRAFTS CO.
770-774 Carnegie Ave.
Cleveland 15, Ohio
15. THE CRAFT SHOP
P. O. Box 3069
St. Louis 5, Mo.
16. CRAFTSMAN SUPPLY
HOUSE
735 Brown's Ave.
Scottsville, N. Y.
17. DEARBORN LEATHER SUP-
PLIES
8625 Linwood Ave.
Detroit 6, Mich.
18. ELCRAFT
1637 Court Place
Denver 2, Colo.

19. FELLOWCRAFTERS, INC.
26-28 Oliver St.
Boston 10, Mass.

20. FELT CRAFTERS
500 Chadwick St.
Plaistow 1, N. H.

21. FLORIDA SUPPLY HOUSE
415 12th St.
Bradenton, Fla.

22. FUN WITH FELT CORP.
118 East 28th St.
New York 16, N. Y.

23. GEBHARDT LEATHER CO.
416 N. Water St.
Milwaukee, Wis.

24. GRIFFIN CRAFT SUPPLIES
5626 Telegraph Ave.
Oakland 9, Calif.

25. GUILDCRAFT OF BUFFALO,
Inc.
1305 Hertel Ave.
Buffalo, N. Y.

26. THE HANDCRAFTERS
Waupun, Wisconsin

27. HIGHLAND HOBBY SHOP
1061 Sixth
Des Moines, Iowa

28. HOBBY MART
604 Penn Ave.
Pittsburgh, Pa.

29. HOUSE OF HOBBIES
1728 Sherman Ave.
Evanston, Ill.

30. HYALINE CORP.
Indianapolis, Ind.

31. J. C. LARSON CO.
820 S. Tripp Ave.
Chicago 24, Ill.

32. LEISURE CRAFTS
907 South Hill St.
Los Angeles 15, Calif.

33. H. LIEBER CO.
24 W. Washington St.
Indianapolis, Ind.

34. MAGNUS BRUSH & CRAFT
MATERIALS
108 Franklin St.
New York 13, N. Y.

35. METAL GOODS CORP., Craft
& Hobby Div.
640 Rosedale
St. Louis 12, Mo.

36. FRED MUELLER, Inc.
1415 Larimer St.
Denver 2, Colo.

37. NASHVILLE PRODUCTS CO.
158 Second Ave., N.
Nashville, Tenn.

38. THE NAUTILUS
Box 1270
Sarasota, Fla.

39. O-P CRAFT CO., Inc.
Sandusky, Ohio

40. PACIFIC RECREATION
SERVICE
P. O. Box 185
San Jose, Calif.

41. PLASTIC PARTS & SALES
1157 S. Kingshighway
St. Louis 10, Mo.

42. PLASTIC SUPPLY CO.
2901 N. Grand Blvd.
St. Louis 7, Mo.

43. ROHM AND HAAS
Washington Square
Philadelphia, Pa.

44. SHELLART STUDIOS
3202 Sixth St., S.
St. Petersburg, Fla.

45. SOUTHERN SHELLCRAFT
SUPPLY
Clearwater, Fla.

46. STROMBECK-BECKER MFG.
CO.
Moline, Ill.

47. THAYER AND CHANDLER
910 Van Buren St.
Chicago, Ill.

48. JOSEPH TORCH
147 W. 14th St.
New York 11, N. Y.

49. UNIVERSAL HANDICRAFT
SERVICE, Inc.
1267 Sixth Ave.
New York 19, N. Y.

50. WESTERN CRAFTS AND
HOBBY SUPPLY CO.
213-215 E. 3rd St.
Davenport, Iowa

NOTES FOR CHAPTERS

NOTES FOR CHAPTER 1

1. As Henry Lewis pointed out at the Northfield Recreation Lab.
2. Documentation for all books referred to in text will be found in Bibliography, alphabetical by titles.
3. Available from Broadman Films, 127 9th Ave., N., Nashville, Tenn. The film was produced by Mrs. Agnes Pylant of the Baptist Church.
4. 8 West 8th St., New York 11, N. Y.
5. Such as the Northland Lab., Loretto, Minn.
6. By Joseph Mallins.
7. Written by Mary Elizabeth McDonald, Coral Gables, Florida, in the style of Kahlil Gibran's *The Prophet*.

NOTE FOR CHAPTER 2

1. Both charts supplied by Harold Hipps, West Market Street Methodist Church, Greensboro, N. C.

NOTE FOR CHAPTER 4

1. Some of the ideas in "Dating Fun" were gleaned from letters to a contest conducted by Don Winkler in the magazine CONCERN on "What to Do on a Date Rather Than Neck."

NOTE FOR CHAPTER 6

1. From *Home Play* (New York: National Recreation Association, © 1945). Used by permission.

NOTES FOR CHAPTER 7

1. See Valerie V. Hunt, *Recreation for the Handicapped* (New York: Prentice-Hall, Inc., © 1955), pp. 45-48.
2. *Ibid.*, p. 47.
3. *Ibid.*, pp. 50-52.
4. *Ibid.*, pp. 77-8.
5. *Ibid.*, p. 61.
6. *Ibid.*
7. Hallowell Davis, ed., *Hearing and Deafness, A Guide for Laymen* (New York: Rinehart & Co., Inc., © 1947), pp. 87-91.
8. Hunt, *Recreation for the Handicapped*, p. 103.
9. *Ibid.*, p. 105.
10. *Ibid.*, p. 128.
11. *Ibid.*, p. 133.
12. *Ibid.*, p. 152.

13. *Ibid.*, p. 151.
14. *Ibid.*, p. 157.
15. *Ibid.*, pp. 80-83.
16. *Ibid.*, pp. 69-70.
17. *Ibid.*, pp. 110-112.
18. *Ibid.*, p. 141.
19. *Ibid.*, p. 154.
20. *Ibid.*, p. 156.
21. *Ibid.*, p. 164.
22. *Ibid.*, pp. 91-95.
23. *Ibid.*, p. 121.
24. *Ibid.*, p. 86.

NOTES FOR CHAPTER 9

1. Bill Jennings, Delaware, Ohio.
2. Johnny Hassler, Magnolia, Ark.
3. Mrs. R. H. DeHanuit, Baton Rouge, La.
4. From Warren W. Willis, Lakeland, Fla.
5. From Mrs. Stell Chappell, Nashville, Tenn.
6. From Miss Wilma Mintier, Pittsburgh, Pa.

NOTES FOR CHAPTER 10

1. Wilma Mintier, Pittsburgh, Pa.
2. As presented at the Ihduhapi Recreation Lab.
3. By Alan Beck in New England Mutual Life Insurance Company house magazine, © 1949.
4. By Roy E. Dickerson.
5. From Dr. Hugh C. Stuntz, President of Scarritt College, Nashville, Tenn.

NOTES FOR CHAPTER 12

1. We are indebted to Harry Edgren, George Williams College, Chicago, Ill., for several interesting contributions to this chapter.
2. Adapted from material by J. Neil Griffith, Indiana, Pa.

NOTES FOR CHAPTER 13

1. From *Bigger and Better Boners* and *Boner Books*. Copyright 1931, 1932, 1951, and 1952 by The Viking Press, Inc. Reprinted by permission of The Viking Press, Inc., New York.
2. Adapted from material sent by Harry Edgren, George Williams College, Chicago, Ill.
3. From *It All Started with Europa*, Richard Armour (New York: McGraw-Hill Book Company, Inc., © 1955).
4. From *It All Started with Columbus*, Richard Armour (New York: McGraw-Hill Book Company, Inc., © 1953).
5. From *The Benchley Roundup*, Nathaniel Benchley (New York: Harper and Brothers, © 1954).
6. From *Cinderella Hassenpfeffer*, Dave Morrah. Copyright 1946, 1947 by The Curtis Publishing Company. Copyright, 1948 by Dave Morrah. Reprinted with the permission of Rinehart & Co., Inc., New York.

7. *Ibid.*

8. From *My Tale Is Twisted,* Col. Stoopnagle (New York: William Morrow-M. S. Mill Co., © 1947). Reprinted by permission.

9. *Ibid.*

10. *Ibid.*

11. *Ibid.*

12. *Ibid.*

13. *Ibid.*

NOTES FOR CHAPTER 14

1. An attractive name tag, made of wood, is available from The Handcrafters, Waupun, Wis., and sells at little more than a cent each in lots of 100 or more. The names could be burned on with a wood-burning tool; or a wax pencil or Tri-Chem (the color in a ball-point tube) can be used.

2. Created by J. Neal Griffith, Indiana, Pa.

3. From Raymond M. Veh, Harrisburg, Pa.

4. From Ardis Stevens, Chester, Vt.

5. From Joe Gibson, Nashville, Tenn.

6. From Irving Elson, Brooklyn, N. Y.

7. From Reverend David Huffines, Lillington, N. C.

8. *Ibid.*

9. From Ardis Stevens.

10. *Ibid.*

11. From Irving Elson, Brooklyn, N. Y.

12. From Rose Shill, Philadelphia, Pa.

NOTES FOR CHAPTER 15

1. By Russell Ames Cook.

2. Idea suggested by Roland Burdick.

3. This is the way it is done by Perry Saito.

4. From Ardis Stevens, Chester, Vt.

5. From Ardis Stevens, Chester, Vt.

6. The songs which follow were selected and arranged for this book by Mary Elizabeth McDonald, Coral Gables, Fla.

7. Credited to Mrs. Dorothy Dicks, Durham, N. C.

NOTES FOR CHAPTER 16

1. "Drama as Recreation" was written by Amy Goodhue Loomis especially for *The Omnibus of Fun.*

2. New York: Friendship Press, © 1947.

3. New York: Oxford University Press, © 1950.

4. From Sue Horne.

5. Used by permission from Sylvania *Beat the Clock* book, © 1951, from television program by same name produced by Mark Goodson and Bill Todman in association with Columbia Broadcasting System, Inc.

6. *Ibid.*

7. *Ibid.*

8. *Ibid.*

9. Adapted from material by Mollie O'Meara in *Fun Fare,* published by Reader's Digest Association. Used by permission.

10. From Mrs. Elmore Brown, Richmond, Va.

11. From Russell Robinson, Waukesha, Wis.
12. *Ibid.*
13. From Beverly Hammock, Dewitt, Ark.
14. From PACK O FUN Magazine, Jan., 1956, by permission of Edna N. and John M. Clapper, Park Ridge, Ill.
15. By Robert C. Yoh, The Southern Union College, Wadley, Ala.
16. From *Handbook for Recreation Leaders* by Ella Gardner (Washington, D.C. Supt. of Documents, 1936).
17. Ihduhapi Recreation Lab. Notes.
18. Suggested by Jane Farwell Hindricks.

NOTES FOR CHAPTER 17

1. Glenn Bannerman, Durham, N. C.
2. Somewhat similar to Stone, Paper, Scissors (see Index).
3. Ruth Wohr Dixon, Massachusetts.
4. Leona Holbrook, Provo, Utah.
5. Howard Ellis, Nashville, Tenn.
6. F. L. McReynolds, Lafayette, Ind.
7. Reynold E. Carlson, Bloomington, Ind.
8. Wilma Mintier, Pittsburgh, Pa.
9. *Ibid.*
10. Ted Budrow, Syracuse, N. Y.
11. Harold W. Ewing, Nashville, Tenn.
12. Richard Bowers, King College, Bristol, Tenn.
13. James McIntyre, Montgomery, Ala.
14. Leona Holbrook, Provo, Utah.
15. Ardis Stevens, Chester, Vt.
16. Mrs. Martha Hammond, Greeley, Colo.
17. Bill Beatty, New Kensington, Pa.

NOTES FOR CHAPTER 18

1. From Wilma Mintier, Pittsburgh, Pa.
2. From *Secret Code Book,* © 1950 by The Seahorse Press, Pelham, N. Y.
3. Howard Irish, Detroit, Mich.
4. John E. Wilson, Forth Worth, Tex.
5. Suggested by Howard Tanner, who travels for The Handcrafters.
6. Reprinted from CORONET Magazine, April, 1949, by permission.

The answers to this quiz are as follows:

1—G	7—T	13—A	19—C
2—N	8—B	14—H	20—Q
3—W	9—U	15—D	21—M
4—I	10—F	16—S	22—J
5—Y	11—R	17—X	23—O
6—K	12—V	18—P	24—L
		25—E	

7. From *The Teachers' Word Book of 30,000 Words,* by Edward L. Thorndike and Irving Lorge, published by Teachers College, Columbia University, New York, N. Y.

NOTES FOR CHAPTER 19

1. Hammatt & Sons, Anaheim, Calif.
2. An original game by Walter C. Cowart, Jr., Canton, N. C.
3. *Ibid.* (See also April, 1950 issue of Popular Science Monthly for Bean Bag Toss, another game by Mr. Cowart.)
4. Neal Griffith, Indiana, Pa.
5. Walter C. Cowart, Jr.
6. W. Randolph Thornton, Chicago, Ill.
7. Bob Tully, Martinsville, Ind.
8. Frank Walkup, Anchorage, Alaska.
9. W. Randolph Thornton.
10. Walter C. Cowart, Jr.
11. Bu Bush, Pacific Recreation Service, San Jose, Calif.

NOTES FOR CHAPTER 21

1. From Edna Ritchie, Ary, Ky.
2. From *Folk Games of Denmark and Sweden.* Copyrighted by Neva L. Boyd. Used by permission.
3. From Pauline M. Reynolds, Fargo, N. D.
4. Jane Farwell Hindricks.
5. A modern singing game, largely developed by Jane Farwell Hindricks and the Folk Dance Campers at Oglebay Park, Wheeling, W. Va.
6. Ivan Immel shared this story for "The Wheat" at Yale Divinity School.
7. As called by Ralph Page.
8. *Ibid.*
9. This call was found among Lawrence Loy's papers by Ardis Stevens, who completed it. It is interesting and not hard.
10. Ruth and James Norris, New York, N. Y.
11. Richard Chase, Beech Creek, N. C.
12. Adapted by Richard Chase from "The Lancers," with the exception of No. 4.
13. We learned the call from Scotty Burns, Hamilton, Ontario.
14. Some of these figures are done by Peter Olsen.

NOTES FOR CHAPTER 22

1. Published by Silva, Ltd., La Porte, Ind., © 1948.
2. This game was prepared many years ago by "Bugs" Cain, naturalist for the Oakland Area Council of the Boy Scouts of America.

NOTES FOR CHAPTER 23

1. West Market Street Methodist Church, Greensboro, N. C.
2. Most of the points of advice are given by Howard Tanner of The Handcrafters, Waupun, Wis., who has helped many people with their craft programs all over the United States.
3. Shadow box frames may be ordered from Magnus Craft Materials Co., 108 Franklin St., New York 13, N. Y.
4. Dr. George Steinman of Abilene, Texas, devised this way of using cans.
5. We are indebted to the 4-H Club Department of the Agricultural Extension Service, Purdue University, Lafayette, Ind., for suggesting this system of cataloguing craft projects and companies.

Bibliography

For the user's convenience the bibliography for *The Omnibus of Fun* presents items alphabetically under the following categories of recreational interests:

Age Group Helps
Camp, Outdoors, Nature Lore
Church and Religious Organizations
Drama, Skits, Stunts
Equipment Sources
Festivals, Folk Material, International Fun

Games, Parties, Banquets
Hobbies, Handcrafts
Leadership, General Books
Music
Publishers, Suppliers
Record Suppliers
Service Projects
Stories to Be Told or Read

AGE GROUP HELPS
(See other sections, particularly Games.)

Child from 1 to 6, The (Washington 25, D.C.: Superintendent of Documents).

Children's Games from Many Lands, Nina Millen (New York: Friendship Press, 1942). International games for children.

Choice Parties for Little Children, Adelle Carlson (Nashville: Broadman Press, 1956). Inexpensive source for good ideas.

Facts of Life and Love for Teen-Agers, Evelyn Millis Duvall (New York: Association Press, rev. ed., 1956). Helps teen-agers think through important relationships. Gives recreation suggestions.

Family Fun Book, Helen and Larry Eisenberg (New York: Association Press, 1954). Hundreds of family fun ideas for home, trips. Family Fun Kit (Service Department, Box 871, Nashville, Tenn.). Collection of leaflets on family fun.

Fun for Older Adults, Virginia Stafford and Larry Eisenberg (Nashville: Parthenon, 1956). Helps for organizing and maintaining an older adult group, especially in fun. Ideas were contributed by older adults.

Games for Boys and Girls, E. O. Harbin (Nashville: Abingdon, 1949). Simply written. Child of 8 or over can take book, play the games.

He Manners, Robert H. Loeb, Jr. (New York: Association Press, 1954). Book on manners for men by a man. Excellent social conduct suggestions.

Here's How and When, Armilda B. Keiser (New York, Friendship Press, 1952). Interesting, creative play and educational activities for children, especially in the vacation church school.

Recreation for Adults, E. O. Harbin, M. Leo Rippy, others (Nashville: Methodist Publishing House, 1950). Principles of planning fun for adults.

Ten Parties for Children 3 to 8 (New York: Hart, 1945). Completely planned parties for little children. Inexpensive.

CAMP, OUTDOORS, NATURE LORE

Campfire Adventure Stories, Allan A. Macfarlan (New York: Association Press, 1952). Wealth of camp, woodcraft, and Indian lore. Twenty-two story hours.

Campfire and Council Ring Programs, Allan A. Macfarlan (New York: Association Press, 1950). Games, stunts, challenges, Indian pageants, magic.

CAMPING MAGAZINE (Bergenfield, New Jersey). Contains articles, helps, advertising of interest in camping.

Camp Program Book, The, Catherine T. Hammett and Virginia Musselman (New York: Association Press, 1950). Very complete source for all phases of camp program planning.

Nature Games, Paul Nesbit (Colorado Springs, Colo). Interesting and instructive nature games.

Nature Lore Manual, Reynold E. Carlson (available at Cokesbury Bookstores, such as 810 Broadway, Nashville, Tenn.). Games, crafts, nature activities.

Services for the Open, Laura Mattoon and Helen Bragdon (New York: Association Press, 1938). Choice poetry and biblical material woven into worship services. Contains the beautiful will of Charles Loundsbury, who died in a mental institution.

Worship Ways for Camp, Clarice M. Bowman (New York: Association Press, 1955). More than 200 worship aids, graces, scriptural passages, benedictions, offerings, poems. Creative approach.

Your Own Book of Campcraft, Catherine T. Hammett (New York: Pocket Books, 1952). Especially written for teen-agers. All phases of campcraft.

CHURCH AND RELIGIOUS ORGANIZATIONS

(Be sure to ask your own organizational or institutional headquarters for leaflets, booklets, books or other aids which they recommend.)

Church Recreation (National Recreation Association, 8 W. 8th St., New York 11, N. Y.). Practical help for a total program of church recreation.

"Church Recreation Bibliography" (Baptist Sunday School Board, Nashville 3, Tenn.). Lists recreation books. Free.

Leisure (Service Department, Box 871, Nashville, Tenn.). A quarterly low-cost bulletin listing new fun publications, leadership training venture for churches.

Playtime, Agnes Durant Pylant (Nashville: Broadman Press, 1951). Suggestions for church-centered play, written by an experienced specialist. Parties and socials for all age groups.

Recreation Bulletin (Youth Department, United Presbyterian Church, 209 9th St., Pittsburgh 22, Pa.). Monthly parties, well planned. Low cost.

Recreation for the Rural Church, Ed Schlingman (Philadelphia: Christian Education Press, 1948). Standard guide for those working with rural churches.

DRAMA, SKITS, STUNTS

Publishers

Samuel French, Inc., 25 W. 45th St., New York 36, N. Y.
Walter H. Baker Co., 569 Boylston St., Boston 16, Mass.
Children's Theatre Press, Anchorage, Ky.
Eldridge Publishing Co., Franklin, Ohio, and Denver, Colo.

Books

Art of Play Production, The, John Dolman, Jr. (New York: Harper, rev. ed., 1950). Basic reference in the art of play producing.

Drama Clubs, Step by Step, Charles F. Wells (Boston: Walter H. Baker, 1932). How to organize a drama club. Also numerous short skits.

Handbook of Skits and Stunts (1953) and *Fun with Skits, Stunts, and Stories* (1955), Helen and Larry Eisenberg (New York: Association Press). Two collections of skits and stunts for all ages from older children through older adults.

Handy Stunts (Delaware, Ohio: Co-operative Recreation Service).

Playmaking with Children, Winifred Ward (New York: Appleton-Century-Crofts, 1940). Widely accepted among those doing dramatics with children.

Play Production Primer (Salt Lake City: Deseret Press). Low-cost manual, very complete, for the new director.

Puppet Theatre Handbook, Marjorie Batchelder (New York: Harper, 1940). Detailed help on making puppets, presenting plays.

Skit Hits, Helen and Larry Eisenberg (Brentwood, Tenn.: Fun Books).

NOTE: The following three sections of the Bibliography were prepared by Amy Goodhue Loomis for her chapter on Drama in this book.

Collections of Plays

Old-Time Church Dramas, Adapted, Phillips Endicott Osgood (New York: Harper).

Seven Plays, George Bernard Shaw (Boston: Walter H. Baker).

Treasury of Religious Plays, A, Thelma Sharman Brown (New York: Association Press).

Full-Length Plays (listed alphabetically by playwrights)

Anderson, Maxwell, "Journey to Jerusalem" and "Key Largo" (New York: Anderson House).

Barrie, Sir James, "The Boy David" and "Dear Brutus" (New York: Samuel French).

Coffee-Cowan, "Family Portrait" (New York: Dramatists' Play Service).

Drinkwater, John, "A Man's House" and "Abraham Lincoln" (Boston: Walter H. Baker).

Frye, Christopher, "The Boy with a Cart" (New York: Dramatists' Play Service).

Housman, Lawrence, "Victoria Regina" (Boston: Walter H. Baker).

Sherwood, Robert, "Abe Lincoln in Illinois" (New York: Dramatists' Play Service).

Sliker, Harold, "The Other Wise Man" (Evanston, Ill.: Rowe, Peterson).

Vane, Sutton, "Outward Bound" (Boston: Walter H. Baker).

One-Act Plays

Barrie, Sir James, "The Old Lady Shows Her Medals" (New York: Samuel French).

Benét, Stephen Vincent, "A Child Is Born" (Boston: Walter H. Baker).

Dyer, Bernard V., "John Doe" (New York: Samuel French).

Eckart, Frances D., "The Builders" (Boston: Walter H. Baker).

Gale, Zone, "The Neighbors" (Boston: Walter H. Baker).

Kelly, George, "The Flattering Word" (New York: Samuel French).

Loomis, Amy G., "Baker's Dozen" (Manuscript—write its author, care of Vincennes University, Vincennes, Ind.).

Millay, Edna St. Vincent, "Aria da Capo" (Boston: Walter H. Baker).

Sterling, Nora, "Temperate Zone" and "The Case of the Missing Handshake" (New York State Committee on Mental Health).

EQUIPMENT SOURCES

Balloons (in quantities)

Rodin Novelty Co., 3211 N. Clark St., Chicago 13, Ill.

Games Made of Wood, Plastic. (Write each for complete list.)

Consolidated Industries, 710 W. Market St., Greensboro, N. C. 4-D Tick-Tack-Toe, Table Soccer, Bop Stick, Skittles, others (all renamed).

Gangler-Gentry Co., 113 Birchwood Road, Catonsville 28, Md. Manufactures Quad, inexpensive plastic 4-D Tick-Tack-Toe.

Hammatt & Sons, 11356 Orangewood, Anaheim, Calif. Sky Pie, metal shuffleboard, X-L tops, others.

World Wide Games, Delaware, Ohio. Table Soccer, Pommawanga, Count and Capture, Skittles.

Playground Equipment. See advertising in RECREATION Magazine or write its publisher, the National Recreation Association, 8 W. 8th St., New York 11, N. Y., for names of suppliers.

Novelties, Supplies

Johnson Smith & Co., 6615 E. Jefferson St., Detroit 7, Mich., has a 10-cent catalogue of 3000 novelties, party tricks, low-cost instruments.

Public Address, Slides, Films, Projectors

Local dealers can supply you. Many national organizations have catalogues, sell to their members. One such catalogue is *The Projector,* 810 Broadway, Nashville, Tenn.
Allied Radio Corporation, 100 N. Western, Chicago, Ill., sells public address equipment at near-wholesale.
Association Films, 347 Madison Ave., New York 17, N. Y., and Brandon Films, 1600 Broadway, New York 19, N. Y., are sources for films—also the National Conference of Christians and Jews, 733 Southern Building, Washington, D.C.
See *The Program Encyclopedia* (New York: Association Press, 1955) for film suggestions.

Roller Skates

Chicago Roller Skates Co., Chicago, Ill.

FESTIVALS, FOLK MATERIAL, INTERNATIONAL FUN

And Promenade All, Helen and Larry Eisenberg (Nashville: Fun Books, rev. ed., 1952). Musical games, folk games for new leaders, piano accompaniments by Mary Lib McDonald. Big set calls by Bert Lyle.
Cowboy Dances, Lloyd Shaw (Caldwell, Idaho: Caxton Printers, 1940). One of the best books of Western calls, profusely illustrated, by the dean of callers.
Folk Dances for All, Michael Herman (New York: Barnes and Noble, 1950). Piano music, side notes, pictures for 19 dances from 15 countries.
Folk Dances for Fun, Jane Farwell Hindricks (Delaware, Ohio: Co-operative Recreation Service, 1952). International folk material, well assorted, helps for presenting.
Folk Dances of Lietuva, Vytautas Beliajus (San Diego, Calif.: Vyts Beliajus, 1952). Lovely collection of dances, some simple, some harder, from Lithuania. (The author also publishes the magazine of folklore, *Viltis.*)
Folk Party Fun, Dorothy Gladys Spicer (New York: Association Press, 1954). Has 25 planned parties with materials, decorations, refreshments.
"Fun and Festival" series of low-cost pamphlets on international and intercultural fun. *Fun and Festival—Among America's Peoples; from Africa; from China; from India; from India, Pakistan, and Ceylon; from Japan; from Southeast Asia; from the Other Americas; from the U.S. and Canada* (New York: Friendship Press).

Games of Many Nations, E. O. Harbin (Nashville: Abingdon, 1952). Choice collection of international games from many nations, especially children's games.

Handy Play Party Book, Handy Folk Dance Book, Handy Square Dance Book—all collected by Lynn Rohrbough (Delaware, Ohio: Co-operative Recreation Service). Well-written collections of materials in the fields respectively of singing games, international folk dances, American square dances.

Old Square Dances of America, Neva L. Boyd (Chicago: Fitzsimmons, 1938). Standard collection of traditional squares, Middle-West style.

Singing Calls, John Marks (Indianapolis: Indiana Farm Bureau, 130 E. Washington Ave., 1952). Fifty modern singing calls with records, references.

Square Dance, The, The Chicago Park District Book (Chicago 57: Best-Ford Co., 5707 W. Lake, rev. ed., 1952). Shows techniques, gives material, photos, diagrams, to help the caller.

GAMES, PARTIES, BANQUETS

Abingdon Party and Banquet Book, Clyde M. Maguire (Nashville: Abingdon, 1956). Nineteen complete plans for any occasion—the directions, menus, quantity recipes.

Active Games and Contests, Mason and Mitchell (New York: A. S. Barnes, 1946). Outdoor and gymnasium games, complete rules, fine points.

Calendar of Parties, A, Jack and Edith Fellows (Nashville: Broadman Press, 1953). Ideas for parties to take groups right through the year.

Choice Socials, series of pamphlets by Agnes Durant Pylant (Nashville: Broadman Press). One each for juniors, intermediates, young people, adults. Also one on Choice Banquets.

Cokesbury Game Book and *Cokesbury Party Book*, each by Arthur M. Depew (Nashville: Abingdon, 1954). Two low-cost books with tried and tested ideas.

Complete Book of Children's Parties, The, Florence Hamsher (Garden City, N. Y.: Hanover House, 1949). One of the best collections of planned parties.

Games for Boys and Men (New York: National Recreation Association, 1956). There is also available *Games for Girls and Women* by Ethel Bowers (same source).

Handbook of Games, Neva L. Boyd (Chicago: Fitzsimmons, 1940). Carefully selected games, especially for school-age children.

Hospital and Bedside Games, Neva L. Boyd (Chicago: Fitzsimmons, 1945). Well selected for this specialized purpose.

Public Speakers' Treasure Chest, H. V. Prochnow (New York: Harper, 1942). All-inclusive book of helps in banquet speaking.

10,000 Jokes, Toasts and Stories, edited by L. and F. Copeland (New York: Garden City, 1940). Extra large, extra good. Bargain.

HOBBIES, HANDCRAFTS

Suppliers. Locally you can often find handcraft supplies available. Here are a few firms:

O. P. Crafts, Sandusky, Ohio. Objects to be decorated, etc.

Consumers Co-operative, 318 E. 10th St., Kansas City, Mo. Special wax for candlecraft.

Dennison, 300 Howard St., Framingham, Mass. Idea service, plus many low-cost pamphlets on use of crepe paper in decorating and crafts.

The Handcrafters, Waupun, Wis. Creative projects of felt, cork, wood. Small looms, enameling.

Eastman Kodak Co., Rochester, N. Y. Many publications on taking and developing pictures.

Larson Leather Co., 820 Tripp Ave., Chicago, Ill. Anything of leather.

Magnus Craft Materials, 108 Franklin St., New York 13, N. Y. Projects of enameling, whittling, bead stringing, molding, plastic, tray making.

Pacific Recreation Service, San Jose, Calif. Art supplies, felt, plastic, jewelry supplies, wood boxes, burning, leather, games, books.

Books, Magazines

The Book of Arts and Crafts, by Marguerite Ickis and Reba Selden Esh (New York: Association Press, 1954). This is an amazing collection of instructions for over 1,000 craft projects, described simply, with copious line drawings. Craft ideas for all ages.

Care and Feeding of Hobby Horses, The, Earnest Elmo Calkins (New York: Sentinel Books, 1932). The standard work in the hobby field, written by one who had to take up hobbies.

Handicraft, by Lester Griswold (New York: Prentice-Hall, Inc.). Includes illustrations and instructions for Basketry, Bookbinding, Ceramics, Leatherwork, Fabric Decoration, Plastics, Lapidary, Metalwork, Cord Weaving, Weaving, Woodwork, and Archery. A wonderful book for the mature crafter.

Here's How and When, by Armilda B. Keiser (New York: Friendship Press). Although this is written for church school teachers, this book is full of clever ideas for small children.

"Hobby Books Division," 154 E. Erie, Chicago 11, Ill., has an interesting catalogue of do-it-yourself books.

MECHANICS ILLUSTRATED Magazine, 67 W. 44th St., New York 36, N. Y. A how-to-do-it publication for the power-tool crowd.

PACK-O-FUN Magazine, edited by John and Edna Clapper (Park Ridge, Ill.). For those working with children in the 7-to-12 bracket. Scrapcraft ideas galore, skits.

PROFITABLE HOBBIES Magazine, 543 Westport Road, Kansas City 11, Mo. Interesting, profitable hobbies shown each month.

For books dealing with specific crafts, inquire at the supply house where you buy your materials.

LEADERSHIP, GENERAL BOOKS

Fun Encyclopedia, The, E. O. Harbin (Nashville: Abingdon, 1940). Giant collection of 1000 pages of twenty-one kinds of social fun.

Handbook for Recreation Leaders (Washington 25, D.C.: Superintendent of Documents, 1936). Low-cost handbook for social fun—active, quiet, singing games.

Philosophy of Recreation and Leisure, Jay B. Nash (St. Louis: Mosby, 1953). Sound guide for thought and discussion on wholesome use of leisure time.

Program Encyclopedia, The, Clement A. Duran (New York: Association Press, 1955). A 640-page gold mine of activity suggestions (recreation and otherwise) for program chairmen of clubs, churches, schools, community organizations.

Recreation for the Handicapped, Dr. Valerie V. Hunt (New York: Prentice-Hall, 1956). Authoritative book entering in detail into the kinds of recreation suitable for handicapped of all ages and stages.

Recreation Leader, The, E. O. Harbin (Nashville: Abingdon, 1952). Excellent guide or textbook for recreation leadership.

MUSIC

(Check local music stores, public library, for song books and records.)

Books

"American Folk Music" bibliography, Sam Hinton (La Jolla, Calif.). An outstanding folklorist has collected the most extensive list of music publications.

Camp Songs 'n' Things (1925 Addison Way, Berkeley, Calif.). Folk and novelty songs for camps, children's and youths' groups.

Christmas Customs and Carols, Ruthella Rodeheaver (Winona Lake, Ind.: Rodeheaver-Hall-Mack, 1944). Background for Christmas customs, also favorite carols.

How to Lead Group Singing, Helen and Larry Eisenberg (New York: Association Press, 1955). Helps for directing, programming, keeping up with music.

Lift Every Voice, edited by Larry Eisenberg and committee (Service Department, Box 871, Nashville, Tenn.). Pocket-size vocal, large accompaniment-background editions. Folk songs, hymns, spirituals, fun songs, especially for church use.

Singing America, A. D. Zanzig (Boston: C. C. Birchard, 1943). Folk songs that America sings. Beautiful accompaniment edition, also vocal edition. Some background material.

Sociability Songs (Dayton, Ohio: Lorenz Publishing Company). Informal songs for community singing. An older book.

Song in the Air, edited by Wally Chappell and others (Delaware, Ohio: Co-operative Recreation Service). Pocket-size collection of familiar and lesser-known carols.

357 Songs We Love to Sing (Chicago: Hall-McCreary, 1940). Large collection of familiar and folk songs, complete with piano accompaniments.
Whole World Singing, The, Edith Lovell Thomas (New York: Friendship Press, 1951). Songs from around the world, especially for children.

Some Publishers

C. C. Birchard, 285 Columbus, Boston 16, Mass. Choral arrangements of folks songs, also collections, especially for public schools. "Twice 55" series.
Co-operative Recreation Service, Delaware, Ohio. Free list. Specializes in pocket-size song books for informal group singing, especially folk.
Hall-McCreary Publishing Co., 434 S. Wabash, Chicago, Ill. Free list. Several "community sing" song books.
Neil Kjos Publishing Co., Chicago, Ill. Publishes the popular arrangements of Bea and Max Krone, especially for use in public schools.

PUBLISHERS, SUPPLIERS

Abingdon Press, 810 Broadway, Nashville, Tenn. Variety of books in social recreation: parties, games, fun activities for churches.
Agricultural Extension Service of your state college of agriculture. Usually furnish free material, mimeographed, on phases of recreation.
American Youth Hostels, 15 W. 8th St., New York 11, N. Y. Materials for hosteling and outdoor fun.
Association Press, 291 Broadway, New York 7, N. Y. Large list of books on camping, social recreation, group work, courtship and marriage, YMCA work.
Athletic Institute, 209 S. State St., Chicago 4, Ill. Books on athletics and recreation. Authoritative source for rules of most athletic games, tennis, archery. Free list.
A. S. Barnes, Publishers, 232 Madison Ave., New York 16, N. Y. Books for school use—games, dances, athletics. Inexpensive series on how to play the popular sports.
Boys' Clubs of America, 381 Fourth Ave., New York 16, N. Y. Publishes pamphlets and material for boys' clubs.
Boy Scouts of America, Inc., New Brunswick, N. J. Scouting books, including fun books. (Often available locally.) Magazine for leaders (SCOUTING) and for Scouts (BOY'S LIFE).
Broadman Press, 127 9th Ave., N., Nashville 3, Tenn. Extensive listing in materials on recreation for churches.
Co-operative Recreation Service, Delaware, Ohio. Feature folk song and game publications, low cost. Subsidiary, "World Wide Games," makes games.
Coronet, 488 Madison Ave., New York 22, N. Y. Publish interesting quizzes and other fun material monthly.
Friendship Press, 257 Fourth Ave., New York 10, N. Y. The "Fun and Festival" series, and other books and booklets for international, intercultural fun.
Girl Scouts of America, 155 E. 44th St., New York 17, N. Y. Nature, games, crafts books for girls, and GIRL SCOUT LEADER for leaders.

Hall-McCreary Co., 434 S. Wabash, Chicago, Ill. Music and books of music for community singing, etc.

National Recreation Association, 8 W. 8th St., New York 11, N. Y. The national nonprofit organization of the movement. Extensive list of low-cost publications in music, drama, social recreation, building plans, etc. Consultation service. Seasonal publications for Christmas, Hallowe'en, Excellent, helpful magazine, RECREATION.

PARENTS' MAGAZINE, 52 Vanderbilt Ave., New York 17, N. Y. Authoritative publisher of reading material for children and youth, especially magazines.

Popular Mechanics Press, 200 E. Ontario, Chicago 11, Ill. How-to-do books for the handy man, especially including hobbies using machine tools.

Zondervan Publishing House, 1415 Lake Drive, S. E., Grand Rapids, Mich. Recreation books for churches, special emphasis on Bible-centered activities.

RECORD SUPPLIERS
(Check locally with record stores.)

Firms Doing Business by Mail

DeLuxe Music Shop, 3965 Milwaukee Ave., Chicago 41, Ill.
The Folk Dancer (Michael Herman), Box 201, Flushing, N. Y.
Ed Kremer's Folk Shop, United Nations Theatre Building, San Francisco, Calif.

The World of Fun Records

This is a series of fifteen 12″ plastic records of music from the Americas, England, Denmark, Finland, Russia, Belgium, Hungary, Lithuania, Germany, and Switzerland. There are four tunes on most. Try your record store or Audio-Visual Department, 810 Broadway, Nashville, Tenn.

M-101 Cshebogar; Kalvelis
Hol-Di-Ri-Di-A; Seven Steps

M-102 Galway Piper; Ace of Diamonds
Come, Let Us Be Joyful; Danish Schottische

M-103 Irish Washerwoman
Captain Jinks

M-104 Red River Valley; Sicilian Circle
Camptown Races; Pop! Goes the Weasel

M-105 Weaving; Troika
Spanish Circle; Chimes of Dunkirk

M-106 Trallen; La Raspa
Green Sleeves; Trip to Helsinki

M-107 Little Brown Jug
Put Your Little Foot; The Fireman's Dance

M-108 Seven Jumps; Korobushka
Gustav's Skol; Crested Hen

M-109 Cumberland Square Eight; Good Humor
Christ Church Bells; Black Nag

M-110 Newcastle; Spinning Waltz
Hopak; Roads to Isles

M-111 Ten Little Indians; Oats, Peas, Beans
Mulberry Bush; Rig-a-Jig-Jig

M-112 Sandy Land; Turn the Glasses Over
Alabama Gal; Sent My Brown Jug Down

M-113 Lili Marlene; Great Big
House
Waltz of the Bells; Ten
Pretty Girls
M-114 Butterfly; Dance Lightly;
Stopp Galopp
Klapptanz; Tampet

M-115 Alfelder; Foehringer Kontra
At the Inn "To the Crown";
Sounderburg; Double
Quadrille

SERVICE PROJECTS

American Friends Service Committee, 20 S. 12th St., Philadelphia, Pa. Excellent projects described for children, youth, adult groups, for U. S. and overseas distribution to the needy.

Meals for Millions Foundation, 115 W. 7th St., Los Angeles 14, Calif. Nonprofit distributors of a 3-cent meal for famine relief and supplementary feeding. Share Banks, Others' Day, Sacrificial Meals. Food available for demonstrations.

UNICEF, United Nations, New York. Publishes pamphlets giving guidance for trick-or-treat collections for the Children's Fund, also festivals.

STORIES TO BE TOLD OR READ

Anthology of Children's Literature, Edna Johnston (Boston: Houghton Mifflin, 1952). Over 1,000 pages of traditional and modern stories, poems.

CHILDREN'S DIGEST, monthly magazine (Parents' Magazine Press, 52 Vanderbilt Ave., New York 17, N. Y.). For children 7 to 12. Stories, poetry.

Cinderella Hassenpfeffer, Dave Morrah (New York: Rinehart, 1948). "Pennsylvania Dutch" dialect stories to be read aloud. (Some in this book.)

Folk Tales of All Nations, F. H. Lee (New York: Tudor, 1934). A classic collection of folk tales from around the world.

Grandfather Tales, Richard Chase (Boston: Houghton Mifflin, 1947). Authentic mountain folk stories for all ages.

It All Started with Columbus (1953) and *It All Started with Europa* (1955), Richard Armour (New York: McGraw-Hill). Hilarious, improbable accounts of American and European history.

Tall Tale America, Walter Blair (New York: Coward-McCann, 1946). Tales of most of America's folk heroes. School age and above.

Treasury of American Folklore, B. A. Botkin (New York: Crown, 1949). Large, authentic collection of stories, "folk say," songs, games.

The "Fun and Festival" series carry stories. (See "Festivals" section.)

Index

I

J